Web Design and Development:

Concepts, Methodologies, Tools, and Applications

Information Resources Management Association
USA

Volume III

Information Science
REFERENCE
An Imprint of IGI Global

Managing Director:	Lindsay Johnston
Managing Editor:	Austin DeMarco
Director of Intellectual Propery & Contracts:	Jan Travers
Acquisitions Editor:	Kayla Wolfe
Production Editor:	Christina Henning
Multi-Volume Book Production Specialist:	Deanna Jo Zombro
Typesetter(s):	Kaitlyn Kulp
Cover Design:	Jason Mull

Published in the United States of America by
Information Science Reference (an imprint of IGI Global)
701 E. Chocolate Avenue
Hershey PA, USA 17033
Tel: 717-533-8845
Fax: 717-533-8661
E-mail: cust@igi-global.com
Web site: http://www.igi-global.com

                    Library of Congress Cataloging-in-Publication Data

Web design and development : concepts, methodologies, tools, and applications / Information Resources Management Association, editor.
     volumes cm
  Includes bibliographical references and index.
  Summary: "This book explores the use of innovative and comprehensive technologies, strategies, and other tools in the creation of quality web pages, focusing on web design in fields such as education, business, government, and more"-- Provided by publisher.
  ISBN 978-1-4666-8619-9 (hardcover) -- ISBN 978-1-4666-8620-5 (ebook) 1. Web site development. I. Information Resources Management Association.
  TK5105.888.W36874 2016
  006.7--dc23
                    2015015771

British Cataloguing in Publication Data
A Cataloguing in Publication record for this book is available from the British Library.

For electronic access to this publication, please contact: eresources@igi-global.com.

List of Contributors

Table of Contents

Volume I

Section 1
Fundamental Concepts and Theories

This section serves as a foundation for this exhaustive reference tool by addressing underlying principles essential to the understanding of web design and development. Chapters found within these pages provide an excellent framework in which to position web design and development within the field of information science and technology. Insight regarding the critical incorporation of global measures into web design and development is addressed, while crucial stumbling blocks of this field are explored. With 17 chapters comprising this foundational section, the reader can learn and chose from a compendium of expert research on the elemental theories underscoring the web design and development discipline.

Section 2
Frameworks and Methodologies

This section provides in-depth coverage of conceptual architecture frameworks to provide the reader with a comprehensive understanding of the emerging developments within the field of web design and development. Research fundamentals imperative to the understanding of developmental processes within web design and development are offered. From broad examinations to specific discussions on methodology, the research found within this section spans the discipline while offering detailed, specific discussions. From basic designs to abstract development, these chapters serve to expand the reaches of development and design technologies within the web design and development community. This section includes 14 contributions from researchers throughout the world on the topic of web design and development.

Volume II

Section 3
Tools and Technologies

This section presents an extensive coverage of various tools and technologies available in the field of web design and development that practitioners and academicians alike can utilize to develop different techniques. These chapters enlighten readers about fundamental research on the many tools facilitating the burgeoning field of web design and development. It is through these rigorously researched chapters that the reader is provided with countless examples of the up-and-coming tools and technologies emerging from the field of web design and development. With 16 chapters, this section offers a broad treatment of some of the many tools and technologies within the web design and development field.

Fernando Ramos, University of Aveiro, Portugal
Marta Pinto, University of Aveiro, Portugal
Dalila Coelho, University of Aveiro, Portugal
Rui Raposo, University of Aveiro, Portugal
Lúcia Pombo, University of Aveiro, Portugal
Luís Pedro, University of Aveiro, Portugal
Pedro Almeida, University of Aveiro, Portugal
João Batista, University of Aveiro, Portugal
Nídia Morais, University of Aveiro, Portugal
Francislê Souza, University of Aveiro, Portugal
Ana Balula, University of Aveiro, Portugal
Margarida Lucas, University of Aveiro, Portugal
António Moreira, University of Aveiro, Portugal

Section 4
Cases and Applications

This section discusses a variety of applications and opportunities available that can be considered by practitioners in developing viable and effective web design and development programs and processes. This section includes 13 chapters that review topics from case studies to best practices and ongoing research. Further chapters discuss web design and development in a variety of settings. Contributions included in this section provide excellent coverage of today's IT community and how research into web design and development is impacting the social fabric of our present-day global village.

Debopriyo Roy, University of Aizu, Japan

Jean-Eric Pelet, IDRAC Business School of Management, Lyon, France & LEMNA, IAE-
    IEMN, Nantes University, France
Jashim Khan, Laureate Online Education B.V., The Netherlands
Panagiota Papadopoulou, University of Athens, Greece
Emmanuelle Bernardin, Audencia Nantes, Pres l'Unam, France

Edita Butrimė, Lithuanian University of Health Sciences, Lithuania
Vaiva Zuzevičiūtė, Mykolas Romeris University, Lithuania

Section 5
Issues and Challenges

This section contains 14 chapters, giving a wide variety of perspectives on web design and development and its implications. Within the chapters, the reader is presented with an in-depth analysis of the most current and relevant issues within this growing field of study. Crucial questions are addressed and alternatives offered along with theoretical approaches discussed.

Section 6
Emerging Trends

This section highlights research potential within the field of web design and development while exploring uncharted areas of study for the advancement of the discipline. Introducing this section are chapters that set the stage for future research directions and topical suggestions for continued debate, centering on the new venues and forums for discussion. A pair of chapters on space-time makes up the middle of the section of the final 5 chapters, and the book concludes with a look ahead into the future of the web design and development field. In all, this text will serve as a vital resource to practitioners and academics interested in the best practices and applications of the burgeoning field of web design and development.

Preface

The constantly changing landscape of web design and development makes it challenging for experts and practitioners to stay informed of the field's most up-to-date research. That is why Information Science Reference is pleased to offer this three-volume reference collection that will empower students, researchers, and academicians with a strong understanding of critical issues within web design and development by providing both broad and detailed perspectives on cutting-edge theories and developments. This reference is designed to act as a single reference source on conceptual, methodological, technical, and managerial issues, as well as provide insight into emerging trends and future opportunities within the discipline.

Web Design and Development: Concepts, Methodologies, Tools and Applications is organized into eight distinct sections that provide comprehensive coverage of important topics. The sections are:

1.   Fundamental Concepts and Theories,
2.   Frameworks and Methodologies,
3.   Tools and Technologies,
4.   Cases and Application,
5.   Critical Issues, and
6.   Emerging Trends.

The following paragraphs provide a summary of what to expect from this invaluable reference tool.

Section 1, *Fundamental Concepts and Theories*, serves as a foundation for this extensive reference tool by addressing crucial theories essential to the understanding of web design and development. Introducing the book is "Get Out of My Sandbox: Web Publication, Authority, and Originality" by Barbara Bordalejo, a great foundation laying the groundwork for the basic concepts and theories that will be discussed throughout the rest of the book. Another chapter of note in Section 1 is titled "The Role of Electronic Signature in the Third Millennium of the Development of International Trade Transactions" by Amir Bagherian and colleagues. Section 1 concludes, and leads into the following portion of the book with a nice segue chapter, "Complex Adaptive Systems Thinking Approach to Enterprise Architecture," by Marc Rabaey. Where Section 1 leaves off with fundamental concepts, Section 2 discusses architectures and frameworks in place for web design and development.

Section 2, *Frameworks and Methodologies*, presents in-depth coverage of the conceptual design and architecture of web design and development. Opening the section is "First Steps in the Development of a Model for Integrating Formal and Informal Learning in Virtual Environments" by Victoria I. Marín and Jesús Salinas. Through case studies, this section lays excellent groundwork for later sections that will get into present and future applications for web design and development, such as: "Designing and

Delivering Web-Based Instruction to Adult Learners in Higher Education" by Mabel C. P. O. Okojie. The section concludes with an excellent work by Evelina Pencheva, titled "Design of Web Services for Mobile Monitoring and Access to Measurements."

Section 3, *Tools and Technologies*, presents extensive coverage of the various tools and technologies used in the implementation of web design and development. Section 3 begins where Section 2 left off, though this section describes more concrete tools at place in the modeling, planning, and applications of web design and development. The first chapter, "Information Architecture for Pervasive Healthcare Information Provision with Technological Implementation," by Chekfoung Tan and Shixiong Liu, lays a framework for the types of works that can be found in this section. Section 3 is full of excellent chapters like this one, including "Supporting Accessible User Interfaces Using Web Services" by Georgios Bouloukakis and colleagues. The section concludes with "Tracing the Use of Communication Technologies in Higher Education" by Fernando Ramos and colleagues. Where section 3 described specific tools and technologies at the disposal of practitioners, section 4 describes successes, failures, best practices, and different applications of the tools and frameworks discussed in previous sections.

Section 4, *Cases and Application*, describes how the broad range of web design and development efforts has been utilized and offers insight on and important lessons for their applications and impact. The first chapter in the section is titled "Using Website Analysis as a Tool for Computer Assisted Language Learning in a Foreign Language Classroom" written by Debopriyo Roy. Section 4 includes the widest range of topics because it describes case studies, research, methodologies, frameworks, architectures, theory, analysis, and guides for implementation. The breadth of topics covered in the chapter is also reflected in the diversity of its authors, from countries all over the globe. Another chapters of note is "Increasing Research Students' Engagement through Virtual Communities" by Maria Limniou, Clare Holdcroft, and Paul S. Holme. Section 4 concludes with an excellent segue into the next section, "Actor Network Theory Applied to Organizational Change: A Case Study" by Carlos Páscoa and José Tribolet.

Section 5, *Critical Issues*, presents coverage of academic and research perspectives on web design and development tools and applications. The section begins with "How Interface Design and Search Strategy Influence Children's Search Performance and Evaluation," by Hanna Jochmann-Mannak, Leo Lentz, Theo Huibers, and Ted Sanders. Chapters in this section will look into theoretical approaches and offer alternatives to curtail questions on the subject of web design and development such as: "From Adoption to Routinization of B2B e-Commerce: Understanding Patterns across Europe" written by Tiago Oliveira and Gurpreet Dhillon. The section concludes with "A Business Motivation Model for IT Service Management" by Marco Vicente, Nelson Gama, and Miguel Mira da Silva.

Section 6, *Emerging Trends*, highlights areas for future research within the field of web design and development, opening with "Challenges, Opportunities, and Trends in Quality K-12 Online Environments" by Marius Boboc. Section 8 contains chapters that look at what might happen in the coming years that can extend the already staggering amount of applications for web design and development. The final chapter of the book looks at an emerging field within web design and development, in the excellent contribution, "'Talking Tools': Sloyd Processes Become Multimodal Stories with Smartphone Documentation" by Annika Wiklund-Engblom and colleagues.

Although the primary organization of the contents in this multi-volume work is based on its six sections, offering a progression of coverage of the important concepts, methodologies, technologies, applications, social issues, and emerging trends, the reader can also identify specific contents by utilizing the extensive indexing system listed at the end of each volume. As a comprehensive collection of research on the latest findings related to using technology to providing various services, *Web Design and Development: Concepts, Methodologies, Tools and Applications*, provides researchers, administrators and all audiences with a complete understanding of the development of applications and concepts in web design and development. Given the vast number of issues concerning usage, failure, success, policies, strategies, and applications of web design and development in countries around the world, *Web Design and Development: Concepts, Methodologies, Tools and Applications* addresses the demand for a resource that encompasses the most pertinent research in technologies being employed to globally bolster the knowledge and applications of web design and development.

Chapter 53

Increasing Research Students' Engagement through Virtual Communities

Maria Limniou
University of Liverpool, UK

Clare Holdcroft
Manchester Metropolitan University, UK

Paul S. Holmes
Manchester Metropolitan University, UK

ABSTRACT

This chapter describes important issues regarding research students' participation in a virtual community. Within a virtual community, university staff can communicate with research students without geographical/space constraints, and research students can exchange views, materials, and experience with their peers and/or academics in a flexible learning environment. Students' participation in virtual communities is mainly based on socio-emotional and informational motivations. Initially, this chapter describes the conditions of research in a traditional environment and the role of students and academics in it, along with the role of pedagogical and psychological aspects in virtual communities. Examples from a university virtual community developed in a Virtual Learning Environment and a Facebook™ closed group are presented. Apart from discussion forums, blended learning activities also increase students' engagement in virtual communities. Technical issues and difficulties based on different learning environments and university members' experience and familiarity with technology are highlighted and discussed.

INTRODUCTION

The word *research* can take on a variety of different meanings. For many students and academic staff, the term can have different implications depending on their research discipline. The term

research evokes a number of connotations: the reading and gathering of information from books, journals, or other printed resources; the undertaking of experiments in a laboratory environment; and the analysis, collection and interpretation of data. Research encompasses all of the above

DOI: 10.4018/978-1-4666-8619-9.ch053

as a process of systematic investigation with the objective of creating new knowledge. According to the Research Excellence Framework (2011; p. 48), research "is defined as a process of investigation leading to new insights, effectively shared," which may include a definite set of procedures and steps, such as problem identification, data gathering and interpretation, action on evidence and result evaluation. The majority of researchers work independently in one or more of the traditional environments, gathering, interpreting and evaluating experimental data in order to complete their research project to create new knowledge. The interaction between students and academics (supervisors) is mainly based on a face-to-face communication. The frequency of communication is dependent, in part, on students' and academics' workload, styles, and requirements in relation to the disciplinary practice. For example, in a Science and Engineering faculty, students and academics may have multiple and frequent informal interactions since research projects may be conducted in laboratory settings, which may require close supervision of specialist techniques. In a Humanities and Social Science faculty, however, student-academic interactions may be less regular and communication usually takes place in formal meetings (Heath, 2002). Research students, during their studies, may also interact with other academics, such as librarians and technicians, in addition to their supervisory team. By developing contacts and interacting with other staff and students, a research student may save time involved in independent research. University personnel who are experts in a scientific topic or a field are often willing to provide research students with relevant information but, in most cases information holders do not meet with the research students who are in need of the information. Part-time research students are faced with their own unique situations, and are often struggling to balance careers and personal responsibilities alongside their research. Thus, they may not visit the University as frequently to

develop their contacts and to determine who is an appropriate expert (academic or not) to assist them (Watts, 2008).

Moreover, although research students need to follow a specific research model that is different for each discipline, they should develop and use a range of transferable skills to achieve their aims, such as careful planning, observation, evaluation and critical reflection, along with presentation and publication skills. For that purpose, the UK organization Vitae, which supports the personal, professional and career development of researchers, has designed a Researcher Development Framework by providing guidance to research students and staff to develop knowledge and skills (Vitae, 2013). The Framework is informed by consultation within academia and industry, and identifies the characteristics that typify an excellent researcher. These characteristics are clustered within four domains:

- Knowledge and intellectual abilities;
- Personal effectiveness;
- Research governance and organization; and
- Engagement, influence and impact.

The aim of the Framework is to encourage "researchers to plan their personal and career development through achievable goals within an action plan; identifying their strengths and developing those areas deemed weaker or important to their career progression to enable them to realize their potential" (Vitae, 2013). Most UK universities have engaged with the principles of the Researcher Development Framework and have organized and delivered workshops in order to assist their research students to obtain the necessary skills.

In a traditional research environment, research students typically learn to conduct research by working closely with their faculty, following a specific research model well supported by their supervisory team; and they often attend face-to-face workshops in order to develop skills and attitudes valuable for their research project. According to Protivnak and Foss (2009), collaboration between students and faculty members is an important factor for successful completion of research studies; and the relationships between students and university staff and the attendance of events and workshops enhance the sense of belonging to a research community. Generally, any group of people who share a physical location, and/or share a common interest or characteristic such as research, belong to a community (Blanchard, 2004). However, according to a recent Postgraduate Research Experience Survey in the UK for research studies, only 54% of respondents expressed that they felt integrated within the Department's research community and 65% considered that their department provided limited opportunities for sharing "campus space" with others and opportunities for interactions with the University staff (supervisors, other academic staff, non-academic staff) and with their peers (Hodsdon & Buckley, 2011). Therefore, it seems that the social ties of a research community are not strong enough, as researchers feel isolated inside the traditional research environment and research students seldom interact with their peers or with University staff. Moreover, they do not seem to have strong relationships before, during, or after their participation in face-to-face workshops with their peers and the workshop tutors. According to Ali (2006), the independent nature of undertaking research and the feelings of isolation have often been associated with higher levels of non-completion.

In order to enhance the sense of belonging to a community, Universities have adopted other modes of communication supported by the extent of technology mediation of interaction (computer-mediated communication). Specifically, the development of the Internet and the World Wide Web (WWW or the Web) gave to the world several advantages over the communication media, including interactivity, user-involvement, time-independence and worldwide access. Through the first-generation of web technologies (Web

1.0), a web server could only deliver information to users. However, the second generation of Web technologies (Web 2.0) supports two-way communication, as users can create and easily upload new information to the Web server. Therefore, the users are not only information consumers, but also information contributors. Web 2.0 technologies allow users to collaborate with others, to share ideas and documents, to create online collaborative documents and to socialize with others (Collis & Moonen, 2008). Collaborative wikis, blogs, photo and slide sharing, and online social networks are used by millions of people in everyday life either for personal/social or professional/organizational purposes (Ponte & Simon, 2011; Shang, Li, Wu & Hou, 2011). These collaborative platforms have many common features, such as content creation and sharing (images, files), provision for discussions related to the content (comments, online posts and forums), user-to-user connections (private messaging) and networks of users based on common interests (Kolbitsch & Maurer, 2006). An example of an online social networking platform is Facebook™, that launched in 2004; it enables users to keep in touch with their (old) friends, classmates, relatives and new friends, whilst sharing resources such as photos, videos and news. Facebook™ also provides layers of common identities via groups that are designed to connect users with a common interest. That specific "group function" of Facebook™ can support and facilitate virtual communities. Overall, Web 2.0 technologies give users the opportunity to engage virtually with a group of people with common interests in order to perform activities in a common cyberspace such as the sharing of ideas, photos, documents and online chat (Beye, Jeckmans, Erkin, Hartel, Lagendijk & Tang, 2010). Any group of people who may or may not meet one another face-to-face, but who have similar interests and try to achieve similar goals by exchanging ideas, views, documents, experience, etc. through online web networks belong to a virtual community (De Moor & Weigand, 2007). Usually, a virtual community-based approach facilitates informal sharing of knowledge available from experienced and skilled people and virtual communities are characterized as unique, addressing issues such as communities of practice, virtual collaboration and knowledge management with different ways, depending on people, shared purposes, policies, and computer systems (Koh & Kim, 2004). The four characteristics (Lee, Vogel & Limayem, 2002) that define a "virtual community are:

- A virtual community is built on a computer-mediated space (cyberspace);
- Activities in the virtual community are enabled by Information and Communication Technology;
- The contents or topics of the virtual community are driven by its participants; and
- The virtual community relationship evolves through communication among members." (p. 2)

However, it is a challenge for people who develop and/or facilitate a virtual community to build a commitment from all the members, as even the most successful online communities fail to engage all the members and to encourage active participation in it. For example, in Wikipedia, 60% of the users never return the benefits that they gain from the community (Panciera, Halfaker & Terveen, 2009). Some members in a virtual community feel greater commitment and they provide content, enforce norms of appropriate behavior, and perform behind-the-scenes work to keep the community going (Farzan, Dabbish, Kraut & Postmes, 2011).

The aim of this chapter is to review important issues regarding the research students' participation in a virtual community. The authors have chosen to provide different examples from a virtual research community under the perspectives of building up a new one. The role of technological resources, the student-teacher interaction, the role of communication, and the enhancement of the

sense of community among the University members through the interactions between academic, students and non-academic staff are discussed.

BACKGROUND THEORY

Students who were born after 1980 belong to the Net Generation and have a fundamentally different way of processing information and ways of communicating compared to generations before. These students feel comfortable with technology and the way that they learn is task-oriented and experiential. Thus, they prefer to receive information quickly and use multiple/multi-modal communication channels to access information and to e-communicate with friends, peers, and teachers (Oblinger & Oblinger, 2005). Many universities have adopted Information and Communication Technology (ICT)-enhanced environments in order to support the teaching that they offer. Virtual Learning Environments (VLEs), such as WebCT©, BlackBoard® and Moodle™ ©, give University staff the opportunity to deliver online courses or to create virtual communities (Blas & Serrano-Fernández, 2009; Limniou, Papadopoulos & Kozaris., 2009; Ngai, Poon & Chan, 2007). VLE systems support teaching and learning by offering tools which enable teachers to embed audios, videos, animations, PowerPoint presentations and/or simulations to the taught courses. In addition VLE systems allow teachers to interact synchronously and/or asynchronously with their students through collaboration tools such as chat rooms and/or discussion boards. Management tools, such as the selective release of the learning material, the students groups' creation and the tracking of students who participate in Virtual Space, offer academic staff extra possibilities to supervise their courses and engage students in teaching and learning. From a pedagogical point of view, by integrating VLEs into the teaching approach, academic staff can engage students in the process of learning through discussions, individual feedback based on students' actions and/or performance and their awareness of their knowledge and areas of weaknesses. Learning activities through discussion boards allow students to exchange views on difficult topics and allow academic staff to create a flexible teaching approach enhancing their communication with their students. Additionally, students can be connected to a community at anytime, anywhere, without being time- or place-constrained (Limniou, 2012). By integrating the technological developments into courses/workshops teachers have the opportunity to design different teaching strategies (Limniou & Papadopoulos, 2011). Generally, the combination of pedagogical approaches, such as behaviorism, socio-constructivism, and cognitivism, with or without instructional technology, can produce an optimal learning outcome (blended learning) (Bliuc, Goodyear & Ellis, 2007; Driscoll, 2002).

Pedagogical and Psychological Aspects Related to Research Studies

Behaviorism is based on the assumption that teachers are able to transfer knowledge to students' minds. Specifically, this model defines learning as a change in observable behaviors due to environmental stimuli, where learners are essentially regarded as passive and shape their behavior through positive or negative reinforcement and punishment (Slavin, 2006). This style promotes a clientele or patronage type of supervision, where supervisors act more as "sage on the stage" rather than a facilitator of learning and research. Thus, the feedback that the supervision team provides to research students is based on the concept of rewards and reinforcements, which are more focused on the technical aspects of the research and the thesis production rather than on how the students are shaped (Zuber-Skerritt & Roche, 2004). However, the supervised student should have the opportunity to receive not only information on correct formats of presenting a thesis, but also information on what to research, how to

argue and arrive at the conclusions, and how to develop critical thinking skills (Deuchar, 2008).

We argue that pedagogical theories other than behaviorism might be more suitable to better assist academics to help their students to process and obtain knowledge and skills. For example, constructivism provides an account of how individual learners obtain knowledge through their interaction with the world. Constructivism advocates that learners learn better when given the opportunity to actively process their own knowledge through feedback by working in a more student-centered learning environment. The constructivism model comprises "cognitive constructivism" and "sociocultural constructivism". According to cognitive learning theories, the amount of supervision depends both on how academics present materials to students and on how the student processes the material (Quan-Baffour & Vambe, 2008). However, it seems that cognitive learning theories, in the cases of supervision and research, cannot fill the gap, which is coming from the social interactions and stressful situations (Mearns, 2009). In a socio-constructivism approach, learners share experiences and one helps the other to learn, so knowledge is essentially developed through social interactions. Collaborative Learning, which is a framework of constructivism, involves the mutual engagement of learners in a coordinated effort to solve a problem or to examine an issue all together. Thus, through the socio-constructivism process, teachers should treat students as learners capable of critically questioning dominant beliefs and mainly the teacher should focus on students' empowerment (Schulze, 2012). According to Biggs (1999), teaching and learning activities based on constructivism can be categorized as teacher-directed (e.g. by ensuring that a presentation is clear), peer-directed, and/or self-directed. Features for peer-directed teaching are:

- "Learning takes place in an active mode;
- The teacher is more a facilitator than "sage on the stage";

- Teaching and learning are shared experiences between teacher and student;
- Students participate in small-group activities;
- Students must take responsibility for learning;
- Discussing and articulating one's ideas enhances the ability to reflect on one's own assumptions and thought processes;
- Students develop social and team skills through the give-and-take of consensus-building; and
- Students experience diversity, which is essential in multicultural democracy". (Kirschner, 2001, pp. 4-5)

Community and Social Learning

Community-based learning is founded on socio-cultural and constructivist learning theories and is focused on the concept of communities such as communities of practice, communities of interest, learning communities and knowledge-building communities (Fischer, Rohde & Wulf, 2007). A community of practice has been defined as a "network of people who share a common interest in a specific area of knowledge and are willing to work and learn together over a period of time to develop and share knowledge" (Sobrero & Craycraft, 2008). A member of a community can act as a knowledge provider to others who act as knowledge recipients. (Kim, Song, and Jones, 2011). Knowledge could be transferred directly by communication between individuals or indirectly from a knowledge archive. Specifically, the way that the members of a community acquire knowledge and information can be through reading, sharing, observing, and experiencing. In addition community members should invest the optimal effort and time in order to obtain the specialized knowledge related to their task and/ or performance. According to social cognitive theories, there are natural tendencies of individuals to alter personal behaviors based on the observed

behavior of others. Learners' behavior is determined by the continuous, reciprocal interaction among behavioral, cognitive, and environmental factors (Bandura, 1986). Specifically, learners play a proactive role in a behavioral adaptation, rather than simply undergoing experiences in which environmental stressors act on their personal vulnerabilities (Bandura, 2001). The three models for learning through observation identified by Bandura are:

- A live model, which involves an actual individual demonstrating or acting out a behavior;
- A verbal instructional model, which involves descriptions and explanations of a behavior; and
- A symbolic model, which involves real or fictional characters displaying behaviors in books, films, television programs, or online media.

Following Bandura's model (2001), the four key elements, which play a significant role in whether social learning is successful or not, are:

- **Attention:** Anything that distracts learners' attention has negative effects on observational learning including distinctiveness, complexity, functional values and one's characteristics such as sensory capacities, perceptual set and past reinforcement;
- **Retention:** The ability to store information and to recall it later that includes symbolic coding, mental images, cognitive organization, symbolic rehearsal, motor rehearsal;
- **Reproduction:** When learners pay attention and retain the information, then they will perform the behavior that they observed, including physical capabilities and self-observation of reproduction; and
- **Motivation:** When learners have a good reason to imitate, including motives such as traditional behaviorism, imagined in-

centives, seeing, and recalling the reinforced model. Bandura (1995) identified the significant role that the internal reinforcements play in learning along with external reinforcement.

Virtual Community and Social Learning

Bandura has identified the outcome expectation and the self-efficacy as the major cognitive forces guiding behavior. For example, if individuals are not confident in their ability to share knowledge, then they are unlikely to perform the expected behavior, especially when knowledge sharing is voluntary (Bandura, 1982). In the case of virtual communities, the previous two cognitive forces, along with the key element of motivation, influence the members' behavior. Specifically, members of virtual communities differ from common Internet users, as these members are brought together by shared interests, goals, needs, or practices; therefore, the barriers of complex knowledge sharing process and extrinsic reward are overcome (Chiu, Hsu & Wang, 2006). Thus, their motivation in learning through Computer-Mediated Communication (CMC) is influenced by the flexible learning environments, learning resources, and active participation in the learning process. Technology can enable and facilitate the communication and transmission of information to the students by providing them with the opportunity to exchange knowledge and resources and to develop mutual understandings. Authentic learning resources can bring reality into the learning environment assisting the students to prepare themselves for real-life situations (Limniou et al., 2009). Additionally, a member's decision in a virtual community to either read or post messages is dependent on whether (s)he believes the benefits of such action outweigh the costs (Ren & Kraut, 2009).

Online support behaviors are associated with a greater Sense of Virtual Community and social connectivity that is related to the reduction of stress (McKenna & Green, 2002). Specifically, informational and socio-emotional support play a significant role for members of a community and are directly related to the motivations that users have in order to actively participate in a virtual community. Socio-emotional motivation refers to comfort, relationship with others, and/or other relationship benefits from online interactions, whilst informational motivation refers to advice, suggestions, and/or recommendations (Welbourne, Blanchard & Wadsworth, 2013). Overall, the Sense of Virtual Community reflects the feeling that individual members have of belonging to an online social group where the members will gain valuable knowledge and improve learning opportunities (cognitive expectations). Although members of virtual community have common interests in the content and the motivation for activity, negative rumors or messages are not easily replaced with positive messages, information, or rewards (Silius, Miilumaki, Huhtamaki, Tebest, Merilainen & Pohjolainen, 2010). Figure 1 illustrates a schematic virtual community Model of Research presenting a connection between social learning theories along with motivations. Through this model, research students could perceive a specific behavior or obtain skills under stressful situations or through interaction with others.

MAIN EMPHASIS OF THE CHAPTER

By following the above model, the authors will describe how a virtual community can be built up based on members' characteristics, technology choices, and University facilities. Additionally, they will provide examples from online discussions, identifying the benefits and the difficulties for the members.

Figure 1. Schematic of the virtual community model

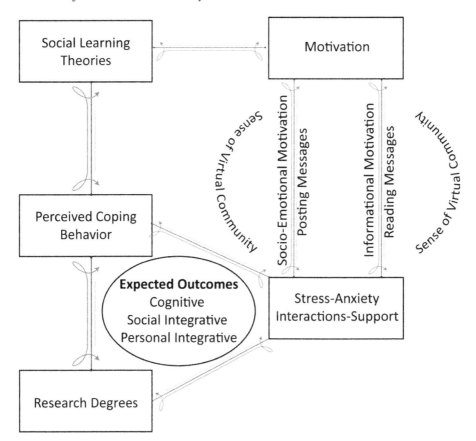

Members' Characteristics

In order to build up a virtual community for Research, we should study the potential members' background, experience and needs. In our case the potential members are university research students and staff. As in any United Kingdom University, Manchester Metropolitan University (MMU) has home (UK), European Union (EU) and overseas students who can follow a part- or full-time research degree course through either face-to-face or distance learning. In all cases, research students work closely with an appointed supervisory team that assists them to formulate their research topic and ensure that students are making progress towards completing the research on time. In each faculty, there are research administrators who provide advice and support to academics, students and applicants and help to organize events such as research symposiums/events for all the research staff and students. The Graduate School manages, monitors, and evaluates the research degrees across the University. It collaborates with research administrators, staff (internal and external), other offices/units that facilitate students' progress, enrolment, admissions, etc. and it is in a close collaboration with research students who are the key stakeholders. Additionally, during their studies, research students have access to a wide range of personal advisers, guidance, and support, including financial and careers advice, disability and counseling support. For example, librarians, technicians, and the international office all need to be in collaboration with the Graduate School in order to ensure that they provide focused and dedicated support to postgraduate research students.

One difficulty that MMU research students usually face in their research projects is the lack of communication between themselves and university staff. In addition, research students need to develop transferable skills such as time management, managing a research project, etc. during their studies. The social interactions between research students and University staff can be enhanced through virtual communities where, through virtual discussions (synchronous and/or asynchronous), research students could discuss issues related to their research with their peers and university research staff such as progression enquiries and research methodologies. In addition, students can find related documents, learning material, and useful external web links related to the research environment. Students could get information and feedback not only from their supervisory teams, but also from other non-academic staff, such as librarians, technicians, research administrators and their peers.

In order to assist research students to develop academic and vocational skills and lead on the governance of postgraduate research degrees in the University, the Graduate School delivers workshops following the Vitae's Researcher Development Framework. The student development program has been created to ensure that postgraduate research students gain transferable skills in addition to all the skills required to successfully manage their research. Some of the workshops that are offered to research students are related to the management of a research project, networking skills, thesis and publication formatting, Cite Rite™ with EndNote™, presentation skills, and qualitative and quantitative research methods. Due to the fact that by following the traditional way of teaching little motivation is given to students in order to solve problems or to collaborate with their peers during the workshop. Vitae recommends the adoption of blended learning activities in order to engage students in the learning process

(Vitae, 2013). In this way, students' motivation is enhanced, allowing teachers to meet students' needs. The activities could support either face-to-face and/or online modes. Figure 2 illustrates the role of the MMU Graduate School in Research.

Developing a Virtual Community

In order to build up a virtual community, key issues such as users' familiarity with ICT, University facilities and technological developments should be taken into account. MMU has recently adopted Moodle™ as a Virtual Learning Environment, and the university policy is that all courses/workshops should have a relevant virtual space. Thus, it is compulsory for university staff to embed Moodle™ into university activities. In each faculty, there is at least one assigned e-learning technologist in order to support teachers to use VLEs and other technologies in their teaching and to verify their content quality. Other Universities often provide similar e-learning support (Limniou & Smith, 2010). Overall, the majority of the university staff has some level of support on the use of VLEs in their teaching. The reasons that Universities follow the above strategy, i.e. to support the teaching staff via e-learning technologists, is because of university staff's lack of familiarity with the use of ICT, their individual workloads, the limitations of the technology in relation to particular tasks, the different way of communications (electronic medium communication vs face-to-face), the limited training, and the lack of a reliable infrastructure (Heaton-Shrestha, Edirisingha, Burke & Linsey, 2005). Even though not all university staff are ultimately persuaded that VLEs could enhance their teaching approach, the majority of research students have previous experience on different VLE platforms and/or on social media. Specifically, regarding their familiarity with new technologies and the use of social media, 85% of research students (strongly) agreed that they have familiarity with new technologies and approximately 72% of them use social

Figure 2. Schematic model for the role of the graduate school in research

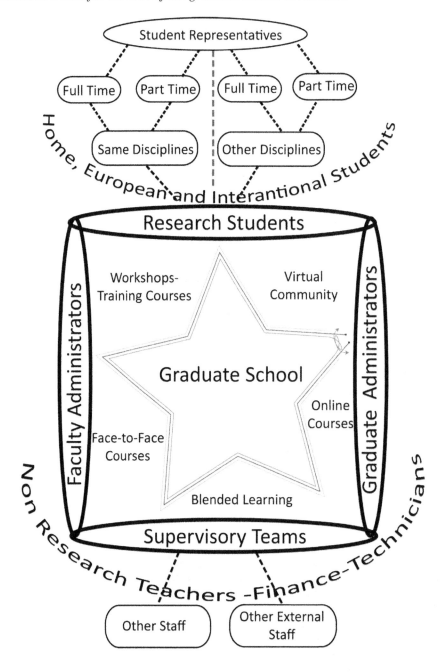

media in their everyday life. Taking into account university staff and research students' previous experiences of new educational technologies, the use of social media and the facilities and support that the University offers, the Graduate School has built up a virtual community on Moodle™ and supplements it with a closed Facebook™ group and a Twitter™ account. Some of Moodle™'s benefits, for educational purposes, are the low cost of ownership, the high level of security, technical support, constant updates, and plug-ins. Also, the source code is available along with the ability for customization.

In the Moodle™ Research Students Community, all the members can discuss issues related to research and workshops. Students and staff with a Facebook™ account can also participate in open discussion related to research and/or to post messages, web links, files, etc. to a closed Facebook™ group through a flexible social network system. Apart from online discussions, workshops are supported by e-assignments, where research students can upload their workshop activities and the tutors can provide them with online feedback. Additionally, by creating a Twitter™ account for Postgraduate Students, the MMU research community can communicate with other intuitions, organizations, and individual Twitter™ users by disseminating information to internal or external researchers on MMU research projects and events, recruiting people for research projects, re-tweeting interesting tweets from other users, and creating a Twitter™ *#hashtag* to provide a means of grouping messages and discussions.

Structure and Promotion of Virtual Community across the University

Initially, all the university staff who participated in the virtual community were informed of the strategy of this initiative and were asked to contribute with relevant research material that they usually used in their workshops or in their supervision. Before launching the virtual community for Research to all the members, key stakeholders (such as librarians, research administrators, research staff and a few of our research students) provided feedback. One major difficulty that the developers had was to design and build a virtual Research Students Community to cover the needs and expectations of all the stakeholders. This virtual group was a heterogeneous mix of people, with mixed familiarity with educational technology and different ages, ethnicities, etc. An additional difficulty was that Moodle™ might be challenging for some users, although it provides an easy way

for academics to present the materials to students, the material can be displayed on the page either as individual items or as items bundled together inside folders. As a result, the entire Moodle™ page can be quite long and course instructors need to spend some time in creating a more user-friendly learning environment. Thus, in order to make the Moodle™ virtual community more user-friendly, the developers created an interactive image in which each section was illustrated. When members of the community enter the Research Students Community, an interactive image was the first item of the virtual community (Figure 3). The users could then click on the circle near to each section and be re-directed to the appropriate section quickly.

In the Induction section of the Moodle™ area, the members of the community could find information for the Induction Day, the only workshop that is compulsory for all the first year research students. Under this section, the virtual members had the opportunity to participate in discussion forums. There was general discussion forum, where all the participants of the Moodle™ space could post messages and discussion forums for specific target groups, for example, forums for faculty, forum for research administrators only, and forum only for student representatives. The Graduate School's policy was for the recently uploaded material to stay in the section entitled *New Material* for one month and then to be placed in the appropriate section. All the information and material regarding the University regulations, student handbook, student journeys, documents for Ethical approval and articles for research such as the role of supervisor, literature review for a thesis, etc. were placed under the section *Resources*. All the relevant information for the University Library (facilities, services and staff) and material for the workshops, such as Cite Right™ with EndNote™, Cited Reference Searching on the Web Science and Scopus™, which librarians delivered to research students, were under the section *Library Services*.

Figure 3. A representation of the sections in the Moodle™ virtual community

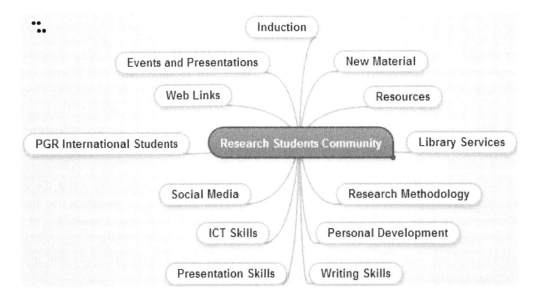

A discussion forum was available in this section providing an opportunity for research students and staff to clarify any issues related to Library services. Under the *section Research Methodology* virtual members could find information regarding a commitment to good research conduct and the relevant workshops which were delivered by the Graduate School such as Quantitative and Qualitative Research Methods. Information about relevant workshops such as Time Management, Team Work, Manage Your Research Project and Critical, Thinking, Reading and Writing, along with group discussions and assignments for research students could be found under the section *Personal Development*. The MMU Research Students Community also contained sections on:

- Writing Skills, where information could be found for plagiarism and copyright issues along with workshop material for writing skills and writing proposals;
- Presentation Skills, where material for the workshop on how research students could improve their presentation skills;
- ICT Skills, where students could find material for specific software such as ad-vanced Microsoft Word, SPSS, etc. along with online assignments and discussion forums; and
- Social Media, discussions and workshops for making research available to other researchers inside and outside the University, for exploring online social media and research networking platforms in order for research students to interact and communicate with other researchers developing networking skills.

Under the section *PGR International Students*, information provided by the International Office were delivered to our international research students along with an appropriate discussion forum for them. Finally, the last sections were designed in order to provide recommended external links to virtual members for further considerations/ reading (Web Links) and to encourage research students' efforts to organize events and actions across the University (Events and Presentations).

In our closed Facebook™ group for researchers, virtual members could upload external web links, documents, and files related to research and invite other members to share their views on the specific digital element that they uploaded. This process was equivalent to asking for an opinion in a face-to-face meeting and it was also an ideal mechanism for promoting internal and external events to the student community. The open discussion that then took place was very useful for educational purposes, as just-in-time information was crucial in the learning process. The other use of the closed Facebook™ group was to take external links that research students and staff thought were valuable for their study and put them in the Moodle™ virtual community, as not all the members wished to be part of the Facebook™ group. In a closed Facebook™ group, anyone could see the members of the group, but only members could see posts, which provided more privacy. In addition, in order to confirm that the Facebook™ user who wanted to join our group was an MMU research student, we checked the Student Record system of the University. In the case that a Facebook™ user had a fake account, the group administrator sent him/her a personal message through Facebook™ asking for more details (his/her name and in which Faculty (s) he is studying for, etc.) to confirm his/her details with the Student Record system.

In order to promote the virtual community across the University, the capabilities of the Moodle™ space, the closed Facebook™ group, and Twitter™ account were presented to first year postgraduate students during the compulsory Induction workshop. In addition, information was circulated through printed brochures, the Graduate School website, training courses (dedicated mainly for second-, third- and fourth-year research students and university staff) and via personal contact with all the potential virtual members.

Discussions in Virtual Communities

In a comparison to a face-to-face classroom contact, virtual interactions lack the social cues such as eye contact, gesture and other expressions. This can be viewed either positively or negatively. For example, females tend to use more emotions than males in a face-to-face interaction (Wolf, 2000), which through virtual discussions, is translated through the use of emotional icons and capital letters. On the other hand, through virtual communications social pressures are reduced, as the participants feel more comfortable (Gilmore & Warren, 2007). Additionally, through asynchronous communication every research student and/or staff member in the virtual community could potentially read and respond to other messages instantly, if these posts were relevant to their interest and/or research. Figure 4 illustrates an example from a research student who posted a message (asking for help) on a Saturday evening, and in a couple of hours other members of the community had sent other messages trying to assist her to resolve the problem. Specifically, they posted fifteen messages in less than 24 hours providing feedback to the initial question. One of the replies on the initial question recommended to the student to use EndNote. While this recommendation did not apply to the student that started the discussion it seemed to apply to another student who was trying to use EndNote but did not know how. Thus, the discussion continued based on one reply that was provided and so there were more than five messages under the same category *Reading log*. The point of this example was that, even if a research student did not start a discussion, (s)he could find the opportunity to ask other questions based on a given response. Overall, they exchanged twenty-two (22) messages on that particular question. The conclusion of the presented example is that an asynchronous discussion within virtual groups can enable multiple people to respond to a message thus increasing research students' motivation not only from an informational point of view but also from a social-emotional one as well.

We have observed that research students who were familiar with social media usually preferred to post messages via Facebook™ rather than via the Moodle™ Community. Figure 5 illustrates an example of an online discussion related to ethics.

Figure 4. Example for an asynchronous discussion with the Moodle™ community

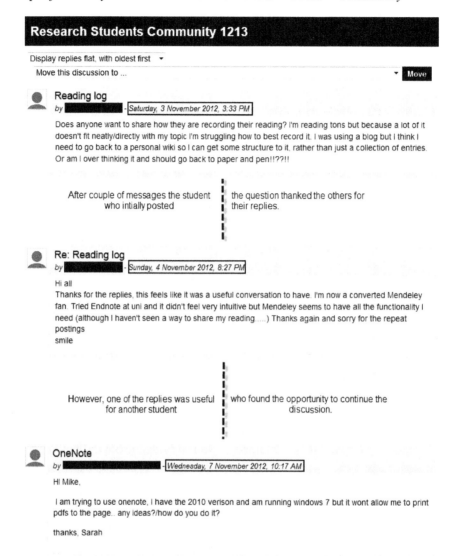

In the case of Facebook™, there were more posts than to Moodle™ Community; and as Facebook™ had the functionality of "Like", this acted as a sort of ranking system for the usefulness and/or the agreement with the specific post by other members. This capability is also present in Moodle™, in which course leaders have a tracking system, but they cannot tell if a specific post, document, resource is valuable for the members of the community. For that purpose, the Facebook™ group acted as a supplementary platform, in order to track posts and responses, and to meet the needs that the members had and what they expected from the community.

Generally, asynchronous communication allows research students to prepare their messages more carefully than in a face-to-face communication. Very often in synchronous communication, research students do not formulate their thoughts well enough through questions and answers, as they try to follow a conversation, which is relatively quick. An international research student, for example, who might struggle due to language barriers on a face-to-face discussion, by participating in an asynchronous virtual communication, might have a better chance of actively contributing in the discussion and might have a better understanding of the message by re-reading it.

Another issue regarding the virtual community was that occasionally members complained about posts because they did not think that were

relevant to their interest. On several occasions, disapproving posts discouraged other members of the community from participating in that particular discussion. For example, as briefly illustrated in Figure 6 below, a member of the Facebook™ group posted an external link that he found useful for his research. However, another member stated that (s)he found the topic and/or the discussions boring or annoying. In this particular occasion, a

Figure 5. Example for an asynchronous discussion in the virtual community's closed Facebook™ group

Figure 6. Someone posted an external link, someone else complained and another replied

student replied and, in effect, isolated the negative comment, and the members continued to post messages, external files, and websites. Negative comments such as the one below might discourage students from continuing posting on the topic and, thus, a potentially constructive discussion might end prematurely.

On the other hand, in the Moodle™ community, when a member did not think that (s)he could contribute more to the discussion or did not wish to follow the discussion anymore, (s)he sent a direct message to the course leader or to the member that initially started the discussion asking to be unsubscribed from the specific discussion. These two different behaviors were mainly because of the difference between social media and Moodle™. In Facebook™ the users knew that they could put items on the Group wall, which is common practice in Facebook™, and also there was no reason to complain as it was their choice to be a member of the Facebook™ group. In the Moodle™, all

research students and staff were provided with access to the Research Students Community following the University policy. They were given the opportunity to unsubscribe themselves in the case that they wished to leave a discussion. In addition, in the Moodle™ community, the members could configure their profile settings and they had three options: (a) to receive e-mails for each discussion post; (b) to receive only one e-mail at the end of the day which would include a digest of all the posts; or (c). to receive a daily e-mail per specific discussion topic.

Engagement in Virtual Community

Apart from uploading e-material for the workshops through the research community, students had the opportunity to facilitate their learning process based on their learning style, characteristics, and the nature of the cognitive topic by participating in online activities and receiving feedback based on their discussion posts and/or formative assignments. The degree of integration of conventional (face-to-face) teaching with computer-based activities (blended learning) varied between the workshops. Figure 7 demonstrates an example of blended learning for the workshop entitled *Thesis and Publication Formatting* which combines online activities along with activities in a computer cluster. Initially, students should have read the handouts and participated in a couple of activities. Through the online discussion forum, the students received feedback by their peers/tutors based on these initial online activities. By using the online assignment tool, the research students could upload the activities before the face-to-face

workshop. Thus, the teachers could easily discover their students' backgrounds; they could make the appropriate changes to e-material and/or change the way that they delivered their workshop. A self-paced online session, in which the research students were able to review concepts and fill the gaps between theory and practical work, built up their confidence before they entered the face-to-face session, strengthening their motivation for learning. The workshops also provided students with the opportunity to meet other research students and academic and administrative staff from across the University, thus enhancing the sense of community.

Figure 7. A blended learning example of research students community in Moodle™

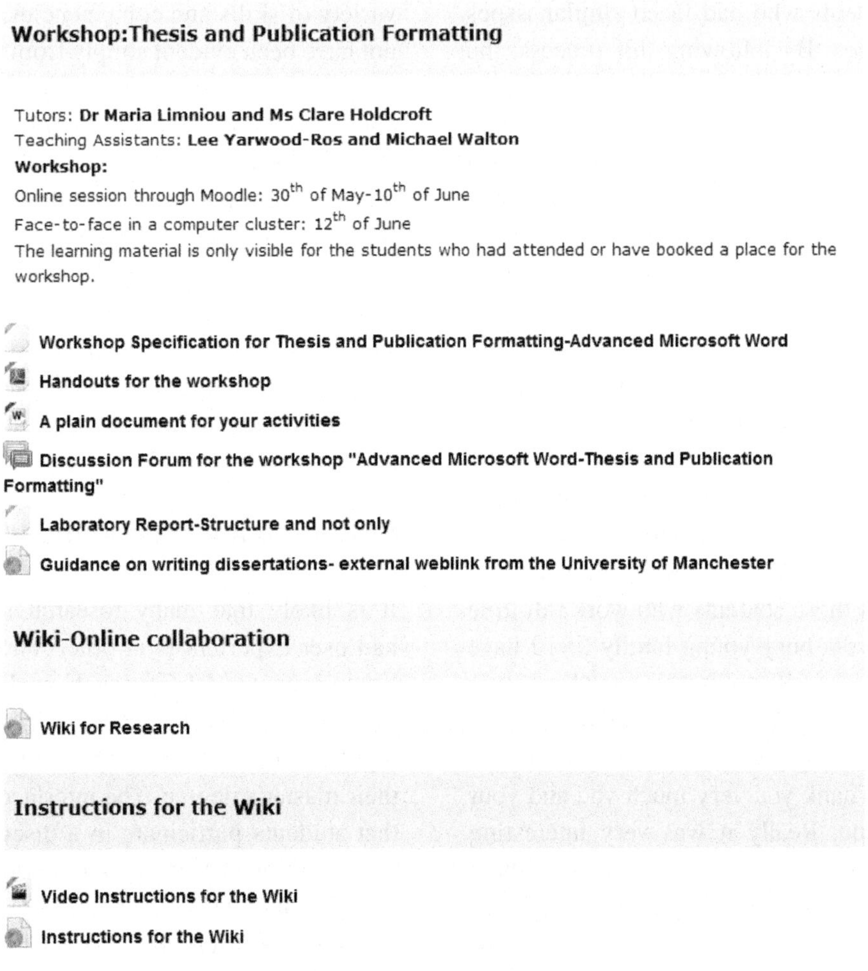

Workshop:Thesis and Publication Formatting

Tutors: **Dr Maria Limniou and Ms Clare Holdcroft**
Teaching Assistants: **Lee Yarwood-Ros and Michael Walton**
Workshop:
Online session through Moodle: 30th of May-10th of June
Face-to-face in a computer cluster: 12th of June
The learning material is only visible for the students who had attended or have booked a place for the workshop.

  Workshop Specification for Thesis and Publication Formatting-Advanced Microsoft Word

  Handouts for the workshop

  A plain document for your activities

  Discussion Forum for the workshop "Advanced Microsoft Word-Thesis and Publication Formatting"

  Laboratory Report-Structure and not only

  Guidance on writing dissertations- external weblink from the University of Manchester

Wiki-Online collaboration

  Wiki for Research

Instructions for the Wiki

  Video Instructions for the Wiki
  Instructions for the Wiki

In addition, in order to increase their sense of belonging in the community, students were provided with the opportunity to be involved in teaching a part of the workshop to their peers, thus they shared their experience and skills of a specific area with their peers. This policy aimed to encourage students to actively participate in the teaching and learning process and to develop skills such as presentation and writing skills. Overall, the research students produced high quality material, had a good attitude towards being of service to the University, and had the desire to learn and share with others. By involving them in the teaching process, they remained motivated and they exhibited self-confidence. Students became engaged; and they reflected learning by real world examples through their participation, while at the same time their peers had examples from other research students who had faced similar issues and difficulties. By following this process, the workshops were conducted in a collaborative environment. In addition, the research students that participated actively in the workshops gained experience as presenters, which will be valuable for them in the future. Some of students' feedback for the workshop *Thesis and Publication Formatting* is the following:

Student 1: I thought I knew quite a lot about Word, but this course has shown me some very useful techniques that will enhance my finished thesis and making [sig.] formatting the document soooooo much easier. A very well presented and run course, that takes into account those students who work full time and have a busy young family life. I have been able, easily, to fit this around my other commitments! Very forward thinking, please please please more like this, well done!!!

Student 2: Thank you very much you and your colleague. Really it was very interesting workshop I wish we could get some of them in near future. Personally I got lot of things I did not know it [sig.] before it really helps

me to organise some of my work. Thank you once again.

Student 3: I thought workshop worked well and liked the individual and group balance. One thing I really liked was the content of the session, the Moodle™ information and the practical work. The administration of the workshop was very professional but very warm and friendly simultaneously.

Student 4: It was really useful - a whole new world of what Word can do!

One challenge that the Graduate School faced was that some of the research students believed that they knew the topics and that the workshops did not have something new to offer them. The reality, however, was far different, as the workshops were very in-depth and offered students a wide variety of skills and competencies, which might not have been evident simply from the workshop title. In order to overcome this difficulty, and to engage students with the learning process, the Graduate School created a standard template for the workshop specification in which the research students could be informed in more detail of the learning outcomes, the activities, and the aim and the objectives of the workshops. By creating such a template, the student could make a more informed decision as to whether or not to attend the workshop and if (s)he would gain new knowledge and experience from it.

Solutions and Recommendations

It is likely that many research students have had user experiences in other Virtual Learning Environments (VLEs), such as BlackBoard®, BlackBoard Vista® and WebCT®, gained during their undergraduate studies or while earning their master's degree. The interface and the way that students participate in a discussion on the aforementioned VLE are slightly different from that of Moodle™. For example, in BlackBoard®, the users need to check the posts without receiving e-mails, but they should enter the online module and search under the module's discussion forums. In the case of Moodle™, the default option is for users to receive e-mail alerts for each post. Therefore, research students, who are unfamiliar with the Moodle™ environment, might complain about the vast number of e-mails that they receive and are, overall, reluctant to use it. In order to tackle this issue, the course leader needs to provide students with a step-by-step instruction booklet where some useful tips on how to configure Moodle™ will be illustrated.

Another issue that needed careful consideration was the university staff's familiarity with the Virtual Learning Environment. In our case, the Graduate School informed the university staff that their role in the Virtual Community would be that of a non-editing teacher. However, later throughout the academic year, many University staff started to complain that they received e-mails from the discussion posts even if they were not in the discussion group. That meant that they did not have a clear idea as to what the role of non-editing teacher entailed in Moodle™. Thus, although the role of the course leaders was not to support the university staff with tutorials and advice as to the role of non-editing teacher, they had to organize dedicated training courses and create supporting documentation to bring the university staff up to speed with the functionalities in Moodle™ that staff should have already been aware of. Another issue related to teachers was that some of them had the misunderstanding that their role in regards to the online course finished upon uploading the learning material. However, the role of teachers in facilitating discussion forums should be more than that of a mere provider of materials. The problem with this simplistic approach was that the teacher lost the continuous communication with students who eventually felt frustrated by the learning process. For that purpose, the course leaders checked regularly the discussion forums in Moodle™ and/or Facebook™ and if they could not respond directly to students' questions, they

forwarded it to the appropriate person and/or encouraged other academics to provide an answer within the discussion forum. University staff are not always aware of technical and pedagogical issues related to virtual communities, the benefits of synchronous and asynchronous communication, and students' preferences for the new technological developments. Thus, apart from the existence of support via e-learning teams, universities are usually training new incoming academics on designing online courses and/or adopting blended learning. In our case, academics worked together in order to enhance teaching with the opportunities of blended learning, the new staff being more familiar with computer information technologies, whereas the senior staff had more experience on research related issues.

Another issue that the authors would like to mention is that some members of the community felt uncomfortable to post messages. There were a few examples where research students, despite the fact that they had access to Moodle™, were afraid to ask a question and they approached their Faculty administrator in order for them to post a question on their behalf. We assumed that the reason for this attitude was mainly that these students were afraid that their question would be deemed to be too simple and as such they would appear ignorant on the subject to their peers. As an example, this question was posted by a research administrator instead of the research student:

There is a question from a research student and we are wondering if you have similar issues or if you have any possible reply. The question: I'm planning a survey for part of my research and wondered if I could have access to a survey tool for collecting data online- does the university subscribe to Survey Monkey or anything similar and how would I get access to it?

In order to enhance the sense of community, and the relationships between university staff and research students, the Graduate School is organizing periodic face-to-face meetings and events in addition to workshops in order to keep the community focused and productive.

FUTURE RESEARCH DIRECTIONS

As the extensive use of ICT in Higher Education has changed the way that students, teachers, and other university staff communicate, one future step is for research students to create their own e-portfolio through their studies. By following this approach, supervision teams, along with research administrators, will have a complete view of the student's progress; individual feedback could be provided on students' projects and their personal development. E-portfolios could initially be restricted to private view and only university staff or other students would have access; but, after finishing their studies; the research students may make them available for public view. Overall, the e-portfolios could enhance the digital demands of research and they could be created by using platforms such as WordPress™ and/or Blogger™.

CONCLUSION

Over the last decades, the rapid growth of Internet access and Computer-Mediated Communication has created new possibilities for researchers to engage in supportive communication with a network of individuals coping with similar issues and challenges. The ability of Computer-Mediated Communication to transcend geographical and temporal constraints, the access to diverse sources, and the facilitation of more heterogeneous supportive relationships are possible through a virtual Research Students Community. University staff can collaborate with students in a flexible digital environment and consciously empower them. Research students could also exchange views and resources with their peers obtaining skills and knowledge and developing attitudes through col-

laboration. Research students will have a stronger sense of community compared with a traditional research environment, as they:

- Know who is the most appropriate person to assist them;
- Share their experience with other members of the community and are informed about other's views; and
- Are better supported in order to overcome their research project difficulties.

The Internet, as a medium for social activities, opens up entirely new features in academic society. However, academics should understand how people learn and how people can be facilitated to learn through ICT in order to create a pedagogically worthwhile virtual course/community. Socio-emotional and informational motivations mainly lead research students to be involved in a virtual community in order to discuss with others and/or collect information about common interests. The research students can discuss with the University staff and their peers, theory related to their research project through online discussion forums; or they can collect information independently by reading the uploaded material and others' messages to discussion forums or by searching on the uploaded web links available to them. Thus, research students do not have their supervisory teams as the only resource for collecting information. One issue for course leaders, however, is to keep students engaged in the process and to continue to pose questions, exchange views and ideas with the members of the community. The university staff have a significant role for students' involvement in a virtual community. They trigger a discussion, adopting an active and stimulating role by posing questions without being the direct provider for the research students' learning, or by posting external web links and/or documents. In a collaborative learning environment, the teaching style is changing from a directive and task-oriented (power-centered) supervision to a more non-directive and process-oriented (facilitation-centered) supervision. However, staff's beliefs, attitudes, and skills are potential points for a successful integration of virtual communities into research degree programs. University members have their own personal style regarding the way that they handle problem identification and solving, feedback, and support given to students, the way that they act as subject experts, and the way that they evaluate and respond to the students' work. The transition from traditional teaching to ICT-enhanced environments is not obvious and many staff are still hesitant or reluctant to adopt technology as part of their teaching. Thus, the participation of new staff along with senior lecturers would be beneficial for their active contribution to discussion forums, the enhancement of teaching with blended learning principles and their experience to overcome course difficulties.

REFERENCES

Ali, A., & Kohun, F. (2006). Dealing with isolation feelings in IS doctoral programs. *International Journal of Doctoral Studies*, *1*, 21–33.

Bandura, A. (1982). Self-efficacy mechanism in human agency. *The American Psychologist*, *37*(2), 122–147. doi:10.1037/0003-066X.37.2.122

Bandura, A. (1986). *Social foundations of thought and action: A social cognitive theory*. Englewood, NJ: Prentice-Hall.

Bandura, A. (1995). Comments on the crusade against the causal efficacy of human thought. *Journal of Behavior Therapy and Experimental Psychiatry*, *26*(3), 179–190. doi:10.1016/0005-7916(95)00034-W PMID:8576397

Bandura, A. (2001). Social cognitive theory: An agentic perspective. *Annual Review of Psychology*, *52*(1), 1–26. doi:10.1146/annurev.psych.52.1.1 PMID:11148297

Beye, M., Jeckmans, A., Erkin, Z., Hartel, P., Lagendijk, R., & Tang, Q. (2010). *Literature overview privacy in online social networks* (Technical Report TR-CTIT-10-36). Centre for Telematics and Information Technology University of Twente, Enschede. Retrieved from http://eprints.eemcs.utwente.nl/18648/

Biggs, J. (1999). *Teaching for quality learning at university*. Buckingham, UK: SRHE and Open University Press.

Blanchard, A. (2004). Virtual behavior settings: An application of behavior setting theories to virtual communities. *Journal of Computer-Mediated Communication*, *9*(2). Retrieved from http://jcmc.indiana.edu/vol9/issue2/blanchard.html

Blas, T. M., & Serrano-Fernández, A. (2009). The role of new technologies in the learning process: Moodle™ as a teaching tool in Physics. *Computers & Education*, *55*(1), 35–44. doi:10.1016/j.compedu.2008.06.005

Bliuc, A. M., Goodyear, P., & Ellis, R. (2007). Research focus and methodological choices in studies into students' experiences of blended learning in higher education. *The Internet and Higher Education*, *10*(4), 231–244. doi:10.1016/j.iheduc.2007.08.001

Chiu, C. M., Hsu, M. H., & Wang, E. T. G. (2006). Understanding knowledge sharing in virtual communities: An integration of social capital and social cognitive theories. *Decision Support Systems*, *42*(3), 1872–1888. doi:10.1016/j.dss.2006.04.001

Collis, B., & Moonen, J. (2008). Web 2.0 tools and processes in higher education: Quality perspectives. *Educational Media International*, *45*(2), 93–106. doi:10.1080/09523980802107179

De Moor, A., & Weigand, H. (2007). Formalizing the evolution of virtual communities. *Information Systems*, *32*(2), 223–247. doi:10.1016/j.is.2005.09.002

Deuchar, R. (2008). Facilitator, director or critical friend? Contradiction and congruence in doctoral supervision styles. *Teaching in Higher Education*, *13*(4), 489–500. doi:10.1080/13562510802193905

Driscoll, M. (2002). Blended Learning: let's get beyond the hype. *E-learning*. Retrieved from http://elerningmag.com/Itimagazine

Farzan, R., Dabbish, L. A., Kraut, R. E., & Postmes, T. (2011). Increasing commitment to online communities by designing for social presence. In *Proceedings of the ACM 2011 Conference on Computer Supported Cooperative Work*. New York, NY: Association for Computing Machinery. doi:10.1145/1958824.1958874

Fischer, G., Rohde, M., & Wulf, V. (2007). Community-based learning: The core competency of residential, research-based universities. *Computer-Supported Collaborative Learning*, *2*(1), 9–40.

Gilmore, S., & Warren, S. (2007). Themed article: Emotion online: Experiences of teaching in a virtual learning environment. *Human Relations*, *60*(4), 581–608. doi:10.1177/0018726707078351

Heath, T. (2002). A quantitative analysis of PhD students' views of supervision. *Higher Education Research & Development*, *21*(1), 41–53. doi:10.1080/07294360220124648

Heaton-Shrestha, C., Edirisingha, P., Burke, L., & Linsey, T. (2005). Introducing a VLE into campus-based undergraduate teaching: Staff perspectives on its impact on teaching. *International Journal of Educational Research*, *43*(6), 370–386. doi:10.1016/j.ijer.2006.07.001

Hodsdon, L., & Buckley, A. (2011). *Postgraduate research and experience survey. The Higher Education Academy.*

Kim, J., Song, J., & Jones, D. R. (2011). The cognitive selection framework for knowledge acquisition strategies in virtual communities. *International Journal of Information Management*, *31*(2), 111–120. doi:10.1016/j.ijinfomgt.2010.05.011

Kirschner, P. A. (2001). Using integrated electronic environments for collaborative teaching/learning. *Research Dialogue in Learning and Instruction*, *2*, 1–9. doi:10.1016/S0959-4752(00)00021-9

Koh, J., & Kim, Y.-G. (2004). Knowledge sharing in virtual communities: An e-business perspective. *Expert Systems with Applications*, *26*(2), 155–166. doi:10.1016/S0957-4174(03)00116-7

Kolbitsch, J., & Maurer, H. (2006). The transformation of the web: How emerging communities shape the information we consume. *Journal of Universal Computer Science*, *12*(2), 187–213.

Lee, S. L., Vogel, D., & Limayem, M. (2002). Virtual community informatics: what we know and what we need to know? In R. H. Sprague (Ed.), In *Proceedings of the 35th Hawaii International Conference on System Sciences*. Los Alamitos, CA: Institute of Electrical and Electronics Engineers Computer Society Press. doi:10.1109/HICSS.2002.994248

Limniou, M. (2012). From present to virtual classroom: A review of the influence of ICT on education. In S. Abramovich (Ed.), *Computers in Education* (pp. 93–119). New York, NY: NOVA Science Publishers.

Limniou, M., & Papadopoulos, N. (2011). Teaching strategies and procedures in chemical education based on blended Learning. In J. P. Henderson & A. D. Lawrence (Eds), Teaching Strategies, 81-111. New York, NY: NOVA Science Publishers.

Limniou, M., Papadopoulos, N., & Kozaris, I. (2009). The role of simulations and real-time applications in collaborative learning. In E. Luzzatto & G. DiMarco (Eds.), *Collaborative learning: methodology, types of interactions and techniques* (pp. 225–255). New York, NY: NOVA Publishers.

Limniou, M., & Smith, M. (2010). Teachers' and students' perspectives on teaching and learning through virtual learning environments. *European Journal of Engineering Education, 35*(6), 645–653. doi:10.1080/03043797.2010.505279

McKenna, K., & Green, A. (2002). Virtual group dynamics. *Group Dynamics, 6*(1), 116–127. doi:10.1037/1089-2699.6.1.116

Mearns, J. (2009). Social learning theory. In H. Reis & S. Sprecher (Eds.), *Encyclopedia of Human Relationships* (Vol. 3, pp. 1537–1540). Thousand Oaks, CA: Sage. doi:10.4135/9781412958479.n506

Ngai, E. W. T., Poon, J. K. L., & Chan, Y. H. C. (2007). Empirical examination of the adoption of WebCT using TAM. *Computers & Education, 48*(2), 250–267. doi:10.1016/j.compedu.2004.11.007

Oblinger, D. G., & Oblinger, J. L. (2005). *Educating the net generation*. Retrieved from http://www.educause.edu/ir/library/pdf/pub7101.pdf

Panciera, K., Halfaker, A., & Terveen, L. (2009). Wikipedians are born, not made: a study of power editors on Wikipedia. In *Proceedings of the ACM Special Interest Group on Computer-Human Interaction*. New York, NY: Association for Computing Machinery. doi:10.1145/1531674.1531682

Ponte, D., & Simon, J. (2011). Scholarly communication 2.0: Exploring researchers' opinions on Web 2.0 for scientific knowledge creation, evaluation and dissemination. *Serials Review, 37*(3), 149–156. doi:10.1080/00987913.2011.10765376

Protivnak, J. J., & Foss, L. L. (2009). An exploration of themes that influence the counselor education doctoral student experience. *Counselor Education and Supervision, 48*(4), 239–256. doi:10.1002/j.1556-6978.2009.tb00078.x

Quan-Baffour, K. P. & Vambe, M. T. (2008). Critical issues in the supervision of post-graduate dissertations in distance education environments. *The Journal for Open and Distance Education and Educational Technology, 4*(1).

Ren, Y., & Kraut, R. E. (2009). A simulation for designing online community: Member motivation, contribution, and discussion moderation. *Organization Studies, 28*(3), 377–408.

Research Excellent Framework (REF). (2011). *Assessment framework and guidance submissions*. Retrieved from: http://www.ref.ac.uk/media/ref/content/pub/assessmentframeworkandguidanceonsubmissions/GOS including addendum.pdf

Schulze, S. (2012). Empowering and disempowering students in student-supervisor relationships, *Koers-Bulletin for Christian Scholarship, 77*(2). Retrieved from http://koersjournal.org.za/index.php/koers/article/view/47/560

Shang, S. S. C., Li, E. Y., Wu, Y. L., & Hou, O. C. L. (2011). Understanding Web 2.0 service models: A knowledge-creating perspective. *Information & Management, 48*(4-5), 178–184. doi:10.1016/j.im.2011.01.005

Silius, K., Miilumaki, T., Huhtamaki, J., Tebest, T., Merilainen, J., & Pohjolainen, S. (2010). Students' motivations for social media enhanced studying and learning. *Knowledge Management & E-Learning: An International Journal, 2*(1), 51–67.

Slavin, R. E. (2006). *Educational psychology: Theory and practice*. New York: Pearson Publishing Ltd.

Sobrero, P. M., & Craycraft, C. G. (2008). Virtual communities of practice: A 21st century method for learning, programming, and developing professionally. *Journal of Extension*, *46*(5). Retrieved from http://www.joe.org/joe/2008october/a1.php

Vitae. (2013). *Vitae Researcher Development Framework*. Retrieved http://www.vitae.ac.uk/researchers/428241/Vitae-Researcher-Development-Framework.html

Watts, J. H. (2008). Challenges of supervising part-time PhD students: Towards student-centred practice. *Teaching in Higher Education*, *13*(3), 369–373. doi:10.1080/13562510802045402

Welbourne, J. L., Blanchard, A. L., & Wadsworth, M. B. (2013). Motivations in health communities and their relationship to community, connectedness and stress. *Computers in Human Behavior*, *29*(1), 129–139. doi:10.1016/j.chb.2012.07.024

Wolf, A. (2000). Emotional expression online: Gender differences in emoticon use. *Cyberpsychology & Behavior*, *3*(5), 827–833. doi:10.1089/10949310050191809

Zuber-Skerritt, O., & Roche, V. (2004). A constructivist model for evaluating postgraduate supervision: A case study. *Quality Assurance in Education*, *12*(2), 82–93. doi:10.1108/09684880410536459

ADDITIONAL READING

Anderson, P. (2007). What is Web 2.0? Ideas, technologies and implications for education: a report for JISC Technology and Standards Watch. Retrieved from http://www.jisc.ac.uk/media/documents/techwatch/tsw0701b.pdf

Anderson, S. (2011). The twitter toolbox for educators. *Teacher Librarian*, *39*(1), 27–30.

Armstrong, J., Franklin, T., McLoughlin, C., Westera, W., Schmidt, S., Kelly, B., & Marwick, A. E. (2008). A review of current and developing international practice in the use of social networking (Web 2.0) in higher education. Retrieved from http://dspace.ou.nl/bitstream/1820/1930/1/the%20use%20of%20social%20networking%20in%20HE.pdf

Bellarby, L., & Orange, G. (2006). Knowledge sharing through communities of practice in the voluntary sector. In E. Coakes & S. Clarke (Eds.), Encyclopedia of communities of practice in information and knowledge management. Hershey, PA: Idea Group.

Blanch, K. (2013). Identity, Facebook and education: Students negotiating identity on a class' Facebook page. Retrieved from http://otago.ourarchive.ac.nz/bitstream/handle /10523/4092/BlanchKeelyF2013MA.pdf?sequence=1

Blanchard, A. (2007). Developing a sense of virtual community measure. *Cyberpsychology & Behavior*, *10*(6), 827–830. doi:10.1089/cpb.2007.9946 PMID:18085972

Bradshow, P. (2008, February 15). Teaching students to twitter: The good, the bad and the ugly. Retrieved from http://onlinejournalismblog.com/2007/02/15/teachingstudentstotwitter the-goodthebadandtheugly/

Cadman, K., & Ha, H. T. (2001). Only connect: Transactional supervision as the "rainbow bridge". In A. Bartlett & G. Mercer (Eds.), *Postgraduate research supervision: Transforming (R)elations* (pp. 215–232). New York, NY: Peter Lang.

Cobb, S. C. (2009). Social presence and online learning: A current view from a research perspective. *Journal of Interactive Online Learning, 8*(3), 241–254. Retrieved from http://anitacrawley.net/ Articles/Social%20Presence%20and%20Online%20Learning%20A%20Current%20View%20 from%20a%20Research.pdf

Dunlap, J. C., & Lowenthal, P. R. (2009). Tweeting the night away: Using Twitter to enhance social presence. *Journal of Information Systems Education, 20*(2), 129–136.

Epp, E. M., Green, K. F., Rahman, A. M., & Weaver, C. G. (2010). Analysis of student-instructor interaction patterns in real-time, scientific online discourse. *Journal of Science Education and Technology, 19*(1), 49-57. doi: 10.1007/s10956-009-9177-z

Hsu, P.-L., & Yen, Y.-H. (2012). Facebook as a teaching enhancement tool to facilitate college student learning: A case study. In *Proceedings of the 11th WSEAS International Conference on Education and Educational Technology (EDU '12)*. Montreux, Switzerland: World Scientific and Engineering Academy and Society Press.

Kraska, M. (2008). Retention of graduate students through learning communities. *Journal of Industrial Teacher Education, 45*(2), 45–70.

Pemberton, J., & Mavin, S. (2007). CoPs: One size fits all. *The International Journal of Knowledge and Organizational Learning Management, 14*(1), 1–3.

Research Excellent Framework (REF). (2011). Assessment framework and guidance submissions. Retrieved from: http://www.ref.ac.uk/media/ref/content/pub/assessmentframeworkandguidanceonsubmissions/GOS including addendum.pdf

Wellman, B., & Gulia, M. (1999). Net surfers don't ride alone: virtual communities as communities. In P. Kollock & M. Smith (Eds.), *Communities in cyberspace* (pp. 331–367). Berkley, CA: University of California Press.

Wenger, E. (1998). Communities of practice: Learning as a social system. *System Thinker.* Retrieved from http://www.co-i-l.com/coil/knowledge-garden/cop/lss.shtml

Wenger, E., McDermott, R. A., & Snyder, W. M. (2002). *Cultivating communities of practice: A guide to managing knowledge.* Boston, MA: Harvard Business School Press.

Wenger, E., White, N., & Smith, J. D. (2009). Digital habitats: Stewarding technology for communities. Portland, OR: CPSquare.

Whittle, J. (1994). A model for the Management of Research degree supervision in a post-1987 university. In O. Zuber-Skerritt & Y. Ryan (Eds.), *Quality in Postgraduate Education* (pp. 38–50). London, U.K: Kogan Page.

Wright, T., & Cochrane, R. (2010). Factors influencing successful submissions of PhD Theses. *Studies in Higher Education, 25*(2), 181–195. doi:10.1080/713696139

Zhang, Y., Fan, Y., Wei, K. K., & Chen, H. (2010). Exploring the role of psychological safety in promoting the intention to continue sharing knowledge in virtual communities. *International Journal of Information Management, 30*(5), 425–436. doi:10.1016/j.ijinfomgt.2010.02.003

KEY TERMS AND DEFINITIONS

Blended Learning: A combination of different pedagogical theories in a face-to-face learning environment with or without technologically mediated interactions between students, teachers and learning resources.

Computer-Mediated Communication: Two or more individuals communicate via separate computers through the Internet or an intranet.

Research: The process of carrying out a systematic and scientific investigation and publishing accurate results.

Social Learning: Occurs when the learners' behavior is changing from the environment through the process of observational learning, i.e. by observing how other learners behave around them.

Social Media: Platforms based on the Web 2.0 technology that allows the sharing of ideas, information and documents among users.

Virtual Community: A group of individuals who share the same interests and interact without geographical limitations through a social network system.

Virtual Learning Environments: E-learning platforms where teachers and learners have access to learning material, assessments, discussions, chat, etc.

This work was previously published in Student-Teacher Interaction in Online Learning Environments edited by Robert D. Wright, pages 50-75, copyright year 2015 by Information Science Reference (an imprint of IGI Global).

Chapter 54

M–Learning in the Middle East:
The Case of Bahrain

Evangelia Marinakou
Royal University for Women, Bahrain

Charalampos Giousmpasoglou
Bahrain Polytechnic, Bahrain

ABSTRACT

The introduction of e-learning in higher education has brought radical changes in the way undergraduate and postgraduate programmes are designed and delivered. University students now have access to their courses anytime, anywhere, which makes e-learning and m-learning popular and fashionable among university students globally. Nevertheless, instructors are now challenged, as they have to adopt new pedagogies in learning and teaching. This chapter explores the adoption of m-learning at universities in the Kingdom of Bahrain, as well as the relevant current developments and challenges related to the major stakeholders (educators and students) in higher education. It mainly investigates the educators' views and perceptions of m-learning, as well as its future potential in higher education. Most of the educators use m-learning tools to some limited extent, and there is still opportunity to reach full integration with curriculum and the blended learning approach. Further, it is proposed that professional development should be provided to instructors to enable them to use the available new technologies in an appropriate and effective way.

INTRODUCTION

The rapid technological advancements in the context of globalization have changed our everyday lives at individual and societal level. Universities worldwide are among the first to embrace these changes and prepare their students with the appropriate tools to enter the 'real' world of work. Two decades ago the technological advancements

infiltrated the traditional classrooms with the introduction of e-learning. The extensive use of Information and Communication Technologies (ICTs) – especially the use of the Internet – revolutionized and changed for good the design and delivery of curricula in universities around the world. During the last decade, an unseen 'revolution' emerged from the introduction of e-learning and even more recently of m-learning tools in the

DOI: 10.4018/978-1-4666-8619-9.ch054

classroom. The magnitude of these information technology developments is still not very well understood, simply because practice has run well ahead theory. In addition, many argue that the m-learning community is still fragmented among the various stakeholders, with different national perspectives, differences between academia and industry, and between the school, higher education and lifelong learning sectors (Al Saadat, 2009). Whether one looks at this phenomenon of e-learning and m-learning as a fad, threat, or a solution to educators' problems in delivering mainstream learning in higher education (Peters, 2009), it is currently a hot issue that needs our attention.

The emergence of the World Wide Web supported the development and the popularity of e-learning (Peng, Su, Chou, & Tsai, 2009). In addition, mobile devices such as mobile phones, laptops have increased drastically and are widely used in e-learning (Iqbal & Qureshi, 2012; Koszalka & Ntloedibe-Kuswani, 2010). The use of e-learning in higher education has grown in the past two decades, transforming the nature of higher education, as the technologies are supplementing the course delivery (Bharuthram & Kies, 2013). There are ongoing debate and criticisms on using e-learning, nevertheless most of the literature has shown a positive impact of e-learning in educational contexts, as the drastic developments in technologies have produced a new revolution in education.

Nevertheless, most studies in e-learning and m-learning focus on its acceptance by students in developing countries (i.e. Rhema & Sztendur, 2013; Wang, 2011), on the challenges and opportunities from the adoption of e and m-learning, but very few focus on its acceptance by instructors or on their perceptions of m-learning and its future potential. Therefore, this chapter discusses the origins of m-learning, its pedagogical value and the current developments and challenges in higher education context; in addition, it presents the instructors' perceptions of m-learning in general

in the Middle East and more specifically in the Kingdom of Bahrain. The chapter is organized as follows: the first part provides a summary of the origins and concepts of e-learning and m-learning. The following section explores the opportunities and challenges from the use of m-learning in higher education, as well the instructors' perception and use of m-learning via the survey results. The final part discusses the current and future status of m-learning followed by the conclusions.

THE ORIGINS AND CONCEPTS OF E-LEARNING AND M-LEARNING

E-Learning in Higher Education

Despite the relative recent appearance in literature, the concept of e-learning has fueled a number of debates regarding its usefulness in higher education and more particular, in the development of learning and teaching strategies. The few theoretical models describing this concept are still not adequate to capture the dynamics of the e-learning and m-learning proliferation in universities globally. The growing body of literature is still too narrow and short-sighted to capture the changes that currently take place in higher education. Nevertheless, the future is here, at least from a technological perspective.

In fact, practice has understandably run well ahead of theory, and in some issues and approaches away from theory, for example, the use of virtual learning environments (VLEs) and the use of applications to support them in mobile devices. A VLE is a set of teaching and learning tools designed to enhance a student's learning experience by including computers and the Internet in the learning process (Demian & Morrice, 2012). The principal components of a VLE package include curriculum mapping (breaking curriculum into sections that can be assigned and assessed), student tracking, online support for both teacher and student, electronic communication (e-mail, threaded discussions, chat, Web publishing), and Internet links to outside curriculum resources. There are a number of commercial and customized VLE software packages available, including Blackboard, Moodle and WebCT. A quick search on the Internet reveals that commercial and customized VLEs have introduced e-learning and m-learning applications to allow ubiquitous access for users (i.e. http://www.blackboard.com/platforms/mobile/products/ mobile-learn. aspx). Big search engines for academic content also adopt and follow this trend (i.e. EBSCO, Science Direct, Emerald) as well as international publishers (i.e. Prentice Hall, McGraw Hill, Springer).

Another recent important development is the use of tablet PCs and e-books as integral parts of the m-learning pedagogy. The optimization of mobile devices such as smart phones, e-book readers and tablet PCs, in conjunction with the digitalization of university libraries currently based mainly on e-books in PDF format, has changed for good the way we perceive study in a university environment. The classic view of a university student spending valuable time in a campus library struggling to borrow the last short-loan copies of the books s/he needs, tends to be an image of the past: virtual or e-libraries allow university students access content and borrow e-books for literary anywhere, anytime they wish for. A recent study undertaken as part of the project of the Open University's Building Mobile Capacity initiative, provides strong indications that e-learning is here for good. Despite the various issues reported in this project, it was found that when combined synergistically, the functionality, portability and comprehensiveness of resources offered by e-books, Internet access and mobile group learning, together facilitate rich learning experiences for students (Smith & Kukulska-Hulme, 2012).

As it has been previously discussed, the availability of mobile and wireless devices enables different ways of course contents delivery in higher education. It has also changed the communication between the teacher and the learner, as teachers nowadays are confronted with digitally literate students. In addition, these devices have created learning opportunities different to those provided by e-learning (Peters, 2009). E-learning is also changing by providing instructors and students with a different educational environment that is enabled with the use of mobile devices such as PDAs, mobile phones and other. According to Sarrab, Al-Shihi, and Rehman (2013) e-learning offers two main facilities to improve the educational system. E-learning happens anywhere anytime where learning and educational activities are offered the individuals and groups the opportunity to work online or offline, synchronously and asynchronously via networked or standalone computers and other mobile devices. The main drawback of e-learning according to Sarrab et al. (2013) is that it is bound to the location of personal computers or laptops, hence there is an issue with usability. Therefore, m-learning has been integrated to help make learning more interesting, widely available, more interactive and flexible.

The Emerging Concept of m-Learning

M-learning or mobile learning is an evolving phase of e-learning (Peng et al., 2009), as e-learning is dependent on desktop computers, whereas m-learning is dependent on mobile devices (Orr, 2010). There are a variety of definitions of m-learning, partly because m-learning is a new concept. Most studies define m-learning as an extension of e-learning which is performed using mobile devices such as PDA, mobile phones, laptops etc. (Sad & Goktas, 2013; Motiwalla, 2007). Others highlight certain characteristics of m-learning including portability through mobile devices, wireless Internet connection and ubiquity. For example Hoppe et al. (2003 in Iqbal & Qureshi, 2012), define m-learning as "using mobile devices and wireless transmission" (p.148). Kukulska-Hulme and Traxler (2007, p.35) suggest that "m-learning emphasizes the ability to facilitate the learning process without being tied to a physical location". In the higher education context, the term mobile learning (m-learning) refers to the use of mobile and handheld devices, such as smart phones, laptops and tablet PCs, in the delivery of teaching and learning. Simply put, m-learning is defined as "the process of learning mediated by a mobile device" (Kearney, Schuck, Burden, & Aubusson, 2012). M-learning can be thought of as a subset of e-learning, which is the "the use of computer network technology, primarily through the Internet, to deliver information and instruction to individuals" (Welsh, Wanberg, Brown, & Simmering, 2003).

Brink (2011) divided m-learning in three main types, formal, informal and well-directed or self-directed. Forma learning includes normal learning, which is triggered by notifications and reminders such as short messages. Informal learning encompasses two-way message exchange, hence an interactive relationship, such as Facebook, blogs, Twitter etc. Finally well-directed or self-directed learning uses reference and media-based materials such as videos and podcasts. For example, Table 1 shows the differences between normal and m-learning.

Although, in higher education, students are regarded as pioneers in forcing the faculty to change and adapt m-learning, the literature suggests that there are significant positive outcomes (Sad & Goktas, 2013). The literature suggests that there are several factors that influence readiness

for m-learning. For example, demographic influences on users' readiness for m-learning such as gender, age and educational level. Others refer to technology acceptance, ease of use, perceived usefulness, quality of services and cultural factors.

A prerequisite for the delivery of e-learning programmes is the use of fixed locations i.e. in a classroom or where a desktop PC and an Internet connection are available. The remedy to this significant e-learning limitation appeared in the mid-2000s with the advent of m-learning applications for a wide variety of uses such as workplace learning, teaching and social networking. Quinn (2001) argues that m-learning intersects mobile computing with e-learning. The unique features of the new mobile technologies and the unlimited potential they offer in terms of flexibility and customization to individual needs, place it also in the framework of flexible learning (Peters, 2009; Sarrab et al., 2013). In this context, students expect training that is "just in time, just enough and just for me" (Rosenberg, 2001), and that can be delivered and supported beyond the boundaries of traditional classroom settings (Kearney et al., 2012). M-learning emphasizes the *mobility* of learning, whereas others place emphasis on the mobility of learners, and the experiences of learners as they learn by means of mobile devices (El-Hussein & Cronje, 2010, p.14). Similarly, Traxler (2007) claims that m-learning is not about 'mobile' or about 'learning' but is part of a new mobile conception of society. Hence, the

Table 1. Difference between normal learning and m-learning

Normal Learning Style	Mobile Learning
Individual assessment, group projects, group discussions and project presentations will be done through quizzes and tutorials.	The use of multimedia elements in conveying information and receive online feedback.
Students will go to a class or lecture hall to attend the lecture.	The learning process can be done anywhere and at any time.
Students will interact face to face to allow them to communicate effectively.	Able to organize meetings and schedules of all team members at the same time.
Using chalk and talk method in delivering information.	Students can get the lecture notes quickly without copying from the board.

Source: Devinder & Zaitun (2006)

definition of m-learning depends on how each member of the society understands and explains mobile learning. For example, other definitions refer to the physical way in which technology is used and others emphasize on what learners experience when they use mobile technologies in education, whereas others refer to how it can be used to make unique contribution to education and e-learning (El-Hussein & Cronje, 2010, p. 14). Figure 1 illustrates the above view.

The mobility of technology refers to the mobile cellular devices that link to the internet and deliver content and instruction and can enable learning to learn at anytime and anywhere in a form that is culturally prestigious among people in the same group (King, 2006; El-Hussein & Cronje, 2010). The mobility of learners is linked to the mobility of the devices and the fact that the learner is connected to the internet, hence learning can occur at any time and any place (Traxler, 2009). Finally, the mobility of learning is unique as it is "received and processed withing the context in which the learner is situated" (El-Hussein & Cronje, 2010, p. 19).

While the technical advancements in m-learning progress rapidly by satisfying a consumer driven demand, there are still many barriers in the development of an appropriate pedagogical framework for its application in teaching and learning. The aging instructor population is apparently one of the primary barriers in the smooth transition to the new era in higher education. The well-established learning theories of the past are based on teaching by the textbook and memorizing information. Educating and persuading older instructors to use m-learning as part of their learning and teaching approach poses as one of the most difficult challenges. Another issue in the use of m-learning in higher education programmes is that learning practices are changing while learning theories that support them are not (El-Hussein & Cronje, 2010). In addition, Wang (2011) found that e-learning (including m-learning) development tends to focus on technical issues of design and ignores organizational, social, and pedagogical aspects that are necessary for effective e-learning programmes in the workplace. Most applications are lacking of pedagogical underpins on the use of m-learning, and fail to understand learning behavior that takes place in the organizational and social context. It is also suggested that locating distinctive features of learning with mobile devices is an evolving process interwoven with the maturation of the relevant technologies (Kearney et al., 2012). The design of m-learning content for higher education is a complex and difficult task.

Figure 1. Mobile learning
Source: El-Hussein and Cronje (2010, p. 17)

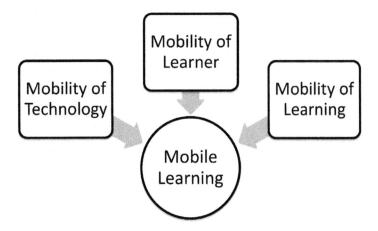

Account still needs to be taken of learner's and instructors' specific needs as well as the environment which learning takes place. What also needs to be done is to include appraisal and evaluation for each programme, tailored to the different cultural and organisational needs (El-Hussein & Cronje, 2010). The way that people and organisations perceive this new era in teaching and learning is the key to shape the new curricula in higher education. Sharples, Taylor, and Vavoula (2007) identify two layers of m-learning, the semiotic (socio-cultural) and technological; they argue that these two layers will eventually converge. This convergence requires though a total rethink and redesign of formal learning as we know it: a more open and collaborative model which places educators as facilitators of learning in a connected and mobile world, where students participate actively in the learning creation process. On the other hand, others believe that m-learning will never fully replace classroom or other electronic learning approaches (Liaw, Hatala, & Huang, 2010). However, if leveraged properly, mobile devices can complement and add value to the existing learning models and frameworks.

M-learning and e-learning also differentiate from a pedagogical perspective in the learning approach. While e-learning is based primarily on the objectivist learning model (Wang, 2011), m-learning is building on a *constructivist* approach. The objectivist approach is based on the transfer of knowledge from the instructor to the learner; on the other hand the constructivist approach views learning as a process in which learners actively construct or build new ideas or concepts based upon current and past knowledge. In this interactive environment, instructors should let learners participate in meaningful activities so that they can generate their own knowledge (Brown & Campione, 1996). M-learning is also linked with the theory of *connectivism* which states that learners are actively attempting to create meaning through engagement in networks; learning is the process of creating connections and developing a

network (Siemens, 2005). King (2006) proposes that the use of m-learning in higher education, reduces the physical walls of the classroom and replaces them with virtual, as the content of the education it delivered by means of a radical new technology, and he adds that "by breaking down the assumptions and process behind writing and speaking, we can go beyond them and find new ways of thinking about the world" (King, 2006, p. 171). Herrington, Herrington, Mantei, Olney, and Ferry (2009) placed m-learning in the context of the *authentic learning* approach. Authentic learning situates students in learning contexts where they encounter activities that involve problems and investigations reflective of those they are likely to face in their real world professional contexts.

Researchers have also explored m-learning perspectives from a wider socio-cultural view. Traxler (2009) described m-learning as noisy and problematic, featuring three essential elements: the personal, contextual and situated. Klopfer, Squire, and Jenkins (2002) propose that mobile devices (handheld computers) "produce unique educational affordances," which are: portability, social interactivity, context sensitivity, connectivity and individuality. Based on the activity theory approach Liaw et al. (2010) investigated the acceptance toward to m-learning as a means to enhance individual knowledge management. They found that factors such as enhancing learners' satisfaction, encouraging learners' autonomy, empowering system functions and enriching interaction and communication activities, have a significant positive influence on the acceptance of m-learning systems. More recently Kearney et al. (2012) presented a framework, which highlights three central features of m-learning: authenticity, collaboration and personalization, embedded in the unique time-space contexts of mobile learning. Sharples et al. (2007, p.4) provide more details on the convergence between learning and technology as shown in the Table 2.

M-learning has attracted attention due to the increasing number of available mobile devices,

Table 2. Convergence between learning and technology

New Learning	New Technology
Personalised	Personal
Learner-centered	User-centered
Situated	Mobile
Collaborative	Networked
Ubiquitous	Ubiquitous
Lifelong	Durable

Source: Sharples, Taylor, and Vavoula (2007, p.4)

which are affordable and their costs are increasingly decreasing making them more accessible to people. At the same time these devices have multiple features and capabilities, such as making phone calls, taking pictures and making videos, storing data and of course accessing the internet (Sarrab, Al-Shihi, & Rehman, 2013). Maccallum and Jeffery (2009) propose that all these capabilities may be used in teaching and learning, for example for classroom activities (Dawabi., 2003). These mobile devices can be used for learning purposes via interactive games, for brainstorming, quizzing and are widely used to support and develop students' own learning and collaborative learning (Iqbal & Qureshi, 2012). Moreover, they are available to users at any time and all time (Giousmpasoglou & Marinakou, 2013). Kukulska-Hulme and Traxler (2007) present several case studies that report and support the experience of educators with mobile technologies in universities. Zawacki-Richter, Brown, and Delport (2009) claim that e-learning and m-learning provide a wide range of opportunities for learners and teachers. However, as it has been previously discussed, Herrington, Mantei, Olney, and Ferry (2009, p.1) claim that it is not still clear whether "m-learning is used in pedagogically appropriate ways".

M-learning is widely used in distance learning as it supports the access to the teaching material for a large number of students, independent of time and space, at low costs. Moura and Carvalho

(2009, p.90) suggest that "the development of m-learning as a new strategy for education has implications on the way students learn, on the role of the teachers as well as in the educational institution". Hence, for the purpose of this chapter m-learning is studied as an element of e-learning and blended learning in general not necessarily as a tool for distance learning, as it also helps in constructing problem-based learning as well as any related assignments and projects that meets the students' interest (Kukulska-Hulme & Traxler, 2007). M-learning allows student-centered learning in which students are able to modify the access and transfer of information to strengthen the knowledge and skills of students to meet their educational goals (Giousmpasoglou & Marinakou, 2013; Sharples et al., 2007). In addition, it can support ubiquitous learning and can make the educational process more comfortable and flexible (Sarrab et al., 2013, p. 828).

Higher education may be presented in a more interactive ways as m-learning provides the support for learning and training. Although, technological developments have made mobile devices strategic tools to the delivery of higher education instruction, these fundamental changes pose new problems, challenges as well as opportunities to the instructors and students as they are discussed in the following.

Opportunities and Challenges from the Use of m-Learning in Higher Education

The introduction of m-learning in universities change radically the way we perceive, design and deliver higher education programmes. In this mobile and always connected world, a number of benefits and challenges arise for both educators and students. Literature indicates that three features are most cited by researchers, practitioners and users: mobility/ubiquity (anytime, anywhere), personalization, and collaboration. Current technology allows learners to disseminate information and complete coursework even when they are away from their desktop PCs and hard-wired Internet connections. A wireless device has the potential to give instant gratification to students by allowing them to interact with the instructors, other students in the course, and access course related content from anywhere wireless connectivity is available. BenMoussa (2003) identifies three key benefits of mobile connectivity for the users. Firstly, mobile devices offer personalized and/or individualized connectivity. Liaw et al. (2010) also suggest that the relationship between the owner and the mobile/handheld device provides a 'one-to-one' interaction in a personalized manner. Secondly, mobile connectivity improves collaboration via real-time or instant interactivity that may lead to better decision-making. And third, mobile connectivity enhances users' orientation or direction. Kearney et al. (2012) argue that m-learners can enjoy a high degree of collaboration by making rich connections to other people and resources mediated by a mobile device. This often-reported high level of networking creates shared, socially interactive environments so m-learners can readily communicate multi-modally with peers, educators and other experts, and exchange information. Learners consume, produce and exchange an array of "content", sharing information and artefacts across time and place. In addition, Motiwalla (2007) suggests that access to information at the point of relevance may make it possible for m-learners to minimize their unproductive time, which may enhance their work-life-education balance.

The challenges generated from the advent of m-learning in higher education programmes affect mostly those responsible for the design and delivery and evaluation of teaching and learning. Wang (2011) argues that the emergence of Web 2.0. related technologies, brought a radical transformation in e-learning (and thus m-learning) environment: the largely central controlled education system turned to an interactive and conversational learning network. As a direct consequence we observe that learning practices are changing very

fast (i.e introduction of e-books instead of traditional textbooks), while the learning theories that support educational practices are not (El-Hussein & Cronje, 2010). Educators are currently unable to follow the needs of the younger generations of learners described as digital natives (Corbeil & Valdes-Corbeil, 2007). These learners do not see technology as something foreign: they readily accept it and consider it as part of their everyday lives; they are totally immersed and addicted to mobile technologies. Young learners also created and use their own language and signs when communicating either via Short Message Service (SMS), e-mail or live chat through a mobile Internet or Wi-Fi connection (El-Hussein & Cronje, 2010); this is how they were called the text generation. Overall, the traditional teacher-centered, classroom situated learning environment, is now challenged by the digitally literate students who view learning as an open collaborate process without boundaries (Peters, 2009).

M-learning provides flexibility in higher education programmes that may result in some challenges that learners may not have imagined (Motiwalla, 2007). For example, a serious implication from the continuous exposure to information and interaction in a connected world can be the creation of confusion and disorientation to m-learners. Then various security issues regarding the information privacy of the users are raised as in any other commercial application. Mobile devices are currently appear to be more vulnerable than PCs, thus personal data are easily traceable for mobile users (Okazaki, 2011). Finally, there are ethical issues reading the use of m-learning in student assessment, where cheating cannot be easily prevented or traced based on the current technologies and learning philosophies (Banyard, Underwood, & Twiner, 2006).

The challenges of the use of m-learning are many for all stakeholders as it may have many technological restrictions. For instructors, m-learning is a challenge as they should be familiar with technology, not only to use it for teaching and learning but also to support developers who are challenged by the limited memory, the lack of keyboard, the small displays especially when compared to computers and laptops (Iqbal & Qureshi, 2012; Wang et al., 2009). Instructors should adapt the design of the courses to integrate ICT; this design should be dynamic, easily scalable and should be applied at all times and places (Marwan, Madar, & Fuad, 2013). Moreover, Marwan et al. (2013) suggest that instructors face the lack of time to prepare for class. There is also concern on the educators' ability to understand and respond to digital learning opportunities, as in many cases they are challenged by the need "to collaborate with a wide range of people such as web developers and programmers to deliver successful web-based education" (Peters, 2007). It is a fact that m-learning enables learning to occur at a less formal setting that is teacher-mediated, hence technical skills are required (Kearney et al., 2012). In addition, m-learning experiences can be customized for the learner to meet different learning styles and approaches, they may provide a high degree of collaboration and making connections to other people, creating further challenges to educators whose roles are changing (Mohammad & Job, 2013; Kearney et al., 2012). Thus, educators should be able to understand and analyze the unique challenges in emerging m-learning environments and facilitate insights to support their design and use of m-learning resources.

Students usually have access to the Internet and other applications via their mobile devices such as Facebook, YouTube, MySpace and other. They are also familiar with its use, hence being well introduced to m-learning may lead to its wide use in their own learning. Nowadays students are active and innovative in terms of their learning, they expect a quick response from the tutor and want an interactive learning, student-centered, authentic, collaborative and effective learning with the use of ICT (Marwan et al., 2013). According to Mirza and Al-Abdulkareem (2011, p. 88) "the

learner's attitude and lack of prior knowledge of IT use are major factors that affect the acceptance of e-learning by students".

Previous research suggests that there are various factors that contribute to the adoption of m-learning by instructors and students. Ju, Sriprapaipong, and Minh (2007) claim that the perceived usefulness influences the intention to adopt m-learning. On top of usefulness, Wang et al. (2009) and Sarrab et al. (2013) identified other factors such as the self-managed pace of learning, the social influence, the performance and the effort expectancy. Venkatesh, Morris, Davis, and Davis (2003) added the available infrastructure to support the use of any m-learning system, and Liu and Li (2010) add the playfulness. The interface makes the use of mobile devices more interesting for students, as the learning is personalized, more fun, spontaneous, and engaging users to contribute and share (Sarrab et al., 2013). Marwan et al. (2013) add the interactive learning process, the integrated learning information and the high learning needs. Thornton and Houser (2002 in Moura & Carvalho, 2009) propose that recordings, communication and access to information in the local set, sending reminders or relevant information for students are good options of the use of m-learning. Attewell (2011) propose that m-learning assists in the development of the learners' literacy and numerical skills. In addition, m-learning students are able to experience a dynamic class via interaction. To understand the factors that contribute to the adoption of m-learning will help stakeholders (educators, software developers and technicians) to incorporate these factors into the design of the m-learning systems.

Challenges and restrictions of the use of m-learning include the lack of standardization, the low bandwidth, the limited processor speed and small screen size, low storage, short battery life, lack of data input capability (Sarrab et al., 2013; Maniar & Bennett, 2002), low display resolution, limited memory and less computational power (Shiau, Lim, & Shen, 2001). Marwan et al. (2013)

claim that classes are difficult to be rescheduled with m-learning. All of the above benefits and challenges of m-learning could be summarized in Table 3.

If students are provided with the educational context in an appropriate and challenging manner, which is exciting and novel, they will be more inclined to use all these mobile devices and m-learning. M-learning has been considered to be a promising approach to complement student learning. At the same time, instructors cannot just be provided with the technology and left on their own; they should be provided with a vision and the necessary resources and support to use e-learning and m-learning.

E-Learning and M-Learning in the Middle East (ME) and Bahrain

Although e-learning has been growing rapidly in the Middle East (ME), North Africa (MENA) region and the Gulf Co-operation Council (GCC) countries, m-learning has been considered as an

alternative learning style and a new fashion. In these countries, according to Hamou, Anwar and Benhadria (2012) several initiatives have been introduced such as proliferation of e-books and e-learning devices, as well as flexible access to distance learning. In fact, the Arab region witnesses an increasing penetration of mobile phones and much faster Internet (Muttoo, 2011). However, these initiatives do not show a clear shift towards e-learning and m-learning in the region.

Nevertheless, there are some good examples and initiatives of educational institutions that have contributed to the development of e-learning and m-learning. For example, Hamdan Bin Mohammed e-University (HBMeU) in the UAE has introduced an effective architecture for e-learning, and also contributed to the development of standards for e-learning programme accreditation (Hadj-Hamou, Anwar, & Benhadria, 2012). The *e-learning Declaration* was drafted at the 2008 e-learning Forum in Dubai, providing a new educational model, which is based on research on active research changing teaching

Table 3. Benefits and challenges of m-learning

Benefits of M-Learning	Challenges of M-Learning
Great for people on the go.	May make it easier to cheat.
Anytime, anywhere access to content.	Could give tech-savvy students an advantage over non-technical students.
Can enhance interaction between and among students and instructors.	Can create a feeling of isolation or of being out-of-the-loop for non-techies.
Great for just-in-time training or review of content.	May require media to be reformatted or offered in multiple formats.
Can enhance student-centered learning.	Might render some content outdated because of rapid upgrades – here today, outdated tomorrow.
Can appeal to tech-savvy students because of the media-rich environment.	Could require additional learning curve for non-technical students and faculty.
Support differentiation of student learning needs and personalized learning.	Many be used by a new high-tech package for the same old dull and boring content.
Reduce cultural and communication barriers between faculty and students by using communication channels that students like.	There are different mobile platforms such as iOS, Android etc.
Facilitate collaboration through synchronous and asynchronous communication.	The wireless network trust ability.
Supports distance learning.	

Source: Corbeil and Valdes-Corbeil (2007, p. 54); Sarrab et al. (2013, p. 835-836)

and learning from the traditional approach to the student-oriented approach. In addition, they have launched an e-book and e-reader device to help learners use their iPad/iPhone for their learning. They support the blended learning approach, where they integrate the face-to-face learning with online collaborative learning and self-paced learning, as they make effective use of ICT to support delivery of the courses. They use Moodle, which enables the online collaborative learning, and asynchronous study is enabled by interactions with the professors via virtual classrooms (with the use of Wimba) and access to electronic teaching material.

Moreover, in Saudi Arabia, the rapid advancement in mobile technologies, wireless networks and the acceptance of new smart devices have increased the interest in m-learning. In fact, the Ministry of Higher Education (MOHE) has launched a national project "AAFQ" to develop a long-term plan for HE in order to address future challenges including m-learning (Garg, 2013). They have also established other projects such as the National Centre for E-learning and Distance Education (NCELDE) with its own learning portal, the Saudi Digital Library and the Saudi Centre for Support and Counseling to all beneficiaries of e-learning among others. The aim of the center is to become "an international leader in research, development and implementation of an e-learning architecture and infrastructure using open standards" (Mirza & Al-Abdulkareem, 2011, p. 91). Many universities in Saudi Arabia are utilizing distance-learning technologies. For example, King Saud University has recently initiated a new service that offers users with the ability to send text messages directly from a PC to a mobile phone (Altameem, 2011, p. 22). There is also the Knowledge International University (http://www.kiu.com.sa/website/index.php) established in Saudi Arabia in 2007, which specializes in online degrees programmes in Islamic studies (Mirza & Al-Abdulkareem, 2011).

In Oman, the Ministry of Education has established ongoing relations with Edutech Middle East to integrate 590 schools around the country with e-learning solutions (Mirza & Al-Abdulkareem, 2011). They also state that the Syrian Virtual University offers various degrees including diplomas, bachelor's and master's in business, technology and quality management.

As the GCC countries are endowed with oil and gas reserves they have turned their attention to education and to the improvement of the quality of education (World Economic Forum, 2010). Although education is a high priority in the GCC countries, considerable ground has to be covered to make progress in terms of enrolment and quality enhancement (Hadj-Hamou et al., 2012, p. 57). Education has strategic significance in the Arab world, but still there are great variations among the Arab states in their literacy rates. In addition, there is limited financial support for education in a large number of Arab countries. According to the World Bank (2007) the rate of total expenditure in education relative to GDP in all Arab countries is nearly 1.3%.

Table 4 shows the education rank of GCC countries among 134 countries.

The same study reports that there is low quality of research, and low number of publications in the GCC countries in comparison to those from fast developing countries. Most universities are teaching-oriented, rather than research-oriented; the rate of researchers in Arab universities as compared with employees is 2.7 per 10.000. Moreover, the report suggests that there is lack of planning and strategies for education at all levels, lack of information and communications technology (ICT) integration into education, there is centralization of education, intellectual migration and weaker linkages between education and labour markets. Hence, decision-makers can respond to these challenges by exploring the potential of electronic communication for spreading education in the countries (Hadj-Hamou et al., 2012, p.60).

Table 4. Education rank of GCC countries

Country	Quality of Primary Education	Secondary Enrolment	Tertiary Enrolment	Quality of Educational System
Bahrain	41	36	74	38
Kuwait	79	62	92	88
Oman	48	70	81	43
Qatar	5	49	106	4
Saudi Arabia	54	43	75	41
UAE	29	46	84	27

Source: World Economic Forum (2010)

Bahrain is one of the countries in the Arab world that have recently considered the potential of distance education with the use of e-learning. A study in the Middle East reveals that only 49% of society members are aware of e-learning (CITC, 2007) and the main reason for the limited use of e-learning and m-learning in the region is the low public and teachers' esteem for online learning (Mirza & Al-Abdulkareem, 2011). The first e-learning project in Bahrain was the Future Project at His Majesty King Hamad's Schools, which was established on January 2005 to serve the public secondary education and at a later level to include the private schools as well. There is also the e-learning center at the University of Bahrain, opened in March 2007 under the patronage of the King's wife, Her Majesty Shaikha Sabeeka Bint Ibrahim Al Khalifa, who is also the President of the Supreme Council for Women. The e-learning center plays a significant role in Bahrain's development as the government of Bahrain takes a regional lead in the launch of a range of egovernment services. The center focuses on promoting the adoption of wireless technology to support teaching and learning programmes across eight university departments. It can be accessed by 8000 students, and both staff and students are benefiting with 145 teaching modules already tailored for delivery on the university's network. The center's facilities include a range of e-learning tools including email, and online university chat and discus-

sion rooms, which enable 24-hour interactivity and access to information for academic staff and students. It ultimately aims to support all University of Bahrain students to become proficient in the use of modern technology in their learning and to develop valuable employment skills. The center has a broader remit to cascade and share the knowledge and expertise acquired through the e-learning and e-teaching with other academic institutes and professionals throughout Bahrain (Albardooli, Alobaidli, & Alyousha, 2006, p. 15).

Moreover, universities in the oil-rich GCC have shown particular interest in m-learning, which currently is treated as fashion (Mohammad & Job, 2013), but at the same time is considered by corporations and educational institutions to be very promising (Sharrab et al., 2013; Unesco, 2012). Nevertheless, there are many challenges identified in the adoption of e-learning and m-learning in the region. Weber (2011) suggests that there are some cultural concerns in the use of the Internet in the region. More specifically, he proposes that cultural taboos prevent or restrict the social interaction of unmarried men and women; hence some of the collaborative tools in the use of e-learning and m-learning "may be at variance with Islamic customs" (Weber, 2011, p. 1). He continues that there might be cultural bias such as language, as in many universities nowadays the communication and teaching and learning language is English. Even the fact that people in this culture are used to communicate mainly orally creates some challenges for the use of m-learning. In his study, Weber (2011) identified women and the issue of literacy as another challenge. He suggests that women's illiteracy in the Arab world is a major concern for women's education and development. Traditional, social and religious affiliations are impacting on women, as they cannot physically attend classes in traditional universities. However, the use of m-learning could be a potential solution to this issue as proposed by Tubaishat (2008) in his study of Zayed University, an all girl university in the UAE.

Finally, Weber (2011) claims that the issue of privacy is also a challenge. Censorship in most ME countries is common practice. There is the fear of misuse of student information similar to this of the use of Facebook. He adds that "Arabian Gulf traditions emphasize the privacy and sanctity of the home and the potential for misuse of online information used in an educational setting is immense" (2011, p. 2). Weber (2011) supports that in the MENA region instructors are concerned about the security of the educational data, and parents are concerned about the use of chats and the safety of the online environment. Mirza and Al-Abdulkareem (2011, p.84) add that exposure to material from the internet "could be considered dangerous to youths and to the religious moral values of those nations".

Moreover, Mirza and Al-Abdulkareem (2011) provide another barrier to e-learning adoption in the ME. They include the passive attitude that some governments took in response to e-learning and the low Internet penetration rate by the general public. They also comment on the conservative religious clerics who were warning of the dangers of the Internet, nevertheless, many adhered to the warning. The low public esteem for online learning was among the reasons for hesitation of many academics to resort to e-learning. This barrier impacted on the lack of online repositories that contain educational material in the Arabic language (Al-Khalifa, 2008).

Although, there is increased interest in m-learning adoption in teaching and learning in the region, there is limited research conducted (Iqbal & Qureshi, 2012; Mirza & Al-Abdulkareem, 2011). Most studies focus on the learners' perceptions and use of m-learning with very little research conducted in the instructors' views (Mirza & Al-Abdulkareem, 2011). Hence, the authors decided to investigate the adoption of m-learning at universities in the Kingdom of Bahrain, and explore the educators' views and perception of m-learning, their intention to use it, as well as its future potential in higher education. This chapter aims to provide an overview of the challenges that instructors face with the use of m-learning and of insights and recommendations on strategies for the use of mobile learning to change and enhance the pedagogies in HE.

SURVEY IN M-LEARNING

This chapter presents the findings of the pilot study of the questionnaire conducted in four out of eight universities in Bahrain; both private and public universities were included in the survey. In order to address the aim and the research questions of the study, Zawachi-Richter, Brown, and Delport (2009) questionnaire titled 'Mobile Learning: From single project status into the mainstream?' was used after having acquired the authors' permission for its use. Instructors were asked to rate the mobile learning and teaching experience of distance educators, the development and growth of mobile learning, the impact of mobile technologies on teaching and learning, mobile learning applications and mobile learning activities, mobile learning and access to (higher) education, and the future development of mobile learning with a 5 Likert scale from (1) strongly disagree to (5) strongly agree.

For the pilot study, a total of 45 questionnaires were collected between April and June 2013, in which educators were asked to provide their attitudes regarding m-learning as a tool in their teaching. The participants in the study were from different faculties such as Business, ICT, Humanities, Art and Design, and from different academic rankings, with the majority being PhD holders (53.3%). 35.6% were female and 64.4% were male.

In order to identify the instructors' perceptions of m-learning frequencies, means and standard deviations were calculated. Moreover to identify the main ideas about the future of m-learning the frequencies of responses were calculated.

M-Learning Survey Results in Bahrain

The current status of the use of m-learning at the institutional level was identified and the results are shown in Table 5. For the purpose of this paper the authors present the most frequent answers or the majority of answers.

It is evident from the above that the majority of the institutions in the study were face-to-face with limited use of e-learning. M-learning was non-existent and most did not have any plans in developing m-learning. In addition, there was no technical support or in the cases that there was, it was limited. However, 31.1% claimed that a new unit within the organisation has been created for the purpose of m-learning. In reference to the current

status on m-learning the participants expressed their opinions on their knowledge on m-learning and on the use of mobile devices. The results are shown in Table 6.

Interestingly, most respondents are aware of m-learning, but only 15.6% are currently doing research and only 4.4% are involved in projects relevant to m-learning. Similarly, 15.6% of the respondents have not heard about mobile learning. The use of mobile devices is shown in Figure 2.

Most of the respondents (43.52%) used a laptop for connecting to the internet, and then their smartphone (22.27%), 16.20% use a tablet PC and only 1.1% use PDAs. Moreover the participants were asked to evaluate their experience in m-learning. The results are shown in Figure 3.

The majority of the responses to this question were towards the strongly disagree (1) area. 28% of the participants have been involved in m-learning projects, however, 22% of them state that these projects are not within their universities. 14% of the participants were not involved in projects on m-learning but were aware of others who were, and still 20% were not exposed to m-learning at all.

Further, respondents were asked to rate the importance of learning tools for students, the learning activities that are appropriate for mobile devices and the importance of applications. The findings are shown in Table 7. The results suggest

Table 5. M-learning status at institution level

	Response (N=45)	Frequency (%)
C1	A traditional face-to-face or contact-based teaching institution	34 (75.6)
C2	Non-existent	27 (60)
C3	No, there are no institutional plans for developing course materials for use on mobile devices	27 (60)
C4.1	No, there is no institutional support.	14 (31.1)
C4.2	Yes, a new unit at the organisation/institution has been created for this purpose.	14 (31.1)

Table 6. Current personal status

	Response (N=45)	Frequency (%)
B1.1	Yes, I am personally doing research on mobile learning	7 (15.6)
B1.2	Yes, but I am not personally doing research on mobile learning	11 (24.4)
B1.3	Yes, I am involved in mobile learning projects	2 (4.4)
B1.4	I have read a number of articles and papers on mobile learning.	4 (8.9)
B1.5	No, but other persons in my institution are knowledgeable.	14 (31.1)
B1.6	No, I have not heard about mobile learning.	7 (15.6)

Figure 2. Mobile devices

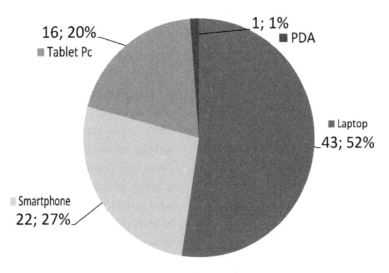

Figure 3. Experience in m-learning

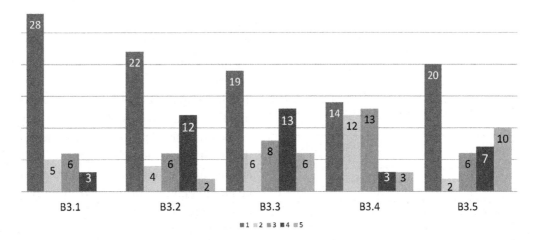

that the respondents found very important 'being connected anywhere, anytime' (B4.5), and 'sharing texts, notes and documents' (B4.4), hence they did not find the text messaging or voice calls and e-mails as highly important tools for students. Moreover, they identified as appropriate learning activities for mobile devices 'coursework' (B5.1), 'collaborative learning' (B5.3) and 'information retrieval' (B5.5). The applications found to be more important were all those included in the questionnaire such as mobile office (B6.1), diary and scheduling (B6.2), audio and video applica-

tions (B6.3), imaging (B6.4), other accessories (B6.5) and online data services (B6.6). Finally, the most useful tools were accessing information such as notes, documents etc (B7.2) and again 'being connected anywhere, anytime' (B7.5).

The respondents were asked to rate the new strategies and methodologies that are facilitated by m-learning. The results are shown in Table 8.

Except the 'assessment' (B8.2, Mean=2.69), the rest of the variables were rated close to agree and strongly agree responses. It was evident that they would use m-learning mainly to assess stu-

Table 7. Importance rating of importance for tools (B4), learning activities (B5), applications (B6) and learning tools (B7)

Item (N=45)	1 (Freq)	2 (Freq)	3 (Freq)	4 (Freq)	5 (Freq)
B4.1	7 (15.6)	7 (15.6)	10 (22.2)	10 (22.2)	11 (24.4)
B4.2	7 (15.6)	8 (17.8)	13 (28.9)	10 (22.2)	7 (15.6)
B4.3		5 (11.1)	12 (26.7)	18 (40.0)	10 (22.2)
B4.4	3 (6.7)	1 (2.2)	5 (11.1)	18 (40.0)	18 (40.0)
B4.5	3 (6.7)	1 (2.2)	3 (6.7)	14 (31.1)	24 (53.3)
B5.1	6 (13.3)	7 (15.6)	10 (22.2)	6 (13.3)	16 (35.6)
B5.2	3 (6.7)	12 (26.7)	5 (11.1)	12 (26.7)	13 (28.9)
B5.3	2 (4.4)	3 (6.7)	7 (15.6)	19 (42.2)	14 (31.1)
B5.4		5 (11.1)	12 (26.7)	18 (40.0)	10 (22.2)
B5.5		4 (8.9)	10 (22.2)	10 (22.2)	21 (46.7)
B6.1	5 (11.1)	5 (11.1)	7 (15.6)	9 (20.0)	19 (42.2)
B6.2	2 (4.4)	6 (13.3)	8 (17.8)	10 (22.2)	19 (42.2)
B6.3	2 (4.4)	4 (8.9)	15 (33.3)	7 (15.6)	17 (37.8)
B6.4	2 (4.4)	7 (15.6)	10 (22.2)	12 (26.7)	14 (31.1)
B6.5	2 (4.4)	1 (2.2)	11 (24.4)	15 (33.3)	16 (35.6)
B6.6	2 (4.4)		2 (4.4)	7 (15.6)	34 (75.6)
B7.1	1 (2.2)	7 (15.6)	12 (26.7)	11 (24.4)	14 (31.1)
B7.2	2 (4.4)	3 (6.7)	11 (24.4)	15 (33.3)	14 (31.3)
B7.3	1 (2.2)	9 (20.0)	10 (22.2)	12 (26.7)	13 (28.9)
B7.4	1 (2.2)	8 (17.8)	8 (17.8)	15 (33.3)	13 (28.9)
B7.5	1 (2.2)	1 (2.2)	5 (11.1)	10 (22.2)	28 (62.2)

dents' knowledge short time before a lecture or a discussion. Interaction (B8.4, Mean=4.02) was the most important of all the strategies that are facilitated by m-learning. Hence, the respondents suggested that m-learning provides more support for collaboration, more support for bottom-up content creation and could be used to consult peers. Next important strategy for m-learning was the resources for m-learning (B8.3, M=3.84). The participants use it for generating information, sharing resources, navigation and other. The major weaknesses of mobile devices that might hinder m-learning were also rated by the respondents as shown in Figure 4.

Most of the respondents agreed or strongly agreed with all the variables except the screen size (B9.2). This showed that the size of the screen of mobile devices was not considered to be a hindering factor for m-learning. On the contrary, the small size of the displays was found to be a challenge for m-learning activities. Similarly, the costs of network, the memory size, the device capabilities and the limited battery time were among the most important challenges for applying m-learning.

When respondents were asked their views on the latest trends and developments in teaching and learning as well as on when m-learning will be an integral part of mainstream in HE, this is reflected in Table 9.

Most of the respondents (51.1%) supported the view that although the technology should impact on the teaching and learning, currently this was not the case. 26.7% agreed that teaching and learning strategies and methodologies adapt to the constant changes in technology. In addition, most of the respondents (75.6%) believed that m-learning will become an integral part of mainstream HE within 5 years.

Finally the participants were asked to present their views on the future trends of m-learning. For the purpose of this paper only the majority of responses are illustrated in Table 10.

The majority of the respondents (55.6%) supported the view that new teaching and learning

Table 8. Strategies and methodologies

Category	Typical Examples	Mean	SD
B8.1 Learning Activities	(Inter)active learning, authentic learning, explorative learning, project orientated learning, situated and informal learning, Qs & As.	3.60	1.286
B8.2 Assessment	Security for testing and evaluation procedures, assessment to determine students' knowledge a day or two before a lecture/discussion to determine which topics need more attention.	2.69	1.411
B8.3 Resources	Generation of information, sharing resources, data sourcing, access to information, navigation, m-library.	3.84	1.127
B8.4 Interaction	More support for collaboration, more support for bottom-up content creation, enhanced social support, consulting peers & experts. Distance Educators will teach again instead of providing teaching material only.	4.02	1.033
B8.5 Personalisation & Individualisation	New strategies might emerge from better knowledge of learner behaviours and study patterns with technology, which were never examined that closely before, just-in-time learning, addressing learner styles or needs, keeping it simple, focus on small 'chunks' of learning, just-in-time support/job aids.	3.76	.957

Figure 4. Major weaknesses

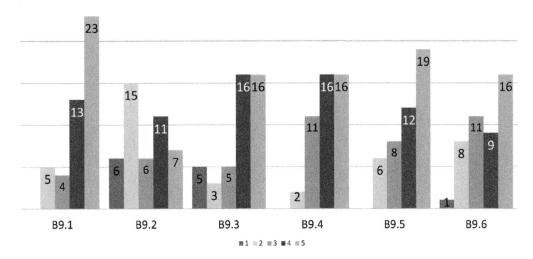

strategies will emerge due to IT developments. In addition, they proposed that they will enhance the teaching and learning, nevertheless, they proposed that the mobile devices will be the preferred device for learning. They also supported that m-learning will widen access to HE, because of the profileration of mobile phones and wireless infrastructure and the devices are expected to be small in size. Most of the respondents (84.4%) agreed that m-learning will facilitate new strategies and methodologies for learner support.

CONCLUSION

M-learning as a relatively recent phenomenon in higher education, enjoys high popularity among university students globally. In the ME region change has already started and e-learning and m-learning are becoming part of the educational system. Some may still be unfamiliar with the technical advancements in e-learning and m-learning, but plans are in place to make these technologies widely known and usable in the near future.

Table 9. Respondents' views on trends and developments in m-learning (and in years)

Responses	Technology changes should not have an impact on our teaching & learning strategies and methodologies.	Technology changes should have an impact on our teaching & learning strategies and methodologies, but this is currently not the case at present.	Teaching and learning strategies and methodologies adapt continuously due to new affordances that technology provides.	Technology changes bring about radical changes to our teaching & learning strategies and methodologies.
Frequency	2	23	12	8
(Percent)	(4.4)	(51.1)	(26.7)	(17.8)

Table 10. Future trends of m-learning

Statement	Frequency N=45	Percent
Teaching and learning theories in 20 years...		
In essence remain the same, but new learning paradigms and learning strategies will emerge because of technological developments.	25	55.6
Change completely with new learning theories replacing behaviourism and constructivism due to the radical impact of future technologies.	15	33.3
The attributes and opportunities that mobile technologies afford will...		
Be very helpful in enhancing teaching and learning independent of time and space.	33	73.3
Mobile devices and applications will in future be...		
Only one of many types of computing devices used.	22	48.9
The preferred access and learning device for any type of learning.	15	33.3
The development of m-learning will have an impact on HE		
It will widen access to (higher) education, because of the proliferation of mobile phones and wireless infrastructure – especially in developing countries.	29	64.4
The ideal mobile devices in the future will be...		
Small but still laptop sized devices because of its all-in-one device nature.	12	26.7

The key opportunity identified in this chapter is the ability of m-learning to provide learning that is "just in time". Mobile devices have the potential to deliver the kind of learning that is embedded in our daily lives, as the use of these devices is well established. Many instructors in higher education, including Bahrain, recognize the benefits of m-learning, but there is limited adoption for educational use. The main challenge identified in the chapter is the age and ability of instructors to use these mobile devices and technologies.

In order to support a strategic response to the opportunities and demands of mobile learners, the higher education sector needs to be informed about the actual use of mobile devices, and about potential future trends in mobile learning. This requires the re-examination and re-design of the foundational assumptions and presuppositions on which all previous understandings of the term "higher education" are constructed. It is imperative that this process foregrounds pedagogy rather than technology. In addition, these on-going structural changes in higher education, provide the potential to make learning more efficient, personal and culturally acceptable for learners. Training and workshops should be provided to increase faculty perception of e-learning and m-learning. This change and the integration of m-learning requires a change in the pedagogical paradigm in agreement with Moura and Calvalho (2009). The authors propose that this change should include transformation in the design and the development of teaching material.

It is also important to introduce by laws that governs the e-learning and distance learning which encourages students to participate at this type of learning. Regardless criticisms and debates, m-learning is now part of the academic curricula; what remains to see is how smooth the transition from the traditional to the contemporary teaching and learning environment can be.

IMPLICATIONS FOR FUTURE RESEARCH

The purpose of this chapter was to investigate the instructors' views on m-learning and its use in teaching and learning in higher education in Bahrain. It is evident from the above that m-learning plays an important role in teaching and learning strategies. Although, most of the participants work in institutions that do not offer m-learning strategies and they use face-to-face teaching, the instructors are considering its use, and some already conduct research in m-learning. Students and faculty will find ways to integrate m-learning in all aspects of their lives including the tasks of teaching and learning. Nevertheless, educational systems should not assume that instructors are proficient in using new technologies. Similarly to Ferry (2008), this chapter proposes that there is a need to integrate appropriate technologies into existing education systems. Professional development programmes should focus not only on the technology, skills and knowledge required to implement m-learning strategies, but also on the targeted use of technologies that support overall learning goals. Hence, further research is required to identify and determine such professional development programmes for instructors in higher

education, especially in the Kingdom of Bahrain and the region.

Moreover, it was interesting that the majority of the respondents have not heard of m-learning.

The findings proposed that m-learning could be considered a continuation of traditional learning methods as well as an alternative to the methods of effective learning. It is mainly used for coursework, information retrieval and collaborative learning. The most important elements of m-learning included the fact that instructors are connected anywhere anytime, and they can share texts with their students, supporting the view of Giousmpa-soglou and Marinakou (2013). Hence, instructors should be cautious when including e-learning as part of their assessment as the infrastructure and the support is not available at the institutions in the study. This study agrees with Venkatesh et al. (2003) that the available support and infrastructure are important for the use of e-learning and m-learning. Similarly to Sarrab et al. (2013), the main weaknesses identified include the small size of displays, the cost of network, the memory size and the mobile devices capabilities. However, the participants proposed that the new technologies should have an impact on teaching and learning in HE, and they believed that new may emerge, as they may enhance the learning and the teaching strategies. Macallum and Jeffery (2009) also propose that mobile devices may enhance m-learning, and the teaching and learning pedagogies.

Understanding the factors that contribute to the effective use of m-learning may help stake-holders to incorporate those in the design and implementation of m-learning. It is necessary to identify the practices in terms of instructional design and adapt them to reflect the number of changes that have taken place in education from the use of e-learning and m-learning. A transformation towards m-learning requires not only the use of the devices but also awareness and familiarity with new technologies (Wang, 2011), hence mobile tools should be aligned with the course objectives, and instructors should be aligned with m-learning requirements. M-learning should be used appropriately in order to be effective (Herrington et al., 2009), thus instructors should have the technical know-how as they are an essential part of m-learning.

This study proposes that informative meetings and instructors' training on m-learning can enhance the perception and the use of m-learning in higher education in Bahrain. Nevertheless, more empirical research is required to test the effectiveness of e-learning. Future studies can focus on identifying the factors, challenges and weaknesses in specific disciplines as the use of technology varies depending on the field of study for example it can be limited in liberal arts. It would also be interesting to explore the above findings in terms of gender differences.

REFERENCES

Al-Khalifa, H. (2008). Building an Arabic learning object repository with an ad hoc recommendation engine. In *Proceedings of the iiWAS* (pp. 390-394). Linz: iiWAS. doi:10.1145/1497308.1497378

Albardooli, M., Alobaidli, O., & Alyousha, F. (2016). *E-mobile, the future of e learning*. Thesis submitted at the University of Bahrain. Retrieved from www.albardooli.com/dlobjects/EmobileMAlbardooli.pdf

Alsaadat, K. (2009). Mobile learning and university teaching. In *Proceedings of the International Conference on Education and New Learning Technologies* (vol. 6, pp. 5895-5905). Barcelona: IATED.

Altameem, T. (2011). Contextual mobile learning system for Saudi Arabian universities. *International Journal of Computers and Applications, 21*(4), 21–26. doi:10.5120/2499-3377

Attewell, J. (2011). *From research and development to mobile learning: tools for education and training providers and their learners*. Retrieved from http://www.mlearn.org.za/CD/papers/Attewell.pdf

Banyard, P., Underwood, J., & Twiner, A. (2006). Do enhanced communication technologies inhibit or facilitate self-regulated learning? *European Journal of Education, 41*(3/4), 473–489. doi:10.1111/j.1465-3435.2006.00277.x

BenMoussa, C. (2003). *Workers on the move: New opportunities through mobile commerce*. Paper presented at the Stockholm Mobility Roundtable. Stockholm, Sweden.

Bharuthram, S., & Kies, C. (2013). Introducing e-learning in a South African higher education institution: Challenges arising from an intervention and possible responses. *British Journal of Educational Technology, 44*(3), 410–420. doi:10.1111/j.1467-8535.2012.01307.x

Brink, J. (2011). M-learning: The future of training technology. *Training & Development, 65*(2), 27.

Brown, A., & Campione, J. (1996). Psychological theory and design of innovative learning environments: on procedures, principles, and systems. In L. Schauble & R. Glaser (Eds.), *Innovations in learning: new environments for education* (pp. 289–325). Mahwah, NJ: Erlbaum.

Corbeil, J. R., & Valdes-Corbeil, M. E. (2007). Are you ready for mobile learning? *EDUCAUSE Quarterly, 30*(2), 51–58.

Dawabi, P., Wessner, M., & Neuhold, E. (2003). Using mobile devices for the classroom of the future. In *Proceedings of Mlearn 2003 Conference on Learning with Mobile Devices* (pp. 14-15). London: Mlearn.

Demian, P., & Morrice, J. (2012). The use of virtual learning environments and their impact on academic performance. *English Education*, *7*(1), 11–19. doi:10.11120/ened.2012.07010011

Devinder, S., & Zaitun, A. B. (2006). Mobile learning in wireless classrooms. *Malaysian Online Journal of Instructional Technology*, *3*(2), 26–42.

El-Hussein, M. O. O., & Cronje, J. C. (2010). Defining Mobile Learning in the Higher Education Landscape. *Journal of Educational Technology & Society*, *13*(3), 12–21.

Ferry, B. (2008). *Using mobile phones to augment teacher learning in environmental education.* Retrieved from http://www.ascilite.org.au/conferences/melbourne08/procs/ferry.pdf

Garg, V. (2013). *The emergence of mobile learning for higher education in Kingdom of Saudi Arabia.* UPSIDE learning blog. Retrieved from http://upsidelearning.com/blog/index.php

Giousmpasoglou, C., & Marinakou, E. (2013). The future is here: M-learning in higher education. *Computer Technology and Application*, *4*(6), 317–322.

Hadj-Hamou, N., Anwar, S. A., & Benhadria, M. (2012). A new paradigm for e-learing in the Arab Middle East: Reflections on e-books and e-Reader devices. In T. T. Goh, B. C. Seet, & P. C. Sun (Eds.), *E-Books & E-Readers for E-Learning* (pp. 92–123). Wellington, New Zealand: Victoria Business School.

Herrington, J., Mantei, J., Olney, I., & Ferry, B. (2009). Using mobile technologies to develop new ways of teaching and learning. In J. Herrington, A. Herrington, J., Mantei, I., Olney, & B. Ferry (Eds.), New technologies, new pedagogies: Mobile learning in higher education (p. 138). New South Wales, Australia: Faculty of Education, University of Wollongong.

Iqbal, S., & Qureshi, I. A. (2012). M-learning adoption: A perspective from a developing country. *International Review of Research in Open and Distance Learning*, *13*(3), 147–164.

Ju, T. L., Sriprapaipong, W., & Minh, D. N. (2007). *On the success factors of mobile learning.* Paper presented at 5th Conference on ICT and Higher Education. Bangkok, Thailand. Retrieved from http://www.mendeley.com/research/success-factors-mobile-learning/

Kearney, M., Schuck, S., Burden, K., & Aubusson, P. (2012). Viewing mobile learning from a pedagogical perspective. *Research in Learning Technology*, *20*(1).

King, J. P. (2006). *One hundred philosophers: A guide to world's greatest thinkers* (2nd ed.). London: Apple Press.

Klopfer, E., Squire, K., & Jenkins, H. (2002). Environmental detectives: PDAs as a window into a virtual simulated world. In *Proceedings for the International Workshop on Wireless and Mobile Technologies in Education* (pp. 95-98). Vaxjo, Sweden: IEEE.

Koszalka, T. A., & Ntloedibe-Kuswani, G. S. (2010). Literature on the safe and disruptive learning potential of mobile technologies. *Distance Education*, *31*(2), 139–157. doi:10.1080/01587 919.2010.498082

Kukulska-Hulme, A., & Traxler, J. (2007). *Designing for mobile and wireless learning.* London: Routledge.

Liaw, S. S., Hatala, M., & Huang, H. M. (2010). Investigating acceptance toward mobile learning to assist individual knowledge management: Based on activity theory approach. *Computers & Education*, *54*(2), 446–454. doi:10.1016/j.compedu.2009.08.029

Liu, Y., & Li, H. (2010). Mobile internet diffusion in China: An empirical study. *Industrial Management & Data Systems, 110*(3), 309–324. doi:10.1108/02635571011030006

MacCallum, K., & Jeffrey, L. (2009). Identifying discriminating variables that determine mobile learning adoption by educators: An initial study. In Proceedings of the conference for Same places, different spaces. Auckland: Ascilite. Retrieved from http://www.ascilite.org.au/conferences/auckland09/procs/maccallum.pdf

Maniar, N., & Bennett, E. (2007). Media influence on m-learning? In S. Iqbal, & I.A. Qureshi. (2012). M-learning adoption: A perspective from a developing country. *International Review of Research in Open and Distance Learning, 13*(3), 147–164.

Marwan, M. E., Madar, A. R., & Fuad, N. (2013). An overview of mobile application in learning for student of Kolejpoly-tech Mara (KPTM) by using mobile phone. *Journal of Asian Scientific Research, 3*(6), 527–537.

Mirza, A. A., & Al-Abdulkareem, M. (2011). Models of e-learning adopted in the Middle East. *Applied Computing and Informatics, 9*(2), 83–93. doi:10.1016/j.aci.2011.05.001

Motiwalla, L. F. (2007). Mobile learning: A framework and evaluation. *Computers & Education, 49*(3), 581–596. doi:10.1016/j.compedu.2005.10.011

Moura, A., & Carvalho, A. (2009). Mobile learning: two experiments on teaching and learning with mobile phones. In R. Hijon-Neira (Ed.), *Advanced Learning* (pp. 89-103). Rijeka, Croatia: InTech. Retrieved from http://www.intechopen.com/download/get/type/pdfs/id/8593

Muttoo, S. (2011). *'Mobile' changes in the Arab world.* Middle East economy and Globalization. Retrieved from http://www.strategicforesight.com/inner-articles.php?id=128£.UiRFZD-BWSo

Okazaki, S. (2011). Teaching students while leaking personal information: m-learing and privacy. In *Proceedings of 4th International Conference of Education, Research and Innovations* (pp. 1659-1664). Madrid: IATED.

Orr, G. (2010). Review of the literature in mobile learning: Affordances and constraints. In *Proceeding of the 6th IEEE International Conference on Wireless, Mobile and Ubiquitous Technologies in Education* (pp. 107-111). Taiwan: IEEE. doi:10.1109/WMUTE.2010.20

Peng, H., Su, Y., Chou, C., & Tsai, C. (2009). Ubiquitous knowledge construction: Mobile learning re-defined and conceptual framework. *Innovations in Education and Teaching International, 46*(2), 171–183. doi:10.1080/14703290902843828

Peters, K. (2009). m-Learning: Positioning educators for a mobile, connected future. In M. Ally (Ed.), Mobile learning: Transforming the delivery of education and training (pp. 113-132). Vancouver: Marquis Book Printing.

Quinn, C. (2001). Get ready for m-learning. *Training & Development, 20*(2), 20–21.

Rosenberg, M. (2001). *E-learning: Strategies for delivering knowledge in the digital age.* New York: MacGraw-Hill.

Sad, S. N., & Goktas, O. (2013). Preservice teachers' perceptions about using mobile phones and laptops in education as mobile learning tools. *British Journal of Educational Technology, 45*(4), 606–618. doi:10.1111/bjet.12064

Sarrab, M., Al-Shihi, H., & Rehman, O. M. H. (2013). Exploring major challenges and benefits of m-learning adoption. *British Journal of Applied Science and Technology, 3*(4), 826–839. doi:10.9734/BJAST/2013/3766

Serin, O. (2012). Mobile learning perceptions of the prospective teachers (Turkish Republic of Northern Cyprus sampling). *TOJET: The Turkish Online Journal of Educational Technology*, *11*(3), 222–233.

Sharples, M., Taylor, J., & Vavoula, G. (2007). *A theory of learning for the mobile age*. London: Sage Publications.

Shiau, K., Lim, E. P., & Shen, Z. (2001). Mobile commerce: Promises, challenges, and research agenda. *Journal of Database Management*, *12*(3), 4–13. doi:10.4018/jdm.2001070101

Siemens, G. (2005). *A Learning Theory for the Digital Age*. Retrieved from http://www.elearnspace.org/Articles/connectivism.htm

Smith, M., & Kukulska-Hulme, A. (2012). Building Mobile Learning Capacity in Higher Education: E-books and iPads. In M. Specht, J. Multisilta, and M. Sharples, (Eds.), *11th World Conference on Mobile and Contextual Learning Proceedings* (pp. 298-301). Helsinki: CELSTEC & CICERO Learning.

Traxler, J. (2009). Learning in a mobile age. *International Journal of Mobile and Blended Learning*, *1*(1), 1–12. doi:10.4018/jmbl.2009010101

Tubaishat, A. (2008). Adoption of learning technologies to alleviate the impact of social and cultural limitations in higher education. In *Proceedings of the 1st E-learning Excellence Forum* (pp. 15-18). Dubai: Academic Press.

Venkatesh, V., Morris, M. G., Davis, G. B., & Davis, F. D. (2003). User acceptance of information technology: Toward a unified view. *Management Information Systems Quarterly*, *27*(3), 425–478.

Wang, M. (2011). Integrating organizational, social, and individual perspectives in Web 2.0-based workplace e-learning. *Information Systems Frontiers*, *13*(2), 191–205. doi:10.1007/s10796-009-9191-y

Weber, A. S. (2011). *Research programme for next-gen e-learning in MENA region*. Paper presented at the 7th International Scientific Conference eLearning and Software for Education. Bucharest, Romania. Retrieved from https://adlunap.ro/else_publications/papers/2011/1758_2.pdf

Welsh, E. T., Wanberg, C. R., Brown, K. G., & Simmering, M. J. (2003). E-learning: Emerging uses, empirical results, and future directions. *International Journal of Training and Development*, *7*(4), 245–258. doi:10.1046/j.1360-3736.2003.00184.x

World Bank. (2007). *World development report*. Washington, DC: Author.

World Economic Forum. (2010). *Global competitiveness report 2010-2011*. Davos: Author.

Zawacki-Richter, O., Brown, T., & Delport, R. (2009). Mobile learning: from single project status into the mainstream? *European Journal of Open, Distance and E-learning*. Retrieved from http://www.eurodl.org/?article=357

KEY TERMS AND DEFINITIONS

Bahrain: The Kingdom of Bahrain is a small island country in the Persian Gulf. Since 2012 was ranked 48th in the world in the Human Development Index, and was recognized by the World Bank as a high income economy. Currently, there are 12 universities.

Blended Learning: A method of learning which uses a combination of different resources, especially a mixture of classroom sessions and online learning materials.

Collaboration (Collaborative Learning): Learners making rich connections and sharing resources to other learners and/or educators; this type of communication is mediated by a mobile device.

E-Learning: Any type of learning conducted via electronic media using specialized software, typically on the Internet.

Higher Education: The education offered after secondary education, usually available through colleges, universities, including vocational training, trade schools and other professional certifications.

Information and Communication Technologies (ICTs): The term stresses the role and importance of unified communications and the integration of telecommunications with computers as well as necessary enterprise software, middleware, storage, and audio-visual systems, which enable users to access, store, transmit, and manipulate information.

M-Learning (Mobile Learning): Any activity that allows learners to be more productive when interacting with, or creating information, mediated through a mobile device that the learner carries on a regular basis, has reliable connectivity, and fits in a pocket, a purse or a handbag.

Teaching and Learning: Teaching is undertaking certain ethical tasks or activities the intention of which is to induce learning, to impact knowledge of or skill of. Learning is the act or process of acquiring knowledge or skill.

Ubiquity: The ability of users to access content "anytime – anywhere" though the use of mobile devices.

Virtual Learning Environments (VLEs): A set of teaching and learning tools designed to enhance a student's learning experience by including computers and the Internet in the learning process.

This work was previously published in Assessing the Role of Mobile Technologies and Distance Learning in Higher Education edited by Patricia Ordóñez de Pablos, Robert D. Tennyson, and Miltiadis D. Lytras, pages 176-199, copyright year 2015 by Information Science Reference (an imprint of IGI Global).

Chapter 55
Implementing Advanced Characteristics of X3D Collaborative Virtual Environments for Supporting e-Learning:
The Case of EVE Platform

Christos Bouras
Research Academic Computer Technology Institute, Patras, Greece & Department of Computer Engineering and Informatics, University of Patras, Patras, Greece

Vasileios Triglianos
Department of Computer Engineering and Informatics, University of Patras, Patras, Greece

Thrasyvoulos Tsiatsos
Department of Informatics, Aristotle University of Thessaloniki, Thessaloniki, Greece

ABSTRACT

Three dimensional Collaborative Virtual Environments are a powerful form of collaborative telecommunication applications, enabling the users to share a common three-dimensional space and interact with each other as well as with the environment surrounding them, in order to collaboratively solve problems or aid learning processes. Such an environment is "EVE Training Area tool" which is supported by "EVE platform". This tool is a three-dimensional space where participants, represented by three-dimensional humanoid avatars, can use a variety of e-collaboration tools. This paper presents advanced functionality that has been integrated on "EVE Training Area tool" in order to support: (a) multiple collaborative learning techniques (b) Spatial audio conferencing, which is targeted to support principle 3 (augmenting user's representation and awareness). Furthermore the paper presents technological and implementation issues concerning the evolution of "EVE platform" in order to support this functionality.

DOI: 10.4018/978-1-4666-8619-9.ch055

INTRODUCTION

The maturation of the Internet and the need for electronic communication formed the basis for the research and development of collaborative applications. Collaborative Virtual Environments (CVE) is a promising form of this type of applications. CVEs might vary in their representational richness from three dimensional 3D graphical spaces, 2.5D and 2D environments to text-based environments (Snowdon et al., 2001). CVEs can enable the users to share a common 3D space and interact with each other as well as with the environment surrounding them, in order to collaboratively solve problems or aid learning processes.

Collaborative Virtual Environments are technologically based on Networked Virtual Environment (NVE) platforms. NVEs allow the communication and interaction of geographically separated users, inside 3D virtual worlds. This paper presents advanced NVE's functionality that has been integrated on EVE platform (Bouras et al., 2001; Bouras & Tsiatsos, 2004; Bouras et al., 2005; Bouras et al., 2006) in order to support. More specifically, the main goal of this paper is to present the evolution of EVE platform in order to support e-learning and e-collaboration scenarios in a more effective manner.

Since the early uses of collaborative virtual environments in learning, researchers have tried to establish a schema that incorporates some well known aspects, issues, elements and principles which should be taken into account during the design process of educational virtual worlds. The rationale behind the designers' decisions can have a significant effect on the appropriateness of the platform for education. Regarding the design adequacy of EVE for online learning purposes, we validated (as presented in the next section) the platform's features, philosophy and policies against the design principles presented in Bouras et al. (2008). These principles are the following:

Principle 1: Design to support multiple collaborative learning scenarios: A useful tool for collaboration would support the execution of many e-learning scenarios. E-learning scenarios can combine one or more instructional methods like role-playing, case studies, team projects, brainstorming, jigsaw and many more, as long as the environment supports their functional requirements;

Principle 2: Design to maximize the flexibility within a virtual space: Space parameters like size, architecture, facilities and the physical environment affect the way learners socialize (Koubek & Müller, 2002). In order foster educational value, virtual environments must fulfil the teacher's expectations for spatial and temporal flexibility. Therefore, due to the need for multiple functions within a collaborative online synchronous session, it should be possible to quickly reorganize the virtual place for a particular activity or scenario;

Principle 3: Augmenting user's representation and awareness: Combining gestures, mimics, user representation, voice and text chat communication, users can share their views and show others what they are talking about;

Principle 4: Design to reduce the amount of extraneous load of the users: The main objective of an e-learning environment is to support the learning process. Therefore, the users should be able to understand the operation of the learning environment and easily participate in the learning process;

Principle 5: Design a media-learning centric virtual space: The virtual space should be enhanced by multiple communication and media layers. Each media type (e.g. text, graphics, sound etc.) has its advantages. The virtual space should integrate many communication channels (e.g. gestures, voice and text chat etc.) in order to enhance awareness and communication among the users;

Principle 6: Ergonomic design of a virtual place accessible by a large audience: The designers of a virtual place should take into account that a virtual place for e-learning could be used by various individuals with different backgrounds and level of expertise in information and communication technologies;

Principle 7: Design an inclusive, open and user-centred virtual place: SL membership is free, anyone above 18 years old can join (there is also a separate world for teenagers) and the virtual content of the world is created by its users;

Principle 8: Design a place for many people with different roles: An e-learning system should support a variety of roles each with different access rights. For example, in a collaborative learning scenario the participants could be moderators, tutors, or learners.

The virtual space should be designed accordingly in order to differentiate these roles.

The previous versions of EVE platform could support the majority of the above principles through the EVE Training Area tool (Bouras & Tsiatsos, 2002; Bouras et al., 2005). This tool is a three-dimensional space where participants, represented by 3D humanoid avatars, can use a variety of e-collaboration tools. However, the previous versions of EVE should be improved in order to support the following functionality:

- Multiple collaborative learning (CL) techniques (i.e. to support principle 1) and flexibility within a virtual space (i.e. to support principle 2);
- Spatial audio conferencing, which is targeted to support principle 3 (augmenting user's representation and awareness).

The improvements that were made and the new functionality that were added to the previous version of EVE platform are focused on the

satisfaction of the above mentioned principles as well as on the enhancement of the EVE platform in terms of performance, compatibility and stability. The advancements presented in this paper concern: (a) full compatibility with the current version of Extensible 3D (X3D) standard (Web3D, 2009) and extension in order to offer X3D event sharing, even for dynamic created shared objects; (b) support for spatial audio conferencing; and (c) integration of a generic non-X3D events management.

This paper is structured as follows. In the next section EVE training area tool is presented and the way that every principle is met in this environment is described. In addition this section introduces the necessary functional as well as technological improvements in EVE platform which are needed for the support of the new functionality. The third section presents the related work done on X3D enabled NVE platforms; protocols for supporting 3D event sharing in NVEs; spatial audio conferencing; and collaborative design applications. The fourth section presents the integration of X3D event sharing mechanism in EVE platform. Afterwards, in fifth section, we present in detail the design of a spatial audio conferencing server and its integration in EVE platform. In the section that follows we describe a server dedicated to handle non-X3D events sharing. Finally, we present some concluding remarks and our vision for future work.

SUPPORTING COLLABORATIVE LEARNING WITH EVE PLATFORM: AFFORDANCES, LIMITATIONS, FUNCTIONAL AND TECHNOLOGICAL EXTENSIONS

In the following paragraphs, EVE training area is presented and the way that every principle is met in this environment is described.

Furthermore, we are discussing the limitations of this tool concerning the support of:

- Multiple collaborative learning techniques and flexibility within the virtual educational space;
- Spatial audio conferencing.

In addition, we are introducing the necessary functional as well as technological improvements in EVE platform which are needed for the support of the new functionality.

EVE Training Area

EVE Training Area is designed and implemented for hosting synchronous e-learning and e-collaboration sessions. As described in Bouras and Tsiatsos (2006), after the user-evaluation, the usability of this tool has been rated positive. It combines 2D and 3D features for providing the users with the necessary communication and collaboration capabilities. The main feature of EVE training area is the 3D representation of a multi-user virtual classroom. The user interface of the training area is depicted in Figure 1. The participants in the virtual classroom can have two different roles: tutor (only one participant) and students. In that way EVE training area meets principle 8.

The users that participate in the virtual classroom are represented by humanoid articulated avatars, which can support animations (such as walking and sitting down) and gestures for non-verbal interaction among the users. EVE's avatars support functions not only for representing a user but also for visualizing his/her actions to other participants in the virtual space, which also satisfies principle 3.

Available functions in EVE Training area are: Perception (the ability of a participant to see if anyone is around); Localization (the ability of a participant to see where the other person is located); Gestures (representation and visualization of others' actions and feelings. Examples are: "Hi",

Figure 1. User interface of the training area

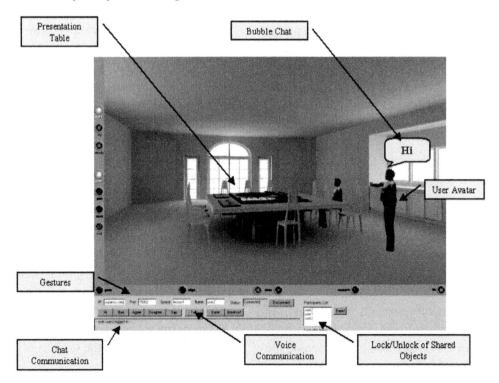

"Bye", "Agree", "Disagree", and "Applause"); Bubble chat (when a user sends a text message, a bubble containing the message appears over his/her avatar).

The virtual classroom is supported by various communication channels (principle 5) such as (a) audio chat, which is the main interaction channel, (b) 3D text/bubble chat, (c) non verbal communication using avatar gestures in order to provide a more realistic interaction among users, expressing, when needed, the emotion of each one to the others (Capin et al., 1999). Furthermore, EVE Training Area supports manipulation of users and shared objects by integrating two specific tools: (a) expel learner/participant and (b) lock / unlock objects. EVE Training Area integrates a "presentation table", which is the central point in the virtual space, in order to provide specific collaboration tools. Using the functionality of this table the users can present their slides and ideas, can comment on slides, upload and view learning material as well as view streaming video. The avatars of all participants in the virtual space can have a sit next to this table, viewing not only what is presented on the table but also the other participants. Furthermore, the user can change his/her viewpoint in order to zoom in and out on the presented material. The presentation table has the following functionality:

- **3D Whiteboard:** The 3D whiteboard supports slide projection, line, circle and ellipsis drawing in a wide range of colors and text input in many sizes and colors. It also offers "undo last action" capability as well the cancellation of all previous actions on the whiteboard;
- **Brainstorming Board:** The brainstorming board can be used in a range of collaborative learning techniques for learners to present their ideas in a structured way. The users can create cards in three shapes (rectangle, circle and hexagon) and five colors

attaching text on them. It should be mentioned that the shape and color of the cards is attached to a defined argument. They can also move and delete a card;

- **Video presenter:** Video presenter is used in order for the user to attend streaming video presentation/movies inside the 3D environment. The users have the capability to start and stop the movie. Supported formats are rm, mpeg, and avi;
- **Library with drag and drop support:** The users have the capability to drag and drop learning material on the table. This material is represented as a small icon on the backside of the table. When the user clicks on the icon the corresponding file is opened either on the whiteboard (if the corresponding file is picture or VRML object), on the video presenter (if the corresponding file is of rm, mpeg or avi type) or on a new pop-up window (if the corresponding file is not supported by the VRML format).

In order to augment the user's representation and awareness (and to satisfy principle 3), the usage of avatars along with gestures and additional icons attached to the avatar could be very helpful (Bouras & Tsiatsos, 2006). Examples of this functionality are the following:

- Bubble chat over the avatars head, which can be used in order to inform the participants of a session about the text chat input of this user. Figure 2a depicts the implementation of a bubble chat;
- User representation and avatar gestures for expressing actions and feelings. In Figure 2b, we can see an avatar of a user to visualize a "Hi" action by a gesture in the EVE training area (Figure 2b).

Concerning awareness of objects and the action on them, there are many solutions. An example is

Figure 2. Examples of augmenting user's representation and awareness

(a)   (b)

depicted in Figure 7, where users can share and see the cards attached in the brainstorming board by their participants.

According to principle 4, the basic functionality of the interface should be accessible in a graphical user interface fashion in the context of a collaborative virtual environments. Furthermore, in order to reduce the amount of extraneous load of the users, EVE training area adopts the following approach:

- It integrates avatars with gestures. In such way the user can see at once who is participating and who is making what contribution. An example is depicted in Figure 3a;

- It separates the shared and not shared areas in order to avoid user's misconception as depicted in Figure 3b. A different design that could maximize the amount of extraneous load of the users is depicted in Figure 3c. In that case there are many areas that contain information fully, partly or not shared. Thus, the user could be overloaded in order to discover what the rest of participants are doing, who is participating, etc.

As previously described e-learning systems, supported by collaborative virtual environments, should be based on three main categories: Content, Learning Context and Communication Media (principle 5). The approach adopted in EVE training area with the concepts of (a) presentation table for sharing information; (b) avatars, audio conferencing and text chat for supporting communication; (c) 3D classroom design along with shared library for integrating learning content has been rated very positively as described in Bouras and Tsiatsos (2006). Thus such a design approach is proposed for supporting principle 5.

Figure 3. Design examples to reduce the extraneous load of the users

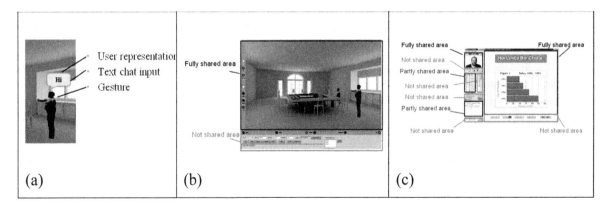

Limitations

EVE Training Area supports almost all the previous defined design principles. Thus, even if the use of virtual reality technology is not a required feature a priori, it seems that the use of collaborative 3D virtual environments and humanoid avatars along with supportive communication channels fit well as a solution for virtual collaboration spaces. Humanoid avatars are a unique solution that 3D-centered tools offer to group communication and learning. It is a fact that persons participating in the virtual learning experience with human like full-body avatars feel more comfortable than in chat or audio-communication (Bouras & Tsiatsos, 2006). The main benefit of the avatars is the psychological feeling of a sense of 'presence'. The sense of 'presence' results in a suspension of disbelief and an increase in motivation and productivity (Bouras & Tsiatsos, 2006). There are a number of important attributes to this experience. The ability to make basic gestures along with a voice or text message strengthens the understanding of the communication context (Redfern & Galway, 2002). Therefore, due to the fact that the user's awareness of the spatial proximity and orientation of others has a strong impact on the dynamics of group communication (Redfern & Galway, 2002), we could say that 3D multi-user virtual spaces have a good potential for supporting learning communities and e-collaboration. In such an environment users feel as though they are working together as a group and tend to forget they are working independently.

However, the previous versions of EVE should be improved in order to support the following functionality:

- **Multiple collaborative learning techniques (i.e. principle 1) and flexibility within a virtual space (i.e. principle 2):** Even though, in the previous versions of EVE, it is feasible to implement and integrate various educational spaces in order to support different collaborative learning techniques, it is not possible to change on the fly the settings of the educational space. A comprehensive and thorough list of collaborative learning techniques is presented in Barkley et al. (2004). Examples are "fishbowl" (where the students form concentric circles with the smaller, inside group of students discussing and the larger, outside group listening and observing), "role play" (where, students assume a different identity and act out a scenario) and "jigsaw" (where, students develop knowledge about a given topic and then teach it to others). Depending on the set objective, the collaborative learning techniques can be used independently of, or in combination with each other. However, the spatial organization of the virtual environment could be very different for each technique. For example the jigsaw CL technique needs various rooms (which are furnished by chairs and a collaboration table) for supporting the discussion and collaboration among the members of jigsaw groups (Figure 4a). On the contrary, fishbowl CL technique could be supported by a hall (Figure 4b), which is furnished by chairs in two concentric cycles and a presentation board.

Furthermore, in the previous versions of EVE platform is possible for the user (teacher) to use and choose various services/virtual tools for supporting the educational process. However, the tutor cannot reorganise the EVE training area in order to support better the learning needs as well as to avoid misunderstandings in the usage by the students. Due to the need for multiple functions within a collaborative online synchronous session, it should be possible to quickly reorganize the virtual place for a particular activity or scenario:

Figure 4. Examples of virtual learning spaces for supporting collaborative learning techniques

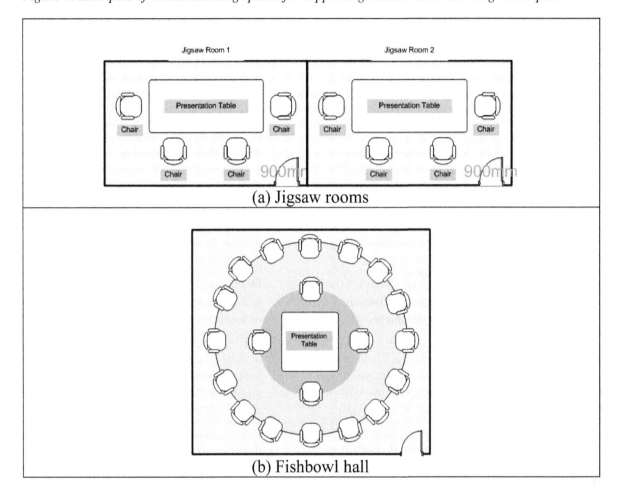

- **Spatial audio conferencing, which is targeted to support principle 3 (augmenting user's representation and awareness):** The spatial audio conferencing support is an important feature of a networked virtual environment that aims to support either distance learning scenarios or e-collaboration (Begault, 1994). According to Barfield et al. (1997) the three primary benefits of auditory spatial information displays are identified as: (a) relieving processing demands on the visual modality; (b) enhancing spatial awareness; and (c) directing attention to important spatial events.

Yamazaki and Herder (2000) refer that, by exploiting spatial audio conferencing, our eyes track a moving avatar on the screen and at the same time a spatialized sound source gives other information without disturbing the visual task. Furthermore, they claim that spatial audio conferencing can enhance the spatial awareness, because the spatial locations of all sound sources let us determine not only the location of other sound sources, but also our own location in space. They also claim that an acoustical event spatialized using a sound source can direct our attention. We tend to agree with the above claims and findings. Spatial audio is of equal importance with visual modality in order for an interactive 3D environment to be realistic. Plain audio conferencing support is an important feature. However, the best results are achieved by integrating spatial audio conferencing.

Functional Extensions

In the following paragraphs, we are presenting the necessary functional improvements in EVE platform for the support of:

- Multiple collaborative learning techniques, spatial collaboration on the implementation of CL techniques and flexibility within the virtual educational space;
- Spatial audio conferencing.

Multiple Collaborative Learning Techniques and Design to Maximize the Flexibility within a Virtual Space

EVE platform has been improved and offers a new module, giving the teacher the ability to design the EVE training area as s/he wants (Bouras et al., 2007). From the users' side this module is a plug-in which is extended by a 2D tool (Figure 5) called "Collaborative Spatial Design Tool". This tool contains a number of panels to provide different functions. Besides the already existing panels from the previous versions of EVE platform (i.e. gesture, chat and lock panels), two new panels is introduced:

- **The "2D Top View Panel" (Figure 5: 2D Top View Panel):** This panel was embedded in the user interface as a tool for re-

Figure 5. User interface of EVE client extended with collaborative spatial design tool

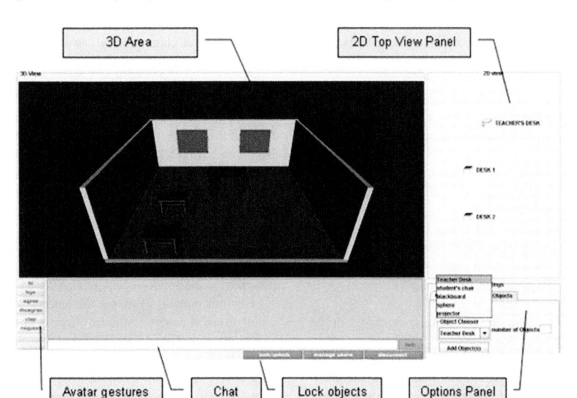

arranging worlds in collaborative spatial designs. It illustrates the floor plan of the world area and its objects. A user can move an object inside the limits of the world thus the limits of the panel and then s/he can watch the corresponding X3D object moving in the virtual X3D world. The introduction of this panel is of great importance. Not only it gives a better inspection of the object arrangement in the world, making it easier for the user to choose the modifications to be applied, but it also functions as lightweight object transporter. The events occurring on that panel are shared with the rest of the online users;

- **The "Options Panel" (Figure 5: Options Panel):** When dealing with collaborative spatial design options (such as object lists and classroom information) are a necessity. For that reason the option panel features options depending on the application. For example, this panel features options such as an object list for choosing virtual objects, a classroom object list, and number of copies of certain objects to be inserted, etc.

Using the Collaborative Spatial Design Tool, depicted in Figure 5, the teacher can design the EVE training area as s/he wants by:

- Using predefined classroom models and having the ability to reorganize the classroom;
- Creating and setting up of a virtual classroom using object library;
- Using spatial collaboration on the implementation of CL techniques.

These usage scenarios are described in the following paragraphs.

Usage of predefined classroom models with classroom reorganization ability: This functionality offers quick classroom setup and the ability to move existing objects or to add new. The procedure that a teacher has to follow is to choose one of the predefined classrooms according to his/her criteria. Once the teacher selects a predefined classroom in which specific objects are placed has two options. The first one is to select new objects, which s/he wants to add, from an object list (Figure 5: Options Panel). The second one is to rearrange already added components. When a teacher loads a classroom a top view is created in a 2D panel next to the 3D world (Figure 5: 2D Top View Panel). Each 3D object has a 2D representation. The teacher can move an object in the 2D view. Accordingly the corresponding X3D object will be re-located in the virtual world. This scenario is preferred when the features and the customization needed for a classroom have to do mainly with objects' location and re-orientation. In that case the avoidance of having to select an empty classroom and fill it with object saves much time.

Creation and set up of a virtual classroom using object library: This functionality supports the teacher to implement multiple learning scenarios. More specifically s/he can change the organization of the virtual classroom and can use different shared objects that can facilitate each learning scenario. For example, s/he may want to select the size or shape of the virtual classroom, add specific objects etc. If that is the case EVE offers the ability to select from a variety of objects stored in a database library (Figure 5: Options Panel). Extended customization is offered by this model enhancing more precise customization. The teacher chooses an empty virtual classroom from a list of virtual classrooms, according to his/her needs. Then s/he adds the kind and number of objects s/he likes. Moving the 3D objects is supported as well, as described in the previous paragraph.

This functionality is giving the teachers the ability to select among a number of empty or already customized classrooms. A list of available objects can be added in the virtual classrooms by the teachers. Moreover, a teacher can move objects in the 2D floor plan. This plan contains a 2D representation of all the objects in the classroom.

Dragging an object in the 2D view moves the corresponding object in the 3D world accordingly. For example, in order to apply the brainstorming/roundtable scenario the tutor can re-organise the classroom area by creating a table with a brainstorming board and seats for the learners around the table, as depicted in Figure 6.

EVE Training Area has been designed in such a way to maximise the flexibility within a virtual space (in order to satisfy principle 2). The tutor can reorganise the EVE training area in order to better support the learning needs as well as to avoid misunderstandings in the usage by the students. In that way, the tutor can either create or re-use virtual rooms for formal classes, group work, etc. For example in the organisation depicted in Figure 6 the only action for the user, in order to participate in the brainstorming session, is to move his/her mouse over a chair and to click on it (Figure 7a). By following these actions the viewpoint of the user is changed and s/he can see the presentation table and the other participants (Figure 7b and Figure 7c). After that the user can cooperate with the rest of participants in the brainstorming session by zooming in the brainstorming table (Figure 7d).

Spatial collaboration on the implementation of CL techniques: During these scenarios an inexperienced teacher in the application of CL techniques could collaborate with an expert in order to rearrange the classroom. This collaboration can be supported by chat communication and 3D objects sharing. Furthermore, the expert can take the control to organize the classrooms adding and rearranging 3D objects. Alternatively, two or more teachers can collaborate concerning the creation and organization of a virtual classroom.

Spatial Audio Conferencing

The integration of spatial audio conferencing in CVE platforms could facilitate the users' communication in terms of immediateness, while at the same time the voice contributes to a more realistic communication and interaction among the users. Spatial audio conferencing contributes to a best perception of the environmental entities,

Figure 6. Organizing the EVE training area for brainstorming

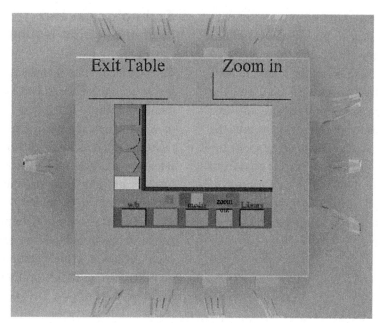

Figure 7. Brainstorming session

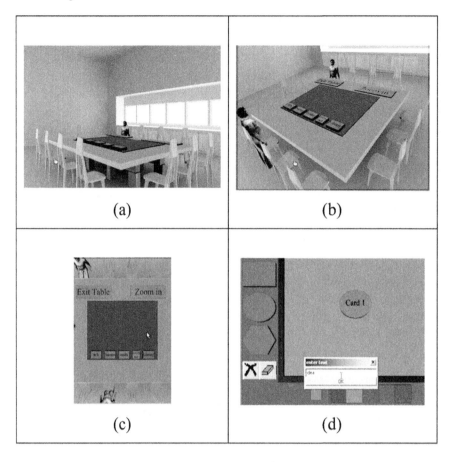

especially when the user has no eye contact with them. The user, by hearing spatial audio, obtains information about the 3D location, and the direction of the entity which emits the sound moves. Moreover, depending on the intensity and the tone of the sound, a user can be aware, to some extent, of the intensions of the entity towards the user as well as the psychological situation of the entity. These psychological effects that arise from the 3D spatial sound along with the perception of space, lead to a very realistic interaction in two fashions: among the users, and between the user and the virtual space.

Technological and Implementation Issues

The advancements presented in this paper were implemented in EVE Networked Virtual Environments platform. Thus, it is essential to present the main characteristics of this platform. EVE is based on open technologies (i.e. Java and X3D). It features a client-(multi) server architecture (Figure 8) with a modular structure that allows new functionalities to be added with minimal effort. The previous version of EVE platform provided a full set of functionalities for e-learning procedures, such as avatar representation, avatar gestures, content sharing, brainstorming, chatting etc.

Figure 8. EVE architecture

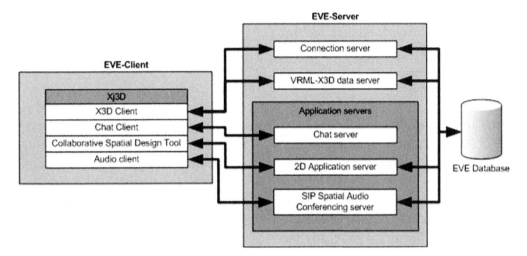

However, the above described functionality for maximizing the flexibility within a virtual space, implies the implementation and integration of a collaborative spatial design application in EVE platform. Such an application requires:

- A flexible way for dynamic 3D world manipulation such as the ability to dynamically load virtual environments and shared objects;
- A generic event's management mechanism for effective non-X3D event handling.

From the technical point of view X3D (Web3D, 2009) is the current open standard for lightweight 3D content description and representation, to build virtual environments. It can be used from desktop to web applications and is the ideal solution for open platforms. However, X3D standard does not support 3D event sharing, which is necessary for the multi-user nature of Collaborative Virtual Environments. The previous version of EVE integrated an X3D event-handling mechanism responsible for serving events related to the virtual world. However, a more robust and complete solution has been implemented in the extended version of EVE platform in order to accomplish the demand for dynamic X3D node loading.

Concerning the integration of the Collaborative Spatial Design Tool, there is a need to handle non-X3D events in order to support:

- The retrieval of new 3D objects or whole virtual worlds from a database, (such as database queries to retrieve objects and 3D environments from a database);
- The manipulation of 3D objects from an external and intuitive 2D interface, which implies the support of java swing events.

These events are called "2D applications events". An additional server called "2D application server" has been developed and integrated in EVE platform for servicing "2D applications events".

Concerning the integration of spatial audio conferencing, EVE platform featured H.323 audio conferencing since it was introduced. However in order to support the spatial audio conferencing a new Audio Conferencing Server is needed. This server features a new algorithmic approach and utilizes the latest session protocols and codec technologies. The main issues concerning the integration of spatial audio conferencing are the following:

- The selection of a networked audio protocol along with algorithms and codecs that will be used to establish sessions and reproduce sound among users;
- The algorithms that will create the illusion of 3D spatial sound.

After the integration of the new features, the client-side of EVE platform is a Java applet that incorporates an X3D browser (based on Xj3D API), and audio and a chat client.

The server-side architecture of the EVE platform consists of five servers as shown in Figure 8. The "Connection Server" coordinates the operation of the other three. The "VRML-X3D Server" is responsible for sending the 3D content to the clients as well as for managing the virtual worlds and the events that occur in them. The "Chat Server" supports the text chat communication among the participants of the virtual environments. The "SIP Spatial Audio Conferencing Server" is used to manage audio streams from the clients and to support spatial audio conferencing. Finally the "2D Application Server" handles the generic (i.e. non-X3D) events.

Both "SIP Spatial Audio Conferencing Server" and "2D Application Server" are the new servers that integrated in EVE platform. More details about this server and the related implementation issues will be described in detail later in this paper.

The rest of the paper is focused on presenting the related work and the work done concerning the technological advancements of EVE platform.

RELATED WORK ON TECHNOLOGICAL ISSUES

This section presents the related work in point of the advancements of EVE platform. Therefore, it is organized in the following parts describing work done on: (a) X3D enabled NVE platforms; (b) protocols for supporting 3D event sharing in

NVEs; (c) spatial audio conferencing; and (d) collaborative design applications.

X3D Enabled NVE Platforms

This paragraph presents an overview of the state of the art on X3D enabled networked virtual environment platforms. Generally speaking, there are many networked virtual environment platforms either commercial products or research platforms. The most significant commercial networked virtual environment platforms are the following: blaxxun platform (http://www.blaxxun.com), Bitmanagement's BS Collaborate (BS Collaborate, 2007), Active Worlds (http://www.activeworlds.com), Octaga (http://www.octaga.com), ParallelGraphics (http://www.parallelgraphics.com), Croquet (http://www.croquetconsortium.org), I-maginer, (http://www.i-maginer.fr/), Second Life (http://secondlife.com) and Workspace 3D (http://www.tixeo.com). The most significant research platforms are the following: DIVE: Distributed Interactive Virtual Environments (Carlsson & Hagsand, 1993; http://www.sics.se/dive), SPLINE: Scalable Platform for Large Interactive Environments (http://www.merl.com/projects/spline), VLNET: Virtual Life Network (Pandzic et al., 1996; Pandzic et al., 1998), SmallTool (Broll, 1998) and EVE (Bouras et al., 2005; Bouras et al., 2006; http://ouranos.ceid.upatras.gr/vr).

However, some of the above platforms are not supporting X3D standard at all and some of them are supporting X3D standard partially (Bouras et al., 2005). The most promising X3D enabled CVE platforms today are Bitmanagement, Octaga and EVE solutions. Almost all these platforms partially support X3D standard, and offer good rendering functionality. However, the first two (i.e. Bitmanagement, and Octaga) solutions are commercial and any extension and or programming, that requires additional technical implementation, cost additionally due to the additional cost of the respective SDKs. Furthermore, a commercial solution may have the risk of a closed solution due to each company's extensions to the standards. Therefore, it is obvious that in order to support X3D collaborative virtual environments the most mature solutions are the commercial platforms. However, the cost in this case is high. Thus, a promising technical solution could be EVE platform. For that reason we have decided to work on the extension of EVE platform in order to accomplish the demand for dynamic X3D node loading.

Protocols for Supporting 3D Event Sharing in NVEs

This paragraph is presenting briefly the main protocols for handling 3D event sharing in NVEs, in order to adopt similar mechanisms (if any) for dynamic X3D node loading. These protocols are VRTP (Virtual Reality Transfer Protocol) (Brutzman et al., 1997), DIS (Distributed Interactive Simulation) protocol (Canterbury, 1995) and SWAMP (Simple Wide Area Multi-user Protocol) (Weber & Parisi, 2007).

VRTP is an application level protocol for Internet based NVE's in a standardized way. It offers four basic functionalities for NVEs communication capabilities: (a) entity state processing, (b) heavyweight objects, (c) network pointers and (d) real-time streams. VRTP framework consists of a protocol collection and an application level protocol that provides the necessary connectivity between the client and the virtual environment. The main problem of VRTP is that its design is focused on the support of the communication needs of VRML-based NVEs; It wasn't designed in order to meet specific networking demands.

The DIS protocol has been designed to support large scale Virtual Environments and is based on the SIMNET standard (Miller & Thorpe, 1995). It consists of a set of protocols. More specifically DIS defines a set of Protocol Data Units (PDUs), which are transmitted to all the participants of the NVE in order to update the current state of each object. DIS is very efficient in supporting many concurrent users. However, it is difficult to be integrated in EVE platform because of its limited scalability and the rigidity caused by embedding its application in its architecture (Wray & Hawkes, 1998).

Finally, SWAMP is a new multi-user protocol which was designed in order to support X3D client-server communication. The philosophy behind its design is the ability to be used in wide area, thus heterogeneous, networks. A great amount of concern has been given to the message exchange speed and safety. SWAMP uses an entity model that is based on the X3D rationale (i.e. nodes and fields). Abstractions of an entity or a total of entities are also supported. The approach of SWAMP for the client-server communication, regards the use of TCP/IP for the establishment of the initial connection as well as for the exchange of low frequency messages and utilizes UDP for exchanging continuous, highly frequent messages. UDP usage involves the use of packages with small overhead, which results in faster transportation. SWAMP integration in the X3D scene graph involves the usage of the X3D Network Component. This features a node named EventStreamSensor that establishes network connections. However, SWAMP is still under development and thus it is not ready for public use.

Our work differs from SWAMP in the type of the events that are sent to the server. Instead of using the EventStreamSensor node to transmit events, each event that occurs in the virtual world is captured by a custom event sharing mechanism and is transmitted to a dedicated server for processing. The mechanism of our solution is more generic, since it allows the sharing of events that occur outside the 3D scene as well. By that way our mechanism can support the dispatch of an event of an external application to the 3D scene. In addition our mechanism is mature and fully functional, offering a variety of events that is a superset of the X3D standard set of events.

Spatial Audio Conferencing

A fair amount of work has been done on spatial 3D sound. The majority of today's 3D games, single or multi-user, features spatial 3D sound. However the sound that is used in this type of applications is pre-recorded. When it comes to CVE's where live streaming sound needs to be converted to spatial 3D sound, little work has been done. Good examples have been presented by Liesenborgs (2000) and Macedonia et al. (1995).

The work done by Macedonia et al. (1995) is based on multicast networks. It features a networked virtual environment that offers low cost 3D sound. We want to avoid this solution due to the fact that multicasting is not available in every network.

Liesenborgs (2000) describes a Voice over IP framework for networked virtual environments. The capture and reconstruction of voice is accomplished by the clients' operating system. The session initiation and the transmission of the voice are carried out by Real-time Transmission Protocol (RTP) and Session Initiation Protocol (SIP) (RFC3261, 2002) libraries written in C++. The spatialization of the audio is performed by an algorithm that mimics the way human ear perceives sound, that is using the Interaural Time Difference (ITD) and the Interaural Intensity Difference (IID) effects. Our work differs from the work done by Liesenborgs (2000) in terms of portability, since our solution is Java based thus platform independent. The second and major difference is that our solution relies on an X3D standard node to perform the audio spatialization in X3D based virtual environments.

Spatial Collaboration Applications

There is some research work done on spatial collaboration using CVE. This work, as described in the following paragraphs, is focused on: (a) the usefulness of multiple representations and the need for additional features to support collaboration across representations; (b) the viewpoints handling; (c) findings concerning intuitiveness and real-time interaction issues in virtual environments for supporting spatial collaboration.

The main example is the work done by Schafer and Bowman (2005), which investigates how to support distributed spatial collaboration activities and presents a novel prototype that integrates both two-dimensional and three-dimensional representations. Our work differs from this project in terms of technological solution as well as from the communication channels included. Our scope is to rely on the use of the combined representations and the findings of Schafer and Bowman (2005), which highlight the usefulness of multiple representations and the need for additional features to support collaboration across representations.

Another example is CALVIN prototype (Leigh & Johnson, 1996; Leigh et al., 1996). This system explores the usage of different virtual reality hardware configurations, such as CAVE and Immersadesk technology, for collaboration. Although our scope is to design and develop a system for desktop CVEs, using only keyboard and mouse as input devices, the findings of this work are useful concerning the viewpoints handling.

Another interesting work concerns VSculpt (Li & Lau, 2003), which is a collaborative virtual sculpting system that enables geographically separated designers to participate in the design process of engineering tools and sculptures. Although this work aims at supporting collaborative virtual sculpting, its findings concerning intuitiveness and real-time interaction are very useful for the extension of our platform.

Furthermore, Li et al (2006) implemented a 3D collaborative system for double-suction centrifugal pump, based on X3D and Java Applet technology. The system allows the assembly of a centrigugal pump by one or more collaborators via a web interface that is embedded in an X3D browser. Our work is different in the way that the 3D objects are externally modified, and that user can move objects inside the 3D scene. Our work is based on the use of a two dimensional ground plan of the scene that displays labels of all the available 3D objects. These labels can be dragged within the 2D ground plan resulting in the movement of the corresponding 3D objects in the 3D scene.

X3D SUPPORT AND EVENT SHARING

This section presents two important features of the EVE platform:

- The support of X3D standard, which is the current standard in the area web based virtual reality applications;
- The extension of X3D by a custom event sharing mechanism, which manages and shares events over the network.

Generic X3D Features

Originally, VRML (Virtual Reality Modeling Language) was used in EVE for 3D content creation and visualization. VRML evolved to, the ISO certified, X3D open standard. X3D supports XML encoding as well as the syntax of the VRML language. Many advantages derive from the use of XML, such as interoperability with other networking applications and familiar syntax to web applications developers. Considering that EVE is a web based platform, the use of an XML based open standard is very important. Moreover, X3D allows lightweight core 3D runtime delivery engine. This is crucial since EVE's client runs within a browser where minimum consumption of resources is required. Furthermore, there is no tradeoff between lightness and quality since X3D graphics are of high quality, while performing in real-time.

In order to dynamically modify 3D content, which is a key feature for the interactive virtual environments, the Scene Authoring Interface

(SAI) was created. SAI is the appropriate API (Application Programming Interface) for user-3D scene interaction. Using SAI programmers can add, remove and modify nodes and their fields from both inside and outside the 3D scene.

Although X3D offers many advantages for visualizing and interacting with web based virtual environments, there is no mature or cost-effective solution for multi-user event sharing over the network, as presented in a previous section. Therefore, the only solution for supporting multi-user virtual environments is the extension of X3D by implementing an event sharing mechanism. This mechanism is described in the next paragraph.

X3D Event Sharing Mechanism

An NVE is based on a mechanism for sharing events that occur in the virtual scenes. This is important in order to maintain 3D content consistency and to allow interaction among users. As said before, X3D currently does not provide a mechanism and/or protocol to share 3D scene events. The event sharing mechanism of the previous version of EVE platform is now improved. In order to accomplish the demand for event sharing support of dynamic created 3D objects (i.e. dynamic X3D node sharing and loading). The previous version of EVE integrated an X3D event-handling mechanism responsible for serving events related to the virtual world. The previous mechanism overrides SAI and EAI (External Authoring Interface) in a way that events are sent to all users connected to the platform. In order to dynamically create nodes a specific event is sent to the VRML-X3D server, containing the node to be added and the parent (default is "root node") to make this node its child. This event is then broadcasted to online users and is added to an X3D representation of the world it belongs. This representation is kept in the server and it is broadcasted to new users that entered later in the virtual world. It should be pointed out that already online and connected users to the platform receive only the newly added nodes. By that way, networking load is significantly reduced. Once online clients receive a shared node they locally add it to their VRML-X3D Scene.

In general, the design of event sharing mechanism is trying to fulfill the following three requirements:

- Event sharing support of many data types and events;
- Easy transformation of a non multi-user X3D virtual world to a multi-user one, based on little code changes to the initial X3D file;
- Selection of efficient and suitable network protocols for good network bandwidth management.

In order to satisfy the above requirements, the event sharing mechanism features an internal Java representation of X3D nodes and fields. Events that are needed to be shared are marked with a "shared" tag, in the corresponding field routes. This method causes a minimum change to the initial X3D file. When a new shared event occurs in a client's virtual world the following steps are followed:

- The event is being transmitted to the VRML-X3D server without affecting the local copy of the virtual world in the client;
- The event is converted to an instance of class responsible for describing event, with all the necessary parameters stored as well;
- The event is processed by the server and is sent back to the clients that the event concerns;
- The event is received by the client, it is transformed via SAI to reflect the change inside the virtual scene.

The network protocol used for the event transmission is, generally, TCP in order to ensure reliability. However, the events occurring from avatars' position or orientation changes are transmitted via UDP. This ensures low network load, while at the same time it does not have impacts on the quality of the user's experience, since packages of such events are very frequently transmitted.

Implementation Issues

The implementation of the above described mechanism involves both 3D content handling and parsing. As EVE is mainly implemented in Java, the Xj3D toolkit is used for the X3D and SAI implementation. We have extended Xj3D's Java library by creating a custom library (called "vrmlx") in order to provide support for shared events. This library contains packages that describe the fields and nodes of the X3D standard (Web 3d, 2007). Every vrmlx node extends a basic node named BaseNode. Similarly, each field extends a basic field named "Field". Each time occuring an event in the virtual world, the event's attributes related to X3D (such as a node or a field) are transformed to a vrmlx library representation. Afterwards, the clients receive the event, convert its vrmlx representation to an Xj3D representation and the event is applied to the 3D scene.

In order to support X3D virtual world loading and dynamic X3D objects' events sharing an X3D parser has been implemented. This parser parses the x3d files and loads the 3D content. The parser has been integrated in EVE platform as a package (called "vrmlx.parser") in the vrmlx library.

EVE'S SIP SPATIAL AUDIO CONFERENCING SERVER

The previous versions of EVE platform featured H.323-based audio conferencing. In order to increase performance and stability as well as to emphasize the distributed nature of the platform a new Audio Conferencing Server was introduced. This server features a new algorithmic approach and utilizes the latest session protocols and codec technologies. The main issues concerning the integration of spatial audio conferencing are the following:

- The selection of a networked audio protocol along with algorithms and codecs that will be used to establish sessions and reproduce sound among users;
- Design and implementation of the algorithms that will create the illusion of 3D spatial sound.

These issues are described in the following paragraphs.

EVE Audio Spatialization Process and Conferencing Architecture

The steps of the audio spatialization process adopted in EVE platform are the following:

- The establishment of the client-server connection;
- The capture of the audio stream by the client;
- The transmission of the audio stream to the server;
- The spatialization process of the audio stream in the virtual world;
- The reception of the audio stream by the rest of clients.

The technologies used in order to support the above process are the following:

- Session Initiation Protocol (SIP) for the session establishment. This lightweight, transport independent protocol has proven to be very reliable and robust thus making it the most popular session protocol nowadays;
- Real Time Protocol (RTP) for audio data transmission (RFC3550, 2003);

- The Java Media Framework API, which provides convenient classes and methods for media manipulation, is used for supporting the audio capture.

Concerning the process for audio spatialization the proposed and implemented solution takes into account issues such as bandwidth consumption, processing costs, complexity, as well as design and implementation issues related to EVE platform.

Audio spatialization is performed by an X3D Sound node (Figure 9). Firstly, the client's side architecture is examined. The establishment of the client-server connection is accomplished via the SIP protocol. The client's applet makes a call to the SIP Spatial Audio Conferencing Server and a server port is reserved for the connection with the client. After the session initiation, an RTP stream, using the JMF API, is established with the server, in order to transmit the audio data stream. At the same time the client's capture device captures audio data, utilizing JMF API's classes, and transmits them through the RTP stream. The X3D browser of the applet receives the audio data encapsulated, by the SIP Spatial Audio Conferencing Server, in X3D AudioClip nodes. The playback of the audio is performed by X3D Sound nodes that use the AudioClip nodes as their sources.

The X3D Sound node features built-in spatialization and attenuation audio algorithms. Regarding the server side, the following procedure takes place: The server is waiting for new SIP calls on a dedicated port. After an incoming call from a client is accepted, a new port is assigned for the communication between a server thread, dedicated in servicing the specific client, and the server. This thread establishes an RTP stream with the client for receiving audio data. Concurrently, the SIP Spatial Audio Conferencing Server acquires information of the user's avatar location and orientation in the virtual world through the VRML-X3D Server. This information will be used to reproduce the sound like it is being emitted from the avatar's mouth.

Figure 9. Audio conferencing architecture

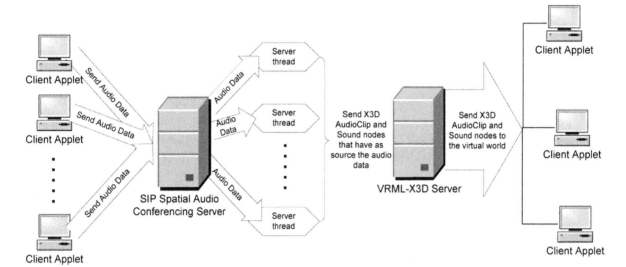

For each user an X3D AudioClip node along with an X3D Sound node are instantiated via the Xj3D API and they are added in the graph scene of the virtual world. A file is created to which the audio data are continuously appended to. The AudioClip node's URL field is given that file as a value, while the Sound node's fields direction, location and source fields are given the values of the avatar's mouth direction, avatar's mouth location and the AudioClip, respectively. The key point in this solution is that the audio spatialization is based on the X3D Sound node. This node can produce spatialized audio by setting appropriate values to the specialized fields.

When the two new X3D nodes are added to the scene, the VRML-X3D server sends them to the client and the client's X3D browser starts immediate playback of the Sound node.

Implementation Issues

In this section the implementation issues (SIP integration, audio streaming, capture and spatialization) are discussed along with the main technologies in which the SIP Spatial Audio Conferencing Server is based on:

- **SIP integration:** A java implementation of the protocol was adopted due to the fact that the EVE platform is Java – Xj3D based. More specifically, JAIN – SIP (JAIN – SIP, 2007) was chosen as an API. This solution helps us to maintain EVE's openness and cross platform characteristics;
- **RTP streaming and audio capture:** The RTP streaming and the audio captured management tasks, is performed by custom code that utilizes the *Java Media Framework API* – JMF. The capture format that is used in this implementation is in linear encoding, has 8000 Hz sample rate, 8 bits of sample size and is monophonic. The streaming format was of the same characteristics. We used these relatively low quality settings in order to save bandwidth;
- **Audio spatialization:** The spatialization of audio is performed by the X3D Sound Node. The Sound node specifies fields that affect the spatialization of the sound. The sound is located at a point in the local coordinate system and it is emitted in an elliptical pattern. The location is specified by the *location* field, while the direction vector

of the ellipsoids is specified by the *direction* field. There are fields that specify the maximum and minimum values to where the sound is audible, that is the maximum and minimum lengths of the two ellipsoids along the direction vector. A very crucial field is the *spatialize* field. If set to *TRUE* the sound is perceived as being directionally located relative to the listener. If the listener is located between the transformed inner and outer ellipsoids, the listener's direction and the relative location of the Sound node is taken into account during playback. In our implementation this field is set to *TRUE*, resulting in a very realistic spatialized audio playback. The sound source specified by the field source is an AudioClip node. The AudioClip node specifies an URL field (that in our implementation is the URL file of the buffer), which is used as source. In order to change between the two sets of nodes, we used an ECMA script which sets the *startime* field of one AudioClip that waits to start, equal to the *stoptime* field of the currently playing AudioClip.

GENERIC EVENT'S MANAGEMENT: EVE'S 2D APPLICATION SERVER

As described before, there is a need to handle non-X3D events in order to support:

- The retrieval of new 3D objects or whole virtual worlds from a database, (such as database queries to retrieve objects and 3D environments from a database);
- The manipulation of 3D objects from an external and intuitive 2D interface, which implies the support of java swing events.

These events are called "2D applications events". Five types of "2D application events" are currently supported:

- SQL Database query (which is a string representing an SQL query);
- JDBC ResultSet (a JDBC ResultSet class);
- Java Swing Component (such as labels, shapes, etc.);
- Java Swing Events (such as altering the location of a Swing Component);
- Ping: Used to verify the connection between the server and the clients.

EVE, as already mentioned, consists of several servers. However, none of them is able to manage 2D events. For that reason an additional server called "2D application server" has been integrated in EVE platform.

The client-server communication operation is described as shown in Figure 10: Firstly a client establishes a connection to the server. This class deals with connection related issues such as sockets server ports etc. Once a connection has been established, two threads (one responsible for sending and one for receiving "2D application event" instances) are created for each client. On the client side, a thread responsible for "2D application event" handling and server communication is created. The receiving thread examines if the event is to be executed in the server (e.g. Database query). In that case, it executes the event and, if necessary, it creates another event (e.g. ResultSet). Otherwise, it enqueues the event in the ClientConnection FIFO queue. After that the sending thread takes the first pending event and sends it to all clients.

FUTURE WORK

Among our next steps, it is to extensive test the newly added features among a various usage scenarios by large groups of users. Also, several

Figure 10. 2D events architecture

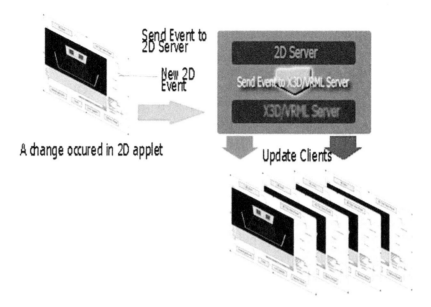

technical aspects of the features need to be thoroughly examined, such as scalability, packet jitter and server load.

In addition, we plan to extend EVE platform in order to support mixed reality applications. Mixed reality applications usually involve the usage of specialized and expensive equipment in order to mix real world with virtual world (i.e. computer generated data). This can be done by utilizing the generic event's management mechanism to handle non-3D data such as video projections.

Concerning spatial collaboration applications, our next step has mainly to do with extended world setup abilities. Particularly, a user will have the abilities to add his/her custom X3D objects, change a classroom's dimensions, and visualize possible collisions. Collisions may occur due to the following reasons: (a) specific spatial setup models; (b) accessibility to emergency exits in case of an emergency situation; (c) routes a teacher follows during class time; and (d) students co-existence problems.

Also, we intend to provide full H-Anim (http://www.h-anim.org/) support in EVE avatars. The H-Anim protocol is a standard way of modeling and animating humanoids, designed to facilitate the sharing of animations between different humanoid models. This will allow the creation of portable avatars that can be transferred from one NVE platform to another. By supporting H-anim standard we will facilitate the users to upload and use their custom H-Anim compliant avatar.

Finally, we plan to evaluate this platform exploiting the framework suggested by Tsiatsos, Konstantinidis and Pomportsis (2010). This framework consists of two consecutive cycles. Each cycle is made up of individual phases consisting of three steps: main phase step, data acquisition step and data analysis step. There are three types of phases: pre-analysis, usability and learning. This evaluation will include the Jigsaw CL technique, the Fishbowl CL technique and the participation of postgraduate students.

CONCLUSION

This paper presented advanced functionality that has been integrated on "EVE Training Area tool" in order to support: (a) multiple collaborative learning techniques (b) Spatial audio conferencing, which is targeted to support principle 3.

Furthermore, the paper presented technological and implementation issues concerning the evolution of "EVE platform" in order to support this functionality.

EVE platform is based on open technologies (i.e. Java and X3D). It features a client – multi-server architecture with a modular structure that allows new functionalities to be added with minimal effort. The previous version of EVE platform provided a full set of functionalities for e-learning procedures, such as avatar representation, avatar gestures, content sharing, brainstorming, chatting etc. However, the above described functionality for maximizing the flexibility within a virtual space, implied the implementation and integration of a collaborative spatial design application in EVE platform. Such an application required: (a) a flexible way for dynamic 3D world manipulation such as the ability to dynamically load virtual environments and shared objects; and (b) a generic event's management mechanism for effective non-X3D event handling. For that reason the X3D standard has been extended by a custom event sharing mechanism over the network, which manages and shares events that occur in the virtual worlds. This mechanism has been integrated in EVE platform.

Another important extension of EVE platform is the design and implementation of a spatial audio conferencing server to support spatial audio conferencing functionality. By that feature EVE can support the three primary benefits of auditory spatial information displays that are identified as: (a) relieving processing demands on the visual modality, (b) enhancing spatial awareness, and (c) directing attention to important spatial events. Concerning the integration of spatial audio conferencing we have faced the following issues: (a) the selection of a networked audio protocol along with algorithms and codecs that will be used to establish sessions and reproduce sound among users; and (b) the design and implementation of the algorithms that will create the illusion of 3D

spatial sound. As far as the protocol is concerned, the Session Initiation Protocol (SIP) was used. The transmission of the audio data utilizes the Real-time Transport Protocol (RTP).

The last technological improvement in EVE platform was the integration of a module for handling non-X3D events in order to support (a) the retrieval of new 3D objects or whole virtual worlds from a database, (such as database queries to retrieve objects and 3D environments from a database); and (b) the manipulation of 3D objects from an external and intuitive 2D interface, which implies the support of java swing events. An additional server called "2D application server" has been developed and integrated in EVE platform for servicing this type of events.

To conclude with, the new version of EVE platform, by integrating the above features can support in a more effective way the EVE training area by offering to its users new tools and flexibility concerning the application of collaborative learning techniques. Now the teacher can design the EVE training area as s/he wants by (a) using predefined classroom models and having the ability to reorganize the classroom; (b) creating and setting up a virtual classroom using object library; and (c) using spatial collaboration on the implementation of CL techniques.

REFERENCES

Barfield, W., Cohen, M., & Rosenberg, C. (1997). Visual, auditory, and combined visual-auditory displays for enhanced situational awareness. *The International Journal of Aviation Psychology*, 7(2), 123–138. doi:10.1207/s15327108ijap0702_2

Barkley, E., Cross, P., & Major, C. (2004). *Collaborative learning techniques: A handbook for college faculty*. Jossey-Bass.

Begault, D. R. (1994). *3-d sound for virtual reality and multimedia*. Academic Press Professional, Inc.

Bouras, C., Giannaka, E., Panagopoulos, A., & Tsiatsos, T. (2006). A platform for virtual collaboration spaces and educational communities: The case of EVE. *Multimedia Systems Journal* [Springer Verlang.]. *Special Issue on Multimedia System Technologies for Educational Tools*, *11*(3), 290–303.

Bouras, C., Giannaka, E., & Tsiatsos, Th. (2008). Exploiting virtual environments to support collaborative e-learning communities. [IGI Global.]. *International Journal of Web-Based Learning and Teaching Technologies*, *3*(2), 1–22. doi:10.4018/jwltt.2008040101

Bouras, C., Panagopoulos, A., & Tsiatsos, T. (2005, December 12–14). Advances in X3D multi - user virtual environments. In *Proceedings of the IEEE International Symposium on Multimedia (ISM 2005)*, Irvine, CA (pp. 136–142).

Bouras, C., Psaroudis, C., Psaltoulis, C., & Tsiatsos, T. (2001, October 9-12). A platform for sharing educational virtual environments. In *Proceedings of the 9th International Conference on Software, Telecommunications and Computer Networks (SoftCOM 2001)*, Split, Croatia (pp. 659–666).

Bouras, C., Tegos, C., Triglianos, V., & Tsiatsos, T. (2007, June 25-29). X3D multi-user virtual environment platform for collaborative spatial design. In *Proceedings of the 9th International Workshop on Multimedia Network Systems and Applications (MNSA-2007)*, Toronto, Canada.

Bouras, C., & Tsiatsos, T. (2002, September 9-12). Extending the limits of CVEs to support collaborative e-learning scenarios. In *Proceedings of the 2nd IEEE International Conference on Advanced Learning Technologies*, Kazan, Russia (pp. 420–424).

Bouras, C., & Tsiatsos, T. (2004). Distributed virtual reality: Building a multi-user layer in EVE platform. [Academic Press.]. *Journal of Network and Computer Applications*, *27*(2), 91–111. doi:10.1016/j.jnca.2003.10.002

Bouras, C., & Tsiatsos, T. (2006). Educational virtual environments: Design rationale and architecture. [Kluwer Academic Publishers.]. *Multimedia Tools and Applications*, *29*(2), 153–173. doi:10.1007/s11042-006-0005-7

Broll, W. (1998). SmallTool - a toolkit for realizing shared virtual environments on the Internet. *Distributed Systems Engineering Journal, Special Issue on Distributed Virtual Environments* (Vol. 5). The British Computer Society, The Institution of Electrical Engineers and IOP Publishing Ltd.

Brutzman, D., Zyda, M., Watsen, K., & Macedonia, M. (1997). Virtual reality transfer protocol design rationale. In *Proceedings of the IEEE Sixth International Workshops on Enabling Technologies: Infrastructure for Collaborative Enterprises (WETICE'97), Distributed System Aspects of Sharing a Virtual Reality workshop* (pp. 179-186). Cambridge, MA: IEEE Computer Society.

Canterbury, M. (1995). *An automated approach to distributed interactive simulation (DIS) protocol entity development*. Master's Thesis, Naval Postgraduate School, Monterey, California.

Capin, T., Pandzic, I., Magnenat-Thalmann, N., & Thalmann, D. (1999). *Avatars in networked virtual environments*. John Wiley & Sons Ltd.

Carlsson, C., & Hagsand, O. (1993). DIVE: A multi user virtual reality system. In *Proceedings of the IEEE 1993 Virtual Reality Annual International Symposium (VRAIS '93)*. Piscataway, NJ: IEEE Service Center.

Collaborate, B. S. (2007). BS Collaborate documentation. *Bitmanagement Software GmbH*. Retrieved September 10, 2009, from http://www.bitmanagement.com/download/BS_Collaborate/BS_Collaborate_documentation.pdf

JAIN – SIP. (2007). *Java API for signaling*. Retrieved September 10, 2009, from https://jain-sip.dev.java.net

Koubek, A., & Müller, K. (2002, November 16–20). Collaborative virtual environments for learning. In *ACM SIG Proceedings*, New Orleans, LA.

Leigh, J., & Johnson, A. E. (1996). Supporting transcontinental collaborative work in persistent virtual environments. *IEEE Computer Graphics and Applications*, *16*(4), 47–51. doi:10.1109/38.511853

Leigh, J., Johnson, A. E., & DeFanti, T. A. (1996). CALVIN: An immersimedia design environment utilizing heterogeneous perspectives. *IEEE International Conference on Multimedia Computing and Systems* (pp. 20-23).

Li, F., & Lau, R. (2003). VSculpt: A distributed virtual sculpting environment for collaborative design. *IEEE Transactions on Multimedia*, *5*(4). doi:10.1109/TMM.2003.814795

Li, H., Yin, G., & Fu, J. (2006). Research on the collaborative virtual products development based on Web and X3D. In *Proceedings of the 16th International Conference on Artificial Reality and Telexistence (ICAT '06)* (pp. 141-144).

Liesenborgs, J. (2000). *Voice over IP in networked virtual environments*. B.A. Thesis, School for Knowledge Technology, Limburgs Universitair Centrum, Belgium, 2000. Retrieved September 10, 2009, from http://research.edm.uhasselt.be/~jori/page/index.php?n=CS.Thesis

Macedonia, M. R., Zyda, M. J., Pratt, D., Brutzman, R., Donald, P., & Barham, P. T. (1995). Exploiting reality with multicast groups: A network architecture for large-scale virtual environments. In *Proceedings of the IEEE Virtual Reality Annual International Symposium (VRAIS'95)*.

Miller, C., & Thorpe, A. (1995). SIMNET: The advent of simulator networking. *Proceedings of the IEEE*, *83*(8), 1114–1123. doi:10.1109/5.400452

Pandzic, I., Capin, T., Magnenat-Thalmann, N., & Thalman, D. (1996). Towards natural communication in networked collaborative virtual environments. In *Proc. of FIVE '96*, Pisa, Italy.

Pandzic, I., Magnenat-Thalmann, N., & Thalman, D. (1998). Realistic avatars and autonomous virtual humans. In R. Earnshaw & J. Vince (Eds.), *VLNET networked virtual environments. Virtual worlds in the internet*. IEEE Computer Society Press.

Redfern, S., & Galway, N. (2002). Collaborative Virtual environments to support communication and community in internet-based distance education. [JITE]. *Journal of Information Technology Education*, *1*(3), 201–211.

RFC3261. (2002). *SIP: Session initiation protocol*. Retrieved September 10, 2009, from http://www.ietf.org/rfc/rfc3261.txt

RFC3550. (2003). *RTP: A transport protocol for real-time applications*. Retrieved September 10, 2009, from http://www.ietf.org/rfc/rfc3550.txt

Schafer, W., & Bowman, D. (2005). Integrating 2D and 3D views for spatial collaboration. In *Proceedings of the 2005 international ACM SIGGROUP Conference on Supporting Group Work* (pp. 41–50).

Snowdon, D., Churchill, E., & Munro, A. (2001). Collaborative virtual environments: Digital spaces and places for CSCW: An introduction. In D. Snowdon, E. Churchill, & A. Munro (Eds.), *Collaborative virtual environments: Digital places and spaces for interaction*. Springer-Verlag. doi:10.1007/978-1-4471-0685-2_1

Sweller, J. (1988). Cognitive load during problem solving: Effects on learning. *Cognitive Science*, *12*(29), 257–285. doi:10.1207/s15516709cog1202_4

Tsiatsos, T., Konstantinidis, A., & Pomportsis, A. (2010). Evaluation framework for collaborative educational virtual environments. *Journal of Educational Technology & Society, 13*(2), 65–77.

Web3D. (2009). *X3D and Related Specifications.* Web3D Consortium. Retrieved September 10, 2009, from http://www.web3d.org/x3d/specifications/

Weber, J., & Parisi, T. (2007). An open protocol for wide-area multi-user X3D. In *Proceedings of the Web3D 2007 Symposium*, University of Perugia, Umbria, Italy.

Wray, M., & Hawkes, R. (1998). Distributed virtual environments and VRML: an event-based architecture. *Comput. Netw. ISDN Syst. 30*(1-7), 43-51. DOI= http://dx.doi.org/10.1016/S0169-7552(98)00022-1

Yamazaki, Y., & Herder, J. (2000). Exploring spatial audio conferencing functionality in multiuser virtual environments (poster session). In *Proceedings of the Third International Conference on Collaborative Virtual Environments*, San Francisco, CA. DOI= http://doi.acm.org/10.1145/351006.351051.

This work was previously published in the International Journal of Distance Education Technologies (IJDET), 12(1); edited by Maiga Chang, pages 13-37, copyright year 2014 by IGI Publishing (an imprint of IGI Global).

Chapter 56

Business Process Design Meets Business Practices through Enterprise Patterns:
A Case Study

Carmelo Ardito
University of Bari, Italy

Antonio Capodieci
University of Salento, Italy

Ugo Barchetti
University of Salento, Italy

Annalisa Guido
University of Salento, Italy

Luca Mainetti
University of Salento, Italy

ABSTRACT

Every day companies deal with internal problems in order to manage human resources during the execution of business processes. The ability to quickly identify and rapidly apply effective business practices to recurring problems becomes crucial in order to improve the efficiency of the organization. To seize the opportunity of adapting their business practices to emerging organizational forms (Extended Enterprise, Virtual Enterprise) and to reuse the expertise of knowledge workers – who are central to an organization's success – companies are required to face several challenges. This paper presents a set of business patterns useful in resolving emerging organizational issues to support the activities of knowledge workers, increase their productivity and their ability to find the information they need, and enable collaboration with colleagues without changing their habits. Also it describes a real case study and a software system that allows companies to introduce these business patterns in the workplace, adopting an Enterprise 2.0 approach.

DOI: 10.4018/978-1-4666-8619-9.ch056

INTRODUCTION

Companies base their success on the use of established business practices to ensure efficiency and effectiveness in the activities related to their core business (Gebauer & Lee, 2008). The introduction of efficient business practices can help resolve recurring problems through proven solutions coming from past experiences (Dietz, 2006). Traditionally, this is achieved through the leadership's ability to empower the workers' productivity in a company, but in reality businesses can benefit from systematic, structured investment in the tools and methods supporting collaboration (Kristensen & Kijl, 20102010).

In the past 50 years, a new form of worker – the 'knowledge worker' (Davenport, 2005) – has become more and more important for companies. The knowledge worker is "one who works primarily with information or one who develops and uses knowledge in the workplace". Typically, knowledge workers operate multiple tasks at the same time. They have different working contexts and different channels to deliver information. (Baars & Kemper, 2008) They are involved in many parallel 'knowledge processes' (Simperl et al., 2010) that are often not codified in formal procedures but are unstructured or semi-structured, collaborative and continuously changing. The advent of Web 2.0 has also amplified the presence of knowledge processes not coded in formal structures because knowledge workers have many basic collaboration tools at work but are not checked by traditional information systems. In this context it is essential to keep coherent knowledge processes (unstructured) and business processes (structured), moving from tacit to explicit knowledge (Alderete, 2012; Jashapara, 2007) and involved in shaping a new kind of information system known as Enterprise 2.0 (Maule & Gallup, 2010).

Researchers have pointed out that process modelling and design practices can represent a way to respond to this new situation. If the Enterprise 2.0 tools can be adapted to Extended Enterprise and Virtual Enterprise organization, they can give flexible support to networked human processes. Moreover, network systems based on technologies and architectures of participation offer a new model for online knowledge sharing, cooperation, and collaboration that is different from the traditional institutional framework (Blau, 2011).

In a networked context, the management of informal processes/activities is a challenging problem. Such activities are often collaborative and, typically, they are not codified or elicited as business practices. Informal processes limit the growth of a company because they are highly dependent on the ability of the knowledge worker to correctly and promptly manage activities and generate the information overload. As Lundqvist, Sandkuhl, and Seigerroth (2011) observe, new organizational and technological approaches are needed to prevent knowledge workers' information overload, by proposing methods of achieving a more pertinent and accurate information supply. A formal definition of business practice contributes to capturing and understand the information demand and roles in organizations. Researchers such as Henkel, Johannesson, and Perjons (2011) suggest that enterprise models and business models as being adequate tools for design and maintenance of processes, which require collaboration in agile and flexible networks.

In trying to address the modelling issues involved in business practices, we have explored the traditional Business Process Management (BPM) approach. In particular, we have attempted to formally describe the collaboration and coordination processes in which knowledge workers in a real Small-Medium Networked ICT Enterprise were involved, integrating them into the information system in order to derive process models efficiently (i.e. consuming less resources and time) and effectively (i.e. at a high quality to meet specific needs). However, the unstructured, adaptable and changing nature of knowledge processes soon became an obstacle to the formalization of large-scale business practices. So we decided to project a smaller impact on the overall organization, modelling only recurring business practice atoms, i.e. patterns. A pattern-based approach can be useful to re-design processes (Drucker, 1959) but also in the design of information systems from scratch. In fact, the concept of pattern has been effective in practical contexts and will probably be suitable in others (Fowler, 1997). The approach has been inherited from the traditional business processes design method (Van Der Aalst, Ter Hofstede, Kiepuszewski, & Barros, 2003) and from the software engineering field (Fowler, 1997). Several studies propose the use of workflow patterns as a means to categorize recurring problems and solutions in modelling business processes (Russell, ter Hofstede, van der Aalst, & Mulyar, 2006), and also to organize collaborative work (Winograd, 1986).

In this paper, we apply a pattern-based approach to knowledge processes as a key factor in quickly identifying and rapidly applying effective business practices to support the activities of knowledge workers, increasing their productivity in the networked workplace without changing their habits. The paper presents a case study highlighting the issues related to the modelling of knowledge processes, demonstrating the difficulty of managing tacit knowledge. To address these issues, we present a set of business patterns which can be useful in modelling collaborative and cooperative activities within business practices. In addition, we propose a software system that allows companies to introduce business patterns in the workplace, and to track tacit knowledge, improving knowledge management and promoting collaboration.

The paper is structured as follows: the next section (Related Work) reports on key related works in the area of analysis, description, identification and application of business practices, mainly to address knowledge workers' emerging needs. The section 'Business Patterns for Modelling the Project Proposal Drafting Process' provides readers with an overview of our pattern-based approach. Each business pattern is identified as a solution

to a recurring problem. The section 'KPeople Software System' describes the evaluation of the software system we deployed to apply the patterns, using them to manage typical business practices within real organizations. The numerical details we obtained using a technique based on the living laboratory approach are shown and the results of a usability test we performed during the experimental phase are reported. Finally, the section on 'Conclusions' summarizes our key messages and sketches future research directions.

Related Work

This section analyzes existing works on explicit modelling of business practices to support collaborative and cooperative semi-structured processes. Business practices are often associated with best practices that companies adopt to manage their internal processes. Therefore, the ability to identify best practices is essential to apply efficient and effective business practices, and to enable the reusing of knowledge and expertise. (Remus, 2012) Companies need to find methods to provide the necessary level of abstraction while modelling daily practices. At the same time, companies must manage and preserve social capital through knowledge workers (Hall & Goody, 2007).

Bhandar, Pan, and Tan (2007) made an interesting study of the importance of 'social capital' is highlighted during the various phases of the development of an information system involving multiple organizations. In doing so, the study suggests innovation through two new perspectives (knowledge integration and inter-organizational relationships) and by leveraging the social capital, a resource based on social relationships that inherently emerges in a collaborative project thanks to the ability of integrating the knowledge bases and knowledge processes of the participating organizations.

The concept of social capital is central. The literature proposes many definitions of social capital and one of them is related to the assets that reside in social relationships (Walker, Kogut, & Shan, 1997) and that emerges or exists in social structures (like projects, hierarchies) through interaction between members (Adler & Kwon, 2002). So, as the authors say "the formation of social capital is supported by the use of social networks" (Burke & Calton, 2009). Conflicts between collaborating organizations, and/or between members of the same organization, can be solved using social capital and can enhance the knowledge integration process by developing cohesion within the structure, aligning stakeholders to the collective goal and reducing the time and the effort related by reaching an agreement within the network of knowledge workers (Briggs, 2003).

A knowledge worker may be categorized by what he/she does with regard to the work processes he or she is involved in Davenport (2005). Knowledge workers are involved on a daily basis in many unstructured activities that are information intensive but not adequately supported by technology. This rapidly leads to an information overload that negatively affects performance. Until now, there have been relatively few studies related to this topic. Andriole attempts to demonstrate how, if properly deployed, new technologies enable companies to cost-effectively increase their productivity and their competitive advantage (Andriole, 2010). To raise their productivity, companies could integrate emerging technologies (mainly coming from Web 2.0) in traditional business processes (McAfee, 2006). In this way, the information system can allow the knowledge worker to use the right information, in the right format, at the right time but it is essential to understand that processes are made up of people, and that people will use the technology to improve their work. To achieve this goal, knowledge workers should be provided with an integrated space where they can retrieve all the information and tools they need.

Some researches in this area have been carried out. Jennings & Finkelstein (2010) authors propose to analyze specific lightweight ad hoc processes,

known as 'micro workflows'; which can occur within a company. Using gestural analysis of human agents within such flexible micro workflows, in combination with social analysis techniques, a new flexibility in business processes can be identified. Thus, the authors provide a helpful way to define how people work in companies and how they can integrate Web 2.0 tools into their daily activities. Stephenson and Bandara (2007) present business process patterns in order to enhance the design of the public health care business process.

The introduction of micro workflows and social software affects Enterprise 2.0 (McAfee, 2006). In this context, the main technological areas through which the Enterprise 2.0 are carried out are the social network/community, unified communication/collaboration and enterprise content management. These areas are particularly important because they show how new trends stimulate collaboration and knowledge sharing. Along with the emergence and the use of Web 2.0 tools, not only in large companies but also in the small and medium enterprises, new operating practices have been introduced to complete the existing ones.

Cook introduces the concept of collaboration process in addition to traditional business processes that define the way a company works (Cook, 2008). Collaboration processes are characterized by a strong and unpredictable collaboration among the participating stakeholders in order to achieve a common goal. This collaboration takes place through the combination of communication tools, both traditional (e-mail, telephone, direct conversation) and Web 2.0 oriented (Sari, Loeh, & Katzy, 2010).

Harrison-Broninski (2005), argue that it is necessary to amplify human-driven processes in order to understand how to formally describe such work, then to capture this knowledge in a software tool. This requires changes in both business process modelling and information systems. The author examines the true nature of work and shows how it can be supported by the next generation of information systems. In order to formally describe human work and the interaction between humans and technology, the identification of patterns can be a useful approach allowing for fine-grained modelling support, as Gschwind, Koehler, and Wong (2008) point out. However, the modelling tools currently available do not fully support the application of patterns, although, as these authors demonstrate it is possible to use an approach through which business users receive help in understanding the context through design patterns.

The concept of pattern (Fowler, 1997) has been useful in a practical contexts and will probably be useful in others. A pattern-based approach has been exploited for many years in the software engineering field but, over the last decade, the concept has been inherited in the business processes area (Desai, Chopra, & Singh, 2009). Mitra and Gupta (2005) point out that most of the analysts who have actually worked on simplifying business process have focused on reusing or identifying some process elements that can be re-applied from one process to another, or at least when similar processes are encountered. This solution, which comes from the methodology of business process patterns, is very helpful in the information system field and is an important step towards creating a structured and systematic way to manage business practices both in real (Barchetti, Capodieci, Guido, & Mainetti, 2012a) and in virtual environments (Di Blas, Bucciero, Mainetti, & Paolini, 2012). The next section addresses this issue by presenting a set of process patterns which can model collaborative and cooperative activities as business practice atoms.

Business Patterns Modelling the "Project Proposal Drafting" Process

In this section, we present a set of business patterns we have identified in a specific case study, namely the 'project proposal drafting' process. The identified business patterns can be used in a other case studies. The case study identification has been carried out in collaboration with 'Webscience S.r.l.' (referred to here as Webscience), an Italian networked company that operates in the ICT field. Webscience is the leading partner of the KPeople research project, which was founded by the Apulia Region and the European Community. The company has 140 employees, who operate in five business units spread around three continents. Ten focus groups have been carried out, involving the top management and the business unit directors. They indicated that the 'project proposal drafting' process would be an interesting testing ground. Indeed, offering a project proposal to the customer is the first step in starting a business. In addition, according to the opinions of the focus group participants, project proposal drafting is a key process for enhancing the efficiency of the company, because it involves aspects of collaboration and coordination activities with high margins of improvement.

The process of drafting a project proposal is made up of two sub-processes: 'proposal writing' and 'budget creation'. The first of these aims to formalise appealing project ideas that may be submitted to potential customers. The second is required to define economic resources in terms of humans, infrastructures, suppliers and external advisors, training and logistics.

The actors involved in both sub-processes are the Managing Director (MD), the Client Manager (CM), the Project Manager (PM), the Head of Human Resources (HR) and the Business Unit Manager (BM). These actors deal with any aspect of the business, from proposal writing to negotiation with the customer to costs approval and resources management.

From the analysis of the data collected during the focus groups, it emerged that the most relevant problem of the considered process is the loss of information exchanged by knowledge workers due to an uncontrolled use of Web 2.0 tools. To provide readers with evidence of the number of collaborative activities and information exchange characterized by a massive use of Web 2.0 tools, in Table 1 we report the data collected about the budget creation sub-process. Data were collected through interviews and focus groups with the Webscience workers and by analyzing the intranet repository used by the company to manage the budget's lifecycle.

Table 1 shows a large information loss (from the point of view of the company knowledge base) during the execution of the budget creation sub-process and a lack of formalization in repetitive and very similar activities. Business practices are left to the ability and the accuracy of knowledge workers. This leads to a decrease in efficiency for the company.

We have decomposed this general problem in three main aspects related to Collaboration, Coordination and Know-how Elicitation. In the following, each of these is analyzed. Business patterns are proposed which aim to overcome difficulties by modelling the involved actors, their collaboration and communication and the activities they perform.

Collaboration

This aspect tackles problems related to the design of the collaboration among people who operate within the company to achieve a specific goal. Even if we pointed out that there is a strong interaction between knowledge workers in the company, current practices lack any of the specific flows that are typical of business process design.

A knowledge worker in the company (CM or PM) can execute the task independently or he/she may decide to ask for a contribution from other knowledge workers. There is not a default number of workers from which the CM or the PM can ask for help, and the number of interactions between the CM or the PM and other employees can be defined on the fly using different communication tools. For example, the CM can ask about the economics of the proposal using an instant message for the first request, then he/she can use e-mail to exchange documents, and subsequently use instant messages to exchange other information about the quotation. Knowledge workers choose the communication tool autonomously, so there is a risk of losing the information exchanged between employees, which could be valuable for other knowledge workers in the company.

The **Collaborative Decision Making Pattern** models a collaborative activity where the goal is to take a decision about certain topics which involves a number of responsibilities. The pattern allows the identification and the codification of the collaboration data stream in the company information system. In this scenario, a moderator is in charge of preparing a proposal draft for

Table 1. Numerical details of the budget creation sub-process

	N.	Source
Collaborative activities	5	Interviews, focus groups
Employees involved in process execution	40	Interviews, focus groups
Budgets / year	350	Intranet repository analysis
Collaborative activities / year	1,750	(N. of collaborative activities) × (N. of budgets/year)
Categories of Web 2.0	3	Interviews, focus groups
Web 2.0 tool uses in the process	100	Analysis of a sample of process activities
Web 2.0 tool uses/year in the process	35,000	(N. of Budgets / year) × (N. of Web 2.0 tool uses in the process)

discussion and/or to modification. After the discussion, the moderator has the task of preparing an artifact that represents the result of decisions made during the collaborative activity. There are two types of decision makers: the Main Decision Maker, involved in the collaboration activity, and Decision Maker(s) (It is possible involve one or more decision makers) that may contribute to the discussion of a topic (He/she is not forced to participate in the discussion). This pattern is explained in detail by Barchetti, Capodieci, Guido, and Mainetti (2011) who present it in the context of the 'budget creation' process. Readers should refer to the cited paper for details.

Coordination

This aspect tackles problems related to the task of making cooperation possible among several people who have different roles within the company and who work in remote places. The activities regarding people with specific roles, and who can cooperate with each other, are often not structured in terms of traditional information systems, although it is useful to keep track of data exchanged among employees during cooperative activities in order to avoid losing information.

During the drafting of the project proposal, the interaction, e.g. mail exchange, between the PM and other knowledge workers is often frenetic. This may be a problem when the people in charge of writing the proposal are too busy with other activities.

The role of the PM is to make cooperation possible among colleagues in order to write the proposal and to ensure the quality of the result. However, there are several situations to consider, which recur many times and are often very chaotic. Such situations are modelled by the 'Coordinate Contribution Pattern' and the 'Retrieve Contribution Pattern' described in what follows.

- **Coordinate Contribution Pattern:**
  During the definition of the project proposal, the PM is in charge of coordinating the contributions of several knowledge workers. He/she periodically reviews the contributions and, if correct, registers them. They can be reused later, when all the contributions will be put together. These activities are modelled by using the Coordinate Contribution Pattern. As shown in Figure 1, the pattern aims to verify and evaluate the received contribution. It allows for coordinating the contributions of other actors. First of all, the system checks whether a Provider has delivered the contribution assigned to him/her. If the contribution has not been received, the system requests the contribution to the Provider. Otherwise, the received contribution is evaluated. It is then registered if it matches quality attributes or, if it does not meet requirements, the system asks the Provider for a new version.

- **Retrieve Contribution Pattern:** Another critical situation occurs when the PM has

Figure 1. The coordinate contribution pattern

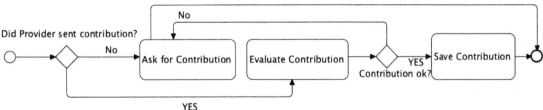

to ask some knowledge workers to write some parts of the documents, depending on their specific expertise. The PM decides a priori who are the involved knowledge workers and sets a deadline to provide the contributions. When the deadline expires, the PM needs to put together all the received documents. These activities are modelled by the Retrieve Contribution pattern. This pattern, as shown in Figure 2, aims to solve the problem of retrieving contributions produced by knowledge workers. It takes into account the need to collect the contributions by a predefined date in order to have time to elaborate them. This pattern aims also to manage situations in which it is necessary to collect contributions before the scheduled deadline. The Retrieve Contribution Pattern foresees the involvement of a Requestor and one or more Providers. The Requestor identifies the resources that will have to provide the contributions, while the Providers produce and send the required contributions. The process is activated by the Requestor who has to identify the involved knowledge workers. Then the Requestor starts the

Coordinate Contribution task, modelled by the previous pattern, which can end for two reasons: (i) the time has expired or, (ii), all the Providers have sent their contributions. Finally, the Requestor evaluates the contributions obtained from the Providers.

Know-How Elicitation

This aspect tackles problems related to practices that are repeated many times and where there is a risk of losing information useful for the company. In the specific case of project proposal drafting, many critical collaborative activities can be performed without an adequate control. Such activities are modelled by the 'Escalation Patterns' and 'Deadline Agreement Patterns' described in what follows.

- **Escalation Pattern:** A typical situation modelled by this pattern happens when the PM has not received the requested contribution from a knowledge worker. Thus, the PM asks his/her own immediate manager to solicit the defaulting knowledge worker to produce the contribution and to send it to the PM. The 'Escalation Pattern' repre-

Figure 2. The retrieve contribution pattern

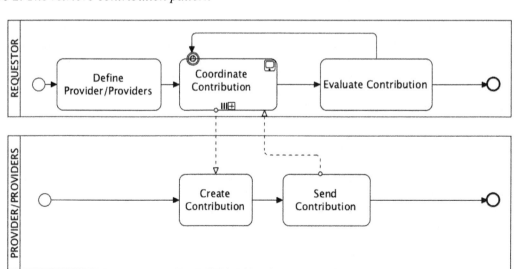

sented in Figure 3 aims at delegating to a manager the responsibility to remind a negligent colleague of the need to obtain more effective and immediate results. The pattern involves the Requestor who requested the contribution, a Provider from whom a contribution has been requested, and a third actor who, given his authority, may be more masterful in requesting the contribution through a reminder. The Requestor can activate the process if the provider does not send the requested contribution by the agreed date and if the Provider continues to not send the required contributions after he/she receives the Requestor's reminder. Then the Requestor prepares a reminder and forwards it to the third actor who, in turn, sends it to the negligent Provider.

- **Deadline Agreement Pattern:** During the project proposal drafting process, there is a delicate issue to be addressed concerning the definition of the deadline for completing a specific task and the job to be assigned to each worker. Work assignation is a crucial activity for the success of projects. This activity can often be affected by factors such as the technical expertise, writing and organizational capability of the people involved. So, in this context, it is important to properly define the work assignation and

to adequately agree on the internal release date of contributions. The PM can decide to agree on these aspects with the knowledge workers. The Deadline Agreement pattern, shown in Figure 4, aims to support the activities related to work planning, work assignation and decisions about the internal release dates for contributions. This pattern aims to create a model according to which the deadline agreement activity can be performed efficiently, taking into account the different needs of the people involved. Two classes of actor characterize the pattern: the Requestor, who is responsible for the whole activity completion, and one or more Providers, who must provide the required contributions. To agree on the work assignation and the internal release date, the Requestor, first of all, defines the date by which any contribution must be provided. Then he/she carries out an initial work assignation of activities. So two collaborative activities ('Work Partitioning' and 'Deadline Collaborative Definition') will begin. Each of them involves a Requestor and the Providers.These collaborative activities deal with assigning the work ('Work Definition' task) and agreeing the internal release dates for each Provider ('Deadline Collaboration Definition' task)

Figure 3. The escalation pattern

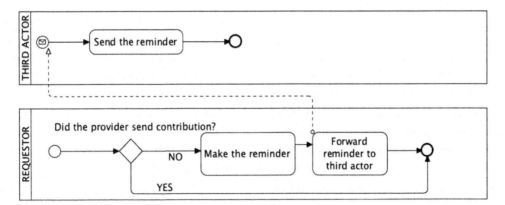

Figure 4. The deadline agreement pattern

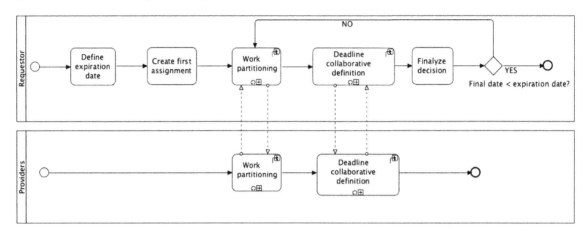

Respectively. The two tasks are sub-processes modelled through the Collaborative Editing pattern. A Decision Team is made up of the Requestor and the Providers who, using collaborative tools, agree on the work assignation and the internal deadline definition. When the Work Partitioning and the Deadline Collaborative Definition are finished, the Requestor, through the 'Finalize decision' task, formalizes the decisions made and he/she defines the latest date against the dates agreed with the Providers as the deadline for the conclusion of their activities. If these deadlines exceed the date defined initially by the Requestor, a new iteration of the two collaborative activities can be carried out.

KPeople Software System

A software demonstrator of the KPeople (Barchetti, Capodieci, Guido, & Mainetti, 2012b) system has been deployed. This focuses on unstructured and complex processes within a networked enterprise environment (such as decisional, collaborative, and creative contexts) in order to improve the management of information and communication, and to optimize the workspace, recovering the time spent in low-value activities, in particular to find

relevant information, execute knowledge tasks, and integrate collaborative workspaces with individual productivity tools (office automation, e-mail, etc.). According to the goals of the project, the KPeople system enables organizations to configure a set of business patterns (those described in the case study) and support the automatic enactment of their workflows. The system exploits collaborative Web 2.0 tools, dynamic process composition methods, and semantic engines to implement the business patterns identified in the case study. In the next subsections, we describe the architecture of the KPeople demonstrator, the Human-Centred approach adopted to design and develop it and the empirical test carried out by adopting the Living Laboratory approach.

Architecture

The KPeople software demonstrator was built upon an event-driven architecture, which – thanks to custom adapters – is able to trace and store events generated by traditional enterprise information systems (CMS, BI, CRM, ERP, etc.), communication tools (e-mail), unified communications & collaboration tools (UCC) and Web 2.0 facilities.

Figure 5 shows the KPeople system architecture. Knowledge workers can collaborate with colleagues by exchanging information, files and

Figure 5. KPeople system architecture

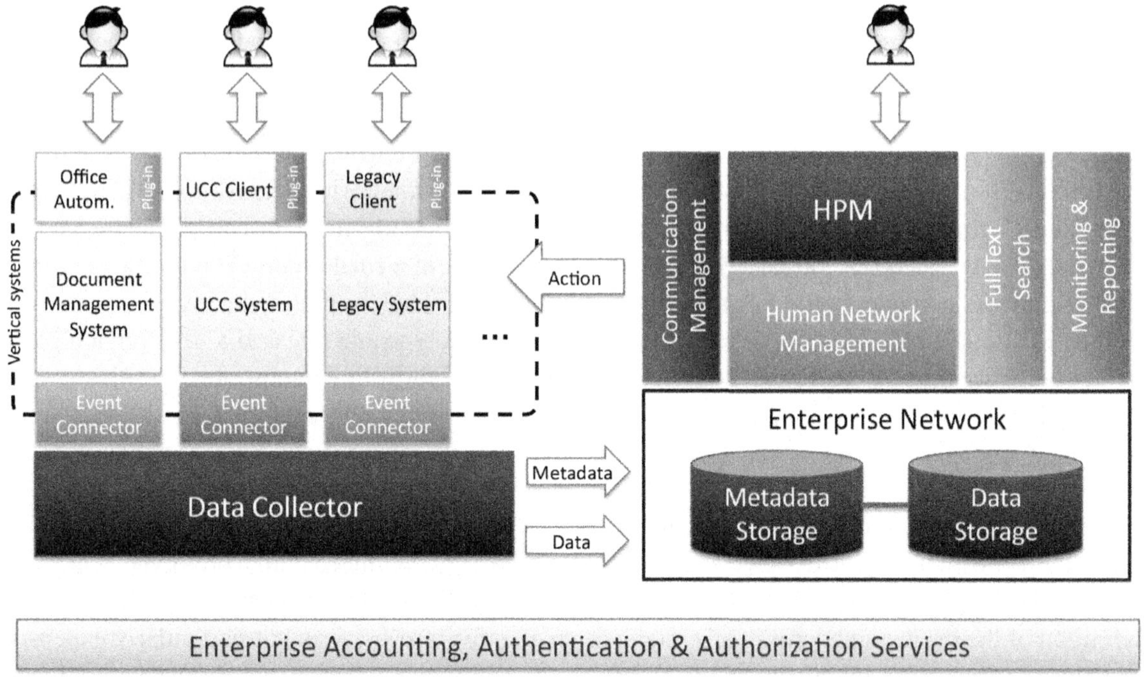

tasks through the HPM (Human Process Management) tool that allows users to apply patterns and examine the progress of the processes, the activities to be completed, the flow of communication, exchanged documents and e-mails, and to examine a set of indicators useful to evaluate performances and to identify bottlenecks. All data, information and documents are collected in a common database (Data Storage) enabling easy data retrieval (through Metadata) for knowledge workers and improving their efficiency. Events are tagged and clustered using a domain ontology. Event streams may be analyzed by social networks analysis tools. For example, during the field studies, the Cytoscape open source platform for complex network analysis and visualization has been exploited.

Human-Centred Design

The software demonstrator of the KPeople system has been designed and developed by adopting an approach based on the Human-Centred Design (HCD) methodology (ISO/IEC 9241-210, 2010). The basic principles of HCD are: 1) to analyze users and task; 2) to design and implement the system iteratively through prototypes of increasing complexity; and 3) to evaluate design choices and prototypes with users. The HCD approach requires that the system be designed by iterating a design-implementation-evaluation cycle. According to Participatory Design, domain experts, representative of end users, and end users themselves have an active role in the whole process (Schuler & Namioka, 1993). They are involved, also, in the requirement analysis. They participate in the evaluation of early paper prototypes and provide feedback. They test the successive system prototypes in the laboratory and then in field settings.

The team created for designing the software demonstrator of the KPeople system was multidisciplinary. It was composed of experts in Human-Computer Interaction, software engineers, and representatives of end users, i.e. a Managing

Director, a Client Manager, a Project Manager, a Business Unit Manager and a Head of Human Resources. These end users' representatives were chosen from the personnel of the business unit of the IT company in Southern Italy which is a partner in the project.

In the early stages of analysis, user profiles were created through meetings, brainstorming sessions, on-site visits for observing users at their workplaces and interviews. The tasks to be performed through the system were analyzed and typical usage scenarios were developed (Rogers, Sharp, & Preece, 2011). Design solutions, consisting of navigation models and schemes were then shaped. Low-fidelity paper prototypes of the main screens of the software demonstrator were sketched and discussed with the whole design team. These were not the same people who participated in the definition of the business patterns.

Later, the system was iteratively designed and developed through the use of prototypes of increasing complexity. Such prototypes were evaluated through user testing and heuristic evaluation, as described in Nielsen and Mack (1994). The prototypes of the KPeople software demonstrator were inspected by five experts in Human-Computer Interaction to assess its compliance with respect to learnability, efficiency, memorability, low error rate, and user satisfaction. The inspectors carried out heuristic evaluations individually and recorded the problems they identified in their own inspection reports. Depending on its seriousness, a rate was assigned to each problem, on a range from 1 (purely aesthetic) to 4 (catastrophic). The inspectors then met together to discuss and aggregate their findings in a final report. The multidisciplinary team received the report, made the corrections to the prototype and released a new version of the KPeople software demonstrator. The iterative process of designing a prototype and its assessment using either heuristic evaluation and user testing with a couple of users (7 users, aged 21-40 years old, were chosen from the outside of the project team) has continued until a prototype, which met the identified requirements, was obtained. This iterative process was not particularly expensive because the interface prototypes used in the evaluations were created easily and evaluated by using methods that required few resources. Table 2 summarizes the types of prototypes employed in the user tests, the tasks executed and the goals.

The final prototype was evaluated through user testing. Ten knowledge workers of the IT company in Southern Italy, aged 21-40 years

Table 2. Prototypes employed in the user tests, tasks executed and goals

Section	Task	Goal
Paper prototypes	• Indicate which processes are assigned to you • Indicate which activities are assigned to you • Indicate which activities you assigned to other workers • Indicate which processes are out of the schedule • Indicate all the open processes • Indicate who are the handlers of the action Z • Search the process X by means of the advanced search form • Show how to create a new process • Show how to add a new activity	Evaluate learnability, efficiency, and low error rate of early prototypes of the KPeople system demonstrator. In order to map users' mental models and processes, stressing the critical ones, they have to 'think aloud' while executing the assigned task through 10 screenshots provided by the demonstrator.
Interactive prototypes	• Create the new process X • Ask a colleague for a contribution • Check process deadlines • Find processes in charge of Mr./Ms. Y that are not yet completed • Find all events and processes related to Mr./Ms. Y • Download the document X • Verify for pending activities	Evaluate learnability, efficiency, and low error rate of interactive prototypes of the system demonstrator. Users have to 'think aloud' while executing 7 concrete tasks to be done using interactive prototypes of the KPeople system demonstrator.

old, were involved. They were observed in individual sessions. Each user performed seven tasks, which required exploiting several of the business patterns and, consequently, of the KPeople system functionalities implementing them (see 'Interactive prototypes' section in Table 2). To avoid a learning effect, the order of task execution was counterbalanced among users. The test demonstrated that the knowledge workers were able to successfully use the system and to detect and correct the few mistakes occurred during the interaction by themselves. The usability problems that emerged during the user test were fixed and the final system was released.

Figure 6 shows a screenshot of one of the KPeople user interfaces. In particular, it implements the Retrieve Contribution pattern. The system is available at http://kpeople.webscience.it.

Field Studies

We introduced the KPeople system in six real organizations: 1) the Italian IT company Webscience; 2) the Italian Association for Computing (AICA); 2) an Italian large-scale public hospital to manage the deployment lifecycle of internal IT products; 3) a Brazilian IT company (Elogroup) specializing in BPM tools; 4) a Hungarian company (John Von Neumann Computer Society) and 5) a Korean company (KPC) that works in the field of computer driving licensing.

Participants

Twenty knowledge workers, characterized by different profiles, were recruited from six companies: 2 MDs, 2 BMs, 4 HRs, 3 PMs, 3 CMs, and 6 developers.

Figure 6. A screenshot of the KPeople system

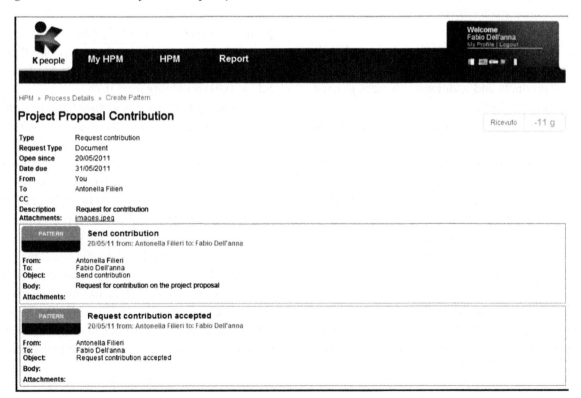

Procedure

The KPeople system was made available to the companies by hosting it on a WebScience server. Minimal modifications were required to customize the application portfolio of each company according to the KPeople system requirements were introduced by means of specific plug-ins. For example, the plug-in for the Microsoft Outlook mail client allows the KPeople system to automatically trace mail exchanges among the people involved in a particular process. This solution also limited the impact of the introduction of a new system in the usual practice of the companies. The trials focused on the planning, development and management of IT applications that support the core business of the companies. In the companies being considered, the realization of these applications is largely outsourced, thus the supervision of the related processes is particularly complex and critical, due to the possible geographical distribution of the actors and to business realities which are extremely different from each other. Thus, the processes considered in the trials were:

- Preparation of the budget dedicated to the development of information technology products and additions / changes to existing products.
- Testing of the applications developed by external suppliers; management of product approvals; management of changes if the products are not approved.
- Management of extra features not planned in the original budget.
- Sharing of reports related to the use of the applications and to the interactions with the help desk.

The trials were conducted over a period of about 3 weeks and involved several users. Within this period, they were enabled to use all the features provided by the prototype simply accessing the system via a web browser. They also installed the plug-in for Outlook.

Data Collection

At the end of the trial, users met again to gather feedback on the3 potential benefits of the tool and its use, its level of usability, areas required for improvement, and implementation of other features. Data collection was performed by means of a questionnaire designed to collect qualitative information concerning the unstructured or semi-structured collaborative activities performed during the trial.

Results

The participants' answers were analyzed according to the following criteria: *Relevance to business goals* was assessed by using a semantic differential scale that required users to judge the KPeople on 12 items. The participants could modulate their evaluation on a (1 = very negative $\div$ 7 = very positive). A user-perceived relevance for business goals index was computed as the mean value of the score across all the 12 items: mean = 5.2, mean S.E. = 0.94, reliability $\alpha = 0.75$.

Degree of utility was measured by the data collected through four questions, asking the participants to judge whether they found KPeople's features for daily work useful and whether they were supported by the implemented business partner. The participants also scored the general degree of utility of the system on a 7-point Likert-scale (1 = very negative $\div$ 7 = very positive). On average, they had a mark of 5.6 (min = 4.1, max = 6.9, reliability $\alpha = 0.83$). A question also asked the participants to globally score the *Perceived degree of efficiency of processes with KPeople* on a 10-point scale (1 = very negative $\div$ 10 = very positive). The global satisfaction was high (mean

= 7.7, mean S.E. = 0.7). The last two questions then asked so the participants could judge their performance as knowledge workers with and without the KPeople system. In particular, they had to indicate the percentage of the processes over which they felt they had adequate control, based on a retrospective analysis of the processes execution. This can be considered as a proxy of confidence (Hornbæk, 2006). On average, the participants stated that they were able to completely control the 94% of the processes executed during the trial (min = 70%, max = 100%, mean S.E. = 10.7%). They also felt very satisfied about their performance (mean = 3.2, mean S.E. = 0.6; on a 4-point scale 1 = very negative ÷ 4 = very positive).

CONCLUSION

Knowledge workers are becoming more and more important for companies, especially for networked organizations. In such a context, knowledge workers operate multiple tasks at the same time, in different working environments involving many parallel knowledge processes that, very often, are not codified in formal procedures and are unstructured, collaborative and continuously changing. Organizations base their success on the quality of the management of informal processes/activities that are not elicited as business practices. Informal processes limit the growth of organizations because they are highly dependent on the ability of the knowledge worker to perform the tasks correctly and promptly. In this paper, in order to meet the challenge of providing a conceptual tool to organize knowledge activities and integrate them within business processes, we presented a pattern-based approach to (re-)design business practices, which involve knowledge-intensive activities. We originally exploited the method of workflow patterns to knowledge processes as a key factor to quickly identify and rapidly apply effective business practices to support the activi-

ties of knowledge workers. By using a real case study, we presented a set of design patterns able to model collaborative activities – Collaborative Decision Making and other patterns that readers can find in Barchetti et al. (2011) – and cooperative activities (Coordinate Contribution, Retrieve Contribution, Escalation, and Deadline Agreement patterns) that represent recurring situations for knowledge workers.

To experiment with and evaluate the usefulness of the identified business patterns in real situations, we developed the KPeople software prototype. According to the Human-Centred Design approach, the system was designed and evaluated involving many stakeholders. Heuristic evaluations and user testing were carried out in order to improve the system usability. The KPeople system was then made available in six different companies spread around the world and twenty knowledge workers, with different roles in their company and who were in the process of project proposal drafting, were involved. The analysis of the data collected through a questionnaire showed that they perceived improved efficiency of the processes carried out with the support of the KPeople system. They felt a reassuring sense of control of the different sub processes, and also rated the system as being highly useful and relevant to the company's business goals.

The proposed approach allows companies to identify and to design collaboration activities recurring in the enterprise practices. The collaboration patterns can coexist with the traditional business process. Compared with the state of the art (Stephenson & Bandara, 2007) our approach is not focused on a specific application domain but can be used in several situations where the problem of managing the collaboration arises. While the state of the art deals mainly with the sociological aspects of collaboration (Briggs, 2003), we identified new collaboration patterns and presented an example of their representation using BPMN.

Future research will concern the collection of new patterns and the comparison of these patterns (derived from an in-field observations of knowledge workers) with those of the social network analysis tool of the KPeople system, which will be automatically gathered through process mining techniques.

ACKNOWLEDGMENT

This research has been supported by the FESR PO Italian funded 4RCPCJ0 KPeople project and Webscience s.r.l.

REFERENCES

Adler, P. S., & Kwon, S.-W. (2002). Social capital: Prospects for a new concept. *Academy of Management Review*, *27*(1), 17–40. doi:10.2307/4134367

Alderete, M. V. (2012). SME e-cooperation: A theoretical team contract analysis under hidden information. [IJeC]. *International Journal of e-Collaboration*, *8*(1), 53–64. doi:10.4018/jec.2012010104

Andriole, S. J. (2010). Business impact of Web 2.0 technologies. *Communications of the ACM*, *53*(12), 67–79. doi:10.1145/1859204.1859225

Baars, H., & Kemper, H.-G. (2008). Management support with structured and unstructured data–an integrated business intelligence framework. *Information Systems Management*, *25*(2), 132–148. doi:10.1080/10580530801941058

Barchetti, U., Capodieci, A., Guido, A. L., & Mainetti, L. (2011). Modelling collaboration processes through design patterns. *Computing and Informatics*, *30*(1), 113–135.

Barchetti, U., Capodieci, A., Guido, A. L., & Mainetti, L. (2012a). Collaborative process management for the networked enterprise: A case study. In *Proceedings of the 26th International Conference on Advanced Information Networking and Applications Workshops (WAINA '12)*.

Barchetti, U., Capodieci, A., Guido, A. L., & Mainetti, L. (2012b). Information systems for knowledge workers: The Kpeople enterprise 2.0 tool. In X. S. Wang, I. Cruz, A. Delis & G. Huang (Eds.), *Proceedings of the Web Information Systems Engineering (WISE 2012)* (Vol. LNCS 7651, pp. 804-807). Berlin Heidelberg, Germany: Springer.

Bhandar, M., Pan, S.-L., & Tan, B. C. Y. (2007). Towards understanding the roles of social capital in knowledge integration: A case study of a collaborative information systems project. *Journal of the American Society for Information Science and Technology*, *58*(2), 263–274. doi:10.1002/asi.20493

Blau, I. (2011). e-Collaboration within, between, and without institutions: Towards better functioning of online groups through networks. [IJeC]. *International Journal of e-Collaboration*, *7*(4), 22–36. doi:10.4018/jec.2011100102

Briggs, R. O. (2003). Collaboration engineering with ThinkLets to pursue sustained success with group support systems. *Journal of Management Information Systems*, *4*, 31–64.

Burke, K., & Calton, J. M. (2009). A framework describing the relationships among social technologies and social capital formation in electronic entrepreneurial networking. In N. Kock (Ed.), *e-Collaboration technologies and organizational performance: Current and future trends* (pp. 25–38). IGI Global. doi:10.4018/978-1-60566-984-7.ch038

Cook, N. (2008). *Enterprise 2.0: How social software will change the future of work*. Ashgate Publishing Company.

Davenport, T. H. (2005). *Thinking for a living: How to get better performances and results from knowledge workers*. Harvard Business Press.

Desai, N., Chopra, A. K., & Singh, M. P. (2009). Amoeba: A methodology for modeling and evolving cross-organizational business processes. [TOSEM]. *ACM Transactions on Software Engineering and Methodology*, *19*(2), 1–45. doi:10.1145/1571629.1571632

Di Blas, N., Bucciero, A., Mainetti, L., & Paolini, P. (2012). Multi-user virtual environments for learning: Experience and technology design. *IEEE Transactions on Learning Technologies*, *5*(4), 349–365. doi:10.1109/TLT.2012.16

Dietz, J. L. G. (2006). *Enterprise ontology: Theory and methodology*. Berlin Heidelberg, Germany: Springer. doi:10.1007/3-540-33149-2

Drucker, P. F. (1959). *Landmarks of tomorrow*. New York, NY: Harper.

Fowler, M. (1997). *Analysis patterns: Reusable object models*. Addison-Wesley.

Gebauer, J., & Lee, F. (2008). Enterprise system flexibility and implementation strategies: Aligning theory with evidence from a case study. *Information Systems Management*, *25*(1), 71–82. doi:10.1080/10580530701777198

Gschwind, T., Koehler, J., & Wong, J. (2008). Applying patterns during business process modeling. In M. Dumas, M. Reichert, & M.-C. Shan (Eds.), *Business process management* (Vol. 5240, pp. 4–19). Springer Berlin Heidelberg. doi:10.1007/978-3-540-85758-7_4

Hall, H., & Goody, M. (2007). KM, culture and compromise: Interventions to promote knowledge sharing supported by technology in corporate environments. *Journal of Information Science*, *33*(2), 181–188. doi:10.1177/0165551506070708

Harrison-Broninski, K. (2005). *Human interactions: The heart and soul of business process management*. Meghan Kiffer Pr.

Henkel, M., Johannesson, P., & Perjons, E. (2011). An approach for e-service design using enterprise models. *International Journal of Information System Modeling and Design*, *2*(1), 1–23. doi:10.4018/jismd.2011010101

Hornbæk, K. (2006). Current practice in measuring usability: Challenges to usability studies and research. *International Journal of Human-Computer Studies*, *64*(2), 79-102. doi: http://dx.doi.org/10.1016/j.ijhcs.2005.06.002 ISO/IEC 9241-210. (2010). *Ergonomics of human-system interaction -- Part 210: Human-centred design for interactive systems*.

Jashapara, A. (2007). Moving beyond tacit and explicit distinctions: A realist theory of organizational knowledge. *Journal of Information Science*, *33*(6), 752–766. doi:10.1177/0165551506078404

Kristensen, K., & Kijl, B. (2010). Collaborative performance: Addressing the ROI of collaboration. [IJeC]. *International Journal of e-Collaboration*, *6*(1), 53–69. doi:10.4018/jec.2010091104

Lundqvist, M., Sandkuhl, K., & Seigerroth, U. (2011). Modelling information demand in an enterprise Context: Method, notation, and lessons learned. *International Journal of Information System Modeling and Design*, *2*(3), 75–95. doi:10.4018/jismd.2011070104

Maule, R. W., & Gallup, S. (2010). Enterprise 2.0 collaboration for collective knowledge and intelligence applications. In T. Sobh (Ed.), *Innovations and advances in computer sciences and engineering* (pp. 567–572). Springer Netherlands. doi:10.1007/978-90-481-3658-2_99

McAfee, A. P. (2006). Enterprise 2.0: The dawn of emergent collaboration. *Management of Technology and Innovation*, *47*(3), 21–28.

Mitra, A., & Gupta, A. (2005). *Agile systems with reusable patterns of business knowledge: A component-based approach.* Artech House, Inc.

Nielsen, J., & Mack, R. L. (1994). *Usability inspection methods.* New York, NY: John Wiley & Sons, Inc.

Remus, U. (2012). Exploring the dynamics behind knowledge management challenges–An enterprise resource planning case study. *Information Systems Management, 29*(3), 188–200. doi:10.1080/1058 0530.2012.687309

Rogers, Y., Sharp, H., & Preece, J. (2011). *Interaction design: Beyond human-computer interaction* (3rd ed.). Wiley.

Russell, N., ter Hofstede, A., van der Aalst, W., & Mulyar, N. (2006). *Workflow control-flow patterns: A revised view.*

Sari, B., Loeh, H., & Katzy, B. R. (2010). Emerging collaboration routines in knowledge-intensive work processes: Insights from three case studies. [IJeC]. *International Journal of e-Collaboration, 6*(1), 33–52. doi:10.4018/jec.2010091103

Schuler, D., & Namioka, A. (1993). *Participatory design: Principles and practices.* CRC / Lawrence Erlbaum Associates.

Simperl, E., Thurlow, I., Warren, P., Dengler, F., Davies, J., & Grobelnik, M. et al. (2010). Overcoming information overload in the enterprise: The active approach. *IEEE Internet Computing, 14*(6), 39–46. doi:10.1109/MIC.2010.146

Stephenson, C., & Bandara, W. (2007). Enhancing best practices in public health: using process patterns for business process management. In *Proceedings of the 15th European Conference on Information Systems.*

Van Der Aalst, W. M. P., Ter Hofstede, A. H. M., Kiepuszewski, B., & Barros, A. P. (2003). Workflow patterns. *Distributed and Parallel Databases, 14*(1), 5–51. doi:10.1023/A:1022883727209

Walker, G., Kogut, B., & Shan, W. (1997). Social capital, structural holes and the formation of an industry network. *Organization Science, 8*(2), 109–125. doi:10.1287/orsc.8.2.109

Winograd, T. (1986). A language/action perspective on the design of cooperative work. In *Proceedings of the ACM Conference on Computer-Supported Cooperative Work*, Austin, TX.

This work was previously published in the International Journal of e-Collaboration (IJeC), 10(1); edited by Ned Kock, pages 57-73, copyright year 2014 by IGI Publishing (an imprint of IGI Global).

Chapter 57
Sacrificing Credibility for Sleaze:
Mainstream Media's Use of Tabloidization

Jenn Burleson Mackay
Virginia Tech, USA

Erica Bailey
Pennsylvania State University, USA

ABSTRACT

This chapter uses an experiment to analyze how mainstream journalists' use of sensationalized or tabloid-style writing techniques affect the credibility of online news. Participants read four news stories and rated their credibility using McCroskey's Source Credibility Scale. Participants found stories written with a tabloid style less credible than more traditional stories. Soft news stories written with a tabloidized style were rated more credible than hard news stories that also had a tabloidized style. Results suggest that online news media may damage their credibility by using tabloidized writing techniques to increase readership. Furthermore, participants were less likely to enjoy stories written in a tabloidized style. The authors conclude by utilizing act utilitarianism to argue that tabloidized writing is an unethical journalistic technique.

INTRODUCTION

There's a journalistic world where old-school objectivity fights for existence against dramatic disasters and fuzzy features. It is a place where journalistic ethics might take a backseat, while reporters or editors douse newspapers with sleaze and entertainment. With little more than a creative selection of verbs and a thirst for a sizzling story, American journalists can venture into tabloid territory.

This technique of spicing up mainstream media news often is called tabloidization. The exact definition of the term varies from one scholar to the next, but it is viewed as a method for attaining audiences in an ever-competitive media environment. Tabloidization has been described as dumbing down the news by giving consumers the stories that they want rather than providing useful public service information (Nice, 2007). The writing tone in these tabloidized stories is designed to be stimulating and exciting (McLachlan

DOI: 10.4018/978-1-4666-8619-9.ch057

& Golding, 2000). Tabloization results in lower journalistic standards, less hard news, and more soft, sensational, or entertaining stories (Kurtz, 1993). It is far too simplistic a notion to assume that tabloidization is a completely negative practice, however. The method also might be utilized to increase the audience of the media and to increase their knowledge of news and information (Gans, 2009).

This chapter is an effort to understand the effects of online news tabloidization on credibility. The study will examine how readers evaluate the credibility of stories written with a tabloidized format compared to how they rate stories written with a more traditional journalistic style. A more traditional reporter's story would stick to the facts and get to the point of the story, whereas a tabloidized story might include sleazy wording or unnecessary intimate details designed to grab the reader's attention rather than inform him or her. In addition, the researchers will consider whether tabloidization is more accepted in certain types of stories, such as feature pieces, as compared to hard news stories. We predict that participants will report a higher level of enjoyment of tabloidized content than non-tabloidized content.

The study also asks how the media should respond to tabloidization pressures. In addition to studying participant responses to tabloidized content, this study will apply normative ethical theory to the tabloidization of the media. By using act utilititarianism, the researchers will examine how journalists should address the challenges of the new media climate and whether utilizing tabloidization for media survival is an acceptable ethical practice.

BACKGROUND

Tabloidization can result from competition, technology, and the desire for circulation. News organizations essentially have restructured, rede-

signed, and degraded their content in an effort to survive. Tabloidization can be viewed as a way of appealing to advertisers above other competing interests (Conboy, 2006). The deregulation of the media is one reason that current affairs programs have become increasingly commercialized. The programs have reverted to a hybrid format that is a combination of news and reality television (Baker, 2006). Not all countries are experiencing the same level of tabloidization, however. Research suggests that the increase of democracy in Brazil resulted in a less tabloidized, and less politically affiliated media (Porto, 2007). An increase in media privatization and deregulation in India, on the other hand, has led to more entertainment news and fewer public service-oriented stories (Rao & Johal, 2006).

Signs of tabloidization can be found in some of the earliest mass media (Tulloch, 2000). Scholars have cited several characteristics as signs of tabloidization. It has been described as an increase in entertainment coverage, a decrease in long stories, an increase in shorter stories with illustrations, and an increase in informal language within news stories. Frank Esser (1999) says the concept "implies a 'contamination' of the so-called serious media by adopting the 'tabloid agenda'" (p. 293). Howard Kurtz (1993) argues that tabloidization results in lower journalistic standards, an increase in sleazy tales in place of thoughtful political pieces, and a transition as to what journalists feel audiences need to know about a politician's capabilities for office. An overall increase in visual elements such as photographs and large headlines are another sign of the tabloidization process (Rooney, 2000).

While many news organizations are developing a tabloid style, mainstream news organizations tend to avoid using the term "tabloid". Journalists have cited the complexities of trying to maintain a serious journalism tradition while reverting to shorter, less complex news stories (Rowe, 2011). Although males and females do not acknowledge it to the same degree, audiences say they enjoy reading tabloid stories. Both sports and celebrity gossip pieces are considered particularly entertaining (Johansson, 2008).

Some scholars argue that those decrying the tabloidization of the media should consider that the media is a complex entity featuring multiple types of journalism. One should not try to distinguish merely between tabloid media and traditional media (Peters, 2011; Harrington, 2008). Furthermore, traditional news stories share some of the same characteristics as tabloid stories. For example, both types of media embrace emotion (Peters, 2011). Tabloidized stories also do not necessarily contain more emotional elements than more traditional news stories (Uribe & Gumter, 2007). While much scholarship criticizes the tabloidization of the media, there is some indication that tabloidization may have positive effects, such as giving the media a way to reach the readers of teen magazines (Nice, 2007). Using journalistic methods to reach out to large groups of people may not be at the heart of the journalist's professional interest, but in a sense, tabloidization or "popularization" could, and perhaps should, be used to increase the audience for news (Gans, 2000, p. 21). Ensuring that the public consumes plenty of news is increasingly important as we operate in a growing global society. It is important for the media to find a way to reach everyone. As Gans (2000) explains: "Although the news media cannot chase away real and imagined demons, and there are other limits to what they can do and whom they can reach, they can try harder to get the news out to the people who may unknowingly need it most" (p. 27). Nonetheless, there are scholars who suggest that sensationalized news has negative effects on audiences. Meijer (2013) conducted an ethnographic inquiry into the relationship between sensationalized news coverage and residents' views of reality using content analyses. Her research revealed that sensationalized and one-dimensional news coverage led readers to feel as though they had lost touch of reality.

Credibility

Information is more believable when it comes from a highly credible source. People are more likely to experience a greater belief change when they receive a message from a highly credible source (Hovland & Weiss, 1951).. Articles from more traditional newspapers such as the *Washington Post* are perceived as more credible than articles from tabloid publications, such as the *National Enquirer.* Highly credible sources also are more believable and accurate (Kaufman, Stasson & Hart, 1999). Audience judgment of credibility may depend on the situation to which credibility is accessed (Kim & Pasadeos, 2007). Media consumers who are liberal and trust the government are more like to trust the media (Lee, 2010).

Credibility often is measured in terms of either the source or the medium. Source credibility emphasizes the reputation of a specific individual who relays a media message (Hovland & Weiss, 1951). Medium credibility emphasizes the reputation of the medium as a whole (Gaziano & McGrath, 1996). This article focuses primarily on source credibility. Source credibility can be measured in terms of multiple dimensions: competence, care, and trustworthiness (McCroskey & Teven, 1999).

Online Credibility

Criteria such as credibility, trustworthiness, and accuracy are among the most important content criteria for online news editors (Gladney, Shapiro, & Castalodo, 2007). Internet credibility research often compares online publications to traditional media outlets. People who trust mainstream media are more likely to use mainstream media websites. Those who are more skeptical of the media are more likely to visit nonmainstream media websites (Tsfati, 2007). Some research suggests that the Internet is as credible as most or all other media (Flanagan & Metzger, 2000; Johnson, Kaye, Bichard & Wong, 2007). However, the credibility of online news websites has dropped during the past decade. One possible explanation for that drop is that audiences are becoming more web savvy (Johnson & Kaye, 2010).

Several factors have been connected to credibility. A higher level of religiosity is associated with a greater trust in the news media than a lower religiosity (Golan & Kiousis, 2010). Age also affects how credibility is rated. College students rated television news more credible than online sources, whereas older participants found online news more credible than television formats (Bucy, 2003). In Westerwick's (2013) investigation of the effects of Web site design appeal, website sponsorship, and search engine ranking on viewers' judgment of online information credibility, website sponsorship was shown to be a significant predictor of credibility ratings. Specifically, a credible website sponsor was shown to be more important for overall information credibility than the website design and the website's ranking within a Google search.

Credibility is important to bloggers (Perlmutter & Schoen, 2007). Heavy blog users find blogs more credible than those who rely less on the medium and individuals interested in politics find blogs somewhat credible (Johnson et. al., 2007; Trammell, Porter, Chung, & Kim, 2006). Blogs are not considered to be fair, but blog users view bias as a strength of the medium (Johnson et al., 2007).

News Type

Research frequently refers to the differences in hard and soft news, but scholarship presents multiple definitions for the terms. Hard news has been defined as stories that need to be reported immediately, whereas soft news refers to stories that do not require such timely publication (Shoemaker & Cohen, 2006). Hard news also has been defined as stories that are important to the audience's understanding of public affairs, while soft news has been classified as "news that typically is more personality-centered, less time-bound,

more practical, and more incident-based than other news" (Patterson, 2000, 3-4).

Research indicates that the media are increasing their soft news coverage and decreasing hard news coverage. This increase in soft, entertaining coverage often is associated with newspaper conglomerate and *USA Today* owner Gannett. The *Arkansas Gazette*'s feature coverage expanded after Gannett purchased the paper (Plopper, 1991). *USA Today*'s style includes an over-emphasis on unimportant soft news stories (Logan, 1985-1996). Media practitioners may rely on this soft news coverage to appeal to larger audiences (Scott & Gobertz, 1992). Soft news attracts viewers who might not otherwise watch the news (Baum, 2002). Individuals who prefer hard news to soft news are better informed about several news issues (Prior, 2003). Some research has suggested that audiences can learn from soft news, but that learning might be limited (Baum, 2002). Boczkowski and Peer (2011) propose that there is a 'choice gap' in what journalists' choose to display as top news stories, and what consumers choose to read. They found that journalists choices in stories tended to be soft in terms of subject matter, and that consumers tended to prefer more hard news stories.

Utilitarianism

John Stuart Mill typically is associated with the normative theory utilitarianism, which proposes "actions are right in proportion as they tend to promote happiness; wrong as they tend to produce the reverse of happiness" (Mill, 2009, p. 55). There are two types of utilitarianism. Act utilitarianism is considered a direct moral theory that emphasizes analyzing actions on the basis of each individual act or situation (Crisp, 1997, p. 102). Rule utilitarianism is an indirect moral theory in that actions are judged on how they conform to something else, namely a rule or norm. The two approaches can resolve ethical issues differently. For example, consider a situation in which a journalist has promised a source – a drug dealer who sells cocaine to youth – confidentiality in exchange for information about the city's drug crisis. In terms of act utilitarianism, breaking that promise might yield the most utility because it allows the authorities to arrest someone who is hurting the city's youth. Act utilitarianism, however, would not suggest that the journalist should always reveal the name of the source. The decision would be based on the circumstances of each act. The act utilitarian approach to decision making asks about the balance of harm versus good that will result from a specific action and endorses the action from which the most utility will result. Rule utilitarianism would consider what would happen if the decision to break a promise to the source became a rule that was consistently followed every time the journalist faced the same set of circumstances. Typically, breaking promises is thought to be morally impermissible. Rule utilitarianism requires me to abide by that rule and keep that promise. Therefore, rule utilitarianism would suggest that the journalists should not break the promise of confidentiality to the source.

For this study, act utilitarianism, rather than rule utilitarianism, is used as a guide for evaluating study results, as ethical decisions in journalism are seldom answered by simply adhering to a rule. We believe that the complexities of practicing journalism require each situation to be evaluated by its specific circumstances.

Utilitarianism requires behavior that promotes happiness. When measuring which action will yield maximum utility, everyone's pleasure is of equal value, including the one doing the act. This begs the question of what is to be considered pleasurable. According to Mill, "pleasures of the intellect, of the feeling and imagination, and of the moral sentiments," should be given "a much higher value as pleasures than those of mere sensation" (Mill, 2009, p. 56). Put another way, "it is better to be a dissatisfied Einstein than a blissfully happy ignoramus" (Christians, 2007, p. 114). This clarification of what is pleasurable makes it easy to see how utilitarianism is applicable to

journalism studies as the aim of journalists is to disseminate information in order to educate the public about important matters.

In journalism ethics research, some scholars argue that utilitarianism is not an adequate method for evaluating ethical decisions in media studies. They argue that other ethical schools of thought are better suited for studying the complexity of media and journalism ethics (Christians, 2007; Quinn, 2007; Ward, 2007). Others argue that utilitarianism often is simplified and therefore misunderstood (Elliot, 2007; Peck, 2006). Nevertheless, utilitarianism is commonly used in journalism ethics research (Christians, 2007; Elliot, 2007; Peck, 2006; Ward, 2007).

Utilitarianism has been used to examine the practice of unnamed sourcing in journalism. Utilitarianism supports the use of unnamed sourcing in particular instances where a greater aggregate good would be achieved. The journalist is required to evaluate whether using the unnamed source is a greater benefit than the harm that can be caused by anonymous sources (Duffy & Freeman, 2011). Utilitarianism has been used to justify the documentary filmmakers' responsibility to prevent harm to his or her subjects. Since documentary filmmaking involves human interaction and is a practice of social institution, filmmakers have a moral obligation to avoid harming subjects (Maccarone, 2010). Some scholars also have argued that utilitarianism is practiced in newsrooms. Editors can justify using gory and controversial images in the news with editors and journalists arguing that gruesome images from car accidents will encourage most people to drive more carefully (Lester, 1999).

While audiences may enjoy reading tabloizied content, this chapter will use act utilitarianism to demonstrate that tabloidization generally is not an ethical journalistic technique. There may be instances where it can be justified, but generally speaking, its usage will not serve the greatest good for the greatest number of people.

MAIN FOCUS OF THE CHAPTER

Issues, Controversies, Problems

Scholars have suggested that sensationalized, tabloid-style writing has cluttered the content of the mainstream media. An experiment was designed to test how audiences respond to these writing techniques. Our goal was to evaluate how tabloidized writing influences the credibility and the enjoyment of news content. We initially posed two research questions and one hypothesis to address these issues. Next, we examined tabloidization through the lens of act utilitarianism.

The media value their own credibility (Gladney et al., 2007). People are more likely to believe information that comes from a credible source (Hovland & Weiss, 1951). Furthermore, audiences find traditional news media more credible that tabloid media (Kaufman, Stasson, & Hart, 1999). Scholarship has not explained what relationship credibility may have to tabloidization.

There also is some question as to whether the news media's use of tabloidization techniques has a positive or negative effect on audiences. On one hand, the increase in personalization and sleaze can be viewed as corruption of professional journalism (Esser, 1999; Kurtz, 1993). On the other hand, tabloidization may help audiences want to consume news (Gans, 2000; Nice 2007).

To explore the relationship between the growing use of tabloidization in the media and credibility, the following research question was proposed:

RQ1: Will participants exposed to tabloidized stories rate the sources of those stories as having lower levels of credibility than participants exposed to traditional news stories?

The media appears to be shifting emphasis from hard news to soft news, which is a characteristic of tabloidization (Esser, 1999). Some scholars believe that the use of soft news lowers the qual-

ity of information (Logan, 1985-1986). This type of news, however, may help the media to attract new audiences (Baum, 2002). If credibility is important to audiences and both tabloidization and the increase of soft news are attempts to garner audiences, then the news media would want audiences to find those soft news stories credible. Yet, the relationship between credibility and different types of news has not been adequately explored. Thus, the following research question was posed:

RQ2: Will readers perceive tabloidized hard news stories as more or less credible than soft news stories?

Scholarship suggests that audiences enjoy reading tabloidized content (Johansson, 2008). Research also suggests that editors have increased the tabloidization of their content because they are responding to audience demands for that type of content. This combined research suggests that audiences enjoy tabloidized material. This leads to the following hypothesis:

H1: Participants who read tabloidized stories will report a higher level of enjoyment than participants that read traditional, untabloidized stories.

Participants for the study came from undergraduate classes at one researcher's institution. Of the 74 participants, about 34% were male and 66% were female. About 53% of the participants were in the traditional group and 47% were in the tabloid group. In regards to media consumption, 33.8% of participants reported they got their news from the newspaper, 35.1% the Internet, 8.1% radio, 36.5% network news, and 31.1% cable news.

Participants viewed a series of mock news stories. The stimuli that participants viewed depended on whether they were randomly assigned to the traditional group or the tabloidized group.

Stimuli

Four fictional news stories were written by one of the researchers. Each story was written in two formats. The first format followed more traditional news writing techniques, such as what is commonly called the inverted pyramid style, a writing format in which the most important information is located at the beginning of the story and the least important details are at the end of the story. The other version kept the same basic facts, but was written in a sensational style. The guidelines for the tabloidized writing style came from Kurtz (1993) and Esser (1999). They included: a decrease in conventional hard news coverage and an increase in soft news and sleaze; a broadened view of the information readers need to determine if a candidate is fit for a political office; lower journalistic standards overall.

Before the experiment began, five current/former journalists were asked to read all eight stories and to evaluate that the stories accurately reflected writing techniques in the way that the researcher intended. The journalists generally agreed that the tabloidized stories were more sensationalized than the traditional stories.

Two mock Web pages were designed for a publication called "The Daily News." The pages were identical, including the story headlines. The only difference was the content of the stories.

The first treatment group stories, which were written in the conventional journalistic style, were placed on one website. The second treatment group's stories were placed on another site. The files for the websites were loaded onto the desktops of several computers.

Both groups of stories were based on the same topics and general information. They also had the same headlines. Two stories used a hard news format and were considered timeline. In other words, these stories contained information that would become outdated if the stories were not published immediately. The other two stories were soft, feature-style stories, the sort of stories that

fulfill an entertainment value and do not need to be published immediately.

The first story on the Web pages focused on a kidnapping incident, where authorities suspected was related to an Internet stalking. The first version of the story was presented in a traditional inverted pyramid format with the most recent information at the beginning of the story, such as the fact that a teen is missing, and her age. In the second version of the story, the same facts are presented, but they are interwoven into a narrative depicting what the stalker and teen might have been thinking and doing just before the disappearance. The second version is highly sensationalized and uses sordid details to grab the reader's attention.

The second story focused on a city council meeting in which officials voted to ban cell phones in downtown businesses. The first version of the story begins with what is traditionally considered the most important information: the fact that the ban was put into action. The least important information, which is related to a heated discussion that occurred after the meeting, is left for the end of the story. In the tabloidized version of the story, the order is changed, allowing the story to immediately emphasize the fight that occurred after the meeting rather than the information about the new law.

The third story was a profile of a candidate for sheriff. Both stories were written as profiles, with the emphasis on informing the reader who the candidate is and what he hopes to do if elected. The tabloidized version highlights details that readers do not necessarily need in order to judge whether the candidate is qualified for the office, such as a physical description of the candidate. Several lines in the story emphasize the candidate's popularity among women. The information is kept to a minimum in the traditional group version of the story.

The final story was a feature about a new teen dance club. The traditional story mostly gave the bare-bones information necessary for the story, whereas the second story was more detailed and sensationalized. Unlike the traditional story, the tabloidized story is more of a narrative that explains how events evolved throughout the night, whereas the traditional group story just gives the essential facts of the story, along with a sprinkling of quotes.

The Instrument

Students were asked to evaluate the source of each news story using James McCroskey's Source Credibility scale (McCroskey & Teven, 1999). The scale measures three dimensions of credibility: competence; caring and goodwill; trustworthiness. The scale has been used in several studies. Reliability of the scale was tested using Cronbach's Alpha. The overall competence alpha was.88; caring,.77; trust,.90.

Participants were asked several demographic questions at the end of the survey. They also were asked to state how enjoyable the stories were and how likely they were to seek out stories similar to the ones that they just read.

Procedure

Participants were recruited from communication classes and randomly assigned to the traditional or the tabloidized group. Participants were asked to read the first story and then answer a series of questions. Then, they were asked to read the next story and answer a series of questions, and so on.

Results

On any of the credibility measures, such as competence, a higher score indicated a higher level of credibility. A probability of.05 was used for all statistical results.

RQ1: Will participants exposed to tabloidized stories rate the sources of those stories as having lower levels of credibility than participants exposed to traditional news stories?

There were statistically significant differences in how the traditional group and the tabloid group rated all three types of credibility. The means on each of the credibility scales are shown in Table 1. The participants reading the traditional stories found the news sources to be more competent with a higher competence factor score than the participants reading the tabloidized stories, $t(72)=3.41$, p. =.00. The sources of the traditional stories also demonstrated more care, as shown with the caring and goodwill scores, $t(72)=2.3$, p.=.02, and more trust with a trustworthiness score, $t(72)=2.28$, p. =.03.

There also was statistical significance in how the traditional participants and the tabloidized group evaluated the credibility of the hard news and the soft news stories. Participants in the traditional group found the sources of the hard news stories more competent than the tabloidized group, $t(72)=4.45$, p. =.00. The traditional group also found the sources of the soft news stories more competent than the tabloidized group, but the relationship was not statistically significant. Traditional participants found the sources of the hard news stories more trustworthy than the tabloidized group, $t(72)=2.61$, p.=.01. The traditional group also found the sources of the soft news stories more trustworthy than the tabloidized group, but

Table 1. Credibility scores for traditional versus tabloidized participants

Credibility Type	Traditional	Tabloidized
Competence overall	165.21*	145.14*
Competence hard news	57.64*	48.97*
Competence soft news	57.49	54.97
Caring/goodwill overall	111.38*	102.69*
Caring/goodwill hard news	55.85*	50.86*
Caring/goodwill soft news	55.54	51.83
Trustworthiness overall	120.77*	111.54*
Trustworthiness hard news	60.77*	54.74*
Trustworthiness soft news	60.00	56.80

*Denotes statistical significance

the relationship was not statistically significant. Traditional participants found the sources of the hard news stories more caring than the tabloidized group, t(72)=2.47, p.=.016. The traditional group found the soft news stories more credible than the tabloidized group, but the relationship was not statistically significant.

RQ2: Will readers perceive tabloidized hard news stories as more or less credible than soft news stories?

There was a statistically significant difference in how the tabloidized group rated the credibility of the hard and soft news stories, t(35) = -3.04, p.=01. Participants found the sources of the soft news stories (54.97) more competent than the authors of the hard news stories (48.97). There was no statistical significance on the caring or the trust factor.

H1: Participants who read tabloidized stories will report a higher level of enjoyment than participants that read traditional, untabloidized stories.

This hypothesis was tested by analyzing participant responses to two questions. One question asked how much the participant "enjoyed reading the style of writing" used on the website. The other question asked how likely the participant would be to "seek out stories that were written in a style similar" to the stories that they viewed. The relationships were tested with Chi-square tests.

There was statistical significance in how participants responded to both questions. Participants in the traditional group were more likely to report a higher level of enjoyment in reading the stories than the tabloidized participants, $\chi^2(3)=9.776$, p=.02. The results are shown in Table 2.

As shown in Table 3, participants in the traditional group also were more likely to report that they would seek out stories written in a similar style than tabloidized participants, $\chi^2(3)=10.739$, p=.01.

The hypothesis was not supported.

Discussion

Tabloidization has become a tool for mainstream journalists (Conboy, 2006). It has been interpreted as a method for attracting younger audiences and as an agent for increasing the audience size overall (Nice, 2007; Gans, 2000). The participants in this study suggested, however, that tabloidized material posted online is less credible than content written in a more traditional journalistic style. Participants were more accepting of sleazy and lurid details when the story was soft news-oriented. While the news media may offer tabloidized content because they believe that audiences want that writing style, the participants in the tabloidized group were less likely to report that they enjoyed reading the stories in this study than participants who read stories written in a more traditional style. While it certainly is possible that participants did not want to admit that they enjoyed reading trashy content and two questions are a limited

Table 2. Enjoyment responses for traditional versus tabloidized participants

Enjoyment level	Traditional (%)	Tabloidized (%)
Very enjoyable	38.5	8.6
Somewhat enjoyable	51.3	68.6
Not very enjoyable	7.7	20
Not enjoyable	2.6	2.9

Table 3. Seek similar content responses for traditional versus tabloidized participants

Seek Likelihood	Traditional (%)	Tabloidized (%)
Very likely	30.8	17.1
Somewhat likely	48.7	28.6
Not very likely	20.5	42.9
Would not	0	11.4

means for accessing enjoyment, this result raises a question as to whether journalists truly are providing audiences with the content that readers want the most. Other scholars have attempted to tackle that question, but more research is needed in this important area. The study did not attempt to ascertain the reasons as to why participants enjoyed a particular style of writing more than another. That is another important question that could be addressed in future research.

Utilitarianism

In addition to studying how audiences responded to tabloidized content, we sought to understand how journalists should address the tabloidization temptation in terms of normative ethical theory. We have chosen to address that issue by applying act utilitarianism to our study results.

Utilitarianism is interested in maximizing utility. The theory suggests that the highest pleasure is that of intellect (Mill, 2009). When applying act utilitarianism, specific actions are evaluated based on the utility that will result from said action. Actual outcomes are difficult to predict, so utilitarians determine the best action based on expected outcomes. If a utilitarian approach is used, journalists should be concerned with providing the highest pleasure for the majority of people. Traditional news stories offer important details and relevant information that might be buried in tabloidized stories. Utilitarianism would suggest that news readers experience more intellectual pleasure by reading stories that stick to the facts rather than sleazy content.

The participants in this study reported that they were more likely to enjoy and seek out stories written in a traditional style rather than tabloidized content. From the perspective of utilitarianism, these participants were more likely to seek out a higher pleasure rather than a lower pleasure. The participants were more interested

in seeking out the material that would maximize utility. Therefore, the best way for journalists to accommodate the enjoyment and overall pleasure needs of the audience is to supply readers with more traditional content more so than tabloidized material. There is some question as to why tabloid content is popular even though participants reported that they were less likely to seek out this type of story. One explanation for the popularity of tabloidized content may be that some people do not have enthusiasm for higher pleasures. Mill argues that people who chose not to enjoy higher pleasures have become incapable of experiencing such pleasures (Crisp, 1997).

Research suggests that people value credibility (Kaufman et al., 1999). Journalists also value credibility. The concept is found throughout journalism textbooks and news organization ethics codes. Participants in this study were more likely to find the journalists who wrote with a more traditional style to be more credible on the basis of competence, trustworthiness, and good will. Utilitarianism calls for one (the journalist) to be impartial to his own happiness when considering actions that yield the most utility (Mill, 2009). Utilitarianism would suggest, therefore, that it would be in the best interest of both the journalist and the audience if content is presented in a more traditional style.

When considering utilitarianism, the news writing styles are relevant not just to journalists, but news consumers as well. Mill suggested that people have a duty ''to form the truest opinions they can'' (Mill, 1859, p. 102). Being informed on matters of concern to society is the best way to do that. Elliot (2007) furthers this point by emphasizing the importance of public discussion in providing the opportunity to compare one's beliefs against others. As such, in most cases, utilitarianism would suggest that journalists should use a more traditional writing style that would appeal to the highest possible intellectual pleasure. There may be instances, however, when the only way to reach the masses may be to use a more tabloidized writing style that will grab the attention of audiences and ensure that they pay attention to a story. Act utilitarianism recognizes that there is no single one-size-fits-all answer to all complex ethical issues. It suggests that decisions should be made on the basis of specific circumstances that the journalist faces. Perhaps the tabloidized style should be utilized when evidence suggests that audiences who have failed to take note of a similar story that was important. Participants here suggested that they were more comfortable with the credibility of writers when they read tabloidized soft news stories than they were with tabloidized hard news stories. This also might suggest that the journalist can have more flexibility in choosing to use a more tabloidized writing style for those feature stories than with breaking news stories, such as homocides and car accidents.

Solutions and Recommendations

The study reconfirms what Mill (2009) suggests, individuals prefer higher intellectual pleasures. Sleazy, sensationalized writing styles appeal to lower pleasures. The participants in this study reported less enjoyment of tabloidized stories. They also tended to find the sources of tabloidized stories less credibile than the sources of more traditional stories.

This study suggests that journalists typically should not rely on tabloidized writing techniques. That writing style may help journalists to grab reader attention, but it interferes with the credibility of the news story and the intellectual pleasures. Journalists should revert to more traditional, tried and true writing styles. That will make their work more ethical and it will satisfy audiences. Futhermore, it will improve the overall credibility of journalists.

FUTURE RESEARCH DIRECTIONS

Future research should consider how tabloidized writing techniques have seeped into mainstream journalism through social media. Certainly, social media outlets such as Twitter have sped up the news consumption process, with information released in some cases before journalists have had time to confirm the facts. Might journalists also reveal more sleazy details through social media than they do in more traditional media? Is tabloidized information, which never makes it into mainstream news stories, revealed in social media or have mainstream news stories become more sleazy as social media has become a significant journalistic tool? Scholars also should consider the type of stories that are being shared through social media. Are audiences more likely to share tabloidized stories through social media sites than they are to share more traditional stories? Are tabloidized stories more frequently shared through some social media sites than they are on other social media sites?

CONCLUSION

New technology gives audiences more access to information than ever before, forcing journalists to compete with one another on a global stage. It can be tempting to add sleazy details to a story in the hopes of garnering some repeat posts on Facebook and other social networking sites. Nonetheless, the participants in this study suggested that they were not fond of tabloidized content and they were less likely to trust the writers of lurid stories. Futhermore, utilitarianism suggests that tabloidization generally is not an ethical way to reach audiences. As journalists continue to ponder their survival in a market that is over-saturated with free content, perhaps they should take a moment to consider not just what they write about, but how they write stories. Perhaps this will help them to appease the ever-technologically savvy audience.

ACKNOWLEDGMENT

The material in this chapter was previously published as a journal article. The original citation is: Mackay, J.B and Bailey, E. (2012). Succulent Sins, Personalized Politics, and Mainstream Media's Tabloidization Temptation. *International Journal of Technoethics*, 3(4), 41-53.

REFERENCES

Baker, S. (2006). The changing face of current affairs programmes in New Zealand, the United States and Britain 1984-2004. *Communication Journal of New Zealand*, 7, 1–22.

Baum, M. A. (2003). Soft news and political knowledge: Evidence of absence or absence of evidence. *Political Communication*, 20, 173–190. doi:10.1080/10584600390211181

Boczkowski, P. J., & Peer, L. (2011). The choice gap: The divergent online news preferences of journalists and consumers. *The Journal of Communication*, 61(5), 857–876. doi:10.1111/j.1460-2466.2011.01582.x

Bucy, E. P. (2003). Media credibility reconsidered: Synergy effects between on-air and online news. *Journalism & Mass Communication Quarterly*, 80, 247–264. doi:10.1177/107769900308000202

Christians, C. G. (2007). Utilitarianism in media ethics and its discontents. *Journal of Mass Media Ethics*, 22, 113–131. doi:10.1080/08900520701315640

Conboy, M. (2006). *Tabloid Britain: Constructing a community through language*. New York, NY: Routledge.

Costera Meijer, I. (2013). When news hurts. *Journalism Studies*, 14(1), 13–28. doi:10.1080/1461670X.2012.662398

Crisp, R. (1997). *Mill on Utilitarianism*. London, UK: Routledge.

Duffy, M. J., & Freeman, C. P. (2011). *Unnamed sources: A utilitarian exploration of their justification and guidelines for limited use*. Retrieved from http://digitalarchive.gsu.edu/cgi/viewcontent.cgi?filename=0&article=1012&context=communication_facpub&type=additional

Elliott, D. (2007). Getting Mill right. *Journal of Mass Media Ethics*, 22, 100–112. doi:10.1080/08900520701315806

Esser, F. (1999). Tabloidization' of news. *European Journal of Communication*, 14, 291–324. doi:10.1177/0267323199014003001

Flanagin, A. J., & Metzer, M. J. (2000). Perceptions of Internet information credibility. *Journalism & Mass Communication Quarterly*, 77, 515–540. doi:10.1177/107769900007700304

Gans, H. J. (2009). Can popularization help the news media. In B. Zeilzer (Ed.), *The changing faces of journalism tabloidization, technology, and truthiness* (pp. 17–28). New York, NY: Routledge.

Gaziano, C., & McGrath, K. (1986). Measuring the concept of credibility. *The Journalism Quarterly*, 63, 451–462. doi:10.1177/107769908606300301

Gladney, G. A., Shaprio, I., & Castaldo, J. (2007). Online editors rate web news quality criteria. *Newspaper Research Journal*, 28, 55–69.

Golan, G. J., & Kiousis, S. K. (2010). Religion, media credibility, and support for democracy in the Arab world. *Journal of Media and Religion*, 9, 84–98. doi:10.1080/15348421003738793

Harrington, S. (2008). Popular news in the 21st century. *Journalism*, 9, 266–284. doi:10.1177/1464884907089008

Hovland, C. I., & Weiss, W. (1951). The influence of source credibility on communication effectiveness. *Public Opinion Quarterly, 15,* 635–650. doi:10.1086/266350

Johansson, S. (2008). Gossip, sport and pretty girls. *Journalism Practice, 2,* 402–413. doi:10.1080/17512780802281131

Johnson, T. J., & Kaye, B. K. (2010). Still cruising and believing? An analysis of online credibility across three presidential campaigns. *The American Behavioral Scientist, 54,* 57–77. doi:10.1177/0002764210376311

Johnson, T. J., Kaye, B. K., Bichard, S. L., & Wong, W. J. (2007). Every blog has its day: Politically-interested internet users' perceptions of blog credibility. *Journal of Computer-Mediated Communication, 13,* 100–122. doi:10.1111/j.1083-6101.2007.00388.x

Kaufman, D., Stasson, M. F., & Hart, J. W. (1999). Are the tabloids always wrong or is that just what we think? Need for cognition and perceptions of articles in print media. *Journal of Applied Social Psychology, 29,* 1984–1997. doi:10.1111/j.1559-1816.1999.tb00160.x

Kim, K. S., & Pasadeos, Y. (2007). Study of partisan news readers reveals hostile media perceptions of balanced stories. *Newspaper Research Journal, 28,* 99–106.

Kurtz, H. (1993). *Media circus: The trouble with America's newspapers.* New York, NY: Times Books.

Lee, T. (2010). Why they don't trust the media: An examination of factors predicting trust. *The American Behavioral Scientist, 54,* 8–21. doi:10.1177/0002764210376308

Logan, R. A. (1985-1986). USA Today's innovations and their impact on journalism ethics. *Journal of Mass Media Ethics, 1,* 74-87.

Maccarone, E. M. (2010). Ethical responsibilities to subjects and documentary filmmaking. *Journal of Mass Media Ethics, 25,* 192–206. doi:10.1080/08900523.2010.497025

McCroskey, J. C., & Teven, J. J. (1999). Goodwill: A reexamination of the construct and its measurement. *Communication Monographs, 66,* 90–103. doi:10.1080/03637759909376464

McLachlan, S., & Golding, P. (2000). Tabloidization in the British press: A quantitative investigation into changes in British Newspapers. In C. Sparks & J. Tulloch (Eds.), *Tabloid tales: Global debates over media standards* (pp. 76–90). Lanham, MD: Rowman and Littlefield.

Melican, D. B., & Dixon, T. L. (2008). News on the net: Credibility, selective exposure, and racial prejudice. *Communication Research, 35,* 151–168. doi:10.1177/0093650207313157

Mill, J. S. (2009). Utilitarianism. R. Crisp (Ed.), J.S. Mill Utilitarianism. New York, NY: Oxford.

Nice, L. (2007). Tabloidization and the teen market. *Journalism Studies, 8,* 117–136. doi:10.1080/14616700601056882

Patterson, T. E. (2000). *Doing well and doing good: How soft news are shrinking the news audience and weakening democracy.* Cambridge, MA: Harvard University Press.

Peck, L. A. (2006). A "fool satisfied"? Journalists and Mill's principle of utility. *Journalism and Mass Communication Educator, 61,* 205–213. doi:10.1177/107769580606100207

Perlmutter, D. D., & Schoen, M. (2007). If I break a rule, what do I do, fire myself? Ethics codes of independent blogs. *Journal of Mass Media Ethics, 22,* 37–48. doi:10.1080/08900520701315269

Peters, C. (2011). Emotion aside or emotional side? Crafting an 'experience of involvement' in the news. *Journalism, 12,* 297–316. doi:10.1177/1464884910388224

Porto, M. (2007). TV news and political change in Brazil: The impact of democratization on TV Globo's journalism. *Journalism, 8,* 263–284. doi:10.1177/1464884907078656

Prior, M. (2003). Any good news in soft news? The impact of soft news preference on political knowledge. *Political Communication, 20,* 149–171. doi:10.1080/10584600390211172

Rao, S., & Johal, N. S. (2006). Ethics and news making in the changing Indian mediascape. *Journal of Mass Media Ethics, 21,* 286–303. doi:10.1207/s15327728jmme2104_5

Rooney, D. (2000). Thirty years of competition in British tabloid press: *The Mirror* and *The Sun* 1968-1998. In C. Sparks & J. Tulloch (Eds.), *Tabloid tales: Global debates about media standards* (pp. 91–109). Lanham, MD: Rowman & Littlefield.

Rowe, D. (2011). Obituary for the newspaper? Tracking the tabloid. *Journalism, 12,* 449–466. doi:10.1177/1464884910388232

Scott, D. K., & Gobetz, R. H. (1992). Hard News/Soft News Content of the National Broadcast Networks, 1972-1987. *The Journalism Quarterly, 69*(2), 406–412. doi:10.1177/107769909206900214

Shoemaker, P. J., & Cohen, A. A. (2006). *News around the world: Practitioners, content and the public.* Oxford, UK: Routledge.

Sparks, C., & Tulloch, J. (2000). *Tabloid tales: Global debates over media standards.* New York, NY: Rowman & Littlefield Publishers, Inc.

Trammell, K., Porter, L., Chung, D., & Kim, E. (2006). *Credibility and the uses of blogs among professionals in the communication industry.* Paper presented to the Credibility divide Communication Technology Division at the 2006 Association for Education in Journalism and Mass Communication. San Francisco, CA.

Tsfati, Y. (2010). Online news exposure and trust in the mainstream media: Exploring possible associations. *The American Behavioral Scientist, 54,* 22–42. doi:10.1177/0002764210376309

Tulloch, J. (2000). The eternal recurrence of new journalism. In C. Sparks & J. Tulloch (Eds.), *Tabloid tales: Global debates about media standards* (pp. 13–46). Lanham, MD: Rowman & Littlefield.

Uribe, R., & Gunter, B. (2007). Are 'sensational' news stories more likely to trigger viewers' emotions than non-sensational news stories? *European Journal of Communication, 22,* 207–228. doi:10.1177/0267323107076770

Ward, S. J. A. (2007). Utility and impartiality: Being impartial in a partial world. *Journal of Mass Media Ethics, 22,* 151–167. doi:10.1080/08900520701315913

Westerwick, A. (2013). Effects of sponsorship, web site design, and google ranking on the credibility of online information. *Journal of Computer-Mediated Communication, 18*(2), 80–97. doi:10.1111/jcc4.12006

ADDITIONAL READING

Arendt, F. (2013). News Stereotypes, Time, and Fading Priming Effects. *Journalism & Mass Communication Quarterly, 90*(2), 347–362. doi:10.1177/1077699013482907

Burgers, C., & de Graaf, A. (2013). Language intensity as a sensationalistic news feature: The influence of style on sensationalism perceptions and effects. *Communications: The European Journal of Communication Research, 38*(2), 167–188. doi:10.1515/commun-2013-0010

Cassidy, W. P. (2007). Online News Credibility: An Examination of the Perceptions of Newspaper Journalists. *Journal of Computer-Mediated Communication, 12*(2), 144–164. doi:10.1111/j.1083-6101.2007.00334.x

Chung, C. J., Nam, Y., & Stefanone, M. A. (2012). Exploring Online News Credibility: The Relative Influence of Traditional and Technological Factors. *Journal of Computer-Mediated Communication, 17*(2), 171–186. doi:10.1111/j.1083-6101.2011.01565.x

Duffy, M. J., & Freeman, C. P. (2011). Unnamed Sources: A Utilitarian Exploration of their Justification and Guidelines for Limited Use. *Journal of Mass Media Ethics, 26*(4), 297–315. doi:10.1080/08900523.2011.606006

Elliott, D. (2007a). [), Taylor & Francis Ltd.]. *Getting Mill Right, 22*, 100–112.

Hendriks Vettehen, P., Beentjes, J., Nuijten, K., & Peeters, A. (2010). Arousing news characteristics in Dutch television news 1990–2004: An exploration of competitive strategies. *Mass Communication & Society, 14*(1), 93–112. doi:10.1080/15205431003615893

Hofstetter, C. R. (1986). Useful news, sensational news: Quality, sensationalism and local TV news. *The Journalism Quarterly, 63*(4), 815. doi:10.1177/107769908606300421

Karlsson, M., & Clerwall, C. (2011). Patterns and origins in the evolution of multimedia on broadsheet and tabloid news sites: Swedish online news 2005–2010. *Journalism Studies*, 1–16.

Lee, S., Stavrositu, C., Yang, H., & Kim, J. (2004). Effects of Multimedia and Sensationalism on Processing and Perceptions of Online News. *Conference Papers -- International Communication Association*, 1.

McChesney, R. W. (2012). Farewell to journalism? *Journalism Studies, 13*(5–6), 682–694. doi:10.1080/1461670X.2012.679868

Molek-Kozakowska, K. (2013). Towards a pragma-linguistic framework for the study of sensationalism in news headlines. *Discourse & Communication, 7*(2), 173–197. doi:10.1177/1750481312471668

Nah, S., & Chung, D. S. (2012). When citizens meet both professional and citizen journalists: Social trust, media credibility, and perceived journalistic roles among online community news readers. *Journalism, 13*(6), 714–730. doi:10.1177/1464884911431381

Netzley, S. B., & Hemmer, M. (2012). Citizen Journalism Just as Credible As Stories by Pros, Students Say. *Newspaper Research Journal, 33*(3), 49–61.

Online News Sensationalism: The Effects of Sensational Levels of Online News Stories and Photographs on Viewers' Attention, Arousal, and Information Recall. (2012). *Conference Papers -- International Communication Association*, 1-29.

Örnebring, H., & Jönsson, A. M. (2004). Tabloid journalism and the public sphere: a historical perspective on tabloid journalism. *Journalism Studies, 5*(3), 283–295. doi:10.1080/1461670042000246052

Parmelee, J. H., & Perkins, S. C. (2012). Exploring social and psychological factors that influence the gathering of political information online. *Telematics and Informatics, 29*(1), 90–98. doi:10.1016/j.tele.2010.12.001

Peck, L. A. (2006). A Fool Satisfied? Journalists and Mill's Principle of Utility. *Journalism & Mass Communication Educator, 61*(2), 205–213. doi:10.1177/107769580606100207

Plassner, F. (2005). From hard to soft news standards? How political journalists in different media systems evaluate the shifting quality of news. *The Harvard International Journal of Press/Politics, 10*(2), 47–68. doi:10.1177/1081180X05277746

Skorpen, E. (1989). Are Journalistic Ethics Self-Generated? *Journal of Mass Media Ethics, 4*(2), 157–173. doi:10.1080/08900528909358341

Sparks, C., & Tulloch, J. (2000). *Tabloid tales: Global debates over media standards*. Lanham, Md: Rowman & Littlefield Publishers.

Sundar, S. S., Knobloch, S., & Hastall, M. (2005/05/26/2005 Annual Meeting, New York, NY). *Clicking News: Impacts of Newsworthiness, Source Credibility, and Timeliness as Online News Features on News Consumption.*

Thorson, K., Vraga, E., & Ekdale, B. (2010). Credibility in Context: How Uncivil Online Commentary Affects News Credibility. *Mass Communication & Society*, *13*(3), 289–313. doi:10.1080/15205430903225571

Vettehen, P. H., Nuijten, K., & Peeters, A. (2008). Explaining Effects of Sensationalism on Liking of Television News Stories: The Role of Emotional Arousal. *Communication Research*, *35*(3), 319–338. doi:10.1177/0093650208315960

Wang, T.-L. (2012). Presentation and impact of market-driven journalism on sensationalism in global TV news. *International Communication Gazette*, *74*(8), 711–727. doi:10.1177/1748048512459143

KEY TERMS AND DEFINITIONS

Act Utilitarianism: Normative ethical theory that considers the consequences that a decision will have when a specific situation is faced. The theory suggests that ethical decisions should be made on a case-by-case basis.

Credibility: The believability of information.

Hard News: Stories that require immediate coverage, such as crime news or stories that assist in an individual's ability to vote intelligently.

Soft News: Stories that generally serve an entertainment function rather than a public affairs function.

Source Credibility: The degree to which an individual source, such as the author of a news story, is considered believable.

Tabloidization: The contamination of tabloid writing techniques into the mainstream news media. It often is associated with less political information and an increase in sleazy details into news stories.

Utilitarianism: Normative ethical theory which suggests that decisions should promote happiness, providing the greatest good to the greatest number of people.

This work was previously published in Evolving Issues Surrounding Technoethics and Society in the Digital Age edited by Rocci Luppicini, pages 97-112, copyright year 2014 by Information Science Reference (an imprint of IGI Global).

Chapter 58
Evaluating Social Interaction and Support Methods over Time

Birgitta Maria Kopp
Ludwig-Maximilians-University, Germany

ABSTRACT

This research focuses on the evaluation of social interaction and support methods for computer-supported collaborative learning over the period of one semester. Specifically, there are three main topics for investigation: first, the subjective evaluation of social interaction and support methods, second, the students' perceptions of these over time, and third, the correlations between social interaction and support methods. Results indicate a specific pattern regarding important aspects of social interaction indicating possible problems in group dynamics (especially relating to taking responsibility). This evaluation pattern remains nearly constant over time. Furthermore, correlation analyses show strong connections between the design of group work and group dynamics, indicating a positive influence of support methods on problematic dimensions of social interaction. As this relation is strongest during the middle phase of collaboration, this study gives a first indication that also CSCL groups may go through the storming and norming stage of collaboration. These findings substantiate the necessity of providing support for computer-based learning.

INTRODUCTION

This research study focuses on three main aspects: (1) The learners' subjective perception of their social interaction and support methods, (2) learner's perceptions of these over a period of time, and (3) the correlations between social interaction and support methods.

Computer-supported collaborative learning (CSCL) is currently implemented in different kinds of education because educators are convinced that such environments allow learners to learn more deeply and meaningfully (Kirschner & Erkens, 2013). CSCL research has also shown that virtual collaborative learning must be supported to provide effective learning in terms of knowledge construction (Pozzi & Persico, 2011). But even when supported, it is not guaranteed that learners who are placed in groups without knowing each other are able to engage in the relevant activities for learning (Lou, Abrami, & d'Apollonia, 2001), for achieving positive learning outcomes (Beers,

DOI: 10.4018/978-1-4666-8619-9.ch058

2005), or for solving tasks together. One key pre-condition for such positive effects lies in the learners' ability to function as team (Kirschner & Erkens, 2013) which implies that learners know each other and specifically draw upon their varied knowledge, information and experiences (Moreland, 1999). Furthermore, "students need to trust each other, feel a sense of warmth and belonging, and feel close to each other before they will engage willfully in collaboration" (Kreijns, Kirschner, & Jochems, 2003). In ad-hoc learning groups, this is often not the case. Therefore, it is of interest to research how learners themselves perceive their learning group in terms of the relevant dimensions of social interaction. This is an issue which has not yet been the subject of investigation.

As support is necessary for fostering the learning process as well as learners' collaborative and individual performance (Kopp & Mandl, 2011a), it is also important to investigate how learners themselves evaluate these support methods. The specific question arises whether learners perceive the support methods as effective for fostering their social interaction and their ability to complete the task at hand.

The next interesting aspect is the development of groups over a period of time. In CSCL research, the premise is that learners function as teams, e.g. "that they trust one another in the team to do what has been agreed upon, know one another's weak and strong points and make use of them, share similar norms for working and goals of the teamwork, and so on." (Kirschner & Erkens, 2013, p. 2). But developing as a team takes time and often there is neither time nor adequate conditions for teams to develop from an ad hoc group to a functioning team. Even though there is a new model for ad hoc learning-team development (Fransen, Weinberger, & Kirschner, 2013), there is no research that evaluates the changes in the development of social interaction. There have mainly been quantitative studies analyzing the learners' contributions in order to gain further insights into cognitive group processes. Thus, this

research also focuses on the development of the perception of social interaction and of support methods over a period of time.

The third issue concerns the interrelationship between social interaction and support methods. To act as a team, it is necessary to plan and coordinate group activities, to keep to a schedule, to work jointly on the group goal, etc. In CSCL environments, support methods are implemented in order to foster such team-building processes and thus improve group dynamics. Various studies in the laboratory and in the field have focused specifically on whether there are differences between learners with support versus learners without support (Kopp & Mandl, 2011b). But research has not yet shown whether there are correlations between support methods and social interaction from the learner's point of view.

In the following three subsections, we describe the theoretical background of the three main purposes of the study in more detail.

SOCIAL INTERACTION AND SUPPORT METHODS

When investigating *social interaction* in virtual collaborative learning, there are two specific levels of interest: The task level and the social level (Kauffeld, 2001). The task level comprises the learners' knowledge about the joint goal and their willingness to solve a task together. This level involves goal orientation and task completion. Goal orientation focuses on the impact of the goal and how it functions as motivator for successful performance (Mento, Locke, & Klein, 1992). As collaborative learning involves the "mutual engagement of participants in a coordinated effort to solve the problem together" (Roschelle & Teasley, 1995, p. 70), an orientation toward the same goal is of utmost importance for effective learning and task solving from a motivational standpoint. Task completion includes activities relevant to completing the task, specifically task-solving strategies (West, 1994) such as task-related conflicts and discussions (Curral, Forrester, Dawson, & West, 2001), the exchange of relevant information (Moreland, 1999), or the coordination of the task solution. As groups tend to disseminate shared knowledge instead of unshared knowledge (Brodbeck, Kerschreiter, Mojzisch, & Schulz-Hardt, 2007), the exchange of relevant information is one main antecedent for groups to outperform individuals. Furthermore, without planning group activities, no joint activities may take place (Erkens, Prangsma, & Jaspers, 2006).

The social level refers to group dynamics and includes group cohesion and taking responsibility. Processes of "getting to know each other, committing to social relationships, developing trust and belonging, and building a sense of on-line community" (Kreijns et al., 2003, p. 342) are part of developing group cohesion. This describes the tendency for a group to stick together and the desire to remain in the group (Kreijns et al., 2003) which is a main reason that group members stay in a group and participate in completing the task. Group cohesion also has an impact on students' satisfaction with collaborative learning (Dewiyanti, Brand-Gruwel, Jochems, & Broers, 2007). Even though meta-analysis of group cohesion showed positive correlations between cohesion and performance mediated by the type of team and the setting (Tannenbaum, Beard, & Sales, 1992), research on the evaluation of group cohesion in virtual learning environments is lacking. Building a community to which all group members belong (Wegerif, 1998) is highly important for virtual collaboration and effective task solving. But the question remains as to whether group members themselves perceive group cohesion when learning together.

The second issue of group dynamics involves taking responsibility which is central to overall collaboration since the group will not be successful without taking responsibility for the task-solving process (Kauffeld, 2001). One key antecedent for feeling responsible is based on the social interdependence theory (Johnson & Johnson, 1998). When group members are interdependent, it means that they are linked to each other in such a way that the individual group member can only succeed unless the others succeed, so that everyone benefits from each other's work (Johnson & Johnson, 1998). This reduces dysfunctional phenomena such as the free-rider or hitchhiking effect (Kerr & Bruun, 1983), social loafing (Latané, Williams, & Harkins, 1979), and the sucker effect (Kerr, 1983). Research on group decision indicates that motivation to participate extensively is necessary for higher effectiveness and greater engagement (Curral, et al., 2001). And vice versa: If group members feel that the sharing of their load is not fair, they will have less motivation for learning and the performance of the group will be impacted negatively (Shen & Wu, 2011). But again, CSCL environments often lack an atmosphere which makes participants feel responsible for collaborative task solving.

In this context, it is necessary to *support* learning in CSCL environments, because building ad hoc learning groups and assigning them tasks does not guarantee the desired positive outcomes (Kirschner & Erkens, 2013). Problems specific to virtual learning environments (e.g. different social presence; a more explicit coordination) occur (Kopp & Mandl, 2011b).Two support methods include designing group work and providing feedback (Kopp, Germ, & Mandl, 2010).

Designing group work includes aspects such as maintaining an adequate group size of between 2 and 5 persons (Lou et al., 2001), a collaborative task that creates social interdependence (Johnson & Johnson, 1998), the assignment of roles (like a rotating moderator), or group rules. The last two aspects are central in this study. In CSCL research, the assignment of roles is specifically used in the scripting approach (Kopp & Mandl, 2010; Pozzi, Hofmann, Persico, Stegmann, & Fischer, 2013). Research on scripts has taken place in different virtual learning environments such as videoconferencing or asynchronous forums. Results were diverse, not decisively proving the efficiency of the support methods in terms of improving learning (e.g. Ertl, Kopp, & Mandl, 2007; Fischer, Kollar, Mandl, & Haake, 2007; Fischer, Kollar, Stegmann, & Wecker, 2013). It is of interest to discover how learners themselves perceive how such support methods affect their collaboration. A second method of designing group work is by providing group rules (Kopp et al., 2010). In CSCL research there has been little investigation into how to provide support in order to organize and plan task solving, but also in order to regulate the social interaction and the way participants interact (e.g. Järvelä & Hadwin, 2013). Group rules may be one possible method of precisely filling this gap in research by focusing on the prevention of dysfunctional group phenomena and harsh or disrespectful contact.

The second method of support, providing feedback, includes feedback on the performance and on the process level, as well as worked examples. Feedback is mainly given on performance, considering the correctness and quality of the respective task solution (Hattie & Timperley, 2007). Such feedback differs in its level of detail, ranging from simple and short answers such as "correct" or "not correct" to elaborated explanations. Elaborated feedback comprises a greater informational content than simple feedback and is more effective for learning (Moreno, 2004). Meta-analyses on performance feedback show that it has a significant effect on the performance improvement (e.g. Tenenbaum & Goldring, 1989). Feedback on the process-level refers directly to the activities that occur during collaboration and task solving. Such kind of feedback focuses on assisting learners in both their task-solving activities and their social interaction. Providing worked examples is a very effective method of increasing learner's performance. Research on worked examples used in different domains, such as medical education (Stark, Kopp, & Fischer, 2011) or mathematics (Lin & Zhang, 2007), often indicated positive effects on learning. Specifically, complete worked examples

seem to be more effective than incomplete worked examples (Lin & Zhang, 2007). Even though, these laboratory studies show positive effects of worked examples, it has not yet been investigated, whether learners evaluate such support methods as positive for their collaboration.

OBSERVING THE SOCIAL INTERACTION OVER TIME

In CSCL environments, research on virtual collaboration over time focused especially on the quantitative analyses of written contributions in group forums. There are different schemes for analyzing these contributions mainly taking cognitive and social processes into account. Regarding cognitive activities, a study by Kopp, Schnurer, and Mandl (2009) revealed no specific trend in the development of cognitive activities such as epistemic activities, conceptual space, the dissemination of distributed knowledge, and conflict-orientation. In contrast, a school class that collaborated for 12 weeks with an online conference showed stronger interaction over time (Hara, Bonk, & Angeli, 1998). In another study, students had problems in the beginning, but increased their activity in the learning environment over time (Heilesen, Thomsen, & Cheesman, 2002). In yet another study by Pena-Shaff and Nicholls (2004) the length of discussions became shorter over time, but group cohesion was stronger (Pena-Shaff & Nicholls, 2004). Overall, analyzing group processes over time did not reveal a clear picture regarding the increase or decrease of specific activities. Furthermore, there has been no research on the perception of social interaction over time that includes group dynamics.

The work of Tuckman (1965) is of interest when looking at the theoretical framework of group development. He distinguishes four phases, namely forming, storming, norming, and performing. In the forming stage, orientation, testing, and dependence are constitutive. Storming comprises conflict and polarization; norming includes the development of in-group feeling and cohesiveness. In the last stage, the groups develop a flexible structure which is supportive for task performance (Tuckman, 1965). A new theoretical model of team development in CSCL also includes the four stages of Tuckman (1965) completed by the stages re-norming, performing 2, and conforming (Fransen, et al., 2013, p. 19). Research in CSCL environments shows no indication of a specific trend in collaboration activities based on these theoretical assumptions on group development (Tuckman, 1965). In this study, it is of interest, whether these stages are reflected in the learners' perception of their social interaction and support methods. If so, it is possible that the evaluation of social interaction may decrease in the storming stage or increase in the performing stage. For the evaluation of support methods, it may be the opposite, indicating an increase in evaluation in storming stages and a decrease in performing stages as support is needed more in the storming stage than in the performing stage.

CORRELATION BETWEEN SOCIAL INTERACTION AND SUPPORT METHODS

CSCL research that focuses on the relationship between support methods and learning are ambiguous, but generally indicates that specific structuring tools such as scripts or content schemes have a positive impact on collaborative learning, specifically on collaborative performance (Fischer, Kollar, Mandl, & Haake, 2007; Kopp & Mandl, 2011a). Research on the effectiveness of feedback also shows that this support method fosters learning and performance (Krause, Stark, & Mandl, 2009). Thus, support methods such as structuring collaboration as well as providing feedback have almost a positive impact on collaboration in terms of learning and performance.

These results from laboratory studies used mostly collaborative task solutions as measure of performance. What is still not clear is whether such support methods positively correlate with the social interaction on a task and a social level from the learner's subjective point of view (Kopp & Mandl, 2011b). As support methods are used to foster social interaction, the main assumption is that there may be positive correlations between support methods and social interaction.

RESEARCH QUESTIONS

Based on this theoretical background, the following questions were examined in this research:

1. How do students evaluate social interaction and support methods?

Ad hoc learning groups initially start to interact with each other to solve tasks together. As learners have to develop as a team (Kirschner et al., 2013) it is assumed that specifically in the beginning of the collaboration, the evaluation of the social interaction in terms of goal orientation, task completion, group cohesion, and taking responsibility may occur to a relatively low degree. Support methods are implemented in order to foster collaboration and the team building process. Therefore, it is expected that learners will react favorably to these methods.

2. To what extent do the evaluations of social interaction and support methods differ over time?

Looking at the team development research, groups may go through the four stages of Tuckman (1965), namely forming, storming, norming, and performing. Depending on these stages, the evaluation of social interaction as well as the perception of support methods may differ over time. It is assumed that social interaction may be perceived more favorably in the norming and performing stages in contrast to the storming stage. Support methods are more relevant in the storming stage and thus likely to be evaluated more favorably in contrast to the norming and performing stages.

3. To what extent do the design of group work and feedback correlate with social interaction over time in terms of:
    a. goal orientation?
    b. task completion?
    c. cohesion?
    d. taking responsibility?

CSCL laboratory research has nearly shown positive interrelationships between support methods and collaboration (Fischer et al., 2007). What is still not known is, whether there are also positive correlations between support methods and social interaction based on the learner's subjective evaluation. As support methods are implemented to foster social interaction, it is assumed that there is a positive correlation. These correlation rates may differ over time indicating a stronger correlation in the storming stage and a lower correlation in the performing stage.

LEARNING ENVIRONMENT

Content

The study was carried out in the seminar "Attachment Theory". The seminar took 14 weeks in the summer semester 2008 from mid April to mid July. The main objective of this course was to introduce the students to the Attachment Theory. Attachment Theory harkens back to John Bowlby (1907-1990) and Mary Ainsworth (1913-1999). It describes the dynamics of long-term relationships between humans, specifically between infants and their primary caregiver, which they need for their normal social and emotional development. The theory is interdisciplinary encompassing the fields of ethnology, cybernetics, information processing, developmental psychology, and psychoanalysis (Bretherton, 1992).

The entire course content was subdivided into three key aspects each with three modules (see Table 1). The course content was delivered virtually using a platform provided by a company called e/t/s. Power Point slides and additional text material was uploaded onto this platform.

Table 1. Course content of the seminar attachment theory

Key Aspect	I: Basics of Attachment Theory	II: Studies, Research and Results of Attachment Theory	III: Support Methods for Fostering the Interaction between Parents and Children
Module I	The beginnings of Attachement Theory (John Bolwby and Mary Ainsworth) and its definition	Bielefelder and Regensburger Longitudinal Study Childhood and Adolescence*	Training of Van den Boom (1994) to manipulate sensitive responsiveness of mothers
Module II	Sensitivity/Tactfulness of the mother	Attachment to the Father	STEEP-Programme
Module III	Effects of Attachment on the Child's Development	Relations outside the Family	Psychotherapeutic advice

Note: *This Longitudinal Study describes the development of attachment from childhood to adolescence in Germany, specifically in the regions of Regensburg and Bielefeld (Grossmann et al., 2003; Spangler & Zimmermann, 2009)

Tasks

Each week, groups received an authentic problem on the platform in the form of a task to be solved collaboratively. For example, learners received a case involving two children, Lisa and Lena, who behaved differently in the Strange Situation based on their different attachment patterns (see Figure 1).

The task related to this case was: *"Analyze the behavior of Lisa's and Lena's mothers and show the relationship between the behavior of the mothers and that of their respective daughters."* The analyses were to be based on the case information and on the theoretical background of the Attachment Theory. The groups had to finalize their tasks virtually within one week and send their final solutions to the e-tutor. The e-tutor gave weekly feedback on these group solutions.

DIDACTICAL DESIGN

The seminar was didactically designed as blended learning. Face-to-face phases for further discussions were alternated with virtual phases for collaboration. Overall, there were three main collaborative virtual phases (3 key aspects in total) each lasting 3 weeks, so that learners had to solve nine collaborative tasks during the seminar. In between, there were three face-to-face phases for learners to get to know each other and for learners to engage in further discussions or ask questions.

Furthermore, the seminar followed a problem-based approach, asking learners to apply their theoretical knowledge to authentic problems from multiple perspectives and contexts in the field. An e-tutor supported the overall collaboration with group rules, a rotating moderator, feedback, and worked examples, as well as emails.

Figure 1. Example of a case task (Key Aspect I, Module 2)

Case 2

Looking at Lisa's and Lena's mothers more closely, we detect differences in their interaction with their kids.

Lisa's mother listens and responds to the needs of her daughter. When Lisa wants to explore her environment, her mother supports her. If her daughter wants to play alone, she does not interrupt her but stays within reach in order to be there when her daughter needs her. As soon as her daughter wants to cuddle up to her on her stomach, her mother takes her and gives her the necessary closeness.

Lena's mother is caring towards her daughter and kisses her, even when the child does not want to be kissed. The mother does not pay attention when Lena explores her environment. She sometimes interrupts the autonomous play of her daughter to show her how to handle specific things. When Lena cries, her mother does not always attend to her. Thus, Lena is accustomed to calling attention to herself loudly and often complains.

The different way of interacting with the children is based on the sensitivity of both mothers. The following explanations highlight this key concept.

Support Methods

In the seminar, there were two dominant support methods: designing the group work and providing learners with feedback (see Table 2 for an overview):

1. The design of the group work included two main principles: the assignment of roles and the definition of group rules:
   a. For every module, groups had to identify a moderator who was responsible for a successful task solution. This moderator role rotated so that every group member functioned as a moderator at least two times;
   b. All groups also had to define specific group rules for planning and organizing their collaboration and for handling social interaction. One example of a rule for the planning and organization of the collaboration was "The tasks could be solved using key words and must be posted to the forum by Sunday at 6pm." Handling social interaction was regulated with rules such as "All group members should be friendly and consider the different points of view and opinions of the other members." These rules were mandatory for all group members;
2. Providing learners with feedback included feedback on the individual group's task solutions as well as worked examples. This feedback was provided by the e-tutor every week immediately after the groups finished the respective collaborative task:

   a. The feedback on group solutions was detailed and comprised aspects relating to the group process and the group results;
   b. For each task, the tutor offered a worked example with all the relevant theoretical concepts and necessary case information (see Box 1).

TECHNICAL DESIGN

The virtual learning environment was technically integrated in the learning platform of the university and run by the company e/t/s, which offers learning software in Germany. All participants in the seminar received access to the virtual learning platform. The students could work at their own convenience from any computer that had an internet connection. The learning platform was equipped with different functions (see Table 3).

First of all, there was a content section for delivering the main content of the "Attachment Theory". All the documents were uploaded in digital format so the students could download the learning material and print it out themselves. The material was presented to students with two modalities: The first modality comprised the most important points for every topic in the form of a PowerPoint presentation. The second modality included additional literature for each of the respective topics. Secondly, there was a collaboration section. The collaboration section was also twofold: There was one section for the whole seminar where all students had the ability to ask general questions regarding the task solving or the technique. In this section, students were also able to upload task solutions and view

Table 2. Support methods

Designing group work	Assignment of roles	Definition of group rules
Providing feedback	Feedback on task solutions	Worked example

Table 3. Functions of the virtual platform

Content Section	Content of attachment theory in PP presentation	Additional literature
Collaboration Section	Seminar forum	Group forums

Box 1. Example solution on the case task (Key Aspect I, Module 3)

Case: Lisa	
Case Information	**Theoretical Concept**
Lisa cries loudly when mother leaves her.	Emotion-specific expression with appeal character.
As soon as the mother appears, she calms down immediately.	Active attachment behavior.
Joyous play with her mother.	Sensitive reaction of the mother to the needs of her child.
Building up a good relationship with her nursery nurse.	Building up a positive internal working model.
Gets along with other kids very well.	Building up a positive internal working model and positive self-concept → competent contact with other kids.
→ All detailed information is evidence of a secure attachment (attachment style B).	
Justification: According to the strange situation test Lisa shows her grief very loudly, as soon as her mother leaves her alone. She has learned to show her needs with this reaction, and her mother reacts adequately to it (emotion-specific expression with appeal character). Therefore, she immediately calms down as soon as her mother appears, because then she feels secure (active attachment behavior). She has built up a positive relationship with her mother. The joyous play shows that she knows that her mother reacts adequately to her needs for closeness and exploration (concept of maternal sensitivity). The ability to form a good relationship with her nursery nurse after an adequate time of acclimatization shows that Lisa has a positive internal working model without being frightened of becoming disappointed by this person. Another hint for a secure relation and of a positive model of Lisa is that she gets along with the other kids very well (competent contact with other kids based on a positive self-concept and working model) and that she feels happy in the day nursery.	

the e-tutor's feedback. The second collaboration section was on the group level. In this section, participants received specific access to their respective group forum for their virtual collaboration and communication.

METHOD

Sample

The participants were undergraduate students majoring in pedagogy. Altogether there were 32 participants in the course, consisting of 30 females and 2 males. Thirty-one students were studying pedagogy; one student was studying pedagogy for students with special needs. Two students were in their sixth semester, 3 in their fifth, 12 in their fourth, 4 in their third, and 11 in their second semester. The participants were divided randomly into eight groups. All groups had four members, with the exception of group 6 with three members and group 7 with five members. The differences in the number of group members was due to the fact that the seminar started with more than fifty

participants comprising 10 groups, each with five or six members. After the first week, there was a significant drop-out rate with several changes in group assignments. This was due to the fact that students were not required to participate in the seminar. Thus, the students did not have to expect negative consequences when they changed their participation and dropped-out without further explanation.

Design of the Study

The seminar was evaluated through a survey with three data collection points. The first data collection was conducted five weeks after the beginning of the seminar from May 14th to May 21st, 2008. The subsequent data was collected two more times every four weeks using an online questionnaire. The second point of measurement was from the 18th until the 25th of June, 2008. The last point of measurement was from the 16th until the 23rd of July, 2008. The students received an online questionnaire per e-mail and were asked to email back their completed questionnaires.

Data Sources

To evaluate collaboration and support methods, we developed a questionnaire that focused on these two aspects (see Appendix). To evaluate collaboration, we used the questionnaire for teamwork by Kauffeld (2001). The Kauffeld questionnaire included four dimensions, namely goal orientation and task completion at the task level and group cohesion and taking responsibility at the social level. Goal orientation was measured with six items on a six-point-Likert scale ranging from 1 ("do not agree") to 6 ("totally agree"). Cronbach's Alpha was between .72 and .86. A sample item is "I identified myself with the group goal." Task completion had 4 items ("The priority was the task solving.") with Cronbach's Alpha between .57 and .72. Regarding the social level, eight items such as "We communicated openly and freely" was used for measuring group cohesion. Cronbach's Alpha was between .65 and .77. Again 4 items were used to measure the dimension "taking responsibility" (Cronbach's Alpha was between .63 and .65). A sample item is "Everyone took responsibility for the joint task solution." Overall, the reliability of the Kauffeld questionnaire was sufficient. As a field study, the external validity of the study is also high.

To measure support methods, we again used a six-point-Likert scale from 1 ("not effective at all") to 6 ("very effective") asking how effective certain aspects were for group work. These aspects were "defining group rules", and "rotating moderator" which were used as methods of group design, and "feedback on group solutions", and "worked examples" as feedback methods. Cronbach's Alpha for group design was between .51 and .63, and for providing feedback between .55 and .79. Again, as field study, the external validity of the study is high.

Data Analysis

The data was analyzed using SPSS 18.0. As a first step, we calculated the descriptive statistics with the mean and standard deviation of the relevant dimensions at the three different points in time. In a second step, we looked at differences between the dimensions on social interaction and the dimensions on support methods at each point of time using t-tests for paired samples. In a third step we again used t-tests for paired samples to calculate the differences between the single dimensions at three points in time. In a fourth step, we correlated the four dimensions of social interaction with the two dimensions of support methods using a Pearson's one-way correlation analysis. The level of significance was .05.

RESULTS

How do Students Evaluate Social Interaction and Support Methods?

Over all three time intervals, students evaluated both social interaction and support methods positively with small standard deviation (See Table 4).

Looking at the social interaction more closely, at the first point of measurement there were signifi-

Table 4. Descriptive data of social interaction and support methods separated by points of measurement

	Time 1		Time 2		Time 3	
	M	*SD*	*M*	*SD*	*M*	*SD*
Goal orientation	4.13	.54	4.09	.67	4.14	.59
Task completion	4.50	.47	4.30	.57	4.36	.53
Cohesion	4.33	.48	4.19	.56	4.26	.53
Taking responsibility	3.96	.65	3.83	.70	3.70	.62
Design of group work	4.45	.61	4.45	.74	4.63	.61
Providing feedback	3.98	.84	4.42	.78	4.53	.60

cant differences between goal orientation and task completion ($t(31)=-3.90$; $p<.01$) and between goal orientation and cohesion ($t(31)=-2.37$; $p<.05$). Furthermore, taking responsibility differed significantly from task completion ($t(31)=-5.65$; $p<.01$) and from cohesion ($t(31)=-4.18$; $p<.01$). These results demonstrate that taking responsibility was evaluated lowest, followed by goal orientation. Both dimensions significantly differed from the other two dimensions of virtual collaboration.

At the second point of time, taking responsibility was evaluated significantly lower than all other three dimensions of virtual collaboration, specifically goal orientation ($t(29)=-2.16$; $p<.05$), task completion ($t(29)=-3.76$; $p<.01$), and cohesion ($t(29)=-3.73$; $p<.01$). There was also a difference between goal orientation and task completion ($t(29)=-2.04$; $p=.051$). The same results occurred at the third point of time with a significant difference between taking responsibility and goal orientation ($t(29)=-3.38$; $p<.01$), task completion ($t(29)=-6.23$; $p<.01$), and cohesion ($t(29)=-5.69$; $p<.01$). Again, goal orientation and task completion differed significantly ($t(29)=-2.24$; $p<.05$).

Regarding support methods, there was only one significant difference between the design of group work and providing feedback at the first point of measurement ($t(31)=2.57$; $p<.05$). At the second and third point in time, both support methods were evaluated positively.

To What Extent do Evaluations of Social Interaction and Support Methods Differ Over Time?

When investigating the development of social interaction, the evaluation remains homogenous. The T-Test showed one significant difference between the first and second point in time, namely between the evaluation of task completion (M(t1)=4.50, SD(t1)=.47, M(t2)=4.30, SD(t2)=.57; $t(29)=2.15$; $p<.05$). Looking at the support methods, there was also one difference between the first and

second point in time in the evaluation of providing feedback (M(t1)=3.98, SD(t1)=.84, M(t2)=4.42, SD(t2)=.78; $t(29)=-2.97$; $p<.01$).

To What Extent Do the Design of Group Work and Providing Feedback Correlate with Social Interaction Over Time in Terms of Goal Orientation, Task Completion, Group Cohesion, and Taking Responsibility?

Looking at Table 5, results show that group design positively correlates with all four dimensions of social interaction at the first and second point in time, and with the two social dimensions of group cohesion and taking responsibility at the third point in time. These correlations are significant. The correlation is on a medium to high level with the highest scores at the second point of measurement.

Providing feedback significantly correlates only once with taking responsibility at the first point of measurement. There were no further correlations between support methods and social interaction.

DISCUSSION

There are three main results for discussion that have been highlighted by this study: First, the evaluation of the social interaction and of the support methods shows a specific pattern. Regarding the four dimensions of social interaction, task completion was evaluated highest at all three points of measurement, followed by group cohesion, goal orientation, and taking responsibility (See Table 4). Significant differences occurred specifically between taking responsibility and the other three dimensions as well as between task completion and goal orientation. This evaluation pattern shows that not all group members share the same sense of responsibility for completing their joint group

Table 5. One-way Pearson-correlations between group design and providing feedback and the four dimensions of social interaction separated by points of measurement

	Time 1		Time 2		Time 3	
	Group Design	**Feedback**	**Group Design**	**Feedback**	**Group Design**	**Feedback**
Goal orientation	.345*	.017	.462*	.136	.219	-.018
Task completion	.493**	.000	.472**	-.069	.218	-.170
Cohesion	.535**	.155	.652**	.181	.344*	.083
Taking responsibility	.574**	.344*	.718**	-.012	.546**	-.056

** p <.01; * p <.05

solution, possibly due to the lack of social presence in virtual learning environments. This is a problem which has often been discussed in virtual learning environments (Kopp & Mandl, 2011b). Since communication takes place only when students are connected with the learning environment and since there are less communication channels, students evaluate the social dimension of taking responsibility lower than all other dimensions of the collaboration process. Nevertheless, task completion does not seem to be negatively affected as it was evaluated the most positively. This means that students internalized the main purpose of the virtual seminar, which was to jointly solve tasks together in order to pass the course.

Regarding support methods, the design of group work was evaluated higher than providing feedback, which also remained stable over time. There was only a significant difference between both dimensions in the beginning. This means that a rotating moderator and obligatory group rules were more effective than the tutor's feedback. One main reason for this result may be that both methods of group design affect social interaction itself, while the feedback that was given after the respective task completion may be of interest to the next task solution, but not directly to the collaboration process. Therefore, in contrast to previous research which revealed the positive impact of feedback on task performance and outcome (Lin & Zhang, 2007; Stark, et al., 2011), this study

revealed a different picture. Thus, the design of group work was evaluated as more effective for social interaction than providing feedback. What we still do not know is whether providing feedback had a positive impact on group performance. This will need to be the subject of investigation in further research.

Second, regarding the development of the virtual collaboration, the evaluation of social interaction and of support methods remained almost stable over time. This means that the same evaluation pattern from the first point of measurement remained consistent at the second and third point of measurement. But there were two interesting changes in evaluation over time: There was a decrease in the evaluation of task completion from the first to the second point of measurement. This could be because the motivation of the learners in completing the task was very high when starting the seminar and was evaluated more realistically at the second and third point of time. Furthermore, there was an increase in evaluating the feedback given from the first to the second point of time. It is possible that learners were more able to transfer the given feedback into their actual task-solving process at the second and third point of measurement than at the first point in time.

Third, the support method of group design correlates with all dimensions of the social interaction at the first and second point of measurement, and with group dynamics in the last evaluation. In contrast to providing feedback, which was given after the task solution, the design of group work directly influenced social interaction. Interestingly, learners also evaluated group design on a higher level than providing feedback, and also evaluated it as more effective. Thus, the correlation analysis confirms the assumption of the first research question. Looking at the extent of the correlation numbers, they are highest at the second point of measurement. This may be explained with the stages in group process by Tuckman (1965). As explained as part of the theoretical framework, there are four stages; forming, storming, norming, and performing. It is possible that in the middle of the semester the groups were in the storming and norming stage. During this stage, concrete rules on how to collaborate and the existence of a moderator who leads the group process are of great relevance for the learners. Because of this, support and social interaction are highly related to one another. This finding is key for CSCL research as until now, there has been no empirical data on group development in such virtual collaborative learning environments (Fransen et al., 2013). There is only one new theoretical approach described by Fransen et al. (2013). The most important aspects involve these first indications that such a development may occur in these environments.

CONCLUSION AND IMPLICATIONS

In conclusion, this study showed a specific evaluation pattern regarding important dimensions of social interaction indicating possible problems in group dynamics (especially relating to taking responsibility). Furthermore, supporting social interaction with the specific design of group work is highly connected to group dynamics, which shows the importance of support methods in virtual learning environments. Interestingly, this correlation is strongest in the middle phase of

collaboration, possibly because support is highly necessary in the storming and norming stage of collaboration. Thus, providing learners with support methods, specifically with role assignment and group rules, fosters learners' interaction according to the subjective evaluation data.

As mentioned, this study highlights many interesting aspects regarding support for collaborative online learning. But there are still some open questions. First, the question remains whether these results could be transferred to different settings and to different samples. Second, objective data such as task performance or contributions in the group forum may be able to validate the results. And third, analyzing the virtual collaboration process with detailed discourse analysis may give further insights into the question regarding why providing feedback was not as effective as assumed.

Overall, results indicate that according to the subjective evaluation data, there is a positive relationship between support methods and social interaction which justifies the necessity of providing support for computer-based learning. Especially problematic dimensions are strongly related to the instructions for group design. Therefore, support is essential in virtual collaboration.

According to our results, further research needs to focus on three issues: First of all, it is key to analyze group performance in order to observe possible interrelations between the support method of providing feedback and group performance. These results may confirm past research and show that support not only functions in the laboratory, but also in field studies. A second issue concerns the analyses of group discussions in the forums. These are necessary to confirm the assumption that groups develop over time according to the stages of Tuckman (1965). Finally, these discourse analyses may yield some further interesting insights into virtual collaboration over time which have not yet been the subject of investigation.

REFERENCES

Beers, P. (2005). *Negotiating common ground: tools for multidisciplinary teams* (Unpublished doctoral dissertation). Open University of The Netherlends, Heerlen.

Bretherton, I. (1992). The origins of attachment theory: John Bowlby and Mary Ainsworth. *Developmental Psychology*, 28(5), 759–775. doi:10.1037/0012-1649.28.5.759

Brodbeck, F., Kerschreiter, R., Mojzisch, A., & Schulz-Hardt, S. (2007). Group decision making under conditions of distributed knowledge: The information asymmetries model. *Academy of Management Review*, 32(2), 459–479. doi:10.5465/AMR.2007.24351441

Curral, L. A., Forrester, R. H., Dawson, J. F., & West, M. A. (2001). It's what you do and the way that you do it: Team task, team size, and innovation-related group processes. *European Journal of Work and Organizational Psychology*, 10(2), 187–204. doi:10.1080/13594320143000627

Dewiyanti, S., Brand-Gruwel, S., Jochems, W., & Broers, N. (2007). Students experiences with collaborative learning in asynchronous computer-supported collaborative learning environments. *Computers in Human Behavior*, 23(1), 496–514. doi:10.1016/j.chb.2004.10.021

Erkens, G., Prangsma, M., & Jaspers, J. (2006). Planning and coordinating activities in collaborative learning. In A. M. O'Donnell, C. E. Hmelo-Silver, & G. Erkens (Eds.), *Collaborative learning, reasoning, and technology* (pp. 233–263). Mahwah, NJ: Erlbaum.

Ertl, B., Kopp, B., & Mandl, H. (2007). Supporting collaborative learning in videoconferencing using collaboration scripts and content schemes. In F. Fischer, I. Kollar, H., Mandl, & J.-M. Haake (Eds.), Scripting computer-supported communication of knowledge – cognitive, computational and educational perspectives (pp. 213-236). Berlin, Heidelberg: Springer. doi:10.1007/978-0-387-36949-5_13

Fischer, F., Kollar, I., Mandl, H., & Haake, J. M. (2007). *Scripting computer-supported communication of knowledge–cognitive, computational, and educational perspectives*. New York: Springer.

Fischer, F., Kollar, I., Stegmann, K., & Wecker, C. (2013). Toward a script theory of guidance in computer-supported collaborative leanring. *Educational Psychologist*, 48(1), 56–66. doi:10.1080/00461520.2012.748005 PMID:23378679

Fransen, J., Weinberger, A., & Kirschner, P. A. (2013). Team effectiveness and team development in CSCL. *Educational Psychologist*, 48(1), 9–24. doi:10.1080/00461520.2012.747947

Grossmann, K. E., Grossmann, K., Kindler, H., Scheuerer-Englisch, H., Spangler, G., & Stöcker, K. etal. (2003). Die Bindungstheorie: Modell, entwicklungspsychologische Forschung und Ergebnisse. [Attachment Theory: model, developmental psychological research and results] In H. Keller (Ed.), *Handbuch der Kleinkindforschung* [*Handbook of infant research*] (pp. 223–282). Bern: Hans Huber.

Hara, N., Bonk, C. J., & Angeli, C. (1998). Content analysis of online discussion in an applied educational psychology. *Instructional Science*, 28(2), 115–152. doi:10.1023/A:1003764722829

Hattie, J., & Timperley, H. (2007). The power of feedback. *Review of Educational Research, 77*(1), 81–112. doi:10.3102/003465430298487

Heilesen, S., Thomsen, M. C., & Cheesman, R. (2002). Distributed CSCL/T in a groupware environment. In G. Stahl (Ed.), *Computer support for collaborative learning: foundations for a CSCL community. Proceedings of CSCL 2002* (pp. 642-643). Hillsdale (NJ): Lawrence Erlbaum Associates. doi:10.3115/1658616.1658764

Järvelä, S., & Hadwin, A. F. (2013). New frontiers: Regulating learning in CSCL. *Educational Psychologist, 48*(1), 25–39. doi:10.1080/00461520.2012.748006

Johnson, D. W., & Johnson, R. T. (1998). Cooperative learning and social interdependence theory. In R. S. Tindale, L. Heath, J. Edwards, E. J. Posavac, F. B. Bryant, & Y. Suarez-Balcazar (Eds.), *Theory and research on small groups* (pp. 9–35). New York: Plenum.

Kauffeld, S. (2001). *Teamdiagnose* [Team Diagnosis]. Göttingen: Verlag für Angewandte Psychologie.

Kerr, N., & Bruun, S. E. (1983). The dispensability of member effort and group motivation losses: Free-rider effects. *Journal of Personality and Social Psychology, 44*(1), 78–94. doi:10.1037/0022-3514.44.1.78

Kirschner, P. A., & Erkens, G. (2013). Toward a framework for CSCL research. *Educational Psychologist, 48*(1), 1–8. doi:10.1080/00461520.2012.750227

Kopp, B., Germ, M., & Mandl, H. (2010). Supporting virtual learning through e-tutoring. In B. Ertl (Ed.), *E-Collaborative knowledge construction: learning from computer-supported and virtual environments* (pp. 213–230). Hershey, NY: IGI Global. doi:10.4018/978-1-61520-729-9.ch012

Kopp, B., & Mandl, H. (2011a). Fostering argument justification using collaboration scripts and content schemes. *Learning and Instruction, 21*(5), 636–649. doi:10.1016/j.learninstruc.2011.02.001

Kopp, B., & Mandl, H. (2011b). Supporting virtual collaborative learning using collaboration scripts and content schemes. In *F. Pozzi, & D. Persico (2011) Eds. Techniques for fostering collaboration in online learning communities. Theoretical and practical perspectives* (pp. 15–32). Hershey: IGI Global.

Kopp, B., Schnurer, K., & Mandl, H. (2009). Collaborative learning in virtual seminars: analyzing learning processes and learning outcomes. In C. O'Malley, D. Suthers, P. Reimann, & A. Dimitracopoulou (Eds.), *Proceedings of 8th international conference on collaborative learning* (CSCL) (pp. 151-160). Athen (Greece): International Society of the Learning Sciences. doi:10.3115/1600053.1600076

Krause, U.-M., Stark, R., & Mandl, H. (2009). The effects of cooperative learning and feedback on e-learning in statistics. *Learning and Instruction, 19*(2), 158–170. doi:10.1016/j.learninstruc.2008.03.003

Kreijns, K., Kirschner, P. A., & Jochems, W. (2003). Identifying the pitfalls for social interaction in computer-supported collaborative learning environments: A review of the research. *Computers in Human Behavior, 19*(3), 335–353. doi:10.1016/S0747-5632(02)00057-2

Latané, B., Williams, K., & Harkins, S. (1979). Many hands make light the work: The causes and consequences of social loafing. *Journal of Personality and Social Psychology, 37*(6), 822–832. doi:10.1037/0022-3514.37.6.822

Lin, H., & Zhang, Q. (2007). Effects of worked example learning on learning algebraic operations. *Acta Psychologica Sinica, 39*(2), 257–266.

Lou, Y., Abrami, P. C., & d'Apollonia, S. (2001). Small group and individual learning with technology: A meta-analysis. *Review of Educational Research, 71*(3), 449–521. doi:10.3102/00346543071003449

Mento, A. J., Locke, E. A., & Klein, H. J. (1992). Relationship of goal level to valence and instrumentality. *The Journal of Applied Psychology, 77*(4), 395–406. doi:10.1037/0021-9010.77.4.395

Moreland, R. L. (1999). Transactive memory: Learning who knows what in work groups and organizations. In L. Thompson, D. Messick, & J. Levine (Eds.), *Shared cognition in organizations: The management of knowledge* (pp. 3–31). Mahwah, NJ: Erlbaum.

Moreno, R. (2004). Decreasing cognitive load for novice students: Effects of explanatory versus corrective feedback in discovery-based multimedia. *Instructional Science, 32*(1/2), 99–113. doi:10.1023/B:TRUC.0000021811.66966.1d

Pena-Shaff, J. B., & Nicholls, C. (2004). Analyzing student interactions and meaning construction in computer bulletin board discussions. *Computers & Education, 42*(3), 243–265. doi:10.1016/j.compedu.2003.08.003

Pozzi, F., Hofmann, L., Persico, D., Stegmann, K., & Fischer, F. (2011). Structuring CSCL through collaborative techniques and scripts. *International Journal of Online Pedagogy and Course Design, 1*(4), 39–49. doi:10.4018/ijopcd.2011100103

Pozzi, F., & Persico, D. (2011). *Techniques for fostering collaboration in online learning communities. Theoretical and practical perspectives.* Hershey: IGI Global.

Roschelle, J., & Teasley, S. (1995). The construction of shared knowledge in collaborative problem solving. In C. O'Malley (Ed.), *Knowledge creation diffusion utilization* (pp. 69–97). New York, NY: Springer. doi:10.1007/978-3-642-85098-1_5

Shen, C.-Y., & Wu, C.-H. (2011). An exploration of students' participation, learning process, and learning outcomes in Web 2.0 computer supported collaborative learning. *International Journal of Online Pedagogy and Course Design, 1*(2), 60–72. doi:10.4018/ijopcd.2011040105

Spangler, G., & Zimmermann, P. (Eds.). (2009). *Die Bindungstheorie: Grundlagen, Forschung, Anwendung [Attachment theory: basics, research, application].* Stuttgart: Klett.

Stark, R., Kopp, V., & Fischer, M. (2011). Case-based learning with worked examples in complex domains: Two experimental studies in undergraduate medical education. *Learning and Instruction, 21*(1), 22–33. doi:10.1016/j.learninstruc.2009.10.001

Tannenbaum, S. I., Beard, R. L., & Sales, E. (1992). Team building and its influence on team effectiveness: an examination of conceptual and empirical developments. In K. Kelley (Ed.), *Issues, theory, and research in industrial/organizational psychology* (pp. 117–153). Amsterdam: Elsevier. doi:10.1016/S0166-4115(08)62601-1

Tenenbaum, G., & Goldring, E. (1989). A meta-analysis of the effect of enhanced instructions: Cues, participation, reinforcement and feedback and correctives on motor skill learning. *Journal of Research and Development in Education, 22*, 53–64.

Tuckman, B. W. (1965). Developmental sequence in small groups. *Psychological Bulletin, 63*(6), 384–399. doi:10.1037/h0022100 PMID:14314073

Van den Boom, D. C. (1994). The influence of temperament and mothering on attachment and exploration: An experimental manipulation of sensitive responsiveness among lower-class mothers of irritable infants. *Child Development, 65*(5), 1457–1477. doi:10.2307/1131511 PMID:7982362

Wegerif, R. (1998). The social dimension of asynchronous learning networks. *Journal of Asynchronous Learning Networks*, 2(1), 34–49.

West, M. A. (1994). *Effective teamwork: practical lessons from organizational research*. Oxford: BPS Blackwell Publishing.

This work was previously published in the International Journal of Online Pedagogy and Course Design (IJOPCD), 4(3); edited by Chia-Wen Tsai and Pei-Di Shen, pages 1-17, copyright year 2014 by IGI Publishing (an imprint of IGI Global).

APPENDIX

Goal Orientation

- We formulated the demands of the task clearly.
- Disseminating information from every group member was important for the joint task solution.
- I identified myself with the group goal to solve the task.
- The goals of the group were clear to everyone.
- We developed criteria to measure the quality of the task solution.
- The targeted goals were achievable.

Task Completion

- The priority was task completion.
- Every group member knew his tasks.
- We coordinated our task solution well.
- We disseminated important information for the task solution in time.

Cohesion

- The group was the center during task completion, not the single group members.
- There was nobody who pushed himself in the foreground at the expense of the others.
- Group members did not compete during task completion.
- We felt as group during task completion.
- We helped each other during task completion.
- I felt myself understood and accepted in the group.
- We communicated open and free.
- Everyone of the group disseminated important information to the discussion.

Taking Responsibility

- We always reflected on improvements for the joint task solution.
- All group members were equally involved in the task solving.
- All group members took full responsibility for the joint task solution.
- Everyone felt responsible for the joint task solution.

Design of Group Work

- Defining group rules was helpful for social interaction.
- A rotating moderator was helpful for social interaction.

Providing Feedback

- The feedback on the task solutions was helpful for social interaction.
- The sample solutions were helpful for social interaction.

Chapter 59
Information Architecture For IS Function:
A Case Study

Nelson Carriço
The University of Trás-os-Montes and Alto Douro, Portugal

João Varajão
University of Minho/Centro Algoritmi, Portugal

Vítor Basto Fernandes
Polytechnic Institute of Leiria, Portugal

Caroline Dominguez
University of Trás-os-Montes e Alto Douro, Portugal

ABSTRACT

Today's complex, unstable and competitive society raises several difficulties to organisations. In this context, Information and Communications Technologies (ICT) and information itself have become resources of vital importance. The pressing need for Information Systems (IS) to meet several business requirements, in addition to the complexity involved in technology and business management, turns the IS Function one of the main areas of influence for success of modern organisations. Through its capacity of representing activities, management objects and corresponding relations, the Information Architecture of the Information Systems Function (IAISF), a technique derived from the well-known Information Architecture but exclusively focused on the Information Systems Function (ISF), allows not only the conceptualization and understanding of the ISF itself, but also of its interactions with other areas within organizations. This paper presents the main results of a case study related to the application of the IAISF technique in a computer service centre of a University.

1. INTRODUCTION

The Information Systems Management (ISM) focuses on information resource management and on the management of all related resources involved in Information Systems (IS) planning, development and exploitation. By other words, it

is responsible for the management of the Information System Function (ISF) (Amaral, 1994). At the CI-UTAD (Computer Service Center of the University of Trás-os-Montes e Alto Douro), the need to supply computer services with guaranteed service levels, requires the effective management of all resources and activities, as well as the moni-

DOI: 10.4018/978-1-4666-8619-9.ch059

toring of performance, in order to deliver efficient and effective services to the organization's units which depend on IS and Information and Communication Technologies' (ICT) infrastructure.

Therefore, an architectural view of the ISF turns to be very useful and necessary, to allow the characterisation of this function and the systematization of its reality.

This work presents the process of construction of the Information Architecture of the Information Systems Function (IAISF) (Varajão, 1997; Varajão, 2002; Varajão, 2005) of CI-UTAD. The performed activities and corresponding management objects are identified, reflecting the overall integration of the Information Systems Planning (ISP), the Information Systems Development (ISD), the Information Systems Exploitation (ISE), and the Information Systems Management (ISM) processes.

Next, in Section 2, it is presented the background; section 3 is dedicated to a generic presentation of CI-UTAD construction process and to the results obtained in the CI-UTAD IAISF case study; finally, some considerations on the conceptualisation process and about the case study are reported.

2. THE INFORMATION SYSTEMS FUNCTION AND THE CHIEF INFORMATION OFFICER

There is no doubt that information systems (IS) are the backbone of today's organizations (Muhic & Johansson, 2014). ISF is seen as the functional area in an organization, responsible for the information resources and for the planning, development, exploitation and management of the IS. It is considered a key area due to the increasing importance of information technology (TI) and to the strategic opportunities promoted by IS and ICT.

ISF includes a set of features and activities that must be tuned to organization's size, culture,

structure and to several business issues like, for instance, environmental aspects. ISM must address all these aspects.

ISF can be conceptually described by four main groups of activities (Varajão, 1998; Varajão, 2005): Information Systems Planning (ISP); Information Systems Development (ISD); Information Systems Exploitation (ISE) and Information Systems Management (ISM).

The ISP is responsible for the identification of systems that the organization need, preceding the ISD which is responsible for their development. The ISE follows, being responsible for ensuring the correct use of the IS. ISM coordinates all the ISF activities.

The ISP allows the creation of a long term vision, identifying the potential systems to be created and defining management policies.

It is assumed that ISP is aligned with business planning, taking into account that ISP itself is a way of planning organisational changes, reachable through ISD (Varajão, 2002).

ISF activities must be "tuned" to each organisation (and its IS), according to its own idiosyncratic, most suitable models, methods and techniques (Reis, 1987).

Due to its nature, ISF can be seen both as cyclic and as continuous (Varajão, 2005): its activities feed each other mutually in every system generation cycle, in a tightly coupled way.

The Chief Information Officer (CIO) is the main responsible for the ISF.

The CIO's profile requires technical skills in the areas of ICT and IS, as well as an in depth knowledge of the organization itself (Trigo, Varajão et al., 2007).

The CIO's importance is today well recognised. It is demonstrated by the position CIOs occupy in most organizations: CIOs report their decisions and activities, to a large extent, to the organisational top manager (CIOMAG, 2007).

Gottschalk and Taylor (Gottschalk & Taylor, 2000; Gottschalk, 2002) identify six types of responsibilities assigned to CIOs: Chief Architect; Project Creator; Technology Manager; Tutor; Operations Strategy Manager.

Trigo, Barroso and Varajão (Trigo, Varajão et al., 2007) discuss a set of eight essential roles for the ISM: Leader; Linker; Monitor; Spokesperson; Entrepreneur; Resources Allocator; Architect of Changes; Technology Planner. In order to succeed, CIOs must develop the adequate skills and capacities to perform their role.

It is possible to find a set of activities which CIOs usually perform (Carvalho et al., 2009): interact with top management (Preston, 2003); take strategic decisions (Bilhim, 1999); plan information systems (Feeny & Willcocks, 1998); manage the process of viability assessment of new systems and technologies (Benamati & Lederer, 2001); analyse, assess and select systems (software/hardware) (Tam & Hui, 2001); systems acquisition (Sutter, 2004; Marshall et al., 2005); manage projects (Gorgone & Gray, 2000; Bhatt et al., 2006); manage the development and the implementation of information systems (Varajão, 2002); manage the maintenance of information systems (Reddy & Reddy, 2002); optimize business processes (Davenport & Short, 1990; Carvalho & Costa, 2007); manage the information systems team (Nelson, 1991); manage the contract services (Rockart et al., 1996; Feeny & Willcocks, 1998); manage crises in the information systems (Varajão, 2002); mediate individual and collective conflicts (Varajão, 2002); define rules and processes for the information systems (Ross et al., 1996); manage the infrastructure of the information system (Bakos, 1992; Singh, 1993); assess the performance of information systems and plan their optimization (Heo & Han, 2003); evaluate the business problems, identifiy opportunities and define solutions for the information systems (Trauth et al., 1993); optimize processes of the information systems function (Gottschalk, 2000); manage the information and guarantee its access and security (Montazemi et al., 1996); follow and explore new technologies

and knowledge (Karimi et al., 1996; Ross et al., 1996); manage the system's integration (Ross et al., 1996); manage the purchase of equipment (Varajão, 2002); develop the competences of final users (Rondeau et al., 2002).

In order to develop the activities he/she is in charge, the CIO needs to get several competences (Portela et al., 2010; Colomo-Palacios et al., 2010; Trigo et al., 2010): capacity of thinking and act strategically (Hawkins, 2004); capacity to mediate conflicts (Varajão, 2002); capacity to lead and motivate teams (Chiavenato, 1994; Lane & Koronios, 2007); capacity to manage projects (Gorgone & Gray, 2000); capacity of communicating (Feeny & Ross, 2000; Smaltz et al., 2006); capacity to follow up technological innovations (Lee et al., 2002; Lutchen, 2003); capacity of personal inter-relating (Katz, 1995; Reis, 1987); capacity of creating teams and structure them (Ward, 1995; Nelson, 1991; Polansky et al., 2004); capacity of negotiation (Reich & Nelson, 2003; Ertel & Gordon, 2007); capacity of adaptation to changes (Amaral, 1994; Rhinesmith, 1996); business knowledge (Keen, 1991; Reis, 1987; Rhinesmith, 1996); technical knowledge (Polansky et al., 2004); capacity of making decisions (Bilhim, 1999).

In this context, IAISF is a management tool for CIOs, which allows them to have a deep understanding of ISF activities and their integration.

3. INFORMATION ARCHITECTURE OF THE INFORMATION SYSTEMS FUNCTION

IAISF is a technique based on the well known Information Architecture (IBM, 1974). It allows the complete and global representation of the planning, development, management and exploitation of the ISF activities.

The relevance of an architectural view of the ISF is based on the need for the existence of tools that must be simultaneously powerful, comprehensive, able to describe the ISF in a wide and integrated manner, and compatible with organisational models and representations.

In the IAISF conceptualization and construction process, it is possible to identify two moments of outmost importance (Varajão, 2005): current characterization of the situation; construction of a global vision for the desired future.

IAISF is both a diagnosis and a management tool that allows the creation of an overview of the ISF in the organization. Therefore the ISP must be the leading activity boosting the emergence of the main orientations for the construction and use of the IAISF (Varajão, 2005).

As a diagnosis and a management tool, IAISF constitutes a reference for ISP, ISD, ISE and ISM contextualization within the organisation. IAISF must therefore address each of these domains of the ISF (Varajão, 2005).

There is not a unique model of management objects or activities that can be applied to all organisations. The process of IAISF construction must be studied and detailed according to each organisation's specificities.

The aim of IAISF is to show how the components of a specific reality fit together and interact. Instead of avoiding other techniques, the architectural approach captures their differences and sets suitable interfaces among them, constructing customised solutions according to the specific problem requirements (Poel, 1989).

Any type of architecture needs a well defined context and a set of known and accepted components (or objects) that allow the architecture construction. After their identification, it is necessary to understand the relations between them. It usually involves modelling and evaluation of the scope of the interacting components options (Tapscott & Caston, 1993).

The early development stage of IAISF enables the comprehension of the *status quo* of the ISF and leads, for instance, to the checking of interface problems between activities, or to the identification of problems that would not be visible otherwise.

In practice, the IAISF design brings benefits to the ISF and contributes significantly to its efficiency and effectiveness (Varajão, 1997).

4. CASE STUDY

In this section we present the case study of CI-UTAD. As a university, UTAD goals are education, research, promotion of local and social development, as well as creation and communication of culture, science and technology.

The organisational structure of UTAD includes administrative and technical units and services, both for teaching and research support.

Of all those services, this study focuses exclusively on the Computer Services Unit (CSU). CSU provides technical services and support related to ICT for academic activities to all departments, degrees and users (professors, staff and students).

CSU infra-structure is complex concerning technology. Its heterogeneity is quite high considering the type of users and provided services.

CSU services include: maintenance and upgrade of network technologies and services; data centre management; helpdesk; education support information systems; students services; intranet; administrative support systems; training; special projects and academic partnerships; etc.

CSU human resources are separated hierarchically in two groups: coordination and technical staff. The coordination group is headed by a coordinator, a vice-coordinator and two technical directors.

The coordination group is assigned with the overall management of the activities, as well as with the human resources management. Although there is one person responsible for each technical sub-unit, goals and milestones are set by the directors together with the coordination team. Each sub-unit and respective services have to report their activities to the coordination team on a regular basis. CSU has an annual plan and budget which is elaborated by the coordination team. This document is included in the overall Engineering School plan and budget.

CSU technical sub-units are composed by four teams defined according to their specialization and the activities they perform: Helpdesk; Systems administration; Network administration; and Systems development.

The Helpdesk unit is composed by five people performing face-to-face support, phone support and support by electronic/Internet means and resources. This unit establishes a more direct contact with users.

The system administration team manages the entire university physical network and support services, email, web, etc. Services based on Window and Linux operating systems are managed by different groups/sub-teams.

The network management team, composed by two employees, is responsible for the maintenance, configuration, monitoring, tuning and upgrading of the technological network's infra-structure.

The system development team, with 13 people, is organised in three groups: one for small size projects, another for medium and big size projects, and another one exclusively devoted to the platform, which is the main support system for teaching activities.

The system development team is responsible for developing internally (inside the university) requested projects, as well as external ones.

CSU staff is composed by permanent staff, as well as temporary hired employees, whose remuneration is assured by specific projects.

CSU human resources internal policies enforce staff training, staff mobility and education, including their participation in MSc and PhD programmes.

5. CI-UTAD INFORMATION ARCHITECTURE

The first stage of the IAISF construction process of CI-UTAD consisted in the identification and the description of the activities needed to manage

IS resources. That allowed the understanding of current skills and of IS assets. The outcome from this first stage was: a list of activities of the ISF; a description of each activity; the knowledge about how each activity is performed inside the organization; and the identification of opportunities for the positioning and development of the ISF.

In a second stage, management objects related to the activities previously identified were defined, as well as the relationships between them.

Like for the activities, the identification of management objects is a basis for the definition of IAISF. The relationships between the activities and the corresponding needed data, lead directly to the identification of the management objects and their relationships.

In the same way it happens with the activities, it is useful to group or split the management objects in order to ensure that only one activity is responsible for a specific management object creation. In this context, "creating" means that the activity is responsible for the initial creation or for the maintenance of a specific management object (Varajão, 2005).

All management objects in this case study were analysed taking the following into account: what it represents; which activity creates it; and which activities make use of it.

Table 1 shows an example of identified management objects for the "Creation of user profile" activity. In the column "Management Objects Used", it is possible to check the data needed for that activity. In the column "Created Management Objects" it is possible to see which data is created by this activity.

Figure 1 shows the relation between each management object and its related activity. It is possible to see, in the intersection of both, a "C", a "U", an "E" or a "S" letter. These letters refer if a management object is created ("C"), is used ("U"), is an input ("E") or an output ("S") of the activity. Whenever any of those situations applies to an activity, it is represented by the respective shadowed letter.

Table 1. Example of management objects analysis

Activity			Creation of user profile		
Management Objects (U - Used by the Activity)			Management Objects (C - Created by the Activity)		
Records of users' needs	E	S	Users' Records	E	S
Requirements records of users	E	S		E	S
Users' manuals for systems	E	S		E	S
Records of systems utilization	E	S		E	S

Legend: E–Input / S–Output

So, the following situations may occur:

- A management object is created ("C" relationship) but it is not an input or an output of the activity (neither "E" nor "S" are shadowed). It is thus an internal object for the activity with no interest for other activities (it is only obtained or developed internally in the context of this activity). It is likely to be relevant and used for the development of other outputs of the activity that creates it;
- A management object is created ("C" relationship) and it is an input ("E" shadowed) and an output ("S" shadowed) of the activity. It means that the activity is not only responsible for its creation, but it also makes the object available for other activities. In addition, the activity uses it after its creation for revision or supervision;
- A management object is created ("C" relationship), it is not an input ("E" is not shadowed), but is an output ("S" is shadowed) of the activity. It means that the object is created by a specific activity which will not use it later in following revisions/redefinitions. But other activities make use of it;
- The management object is used ("U" relationship) but is not an output ("S" not shadowed) of the activity. It means the activity needs the object as a reference, but does not change it;

- The management object is used ("U" relationship) and is an output ("S" shadowed) of the activity. It means the activity not only needs the object but also changes it.

6. DISCUSSION

The construction of the IAISF for CI-UTAD made the management of the IS of the organization more comprehensive, through the identification and description of the ISF activities, their respective management objects, and the relations and interactions between the activities.

The most relevant contributions of IAISF construction to the IS comprehension can be enumerated as follow:

- Identification of the integration/alignment of ISP, ISD and ISP group of activities that constitute de ISF, and the evaluation of their complementarity, continuity and interdependence;
- Identification of activities and the management objects created by them, allowing to improve the overall ISM, as well as the management of each one of the activities;
- Clarification of the actual role and position of the ISM inside the organisation, with positive reflexes on strategic alignment;
- Removal of some redundant tasks inside the organisation, facilitating the identifica-

Figure 1. IAISF for CI-UTAD

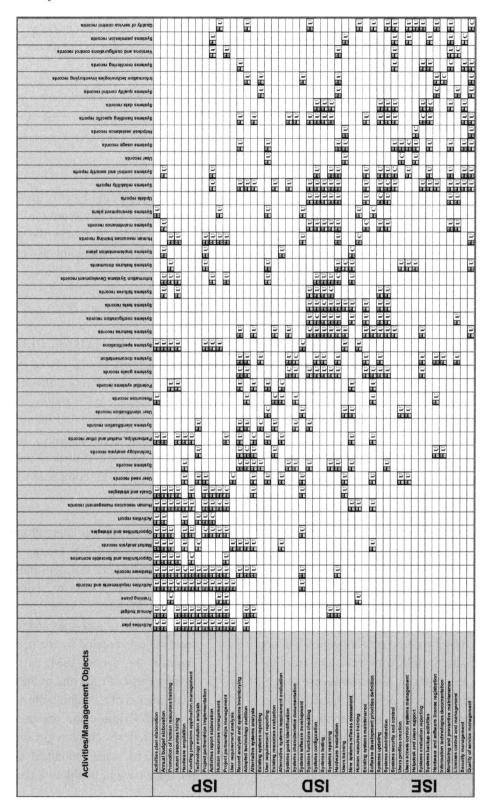

tion of relationships and interdependences among activities;

- Creation of unknown/not used management objects, that are important for the ISD;
- Improvement of the communication between the business areas and the ISM.

It is important to mention that some difficulties were encountered as the work was being developed. For example, since most of the activities involved ICT which are deeply disseminated in the organization, sometimes it was difficult to identify which activities laid within the ISF scope and which not.

It must be underlined that the IAISF development does not end after its initial construction. Like the ISF, it is a continuous and an ongoing process. The IAISF has to be constantly re-evaluated and improved in order to reflect, at any time, a true image of the ISF of the organisation (Varajão, 1997).

7. CONCLUSION

In response to the increasingly competitive environment, organizations are under pressure to become more agile in their operations, accelerate their innovation process, and deliver products within shorter cycles while minimizing cost (Mikalef et al., 2014).

In this context ICT can be an important ally since it is one of the main drivers of changes and innovations in corporations (Bach, Zoroja et al., 2013), being important that organisations improve permanently the use and the management of information as a resource. It is the role of the ISF, usually materialized in the Information Systems Departments, to guarantee that IT are adopted and managed in a contextualised and customised way to serve efficiently the purpose of the organisation (Varajão, 2006).

The IAISF of CI-UTAD allows the visualization of ISF as a whole, constituted of clearly described, integrated and interdependent activities, as well as the management objects related and used by them.

The process that was followed in the construction of the IAISF of CI-UTAD was considered essential for the comprehension and positioning of the ISF. Therefore top management considered it an important contribution for ISM and for the organisation's improvements. This process resulted in the recognition of the IAISF as a relevant instrument of diagnose and planning of the ISF activities within the organisation.

IAISF proved to be a useful management tool for the CIO, allowing him to have a deep understanding of ISF activities and their integration. It is also a valuable tool for the other IT professionals because it enables a better understanding of the activities being developed at several levels (ISP, ISD, ISE, ISM) and of the management (informational) objects.

REFERENCES

Amaral, L. A. M. (1994). *PRAXIS: Um Referencial para o Planeamento de Sistemas de Informação*. Departamento de Informática, Universidade do Minho.

Bach, M., Zoroja, J., & Vukšić, V. (2013). Review of corporate digital divide research: A decadal analysis (2003-2012). *International Journal of Information Systems and Project Management*, *1*(4), 41–55.

Bakos, Y. J., & Kemerer, C. F. (1992). Recent applications of economic theory in information technology research. *Decision Support Systems*, *8*(5), 365–386. doi:10.1016/0167-9236(92)90024-J

Benamati, J., & Lederer, A. L. (2001). Coping with rapid changes in IT. *Communications of the ACM*, *44*(8), 83–88. doi:10.1145/381641.381664

Bhatt, P., Shroff, G., Anantaram, C., & Misra, A. K. (2006). An influence model for factors in outsourced software maintenance. *Journal of Software Maintenance and Evolution: Research and Practice*, *18*(6), 385–423. doi:10.1002/smr.339

Bilhim, J. (1999). *Metodologias e Técnicas de Avaliação, Avaliação na Administração Pública*. Lisboa: INA.

Carvalho, J. Á., & Amaral, L. (1993). Matriz de Actividades: Um Enquadramento Conceptual para as Actividades de Planeamento e Desenvolvimento de Sistemas de Informação. Sistemas de Informação: Revista da Associação Portuguesa de Sistemas de Informação (pp. 37-48).

Carvalho, R., Portela, L., Varajão, J., & Magalhães, L. (2009). *Actividades do Gestor de Sistemas de Informação*. Congresso Internacional de Administração, Gestão Estratégica em Tempo de Mudanças. *Revista ADM*, 2009.

Carvalho, R. A., & Costa, H. G. (2007). Application of an integrated decision support process for supplier selection. *Enterprise Information Systems*, *1*(2), 197–216. doi:10.1080/17517570701356208

Chiavenato, I. (1994). *Gerenciando pessoas* (2nd ed.). São Paulo, Brazil: Makron.

CIOMAG. (2007). *The state of the CIO '07*. CIO Magazine's.

Colomo-Palacios, R., Tovar-Caro, E., García-Crespo, A., & Gómez-Berbis, M. J. (2010). Identifying technical competences of IT professionals. The case of software engineers. *International Journal of Human Capital and Information Technology Professionals*, *1*(1), 31–43. doi:10.4018/jhcitp.2010091103

Davenport, T. H., & Short, J. E. (1990). The new industrial engineering: Information technology and business process redesign. *Sloan Management Review*, *31*(4), 11–27.

Ertel, D., & Gordon, M. (2007). *The point of the deal: How to negotiate when yes is not enough*. Boston, MA: Harvard Business School Press.

Feeny, D., & Ross, J. (2000). The evolving role of the CIO. In R. Zmud (Ed.), *Framing the domains of IT management research, glimpsing the future through the past*. Cincinnati, OH: Pinnaflex Educational Resources.

Feeny, D. F., & Willcocks, L. P. (1998). Core IS capabilities for exploiting information technology. *Sloan Management Review*, *39*(3), 9–21.

Gorgone, J. T., & Gray, P. (2000). MSIS 2000: Model curriculum and guidelines for graduate degree programs in information. *Communications of the AIS*, *3*(1), 1–52.

Gottschalk, P. (2000). Studies of key issues in IS management around the world. *International Journal of Information Management*, *20*(3), 169–180. doi:10.1016/S0268-4012(00)00003-7

Gottschalk, P. (2002). The chief information officer: A study of managerial roles in Norway. In *Proceedings of the 35th Hawaii International Conference on Systems Science*. doi:10.1109/HICSS.2002.994350

Gottschalk, P., & Taylor, N. (2000). Strategic management of IS/IT functions: The role of the CIO. In *Proceedings of the 33rd Hawaii International Conference on Systems Sciences*. doi:10.1109/HICSS.2000.926956

Hawkins, B. L. (2004). A framework for the CIO position. *EDUCASE Review*, *39*(6), 94–102.

Heo, J., & Han, I. (2003). Performance measure of information systems (IS) in evolving computing environments: An empirical investigation. *Information & Management*, *40*(4), 243–256. doi:10.1016/S0378-7206(02)00007-1

IBM. (1984). *Business systems planning: Information systems PlanningGuide*. IBM Corporation.

Karimi, J., Gupta, Y. P., & Somers, T. M. (1996). The congruence between a firm's competitive strategy and information technology leader's rank and role. *Journal of Management Information Systems*, *13*(1), 63–88.

Katz, R. L. (1955). Skills of an effective administrator. *Harvard Business Review*, *33*(1), 33–42.

Keen, P. G. W. (1991). *Shaping the future: Business design through information technology*. Boston, MA: Harvard Business School Press.

Lane, M. S., & Koronios, A. (2007). Critical competencies required for the role of the modern CIO. In *Proceedings of the 18th Australasian Conference on Information Systems (ACIS 2007)* (pp. 1099-1109).

Laudon, K. C., & Laudon, J. P. (1994). *Management information systems: Organization and technology*. MacMillan.

Lee, S., Koh, S., Yen, D., & Tang, H. L. (2002). Perception gaps between IS academics and IS practitioners: An exploratory study. *Information & Management*, *40*(1), 51–61. doi:10.1016/S0378-7206(01)00132-X

Lutchen, M. D. (2003). *Managing IT as a business: A survival guide for CEO*. Hoboken, NJ: John Wiley & Sons.

Marshall, P., McKay, J., & Pranato, A. (2005). Business value creation from IT investments: Towards a process theory of IT governance. *Australasian Journal of Information Systems*, *12*(5), 192–206.

Mikalef, P., Pateli, A., Batenburg, R., & Wetering, R. (2014). Business alignment in the procurement domain: A study of antecedents and determinants of supply chain performance. *International Journal of Information Systems and Project Management*, *2*(1).

Montazemi, A. R., Cameron, D. A., & Gupta, K. M. (1996). An empirical study of factors affecting software package selection. *Journal of Management Information Systems*, *13*(1), 89–105.

Muhic, M., & Johansson, B. (2014). Sourcing motives behind sourcing decisions exposed through the sourcing decision framework. *International Journal of Information Systems and Project Management*, *2*(1).

Nelson, R. R. (1991). Educational needs as perceived by IS and end-user personnel: A survey of knowledge and skills requirement. *Management Information Systems Quarterly*, *15*(4), 503–525. doi:10.2307/249454

Poel, P. A. M. M. d. (1989). *Framework for architectures in information planning. R. M. C. v. Waes*. Elsevier Science Publishers.

Polansky, M., Inuganti, T., & Wiggins, S. (2004). The 21st century CIO. *Business Strategy Review*, *15*(2), 29–33. doi:10.1111/j.0955-6419.2004.00310.x

Portela, L., Carvalho, R., Varajão, J., & Magalhães, L. (2010). A review of Chief Information Officer' main skills. In *Proceedings of the WSKS 2010*, Corfu, Greece (pp. 22-24). Springer-Verlag.

Preston, D. (2003). Shared mental models between the CIO and CEO: Towards information systems strategic alignment. In *Proceedings of the 9th Americas Conference on Information Systems (AMCIS)* (pp. 3375-3381).

Reddy, S. B., & Reddy, R. (2002). Competitive agility and the challenge of legacy information systems. *Industrial Management & Data Systems, 102*(1), 5–16. doi:10.1108/02635570210414613

Reich, B. H., & Nelson, K. M. (2003). In their own words: CIO visions about the future of in-house IT organizations. *ACM SIGMIS Database, 34*(4), 28–44. doi:10.1145/957758.957763

Reis, C. (1987). *Planeamento Estratégico de Sistemas de Informação*. Editorial Presença.

Rhinesmith, S. H. (1996). *Managers guide to globalization: Six skills for success in a changing world*. McGraw-Hill.

Rockart, J. F., Earl, M. J., & Ross, J. W. (1996). Eight imperatives for the new IT organization. *Sloan Management Review, 38*(1), 43–55.

Rondeau, P. J., Vonderembse, M. A., & Ragu-Nathan, T. S. (2002). Investigating the level of end-user development and involvement among time-based competitors. *Decision Sciences, 33*(1), 149–160. doi:10.1111/j.1540-5915.2002.tb01640.x

Ross, J. W., Beath, C. M., & Goodhue, D. L. (1996). Develop long-term competitiveness through IT assets. *Sloan Management Review, 38*(1), 31–42.

Singh, S. K. (1993). Using information technology effectively: Organizational preparedness models. *Information & Management, 24*(3), 133–146. doi:10.1016/0378-7206(93)90062-X

Smaltz, D. H., Sambamurthy, V., & Agarwal, R. (2006). The antecedents of CIO role effectiveness in organizations: An empirical study in the healthcare sector. *IEEE Transactions on Engineering Management, 53*(2), 207–222. doi:10.1109/TEM.2006.872248

Sutter, J. (2004). *The power of IT: Survival guide for the CIO, North Charleston*. North Charleston, SC: BookSurge.

Tam, K. Y., & Hui, K. L. (2001). A choice model for the selection of computer vendors and its empirical estimation. *Journal of Management Information Systems, 17*(4), 97–124.

Tapscott, D., & Caston, A. (1993). *Paradigm shift: The new promise of information technology*. McGraw-Hill.

Trauth, E. M., Farwell, D. W., & Lee, D. (1993). The IS expectation gap: Industry expectations versus academic preparation. *Management Information Systems Quarterly, 17*(3), 293–303. doi:10.2307/249773

Trigo, A., Varajão, J., & Barroso, J. (2007). Os papéis do gestor de Sistemas de Informação. In 4º Congresso Internacional de Gestão de Tecnologia e Sistemas de Informação (CONTECSI 2007), São Paulo, Brasil.

Trigo, A., Varajao, J., Barroso, J., Molina-Castillo, F. J., & Gonzalvez-Gallego, N. (2010). IT professionals: An Iberian snapshot. The case of software engineers. *International Journal of Human Capital and Information Technology Professionals, 1*(1), 61–75. doi:10.4018/jhcitp.2010091105

Varajão, J. (2006). *Gestão da função de sistemas de informação*. *Dirigir - Revista para a chefia e quadros* (pp. 3–9). IEFP.

Varajão, J., & Amaral, L. (1999). *Gestão de Sistemas de Informação: Uma Abordagem Arquitectural*. Revista da Associação Portuguesa de Sistemas de Informação, APSI, 1.

Varajão, J. E. Q. (1997). *A Arquitectura da Gestão de Sistemas de Informação*. Departamento de Sistemas de Informação, Universidade do Minho.

Varajão, J. E. Q. (2002). *Funçāo de Sistemas de Informação: Contributos para a melhoria do sucesso da adopção de tecnologias de informação e desenvolvimento de sistemas de informação nas organizações*. PhD thesis, Universidade do Minho.

Varajão, J. E. Q. (2005). *A Arquitectura da Gestão de Sistemas de Informação* (3rd ed.). FCA.

Ward, J. (1995). *Principles of information systems management*. Routledge.

Wright, M. A. (1994). Protecting information: Effective security controls. *Review of Business, 16*(2), 24–28.

Wu, J. H., Chen, Y. C., & Lin, H. H. (2004). Developing a set of management needs for IS managers: A study of necessary management activities and skills. *Information & Management, 41*(4), 413–429. doi:10.1016/S0378-7206(03)00081-8

This work was previously published in the International Journal of Human Capital and Information Technology Professionals (IJHCITP), 5(2); edited by Ricardo Colomo-Palacios, pages 28-37, copyright year 2014 by IGI Publishing (an imprint of IGI Global).

Chapter 60
Actor Network Theory Applied to Organizational Change:
A Case Study

Carlos Páscoa
Portuguese Air Force Academy, Portugal

José Tribolet
Technical University of Lisbon/Instituto Superior Técnico, Portugal

ABSTRACT

There are various models proposed in the literature to analyze trajectories of enterprise change projects in terms of success and failure. Yet, only the Actor-Network Theory (ANT) perspective considers the interaction factors among network actors and actants. In 2009, with an initiative started in 2007, the Portuguese Air Force developed and carried on a Change project. The aim of this project was to obtain better information to support decision processes. This chapter proposes the ANT for approaching the Portuguese Air Force change process initiative as a case study. In doing so, it provides valuable insight in terms of both local and global actor networks, which surround the initiative.

INTRODUCTION

Enterprise change initiatives are expected to result in better delivery of services to citizens, improved interactions with business and industry, citizen empowerment through access to information, and more efficient government management. In addition, other expected side benefits involve less corruption, increased transparency, greater convenience, revenue growth, and cost reductions. All and all, enterprise changes need to uncover new ways of getting competitive advantage through better objective analysis and definition processes. It all comes to better information that can lead to better decision. The United States Air Force defines information superiority as "the degree of dominance in the information domain which allows friendly forces the ability to collect, control, exploit, and defend information without effective opposition (USAF, 2005). When applied to organizations the information concept has exactly the same importance as it conveys acquiring context

DOI: 10.4018/978-1-4666-8619-9.ch060

and relevant information to allow comprehensive decisions that allow gaining competitive advantage over competitors.

This chapter aims to uncover the trajectories of the Portuguese Air Force change initiative. When conducting a project, there are a lot of factors that influence how it is done and how its outcome is influenced by. For instance, prior similar experiences, IT regulations and capabilities and so forth are some key influencers. All of these factors are related or connected to how parties involved in the project act. Change projects cannot be developed in a total vacuum but rather under the influence of a wide range of surrounding factors.

The acts parties have carried out, and all of these influencing factors, should be considered together. This is exactly what the term actor-network theory accomplishes. An actor network is "the act linked together with all of its influencing factors in building a network" (Suchman, 1987; Hanseth and Monteiro, 1998).

The theoretical framework for Portuguese Air Force change process analysis must be sufficiently rich to comprehend the complexities of all network actors' interactions. The Actor-(or actant) Network Theory (ANT) of Latour and Callon (Callon, 1986; Latour, 1988; Latour, 1992; Latour, 1993) offers a set of analytical resources for this purpose (Frohmann, 1995). ANT has been previously employed by Heeks and Stanforth (2007) to explain the trajectories of the Integrated Financial Management Information System (IF-MIS) development–an application of IT in the Sri Lankan Government.

The remainder of this chapter is organized as follows:

- The following section introduces "Actor-Network Theory" through a review of associated literature.
- Section "Case Overview and Application" explains the Portuguese Air Force change process initiative.

- Section "Using Actor Network Theory" compares the PRT AF change project in light of the ANT theory.
- "Conclusion" and "Future Work" sections constitute the last section of the paper.

ACTOR NETWORK THEORY

The Actor Network Theory (ANT) is a coherent theory that deals with "emergent social processes" (Holmstrom & Robey, 2005) involving technology and organizational change, considering that human and non-human actors are linked together in a web of relationships, referred to as an actor network, where their interests are translated and inscribed into technical and social arrangements (Holmstrom & Robey, 2005) that stabilize the network.

ANT is an established approach (Stanforth, 2006; Jarke, 2007) to explain application of IT projects in developing countries (Stanforth, 2006).

As underlined by Heeks and Stanforth (2007), a great number of projects result in failure. Therefore, it is crucial to examine projects closely to draw lessons for future. Popularity of ANT is increasing to better understand the trajectories of projects as defended by Trusler (2003), Avgerou, Ciborra et al., 2006; Heeks and Stanforth, 2007; Johanes and Kwong, 2007; Hardy and Williams, 2008; Muganda-Ochara and Belle, 2008).

ANT can be applied to empirical studies, on the IT field, guiding the investigation of networks of people, organizations, software and hardware (Latour, 1986; Walsham, 1997), and showing evidence on how social and technology aspects are mutually dependent (Holmstrom & Robey, 2005).

ANT is divided into three main phases (see Figure 1), Translation (which includes Problematization, Interessment, Enrollment and Motivation), Mobilization and Inscription.

Translation is the process of the alignment of the interests of a diverse set of actors with the

Figure 1. ANT phases (source: Research authors)

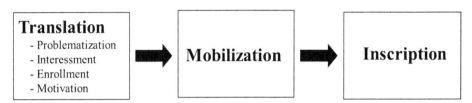

interests of the focal actor. It can be seen as the process of negotiation whereby actors deliberately assume the authority to act and speak on behalf of other actors (Callon and Latour, 1981), attempting to influence others to accept renditions of problem definitions and potential solutions as valid and legitimate (Holmstrom & Robey, 2005).

Translation encompasses the creation of an actor-network. Numerous actors within an organization may be involved in a different process of translation, each with its own unique characteristics and outcomes.

For purposes of clarity, it is useful to focus on a single actor, from whose vantage point we wish to see the process of translation (Callon, 1986; Walsham, 1997), described in the working definitions of ANT central concepts (Sarker, Sarker et al., 2006, p.6).

This process consists of four major stages: Problematization, Interessement, Enrolment and Motivation (Callon, 1986).

- Problematization can be defined as "The first moment of translation during which a focal actor defines identities and interests of other actors that are consistent with its own interests, and establishes itself as an obligatory passage point (OPP), thus 'rendering itself indispensable'" (Callon, 1986; Sarker, Sarker et al., 2006, p.6). In Problematization, certain actors establish themselves as an OPP (Callon, 1986) while defining the problem, proposing solutions and identifying and establishing roles and identities for other actors in the network (Holmstrom & Robey, 2005).

- Interessement stands as the second moment of translation which involves a process of convincing other actors to accept definition of the focal actor (Callon, 1986; Sarker, Sarker et al., 2006, p.6). *Interessment* involves "actions by which an entity attempts to impose and stabilize the identification for other actors it defines through its problematization" (Callon, 1986).

- Enrollment is the third moment of translation, wherein other actors in the network accept (or get aligned to) interests defined for them by the focal actor (Callon, 1986; Sarker, Sarker et al., 2006, p.6). Enrollment encompasses a set of strategies in which initiators seek to convince other actors to join them in a multilateral political process (Holmstrom & Robey, 2005). It can be described as enrollment designates the device by which a set of interrelated roles is defined and attributed to actors who accept them. Enrolment describes the group of multilateral negotiations, trials of strength and tricks that accompany the interessments and enable them to succeed" (Callon, 1986).

- Motivation, termed as "ideological control", is central to enrolment and occurs by influencing actors.

Mobilization is a set of methods proposed by initiators to make sure that the other actors do not betray their interests. Stabilization of a technology implies that its content is institutionalized, that is, no longer controversial (Holmstrom & Robey, 2005).

Inscription "is the process whereby technical objects are treated as a program of action that coordinates a network of social roles" (Holmstrom & Robey, 2005). It encompasses "technical objects being treated as a program of actions that coordinates a network of social roles" (Holmstrom & Robey, 2005). Latour (1992) states that "Inscription is a process of creation of artifacts that would ensure the protection of certain interests".

ANT delivers a concept of the OPP which is introduced on the circuits of power where the social integration (intangible things) and the system integration (technology) are present.

To understand ANT, some important concepts presented by Aykac et al (2009) citing Sarker et al (2006) need to be clarified:

- **Actor:** Any element which bends space around itself, makes other elements dependent upon itself and translate their will into the language of its own. Common examples of actors include humans, collectivities of humans, texts, graphical representations, and technical artifacts. Actors, all of which have interests, try to convince other actors so as to create an alignment of the other actors' interests with their own interests. When this persuasive process becomes effective, it results in the creation of an actor-network (Callon and Latour, 1981, p.286).
- **Actor Network:** Heterogeneous network of aligned interests, including people, organizations and standards (Walsham and Sahay, 1999, p.42).
- **Punctualization:** Treating a heterogeneous network as an individual actor to reduce network complexity (Law, 2003).
- **The Obligatory Passage Point:** Broadly referring to a situation that has to occur in order for all the actors to satisfy the interests that have been attributed to them by the focal actor. The focal actor defines the OPP through which the other actors must pass through and by which the focal actor becomes indispensable (Callon, 1986).

- **Speaker/Delegate/Representative:** An actor that speaks on behalf of (or stands in for) other actors (Callon, 1986; Walsham and Sahay, 1999).
- **Betrayal:** A situation where actors do not abide by the agreements arising from the enrollment of their representatives (Callon, 1986).
- **Irreversibility:** Degree to which it is subsequently impossible to go back to a point where alternative possibilities exist (Walsham and Sahay, 1999, p.42).

ANT has been widely used in several countries as a mean of investigating and concluding about transformational processes in several organizations. Examples are:

- The inscription of organizational change with information technology (Holmstrom & Robey, 2005) where the authors describe the implementation of the Powerplay project in a municipal agency in Sweden:
  ○ The main point was centralized on the existence of non-paid services and the need to reducing costs;
  ○ A system reform changed the concept of service rendering that was setup to follow the logic of cost optimization;
  ○ The inscription concept (to inscribe social objectives in technology in a way that they merge and cannot be separated) has changed the way of thinking in the public services;
  ○ The problem was identified as the existence of excess of information and the inability of performing near-real time analysis;

- The initiators are referenced as being the main actors and they were very careful in separating the IT department from the project;
- There were positive controllers (in the bigger departments) and negative controllers (in the smaller departments). The positive controllers had objectives and the skeptics had to be convinced;
- There were several servers that were used by several actors. For example, politicians used the web services because they wanted to work at home and they were also interested that the public in general could also access the information.
- On the motivation phase (loyalty assurance) the project was financed by politicians. This is, therefore, a case of success.
- The change of mindset is never referred; instead the problem is defined as a lack of timely information that could help decisors.
- The description of "power: the network of force relation" (Holmstrom & Robey, 2005), where the authors present and discuss the application of the London Ambulance Service (LAS) Computer Aided Dispatch System";
    - In the LAS there are no mobilization and social and technical stabilization. The case integrates two methods: circuits of power and ANT;
    - The project objective aims at centralizing and managing the LAS. The project was imposed in order to save money;
    - The two key players had different point of views about the system which resulted in a divorce among them; the

management wanted a quick implementation; the union was favorable to participation;
    - Enrollment and interessment phases were not carefully elaborated and the obligatory passage points were the network control points;
    - Tacit knowledge was not considered or thought relevant. The system was a complete failure and brought chaos to the LAS.
- The approach of the Turkish E-Government Gateway Initiative (Aykac et al., 2009), where the authors discuss the steps taken to create E-Government in Turkey.

CASE OVERVIEW AND APPLICATION

The case study was conducted in the Portuguese Air Force. The leadership promoted the development and use of IT infrastructure attempting to standardize the way that operational critical information is handled by the organization. Operational information encompasses several entities: aircraft, crews and missions, both on the operational and maintenance environments.

The following sections describe the organization's macro structure and the change project where ANT was included.

Organization Structure

The Portuguese Air Force (PRTAF) macro structure, shown in Figure 2, is composed by the Chief of Staff (Air Force Commander–AFC), the Air Staff headquarters, the Finance Directorate, the Inspection and three Commands: Personnel, Operational and Logistics. The AFC has organs of council for dealing with different matters.

Figure 2. The Portuguese Air Force macro structure (source: Research authors)

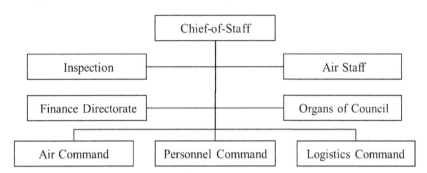

The AFC has the authority to decide about all matters that concern the Air Force. His cabinet is composed by a general (chief of cabinet) and a colonel that directly assist the chief-of-staff. The staff is also composed by several officers and non-commissioned officers that perform clerk duties.

The Air Staff, commanded by a three star general, gives direct support to the AFC in several matters, including human resources, intelligence, operations, logistics, planning, communications and IT systems.

The Personnel Command is responsible for the human resources in the recruitment and overall management phases and also for the formation and training phases. The Air Command is responsible for operating the Air Force assets and the Logistics Command handles all the support items such as aircraft maintenance, IT infrastructure, physical infrastructure and logistics chain. Finance is a centralized Ministry of Defense responsibility and therefore the Air Force owns a Finance Directorate that responds directly to the AFC.

Project Setup

Project set-up was done through five phases not completely independent between each other. The fifth step culminating with the AFC signature on the directive that laid down the execution planning.

As a military organization, the Air Force has a Mission, defined by the Government (PG, 2009),

a Vision, defined by the AFC, a set of goals and objectives (PRTAF COS, 2008) and a strategy to achieve them.

Looking at the Air Force as a system, the input can be considered as the financial budget that is given annually and the output is the capability to perform the Mission. As simple as it seems, being able to perform the Mission, is actually a very complex statement as it comprehends the state of military readiness: clear definitions of what the actions are, qualified and trained human resources and non-human resources ready for action. This implies crew and aircraft readiness to fulfill the Mission needs.

The IT infrastructure is build upon a set of rules and constraints that are transversal to the organization. On the support side, aircraft maintenance is also a complex process that is bound by a specific set of tight environmental, organizational and stakeholder actors and rules.

The Superior Council composed by the chief of staff and the three star generals analyzed a set of reports developed by the Air Staff about the application of IT through the organization and concluded that the organization could be improved to better align it architectural principles to the latest knowledge and technology.

In 2007, the necessity for improving organization self-awareness was recognized by the Air Staff (Operations Division) as a result of observing repository data related to the operational and support dimensions. Although procedures were set, there were still some inconsistencies related from inadequate policy, doctrine and procedures. After around a year of observations, findings included:

- The IT System was not coherent with the registration of maintenance working hours; a lack of information alignment, regarding the number of hours necessary to do maintenance tasks, existed and needed to be corrected;
- Decisions on how to go about the system were taken at each level of execution in different spots; people had different information at each level of execution which caused different decisions taken by different actors at the same level of execution;
- There was an agreed understanding that the official system was not satisfying information needs, which caused the appearance of local systems of information;
- Multiple standalone Excel, Access and Word files created at every levels with problematic consequences at the management level that could not get the necessary information; tactic and strategic managers had the official information system, however it was not updated due to the proliferation of local systems at the operational level;
- There was a lack of understanding of some terminology due to the inexistence of a glossary of terms and definitions;
- There were multiple local repositories containing the same type of information with an evident lack of consistency;
- Doctrine was old and inadequate;
- Centralized objectives were dispersed and could be confused with entities competences;
- Existence of IT non-integrated proprietary systems were creating lack of information at the different organization levels.

All the findings had a key term: information. The absence of context relevant information and the lack of standardization was in the origin all of the problems detected.

A transformation plan for the Air Force (PRTAF COS, 2009), based on the rules depicted by Kotter (1996), was delineated and the Air Staff begun to build up the necessary arrangements for its execution and accomplishment. The transformation plan included strategic thinking, reorganizing, new paradigms and technology utilization and the development of business policy and plans that would enable the creation of the dynamic and flexible organization.

The first stage intended to determine the Organization AS IS. Stage 2 intended to consolidate all the activities and lay down the basis for the TO BE setup.

The plan, approved by the AFC delineated actions in three major areas complemented by other three actions as subsidiary actions, all using the principles of organizational and design engineering (ODE) as laid down by the Center for organizational and design engineering (CODE) which precludes the use of computers in the organization, as an essential tool to achieving the strategy of the areas of managing their own information and decision support, and requires the determination of Architecture Information Systems (ASI), which consists of five sub-models (Abreu & Tribolet 2008).

- **Enterprise Architecture (EA):** Deals with aspects of the organization that are not directly related to the specific business and its operations, such as 'Mission', 'view', 'strategy', and 'organizational goals';
- **Business Architecture (BA):** Deals with the materialization of business strategy, defined in business processes, representing the objects "business process" and "business purpose";

- **Information Architecture (IA):** Deals with what the organization needs to know to perform the operations, as defined in business processes characterized in EA. and provides an abstraction of the information needs of the organization, regardless of technology; contemplates the objects "feature", "actor", "observable state" and "activity";
- **Application Architecture (AP):** Deals with the needs of applications in data management and support of business, being independent of the software used to implement the different systems and includes the objects "Information Systems (IS) component–IS" ("block IS") and "Service";
- **Technological Architecture (TA):** Handles all the technology behind the implementation of the applications as defined in the AP, as well as the necessary infrastructure for the production of support systems, business processes, and considers concepts such as "Information Technology (IT) component" ("IT block") and "IT Services".

Complementary to these actions the Air Staff had been creating/updating a set of business rules that would enable the organization to better sense a feeling of self-awareness. At the same time, the doctoral curricular units that were taken at Technical University of Lisbon, Instituto Superior Técnico (UTL/IST) provided the insight for the development of a Change plan (PRTAF COS, 2009), which was presented and approved by the Air Force Commander.

Along with this process that Air Force was already in a self-centered transformation: the organization was changed to reflect supervening concepts and the actual needs, units were changed in its location and the training processes were also updated to allow adopting new technologies.

The plan of aligning the Information Technology Systems with the Air Force strategy comprehended six main actions.

- The development of operational and maintenance doctrine (concepts and procedures) including a glossary of acronyms and definitions;
- The identification of operational and maintenance processes and activities done using ASI concepts;
- The creation of indicators and metrics on the IT systems that allow decision support;
- Information repositories standardization;
- Model integration and standardization;
- Control mechanisms creation.

Table 1 shows the transversal nature of the plan by relating activities with entities.

The project was set to start in March 2009 with thirteen months duration. It comprehended the creation of several artifacts (a centralized di-

Table 1. Organization macro structure and activities distribution (source: Research authors)

	Doctrine	Processes	Indicators	Repositories	Model Integration	Control Mechanisms
Air Staff	X		X			X
Inspection		X				X
Air	X	X	X	X	X	X
Personnel		X	X			X
Training		X	X			X
Logistics	X	X	X	X	X	X

rectory, an internet forum and a tool for process modeling) in order to help the dissemination of knowledge throughout the organization. Also, to foster rapid reactions to changing events, it was necessary to build a governance capstone that was encompassed by producing basic doctrine that could evolve main problems and creating the basic strategic documents, mission, effort and doctrine related, including:

- **WHAT:** Updating/Creating the "What is the Mission for each Operational Unit";
- **WHO:** Updating/Creating the "Crews, aircraft and maintenance needs " for each Operational Unit;
- **WHEN, HOW, WHERE:** Creating the "Doctrine Framework";
- Creating the Glossary of Terms and Definitions in order to align organizational semantic.

In any project intended to succeed, leadership has to become an active asset. Using Governance artifacts, the next step was to make leadership aware of problems that could arise from the lack of artifacts. A comprehensive communications plan inside an Execution Directive was established and presented to the AFC through the Air Staff. The actions included:

- Briefing to the AFC (setting up Strategy Directive 1/2009–Air Force Strategy–Goals and Objectives);
- Bringing in AFC's approval for posterior activities;
- Defining Project Objectives Calendar and artifacts (Directive 2/2009, 2nd March 2009);
- Getting Project Approval.

The plan, in form of directive, also outlined a communication plan that comprehended several presentations at the different organization levels

that would allow people to learn and understand the project objectives. Initiatives included setting up presentations in order to reach people:

- Briefing to the higher level (AFC and 3-star Generals), 7 persons, 06Nov08;
- Briefing to the higher level (two-star level), 18 persons, 23Jan09;
- Briefing to the Intermediate level (Colonels, Commanders, etc…), 126 people, 16Feb09;
- Interview between an UTL/IST teacher and AFC, 31Mar09;
- Briefing by an UTL/IST teacher to all the Generals and Division Commanders, 30 persons, 21May09;
- Numerous meetings with each organization's POC.

Involving the Ministry of Defense (MOD) and Academia seemed like the correct approach to enlarge project scope and setting up organizational knowledge[1] and self-awareness aiming at forming the younger people and facilitating processes.

- **Technical University of Lisbon, Instituto Superior Técnico:**
  - Frequency of a doctoral degree in organizational and design engineering.
- **Air Force Academy:**
  - Setting the Organizational Engineering Area, composed of three disciplines for Masters thesis: six students–September 2008 to March 2010, six students–September 2009 to March 2011, six students–September 2010 to March 2012 and four students –September 2011 to March 2013);
  - Setting up twelve Master Thesis on Organizational and Design Engineering (eighteen consolidated, four ongoing);

- Setting two briefings on the Course to Captain.
- **Joint Staff College:**
  - Two senior office course on developing process architecture for operational command and operational units (Sep 08–Jun 09);
  - Two senior office course on developing meta-models on aligning maintenance activities with maintenance process (Sep 08–Jun 09);
  - One colonel on mastering organizational competences.
- **MOD (Simplex 2009):**
  - Measure M177 (connecting the Air Force with the Social Security in order to get automated declarations);
  - Measure M180 (developing a corporate web site where people can check information and download, among others, salary receipts and IRS declarations).

To increase organizational self-awareness, before the start of the process, the Air Force has developed/updated business rules that allowed the update of:

- Mission of the Air Units to reflect the changes expressed in the Strategic Concept of National Defense and the Military Strategic Concept, aligning the elements of the mission with NATO doctrine and defining the mechanisms required to obtain indicators related to air activity (PRTAF COS, 2007).
- The definition of dynamic and flexible mechanisms that would keep constantly updated the information about the amount of personnel needed for the operation and maintenance of weapons systems (PRTAF COS, 2008b), in three configurations, for the purpose of:

- Automatically calculating, following the given assumptions, the amount of personnel (operation and maintenance) for the various Air Units.
- Assessing the existing information on weapons systems and, if necessary, the methodology and verification of information integration, correcting methods and procedures.
- Quantifying variations caused by specific features of the Air Units.
- Comparing execution to planning.
- Defining and establishing appropriate planning and management planning, integrating information from different systems.
- The legal publications for operation and maintenance, which establish the Air Force operational publications framework (PRTAF COS, 2008a) and define the responsible entities for developing and updating. It underpins all the actions proposed by the plan regarding doctrine changes.

The doctrine, military term similar to business rules, based on experience, best practices and lessons learned (USAF, 2003), defines how it is expected to employ existing capabilities in a particular operation. The military doctrine is also the basis for future thought integrating new technology and new capabilities (USAF, 2003). Development of operating and maintenance publications, creating a doctrinal framework, standardized and aligned the operational publications with the Organization's strategy.

Approaching the business process methodology represented a new paradigm in the PRTAF. While the doctrine says how to do, the business process, through activity identification, says exactly what it is done, in reality. The Information Architecture provides a real-time layout of what is the essential information to run the PRTAF's core business. The creation of metrics and mechanisms for decision support presupposes the existence of goals and objectives. The standardization of repositories and integration of information artifacts, are essential elements to assure knowledge. The creation of control mechanisms allows the definition of the control points necessary to achieve the objectives.

To create organizational knowledge, based on relevant and contextual information, there were two different repositories for exchanging ideas: a directory on the internal network for staff directly involved and a forum in Internet that allowed global access to information that was being produced.

Change also included other acts, such as the spread of organizational engineering at the Academy and at the various Promotion Courses. At the Academy level, a new master's area on organizational engineering was created comprehending three curricular units across 3 semesters.

One of the key actions to obtain success was the inclusion of the Business Process Architect (BPA) as the tool to identify the business processes and relevant information (the glossary of terms and definitions is an example). This tool was centralized by a group of people at the staff level and disseminated across the Organization with very good results, not only within the coherence level, but also on the organizational memoir domain.

Project monitoring and control was done by providing monthly reports on a graphical dashboard that indicates the several topics, the percentage of work accomplished and corrective actions when necessary. Each month, the AFC approved the report and the corrective actions required. Upon approval, information update was put out on the internal directory and on the forum. Overall, a significant number of people were involved in the several phases and tasks.

Overall, in 3 years, 66 business policy and business rules manuals were produced, 470 business processes and key performance indicators were identified and 18 master thesis were developed. As a result, 18 master thesis were produced, each in close coordination with the staff headquarters

and with immediate application on current organization problems on a direct link between the research and operational domains. A set of almost 30 scientific articles (Páscoa, 2012; Páscoa et al, 2012; Páscoa et al, 2011; Páscoa et al, 2011a; Páscoa et al, 2011b; Páscoa & Tribolet, 2010; Páscoa et al, 2010; Páscoa et al, 2012a; Páscoa et al, 2011b; Páscoa et al, 2010a; Páscoa et al, 2012b; ; Páscoa et al, 2010b; Páscoa et al, 2012c; Páscoa et al, 2011c; Páscoa et al, 2011d; Páscoa et al, 2010c; Páscoa et al, 2009) provided the theoretical basis for the activities being conducted at the organizational level.

The work created by the Air Force, as previously said, entails different configurations for allowing situational awareness and near real time steering, enhancing information quality, standardization and availability allowing for informed decision processes.

USING ACTOR NETWORK THEORY

The next paragraphs describe the several stages of ANT, as shown in Figure 1, and its application to the organization transformation project described before.

As the necessity for improving organization self-awareness was recognized, it provided the insight for the development of a Change plan that was presented and approved by the AFC, in March 2009. The plan, supported by the artifacts developed previously, identified the problem and defined a desired end state and a course of action to "align IS with the Air Force strategy." (PRT AF, 2009). The plan also identified:

- A number of deliverables and the strategy to obtaining them, presenting a calendar, a communication plan, instrument artifacts (internet page and internal directory) and control tools.
- A set of actions to be made at the Air Force Academy level.

As the plan, in form of a directive, was approved, the first phase of Translation (*Problematization*), in the ANT context, was completed.

The communication plan initiated, in the ANT context, the *Interessement* phase of Translation. The Change directive was first presented to the 3 star general at the superior council and approved. In a second moment, the plan was presented to all the 2 star generals. Endorsed by the AFC, the plan was later presented to the intermediate level officers, including Divisions chiefs, Base commanders, operations, personnel and logistics deputy directors, action officers, data administrators, etc. This presentation had all the necessary detail to start execution.

At this stage, individual meetings were conducted with the representatives (point of contact–POC) for each entity. The plan had an immediate interest by the data administrators at each Command, who were appointed as POC and had the responsibility to coordinate all the actions at their level. At this stage the *Enrollment* phase was being initiated. In some circumstances, POC took advantage of the artifacts created and inserted, at their level and other actions to be completed.

For instance, at the Air Staff level, the Communication and Information Systems (CIS) Division developed a plan to acquire BPA, rather than use VISIO, as initially planned, and the CIS Directorate, developed, in two weeks, the internet forum and gave access to the directories created. The CIS Division, extended the scope of work to a transversal business process identification (rather than the operational and maintenance business processes) and developed a plan for the change of the IS systems based on the overall process identification (PRTAF COS, 2009a), adopting the high level business process level that served as a basis for launching the operational and maintenance business process identification. In the early stage, the CIS Division coordinated business process identification training in BPA for more than 300 persons. The high level business process was developed on a doctoral curricular unit, in 2008, and was later approved by the AFC. At this time, the Operations Division had extended its influence and interest not only to the Air Force Commander but also to the data administrators, at the different entities and to the other Air Staff Divisions. In the ANT context, the last phases of *Translation*, the *Enrollment* phase and the *Motivation* phase, were completed.

Each POC had to make a monthly report, indicating the progress and deviations in relation to what was planned. The reports allowed observing a significant delay in the beginning of the actions and the plan took a delay in the planned calendar. As monthly reports were coordinated and presented to the AFC on a monthly basis, the deputy commander was appointed to be responsible for the coordination and verification of the execution of the plan. This action produced rapid results as the POC had to boost the entity's participation in fulfilling what was expected. In the ANT context, the *Mobilization* phase was initiated.

After the second month, the Operations Division inserted a planned deliverable dashboard which immediately made clear how the execution was proceeding. Until the end of the main project, which occurred by May 2010, the dashboard and the monthly reports proved to be essential artifacts. This completed the *Mobilization* phase, as these tools were essential to maintaining focus of plan execution.

Based on ANT theory, the Operations Division, with the endorsement of the AFC, became the *Obligatory Passage Point*. If this was true for the setting up phase, it also can be true that after the deputy Air Force commander took responsibility, the OPP became successful plan implementation as it was used, successfully, to translate staff behavior in line with the demands for improved efficiency and effectiveness and thus, increased situation-awareness and rapid response to influencer actions.

As an overall result, the PRT AF improved substantially its self-awareness and developed a new set of standards at the strategic, tactic and operational levels.

CONCLUSION

Actor-Network Theory is a well established approach to explain application of IT projects in developing countries.

In this chapter, we have proposed to use ANT perspective to provide a brief overview of Portuguese Air Force change case study.

For that, we have presented a literature review of ANT and explained its central concepts followed by a description of the context, objectives and actions of the PRT AF in the transformation process.

We finalized by applying the ANT theory to the PRT case study explaining, in detail, where, how, and when the circumstances matched the several ANT phases.

The actions involved working in several areas. As personnel became aware of what was requested, some of them could see immediate advantage while others considered the extra work to be only an additional burden on the daily activities. For example, the development of operations and maintenance manuals (business rules), from the strategic to the operational level (strategy to task) produced a high degree of standardization and alignment, which caused different ways of operation to surge (transforming tacit knowledge in organizational knowledge). This was not easily implemented due to the fact that it touched people's zone of comfort.

Although the planned deliverables were not completely accomplished, a lot was carried out. The Air Force Academy played a significant role with the inclusion of general officers and action officers in the master thesis juries. In this way, a change proposal, made to a specific entity had the action officer as discussion member and the directing general as the jury president. This re-vealed to be very useful, since it facilitated the comprehension of the work being done in the organization.

IT shaping was one of the main objectives for the change process. An IT change plan was prepared and the actions to identify the AS IS comprehended software acquisition to model business architecture and specification, information architecture. The following phase will determine the TO BE and the design of a new architecture, using service-oriented architecture.

IT also played an essential role on personnel training and the setup of an internal directory and an Internet Forum where, upon registration, people could consult the "things" that have been done and provide feedback.

Indeed, the change process resulted from the detection that information was not a valuable asset to the Organization due to the lack of synchronization and the proliferation of local information systems. The change process, not only brought information synchronization at all levels of the Organization, but also improved the decision process. Relevant and contextual information brings near real time situation-awareness which, in turn, leads to superior understanding and better decision making which attains competitive advantage.

FURTHER RESEARCH

Further research should focus on developing a deep and detailed case study by collecting primary data from the project network human actants. In terms of non-human actants, an interesting current issue raises opportunities for research.

In all this process, initiated to improve information quality, the importance of information, as an essential asset to foster organizational self-awareness, is stressed. Therefore, further research also includes using ASI potentialities to continue improving the quality of information associated to the PRTAF IS.

REFERENCES

Abreu, M., & Tribolet, J. (2008). Considerações sobre a medição de factores soft nas organizações. In *Proceedings of the 8ª Conferência da Associação Portuguesa de Sistemas de Informação* (CAPSI 2008). CAPSI.

Avgerou, C., Ciborra, C., Cordella, A., Kallinikos, J., & Smith, M. L. (2006). *E-government and trust in the state: Lessons from electronic tax systems in Chile and Brazil*. London: London School of Economics and Political Science.

Aykac, D., Kervenoael, R., & Kasap, N. (2009). *An actor-network theory (ANT) approach to Turkish e-government gateway initiative*. Paper presented at the International Conference on eGovernment & eGovernance. Ankara, Turkey.

Callon, M. (1986). Some elements of a sociology of translation: Domestication of the scallops and the fishermen of St Brieuc Bay. In J. Law (Ed.), *Power, Action & Belief: A New Sociology of Knowledge?* (pp. 196–229). London: Routledge & Kegan Paul.

Callon, M. (1999). Actor-network theory–The market test. In J. Law & J. Hassard (Eds.), *Actor Network Theory and After* (pp. 181–195). Oxford, UK: Blackwell Publishers.

Callon, M., & Latour, B. (1981). Unscrewing the big leviathan: How actors macro-structure reality and how sociologists help them to do so. In K. D. Knorr-Cetina (Ed.), *Advances in Social Theory and Methodology: Towards an Integration of Micro and Macro-Sociologies* (pp. 277–303). London: Routledge and Kegan Paul.

Frohmann, B. (1995). *Taking information policy beyond information science: Applying the actor network theory*. London, Canada: University of Western Ontario.

Hanseth, O., & Monteiro, E. (1998). *Understanding information infrastructure*. Retrieved from http://heim.ifi.uio.no/oleha/Publications/bok.html

Hardy, C. A., & Williams, S. P. (2008). E-government policy and practice: A theoretical and empirical exploration of public e-procurement. *Government Information Quarterly*, 25(2), 155–180. doi:10.1016/j.giq.2007.02.003

Heeks, R., & Stanforth, C. (2007). Understanding e-government project trajectories from an actor-network perspective. *European Journal of Information Systems*, 16(2), 165–177. doi:10.1057/palgrave.ejis.3000676

Holmström, J., & Robey, D. (2005). Inscribing organizational change with information technology: An actor network theory approach. In B. Czarniawska & T. Hernes (Eds.), *Actor-Network Theory and Organizing* (pp. 165–187). Malmö: Liber.

Jarke, J. (2007, November). Knowledge sharing in a distributed community of practice: A case study of ePractice.eu. *European Journal of ePractice*.

Johanes, P. E., & Kwong, H. C. (2007). *ANT and e-government research in developing countries: A case in BIMP-EAGA*. Lumut, Malaysia: Managing Knowledge in the Borderless World.

Kotter, J. P. (1996). *Leading change*. Boston: Harvard Business School Press.

Latour, B. (1988). *The pasteurization of France*. Cambridge, MA: Harvard University Press.

Latour, B. (1992). One turn after the social turn. In E. McMullin (Ed.), *The social dimensions of science* (pp. 272–294). South Bend, IN: University of Note Dame Press.

Latour, B. (1993). *We have never been modern* (C. Porter, Trans.). Hemel Hempstead, UK: Harvester Wheatsheaf.

Latour, B. (1996). *Aramis or the love of technology*. Cambridge, MA: Harvard University Press.

Laudon, K., & Laudon, J. (2006). *Management of information systems: Managing the digital firm* (9th ed.). Upper Saddle River, NJ: Pearson / Prentice Hall.

Muganda-Ochara, N., & Belle, J.-P. V. (2008). Adoption processes of egovernment: The case of local councils in Kenya. In *Proceedings of the 10th IBIMA Conference*. Kuala Lumpur, Malaysia: International Business Information Management Association.

Páscoa, C. (2012). *Organizational and design engineering of the operational and support dimensions of an organization: The Portuguese air force case study*. (Unpublished Doctoral thesis). Technical University of Lisboa, Instituto Superior Técnico, Lisboa, Portugal.

Páscoa, C., Alves, A., & Tribolet, J. (2010a). Modeling the effort regime for the air force. In *Proceedings of the CENTERIS 2010 Conference on ENTERprise and Information Systems* (CCIS). Berlin: Springer.

Páscoa, C., Alves, A., & Tribolet, J. (2012a). EX-ANTE and EX-POST model applied to the Portuguese air force flying regime. In *Organizational Integration of Enterprise Systems and Resources: Advancements and Applications*. Hershey, PA: IGI-Global. doi:10.4018/978-1-4666-1764-3.ch010

Páscoa, C., Aveiro, D., & Tribolet, J. (2012). Organizational configuration actor role modeling using DEMO. In *Proceedings of the Conference on Enterprise Engineering* (LNPIB). Berlin: Springer.

Páscoa, C., Belo, N., & Tribolet, J. (2010b). Value model for enterprise and process architect. In T. Oliveira, C. Páscoa, & J. Tribolet (Eds.), *A Strategy Map applied to a Military Organization (CCIS)*. Berlin: Springer.

Páscoa, C., Belo, N., & Tribolet, J. (2012b). *Business objectives and business processes: Alignment and verification*. Information Resources Management Journal Advancements and Applications. doi:10.4018/irmj.2012040104

Páscoa, C., Costa, R., & Tribolet, J. (2011a). Changing the air force. In *Proceedings of CENTERIS 2011 Conference on ENTERprise and Information Systems* (CCIS). Berlin: Springer.

Páscoa, C., Leal, P., & Tribolet, J. (2010c). A business model for the Portuguese air force. In *Proceedings of the Conference on ENTERprise and Information Systems* (CCIS). Berlin: Springer.

Páscoa, C., Leal, P., & Tribolet, J. (2012c). Organization identity: The business model. In *Organizational Integration of Enterprise Systems and Resources: Advancements and Applications*. Hershey, PA: IGI-Global. doi:10.4018/978-1-4666-1764-3.ch006

Páscoa, C., Oliveira, T., & Tribolet, J. (2011b). A strategy map applied to a military organization. In *Proceedings of CENTERIS 2011 Conference on ENTERprise and Information Systems* (CCIS). Berlin: Springer.

Páscoa, C., Pinto, S., & Tribolet, J. (2011c). Ontology construction: Portuguese air force headquarters domain. In *Proceedings of the Practice-driven Research on Enterprise Transformation (PRET) Conference on Enterprise Engineering* (LNPIB). Berlin: Springer.

Páscoa, C., Santos, P., & Tribolet, J. (2011b). Cost per flying hour–Use of information from the integrated management system. In *Proceedings of CENTERIS 2011 Conference on ENTERprise and Information Systems* (CCIS). Berlin: Springer.

Páscoa, C., Soares, J., & Tribolet, J. (2010). Modeling the flight hour cost for the air force. In *Proceedings of the Conference on ENTERprise and Information Systems* (CCIS). Berlin: Springer.

Páscoa, C., Sousa, P., & Tribolet, J. (2009). Ontology construction: Representing dietz process and state models using BPMN diagrams. In *Enterprise Information Systems Design, Implementation and Management: Organizational Applications* (pp. 56–71). Hershey, PA: IGI-Global.

Páscoa, C., & Tribolet, J. (2010). Organizational and design engineering of the operational and support components of an organization: The Portuguese air force case study. In *Proceedings of the Conference on Enterprise Engineering* (LNPIB). Berlin: Springer.

Portuguese Air Force Chief-of-Staff. (2007). *Mission for the air units*. Lisbon, Portugal: Portuguese Air Force.

Portuguese Air Force Chief-of-Staff. (2008a). *Planning directive for 2008-2010*. Lisbon, Portugal: Portuguese Air Force.

Portuguese Air Force Chief-of-Staff. (2008b). *Normative for operational publications*. Lisbon, Portugal: Portuguese Air Force.

Portuguese Air Force Chief-of-Staff. (2008c). *Operational and maintenance personnel for the air units*. Lisbon, Portugal: Portuguese Air Force.

Portuguese Air Force Chief-of-Staff. (2009a). *Directive for change*. Lisbon, Portugal: Portuguese Air Force.

Portuguese Air Force Chief-of-Staff. (2009b). *Planning directive for the new generation of IS*. Lisbon, Portugal: Portuguese Air Force.

Portuguese Air Force Chief-of-Staff. (2010). *Flying rules for crews*. Lisbon, Portugal: Portuguese Air Force.

Portuguese Government. (2009). *Law of the air force organization*. Lisboa, Portugal: Author.

Sarker, S., Sarker, S., & Sidorova, A. (2006). Understanding business process change failure: An actor-network perspective. *Journal of Management Information Systems, 23*, 51–86. doi:10.2753/MIS0742-1222230102

Stanforth, C. (2006). Using actor-network theory to analyze e-government implementation in developing countries. *Information Technologies and International Development, 3*(3), 35–60. doi:10.1162/itid.2007.3.3.35

Suchman, L. A. (1987). *Plans and situated actions: The problem of human-machine communications*. Cambridge, UK: Cambridge University Press.

Trusler, J. (2003). South African e-government policy and practices: A framework to close the gap. In R. Traunmüller (Ed.), *Electronic Government: Second International Conference* (Egov 2003), (pp. 504-507). Prague, Czech Republic: Springer.

United States Air Force. (2003). *Air force basic doctrine*. Washington, DC: United States Air Force Doctrine Centre.

United States Air Force. (2005). Air force doctrine document 2-5 (changed to 3-13 in 2010). Washington, DC: United States Air Force Doctrine Centre.

Walsham, G. (1997). Actor-network theory and IS research: Current status and future prospects. In A. S. Lee, J. Liebenau, & J. I. DeGross (Eds.), *Information Systems and Qualitative Research* (pp. 466–480). London: Chapman and Hall. doi:10.1007/978-0-387-35309-8_23

Walsham, G., & Sahay, S. (1999). GIS for district-level administration in India: Problems and opportunities. *Management Information Systems Quarterly*, 23(1), 39–66. doi:10.2307/249409

WE. (2005). *Semiotics*. World Encyclopedia.

ENDNOTES

[1] Organizational Knowledge–Process that amplifies within the organization the knowledge crated by individuals and crystallizes it as a part of the organizational knowledge network (Magalhães, 2008).

This work was previously published in Rethinking the Conceptual Base for New Practical Applications in Information Value and Quality edited by George Leal Jamil, Armando Malheiro, and Fernanda Ribeiro, pages 233-248, copyright year 2014 by Information Science Reference (an imprint of IGI Global).

Section 5
Issues and Challenges

This section contains 14 chapters, giving a wide variety of perspectives on web design and development and its implications. Within the chapters, the reader is presented with an in-depth analysis of the most current and relevant issues within this growing field of study. Crucial questions are addressed and alternatives offered along with theoretical approaches discussed.

Chapter 61

How Interface Design and Search Strategy Influence Children's Search Performance and Evaluation

Hanna Jochmann-Mannak
University of Twente, The Netherlands

Theo Huibers
University of Twente, The Netherlands

Leo Lentz
Utrecht University, The Netherlands

Ted Sanders
Utrecht University, The Netherlands

ABSTRACT

This chapter presents an experiment with 158 children, aged 10 to 12, in which search performance and attitudes towards an informational Website are investigated. The same Website was designed in 3 different types of interface design varying in playfulness of navigation structure and in playfulness of visual design. The type of interface design did not have an effect on children's search performance, but it did influence children's feelings of emotional valence and their evaluation of "goodness." Children felt most positive about the Website with a classical navigation structure and playful aesthetics. They found the playful image map Website least good. More importantly, children's search performance was much more effective and efficient when using the search engine than when browsing the menu. Furthermore, this chapter explores the challenge of measuring affective responses towards digital interfaces with children by presenting an elaborate evaluation of different methods.

INTRODUCTION

There is a trend in digital media for children to design digital products that are 'cool' and 'playful'. Part of taking a 'playful' approach in designing digital products for children is creating age-appropriate graphics, or graphics that children

can relate to (Meloncon, Haynes, Varelmann & Groh, 2010). In a corpus study of 100 informational Websites for children, we recognized this playful design approach in many of the analyzed interfaces (Jochmann-Mannak, Lentz, Huibers & Sanders, 2012). More specifically, we identified three types of interface design for children, ranging

DOI: 10.4018/978-1-4666-8619-9.ch061

from 1) classical interface design with a classical interaction style and without playful graphics, 2) interface design with playful graphics, but a classical interaction style and 3) playful interface design with playful graphics and a playful interaction style. In this study, we analyzed what the effects are of these different design approaches of an informational Website on children's interaction with these interfaces and on children's affective responses towards these interfaces.

The second important objective in this experiment, is to explore the effects of children's use of a search engine on children's search performance and affective responses. Conducting an experiment by letting children interact with digital interfaces is a big challenge. However, measuring children's affective responses towards these interfaces is an even greater challenge, as will be described in this chapter.

THEORETICAL BACKGROUND

Children's Informational Interface Design

Interactive products for children can be classified in entertainment, educational and enabling products (Markopoulos, Read, MacFarlane & Hoysniemi, 2008). Websites for children as a specific group of interactive products can also be classified in these three genres. Most Websites for children are aimed at entertaining children, for example by providing computer games. For our study with children's informational Websites, both educational and enabling Websites are relevant, because most informational Websites are educational and search engines that help children in finding relevant information, can be classified as enabling.

Researchers propose some guidelines for children's Web design (Nielsen & Gilutz, 2002; Meloncon, et al., 2010). Most of these guidelines

were tested and validated with children, but many of the guidelines are not specifically aimed at children, and similar to standard Web design practices for adult Websites. In a large corpus study with children's informational Websites we identified current design conventions for children (Jochmann-Mannak et al., 2012). This study also showed that designers of children's Websites often follow general Web design guidelines. A closer look at the data in this study did reveal three categories of informational Websites especially designed for children. The first category is a Classic design type in which the layout of the pages is kept minimal and the design is aimed at simplicity, consistency and focus. We called the second category 'the Classical Play design type' in which a classic design approach for the navigation structure is combined with a playful, visual design approach. More effort is spent on the design of graphics, colors and games (Meloncon et al., 2010). The third category was called the 'Image Map design type' in which no classic Web design characteristics are used. The visual design and navigation structure on the Websites of this type are based on Image maps that incorporate objects or locations that children know from real life or from fiction. Children can explore this tableau of real life or fictional objects, which makes information-seeking a playful experience (Meloncon et al., 2010). This Image map web design can be compared to 'spatial metaphors', which can be employed to visually represent information, using the universe, the solar system, galaxies, and so on through which the user navigates to locate information (Chen, 2006).

In their study to develop a visual taxonomy for children, Large, Beheshti, Tabatabaei, and Nesset (2009) emphasized the importance of movement and color in any visualization designed for children. They argue that "such characteristics do not necessarily influence positively the effectiveness of a taxonomy, but the affective reaction of users, and especially of children, that should never be underestimated. If the presentation is not interesting and fails to catch the attention of users, it is unlikely to invite their repeat visits. It also might be argued that intrinsic to visualization schemes is the ability to provoke interest and even fun" (p. 1818).

Two Search Strategies: Keyword Searching and Browsing

In the beginning of the Internet era a general assumption was made by researchers that browsing-oriented search tools, relying on recognition knowledge, were better suited to the abilities and skills of children than keyword search tools. The argument was that browsing imposes less cognitive load on children than searching, because more knowledge is needed to retrieve terms from memory when searching than simply to recognize offered terms when browsing (Bilal, 2000, 2001, 2002; Borgman, Hirsh, Walter & Gallagher, 1995; Large & Beheshti, 2000; Large, Beheshti, & Moukdad, 1999; Schacter, Chung & Dorr, 1998; Bilal & Watson, 1998).

Schacter et al. (1998) found that with both highly specific and vague search tasks, children sought information by using browsing strategies. In their research on children's internet searching on complex problems with thirty-two children in the age of 10 to 12 years, they reported: "Children are reactive searchers who do not systematically plan or employ elaborated analytic search strategies" (p. 847).

Bilal (2000) found in her research on the use of the Yahooligans! Web Search Engine that most of the children (she observed twenty-two children in the age of 12 to 13 years) used keyword search. Only 36% of the searches were performed by browsing under subject categories. This finding may have been affected by the type of search task that was given in this research: a fact-driven query that automatically stimulated children to use keyword search instead of browsing the categories.

Revelle, Druin, Platner, Bederson, Hourcade and Sherman (2002) report on the development of a visual search interface to support children in their efforts to find animals in a hierarchical information structure. To examine searching and browsing behavior, 106 children (aged 5 through 10) participated in an experiment on this visual search interface. The researchers found that: "(…) even young children are capable of efficient and accurate searching. With the support of a visual query interface that includes scaffolding for Boolean concepts, children can use a hierarchical structure to perform searches and construct search queries that surpass their previously demonstrated abilities with the use of traditional search techniques" (p. 56).

By tracking the web logs of The International Children's Digital Library (ICDL), Druin (2003) found that, of 60,000 unique users between the ICDL's launch in November 2002 and September 2003, approximately 75% of the searches used category search (browsing), 15% used place search (by selecting a place using a world interface) and just over 10% of the searches used keyword search.

Hutchinson, Bederson and Druin (2006) found that children are capable of using both keyword search and category browsing, but generally they prefer and are more successful with category browsing. They explain this finding in relation to children's 'natural tendency to explore'. Young children tend not to plan out their searches, but simply react to the results they receive from the Information Retrieval system. Generally, their search strategies are not analytical and do not aim precisely at one goal. Instead, they make associations while browsing. This is a trial-and-error strategy.

It is clear that research results are very diverse when it comes to search strategies used by children. The results seem to depend on the type of interface used in the studies and the type of search task that was given to children. However, the trend in literature is that browsing is more suited for children than using a search engine.

Difficulties with Keyword Searching and Browsing

Formulating a search query might be difficult for children, because they have little knowledge to base 'recall' on (Borgman et al., 1995; Hutchinson, Druin, Bederson, Reuter, Rose & Weeks, 2005). Besides, for searching relevant documents using keyword search, correct spelling, spacing and punctuation are needed. Children have difficulty with spelling and often make spelling errors (Borgman et al., 1995; Druin, Foss, Hatley, Golub, Leigh Guha, Fails, 2009). That is why an information retrieval system should be able to handle spelling errors, to help children find relevant documents using keyword search. Deciding on a single keyword is also difficult for a child, because children tend to use a full natural language query, especially with complex search tasks (Marchionini, 1989; Druin, et al., 2009). Thus, a system should also be able to handle natural language queries to find relevant information. In a comparison study between children and adults, Bilal and Kirby (2002) found that when children employed keyword search, most of their queries were single or multiple concepts, just like adults do. However, adults employed advanced search syntax, while children did not use this.

Browsing taxonomies may also be difficult for a child, because taxonomies in children's Web portals such as Kidsclick.org and Dibdabdoo.com use hierarchically structured taxonomies that may impose considerable cognitive load. Only a part of the hierarchy is displayed at any one time, and users must guess which route might eventually take them to the relevant term within the hierarchy (Large, Beheshti, Nesset & Bowler, 2006). With category search (i.e. browsing), children also have trouble finding the right category, because they have little domain-knowledge to decide which category is optimum. In addition, problems with browsing tools are mostly the result of a lack of vocabulary knowledge. Children often have difficulties understanding abstract, top-level headings, because their vocabulary knowledge is not yet sufficient to understand such terms (Hutchinson et al., 2006). Therefore, formulation of headings should be adjusted to children's vocabulary knowledge, using simple, concrete search terms.

Children may not think hierarchically like adults and may have trouble understanding the way in which hierarchically based categories are constructed. Knowing what their understanding of categories is, can therefore be of great value in designing browsing tools. Bar-Ilan and Belous (2007) tried to understand what browsable, hierarchical subject categories children create by conducting a card sorting experiment with twelve groups of four children in the age of 9 through 11 years. They suggested terms to the children through 61 cards. The children were free to add, delete or change terms. The researchers found that the majority of the category names used by existing directories were acceptable for the children and only a small minority of the terms caused confusion. Finally, often information in browsing systems is alphabetically displayed, requiring good alphabet skills. Many children have problems with alphabetizing and therefore have trouble finding information in such browsing systems (Borgman et al., 1995).

Children's Search Behavior Characteristics

Bilal (2000) found in her research on the use of the *Yahooligans! Web Search Engine* that children were chaotic in their search performance: they switched frequently between types of searching (i.e. keyword search or browsing), they often looped their keyword searches and selected hyperlinks, and they frequently backtracked. These findings suggested that children want to combine different search strategies during one search task.

Bilal and Kirby (2002) also found that children were more chaotic in their search performance than adults. In their research, they compared search behavior between twenty-two children (aged 12 through 13) and twelve graduate students. Children made more web moves, they looped searches and hyperlinks more often, they backtracked more often, and they deviated more often from a designated target. The researchers concluded that adults adopted a "linear or systematic" browsing style whereas most children had a "loopy" style. They explain that this "loopy" style can be caused by children's lower cognitive recall, because the web imposes memory overload that reduces recall during navigation. They also found that children scrolled result pages less often than adults.

We should keep in mind however, that most of these studies were conducted in a time that children did not make use of computers and the Internet as much as they do anno 2013. Children nowadays are much more experienced users of digital interfaces because of iPads, Facebook, online gaming, etc., which makes it difficult to apply these research results to children's current information-seeking and navigation behavior on digital interfaces.

What we have learned so far from this theoretical background is that playful interface design emerges in the genre of children's informational Websites. Literature on children's search behavior and on problems and successes that children experience during information-seeking, especially engages in pragmatic issues such as query handling and comprehensibility of taxonomies. However, the emergence of playful interface design asks for a broader focus than pragmatic issues. Also hedonic issues of playful interface design should be studied. It is assumed that product characters can be described by two attribute groups: pragmatic and hedonic attributes. Pragmatic attributes are connected to the users' need to achieve goals (e.g. finding information on an informational Website). Hedonic attributes are primarily related to the users' self. A product can be perceived by users as hedonic because it provides stimulation by its challenging character or identification by communicating personal values to relevant others

(Hassenzahl, 2004). Hedonic issues of interface design will be discussed in the next part of the theoretical background.

Fun and Engagement

From the beginning, research on interaction with digital interfaces is dominated by pragmatic issues such as the utility and usability of these systems (Thüring & Mahlke, (2007). This is the same for research on children's interaction with digital interfaces (Borgman et al., 1995; Bilal, 2000; Druin, 2003; Hutchinson, 2005). Usability, in particular, is a key concept for capturing the quality of use of digital products in which effectiveness and efficiency of system use is measured. The third component of the usability concept is 'user satisfaction'. Although this is measured using subjective judgments of users, these are mostly based on efficiency and effectiveness of interface usage.

In the field of Interaction Design for Children (IDC), there is a strong downplay in research about efficiency and task completion (Yarosh, Radu, Hunter & Rosenbaum, 2011). Instead of usability and satisfaction, that are goal related, desirability (being 'cool') has become very relevant in the community, which is not goal related. Malone (1980) pioneered the study of fun as an important aspect of software, and published guidelines designing for fun (Malone, 1984). According to his constructivist view, children acquire knowledge through experience. But for many years the study of fun in software was of marginal interest. In recent years there has been increasing interest in fun (Read, MacFarlane & Casey, 2002). Yarosh et al. (2011) report that 'enjoyment' and 'fun' are the most important values in 24% of the papers presented on the yearly Conference on Interaction Design & Children. They even claim that the values enjoyment and fun are that ubiquitous in the community, that they are no longer explicitly discussed, but that they became general assumptions when designing interactive products for children.

User Experience

Also in the general field of Human Computer Interaction (HCI) researchers argue for a broader perspective on user experience (UX) (Hassenzahl & Tractinsky, 2006; Thüring & Mahlke, 2007) which can include, - besides perceived usability - beauty, overall quality and hedonic, affective and experiential aspects of the use of technology (van Schaik & Ling, 2008). Considering this broader perspective on UX, the reason for designing playful interfaces for children – as described in the Introduction of this chapter - becomes more clear. Playful design might have a positive effect on children's overall appraisal of a digital interface. This hypothesis is based on the idea that overall appraisal of a digital product is influenced by perception of both instrumental qualities (for example, effectiveness of a product) and non-instrumental qualities (for example, beauty of a product) as proposed by the Components of User Experience model (Thüring & Mahlke, 2007). Following this idea, playful design might have a positive effect on children's perception of hedonic quality, because children might feel stimulated by the creative and innovative interaction style or they might be able to easily identify with the playful environment. These are the hedonic attributes of stimulation and identification that are primarily related to the users' self as described by Hassenzahl (2004). Thüring and Mahlke (2007) propose that both perception of instrumental and non-instrumental qualities have an influence on users' emotional reactions (such as subjective feelings, motor expressions or physiological reactions), which also has influence on overall appraisal of a system. For example, a slow working system (instrumental quality) may lead to frustration (negative emotion). At the same time, this slow working system might be presented with a creative interface design that may lead to enjoyment (positive emotion). Both experienced emotions have an influence on the overall appraisal of the system.

The Interplay between Components of User Experience

What is interesting to know for designers of digital products is how the overall quality of an interactive product is formed. Evaluating interactive products is very complex, because many factors influence the quality of an interactive product: usability, beauty, overall quality, hedonic quality, and affective and experiential aspects of the use of a product.

Tractinsky, Katz and Ikar (2000), conducted an experiment to test the relationship between user's perceptions of computerized system's aesthetic beauty and usability. Perceptions were measured before and after actual use of the system. Both pre- and post-use measures indicated strong correlations between perceived aesthetics and usability. Post-use usability ratings were not affected by actual usability (i.e. objective measured usability), which made Tractinsky et al. (2000) conclude that a product's beauty is a stronger indicator for its perceived usability than its actual usability. In other words, they claimed that "what is beautiful is usable". Tractinsky et al. (2000) propose the occurrence of a so-called *halo-effect*. Beauty of an interface overrules all other interface characteristics and therefore influences users' overall evaluation of the system.

Hassenzahl (2004) also studied the relation between perceived aesthetics and usability. He investigated the interplay between two product evaluations, beauty and goodness and the following perceptions of product attributes: pragmatic quality (i.e. usability as perceived by the user), hedonic quality of stimulation (personal) and hedonic quality of identification (social). He found that beauty as an evaluation was related to the hedonic quality of identification (e.g. a product is perceived as professional, valuable or presentable, etc.). Hassenzahl (2004) found that goodness was more closely related to attributes of pragmatic quality (e.g. a product is perceived as simple, practical, clear, predictable, etc.), especially when participants also interacted with the product under evaluation. These results of Hassenzahl (2004) contradict to the results of Tractinsky et al. (2000), because Tractinsky et al. (2000) found no significant main effect of usability on post-use ratings of usability and beauty. In contrast, Hassenzahl (2004) did find an effect of actual usability on perceptions of usability. Hassenzahl (2004) explains this contradiction in results by the fact that Tractinsky's manipulation of usability was unlikely to induce stress for the participants, which makes any impact on post-use ratings of usability unlikely.

To study how the overall quality or goodness of an interactive product is formed, van Schaik and Ling (2008) also conducted an experiment on the interplay between components of UX. They found that all measures (i.e. evaluation of goodness, attributes of hedonic and pragmatic quality, task performance and mental effort) except evaluation of beauty, were sensitive to manipulation of web design. Evaluation of beauty was influenced by hedonic attributes (identification and stimulation), but evaluation of goodness was influenced by both hedonic and pragmatic attributes as well as task performance and mental effort. Attributes of hedonic quality were more stable with experience (i.e. using the interactive product) than attributes of pragmatic quality. Evaluation of beauty was more stable than evaluation of goodness.

Hartmann, Sutcliffe, and DeAngeli (2008) found a link between aesthetics and usability. When users' usability experience was poor, positively perceived aesthetics could positively influence overall appraisal of a system, suggesting that "aesthetics could be an important determinant of user satisfaction and system acceptability, overcoming poor usability experience." (p. 176) Furthermore, they argued that the relative importance of aesthetics is related to the user's background and task. When the user's task is goal-oriented, then usability factors will weigh more than aesthetic considerations. When the user's task is action-

oriented (the experience is more important than the goal), users choose designs based on a general impression of aesthetics and engagement.

Tuch, Roth, Hornbaek, Opwis and Bargas-Avila (2012) gave an overview of the current state of research on the aesthetics-usability relation. They made a distinction between correlative studies in which aesthetics and usability were not systematically manipulated as independent experimental factors and experimental studies in which these factors were systematically manipulated. The correlative studies showed some evidence for the relation between usability and aesthetics. However, there was only limited inference on the direction of any causality between aesthetics and usability. In the experimental studies, a pure "what is beautiful is usable" notion was only partially supported. Tuch et al. (2012) reported that there was also some evidence that in certain cases the relation is best described as "what is usable is beautiful" (p. 1598). Tuch et al. (2012) conducted an experiment on the aesthetics-usability relation and also found under certain conditions evidence for the relation "what is usable is beautiful". They found that the frustration of poor usability lowers ratings on perceived aesthetics.

Note that in none of the discussed studies so far children were involved. However, Hartmann et al. (2008) suggest that a metaphor-based interface style, such as an Image map Website type (considered more aesthetically pleasing and engaging), would be better for children than a menu-based style when they were interacting with it in their leisure time. They were undecided about this if the interface was to be used in the classroom within a formal educational context. Their reason for this assumption was that a metaphor-based style would likely prove more engaging but perhaps at the expense of usability.

In a study to validate the Fun Toolkit, a tool to evaluate technology with children, Sim, MacFarlane and Read (2005) did try to relate the constructs 'fun' and 'usability'. They report that children experience less fun when there were more usability problems. They conclude that it is not all about fun for children and that usability does matter to them.

We now learned that conducting research on hedonic issues such as fun and engagement became more important in the field of child-computer interaction in recent years. The study of pragmatic and hedonic issues of interface design with adult users from a subjective user-centered perspective on quality of use, is called 'user experience' (UX). An important topic in this field of research is the interplay between components of UX, such as usability, beauty and goodness. We think that this topic is also relevant for our research on children's informational Websites and especially concerning the emergence of playful interface design in this genre. However, methods used in studies with adults are mostly not suitable for studies with children. Current applied methods should be reflected on whether they are suited for children. Therefore, we will now discuss literature on the methods used in this field of research with adults and the methods used to measure hedonic components of UX with children.

Methods to Measure the UX Components

As mentioned before, research on interaction with digital interfaces was dominated by pragmatic issues such as the utility and usability of these systems. Methods to measure usability are measuring effectiveness (the accuracy and completeness with which specified tasks can be conducted in a particular environment), efficiency (for example, the amount of time or digital events required to reach a specified goal) and satisfaction in using the system (based on instrumental qualities of the system). The same methods to measure these factors of usability that are validated in research with adults, can be used well in research with children, as we experienced in a prior explorative study on children's search behavior (Jochmann-Mannak, Huibers, Lentz and Sanders, 2010).

The evaluation of subjective aesthetic preferences and emotional experiences is more difficult to measure than objective usability scores. According to Laarni (2004), this is one of the reasons why these non-instrumental qualities have played a marginal role in human-computer interaction (HCI) research. Particularly with children, measuring subjective, non-instrumental qualities of a system, for example, with a survey method by asking children to rate product evaluations (such as fun, beauty and goodness) is very difficult, because of risks of satisficing, children's tendency to say yes irrespective of the question and children's tendency to indicate the highest score on the scale when scales are used to elicit opinions about software (Markopoulos et al., 2008).

Horton, Read and Sim (2011) report a study in which the reliability of children's responses on a pictoral questionnaire is tested by asking the same questions about children's technology twice one week after the other. None of the children produced the same results for a question after one week, which proves the difficulty of using survey questions with children and the issues with the validity and reliability of questionnaire answers given by children.

Read, MacFarlane and Casey (2002) developed the Fun Toolkit to measure children's opinions of technology which reduces the mentioned risks of evaluating products with children. The Fun Toolkit consists of four tools: a Funometer, a Smileyometer, a Fun Sorter and an Again-Again table. The Toolkit has been validated in several studies with children (Read & MacFarlane, 2006; Sim, MacFarlane & Read, 2006; Read, 2008).

Visual Analogue Scales (VAS) are often used in survey studies with children. With a VAS, children can identify and visualize their answers, feelings or opinions through pictorial representations instead of textual labels (Markopoulos, et al., 2008). The Smileyometer (Read et al., 2002) is an example of a VAS. But even with such a simple question-answering style like VAS, a child still needs to understand the question, needs to recall relevant information from memory, needs to decide what response is appropriate, needs to translate this response by deciding which pictogram from the VAS is relevant, and requires to physically act to make the selection. All of these steps put high cognitive load on children's working memory that can be problematic for a child.

An often used subjective method that uses VAS to measure emotional valence and arousal is the Self-Assessment Manikin (SAM) (see Figure 6 in the Method section), developed by Lang (1980). The SAM is a non-verbal pictorial assessment technique that measures the pleasure, arousal, and dominance associated with a person's affective reaction to a wide variety of stimuli (Bradley & Lang, 1994) which is based on the dimensions of valence, arousal and dominance (Russell, 1980). The use of SAM with children was validated by Greenbaum, Turner, Cook and Melamed (1990).

To measure users' perceptions of three product attributes (pragmatic quality, hedonic quality– identification and hedonic quality– stimulation) and two product evaluations (beauty and good-ness), Hassenzahl, Burmester and Koller (2003) developed the AttracDiff 2 questionnaire. Each of the three product attributes is represented by seven 7-point semantic differential scales (e.g. professiona)– amateurish) and the two product evaluations by one 7-point semantic differential scales each (e.g. good– bad). To the best of our knowledge, the AttracDiff 2 questionnaire is not yet validated in survey studies with children.

RESEARCH QUESTIONS

As we learned from the literature, there is a general assumption that digital products or systems for children should be fun and engaging (Yarosh et al., 2011). Non-instrumental product attributes - like beauty and fun- are expected to have an influence on overall appraisal of a digital product, just as

instrumental product attributes such as effective-ness and learnability (Thüring & Mahlke, 2007; Van Schaik & Ling, 2008).

It seems that designers of children's interactive products make their products fun and engaging by adding playful design characteristics, both in visual design as in navigation design (Jochmann-Mannak et al., 2012). Therefore, we are inter-ested whether the adding of playful design has a positive influence on children's perceptions of hedonic quality and on their overall appraisal of the system. We are also interested in the relation between children's perception of hedonic quality with their perception of usability and actual task performance.

In a previous explorative study, we did find a positive influence of playful interface design on children's perceptions of hedonic quality, mea-sured by observing children's emotional expres-sions while working with informational Websites in a school setting (Jochmann-Mannak et al., 2010). However, most emotional expressions were based on pragmatic product attributes instead of hedonic product attributes. From this study, we concluded that playful design does not have a large influence on children's overall appraisal of informational interfaces. Usability seems much more important for children than non-pragmatic qualities, such as fun and beauty. However, that study was not set up as an experiment. Therefore, in this follow-up study, we want to test these initial results under controlled experimental conditions.

These are the research questions in our study:

1. What are the effects of different interface design types on...
    a. What are the effects of different design types of informational Websites on children's search behavior?
    b. What are the effects of different design types on children's attitude towards informational Websites (emotions,

perceptions of pragmatic and hedonic quality and product evaluations, such as beauty, goodness and fun)?

c. What is the relation between performance (objective usability) and attitude (subjective user-centered perspective on quality of use)?

d. Is there an interaction between different interface design types with the chosen search strategy (searching with the search engine or browsing the main categories)?

2. If any, what problems and successes do children experience when searching with a search engine or when browsing main categories?

a. Do these problems and successes relate to design characteristics of the different design types?

b. Do these problems and successes relate to the quality of the search engine?

c. Do these problems and successes relate to characteristics of the children?

3. Are existing methods to measure feelings and perceptions of pragmatic and hedonic quality that are used in research with adults also suited for research with children?

RESEARCH METHOD

Experimental Design

The experiment used a 3 x 2 between groups design with two factors: interface design and use of the search engine. Three versions of the same Website varied in aesthetics and navigation style. We did not want to have an influence on children's natural search behavior by telling them to search by using the search engine or to browse by using the navigation to find information. Therefore, the use of the search engine was manipulated by presenting the Websites with or without a search engine.

For each of the three Web design conditions, half of the children used the search engine and half of the children did not use the search engine.

Both independent variables were between-subjects; each child participant used one of the three interface designs and did (at least for one of the search tasks in the experimental session) or did not make use of the search engine at all. Outcome measures included perceptions of product attributes (pragmatic and hedonic quality), evaluations of the Websites (beauty, goodness and fun), objective performance measures, subjective emotion measures and objective emotion measures.

Participants

There were 158 children in the age of 10 to 12 years old that took part in the experiment (70 boys and 88 girls, see Table 1a), with an average age of 10.80 (SD =.65). From these children, 67 were in the fifth grade and 91 were in sixth grade. The children were tested on four different primary schools in the Netherlands. Children were randomly assigned to the three types of Websites concerning age, gender, school, grade and experience with the internet, based on randomization checks. The number of children that used the three different Website versions and the number of these children that did or did not use the search engine are presented in Table 1b.

Materials and Equipment

For the manipulation of the interface design, an existing online encyclopedia for children was used (i.e. Junior Winkler Prins online encyclopedia). By using a fully working, existing Website, ecological validity is higher than by building a prototype Website for the experiment. The disadvantage of working with an existing Website is that the Website comes with real life flaws. For example, the search engine on the Website in our experiment did not provide query suggestions or spelling

Table 1. (a) Age and gender of the participants. (b) Distribution of children over Website versions and use and non-use of the search engine

Age	Male	Female	Total
9	1	0	*1*
10	15	34	*49*
11	44	44	*88*
12	10	10	*20*
Total	*70*	*88*	*158*
Website Version	**Number of Children that Used the Search Engine**	**Number of Children that did *not* Use the Search Engine**	*Total*
Classic version	26	25	*51*
Classical play version	26	26	*52*
Image map version	25	30	*55*
Total	*77*	*81*	*158*

suggestions. Besides the existing version of the Website, two other fully working versions of this same Website were created; each of the three versions with a different interface design. Further, for each of the three versions, again there were two versions: one version with and one version without a search engine. In total, there were six different versions of the same Web site in the experiment.

The Classic version was presented with classical aesthetics and with a classical navigation style (see Figure 1). The Classical Play version (see Figure 2) was presented with expressive aesthetics, but with a classical navigation style. The Image Map version (see Figure 3) was presented with both expressive aesthetics and a playful navigation style. The three Website versions were identical concerning the main categories and subcategories, the menu structure, the content and the logo, to control for effects of these factors. Also, on the deepest navigation level, all three Website versions referred to the same target pages with the same lay out for each of the three versions (see Figure 4).

The experiment ran on a laptop (Intel Core, 2,27 GHz, 4,0 GB RAM, Microsoft Windows 7 operating system) with a remote 20" monitor where the children worked on (Figure 5). The screen activities were recorded with Morae usability software (Techsmith) and video and audio recordings were made with a webcam. The children filled out an online questionnaire developed in PX Lab, an open source collection of Java classes and applications for running psychological experiments (Irtel, 2007). Childrens' electrodermal responses (physiological measure of emotional arousal) were measured with a Q Sensor (Affectiva) (Poh, Swenson, Picard, 2010).

Data Collection

Measuring Performance

Each child conducted the same five fact-based tasks (see Appendix A for the full task descriptions). We tested ten tasks in a pilot test with a group of 14 children. Based on the results of this pilot test, we selected five tasks for the final experiment that varied in difficulty of conducting the task with the search engine or by browsing the categories. The task about Columbus, for example, was difficult to conduct both by using

Figure 1. Classic Website version

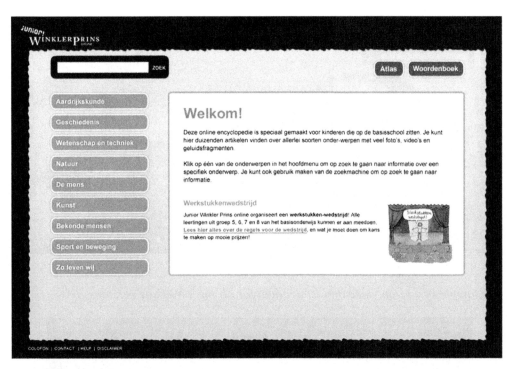

Figure 2. Classical play Website version

Figure 3. Image map Website version

Figure 4. Example of a target page that is identical for all three Website versions

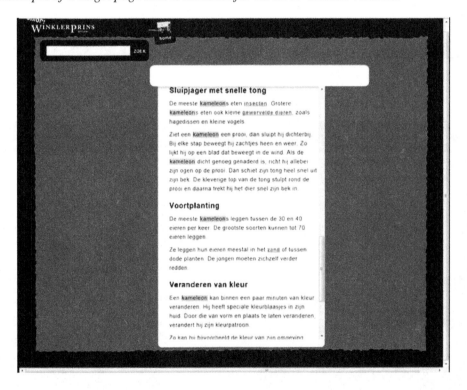

the search engine or by browsing the categories, because children had to find out which nation had discovered America 500 years before Columbus discovered America. The answer to this question was not mentioned on the content page about 'Christopher Columbus', but only on the content page about 'Discoveries' or at the content page about the 'Vikings'.

Task performance was measured by logging the amount of time and clicks needed to conduct

Figure 5. Experimental setting

Figure 6. SAM 5-point bipolar scales for valence (A) and arousal (B)

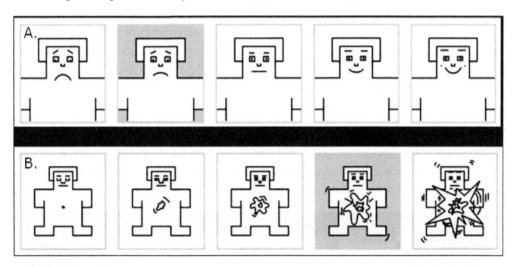

the tasks. Also, per task was analyzed whether the relevant Web page was found and if and - if so - what type of help was offered. Recordings of the screen activities and video (see, for example, Figure 10) and audio recordings of the children were qualitatively analyzed, for example, to indicate what problems children experienced with particular design characteristics.

Measuring Affectivity

The children gave responses to an online questionnaire to measure their feelings, that consisted of three parts: 1) the Self-Assessment Manikin (SAM) (Lang, 1985) to measure children's valence and arousal concerning the Website versions, 2) an adaptation of the AttracDiff 2 (Hassenzahl et al., 2003) to measure children's perceptions of pragmatic and hedonic quality and 3) a questionnaire to measure children's evaluations of beauty, goodness and fun by giving a report mark from 1 (= lowest score) to 10 (= highest score). Each of the items in the questionnaire was presented underneath a picture of the homepage of the Website version that the child had used to conduct the search tasks and that had to be evaluated by the child (for example, Figure 7). An added bonus to this study is that we can also evaluate whether this method is suited to measure product affectivity with children.

In the first part of our questionnaire, we used the same 5-point bipolar scale version of the SAM as used by Greenbaum et al. (1990) (see Figure 6) instead of the original 9-point bipolar scale (Lang, 1980). We decided to only measure the dimensions of valence and arousal and to leave out the dimension of dominance, as Thüring and Mahlke (2007) also did.

For the second part of our questionnaire, we developed Visual Analogue Scales (VAS) based on the AttracDiff 2 questionnaire (Hassenzahl et al., 2003). We translated 15 of the 21 bipolar verbal anchors for the product attribute groups from the AttracDiff 2 questionnaire in bipolar picture anchors as presented in Appendix B (for example, Figure 7: bipolar picture anchor of the semantic differential scale 'Clear – Confusing').[1]

We used these 15 items in the pilot test and asked the children to explain the meaning of the pictures in the visual versions of the semantic differential scales. We decided to remove four of the items from the questionnaire (marked with an asterisk in Appendix B), because none of the children could give a meaning to the pictures that was close to the original meaning of the semantic differential scales. We decided to use 5-point scales instead of 7-point scales. Younger children tend to respond in an extreme matter when asked to use Likert rating scales, whereas older children are more capable of providing graded ratings in the middle of the scale. As tasks become more subjective and emotion focused, as is the case in our study, children's extreme scores, regardless of age, increase (Chambers & Johnston, 2002). Therefore, although the children in our study were between 10 and 12 years old, providing them with more than three ratings in the middle of the scale, would not add value to the rating scales. For younger children, 3-point

Figure 7. Example of the bipolar picture version of the semantic differential scale 'Clear – Confusing' presented underneath the homepage of the Website version under evaluation. (The scores entered by placing the yellow cursor somewhere on the scale, were automatically recorded by the PX Lab software. The left end of the scale was scored as 1 and the right end of the scale as 5.)

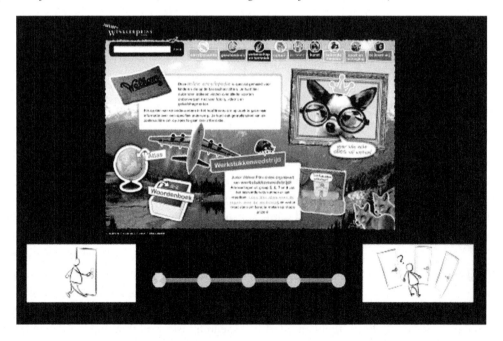

scales would probably be most suited, because of their tendency to give extreme ratings. However, children in the age of our study (i.e. 10-12 years old) are capable of differentiating between more and less extreme ratings on a 5-point scale. We did not use bipolar picture anchors for the product evaluations of beauty, goodness and fun. Instead of that, in the final part of the questionnaire we asked the children to give report marks for beauty, goodness and fun of the Websites.

Product experience is a multi-faceted phenomenon that involves feelings, behavioral reactions, expressive reactions, and physiological reactions (Desmet & Hekkert, 2007). We measured feelings using the online questionnaire as described in the beginning of this section. We also made audio- and video recordings of the children, through which behavioral and expressive reactions could be observed and analyzed[2].

However, because of risks of effects of satisficing (children's tendency to give superficial responses that generally appear reasonable or acceptable), suggestibility (the influence of the interviewer or evaluator on the children's question-and-answer process) and children's tendency to give extreme scale ratings (Markopoulos et al., 2008), we also used a more objective method to measure product experience by measuring physiological reactions. We measured children's physiological emotional arousal with the Q Sensor.

The Q Sensor is a wearable, wireless biosensor that measures emotional arousal via skin conductance (SC), a form of electrodermal activity (EDA) that grows higher during states such as excitement, attention or anxiety and lower during states such as boredom or relaxation. The sensor also measures temperature and activity (Affectiva.com). Typically EDA is recorded as skin conductance by applying a direct current (with two silver electrodes) to the skin (i.e. exosomatic method). Central to this measure is the electrodermal response (EDR). The EDR constitutes a sharp rise in the SC value, followed by a slower drop in conductance. For example, a sudden loud burst of noise will result an EDR 1-2 seconds later, and this is easily visible in the raw data signal. In general, changes in SC are closely linked to activity of the sympathetic part of the autonomic nervous system. Therefore, researchers and practitioners have taken EDA measurements as further operationalization for constructs such as attention, stress, anxiety, workload, pain, and arousal (Noordzij, Scholten & Laroy-Noordzij, 2012). When children emotionally react differently on the three types of Websites, this might be signaled by differences in the number of EDR and the total amplitude of these EDR per minute during task performance between the three Websites. In Figure 8 an example is presented of the output of the Q Sensor, in which can be seen that the device measures three physical properties at the same time: Electrodermal activity, Electrode Temperature and Acceleration.

Procedure

The study was carried out in the fifth and sixth grades of four different primary schools in the Netherlands in the period of September – November 2011. Only children that could hand in a signed consent form by their parents, could co-operate in the study. All children that co-operated in our study filled out a profile survey in the class room in which we asked about their media use, such as their favorite video game, Website or television show, and the amount of time they spent on the Internet, on video games, or on watching television. Half an hour before a child contributed to our study, the test instructor (i.e. the first author of this chapter) put on the Q Sensor on the child's wrist. In that way, the Q Sensor would be accustomed to the child while the child stayed in his class room. After half an hour, the test instructor came back in the class room to take the child to the room in which the experiment was conducted. Before the child started the actual task performance, first, the child was asked to run up and down the stairs three times to activate the Q Sensor. After that,

Figure 8. Example of the Q-sensor's output for Electrodermal Activity, Electrode Temperature and Acceleration

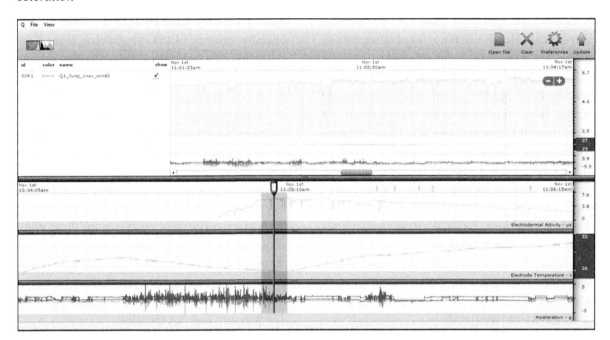

half of the group of children was asked to watch a short animation film (Disney Pixar – "For the Birds") to record a base line for the Q sensor that was the same for all 158 participants. The other half of the group of participants watched the film at the end of the session to control for a potential order effect of watching the film before or after task performance on the experimental Website.

Before the actual task performance started, the test instructor explained that the child would be asked to conduct five search tasks on a Website, because the designer of the Website wanted to know how children feel about the Website and if children can easily find information. The test instructor emphasized that "the child was not tested in this study, but that the Website was tested". The five search tasks were provided to the child in random order on separate sheets. When the child received the first search task, the test instructor started recording the screen activity and the video and audio recording of the child. The test instructor sat next to the child during the task performance and offered help when appropriate. Avoiding help

and social interaction can make the child feel uncomfortable (Markopoulos et al., 2008). We listed the type of help that was offered for each conducted search task. Types of help were help in choosing the right category or sub-category, help in operating the navigation tools, help with spelling or formulation of a search query, or help in finding the right information on a particular content page. The effects of interface design on children's search performance were corrected for the help that was offered to the children. After the search tasks were completed, the test instructor started the online questionnaire and asked the child to read and answer the questions presented in the questionnaire.

Data Analyses

To measure the effects of interface design and search engine use on children's Website performance and attitude towards the Website, a multilevel model was constructed. Independent variables were the type of interface design (Classic, Classical play and Image map) and the use (or non-use) of the search engine. Dependent variables were the percentage of children that were successful in finding the right answers to the search questions (i.e. the chance for success in our multilevel model), the time needed, and the number of clicks needed to find the right information. The model also estimates task variance (because one task can be more difficult than another task), between-children variance (because one child can be more or less skilled in searching information) and residual variance (for example, one child can have more difficulties with task 1, whereas another child can have more difficulties with task 2). By measuring these variances, we can estimate the extent to which we can generate over tasks and children. When we do not take into account this task variance, between-children variance and residual variance, than the probability of falsely rejecting the null hypothesis is greater than 0,05 (Snijders & Bosker, 2012).

RESULTS

Reliability and Validity of the Affective Response Questionnaire

Before we report the results concerning the effects of interface design and search strategies on children's search performance and affectivity towards the interfaces, we will first report about the reliability and validity of the used methods.

We measured actual perceptions of hedonic and pragmatic quality using an instrument that was derived from the AttracDiff 2 questionnaire as composed by Hassenzahl et al. (2003). Cronbach's alphas for the two clusters of bipolar verbal anchors for the constructs of hedonic and pragmatic quality are shown in Table 2. A Cronbach's alpha of 0.6 is usually regarded as the lower bound of an acceptable reliability for experimental purposes. Both clusters measure the underlying constructs in a reliable way (see Table 2). However, the average scores and standard deviations show that most children chose the center of the scales instead of the extreme scale ratings, which makes the reliability scores less meaningful. Apparently, children chose the safe, neutral ratings (the center) of the scales, for reasons that we will discuss in the following of this section.

The validity of the questionnaire was studied by a qualitative analysis of the recordings of all respondents that filled out the questionnaire.[3] In total, 2054 items were filled out by the 158 children and 151 of these children uttered a verbal or non-verbal interpretation of at least one of the 13 items from the questionnaire. These 151 children uttered 693 verbal or non-verbal interpretations of the items, which is 33,7% of the total items that were filled out in the experiment. The items from the questionnaire to measure beauty, goodness and fun were left out of this qualitative analysis, because none of the children indicated having problems with the meaning of these items. Of the 693 utterances in total, 224 utterances represented correct interpretations of the items (as intended by Hassenzahl et al., 2003) and 330 utterances represented incorrect interpretations of the items. For example, about the emotional arousal SAM-

Table 2. Cronbach's alphas of the constructs of hedonic and pragmatic quality (using 5-point Likert scales from 1 to 5)

Cluster	Scale	$N_{semantic\ differentials}$	Cronbach's alpha
Hedonic quality	5-point	5	.63
Pragmatic quality	5-point	6	.72
All semantic differentials	5-point	11	.80

scale, many children gave the following incorrect interpretation: "I think this is about how easy or difficult the Website is". Another 84 utterances were verbal indications of incomprehension of the meaning of the items (e.g. "I don't get it.") and 33 utterances were non-verbal indications of incomprehension (e.g. by frowning). While filling out the questionnaire, the test instructor helped the children when they asked for help, as discussed in the Method section. Most help was offered by asking a counter-question, for example: "What do you think the picture stands for?" Although, only a third of the items represent children's interpretations of these items, we think that these interpretations can be related to the entire set of items that were filled out in the experiment. The interpretations of the items will be discussed in the next section.

Interpretations of the SAM-Scales for Emotional Valence and Arousal

Most children (138 of the 158 children) did not utter verbal or non-verbal interpretations of the valence scale (see Figure 6A). Children also did not ask many questions concerning this item. Most interpretations of this item were correct and were related to positive and negative emotional feelings, such as "The Website is kind of fun". Apparently, children understood the meaning of this valence scale with a more or less smiling manikin, which is related to the Smileyometer of the Fun Toolkit (Read et al., 2002). Therefore, we decided that the valence scale was a valid method to measure children's emotional valence towards a Website in our study.

The SAM scale for emotional arousal (see Figure 6B) caused much more problems than the scale for emotional valence. In total, 85 children uttered an incorrect interpretation or an indication of incomprehension concerning this scale and 32 children uttered a correct interpretation. Most conspicuous interpretations of the SAM-scale of arousal were: "I don't get it! Why is his belly

exploding?" (while he points at the picture for highest arousal), or "I haven't got a clue. It looks like a baked egg on his belly, or something like that". Obviously, for most children the meaning of the SAM-scale for arousal was not clear at all and therefore, in our experiment, the arousal scale has proved to be an invalid method to measure children's emotional arousal towards a Website.

Interpretations of the Bipolar Picture Anchors for Pragmatic Quality

The picture anchors for the semantic differential 'technical– human' were most problematic of all pragmatic semantic differential items for the children as can be seen in Table 3. Only one child gave the correct interpretation of the picture anchors. Many children associated the hearts and flowers with hedonic concepts of 'love' and 'fun', while it was intended as a pragmatic concept. Also, making a direct translation of these pictures to working with a Website, was very difficult for the children. The reliability of the pragmatic scale items increased to .72 if this problematic item 'technical– human' was deleted from the list.

Almost half of the interpretations uttered on the picture anchors for the concept 'complicated-simple' were incorrect. Many children (27) asked for help interpreting these pictures, which also stresses the difficulty of these pictures. Some children gave a literal meaning to the pictures, such as 'neat or scratchy lines' and associated this with hedonic concepts. They could not make a translation to the pragmatic concepts of 'simple' and 'complicated'.

The same problem of literal translation of the pictures was the case with the picture anchors for 'impractical– practical'. Children asked what "tripping over a stone has to do with searching on a Website?" The interpretation 'easy– difficult' was often given to these picture anchors.

Although many children seemed to understand the meaning of the picture anchors for clear– confusing, they interpreted the meaning quite literally,

Table 3. Frequency table of uttered interpretations of the pragmatic semantic differential items (N = absolute amount of children that gave the interpretations)

	Technical-Human (N=158)	Complicated – Simple (N=158)	Impractical – Practical (N=158)	Confusing – Clear (N=158)	Cumbersome – Direct (N=158)	Unruly – Manage-Able (N=158)
Incorrect interpretations	38	28	15	17	11	8
Correct interpretations	1	27	20	24	35	34
Verbal indication of incomprehension	18	2	2	2	1	0
Non-verbal indication of incomprehension	8	1	1	3	2	1
No utterances	90	98	118	112	106	118
Missing values	3	2	2	0	3	0

by saying that the main- and submenus offered many options to choose from. However, they did not give their opinion about whether these options were clear or confusing.

Most children gave a correct interpretation of the picture anchors for 'cumbersome– direct'. However, often help was asked from the test instructor and 25 children received help by giving them a counter-question or by explaining the meaning of the picture anchors. Many children gave the correct interpretation "whether you can find it directly or with a detour." However, most of them based their answer on their own performance instead of on the directness or cumbersomeness of the Website.

The pragmatic item that was least problematic for the children was the semantic differential 'unruly – manageable'. Most interpretations given for this item were correct and little help was offered by the test instructor. The reason for this is that a literal translation of the picture anchors can directly be related to a Website, because a Website can look neat or unruly.

Interpretations of the Bipolar Picture Anchors for Perceived Hedonic Quality

The hedonic items were even more problematic than the pragmatic items (see Table 4), because

the interpretations of these concepts were often even more difficult to translate to the use of a Website. The picture anchors 'easy–challenging' were given the most incorrect interpretations by the children, that is 'easy– difficult'. To strictly test the validity of the questionnaire, we decided to score these interpretations as incorrect, because 'easy–difficult' is a pragmatic concept as opposed to the hedonic concept 'easy– challenging'. The reliability of the hedonic scale items increased to .73 if this problematic item 'easy–challenging' was deleted from the list.

The picture anchors for 'cheap– valuable' caused a lot of problems for the children, because first of all, they did not understand the meaning of the paper hat versus the crown. When the test instructor asked: "What do you think is the difference between the two hats?" children gave the interpretation of 'poor versus rich'. However, they did not understand how a Website could be 'poor or rich'.

The children did not understand the picture anchors for 'amateurish– professional' at all. They often thought it was about 'a drilling machine versus a hammer' and they could not relate these concepts to a Website.

The picture anchors for 'presentable– unpresentable' evoked a lot of questions for the test instructor. When children gave the interpreta-

Table 4. Frequency table of uttered interpretations of the hedonic semantic differential items

	Easy – Challenging (N=158)	Cheap – Valuable (N=158)	Amateurish – Professional (N=158)	Unpresentable – Presentable (N=158)	Lame – Exiting (N=158)
Incorrect interpretations	51	34	33	24	8
Correct interpretations	2	6	3	15	15
Verbal indication of incomprehension	7	16	5	2	2
Non-verbal indication of incomprehension	2	4	3	3	2
No utterances	95	97	113	113	127
Missing values	1	1	1	1	4

tion of an 'old or new present', or maybe even a 'beautiful or ugly present', they could not relate this 'present' to the Website.

Finally, also the picture anchors for 'lame–exciting' were problematic for the children. Again, the children had trouble understanding the meaning of the two types of 'cycling' to 'lame and exciting.' When the test instructor gave help with this first step, most of the time the children gave their opinion about whether searching for information is lame or exciting and not whether the Website was lame or exciting.

Distinction between Perceptions of Pragmatic and Hedonic Quality

We also measured the reliability of all semantic differentials together and it turned out that Cronbach's alpha for all semantic differentials is .80 (see Table 2). It seems that the children perceived all items as the same construct, for example as the construct 'good or bad'. One child said: "It's all a bit the same to me" and often children asked for confirmation: "So this means good and this means bad, right?" In other words, the children did not make a distinction between hedonic and pragmatic constructs or between fun and usability.

And although children did not indicate having problems with the report marks for beauty, goodness and fun, it can be expected that these concepts were evaluated as the same construct. This was also reported by Read et al. (2002) concerning the Fun-Sorter in which children needed to sort products by concepts as 'worked the best', 'liked the most', 'most fun' and 'easiest to use'. They say: "This was quite difficult for the children with the result that some constructs turned out to be quite similar."

Conclusion Validity Questionnaire Items

From the qualitative analysis of children's interpretations of the questionnaire items, we can conclude that, although the construct reliability of the questionnaire items is high, the questionnaire is not a valid method to measure children's perceptions of pragmatic and hedonic quality. The content validity cannot be guaranteed, because often children gave another explanation to the items than was intended by the designers of the questionnaire. Also, construct validity cannot be guaranteed, because items that should measure pragmatic quality, were associated with hedonic quality and vice versa. Besides that, it seems that children do not make a distinction between pragmatic and hedonic constructs at all. Also the SAM-scale for arousal has not proven to be a valid method to measure emotional arousal with children.

The most important problem that children experience with the questionnaire is that they have to interpret the picture anchors and to relate its meaning to using a Website. Because children tend to take the picture anchors very literally, translating them to a more abstract concept is very difficult for them. The cognitive load of this task on children's working memory is too heavy for children to cope with. Furthermore, children tend to relate the picture anchors to their own performance or preferences instead of to the Website under evaluation. Finally, satisficing is a relevant problem in our experiment. Children are prone to satisficing as they find survey participation difficult (Markopoulos et al., 2008), as was the case in our study. From the recordings, we saw that children tend to ask questions about the first four or five items in the questionnaire, but after that fill out the questionnaire very quickly. It is clear that the children gave more or less superficial responses that generally appear acceptable, but without going through all the steps involved in the question-answer process.

Based on the validity analyses of the affective survey question, unfortunately, we can only work with a few items for further qualitative analysis of the affective data. We will work with the results from the SAM-scale for emotional valence, with the semantic differential scale for unruly-manageable and with the report marks for the product evaluations beauty, goodness and fun.

Effects of Interface Design and Used Search Strategy

We will first report the pragmatic effects on children's search performance of differences in interface design (i.e. Classic, Classical Play and Image map) and the used search strategy (i.e. keyword searching or browsing). After that, we will report the effects on children's emotional feelings, perceptions of hedonic quality and product evaluations of interface design and the used search strategy.

What are the Effects on Task Performance of Playful Interface Design and Use of the Search Engine?

To establish whether there is a difference between task performance on the three different versions of the Website and between use and non-use of the search engine, the mean percentages for success were compared (see Table 5). Non-use of the search engine occurred in two situations; 1) when the search engine was not offered, children logically could not use the search engine and 2) when the search engine was offered, some children

Table 5. Percentages of success (logits between brackets) in using the different versions of the Website for use and non-use of the search engine and for help provided yes (grey colored) or no

Website Version	Search Engine Used		Search Engine not Provided		Search Engine Provided, but not Used	
	No Help	Help	No Help	Help	No Help	Help
Classic	.82 (1.53)	.83 (1.61)	.63 (.52)	.68 (.75)	.57 (.30)	.67 (.69)
Classical play	.84 (1.62)	.63 (.51)*	.63 (.54)	.58 (.32)	.49 (-.03)	.56 (.22)
Image map	.92 (2.42)	.76 (1.18)*	.52 (.10)	.25 (-1.10)	.61 (.44)	.54 (.17)

Note. In all cases, a higher mean score represents a higher percentage for success in finding the right information for the search task. The answers for the binomial success-score (1= successful, 0= unsuccessful) are given in Logits that are used for the data analysis (between brackets).

* There is a significant effect of provided help on the mean percentage of success. The percentage of success in finding the right information was significantly lower for the children that used the search engine and received help from the test instructor for both the Classical play Website and the Image map Website (t ≥.2.01; p ≤.04).

did not use it to search for information. We also compared the mean percentages of finding the right answer when help was offered and when no help was offered by the test instructor and we found significant effects of provided help (see * in Table 5). The following data analyses for the mean percentages for success are therefore corrected for help (mean percentages for help are grey colored in Tables 5, 6 & 7).

No main effect on task performance was observed for the design type of the Websites: there is no significant difference for the percentage of success in finding the right information between the three Website versions ($\chi^2 = 1.02$; df = 2; p = 0.31). However, a main effect was found for the

use of the search engine ($\chi^2 = 43.19$; df = 2; p <.001): the percentage of success was much larger when the search engine was used than when the search engine was not offered ($\chi^2 = 27.33$; df = 1; p <.001) and when the search engine was not used ($\chi^2 = 40.63$; df = 1; p <.001). There is no significant difference between the percentage of success when the search engine was not offered and when the search engine was not used ($\chi^2 = 0.41$; df = 1; p =.52). No interaction-effect was found for the use of the search engine and the three Website versions ($\chi^2 \leq 3.04$; df = 2; p $\geq$ 0.080). In other words, the differences between use and non-use of the search engine for success are the same for the three Website versions.

Table 6. Mean time needed in seconds (ln between brackets) using the different versions of the Website, for use and non-use of the search engine and for help provided yes (grey colored) or no

Website Version	Search Engine Used		Search Engine not Provided		Search Engine Provided, but not Used	
	No help	Help	No help	Help	No help	Help
Classic	139.9 (4.94)	247.4 (5.51)*	168.3 (5.13)	264.4 (5.58)*	157.9 (5.06)	300.1 (5.70)*
Classical play	149.7 (5.01)	257.0 (5.55)*	141.6 (4.95)	283.9 (5.65)*	142.7 (4.96)	221.2 (5.40)*
Image map	112.8 (4.73)	236.0 (5.46)*	170.4 (5.14)	164.1 (5.10)	148.5 (5.00)	279.7 (5.63)*

Note. The distribution of the raw data for time was not comparable to the normal distribution. Therefore, we took the natural log of the search times that did show a normal distribution.

* There is a significant effect of provided help on the mean amount of time needed. The amount of time needed to conduct the tasks was significantly higher for children that received help from the test instructor (t $\geq$ 3.73; p $\leq$.001).

Table 7. Mean number of clicks (ln between brackets) using the different versions of the Website, for use and non-use of the search engine and for help provided yes (grey colored) or no

Website Version	Search Engine Used		Search Engine not Provided		Search Engine Provided, but not Used	
	No Help	Help	No Help	Help	No Help	Help
Classic	4.2 (1.44)	7.4 (2.00)*	9.8 (2.29)	17.0 (2.83)*	7.7 (2.04)	17.6 (2.87)*
Classical play	4.7 (1.55)	8.1 (2.09)*	7.7 (2.04)	14.9 (2.70)*	7.9 (2.07)	8.5 (2.14)*
Image map	3.3 (1.20)	7.2 (1.97)*	9.0 (2.20)	8.3 (2.12)	6.3 (1.85)	14.4 (2.67)*

Note. The distribution of the raw data for number of clicks was not comparable to the normal distribution. Therefore, we took the natural log of the number of clicks that did show a normal distribution.

* There is a significant effect of provided help on the mean number of clicks. The number of clicks needed to conduct the tasks was significantly higher for children that received help from the test instructor (t $\geq$ 2.85; p $\leq$.004).

What are the Effects of Playful Interface Design and Use of the Search Engine on Time and Clicks Needed to Conduct the Tasks?

We also compared the mean amount of time and clicks children needed to conduct the tasks between the three Website versions and between the use and non-use of the search engine (see Table 6 and 7). Because we also found significant effects of the provided help for these factors (see * in Table 6 and 7), we corrected the data for provided help.

No main effect was observed for the design of the Website versions: there is no significant difference in time needed to conduct the tasks between the three Website versions ($\chi^2 = 2.00$; df $= 2$; p $= 0.37$). However, a main effect was found for the use of the search engine ($\chi^2 = 8.10$; df $= 2$; p $=.017$): less time was needed when the search engine was used than when the search engine was not offered ($\chi^2 = 6.88$; df $= 1$; p $=.009$) and when the search engine was not used ($\chi^2 = 4.27$; df $= 1$; p $<.039$). There is no significant difference between the time needed when the search engine was not offered and when the search engine was not used ($\chi^2 = 0.88$; df $= 1$; p $=.35$).

No interaction-effect was found for the use of the search engine and the three Website versions ($\chi^2 \leq 2.97$; df $= 1$; p ≥ 0.16). In other words, the differences between use and non-use of the search engine for the time needed to conduct the search tasks are the same for the three Website versions.

No main effect on clicks was observed for the design of the Website versions: there is no significant difference in the number of clicks between the three Website versions ($\chi^2 = 4.08$; df $= 2$; p $= 0.13$). However, a main effect was found for the use of the search engine ($\chi^2 = 257.56$; df $= 2$; p $<.001$): the number of clicks needed when the search engine was used was lower than when the search engine was not offered ($\chi^2 = 80.27$; df $= 1$; p $<.001$) and when the search engine was not used ($\chi^2 = 66.52$; df $= 1$; p $<.001$). The number of clicks is also significantly higher when

the search engine was not offered than when the search engine was not used ($\chi^2 = 212.78$; df $= 1$; p $<.001$). A reason for this could be that children in the condition without a search engine were normally used to working with a search engine and therefore, were less experienced and needed more clicks to find the information using the navigation structure.

No interaction-effect was found for the use of the search engine and the three Website versions ($\chi^2 \leq 3.77$; df $= 1$; p $= 0.052$). In other words, the differences between use and non-use of the search engine for the clicks needed to conduct the search tasks are the same for the three Website versions.

In conclusion, children that used the search engine instead of browsing the categories, were more successful in finding the right information and they needed less time and clicks. There were no significant differences for task performance (i.e. success, time and clicks) between the three Website versions. Apparently, interface design of the search environments is less determinant for task performance than the search strategy (i.e. searching or browsing). The differences that we found between the conditions (independently of the used search method; searching or browsing) cannot be assigned to our manipulations of the interface design. These differences should be assigned to the differences between the children that participated in our experiment. In other words, differences in child characteristics, such as their information skills, domain knowledge, operational skills, etcetera, cause more variance in children's search performance than variation in interface design.

What is the Effect of Interface Design on Emotional Valence and on the Evaluation of Beauty, Goodness, and Fun

To test whether there is an effect of design on children's affective responses, we computed both between groups and within groups analyses of variance. In that way, we took into account the "effect variation" and the "individual variation". Individual variation is the variation within condition differences called "error", because we cannot explain the fact that children who were in the same two conditions - who were all treated the same two ways – have different scores. In this way, we also took into account the "subject variation", which is the variation due to subject variability. For these tests on children's affective responses, we could only use a limited set of variables that proved to be valid (see Table 8).

There were significant differences for children's emotional valence and their evaluation of goodness between the three Website versions. The children judged their feeling with the Classical play Website as more positive than with the other two Websites ($F_{2,155}$ = 3.28; p =.040). Still, all scores are between 4 and 5 on a scale from 1 to 5, so the children are very positive about their feelings with all three types of Websites.

The children evaluated the Image map Website as least good ($F_{2,155}$ = 3.45; p =.034) of the three Websites. We do not use the word 'worst', because with the 'least good' Image map Website, the children evaluated the goodness of the Image map Websites with an 8.2 on a scale from 1 to 10, which is still a very high score (see Table 8). There were no significant differences between the children's perceptions of hedonic quality (i.e.

unruly-manageable) and between their evaluations of fun and beauty of the three Websites.

What is the Effect of Playful Interface Design on Physiological Measurements of Emotional Arousal

We also used a more objective method to measure children's feelings towards the three Website types by measuring electrodermal activity (EDA). From the EDA-data, we computed the number of Electrodermal Responses (EDR) per minute and the total amplitude of the EDR per minute for the period of watching the film and the period of the actual task performance on the experimental Website. Watching the film served as a benchmark, because this was the same over all three conditions. To measure whether there is a difference in EDA between conditions, we computed the difference in number of EDR per minute between the task performance and watching the film for the three conditions. Unfortunately, the EDR data (both number of EDR per minute during the task performance and while watching the film, and the difference between these two variables) were not normally distributed. Therefore, we could not use a parametric test to compute the difference in EDA between conditions and we were constrained to using a non-parametric test.

Table 8. Mean scores for emotional valence (5-point scale), the semantic differential 'unruly-manageable' (5-point scale) and the product evaluations for beauty, goodness and fun (report mark from 1-10) for the different versions of the Website (SD between brackets)

Website Version	Valence	Unruly-Manageable	Goodness	Fun	Beauty
Classic (N = 51)	4.12 (.77)	4.25 (.95)	8.66 (1.31)	8.29 (1.56)	8.37 (1.42)
Classical play (N = 52)	4.38 (.66)*	4.10 (.79)	8.71 (.84)	8.50 (1.19)	8.86 (1.05)
Image map (N = 55)	4.05 (.68)	3.90 (.91)	8.22 (1.04)*	8.13 (1.10)	8.42 (1.03)

* There is a significant effect of the type of design on the affective responses.

First of all, we did not measure any EDA during the actual task performance with 47 children. We did not measure any EDA with 64 children while they watched the film. Apparently, for many children, this type of scholarly tasks on a computer did not activate any electrodermal activity at all. Second, using a Wilcoxon signed rank test, there was no significant difference in EDA between task performance and watching the film.

According to an independent samples Kruskal-Wallis test, there was no significant difference in EDA between the three conditions. There was, however, a significant order-effect in our study. According to an independent samples Kruskal-Wallis test, there was a significant difference in EDA between children that watched the film before or after performing the actual search tasks. Children that watched the film after the search task performance showed a higher number of EDR per minute during the task performance than children that watched the film before the search task performance. A regular univariate analysis of variance also showed no significant differences in EDA between the three conditions and it also did show a significant order-effect of watching the film before or after the search tasks $(F(1,135)=23,03,\ p <.05)$. Apparently, children were less aroused by the use of the search interface when they first saw the film, than when they saw the film afterwards.

What is the Effect of Playful Interface Design on Verbal Emotional Utterances?

Of the children that used the Image map Website, 25 video recordings were studied to collect the verbal emotional utterances about the pragmatic and hedonic quality of the Website. In total, 58 utterances were made. Of these utterances, 55 were related to pragmatic quality and 3 utterances were related to hedonic quality of the Image map Website (see Table 9).

As can be seen in Table 9, most verbal utterances were negative. These utterances were mostly related to the difficulty and inaccessibility of the Website for finding relevant information, such as "I can't find it at all" or "I find it difficult to search on". There are only a few positive utterances, such as "This is not really difficult or anything" and "I found it quite fast". Verbal hedonic utterances are very rare and are more related to pictures on the Website than to the design of the Website itself, such as a child that says: "What an ugly man" (about Columbus). Apparently, children tend to say more about their search activities than about the design of the Website and verbal utterances are almost exclusively related to their perception of the Websites' pragmatic quality.

Relation between Factors

What is the Relation between Children's Performance on the Websites and their Attitude Towards these Websites?

To answer this question, we tested the difference for children's affective responses between tasks that were completed successfully and tasks that were not completed successfully. There was a significant difference between the successful and unsuccessful tasks for children's ratings of emotional valence $(F = 5.07;\ df = 1;\ p =.025)$. Children expressed more positive feelings for tasks conducted on all three Website versions when the tasks were completed successfully than when the tasks were completed unsuccessfully (see Figure

Table 9. Number of positive and negative verbal utterances related to pragmatic and hedonic quality of the Image map Website

Quality	Number of Utterances	
	Positive	**Negative**
Pragmatic	7 (12,1%)	48 (82,8%)
Hedonic	0 (0%)	3 (5,2%)

9). There was no significant interaction-effect between the Website version and whether the tasks were completed successfully or not for the ratings of emotional valence. Furthermore, there were no significant differences for children's product evaluations (beauty, goodness and fun) between tasks that were completed successfully and tasks that were not completed successfully.

Further Diagnosis of Children's Search Behavior

Searching versus Browsing in our Experiment

It is not clear from previous research results whether children in general use more searching or browsing strategies. However, most of the results suggest that children prefer to use search engines, but that they are more successful with browsing categories. Even recently, Meloncon et al. (2010) recommended not to include a search engine on a children's Website, because children have not yet fully developed the intellectual ability necessary to generate relevant search terms (Druin et al., 2009). In addition, giving children the option to search would undermine the process of having them read through the information and explore the Website (Meloncon et al., 2010). In other words, the search engine is seen as a distraction on a children's Website.

In our data, searching with the search engine scores better than browsing the main categories for almost all components of UX that we have

Figure 9. Estimated marginal means of valence (0 = negative feeling; 5 = positive feeling) plotted for the three Website versions with successful and unsuccessful tasks presented on separate lines

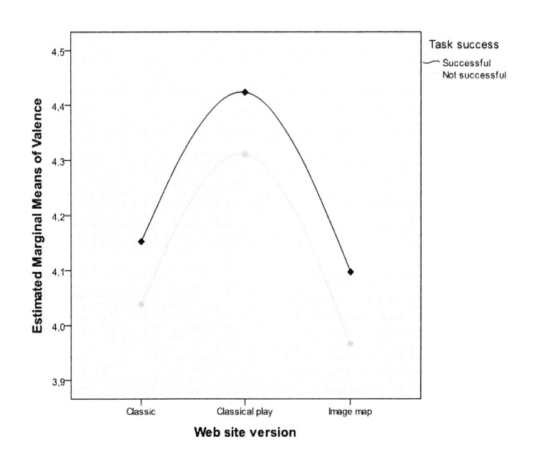

measured. Children were more successful in finding the right content page when they had used the search engine. They also needed significantly less time and clicks to find the information when they had used the search engine than when they had browsed the main categories.

These results are in contrast to results from previous studies on children's search behavior (Borgman et al., 1995; Schacter et al., 1998; Bilal, 2000). This difference might be caused by a better functioning search engine in our study, although we think that is hard to believe, because the search engine in our study did not work as well as Google, for example. The search engine in our study did not provide query suggestions or spelling corrections while typing a search query. Also, most natural language queries could not be processed by the search engine.

The main reason for the results in our study in comparison to previous research, is most likely caused by children's increased experience and skills in using a search engine with respect to a few years ago. Children now are members of the "Google generation" (Rowlands, 2008) and more familiar with the use of search engines. In the Netherlands, almost 80% of children ages 8-12 in 2008 used the Google search engine to find information on the Internet (Pijpers et al., 2008).

In our experiment, initially 115 children were offered a Website version with a search engine and 43 children without a search engine (see Table 10). This inequality was caused by the fact that many children that were offered a search engine, did not use the search engine at all. We offered children a version with a search engine as much as was necessary, to reach an equal amount of children that used the search engine and children that browsed the main categories. In our research, we found it very important to compare searching with a search engine with browsing the main categories.

Therefore, we aimed at an equal distribution of children that did and did not use the search engine. We kept offering a Website version with a search engine until the distribution between use and non-use of the search engine was equal over the three Website versions (see Table 10). In total, 77 of the 115 children that were offered a search engine (67%), used the search engine for at least one of the five search tasks. The children that used a search engine, did not automatically use the search engine for all five tasks. Therefore, the percentage of search engine use per task that was conducted on a Website version with a search engine is lower. In total, 294 tasks were conducted by using a search engine, which is 51% of all tasks that were conducted on a Website version with a search engine.

As can be seen in Table 10, the search engine on the Image map was the least inviting to use for the children, because 25 of the 50 children that were offered a search engine on the Image map Website, did not use it at all. The non-conventional visual design of the Image map version might have distracted the children's attention from the search engine as can be seen in Figure 3.

Another explanation for the low percentage of search engine use when a search engine was offered, can be children's infrequent use of search engines. We asked children how much time they spend using the Internet and most children used

Table 10. Number of children that were offered a search engine and number of children that used the search engine

Website Version (N=158)	Presence of the Search Engine		Use of the Search Engine	
Classic version	Present:	32	Used:	26
	Not present:	19	Not used:	6
Classical play version	Present:	33	Used:	26
	Not present:	19	Not used:	7
Image map version	Present:	50	Used:	25
	Not present:	5	Not used:	25

the internet less than one hour on both week days and weekend days. When we asked what type of activities they conducted on the Internet, than the activities can be ranked from most to least frequently conducted by most children as following:

1. Hyves (a Dutch social network).
2. Playing games.
3. Listening to music/watching video clips.
4. Watching you tube movies.
5. Searching information for myself.
6. Searching information for school work.

Internet activities for which a search engine is required (by searching information for themselves or for school work) are conducted least frequently according to children's self-reports. The children probably do not use a search engine for the Internet activities that are conducted most frequently, such as using Hyves or playing games. The fact that children do not use search engines frequently is a plausible cause of the fact that many children did not use a search engine in our study, even though a search engine was provided in many of these cases.

Search Engine Strategies

In this section, we will analyze children's strategies and skills using a search engine. What makes keyword searching in our experiment successful? Do children experience the same problems or not with key word searching as reported in previous research? We will describe whether children are able to formulate a query and to select a search result that is coherent with the search task. For this qualitative study of submitted queries and selected search results, we have analyzed the submitted queries of the children that used the search engine on two of the three Website types: the Classical play Website (26 children) and the Image map Website (25 children).

For the qualitative data analysis of search engine use, we analyzed 190 search tasks conducted

with the search engine[4]. These 190 search tasks existed of 322 search attempts to formulate a query. Most search tasks (N = 117) existed of one query attempt, but some children required more attempts to formulate a search query within one search tasks (40 * 2 attempts, 20 * 3 attempts, 7 * 4 attempts, 3 * 5 attempts, 2 * 6 attempts and 1 * 10 attempts).

Quality of Query Attempts: Most queries existed of one word (117 query attempts) or more than one word (165 query attempts) and 40 queries existed of a whole sentence. Natural language querying is not as frequently applied by the children in our study as reported in previous studies (Marchionini, 1989; Druin, et al., 2009).

Most query attempts did not require any help with query formulation or spelling help from the test instructor (87% of all query attempts). The children had less problems with query formulation and spelling than expected from the literature (Borgman et al., 1995; Hutchinson, 2005). This was also shown by the fact that 79,5% of the query attempts were spelled correctly. An important reason was that the children in our study received the search tasks written on a task sheet, so they could use the correct spelling of words from the written task sheet. However, still spelling mistakes were made, although children could read the correct spelling from the task sheets.

Correct spelling does not automatically lead to finding the right content page, because almost half of the correctly spelled queries (44,5%) did not lead to a successful search result. Of course, the success of a search query also depends on the relevancy of the search query and the quality of the search engine.

A way to evaluate the quality of the search queries is to compute their latent semantic analysis (LSA) scores in comparison to the search task, following the example of Kitajima, Blackmon, and Polson (2000) that used LSA to simulate Web navigation. LSA is a technique in natural language processing, in particular in vectorial semantics, of analyzing semantic coherence between a set of documents and the terms they contain by producing a set of concepts related to the documents and terms. LSA assumes that words that are close in meaning will occur in similar pieces of text. Values close to 1 represent high semantic coherence while values close to 0 represent low semantic coherence. For the calculation of LSA-scores, spelling mistakes were corrected. We did not find an effect of high LSA-scores on task success. The mean LSA-score of the successful search queries was .26 and the mean LSA-score of the unsuccessful search queries was .24. LSA-scores do not predict the quality of search queries in our study very well. We will illustrate this with the task about Columbus (see Table 11). The query 'Columbus' had the highest LSA-score, but did not lead to success, because the answer to the search task was not mentioned on the content page about Christophorus Columbus, but on the content pages about 'Discoveries' or about 'Vikings'.

Quality of Search Results' Selection: When we look at the behavior of the children in selecting search results, we first of all see that most children tended to directly choose the first search result from the list. From the search attempts in which children actually selected a search result (N=216), 110 selected search results were the first result from the results list. Further, almost all selected search results (211) were selected from the first 10 results that were presented in the results list. This tendency to select the first search result or a search result from the first 10 search results presented was also reported in previous studies (Bilal, 2000; Druin et al., 2009).

The children were not inclined to select more than one search result from the search results that were presented for one search query. Most children only selected one search result (86% of the search attempts). Two search results were selected within 11% of the search attempts and more than two search results were selected within 3% of the search attempts.

Of all analyzed search tasks that were conducted with the search engine (N=190), 83% (after one or more unsuccessful search attempts) were successful and led to the right content page. Within 96% of the selected search results no help was provided by the test instructor. From our analysis it is not entirely clear what the main reason is for the unsuccessful search tasks. A possible explanation is the fact that often children chose high scent incorrect links. However, our research was not concerned with the quality of the search engine and therefore we did not further analyze the relevancy of the provided search results by the search engine.

Navigation and Browsing Categories

In this section, we will analyze children's navigation behavior. What makes browsing successful or unsuccessful? Do children experience the same problems or not with browsing as reported in previous research? For this qualitative study of selected main and subcategories and content pages, the navigation paths for the five search tasks of 46 children were analyzed that were either successful or unsuccessful in completing the

Table 11. LSA scores of the most frequently entered search queries for the search task about Columbus

Search Task	Frequent Search Queries (N)	LSA-Score	Successful?
"It is often said that Christopher Columbus discovered America. Some say that this is not true. They say that another nation discovered America 500 years before Columbus did. *Can you find out what people discovered America before Columbus did at Junior Winkler Prins online?"*	- America (19) - Discovery America (17) - Columbus (10) - Christopher Columbus (7) - Vikings (3)	0.27 0.27 0.30 0.33 0.13	No Yes No No Yes

search tasks by browsing the categories[5]. We will describe problems with the layout of the Websites, problems with the information structure of the Websites and operational navigation problems. The problems presented are not an exhaustive list of all problems, but give an illustration of the most important navigation problems.

Problems with the Location of the Search Box: The most important problem in our view with the layout of the Websites, and particularly with the Image map Website, is the location of the search box. Many children did not use the search engine when it was provided. We do not know for sure if these children were not familiar with using a search engine or whether they did not notice the search box at all. The unconventional layout of the Image map Website and the unconventional location of the search box in the top left corner may have caused the search engine to have been unnoticed by many children (see Figure 10). In a

corpus study of children's informational Websites Jochmann-Mannak et al. (2012) reported that 43% of the Websites with a search engine, presented the search engine in the top right corner of the page and 24% presented the search box in the top center of the page. Therefore, the top left corner is a non-conventional location for children's informational Websites. However, on the other two versions, the search box was also placed on the top left side, but on these two versions more children used the search engine when offered than on the Image map version.

Problems with the Layout: Most problems with the layout were experienced with the Image map Website, most likely because of the unconventional interface design. When parsing the homepage, children directly focused on a particular part (mostly on the main menu) of the Classic Website and the Classical play Website. This was in contrast to children's parsing behav-

Figure 10. The unconventional location of the search box and the main category links as images at the Image map Website

ior on the Image map. Most children parsed the entire homepage of the Image map and all main category links were looked at extensively. This was caused by the fact that the main menu covers the entire homepage of the Image map. There were many problems with the main category links on the Image map Website, because children had to 'mine sweep' the images to see the verbal link labels. However, many children did not directly recognize the main category links as such and did not notice their click ability, as can be seen in Figure 10.

Problems with the Information Structure: Problems with selecting the right main and sub categories occurred at all three type of Websites, but mostly at the Classic and the Image map Website. Especially choosing the right main category was problematic for many children, as was also reported by Hutchinson et al. (2006). Often, children had wrong expectations of the content behind main category links. For example, the main category link label 'human' was often selected for tasks about the first astronaut or about Columbus, because humans were mentioned in the task description.

However, in fact the main category 'human' was about the human body.

Children did benefit from the addition of images with the main and subcategory link labels at the Classical play Website in comparison to the Classic Website (see Figures 11 and 12). The images helped children to choose the right main and sub categories and the children used more trial-and-error in choosing the right categories at the Classic Website.

The addition of images at the Image map Website often had an opposite effect on children's navigation behavior, because the images without the verbal link labels often did not speak for themselves (see Figure 10). In other words, addition of images to the category labels helps children in navigation, but corresponding text labels with the images are essential for quick understanding of the link labels.

Operational Navigation Problems: Children needed more assistance in operating the navigation tools on the Image map than on the other Website versions. The sub category link labels on the Image map appeared in a pop up layer across

Figure 11. The main and subcategory labels without addition of images at the Classic Website

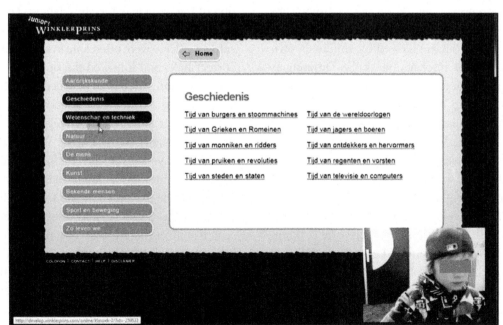

Figure 12. The main and subcategory labels with addition of images at the Classical play Website

the homepage and often children did not know how to get out of this pop up layer (see Figure 13). There were no navigation tools provided to go back to the homepage, as was the case at the other two Website versions. Children had to find out for themselves that they had to click somewhere on the screen next to the popup layer to make the popup layer disappear.

Children's Navigation Skills: Many problems that children experienced on the Websites cannot be attributed to the design characteristics of the Websites, but are caused by children's own navigation and information skills. Differences between children's navigation and information skills are more determinant for differences in search performance than differences between Web design characteristics. We will illustrate this by describing differences between search behavior of children that were successful and unsuccessful in finding the right information on the Websites.

Where successful children showed a clear pattern in link selection, less successful children lacked such a clear pattern. Less successful children especially had problems with the interpretation of the main category link labels. They often selected high scent incorrect links and they almost

never selected low scent correct links. They often lacked domain knowledge to select a relevant category link or did not keep the initial search task in mind. Also, less successful children often did not recognize when they selected the wrong main category link and got lost in the Website's menu structure.

Successful children did keep the initial search task in mind and had less problems with interpretation of the main category link labels. They were well aware when they had selected a wrong main category. They were often able to select low scent correct links and followed the optimum navigation path more often than unsuccessful children.

Browsing Strategies: Successful children used both a trial-and-error strategy and a 'think-than-act' strategy on the Classic Website. On the Classical play Website, successful children only used one strategy: the 'think-than-act' strategy. This might be explained by the fact that the link labels on the Classical play Website were presented with a picture that visually represented the textual link label, allowing children to make a better interpretation of the meaning of the link labels. This made the 'trial-and-error' strategy less necessary.

Figure 13. The sub category link labels at the Image map Website appear in a popup layer across the homepage

Less successful children exclusively used a trial-and-error strategy to find information on all three Website versions. They often only used one strategy and had no plan B, when plan A did not lead them to the right content page. They had trouble keeping the search task in mind and often applied a 'loopy' navigation style, which means that they selected the same incorrect main and sub category links again and again. This looping navigation behavior was also reported by Bilal (2000).

Another problem that occurred with some children while using the Image map Website was that they were hesitant to click on the main and sub category links. The playful lay out of the Image map Website made them insecure to click on the links.

Processing the Content Page: Successful children often asked for assistance in understanding the content. Less successful children did not ask for help, but just gave a wrong answer. Reasons for giving wrong answers were because of a wrong interpretation of the text, not recognizing internal hyperlinks to a relevant content page, because of

low literacy skills, scanning the text too quickly or by not keeping the initial search task in mind. Successful children mostly had the capacity to reflect on the initial search task and made sure that they kept the search task in mind.

Processing Problems: It was noted that children experienced more problems on all areas of navigation on the Image map than on the other Website versions. Children even had trouble understanding the search tasks correctly when using the Image map Website, which did not occur with the other Website versions. This might be explained by the 'cognitive load theory' (Sweller, Merrienboer & Paas, 1998). Processing the Image map Website might have taken that much cognitive energy from the children, that there was too little cognitive energy left to interpret the search task.

Game-Experience: Finally, we found some clues that game-experience influences children's navigation behavior. Children with little game-experience (mostly girls according to the results of the profile survey) often think first before they act. Children with much game-experience (mostly boys) use the trial-and-error search strategy. This trail-and-error strategy is provoked when children do not know exactly where to go, which is often the case on the Image map Website. Therefore, the use of the Image map seems more suited for children with a lot of game-experience.

CONCLUSION AND DISCUSSION

Validation of the Used Methods

In this section we will answer our research questions. The first question is about the suitability of existing methods for research with children to measure feelings and perceptions of pragmatic and hedonic quality that are used in research with adults. We experienced that methods such as the SAM-scale for emotional arousal and the AttracDiff 2 questionnaire are not valid methods in research with children. Unlike Greenbaum et al. (1990), we could not validate the use of the SAM-scale for emotional arousal with children. These opposite results might be caused by the different settings in which the method was used. The pictures in the SAM-scale for emotional arousal might be related easier to 'fear for the dentist' by children (which was the case in the research of Greenbaum et al., 1990) than the feeling experienced with using a Website. We could, however, validate the SAM-scale for emotional valence with children.

Almost all picture anchors for the semantic differential scales for the pragmatic and hedonic items could not be validated for use with children in our experiment (which we did not expect based on our pilot test of the semantic differential scales with 14 children). The children in the experiment did not interpret the picture anchors as intended by the developers of the AttracDiff 2 questionnaire (Hassenzahl et al., 2003). The children only made a clear distinction between what end of the scale was intended as positive and what end of the scale as negative in their opinion. The children were not able to make a distinction between perceptions of

hedonic and pragmatic quality of the Websites. The pragmatic and hedonic items were all seen as the same construct of valence (i.e. positive versus negative).

Although we did find differences in scores for the product evaluations beauty, goodness and fun, we doubt whether children were able to make a clear distinction between these concepts, as was also reported by Read et al. (2002). Fortunately, we were able to use an objective method to measure emotional arousal by using the Q-Sensor. This method turned out to be valid to measure emotional arousal with children in contrast to the subjective methods used in our experiment.

Based on this experiment, we cannot judge whether the UX models presented in research with adults (Hassenzahl, 2004; Thüring & Mahlke, 2007; van Schaik & Ling, 2008) can also be applied to children's UX. Although we could not entirely reproduce UX research concerning perceptions of pragmatic and hedonic quality in our experiment, we did show the difficulty of reproducing UX research with children. More research is needed to develop valid methods to measure children's perceptions of pragmatic and hedonic quality.

Effects of Different Design Types

We did not find any effects on children's search performance on informational Websites of the different design types. The variation in design of the Websites did not have an effect on search success and efficiency. As opposed to the performance scores, there were differences in the subjective scores measured. Children were most positive about the Classical play Website according to their scores on the SAM-scales for valence. This positive score is most likely not based on pragmatic issues, because both children that were successful and unsuccessful in finding the right information on the Classical play Website, gave this Website higher scores than the other two Website versions. Apparently, their feelings about the Website is based on more hedonic issues, such as whether they are attracted to the interface design of the Website. Surprisingly, we saw the same pattern for children's evaluations of goodness: both successful and unsuccessful children evaluated the Image map version as less good than the other two Website versions. There were no significant differences between children that were successful and children that were unsuccessful in finding the right information. Apparently, search success was not determinant for children's evaluation of goodness.

The Relation between Performance and Attitude

We did not find evidence for a strong relation between affectivity and usability in our study. Children's affective responses are not based on the effectiveness of search performance on the Websites. However, their affective responses could be based on pragmatic issues besides the final success in finding the information. For instance, their affective responses could be based on the ease of use while interacting with the interface, as was reported by Sim et al. (2006) who found that children appeared to have less fun when their interactions had more usability problems. However, in our study children's affective responses towards the search systems seem to be independent from their actual search behavior and most likely based on perceived hedonic quality and aesthetics of the interface. This could be best tested by a pre- and post measure of affective responses, to see whether actual behavior changes children's attitude towards product evaluations such as beauty, goodness and fun (van Schaik & Ling, 2008). Because of time constraints it was not feasible in our experiment to conduct both pre- and post tests to measure affective responses.

We did find some prove that the children's affective responses were based on the ease of use while interacting with the interface (i.e. pragmatic quality). An analysis of verbal utterances of 25 children that used the Image map Website, showed that most of the utterances were negative and related to the Websites' low pragmatic quality. This result supports the fact that the children's valence scores and evaluation scores for goodness were lowest for the Image map Website and that these scores are based on perception of pragmatic quality. The fact that almost no hedonic utterances were made, supports the fact that playfulness and expressive aesthetics do not have a large influence on children's attitude towards and evaluation of the Website.

The fact that we did not find a relation between beauty and usability in our experiment can also be caused by children's tendency to indicate the highest score on the scale (Markopoulos et al., 2008). Most children felt very positive about the three Websites and little frustration was uttered. Therefore, we did not find evidence that pragmatic frustrations lower children's perception of aesthetics as Tuch et al. (2012) found in their research with adults. This is most likely also caused by children's tendency to give socially desirable answers. Although they were often not successful at all in conducting a search task, children found it difficult to be negative about the system and tended to blame themselves instead of the system. This was also reported by Serenko (2007), who studied the self-serving biases of interface agent users. He found that adult users may attribute their success to an interface agent and hold themselves responsible for task failure, just like the children may have done in our experiment.

Interaction with the Chosen Search Strategy

From this experiment we can conclude that the search strategy that is used by children is much more determinant for their search performance than the interface design of the search environment. Searching with a search engine proved to be much more effective and efficient than browsing the navigation structure. This was the case for all three types of Websites in our experiment.

We found that there was a significant difference in success scores when children received help from the test instructor. However, this difference meant that children were less successful. In other words, children did not become successful because of the help they received. These findings prove that help was only offered to motivate and reassure children during the search process (as recommended by Markopoulos et al., 2008) and offered help did not have a significant effect on children's success in finding the right information.

It turned out that searching with the search engine is more effective and efficient than browsing the categories. This is quite logical when considering the fact that children nowadays are member of the 'Google-generation' (Rowlands, 2008). However, we did not look at the long-term effects of the fact that children prefer and are better in searching than in browsing. Searching instead of browsing might, for example, have a negative effect on children's knowledge of information taxonomies. The search engine can be compared to a 'black box' that does not give insight in how information is related in a taxonomy. Future research is needed to study long-term effects on children's knowledge of information architectures of searching with a search engine in comparison to browsing categories.

Search- and navigation behavior on the Web is constantly changing. Currently, traditional search engines as Google are loosing 'traffic', because people more and more use social media such as Facebook and Twitter as their primary Web entrance to find information (Xiang and Gretzel, 2010). This might also cause changes in children's search and navigation behavior.

Children's Navigation and Information Skills

When studying children's search performance in more detail, we found that many problems that children experienced on the Websites cannot be attributed to the design characteristics of the Websites, but are caused by children's own lack of navigation and information skills. In other words, children's navigation and information skills are a better predictor of children's search success than the type of design characteristics of the search interface. Children with a lot of internet experience, encounter less problems with searching and browsing than children with little internet experience. Also, children with a lot of domain knowledge are more successful in formulating relevant search queries, selecting relevant search results, or selecting relevant main- and subcategories. Children that are able to check and monitor their own activities, termed metacognition (i.e. the voluntary control an individual has over his own cognitive processes) (Brown & DeLoache, 1978) are more capable of keeping the initial search task in mind, or of recognizing when they select the wrong main- or sub category link.

However, particular search characteristics might support particular groups of children. For example, our research provides indications that children with a lot of game experience are better off with the Image map Website, because this interface type is based on exploring and a trial-and-error strategy. Our research also provides clues that children with little internet experience are better off with the Classic Website, because there are not so many visual stimuli to distract these children from their navigation path.

An important lesson learned from this experiment is that the variance between children is much more determinant for differences in search success and performance than the variance between search interfaces. This makes the challenge for designers to design interfaces that support children in effective information-seeking even greater. It also stresses the importance of educating children in navigation and information skills. However, the most important lesson learned from this experiment is the fact that children's search success and search efficiency is much larger when they use a search engine, than when they browse the main categories of the Website.

ACKNOWLEDGMENT

We would like to thank the children that cooperated in this study. We would also like to thank Matthijs Noordzij of the University of Twente for his help processing the data of the Q-sensor and MA students, Jiske Naber, Marjolein Makkinga, Aafke Ariaans, Yvonne Joosten and Amy Mooij, for their assistance in conducting the qualitative analyses of the experimental data. The research is funded by the Netherlands Institute for Public Libraries (SIOB) and the European Community's Seventh Framework Programme FP7/2007-2013 under grant agreement no. 231507, named 'PuppyIR'.

REFERENCES

Bar-Ilan, J., & Belous, Y. (2007). Children as architects of web directories: An exploratory study. *Journal of the American Society for Information Science and Technology*, 58(6), 895–907. doi:10.1002/asi.20566

Bilal, D. (2000). Children's use of the yahooligans web search engine: I. cognitive, physical, and affective behaviors on fact-based search tasks. *Journal of the American Society for Information Science American Society for Information Science*, 51(7), 646–665. doi:10.1002/(SICI)1097-4571(2000)51:7<646::AID-ASI7>3.0.CO;2-A

Bilal, D. (2001). Children's use of the yahooligans! web search engine: II. cognitive and physical behaviors on research tasks. *Journal of the American Society for Information Science and Technology*, 52(2), 118–136. doi:10.1002/1097-4571(2000)9999:9999<::AID-ASI1038>3.0.CO;2-R

Bilal, D. (2002). Children's use of the yahooligans! web search engine. III. cognitive and physical behaviors on fully self-generated search tasks. *Journal of the American Society for Information Science and Technology*, 53(13), 1170–1183. doi:10.1002/asi.10145

Bilal, D., & Kirby, J. (2002). Differences and similarities in information seeking: Children and adults as web users. *Information Processing & Management*, 38(5), 649–670. doi:10.1016/S0306-4573(01)00057-7

Bilal, D., & Watson, J. S. (1998*). Children's paperless projects: Inspiring research via the web.* Paper presented at the 64th General Conference of the International Federation of Library Associations & Institutions. Amsterdam, the Netherlands.

Borgman, C. L., Hirsh, S. G., Walter, V. A., & Gallagher, A. L. (1995). Children's searching behavior on browsing and keyword online catalogs: The science library catalog project. *Journal of the American Society for Information Science American Society for Information Science*, 46(9), 663–684. doi:10.1002/(SICI)1097-4571(199510)46:9<663::AID-ASI4>3.0.CO;2-2

Bradley, M. M., & Lang, P. J. (1994). Measuring emotion: The self-assessment manikin and the semantic differential. *Journal of Behavior Therapy and Experimental Psychiatry*, 25(1), 49–59. doi:10.1016/0005-7916(94)90063-9 PMID:7962581

Brown, A. L., & DeLoache, J. S. (1978). Skills, plans, and self-regulation. In R. S. Siegler (Ed.), *Children's thinking: What develops?* (pp. 3–35). Hillsdale, NJ: Erlbaum.

Chambers, C. T., & Johnston, C. (2002). Developmental differences in children's use of rating scales. *Journal of Pediatric Psychology*, 27(1), 27–36. doi:10.1093/jpepsy/27.1.27 PMID:11726677

Chen, C. (2006). *Information visualization: Beyond the horizon.* London: Springer.

Druin, A. (2003). What children can teach us: Developing digital libraries for children with children. *The Library Quarterly*, 75(1), 20–41. doi:10.1086/428691

Druin, A., Hutchinson, H., Foss, E., Hatley, L., Golub, E., Leigh Guha, M., & Fails, J. (2009). *How children search the internet with keyword interfaces.* Paper presented at the 8th International Conference on Interaction Design and Children. Como, Italy.

Greenbaum, P. E., Turner, C., Cook, E. W. III, & Melamed, B. G. (1990). Dentists' voice control: Effects on children's disruptive and affective behavior. *Health Psychology, 9*(5), 546–558. doi:10.1037/0278-6133.9.5.546 PMID:2226384

Hartmann, J., Sutcliffe, A., & Angeli, A. D. (2008). Towards a theory of user judgment of aesthetics and user interface quality. *ACM Transactions on Computer-Human Interaction, 15*(4), 15:1-15:30.

Hassenzahl, M. (2004). The interplay of beauty, goodness, and usability in interactive products. *Human-Computer Interaction, 19*(4), 319–349. doi:10.1207/s15327051hci1904_2

Hassenzahl, M., Burmester, M., & Koller, F. (2003). AttrakDiff: Ein fragebogen zur messung wahrgenommener hedonischer und pragmatischer qualitat. In J. Ziegler & G. Szwillus (Eds.), *Mensch & computer: Interaktion in bewegung* (pp. 187–196). Stuttgart, Germany: B.G. Teubner. doi:10.1007/978-3-322-80058-9_19

Hassenzahl, M., & Tractinsky, N. (2006). User experience–A research agenda. *Behaviour & Information Technology, 25*(2), 91–97. doi:10.1080/01449290500330331

Horton, M., Read, J. C., & Sim, G. (2011). Making your mind up? The reliability of children's survey responses. In L. Little & L. Coventry (Eds.), *25th BCS Conference on Human-Computer Interaction* (pp. 437-438). Swinton, UK: British Computer Society.

Hutchinson, H., Druin, A., Bederson, B. B., Reuter, K., Rose, A., & Weeks, A. C. (2005). *How do I find blue books about dogs? The errors and frustrations of young digital library users.* Paper presented at the International Conference on Human-Computer Interaction (HCI). Las Vegas, NV.

Hutchinson, H. B., Bederson, B. B., & Druin, A. (2006). *The evolution of the international children's digital library searching and browsing interface.* Paper presented at the 2006 Conference on Interaction Design for Children. Tampere, Finland.

Irtel, H. (2007). PXLab: The psychological experiments laboratory (2.1.11 ed.). Mannheim, Germany: University of Mannheim.

Jochmann-Mannak, H., Huibers, T., Lentz, L., & Sanders, T. (2010). *Children searching information on the internet: Performance on children's interfaces compared to Google.* Paper presented at the 33rd Annual International ACM SIGIR Conference on Research and Development in Information Retrieval at the Workshop Towards Accessible Search Systems. Geneva, Switzerland.

Jochmann-Mannak, H., Lentz, L., Huibers, T., & Sanders, T. (2012). Three types of children's informational websites: An inventory of design conventions. *Technical Communication, 59*(4), 302–323.

Kitajima, M., Blackmon, M. H., & Polson, P. G. (2000). *A comprehension-based model of web navigation and its application to web usability analysis.* Paper presented at the 14th Annual Conference of the British HCI Group (HCI 2000), People and Computers XIV: Usability Or Else! Sunderland, UK.

Laarni, J. (2004). *Aesthetic and emotional evaluations of computer interfaces.* Paper presented at the Nordi CHI 2004 Workshop: Aesthetic Approaches to Human–Computer Interaction. Aarhus, Denmark.

Lang, P. J. (1980). Behavioral treatment and biobehavioral assessment: Computer applications. In J. B. Sidowski, J. H. Johnson, & T. A. Williams (Eds.), *Technology in mental health care delivery systems* (pp. 119–137). Norwood, NJ: Ablex Publishing.

Large, A., & Beheshti, J. (2000). The web as a classroom resource: Reactions from the users. *Journal of the American Society for Information Science American Society for Information Science, 51*(12), 1069–1080. doi:10.1002/1097-4571(2000)9999:9999<::AID-ASI1017>3.0.CO;2-W

Large, A., Beheshti, J., & Moukdad, H. (1999). *Information seeking on the web: Navigational skills of grade-six primary school students.* Paper presented at the ASIS Annual Meeting. Washington, DC.

Large, A., Beheshti, J., Tabatabaei, N., & Nesset, V. (2009). Developing a visual taxonomy: Children's views on aesthetics. *Journal of the American Society for Information Science and Technology, 60*(9), 1808–1822. doi:10.1002/asi.21095

Large, A., Nesset, V., Beheshti, J., & Bowler, L. (2006). Bonded design: A novel approach to the design of new technologies. *Library & Information Science Research, 28*(1), 64–82. doi:10.1016/j.lisr.2005.11.014

Malone, T. W. (1980). *What makes things fun to learn? A study of intrinsically motivating computer games* (Technical Report No. CIS-7 SSL-80-11). Palo Alto, CA: Xerox Palo Alto Research Center.

Malone, T. W. (1984). Heuristics for designing enjoyable user interfaces: Lessons from computer games. In J. C. Thomas & M. L. Schneider (Eds.), *Human factors in computer systems* (pp. 1–12). Norwood, NJ: Ablex Publishing.

Marchionini, G. (1989). Information-seeking strategies of novices using a full-text electronic encyclopedia. *Journal of the American Society for Information Science American Society for Information Science, 40*(1), 54–66. doi:10.1002/(SICI)1097-4571(198901)40:1<54::AID-ASI6>3.0.CO;2-R

Markopoulos, P., Read, J., MacFarlane, S., & Hoysniemi, J. (2008). *Evaluating children's interactive products.* Burlington, UK: Elsevier.

Meloncon, L., Haynes, E., Varelmann, M., & Groh, L. (2010). Building a playground: General guidelines for creating educational websites for children. *Technical Communication, 57*(4), 398–415.

Nielsen, J., & Gilutz, S. (2002). *Usability of websites for children: 70 design guidelines based on usability studies with kids.* Nielsen Norman Group.

Noordzij, M., Scholten, P., & Laroy-Noordzij, M. (2012). *Measuring electrodermal activity of both individuals with severe mental disabilities and their caretakers during episodes of challenging behavior.* Paper presented at the 8th International Conference on Methods and Techniques in Behavioral Research: Measuring Behavior. Utrecht, The Netherlands.

Pijpers, R., Marteijn, T., Bosman, M., & Berg, V. D. W., & Dijkerman, E. (2008). Klik en klaar: Een onderzoek naar surfgedrag en usability bij kinderen (No. 111). Den Haag, The Netherlands: Stichting Mijn Kind Online.

Poh, M., Swenson, N. C., & Picard, R. W. (2010). A wearable sensor for unobtrusive, long-term assessment of electrodermal activity. *IEEE Transactions on Bio-Medical Engineering*, 1243–1252. PMID:20172811

Read, J. C. (2008). Validating the fun toolkit: An instrument for measuring children's opinions of technology. *Cognition Technology and Work*, *10*(2), 119–128. doi:10.1007/s10111-007-0069-9

Read, J. C., & MacFarlane, S. (2006). *Using the fun toolkit and other survey methods to gather opinions in child computer interaction.* Paper presented at the International Conference on Interaction Design and Children. Tampere, Finland.

Read, J. C., MacFarlane, S. J., & Casey, C. (2002). *Endurability, engagement and expectations: Measuring children's fun.* Paper presented at the International Conference on Interaction Design and Children. Eindhoven, The Netherlands.

Revelle, G., Druin, A., Platner, M., Bederson, B. B., & Sherman, L. (2002). A visual search tool for early elementary science students. *Journal of Science Education and Technology*, *11*(1), 49–57. doi:10.1023/A:1013947430933

Rowlands, I. (2008). *Information behaviour of the researcher of the future.* British Library JISC. doi:10.1108/00012530810887953

Russell, J. A. (1980). A circumplex model of affect. *Journal of Personality and Social Psychology*, *39*(6), 1161–1178. doi:10.1037/h0077714

Schacter, J., Chung, G. K. W. K., & Dorr, A. (1998). Children's internet searching on complex problems: Performance and process analyses. *Journal of the American Society for Information Science American Society for Information Science*, *49*(9), 840–849. doi:10.1002/(SICI)1097-4571(199807)49:9<840::AID-ASI9>3.0.CO;2-D

Serenko, A. (2007). Are interface agents scapegoats? Attributions of responsibility in human-agent interaction. *Interacting with Computers*, *19*(2), 293–303. doi:10.1016/j.intcom.2006.07.005

Sim, G., MacFarlane, S., & Read, J. (2006). All work and no play: Measuring fun, usability, and learning in software for children. *Computers & Education*, *46*(3), 235–248. doi:10.1016/j.compedu.2005.11.021

Snijders, T., & Bosker, R. (2012). *Multilevel analysis: An introduction to basic and advanced multilevel modeling* (2nd ed.). London: Sage Publishers.

Sweller, J., van Merrienboer, J. J. G., & Paas, G. W. C. (1998). Cognitive architecture and instructional design. *Educational Psychology Review*, *10*(3), 251–296. doi:10.1023/A:1022193728205

Thuring, M., & Mahlke, S. (2007). Usability, aesthetics and emotions in human-technology interaction. *International Journal of Psychology*, *42*(4), 253–264. doi:10.1080/00207590701396674

Tractinsky, N., Katz, A. S., & Ikar, D. (2000). What is beautiful is usable. *Interacting with Computers*, *13*(2), 127–145. doi:10.1016/S0953-5438(00)00031-X

Tuch, A. N., Roth, S. P., Hornbæk, K., Opwis, K., & Bargas-Avila, J. A. (2012). Is beautiful really usable? Toward understanding the relation between usability, aesthetics, and affect in HCI. *Computers in Human Behavior*, *28*(5), 1596–1607. doi:10.1016/j.chb.2012.03.024

van Schaik, P., & Ling, J. (2008). Modelling user experience with websites: Usability, hedonic value, beauty and goodness. *Interacting with Computers*, *20*(3), 419–432. doi:10.1016/j.intcom.2008.03.001

Xiang, Z., & Gretzel, U. (2010). Role of social media in online travel information search. *Tourism Management, 31*(2), 179–188. doi:10.1016/j.tourman.2009.02.016

Yarosh, S., Radu, I., Hunter, S., & Rosenbaum, E. (2011). *Examining values: An analysis of nine years of IDC research.* Paper presented at the 10th International Conference on Interaction Design and Children. Ann Arbor, MI.

KEY TERMS AND DEFINITIONS

Browsing: Browsing is a search method in which the user selects a relevant subject category from a menu. The user can 'recognize' a relevant category from the provided categories in the menu.

Classic Interface Design: Classic interface design aims at simplicity, consistency and focus. The layout of classic interfaces is kept minimal with little graphic elements; key elements of the interfaces are the center of attention and different pages have the same layout. Page components are located on conventional locations. The navigation is a basic, textual menu of categories presented in a horizontally or vertically presented list.

Emotional Arousal: The extent to which the user gets exited (by interacting with an interface).

Emotional Valence: The extent to which the user's feelings (towards an interface) are positive or negative.

Keyword Search: Keyword search is a search method in which a search engine is used to search for information in a vast information space by submitting a search query. The search engine matches this query to information elements in the information space and presents search results from which the user can select a result that is relevant for his search task. The user has to 'recall' and formulate a search query from his memory.

Perception of Hedonic Quality: The user's perception of the extent to which interacting with an interface is stimulating for the user and the extent to which the user can identify with the interface (i.e. pleasure-producing quality of an interface).

Perception of Pragmatic Quality: The user's perception of how user-friendly an interface is and how effective and efficient search performance is when using this interface (i.e. user-perceived usability).

Playful Interface Design: Interface design can be made playful both in design of navigation as in visual design. With a playful navigation approach, category labels are integrated in a screen filling image, often without textual labels. Users have to 'explore' the screen image in search of categories, which makes interacting with the interface a playful experience. Visual design can be made playful by adding many different colors, images and animations to the interface and by playfully arranging visual elements on the screen.

Search Performance: The effectiveness and efficiency (for example in amount of time and clicks needed) with which a user can search and find relevant information by interacting with a digital interface.

User Experience: The research field of User Experience (UX) argues for a broader perspective for evaluation of systems or interfaces than usability. Besides instrumental qualities (i.e. pragmatic quality/usability), also non-instrumental qualities are important, such as visual aesthetics, hedonic quality or haptic qualities.

ENDNOTES

[1] Six of the AttractDiff 2 items were not used in our study, because these verbal anchors were too difficult to translate in a picture that we thought could be well-interpreted by children: isolating – integrating, gaudy – classy, takes me distant from people – brings me closer to people, typical – original, conservative – innovative, commonplace – new.

2 Jiske Naber and Marjolein Makkinga (students of the Master Communication studies) assisted the authors by analyzing verbal utterances of 25 children that conducted search tasks on the Image map Website.

3 Aafke Ariaans (MA student) assisted the authors by analyzing the reliability and validity of the data.

4 Yvonne Joosten (MA student) assisted the authors by conducting qualitative analyses of search engine use.

5 Amy Mooij (MA student) assisted the authors by conducting qualitative analyses of the children's navigation paths.

This work was previously published in Evaluating Websites and Web Services edited by Denis Yannacopoulos, Panagiotis Manolitzas, Nikolaos Matsatsinis, and Evangelos Grigoroudis, pages 241-287, copyright year 2014 by Information Science Reference (an imprint of IGI Global).

APPENDIX 1

"How interface design and search strategy influence children's search performance and evaluation"

Task Descriptions Translated from the Original Dutch Versions with the Optimum Navigation Path Presented for Each Task

Task 1

You've seen a chameleon in the zoo and you saw that he was moving very slowly.
Now you wonder how a chameleon captures its prey, because he seems far too lazy for that.
Can you find out how a chameleon catches its prey at Junior Winkler Prins online?

Optimum Navigation Path Task 1:
- **Correct Main Category:** Nature
- **Correct Subcategory:** Reptiles and amphibians
- **Correct Content Page:** Chameleon

Task 2

You would like to become an astronaut and explore space in search of alien planets, like in the movies.
Can you find out who was actually the first living creature that traveled through space at Junior Winkler Prins online ?

Optimum Navigation Path Task 2:
- **Correct Main Category:** Science and technology
- **Correct Subcategory:** Space and Space travel
- **Correct Content Pages:** Space/ Astronaut

Task 3

You spend your holiday in Friesland with your parents and your father told you that he participated in the famous Dutch skating tour named 'Elfstedentocht' once.
He also told you that he met the Dutch crown prince Willem-Alexander during the tour.
Can you find out under what name Willem-Alexander participated in the scating tour that day?

Optimum Navigation Path Task 3:
- **Correct Main Category:** Sports and exercise
- **Correct Subcategory:** Stadiums & Tournaments
- **Correct Content Page:** "Elfstedentocht"

Task 4

It is often said that Christopher Columbus discovered America. Some say that this is not true. They say that another nation discovered America 500 years before Columbus did.
Can you find out what people discovered America before Columbus did at Junior Winkler Prins online?

Optimum Navigation Path Task 4:
- **Correct Main Category:** History
- **Correct Subcategories:** Time of cities and states/ Time of discoverers and reformers/ Time of monks and knights.
- **Correct Content Pages:** Vikings/ Discoveries.

Task 5

Isaac Newton invented a device to be able to see the stars better. Can you find out what the name of that device is at Junior Winkler Prins online?

Optimum Navigation Path Task 5:
- **Correct Main Category:** Famous people / Science and technology.
- **Correct Subcategories:** Inventors and scientists/ Space and space travel/ Measuring, weighing or counting/ How it works.
- **Correct Content Pages:** Isaac Newton/ Star/ Telescope.

APPENDIX 2

Bipolar Picture Anchors for Pragmatic and Hedonic Quality from the AttracDiff 2 Questionnaire

Pragmatic Quality (PQ)

Figure 14. Technical – human

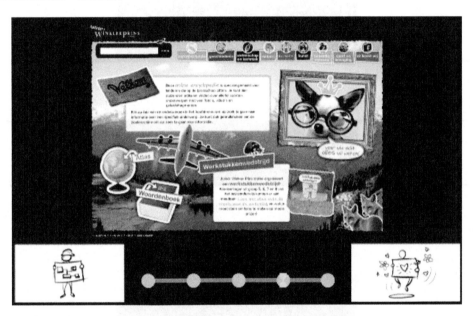

Figure 15. Complicated – simple

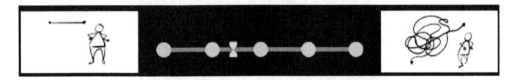

Figure 16. Impractical – practical

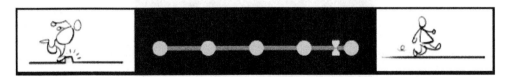

Figure 17. Cumbersome – direct

Figure 18. Unpredictable – predictable*

Figure 19. Confusing – clear

Figure 20. Unruly – manageable

Hedonic Quality – Identification (HQI)

Figure 21. Amateurish – professional

Figure 22. Cheap – valuable

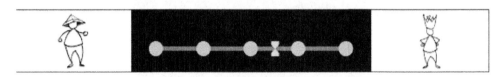

Figure 23. Non-inclusive – inclusive*

Figure 24. Unpresentable – presentable

Hedonic Quality – Stimulation (HQS)

Figure 25. Standard – creative*

Figure 26. Cautious – courageous*

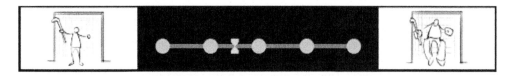

Figure 27. Lame – exciting

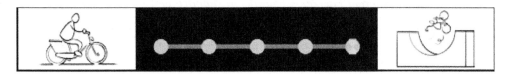

Figure 28. Easy – challenging

* Picture anchors that were left out of the final experiment based on the results of the pilot study

Chapter 62
Creating a Community of Practice in Learning

Ebenezer Uy
De La Salle – College of Saint Benilde, Philippines

Eusebio Yu
De La Salle – College of Saint Benilde, Philippines

ABSTRACT

Social media plays a huge part in Filipinos' lives. In the area of learning, the proponents observed the emergence of an online community of practice using Facebook groups that has over 350 members. The aim of the chapter is to answer the question: How do online communities of practice engage students to learn and build new knowledge? The objective is to propose a framework that will guide readers to build their own online community of practice based on its learning context. To achieve the objective, the proponents use the inductive approach of grounded theory using action research. Results show that community members used different Facebook features to support their ongoing community of practice. Further studies may also assess the applicability of the framework in other areas of development.

INTRODUCTION

Creating a Facebook group for every new class is becoming a common practice. One of the top reasons for doing so is because the students are already on Facebook regularly. While being inside Facebook, they could be notified of group posts. Posts could include class announcements, lecture/presentation materials, questions/comments from students, links to videos and other resources for the class, etc.

Usually, a new Facebook group is made for every section for every subject. Let's say one professor is teaching 3 sections of the same subject. He will create 3 separate Facebook groups for each of the sections, even if they're all the same subject.

It makes the groups very focused. The group is applicable for a specific section and will probably be active for only a specific term. After the term ends, the group will become inactive since students are already done with that subject. In addition, the interactions in the group are very section-specific. A question raised in a particular class may not be the same question raised in the other classes.

DOI: 10.4018/978-1-4666-8619-9.ch062

There is an alternative to the scenario above. Instead of creating a new Facebook group for every section, only one group is created for all the sections of the same subject. And not only is the group active for a specific term only, it will be the same group that would be used for succeeding terms that the subject would be offered. Because of which, an online Community of Practice (CoP) is formed for that particular subject. Students who have already finished the course could still participate and even serve as mentors for the current students.

REVIEW OF RELATED LITERATURE

Communities of Practice

Every year, corporations spend millions of dollars on training and educating their employees. According to the American Society for Training and Development, these corporations spend approximately one thousand dollars per employee per year in 2005. The investment in training and education stems from the current trend that businesses are continuing to stay on the cutting-edge to maintain their competitive advantage over other organizations. Given that knowledge-based organizations will continue to be the driving force of economy, it is essential for organizations to support the knowledge and information needs of their workers (Hara, 2009).

In the past, professional development was discussed within the context of traditional learning. However, traditional learning methods have been criticized for focusing on transmission of explicit knowledge. As a result, administrators have a difficulty in determining the tangible impact of traditional learning methods because of the inherent difficulties of applying knowledge learned in a traditional setting to the work environment (Hara, 2009).

Current research supports the assertion that learning must take place within an organiza-tional context for it to be considered useful. Consequently, a shift from traditional methods to a system of learning founded on collaboration and experience should be considered. Such learning can best be supported through communities of practice (COPs) (Hara, 2009).

Concept of Communities of Practice

Communities of Practice (COPs) are "collaborative, informal networks that support professional practitioners in their efforts to develop shared understandings and engage in work-relevant knowledge building" (Hara, 2009). In other words, these are groups of people who share a common goal, problems or passions about a given topic and want to deepen their knowledge and expertise in one area on an ongoing basis (Clark, 2006).

The ability of COPs to foster a friendly environment for discussing common subject matters and concerns encourages the creation and transfer of new knowledge. It also assists in connecting experts and practitioners with a common professional interest and similar experiences and expertise. COPs use face to face meetings, workspaces, maps and networks to promote peer interaction and address the various needs in all levels of an organization (Clarke, 2006).

Background on Communities of Practice

The term, communities of practice, originated from Lave and Wenger in 1991. Their original definition emphasized "legitimate peripheral participation", a form of apprenticeship which allows newcomers to participate while learning the lingo and develop a shared identity of the community. The end result of the process is the assimilation into the community for the newcomer (Hara, 2009).

The following is the original definition of communities of practice as defined by Lave and Wenger (2006):

A community of practice is a set of relations among persons, activity, and world, over time and in relation with other tangential and overlapping communities of practice. A community of practice is an intrinsic condition for the existence of knowledge, not least because it provides the interpretive support necessary for making sense of its heritage. Thus, participation in the cultural practice in which any knowledge exists is an epistemological principle of learning. The social structure of this practice, its power relations, and its condition for legitimacy define possibilities for learning (i.e., legitimate peripheral participation).

Other definitions of communities are a derivation from the original definition given by Lave and Wenger. Of course, not all scholars have reacted positively to the concept of communities of practice. A handful like Henriksson (2000) criticized that COPs may not represent organizational reality and suggested that the concept should be kept in alignment with existing organizational research. In addition, Fox (2000) criticized the lack of discussion about individuals or group abuse of power in the research of communities of practice. Regardless of the negative reactions, the concept is still extremely useful for articulating collective knowledge creation within organizations (Hara, 2009).

Attributes of Communities of Practice

The following section discusses five attributes of communities of practice. These are as follows: (1) a group of professional practitioners (2) development of shared meaning (3) informal social networks (4) supportive culture and (5) engagement in knowledge building.

1. **Group of Professional Practitioners:** A community, by definition, involves at least two members. However, Orr (1996) pointed out that professionals prefer autonomy. In addition, studies showed that professionals will work in groups. It is essential that professionals share knowledge collectively if a community of practice is to be fostered.

2. **Development of Shared Meaning:** "As people work together, they not only learn from doing, they develop a shared sense of what has to happen to get the job done" (Hara, 2009). The information exchanged in community of practice is communicated among its members. This most basic social process results in the development of shared meanings. In order for the professionals to communicate effectively, the development of shared meaning and means to knowledge exchange is essential (Wenger, 1998). Since each communities of practice exists within a certain context, the shared meanings that evolved should also exist within the same context (Hara, 2009).

3. **Informal Social Network:** Communities of practice are sometimes difficult to identify and isolate for a given study. They exhibit organizational patterns that are not reflected in traditional organizational charts. This is because communities of practice are informal networks that evolve organically. Wenger (1992) supported the claim by stating that "there is no distinction between learning [within communities of practice] and social participation" (Hara, 2009).

4. **Supportive Culture:** Communities of Practice also foster a supportive culture. More importantly, the members of the communities of practice should trust each other – at the very least – on a professional level (Hara, 2009).

5. **Engagement in Knowledge Building:** Learning is a process of acquiring and identifying relationships between facts and ideas. Communities of practice represent systems whereby members may be able to acquire and share information. It will thrive if the community is based on people caring about and

taking responsibility for the other members and for the well-being of other members of the community. In other words, communities of practice are based on the cultivation of trust and mutual respect (Hara, 2009).

In a related study, Wenger identified three dimensions of the relationship of practice as a source of coherence of a community (Roberts, 2011).

1. First, community members interact with one another, establishing relationships and norms through mutual engagement;
2. Second, members are bound together by a mutual understanding of a sense of joint enterprise; and
3. Finally, members develop a shared repertoire over time. This includes communal resources such as include languages, routines, artifacts and stories.

Wenger (2002), in addition, distinguishes the three modes of belonging to a social learning system like communities of practice.

1. First, engagement is achieved by doing things together. An example will be taking and producing artifacts.
2. Second, imagination is involved in creating an image of the community, ourselves and of the world in order to reflect on the current situation, orient ourselves and explore possibilities.
3. Third, alignment is involved in making sure that the local activities are aligned with other processes so that they can be effective beyond our own engagement.

These methods are displayed in the characteristics of communities of practice as stated by Wenger in Table 1.

There are four classifications of Communities of Practice that the study identified: (1) Internal

communities of practice (2) Communities of Practice that are linked through mergers and acquisitions (3) formal networks that span organizations but are not part of any formal relationships and (4) self-organizing networks of individuals (Archer, 2006).

1. **Internal Communities of Practice:** Internal Communities of Practice are COPs that occur entirely within the individual organization. These communities handle explicit knowledge or intellectual capital, adopt a set of rules for managing knowledge and provide opportunities for sharing knowledge among community members (Archer, 2006).
2. **Communities of Practice in Network Organizations:** A network organization is a relationship among independent organizations. Such networks have been growing rapidly in number and scope with majority of business organizations now belonging to one type of network. Member organizations in a network work in close collaboration and

Table 1. Characteristics of communities of practice (Roberts, 2011), classification of communities of practice

Sustained mutual relationships – Harmonious or conflictual
Shared ways of engaging in doing things together
The rapid flow of information and propagation of innovation
Absences of introductory preambles
Very quick setup of problem to be discussed
Substantial overlap in participants' description of who belongs
Knowing what others know, what they can do, and how they can contribute to an enterprise
Mutually defining identities
The ability to assess the appropriateness of actions and products
Certain styles recognized as displaying memberships
A shared discourse reflecting a certain perspective on the world

continuous cooperation on certain projects or processes, common products and even a common strategy (Archer, 2006). Some of the advantages of building network organizations include:

a. Faster time to market
b. Ability to concentrate on core competencies
c. Increase in competencies due to networking with business partners
d. Need to guarantee availability of resources and materials
e. Risk and cost mitigations
f. Fresh insights derived from cross boundary and cross organization partnerships

From a communities of practice standpoint, an important question to decide on is which organizations should be connected. Networks of practice make it easier for inter-organizational exchanges to happen and shared practice among the organizations provides a channel to share knowledge more efficiently (Brown and Duguid, 1991). Learning and knowledge exchange through networks may serve as a resource generator to enhance learning.

Powell, Koput, and Smith-Doer (1996) suggested that the focal innovation of an industry that is operating using complex processes will be found in inter-organizational networks of learning rather than within individual firms (Archer, 2006).

In a network organization, knowledge sharing is encouraged through a network agreement, aided by knowledge transfer and learning through various channels such as communities of practice. With such networks, there is always a risk of knowledge leakage to other competing organizations (Archer, 2006).

3. **Network of Practice:** Network of Practice is an open activity system focused on work practices and may exist primarily through electronic communication. People participating in a network of practice normally work on similar occupations and have similar interests. They gather to engage in knowledge exchange about problems and issues that are common to their occupations and shared practice (Archer, 2006).

4. **Formal Network of Practice:** A formal network of practice differs from network of practice since the former has a membership that is controlled by fees/ and or acceptance through some central authority that also assist in organizing, facilitating and supporting member communications, events and discussion topics. This is similar to a professional or non-profit association, although they are classified more as an affinity network (Archer, 2006).

5. **Self-Organizing Network of Practice:** A self-organizing network of practice is a loosely organized and informal network that has no central management authority or sponsor. Membership is voluntary and there is no explicit commitment. Most of these types of networks operate virtually, so communication strategy is primarily based on knowledge codification. People participate in such networks due to their affiliation with a profession rather than an organization. A good example of such network is Usenet groups (Archer, 2006).

Differences among the Classifications

Major differences of note among the classifications were seen in the following characteristics: (Archer, 2006)

a. The type of knowledge transferred and the desired objective or outcome;
b. Funding;
c. Intellectual property;
d. Dispute Resolution;
e. Potential Knowledge contribution;
f. Professional expertise;

g. Potential problems including maintaining interest and contribution; and

h. Remediation of operational problem

FRAMEWORK FOR USE OF ICT IN COMMUNITIES OF PRACTICE

According to Wenger (1998), the purpose of the existence of communities of practice is to create a common area for individual meetings in order to interact, exchange and assimilate experiences around application areas with clearly defined objectives. These interactions lead to the innovation and development of the core competencies of the company (Campus et al, 2011).

The common area, therefore, should use the cycle of knowledge reception, diffusion, assimilation and renovation in the organizational database, structuring experience and facilitating its members' contributions. In this manner, we may be able to apply to COP, as an agent, the whole knowledge governance model based on the seven strategies defined below: technology and market watch, tacit knowledge management, communications model, individual and organizational learning; quality and Research and development (Campus et al, 2011).

On the other hand, COPs should also facilitate the relation among community members beyond just information exchange. The dynamic exchange is only possible if the internalization of mission and objective occurs within the context of the community. This is because the internalization would facilitate the flow of the interaction. As a result, it will encourage cohesion amongst its members (Campus et al, 2011).

COPs hinge on three pillars which is the basis on the management framework and the necessary tools to support it (Campus et al, 2011).

• Technology provides COPs with the necessary tools to create effective areas of collaboration from the operational standpoint.

• The necessary culture and environment to meet the objectives of the community, the organization and its individuals. The goal is to achieve an identity and generate policies and appropriate management models grounded on training, awareness and motivation

• And the management model through which the rules of the game are established, the work processes, the role of actors, knowledge types and the associated taxonomy.

The creation of COP is linked to two approaches: push and pull (Campus et al, 2011).

The push approach, declared by the organization, is communities of practice that is decided and chosen by the leaders based on the strategic direction of the organization.

The pull approach, is based on providing resources and support the group in developing successful collaboration within the organization.

The challenge is to find a reasonably grounded and practically applicable theoretical foundation for developing and evaluating knowledge management process and information technology in the area of volunteer sector. Research that focuses on the pull approach is still lacking and important in order to fully understand both approaches (Campus et al, 2011)

More recently, Dube, Bourhis and Jacob (2006) developed a typology of online communities of practice that has four dimensions: demographics, organizational context, members and technological environments. However, the typology they developed was developed independent of face – to – face communities of practice (Hara, 2009).

When considering online communities of practice, it is evident that there is a need to investigate how online COPs differ from face-to-face communities of practice.

Another known framework to study online knowledge sharing is Cyber Ba, Literally "cyber place" (Nonaka and Konno, 1998). Basically, Cyber Ba is an environment for distributing explicit knowledge to other members. It supports internalization phase whereby focused training with senior mentors and colleagues consists primarily of continued exercises that stress patterns and working on those patterns. However, it does not address the issues of collective learning and identity formation (Hara, 2009).

IT plays an important role in supporting communities of practice. The proponents distinguish three categories: (1) supporting social actions inherent in COPs, (2) supporting different stages of COPs' lifecycles, and (3) adaptive use of collaborative technologies that assist knowledge management issues and requirements.

Supporting Social Actions Inherent in COPs

Ngwenyama and Lyytinen proposed a framework that indicates four cluster areas that identifies what type of ICT tool would be appropriate for the tasks needed. The cluster areas are as follows: Instrumental action or research tools (example: document management system), communicative action or communication tools (example: email), discursive action or groupware tools (example: online messaging) and strategic action (intelligent agents). (DOTSIKA, 2006) Please refer to figure 2 on the next page for the structure of the framework.

According to Wenger's Communities Evolution model, five stages were identified: potential, coalescing, active, dispersed and memorable. At the end of the model, the community disappears but the knowledge remains in stories and artifacts. (Dotsika, 2006) Table 2 maps the five stages with their main functions and possible relevant technologies.

Another set of ICT used in support of COPs are tools that usually support the above action categories and different stages of the lifecycle. The tools are as follows: knowledge management suites, portals and collaboration tools or groupware (Dotsika, 2006).

Frameworks identified for communities of practice mainly adhere to the push approach. Two such frameworks are used as basis for Systems Defense and Engineering Firm (SDE) and the Spanish nuclear power plants (Campus et al, 2011).

The Use of ICT in Communities of Practice

According to Checkland and Holwell (1995), the main role of an information system is that of a support function that assists people in their different activities of actions. However, many of today's information systems are difficult to learn and awkward to use; the current informa-

Figure 1. Supporting social actions supporting different stages of a COP's lifecycle

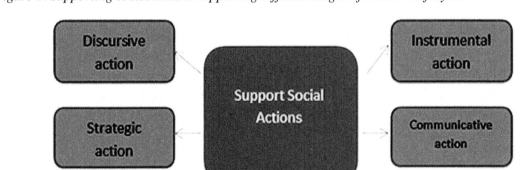

Figure 2. Detailed research design and strategy

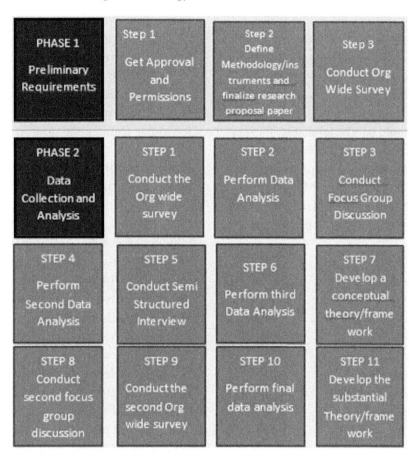

Table 2. Wegner's five stages of COP adaptive use of collaborative technologies

Stages	Main Functions	IT Enabling technologies
1	Connect, plan, commit	Email, e-conferencing, list servers, online forums, corporate intranet
2	Form framework, create context	Same as above, plus remote login, facilities transfer and info repositories
3	Operate, collaborate, grow	Same as above plus online directories, analytical tools, intelligent agents, feedback facilities and portals
	Sustain, renew, maintain, wind down	
4	Shut down	Knowledge repositories may remain for future communities

tion systems change the users' activities in ways that the users do not want. Therefore, the use of information technology in communities of practice must be flexible and employees should be able to adapt technologies based on the local needs. Much research examines the role of ICT in supporting work activity (e.g. Galegher, Kraut and Egido, 1990), the interest is mainly focused on how ICT

can support distributed communities of practice which has grown with the widespread use of the Internet (Hara, 2009).

Despite the enthusiasm of some scholars, online communities of practice have a tendency to be a hit or miss proposition. Some are successful while some are not. INDISCHOOL is one example of the successful online communities of practice that generated over 87000 teachers as of December 2005 (Hara, 2009).

There are also evidences that ICT-supported strategies for COP development work better than ICT-led strategies. (Kling and Courtright, 2003) ICT moves from being an underlying infrastructure to the linking mechanism. Giles Grant of BNFI states that "IT should only be an enabler for sharing and collaboration. It isn't the community. The community is the people". Therefore, the best software to use, according to Nick Milton of Knock (KMOnline, 2004), is the one that the community is most familiar with and is most prepared to use (Clarke, 2006).

1. Ongoing interactions;
2. Work;
3. Social structures;
4. Conversation;
5. Fleeting interactions;
6. Instruction;
7. Knowledge exchange; and
8. Documents

REVIEW OF RELATED SYSTEMS

These program suites include – Tomoye, community Zero, iCohere, and Communispace – were strongly oriented towards fleeting interactions and instructions. However, they have weak support of social structures, knowledge exchange and documents. It also includes a local search, an

expert's database, discussion and events notification facility. None provided video and audio supported meetings or webinars. All, except Tomoye, provided community governance and polls (See Table 3 for the features of COP software).

The next section will showcase three different Communities of Practice software packages and its diverse features and offerings.

ICohere Communities of Practice Software

ICohere provides a platform for engaging and building sustainable collaborative communities of practice. By creating focused connectivity across geographic, business and cultures, COPs use the collective knowledge to arrive at new ideas to move organizations forward. (iCohere, 2011).

The web community software draws on four key areas of strengths: Relationship building, collaborative learning, collaborative knowledge sharing and project collaboration. These areas are integrated within a set of transformational strategies and engaging face to face and online facilitation. (iCohere, 2011) Please see Table 4.

Table 4. iCohere process (iCohere, 2011)

Traditional Strategies	Engaging Group Processes and Facilitation
- Relationship Building - Collaborative Learning	- Collaborative Knowledge Sharing - Project Collaboration

Table 3. Features of COP software (Clarke, 2006)

Relationships	Learning	Knowledge	Action
Member networking profiles; Member directory with "relationship-focused" data fields; Subgroups that are defined by administrators or that allows members to self-join, Online meetings, online discussions	Recorded PowerPoint presentations; e-learning tools; Assessments; Web Conferencing; Online meetings; Online discussions; Web site links	Structured databases; Digital Stories; Idea banks; Web conferencing; Online meetings; Online discussions; Expert database and search tools; Announcements; web links	Project management; Task management; Document collaboration; File version tracking; File check-in and check-out; Instant messaging; Web conferencing; ; Online meetings; Online discussions; Individual and group calendars

ICohere platform combines traditional features like online discussions, instant messaging, document management and searchable member profiles with simple and powerful tools like web conferencing and streaming that will sustain and energize the community involved.(iCohere, 2011)

Communispace Software

Communispace is a communities of practice software that helps organizations deeply engage with their customers through delivering insights and thus creating business results. The company was started in 1999 and it offers full service community capabilities from customer insights, expert facilitation, member recruitment and analysis reporting. Features that aid in ensuring full service community are web 2.0, social networking and online communities.

Community Zero

Community Zero is a web based platform that allows organizations to build secure, scalable and online communities to engage the customers and improve business performance. With over a decade of offering hosted service and used by more than 2 million users, community zero easily scales to support multiple communities and addresses the organization's various collaboration and information requirements (Community Zero, 2011).

The features of Community Zero are as follows:

- Collaboration through centralized calendars, polls and member directories;
- Communication through email, polls and RSS feeds;
- Control and Customization through personalized site URL's, community tools and content moderation;
- Reports and Analytics through Google analytics and detailed reports; and
- Architecture and Security through SSL certification and persistent storage.

Future Trends of Communities of Practice

There is increasing evidence that COPs are being formalized into organizational structures with budgets, resources and tasks and thus become more like project teams with an aim and strategy (Hara, 2009).

There has also been significant growth in the number of network organizations in their various forms, due to a variety of influences. This is a trend that will continue and communities of practice encouraging learning and sharing knowledge within and among firms are an important aspect of success in this endeavors. All of these forms of communities of practice will continue to grow in order to encourage the application of knowledge through sharing and collaboration (Hara, 2009).

In the next section, the proponents looked at the area of social media in the field of education and learning.

THE INTERNET AND SOCIAL MEDIA

Without a doubt, the Internet is impacting people from all walks of life. There is a whole generation today who have grown up being connected to the Internet. Charles H. F. Davis calls them digital natives – people who have never experienced not having the Internet. These are the men and women who were born in the 1990's where the popularity of the World Wide Web exploded. They are now in their late teens to early 20's and currently university-level students.

Social networking or social media came in the early 2000's. Popular social networking sites include: Friendster (2002), MySpace (2003), LinkedIn (2003), Facebook (2004), Twitter (2006). As of October 2012, there are 1 billion active Facebook users worldwide (Dan Rohr, 2013). The Philippines has 31 million Facebook users which is equivalent to a 30.12% penetration rate (Market Insight, 2013). According to a study done by the Harvard Institute of Politics in 2011, 90% of college students have profiles on Facebook.

Usage of Social Media

Social media refers to web-based and mobile applications that allow people to easily create content, share information or resources, and to engage with other people in online conversations. The content can be in the form of plain text, images, audio or video podcasts, and even live streaming of audio or video.

Most usage of social media are people sharing personal information about themselves, their family, work, or things that interest them. The social media platform allows people to let others know their connections with others (Boyd, 2012). These connections could range anywhere from bosses, work colleagues, friends, acquaintances, to close family members such as siblings or spouse. In Facebook, people regularly upload pictures with their friends and re-live the experience that they had when the picture was taken. Conversations that begun during the offline experience are continued online via comments made on the picture.

It is only in the last couple of years that businesses took notice that people were spending a lot of time on social media. They realized that their customers as well as prospective customers were on the social media platform and they could actually engage with them personally. The era of social media marketing came about with companies putting up their own Facebook pages left and right. Lots of books were written to give companies tips and tricks on how to do social media marketing (Safko, 2010). Even the traditional mass media big-three of TV networks, radio stations, and print (newspapers and magazines) are now interacting with their audience on social media. Live TV shows get immediate feedback and comments from people via Twitter & Facebook posts and even broadcast them back on air.

Social Media and Educational Institutions

Since businesses have jumped on the bandwagon of social media, educational institutions are not to be outdone. Universities and colleges have created their own blogs to highlight stories of their current students and graduates. The life and culture of the school are shared through personal stories. This helps prospective students decide whether or not they want to enroll in that institution. The usage of social media here is more for marketing purposes.

Educational institutions are also using social media for broadcasting announcements. For example, if there is a suspension of classes, the administrator could simply post a status on their Facebook page and the students who are online would immediately see the announcement and could share it with their friends in just a few mouse clicks. In addition, reminders or upcoming events could also be advertised to the student body. The usage of social media here is more for notification purposes.

Social media technology is also being used to bridge the gap between the academic and social dimensions of a person (Lang, 2012). In particular, when a student goes to a foreign country, he has to make new social connections. Social media technology can aid in this aspect and indirectly impact the learning process of the student.

Social Media and Learning

The idea of using social media to aid in the learning process has not been explored that much yet. One obvious reason for such is that social networking sites have only been around for just a little more than a decade. Distance education and online learning have been existing for a longer time but they usually use systems which are separate from social networking sites. Recent research is beginning to show how social media is helping adult learners learn in an informal learning environment (Heo, 2013).

A Facebook group was also used in supporting a group of business education students undertaking teaching practicum. The study found that there was a good amount of user engagement/posts in the group (English, 2008).

But in general, there is still a lack of research in the usage of social media for learning. Furthermore, there is a need to create a framework to assess the impact of social media in IT Education. (Davis, 2012).

Being teachers in a higher education institution, this challenge led us to wonder if we could aid the learning process by supplementing classroom discussions with an online community via social media. Will the students learn more? Will the sharing of online resources motivate students to learn the subject? Will peer-to-peer interaction via social media encourage students not to get passive or get stuck? These questions drove us to create an online community of practice using social media technology.

CREATING AN ONLINE COMMUNITY OF PRACTICE USING SOCIAL MEDIA TECHNOLOGY

The Facebook group was created way back in 2011. The subject was about web design technologies. It was initially created to allow the students to have a medium to check requirements and announcements. Term after term, students were added to the group. It eventually developed into a community composed of current students, past students, alumni, and instructors. There are now over 350 members in the group.

The instructors are the group administrators and the prime movers of the group. They share resources and encourage the students to contribute and interact with each other. The members of the group are motivated to share information about web design voluntarily. The alumni are encouraged to help the students who are just new to learning web design. Professors and alumni help one an-

other as peers in order to deepen their expertise and knowledge of the subject areas.

Some of the knowledge shared include: technical information, technology trends and developments, Massive Online Open Courses (MOOC's), job and career opportunities, Youtube videos, quizzes, and Student-Alumni coaching sessions.

ISSUES, CONTROVERSIES, PROBLEMS

Although there is a clamour for social media in education, literature has discovered gaps within the system that may hinder collaboration and knowledge sharing in the area of social media

- Lack of Research in the area of social media and it's use and purpose in postsecondary education (Davis, 2012)
- Need for framework for evaluating impact of Social Media in IT Education (Davis, 2012)

Given the research gaps, the proponents seek to address the given research questions:

- How do online communities of practice engage students to learn and build new knowledge?

SOLUTIONS AND RECOMMENDATIONS

In order to achieve its research objectives and targets, the proponents adhere to the constructivist approach in qualitative research, based on the systems thinking school. In addition, the research used the hybrid approach based on Checkland's soft systems methodology and Strauss and Corbins' version of grounded theory.

The hybrid methodology allows the proponent to develop a framework on communities of practice that is acceptable to all the participants. Therefore, the methodology used is both participant and researcher centered. In order to complement the research methodology, the proponent used single case embedded design to analyze the given phenomenon. Results are collected using data triangulation in the form of interviews, focus group discussions, and participant observations.

Using the approach, the proponents merged the seven phases of the two methodologies into a five-step process as used in the inductive-hypothetical research strategy.

The next section shows the detailed research design that the research project adhered to.

DETAILED RESEARCH DESIGN AND STRATEGY

In order to create a framework that represents the communities of practice that exist in the Facebook group, the proponents used the hybrid methodologies of grounded theory and soft systems methodology and did the following: 1. Assess the existence of communities of practice using codes identified 2. Identify common themes and categories 3. Create a paradigm model to describe

the communities of practice and 4. Create a framework that guides educators in creating their own communities of practice.

QUALITIES OF COMMUNITIES OF PRACTICE

The first element that the proponents evaluated is the existence of the communities of practice. In order to evaluate if the communities of practice existed in the Facebook group, the proponents compared different definitions of communities of practice with the codes identified in the web design Facebook group.

Taking into consideration four different definitions of Communities of practice, it validates the existence of the communities of practice in the online web design group.

The next step taken by the proponent is to analyze the qualities of the communities of practice and identify common themes from the codes taken using data analysis.

Table 5. Comparison of definition of communities of practice

Author	Definition	Web Design Communities of Practice
Wenger	Groups of people that share a concern, a set of problems, or a passion about a topic and who deepen their knowledge and expertise in this area on an ongoing basis	The members of the community share the common objective of learning more about web design technologies and solving complex problems on technology
Sergio Vasquez	Group of people linked by a common, recurring and stable practice whereby they learn in this common practice	The web design community of practice is a group that constantly and consistently engaged with its members on the topic of web technologies
Lesser and Storck	A group whose members regularly engage in sharing and learning based on their common interests	The web design community of practice constantly updates the Facebook group with relevant information regarding web design and applications
John Brown	Group of people with different functions and viewpoints, committed to joint work over a significant period of time during which they construct objects, solve problems, invent, learn and negotiate meaning and develop a way of reading mutually.	The web design community solves Web related problems & shares opinions in solving complex problems

Evaluation of the Online Community of Practice

To evaluate the online community of practice, the proponents performed interviews, focused group discussions, participant observations, and surveys. The proponents used the Grounded Theory by Corbin and Strauss and performed Open Coding and Axial Coding of the data we have gathered from the surveys and interviews.

The main categories that came out of Open Coding include the following:

1. Community Engagement
2. Effectiveness
3. Commitment to Sharing and Learning
4. Self-improvement

Community Engagement

Many of the members indicated that the online community of practice motivated them to study because there is a strong sense of belongingness in the group. By knowing that other like-minded peers are there, studying alongside you, and willing to help you out when you get stuck, they are encouraged to push forward.

In addition, members are motivated to share knowledge to other members since there is a common topic and perhaps there is a "pay-it-forward" effect of sharing. When one benefits from a resource shared by another, that person is motivated to share other resources that he has also found to be helpful.

Finally, the shared resources serve as a form of reference for the members. When members encounter problems in doing their projects, they can come back to the Facebook group, look at the references, solve their own problems, and move forward in completing their projects.

Effectiveness

The second category that was uncovered from the data analysis is effectiveness. The surveyed members said that the online community of practice was helpful for them. For the current students, they had higher motivation to learn and work on their projects compared to another class which had their own Facebook group but didn't have that group serve as an online community of practice.

This effectiveness was driven by mutual trust among members. Since they knew that they were on this journey of learning web design together and that they were there for each other, they were motivated to study and learn. In addition to that, they knew that those who went ahead of them including those who have passed the course already

Figure 3. Themes of communities of practice

or who have graduated and are already in the IT industry, are also in the group willing to help them anytime they had a hard time finishing their work.

Commitment to Sharing and Learning

The third category that came out of the data analysis is that there is a commitment to sharing and learning within the Community of Practice. Some members continue to share resources even if they are not part of the ongoing class anymore. These members include past students, present and past faculty, and even those who have graduated already.

One factor that has greatly contributed to this is that the instructor himself exhibits an attitude of continuous learning. Although he is already a teacher, he also takes the role of a continuous learner. The instructor actively contributes to the group and as a result, encourages the students to share as well.

On the part of the alumni, there is also a willingness to share and mentor current students. Being those who have been on the receiving end of mentoring in the past, they now want to mentor others in return.

Self-Improvement

Finally, a desire of self-improvement is evident among the members of the group. This serves as the underlying motivation why they want to learn more. They want to learn more about web design because ultimately, they improve in their skills and would be more employable in the future.

Besides learning about web design, they also learn about the latest job or career opportunities and the latest trends / technologies of web design. Finally, they are also able to build relationships with peers who may become colleagues or even possible business partners in the future.

Model Paradigm

In order to properly explain the community of practice that is present in the web design group, the proponents used the model paradigm prescribed by axial coding of Grounded theory to discuss the phenomenon of community of practice.

The paradigm model is divided into five conditions: causal conditions, the phenomenon, context, intervening conditions and consequences. The model allows the proponents to identify the relationships between the categories and the subcategories.

In addition, the reasons why the community of practice is present are due to the continuous community engagement and the commitment to learning and sharing. The strategies that the community used include encouraging members to contribute by giving incentives and moderating posts to ensure quality. Please see Figure 5 for the paradigm model of the community of practice.

The Community of Practice framework takes into account inputs, four main elements and outputs. The inputs to the framework include information that the members contribute to the community. It also takes information that the learners share on the topic of web design.

There are four elements that are integral in a COP's success. These elements are as follows: area of responsibility/activities, types or modes of knowledge passed, technology support features and actions that the COP's do in the area of learning.

The output contributes to the process of new knowledge and best practices that may be useful for other community members. Given the model paradigm and themes identified, the proponents were able to create a technology framework that depicts the creation of the online community of practice through social media.

Important aspects of the technology framework include five components: (1) activities done in

Figure 4. Paradigm model of communities of practice

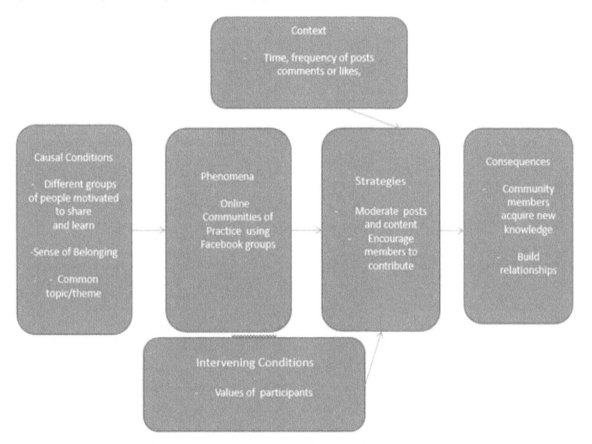

the community (posts, videos, alumni-student coaching, games, sharing best practices among others), (2) technology support features (timeline, files, likes, ask question feature among others), (3) qualities of COP's (community engagement, effectiveness, self-improvement and commitment to sharing and learning), (4) different knowledge types and modes (socialization, externalization and combination) and actions taken (communicate, collaborate and integrate knowledge). By combining these elements, the community will be able to gather best practices in web design, solve problems and create new insights and knowledge.

FUTURE RESEARCH DIRECTIONS

The current research is a good initial study in the area of communities of practice using social media. The next step of the research includes validating the results of the study with an external audience and other experts in the field of communities of practice and collaboration.

Subsequently, further studies may be conducted to examine the impact of behavioral characteristics (power and position) in the dynamics of collaboration inside the group. A comparative study may also determine if the framework can be

Figure 5. Technology framework of community of practice

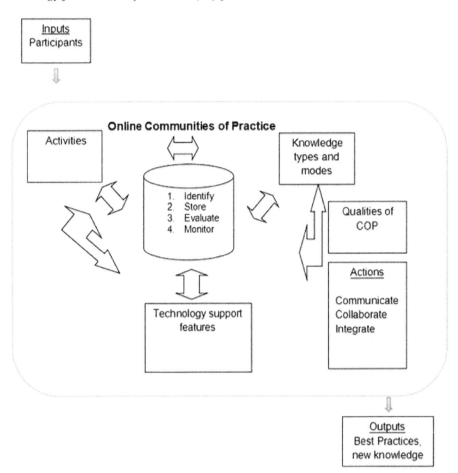

similarly applied to other social media groups like Google+, LinkedIn, or any similar social media platform. Other similar sectors like training and development or government agencies may also adopt the framework and evaluate if it is effective in knowledge sharing and innovation.

CONCLUSION

The communities of practice present in the Web Design Facebook group is an informal group that was formed due to the commitment of learners to learning and acquiring new knowledge, effectiveness of collaborative activities and commitment to sharing and self-improvement.

Based on the hybrid implementation of grounded theory and soft systems methodology, the proponents were able to identify core categories and best practices in the organization. In order to establish the relationship between the categories, the proponents were able to create a model paradigm that effectively analyzes the given phenomenon. Using these categories and existing literature, the proponents were able to create a technology framework that provides a guide for communities of practice to collaborate effectively using Facebook groups.

The framework shows that the communities of practice inside the Web Design Facebook group are composed of five different elements: qualities of the communities of practice, areas and activities where knowledge building and collaboration is delivered, types of knowledge generated and the role of technology in supporting the different activities of the communities of practice.

REFERENCES

Archer, N. (2006). A classification of Communities of Practice. In *Encyclopedia of Communities of Practice in Information and Knowledge Management* (p. 21). London: Idea Group. doi:10.4018/978-1-59140-556-6.ch005

Boyd, D. M., & Ellison, N. B. (2012). Part VIII: Social Network Sites. Online Communication and Collaboration. *Reading (Sunderland)*.

Campos, et al. (2011). *Sharing Knowledge through Communities of Practice*. Hershey, PA: IGI Global.

CheckLand. (1999). *Systems Thinking Systems Practice*. Chichester, UK: John Wiley.

Clarke, C. a. (2006). The Concept of Communities of Practice. In *Encyclopedia of Communities of Practice in Information and Knowledge Management* (p. 92). London: Idea Group. doi:10.4018/978-1-59140-556-6.ch010

Clarke, E. C. (2006). *Encyclopedia of Communities of Practice in Information and Knowledge Management*. Hershey, PA: Idea Publishing.

Communispace. (2011). *Communispace Official Website*. Retrieved October 20, 2011 from http://www.communispace.com/home.aspx

CommunityZero. (2011). *Community Zero Official Website*. Retrieved October 19, 2011 from http://www.communityzero.com

Davis, C. (2012). *Social Media in Higher Education: A Literature Review and Research Directions*. The Center for the Study of Higher Education at The University of Arizona and Claremont Graduate University.

Dotsika, F. (2006). Article. In E. Coakes & S. Clarke (Eds.), An IT Perspective on Supporting Communities of Practice, Encyclopedia of Communities of Practice in Information and Knowledge Management (pp. 257–263). Idea Group Inc.

English, R., & Duncan-Howell, J. (2008). Facebook© goes to college: Using social networking tools to support students undertaking teaching practicum. *Journal of Online Learning and Teaching, 4*(4).

Hara, N. (2009). *Communities of Practice Fostering Peer to Peer learning and Informal Knowledge Sharing in the Workplace*. Springer.

Heo, G. M., & Lee, R. (2013). Blogs and Social Network Sites as Activity Systems: Exploring Adult Informal Learning Process through Activity Theory Framework. Journal of Educational Technology & Society, 16(4).

iCohere. (2011, August 24). *Icohere information*. Retrieved August 24, 2011, from Icohere official website: http://www.icohere.com/webcommunities.htm

Market Insight. (2013). Socialbakers. In *Philippine Facebook Statistics*. Retrieved March 25, 2013, from http://www.socialbakers.com/facebook-statistics/philippines

Roberts, J. (2011). *A Communities of Practice Approach to Management Knowledge Dissemination*. Hershey, PA: IGI Global. doi:10.4018/978-1-60566-802-4.ch001

Safko, L. (2010). *The Social Media Bible: Tactics*. Tools, and Strategies for Business Success.

Socialbakers. (2013). In *Philippine Facebook Statistics*. Retrieved March 25, 2013, from http://www.socialbakers.com/facebook-statistics/philippines

Vicedo, K. (2011). *Proceedings of Knowledge Management Workshop*. Philippines: CNDR.

Wenger, E. (2002). *Cultivating Communities of Practice*. Harvard Business Review Press.

KEY TERMS AND DEFINITIONS

Axial Coding: "A set of procedures whereby data are put back together in new ways after open coding, by making connections between categories." They proposed a "coding paradigm" that involved "conditions, context, action/ interactional strategies and consequences" (Strauss & Corbin, 2008).

Communities of Practice: Collaborative, informal network that support professional practitioners in their efforts to develop shared understandings and engage in work-relevant knowledge building.

Formal Network of Practice: Network of practice that requires membership that is controlled by fees/ and or acceptance through some central authority that also assist in organizing, facilitating and supporting member communications, events and discussion topics.

Open Coding: Includes labeling concepts, defining and developing categories based on their properties and dimensions (Khandkar, 2013).

This work was previously published in The Evolution of the Internet in the Business Sector edited by Pedro Isaías, Piet Kommers, and Tomayess Issa, pages 259-277, copyright year 2015 by Business Science Reference (an imprint of IGI Global).

Chapter 63

Toward An Effective Virtual Learning Environment:
From a Social Presence Perspective

Marie A. Valentin
Texas A&M University, USA

Junhee Kim
Texas A&M University, USA

Helen M. Muyia
Texas A&M University, USA

Celestino Valentin
Texas A&M University, USA

ABSTRACT

In this chapter, the authors present an Effective Virtual Learning Model and answer the research questions, What is the perception of social presence on virtual learning? What role does social presence play in student engagement in virtual learning? and, What are the social presence factors influencing the effective learning environment? The method used to answer the pending research questions was the integrative literature review utilizing a six-step format. Authors conducted a literature review search utilizing the descriptors of virtual learning and social presence. From there articles were identified, selected, and synthesized according to the research questions. This research was informed by the Community of Inquiry Framework as the theoretical foundation from which the results were concluded. Based on results of emerging themes, the authors present the Effective Virtual Learning Model as a foundational basis for theory, research, and more importantly, practice.

BACKGROUND

The concept of learning in a virtual environment has gained vast attention in recent years (Allmendinger, 2010; Shea & Bidjerano, 2012Taghizadeh & Vaezi, 2011), and is the focus of many recently published articles. Allmendinger (2010) indicated "Computer supported collaborative learning give rise to new challenges in terms of mutually constructing meaning, establishing and maintaining the users motivation, as well as structuring social interaction in learning situations" (p. 41). Taghizadeh and Vaezi (2011) called for a deeper understanding of the potential of education and elearning. They further explored elearning in terms of transforming the current state of education and

DOI: 10.4018/978-1-4666-8619-9.ch063

claim that strategic development is necessary for transforming education. To do this, a strong foundation based on theory will be required.

Shea and Bidjerano (2012) found that "between the years of 2008 and 2009, over one million students took courses offered online for the first time" (p. 316), this brought the total number of online students to over 5.5 million in the United States alone. This growth exceeded the growth of normal traditional courses by a rate of 20%, and the U.S. Department of Education reported that over 11, 200 college level programs are being delivered fully online (Shea & Bidjerano, 2012). Condon (2012) argued that technological advancements are rapidly increasing and are becoming obsolete even before they get to the market place, thereby making online access more available. An increasing number of universities are offering online courses to a global audience (Franceschi, Lee, Zanakis, & Hinds, 2009), however, these offerings do not come without problems. Research on the topic of social presence (Weinel, Bannert, Zumbach, Hoppe, & Malzahn, 2011) and sense of community (Tonteri, Kosonen, Ellonen, & Tarkiainen, 2011) may serve to inform effective online collaborations which lead to social presence and online learning (Ke F., 2010). Effective virtual communities serve to provide an exchange of knowledge and deep learning (Ke F., 2010). Shea and Bidjerano (2012) explained that "there is a longstanding belief that distance education requires a greater degree of self-directedness and self-reliance and it seems probable that learners in asynchronous, largely text-based online courses face challenges requiring persistence and determination" (p. 316). These shortcomings of online course offerings have been a source of concern for all stakeholders involved (Franceschi, Lee, Zanakis, & Hinds, 2009).

Social presence is a measure of the feeling of community that learners experience in an online environment (Tu, & McIsaac, 2010). It is argued as the most important perception that occurs in an online environment. Social presence or the lack there of, may serve as an indicator of online course offering success as well as serve to create "the conditions of inquiry and quality interaction; in online learning contexts where learners feel secure to openly communicate with each other and develop a sense of community" (Taghizadeh & Vaezi, 2011, p. 121). Furthermore, social presence may be a predictor of course satisfaction (Weinel, Bannert, Zumbach, Hoppe, & Malzahn, 2011), and a determinant of successful communication in a virtual setting (Allmendinger, 2010). Furthermore, several gaps in research have been found, for example, there is a lack of empirically based information as to how, or what aspects of virtual learning, facilitate learning (Traphagan, et al., 2010) and guarantee student engagement (Bulu, 2012). The intent of this research is to explore what components are necessary in an effective virtual learning environment to ensure student success. Therefore, the purpose of this review of literature is to explore through literature what components need to be present in order to facilitate student engagement and learning in an effective learning virtual environment through the lens of social presence.

The difficulty in obtaining student engagement in a virtual learning environment and social presence are the guiding factors related to the review of literature. We have identified three fundamental research questions that have been found to be important to our literature review process and will serve to guide this review of literature.

Research Questions

The following questions guided this review of literature:

1. What is the perception of social presence on virtual learning?
2. What role does social presence play in student engagement in virtual learning?
3. What social presence factors influence an effective virtual environment?

These questions are addressed throughout the literature review and tables have been created to assist in making correlations easier to understand with regard to components of effective virtual learning environment and components influencing social presence in a virtual learning environment.

Literature Review

To address the research questions, a comprehensive review of literature was conducted using Machi and Mc Evoy (2012) model. In their book, *The Literature Review, Six Steps to Success,* (Machi & Mc Evoy (2012), outline six steps to writing the literature review: Step1. Select a Topic, Step. 2. Search the literature, Step 3. Develop the argument, Step 4. Survey the literature, Step 5. Critique the literature, and Step 6. Write the review. The process of researching and writing the literature review followed the model as described in the book as follows: Step 1. Select a Topic – (Virtual Learning and Social Presence), Step 2. Search the literature (we researched key words), Step 3. Develop the argument (We created a problem statement and developed research questions in relation to virtual learning and social presence), Step 4. Survey the literature (We identified, read, and selected only relevant articles related to the topic), Step 5. Critique the literature (we searched the literature and identified key components and sections of the topic) and Step 6. Write the review (We synthesized findings, developed tables, and cultivated a model for effective virtual learning environments).

The process utilized to create the literature research and search criteria were to identify the resources that would assist in obtaining relevant peer reviewed articles. A basic internet search was conducted using the university library search engine to help identify articles with key words entered as -virtual learning and social presence- which resulted in a total number of peer-reviewed journals (31,327). The search was further narrowed to include only those that were peer reviewed

articles with a criterion date of after 2001, which resulted in (10,638) articles. The authors therefore preformed an advanced search utilizing the university library search engine using-virtual learning and social presence- in subject only and from 2006 to 2012. This resulted in having a reasonable number of peer reviewed articles selected to a feasible amount of (20). The refined search included articles from the following databases- ERIC, M.E. Sharpe, Arts & Sciences JSTOR, Dialnet, DOAJ, Medline, and Social Sciences Citation Index. The articles were then reviewed individually for content -related material and in the written language of English which revealed a further reduction of peer review articles to only 16 in total which were used as part of this review of literature.

Theoretical Framework

Our research was informed by the Community of Inquiry framework model (Garrison, 2007), which combines three elements into the framework of online learning in higher education. These elements consist of cognitive presence, teaching presence and social presence as depicted in Figure 1. The "Community of Inquiry model outlines the behaviors and processes required to enable

Figure 1. Community of inquiry framework; adapted from Garrison (2007)

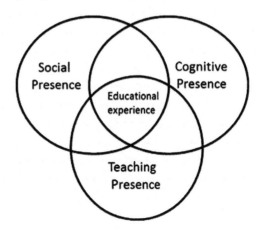

knowledge construction in asynchronous online environments through the development of various forms of 'presence'-cognitive, teaching and social" (Shea & Bidjarano, 2012, p. 317).

Social presence may be categorized as effective expressions (e.g. open communication and group cohesion) and indicators include: risk free expression and encourage collaboration. Whereas, Cognitive presence is categorized as a triggering event (e.g. exploration, integration, and resolution) and indicators include: sense of puzzlement: information exchange, connecting ideas, and applying new ideas. Teaching presence on the other hand may be categorized as design and organization (e.g. facilitating discourse and direct instruction) and indicators for teaching presence include setting curriculum and methods: sharing personal meaning and focusing discussion. Utilizing social presence, cognitive presence, and teaching presence create a positive and rewarding educational experience for the student participant according to Garrison (2007). The focus of this review of literature is to take a -social presence-perspective therefore we have selected -social presence- as the focus.

LITERATURE REVIEW RESULTS

While conducting the review of literature the following components emerged: (a) social presence and its effect on student engagement, (b) components and indicators of social presence, establishing social presence, (c) current state of student engagement in virtual learning environments, (d) effective virtual learning environment components, and (f) influencing social presence in an effective virtual learning environment. We synthesized the findings from the review of literature and these emerging themes and proposed the conceptual effective virtual learning model for recommendation in eLearning virtual environments.

Social Presence and Student Engagement

Social presence according to Allmendinger (2010) is a social factor and specifically addressed "the feeling of being present with another person in a virtual environment (p. 41). Taghizadeh and Vaezi (2011) argued that social presence can be defined as "the ability of participants to identify with the community (e.g. course of review of literature), communicate purposefully in a trusting environment and develop interpersonal relationships by way of projecting their individual personalities (p. 121). Weinel, Bannert, Zumbach, Hoppe, and Malzahn (2011) argued that "social presence is the degree to which a person is aware of another person in technology-mediated communication settings" (p. 513). Social presence consists of effective communication, open communication and group cohesion (Garrison, 2007, p. 63). Short et al. (1976) originally investigated the issues of social presence in the area of telecommunications and Allmendinger (2010) regarded "social presence as a single dimension representing a cognitive syntheses of several factors that occur naturally in face-to-face communication" (p. 46), moreover Allmendinger presented this 38 years ago and still stands true today. Weinel et al. (2011) posited that social presence is that ability for a student to "project themselves socially and emotionally in a community of inquiry" (p. 513).

It is argued that social presence has been found to be one of the most important challenges for online teaching and warrants the importance of its establishment in effective virtual learning environments. This is the case primarily because it has been proven empirically that social presence has a strong connection with student satisfaction and perceptions in online learning (Taghizadeh & Vaezi, 2011) as well as, perceptions of being connected in an interpersonal environment (Allmendinger, 2010). Furthermore, it is important that students are accepted and this acceptance is an integral part of a learning community (Taghizadeh & Vaezi, 2011). Behm-Morawitz (2013) argued that social presence is dependent upon the individual's investments and immersion in online learning. However, to illicit this type of investment and immersion we delved more deeply into the portent of social presence and its components.

Components and Indicators of Social Presence

Mayer and Sung (2012) indicated that there are two components to social presence that are directly linked to cognitive and effective learning: Intimacy and Immediacy.

- **Intimacy:** consists of nonverbal factors (i.e. eye contact, smiling, facial expressions) that can be easily picked up on in a face-to-face setting and can be exhibited in a virtual setting as: feedback, cognitive support, and the communication of emotions (Allmendinger, 2010).
- **Immediacy:** consists of the psychological distance between sender and receiver of the communication and can be exhibited in a virtual setting in terms of time and space between the communicator and the recipient of the communication (Mayer & Sung, 2012).

Furthermore, Rourke, Anderson, Garrison, and Archer (2001) proposed three categories of indicators of social presence which include, affective indicators, interactive indicators, and cohesive indicators:

- **Affective Indicators:** "Expressions of emotions, feeling, and moods and can be exhibited in virtual environments as use of humor and self-disclosure; expression of emotion, feelings, beliefs, and values" (Mayer & Sung, 2012, p. 1739).

- **Interactive Indicators:** "Evidence that someone is actively attending to you in an online communication and exhibited by continuing a thread, quoting from other's messages, referring explicitly to others messages, asking questions, complimenting, expressing appreciation, expressing agreement" (Mayer & Sung, 2012, p. 1739).
- **Cohesive Indicators:** "Exemplified by activities that build and sustain a sense of group commitment and exhibited by vocatives, addressing a person or group by name, phatics, and salutations" (Mayer & Sung, 2012, p. 1739).

These components and indicators can be used as a measure of social presence in any virtual environment. More importantly, they must be included in a community of inquiry to ensure student engagement and participation. However, as important as they may be are sometimes very difficult to attain if not planned for in advance.

Establishing Social Presence

Social presence is not easily established in a virtual learning environment and can be mediated dependent on the amount and quality of information provided (Moskaliuk, Bertram, & Cress, 2013) as well as by utilizing techniques that support social presence and interaction from student participants. Such as course design, instructor strategies, and participant strategies (Mayer & Sung, 2012). DiBlas and Poggi (2007) indicated that "realism" in a virtual environment should be considered, where as, Bosch-Sijtsema and Sivunen (2013) argue that synchronous and asynchronous communication support is a tool that can support social presence. Taghizadeh and Vaezi (2011) posited that open reciprocal and respectful communication is core in establishing social presence. Behm-Morawitz (2013) likewise argued that spatial, virtual and physical presence is crucial to complete immersion from the student participants and result in the establishment of social presence. Spatial presence may be viewed as the level of immersion in a virtual environment. Whereas, virtual presence is viewed as sensory immersion, and physical presence is viewed as cognitive and emotional immersion.

Malik (2012) discussed that there are several challenges that must be considered in establishing social presence in a virtual learning environment, which may range from motivation of the student participant, to the type of learning materials, and course design. However, Boettcher (2010) presented a list of the top ten best practices associated with creating online social presence. At the top of the list was -be present at the course site- which is somewhat as simple as that. Social presence cannot be established if neither the student participant nor the instructor is present in the virtual environment.

Boettcher (2010) described the top ten best practices for practitioners/instructors which are as follows:

1. Be present at the course site.
2. Create a supportive online course community.
3. Share a set of very clear expectations for students and yourself.
4. Use a variety of: large group, small group, and individual work experiences.
5. Use both synchronous and asynchronous activities.
6. Early in the term, ask for informal feedback.
7. Prepare discussion posts that invite questions, discussions, reflections and responses.
8. Focus on content resources and applications and links to current events and examples that are easily accessed.
9. Combine core concept learning with customized and personal learning.
10. Plan a good closing and wrap activity for the course.

Utilizing even some of these ten, if not all, best practices will establish social presence and increase effectiveness in an online virtual learning environment.

Current State of Student Engagement in Virtual Learning environments

In determining the current state of student engagement we must first understand the virtual learning environment (VLE) and its fundamental definition. Tassos A. Mikropolous, defined VLE as being, "a virtual environment that has one or more educational objectives, pedagogical metaphors, provides users with experiences they would otherwise not be able to experience in the physical world and leads to the attainment of specific learning outcomes" (Mikropoulos, 2006, p. 198). Student engagement in virtual learning comes in many forms and is described by various authors in diversified manners such as, telepresence which is defined as "the extent to which one feels present in the medicated environment, rather than in immediate physical environment" (Steuer, 1992, p. 76-77).

Other forms of virtual learning environments to help promote student engagement come in the form of actually creating an environment in which is a means of: creating social and professional relationships, which are all too often absent in virtual environments (Condon, 2012; Phillips, Shaw, Sullivan, & Johnson, 2010). Students engage with others to form a community, which can be both virtual and real so that, "a set of people sharing certain purposes, policies, and resources, including the infrastructure that allows them to meet, may support each other in the achievement of their goals" (Di Blas & Poggi, 2007, p.130). The virtual online environment engagement opportunities are boundless because the "internet allows people with common interest and goals to meet regardless of their geographical location, and other barriers such as age, social status, ethnical group, etc., become easier to overcome" (Di Blas & Poggi, 2007, p. 130).

Furthermore, there are open culture virtual worlds that, "offer a different experience to their users, a more flexible experience than their counterparts. As a result, their sources of engagement are different" and they "do not limit the user experience through the use of narratives or a fixed fantasy setting" (Franceschi, Lee, Zanakis, & Hinds 2009, p. 79). Two key indicators for student engagement in virtual worlds stem from, (1) virtual generation students embrace of technology for open interaction (Chen, Siau, & Nah, 2012; Pew Research, 2009) and (2) open involvement for relationship building within the open society (Siau, & Nah, 2012).

Effective Virtual Learning Environment Components

The effective virtual learning environment may be well represented by the Sense of Virtual Community (SOVC) concept that leads to student engagement such as helping others and collaboration to achieve a certain learning objective (Tonteri et al., 2011). In a virtual environment, sense of community can be defined as "the feeling members have of belonging to a community, the belief that members matter to one another and to the community, and a shared faith that their needs will be met through their commitment to the community" (Tonteri et al., 2011, p. 2216). Although there is still lack of a universal agreement on conceptualization, researchers and scholars commonly suggest that the concept of SOVC involves a shared emotional connection and the dimensions of membership (Blanchard, 2008; Ellonen et al., 2007). Thus, one of the most relevant theoretical frameworks to illuminate the complex phenomenon in virtual learning environments may be the Community of Inquiry framework that offers three dimensions of membership for effective learning: teaching

presence, social presence, and cognitive presence (Taghizadeh & Vaezi, 2011).

Out of the 16 articles that met the selection criteria and were reviewed, nine were based on the Community of Inquiry framework by examining one or two of the three dimensions of membership (Bulu, 2012; Mikropoulos, 2006; Moskaliuk et al., 2013; Weinel et al., 2011) or all of them (Ke, 2010; Shea & Bidjarano, 2012; Taghizadeh & Vaezi, 2011; Tonteri et al, 2011; Traphagan et al., 2010). Although each article had different research purposes, all of them provided characteristics of effective virtual learning environment. The methods used in the literature to identify the components of effective virtual learning environment were diverse: six articles employed an experiment (Allmendinger, 2010; Chen, 2012; Franceschi et al., 2009; Mikropoulos, 2006; Moskaliuk et al., 2013; Weinel et al., 2011); two were mixed method articles (Di Blas, 2007; Traphagan et al., 2010); two employed literature review (Baylor, 2009, 2011); one was based on case review of literature (Ke, 2010); four took quantitative approach such as regression and correlation analysis (Bulu, 2012; Shea & Bidjerano, 2012; Taghizadeh & Vaezi, 2011; Tonteri et al, 2011), and the remaining one employed interview methods (Bosch-Sijtsema & Sivunen, 2013). In the seven articles that did not use the Community of Inquiry framework, also presented were synchronous and/or asynchronous interaction (Di Blas, 2007), avatars (Allmendinger, 2010; Baylor, 2009, 2011), structured tasks to measure group engagement (Franceschi et al., 2009), interactivity (Chen, 2012), and effective features of the virtual learning tool (Bosch-Sijtsema & Sivunen, 2013). More details of this literature are shown in Table 1.

Influencing Social Presence in an Effect Virtual Learning Environment

To capture the complex relationships among the components of effective virtual learning environments, we set the concept of social presence as the

Table 1. Components of effective virtual learning environment

Year	Lead Author	Components of Effective Virtual Learning Environment	Methods
2006	Mikropoulos	• Avatar as the pupils' representation • Personal presence • Social presence	Experiment
2007	Di Blas	• Community and sub-groups with specific tasks and common goals • Synchronous and/or asynchronous interaction • Activities requiring interaction • Informal social interaction, friendly competition, the cultural discussions, the pictures visible in the 3D environment, the HTML content, the messages and directions, the playing of team games	Mixed methods
2009	Baylor	The way in which students are represented by avatars	Lit. Review
2009	Franceschi	• Getting to know you (Group formation or community building) • Sense of being together in the same place • Voice communication • Gesture and body language • Support for student creativity • Structured tasks to measure group engagement	Experiment
2010	Allmendinger	Basic avatars (photos or robotic heads)	Experiment
2010	Ke	• Sense of community • Teaching presence (course design, facilitation, and instruction) • Cognitive presence • Social presence	Case review of literature
2010	Traphagan	• Cognitive presence • Teaching presence • Social presence	Mixed methods
2011	Baylor	A peer model agent with similar level of competence to the learner	Lit. Review
2011	Taghizadeh	• Cognitive presence • Teaching presence • Social presence	Descriptive statistics
2011	Tonteri	• Cognitive benefit • Social integrative benefit • Personal integrative benefit • Hedonic benefit • Activities of participating in learning	Regression analysis
2011	Weinel	Social presence	Experiment
2012	Bulu	• Place presence (personal presence) • Social presence • Co-presence	Correlation analyses
2012	Chen	Interactivity	Experiment
2012	Shea	• Teaching presence • Social presence • Cognitive presence • Learning presence (Learners' self-regulatory cognitions and behaviors)	Regression analysis
2013	Bosch-Sijtsema	• The feature of visualization, use of professional avatars, video, 3D models, and scenarios and real-life situations not restricted by physics laws or scale • The ability to share and edit information, files and documents • Ability to store documents files, whiteboards and sticky notes, possibility to record sessions and discussions • Possibility to make connections to other internal systems in the organization • Options to have more private conversations in either chat or in silent areas	Interview
2013	Moskaliuk	• Feeling of being present (personal presence) • Social context (social presence) • Learning motivation • Perspective-taking	Experiment

frame of reference by means of which we examined the empirical findings and integrated them into a conceptual model. As shown in Table 2, nine studies addressed the components that influence social presence in virtual learning environments.

There were four articles that utilized the experiment methodology for components influencing social presence engage the use of presence such that of an Avatar as the pupils' representation, personal presence, teaching presence, synchronous chat, affective, experience with information and communication technology (ICT), perception of self as part of environment (Mikropoulos, 2006; Moskaliuk, 2013; Ozturk, 2011; Weinel, 2011). There was one article that incorporated a case review of literature in terms of group discussions, synchronous communication and tool as components influencing social presence (Ke, 2010). Furthermore, three articles utilized quantitative (correlation analysis & descriptive statistics), qualitative and/or a mixed method approach to components influencing social pres-

ence which were tasks, group collaboration, open communication, group cohesion, representation through avatars, verbal and non-verbal communication channels, and perception of self as a part of environment (Bulu, 2012; Taghizadeh, 2011; Traphagan, 2010). The final article reviewed for components influencing social presence was done as a literature review with contents including a caring co-learner agent (Baylor, 2011).

The Effective Virtual Learning Model

Developing a conceptual model for an effective virtual learning environment from a social presence perspective necessitates the integration of previous research findings (see Table 1 and 2) and a theoretical framework (i.e., Community of Inquiry). As noted earlier, Community of Inquiry suggests that effective virtual learning environments should have three types of presence: teaching, social, and cognitive. In his research based on Community of Inquiry, Ke (2010) found that the

Table 2. Components influencing social presence in virtual learning environment

Year	Lead Author	Components Influencing Social Presence	Methods
2006	Mikropoulos	• Avatar as the pupils' representation • Personal presence	Experiment
2010	Ke	• Teaching presence (course design approach) • Group discussions • Synchronous communication	Case review of literature
2010	Traphagan	• Tool • Tasks • Group collaboration	Mixed methods
2011	Baylor	A caring co-learner agent	Lit. Review
2011	Öztürk	Synchronous chat	Experiment
2011	Taghizadeh	• Affective • Open communication • Group cohesion	Descriptive statistics
2011	Weinel	Experience with Information and Communication Technology (ICT)	Experiment
2012	Bulu	• The representation through avatars • Verbal and non-verbal communication channels	Correlation analyses
2013	Moskaliuk	• Perception of self as part of environment • Avatars representing real colleagues • Branded equipment	Experiment

content and discussion design features (i.e., teaching presence) predicted 21% of the variability in students' performance of knowledge-constructive interactions (i.e., cognitive presence). Furthermore, he found that the content and discussion design features predicted 23% of the variability in students' performance of social interactions (i.e., social presence). In addition, Shea and Bidjarano (2012) found the moderating effect of learning presence between teaching/social presence and cognitive presence, where learning presence was defined as learner's online self-regulatory cognitions and behaviors. According to Moskaliuk et al. (2013), students' learning motivation is a pivotal prerequisite of higher extent of exploration behavior such as engagement. Thus, learning motivation plays the role of mediator between other situational variables and students' learning or engagement. As shown in Figure 1, a conceptual model for effective virtual learning environment from a social presence perspective was developed

through the integration of these empirical findings and Community of Inquiry. In particular, various components such as the use of an avatar and personal presence that influence social presence were included in the model.

We developed the design of the -Effective Virtual Learning Environment- as a holistic approach to incorporate steps needed in order to transition from a teaching presence through student engagement as a result of the virtual learning experience. Key components in the social presence have been identified through the research documentation process of collecting and analyzing of the data during the literature review process. Identified in the model are six main components of the flow diagram: Teaching presence, Social Presence, Learning Presence, Cognitive presence, Learning motivation and concluding with Student engagement.

Overview based on the Effective Virtual Learning Environment flow diagram conceptual model

Figure 2. A conceptual model for effective virtual learning environment from a social presence perspective

Effective Virtual Learning Environment

- Avatar as the representations of pupil and self
- Personal presence (Perception of self as part of environment)
- Group discussion/cohesion/collaboration
- Synchronous verbal and/or nonverbal communication/chat
- Tool and tasks
- Affective and open communication
- Experience with ICT
- Branded equipment

Teaching Presence → Social Presence → Cognitive Presence → Learning Motivation → Student Engagement

Learning Presence

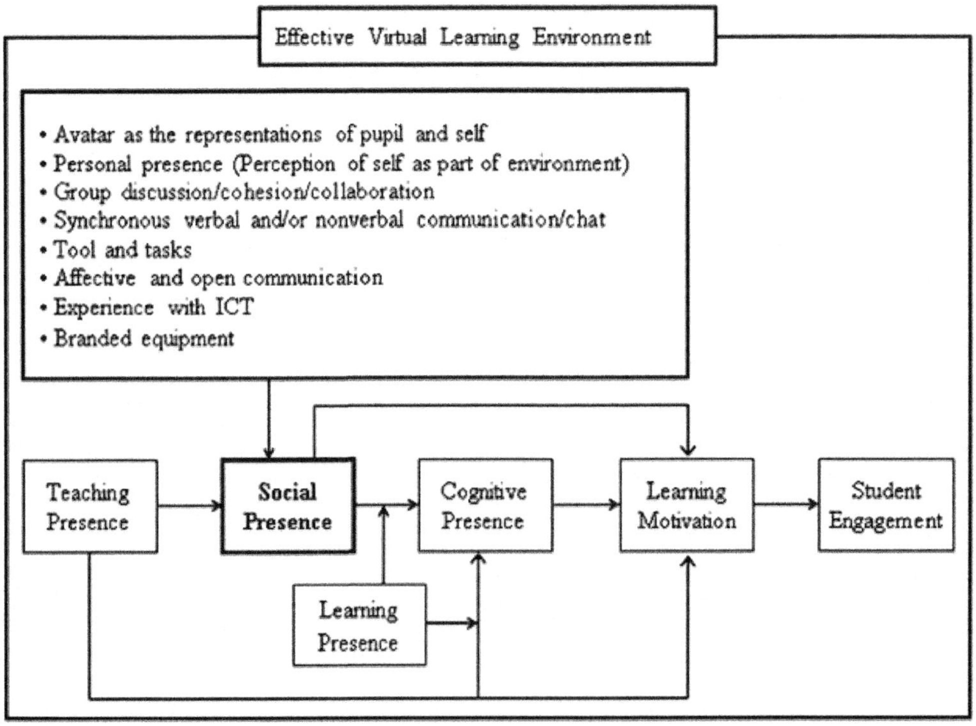

and the directional influence from its first step of teaching presence to the final step of student engagement. The overarching effect of learning presence is an apparent key indicator in the process of effective virtual learning and student engagement in an online environment.

- *Teaching presence* provides an input opportunity for social presence, cognitive presence and learning motivation for the student in an online environment.
- *Social presence* within an effective virtual learning environment has an input of teaching presence and an output of cognitive presence and learning motivation which leads to student engagement.
- *Cognitive presence* within an effective virtual learning environment has an input of social presence and teaching presence and an output of learning motivation which leads to student engagement.
- *Learning motivation* within an effective virtual learning environment has an input from teaching presence, social presence, cognitive presence and learning presence as direct result for student engagement.
- *Student engagement* within an effective virtual learning environment has an input of teaching presence, social presence, learning presence, cognitive presence, and learning motivation.
- *Learning presence* as stated by Shea and Bidjerano is, "interdependence of processes, cognitive, social presence, and teaching presence" (2012, p. 318).

CONCLUSION

As the literature presented in this chapter demonstrates, social presence is important for those involved in designing and delivering virtual learning environments. The value of having a virtual learning environment and social presence in gen-

eral has been reviewed based on literature that has been peer reviewed and available through various databases. The results of the search include the creation of tables for components of effective virtual learning environment, components influencing social presence in virtual learning environment and a model which incorporates social presence, a conceptual model for effective virtual learning from a social presence perspective. These include the use of avatars, group discussions, synchronous verbal and/or nonverbal communication, affective and open communication, experience with ICT and branded equipment to view virtual learning in social presence. Moreover, the questions guiding the literature review assisted in providing an overview of what it means to be engaged as a student and a virtual participant in online activities. Addressed in the body of literature included, what is perception of social presence on virtual learning, what role does social presence play in student engagement in virtual learning and what are the social presence factors influencing the effective virtual environment.

The content in which the materials were analyzed revealed the various methods in which scholars and practitioners view and report on virtual learning. The methods were inclusive of quantitative, qualitative and mixed methodologies as derived from the peer review article search from the databases. We created a model for an effective virtual learning environment based on the findings derived from the review of literature (see Figure 2). The model serves as a springboard from which theorizing may emerge from; in terms of the effects of social presence in a virtual learning environment. Furthermore, recommendations and implications have been derived based on the literature findings.

FUTURE DIRECTIONS

This review of literature has implications for recommendations for establishing an effective virtual learning environment from a social presence perspective. The following recommendations are derived from the review of literature and focus on the three main categories of recommendations for: theory, research and practice.

Social presence has proven to be an integral link to student satisfaction, perceived learning and a less anxiety-provoking environment (Yildiz, 2008). Additionally, social presence reveals benefits that may not be available for international participants in face-to-face communication, they are availed the ability to speak more freely about their personal beliefs, values, and attitudes (Yildiz, 2008). In cases of absence of social presence in a virtual environment there are less positive effects on student participation and learning resulting in a lack of satisfaction and often times hinders learning. The lack of social presence in a virtual environment may be construed as the inability to interact and support knowledge creation (Shea & Bidjerano, 2012), which is vital to a community of inquiry.

Theory

Based on the review of literature we call for the development of other theoretical frameworks for effective virtual learning environments that focus on social presence and the outcomes of student engagement and learning. For example, a model that incorporates learning theories –(social aspects) of learning in the design and delivery of virtual learning environments is most welcome. The model presented may serve as the foundational premise from which theory building may be expanded and validated. Additionally, we call for research that goes beyond the efforts of Mayer and Sung (2012), which proposed the components and indicators of social presence of intimacy and immediacy and further the theoretical frameworks of social presence and cognitive and effective learning.

Research

Research is required to determine the components of social presence and its effect on student engagement and its influence on student satisfaction. Our review presented herein is a start in developing an effective virtual environment by presenting an effective virtual learning model to be applied to theory, research and practice. Furthermore, according to Yildiz (2008) it is unclear what the connections are between social presence and learning, however it serves to only open more questions that need further investigation. This would create an awareness of the implications of social presence in the constructs of knowledge in a virtual environment.

We also call for further exploration into the effects of multinational comparisons which may include cultural influences with regards to social presence, positive learning effects, teaching effects, cognitive effects, and the full educational experience in a virtual environment.

Finally, we call for research into the components found to be associated with social presence from the model that was aforementioned. In doing so, this research may serve as a foundational basis from which to enhance social presence in online communities.

Research also needs to be conducted in the area of social presence as it pertains to both traditional learning and blended learning environments. Also, research need to be conducted on the use of social media in enhancing student engagement in virtual learning environments.

Practice

The effective virtual environment model offered by the authors serves to allow practitioners a roadmap that leads to student engagement and learning. Furthermore, practitioners should consider the components of an effective virtual learning environment when developing course offerings. Careful consideration should be given in virtual learning environments by utilizing as many components of an effective virtual learning environment to illicit social presence which will ensure the outcomes of student engagement and online learning. Those components include:

- Avatar as the representations of pupil and self
- Personal presence (Perception of self as part of environment)
- Group discussion/cohesion/collaboration
- Synchronous verbal and/or nonverbal communication/chat
- Tool and tasks
- Affective and open communication
- Experience with ICT
- Branded equipment

Furthermore, components that result in social presence (Tu & McIsaac, 2010) should also be considered by practitioners when developing course offerings. Online interactions mandate the use of forward planning to ensure social presence is experienced by online participants. Social presence is much more complicated, and may require input from various stakeholders. There is need for online instructors to seek input from their learners as to which appropriate interactions are needed to enhance social presence in virtual learning environments. Also, while designing virtual learning environments, we recommend that Quality matters model be incorporated in the course design to ensure quality of online courses. Moreover, further research is required on the topic of social learning as a means of fostering and enhancing social interactions that result in positive learning effects in an online community.

Class size was not an area explored in the current review of literature. However, it necessitates further research in terms of social presence. This may be an area that can be further studied and added

to the considerations when aspiring toward an effective virtual learning environment. A question to explore should include: Does class size affect effective virtual learning environment? Finally, we call for more research and analysis of online courses that can document benchmark methods that exhibit positive social presence in an online virtual environment which can be replicated and implemented by institutions who offer on-line courses.

REFERENCES

Akyol, Z., & Garrison, D. (2011, March). Understanding cognitive presence in an online and blended community of inquiry: Assessing outcomes and processes for deep approaches to learning. *British Journal of Educational Technology, 42*(2), 233–250. doi:10.1111/j.1467-8535.2009.01029.x

Allmendinger, K. (2010). Social presence in synchronous virtual learning situations: The role of nonverbal signals displayed by avatars. *Educational Psychology Review, 22*(1), 41–56. doi:10.1007/s10648-010-9117-8

Baylor, A. L. (2009). Promoting motivation with virtual agents and avatars: Role of visual presence and appearance. *Philosophical Transactions of the Royal Society B: Biological Sciences, 364*(1535), 3559–3565. doi:10.1098/rstb.2009.0148 PMID:19884150

Baylor, A. L. (2011). The design of motivational agents and avatars. *Educational Technology Research and Development, 59*(2), 291–300. doi:10.1007/s11423-011-9196-3

Behm-Morawitz, E. (2013). Mirrored selves: The influence of self-presence in a virtual world on health, appearance, and well-being. *Computers in Human Behavior, 29*(1), 119–128. doi:10.1016/j.chb.2012.07.023

Blanchard, A. L. (2008). Testing a model of sense of virtual community. *Computers in Human Behavior*, *24*(5), 2107–2123. doi:10.1016/j.chb.2007.10.002

Boettcher, J. V. (2010). *Ten best practices for teaching online*. Retrieved 2012, from Design for Learning: http://www.designingforlearning.info/services/writing/ecoach/tenbest.html

Bosch-Sijtsema, P. M., & Sivunen, A. (2013). Professional virtual worlds supporting computer-mediated communication, collaboration, and learning in geographically distributed context. *IEEE Transactions on Professional Communication*, *56*(2), 160–170. doi:10.1109/TPC.2012.2237256

Bulu, S. T. (2012). Place presence, social presence, co-presence, and satisfaction in virtual worlds. *Computers & Education*, *58*(1), 154–161. doi:10.1016/j.compedu.2011.08.024

Chen, P.-S., Lambert, A., & Guidry, K. (2010, May). Engaging online learners: The Impact of web-based learning technology on college student engagement. *Computers & Education*, *54*(4), 1222–1232. doi:10.1016/j.compedu.2009.11.008

Chen, X., Siau, K., & Nah, F. H. (2012). Empirical comparison of 3-D virtual world and face-to-face classroom for higher education. *Journal of Database Management*, *23*(3), 30–49.

Christidou, V., Hatzinikita, V., & Garvani, M. (2012). Pedagogic practices promoted by distance learning educational material in adult education. *Procedia: Social and Behavioral Sciences*, *46*, 1988–1996. doi:10.1016/j.sbspro.2012.05.416

Condon, B. B. (2012). The present state of presence in technology. *Nursing Science Quarterly*, *26*(1), 24–28. doi:10.1177/0894318412466738 PMID:23247344

Darabi, A., Arrastia, M., Nelson, D., Cornille, T. L., & Liang, X. (2011, June). Cognitive presence in asynchronous online learning: A comparison of four discussions strategies. *Journal of Computer Assisted Learning*, *27*(3), 216–227. doi:10.1111/j.1365-2729.2010.00392.x

Dasgupta, S. (2010). Expanded view of universities would be more realistic. *Nature*, 26–32. PMID:20130631

DiBlas, N., & Poggi, C. (2007). European virtual classrooms: Building effective "virtual" educational experiences. *Virtual Reality (Waltham Cross)*, *11*(2-3), 129–143. doi:10.1007/s10055-006-0060-4

Ellonen, H. K., Kosonen, M., & Henttonen, K. (2007). The development of a sense of virtual community. *International Journal of Web Based Communities*, *3*(1), 114–130. doi:10.1504/IJWBC.2007.013778

Fain, P. (2012, October 10). Nonprofit colleges spark new competition online, study finds. *Inside Higher Education*, 1–2.

Franceschi, K., Lee, R. M., Zanakis, S. H., & Hinds, D. (2009). Engaging group e-learning in virtual worlds. *Journal of Management Information Systems*, *26*(1), 73–100. doi:10.2753/MIS0742-1222260104

Gamage, V., Tretiakov, A., & Crump, B. (2011). Teacher perceptions of learning affordance of multi-user virtual environments. *Computers & Education*, *57*(4), 2406–2413. doi:10.1016/j.compedu.2011.06.015

Garrison, D. R. (2007). Online community of inquiry review: Social, cognitive, and teaching presence issues. *Journal of Asynchronous Learning Networks*, *11*(1), 61–72.

Hakan Isik, A., Karakis, R., & Guler, I. (2010). Postgraduate students' attitudes towards distance learning (The case study of Gazi University). *Procedia: Social and Behavioral Sciences, 9,* 218–222. doi:10.1016/j.sbspro.2010.12.139

Hobbs, M., Brown, E., & Gordon, M. (2006). Using a virtual world for transferable skills in gaming education. *Virtual World Environments, 5*(3), 58-70.

Hulma, E., Green, D. T., & Ladd, K. S. (2013). Fostering student engagement by cultivating curiosity. *New Directions for Student Services,* (143), 53-64.

Hung, S.-W., & Cheng, M.-J. (2013). Are you ready for knowledge sharing? An empirical study of virtual communities. *Computers & Education, 62,* 8–17. doi:10.1016/j.compedu.2012.09.017

Inderbitzin, M. P., Betella, A., Lanata, A., Scilingo, E. P., Bernardet, U., & Verschure, P. R. (2013). The social perceptual salience effect. *Journal of Experimental Psychology, 39*(1), 62–74. PMID:22612058

Kahu, E. (2013). Framing student engagement in higher education. *Studies in Higher Education, 38*(5), 758–773. doi:10.1080/03075079.2011.598505

Ke, F. (2010). Examining online teaching, cognitive, and social presence for adult students. *Computers & Education, 55*(2), 808–820. doi:10.1016/j.compedu.2010.03.013

Ke, F. (2010, September). Examining online teaching, cognitive, and social presence for adult students. *Computers & Education, 55*(2), 808–820. doi:10.1016/j.compedu.2010.03.013

Kim, J., Kwon, Y., & Cho, D. (2011, September). Investigating factors that influence social presence and learning outcomes in distance higher education. *Computers & Education, 57*(2), 1512–1520. doi:10.1016/j.compedu.2011.02.005

Kupezynski, L., Mundy, M. A., Goswami, J., & Meling, V. (2012). Cooperative learning in distance learning: A mixed methods study. *International Journal of Instruction,* 81-90.

Lama, S., Kashyap, M., & Kkhsou, R. (2012). Empowering the human resources and the role of distance learning. *Turkish Online Journal of Distance Education,* 239-246.

Lin, H., Dyer, K., & Guo, Y. (2012). Exploring online teaching: A three year composite journal of concerns and strategies from online instructors. *WestGate Education,* 1-6.

Machi, L., & Mc Evoy, B. (2012). The literature review, six steps to success (2nd ed.). Thousand Oaks, CA: Corwin - Sage Publications.

Malik, S. (2012). Challenges encountered by a distance learning organization. *Turkish Online Journal of Distance Education,* 17-20.

Mayer, R. (2014). Incorporating motivation into multimedia learning. *Learning and Instruction, 29,* 171–173. doi:10.1016/j.learninstruc.2013.04.003

Mayer, R. E., & Sung, E. (2012). Five facets of social presence in online distance education. *Computers in Human Behavior,* 1738–1747.

Mikropoulos, T. A. (2006). Presence: A unique characteristic in educational virtual environments. *Virtual Reality (Waltham Cross), 10*(3-4), 197–206. doi:10.1007/s10055-006-0039-1

Moskaliuk, J., Bertram, J., & Cress, U. (2013). Training in virtual environments: Putting theory into practice. *Egronomics, 56*(2), 195–204. PMID:23231585

Öztürk, E., & Deryakulu, D. (2011). The effect of type of computer mediated communication tools on social and cognitive presence in online learning community. *H. U. Journal of Education, 41,* 349–359.

Parsons, S., Nuland, L., & Parsons, A. (2014, May). The ABCs of student engagement. *Phi Delta Kappan, 95*(8), 23–27. doi:10.1177/003172171409500806

Pew Research. (2009, April). *A portrait of "generation next" - How young people view their lives, futures, and politics.* Retrieved from Pew Research Center: http://people-press.org/report/300/a-portrait-of-generation-next

Phillips, B., Shaw, R., Sullivan, D., & Johnson, C. (2010). Using virtual environments to enhance nursing distance education. *Creative Nursing, 16*(3), 132–135. doi:10.1891/1078-4535.16.3.132 PMID:20879622

Preece, J. (2000). *Online communities: Designing usability, supporting sociability.* Wiley.

Reysen, S., Lloyd, J., Katzarska-Miller, I., Lemker, B., & Foss, R. (2010, November). Intragroup status and social presence in online fan groups. *Computers in Human Behavior, 26*(6), 1314–1317. doi:10.1016/j.chb.2010.04.003

Rourke, L., Anderson, T., Garrison, D. R., & Archer, W. (2001). Assessing social presence in asynchronous text-based computer conferencing. *Journal of Distance Education, 14*(2), 50–71.

Shea, P., & Bidjerano, T. (2010, December). Learning presence: Towards a theory of self-efficacy, self-regulation, and the development of a communities of inquiry in online and blended learning environments. *Computers & Education, 55*(4), 1721–1731. doi:10.1016/j.compedu.2010.07.017

Shea, P., & Bidjerano, T. (2012). Learning presense as a moderator in the community of inquiry model. *Computers & Education, 59*(2), 316–326. doi:10.1016/j.compedu.2012.01.011

Steuer, J. (1992). Defining virtual reality: Dimensions determining telepresence. *Journal of Communication, 42*(4), 73–93. doi:10.1111/j.1460-2466.1992.tb00812.x

Sung, E., & Mayer, R. (2012, September). Five facets of social presence in online distance education. *Computers in Human Behavior, 28*(5), 1738–1747. doi:10.1016/j.chb.2012.04.014

Svinicki, M., & McKeachie, W. J. (2011). *McKeachie's teaching tips.* Wadsworth Cengage Learning.

Taghizadeh, M., & Vaezi, S. (2011). Exploring social presence in virtual learning environments. *World Applies Sciences Journal, 15*(1), 120–128.

Tonteri, L., Kosonen, M., Ellonen, H.-K., & Tarkiainen, A. (2011). Antecedents of an experiences sense of virtual community. *Computers in Human Behavior, 27*(6), 2215–2223. doi:10.1016/j.chb.2011.06.018

Torraco, R. J. (2005). Writing integrative literature reviews: Guidelines and examples. *Human Resource Development Review, 4*(3), 356–367. doi:10.1177/1534484305278283

Toshalis, E., & Nakkula, M. (2012). Motivation, engagement and student voice. *Education Digest: Essential Readings Condensed for Quick Review, 78*(1), 29-35.

Traphagan, T. W., Chiang, Y.-V., Chang, H. M., Wattanawaha, B., Lee, H., Mayrath, M. C., & Resta, P. E. et al. (2010). Cognitive, social and teaching presence in a virtual world and a text chat. *Computers & Education, 55*(3), 923–936. doi:10.1016/j.compedu.2010.04.003

Tu, C.-H., & McIsaac, M. (2010). The relationship of social presence and interaction in Online classes. *American Journal of Distance Education, 16*(3), 131–150. doi:10.1207/S15389286AJDE1603_2

Weinel, M., Bannert, M., Zumbach, J., Hoppe, H. U., & Malzahn, N. (2011). A closer look on social presence as a causing factor in computer-mediated collaboration. *Computers in Human Behavior, 27*(1), 513–521. doi:10.1016/j.chb.2010.09.020

Yildiz, S. (2008). Social presence in the web-based classroom: Implications for intercultural communication. *Journal of Studies in International Education*, *1*(1), 1–21.

ADDITIONAL READING

Anderson, T., Rourke, L., Garrison, D. R., & Archer, W. (2001). Assessing teaching presence in a computer conferencing context. A paper presented at the Annual Meeting of the American Educational Research Association, Seattle, WA.

Cameron, B. A., Morgan, K., Williams, K. C., & Kostelecky, K. L. (2009). Group projects: Student perceptions of the relationship between social tasks and sense of community in online group work. *American Journal of Distance Education*, *23*(1), 20–33. doi:10.1080/08923640802664466

Coppola, N. W., Hiltz, S. R., & Rotter, N. (2001). Becoming a virtual professor: Pedagogical roles and ALN, HICSS 2001 Proceedings, IEEE Press.

Dobbs, R. R., Waid, C. A., & Carmen, A. D. (2009). Students' perceptions of online courses: The effect of online course experience. *The Quarterly Review of Distance Education*, *10*(1), 9–26.

Gagne, R., Briggs, L., & Wager, W. (1988). *Principles of Instructional design*. New York: Holt Reinhardt & Winston.

Hiltz, S. R. (1994). *The virtual classroom: Learning without limits via computer networks*. Norwood, NJ: Ablex.

Hmelo, C. E., Guzdial, M., & Turns, J. (1998). Computer support for collaborative learning: Learning to support student engagement. *Journal of Interactive Learning Research*, *9*(2), 107–129.

Janicki, T., & Liegle, J. O. (2001). Development and evaluation of a framework for creating web-based learning modules: A pedagogical and systems approach. *Journal of Asynchronous Learning Networks*, *5*(1), 100–110.

Jiang, M., & Ting, E. (2000). A study of factors influencing students' perceived learning in a web-based course environment. *International Journal of Educational Telecommunications*, *6*(4), 317–338.

Kearsley, G. (2000). *Online education: Learning and teaching in cyberspace*. Belmont, CA: Wadsworth.

LaRose, R., & Whitten, P. (2000). Rethinking instructional immediacy for web courses: A social cognitive exploration. *Communication Education*, *49*(4), 320–338. doi:10.1080/03634520009379221

Leonard, J., & Guha, S. (2001). Education at the crossroads: Online teaching and students' perspective on distance learning. *Journal of Research on Technology in Education*, *34*(1), 52–57.

Levin, J. A., Kim, H., & Riel, M. M. (1990). In L. Harasim (Ed.), *Analyzing instructional interactions on electronic message networks,' In online education: Perspectives on a new environment* (pp. 16–38). New York: Praeger.

Lyons, A., Reysen, S., & Pierce, L. (2012). Video lecture format: Student technological efficacy and social presence in online courses. *Computers in Human Behavior*, *28*(1), 181–186. doi:10.1016/j.chb.2011.08.025

Mayne, L. A., & Wu, Q. (2011). Creating and measuring social presence in online graduate nursing courses. *Nursing Education Perspectives*, *32*(2), 110–114. doi:10.5480/1536-5026-32.2.110 PMID:21667793

Rhode, J. (2009). Interaction equivalency in self-paced online learning environments: An exploration of learner preferences. *International Review of Research in Open and Distance Learning, 10*(1), 1–23.

Richardson, C. J., & Swan, K. (2003). Examining social presence in online courses in relation to students' perceived learning and satisfaction. *Journal of Asynchronous Learning Networks, 7*(1), 68–88.

Salmoni, A. J., & Gonzalez, M. L. (2008). Online collaboration learning: Quantifying how people learn together online. *Medical Teacher, 30*(7), 710–716. doi:10.1080/01421590802047281 PMID:18608969

Swan, K. (2001). Virtual interaction: Design factors affecting student satisfaction and perceived learning in asynchronous online courses. *Distance Education, 22*(2), 306–331. doi:10.1080/0158791010220208

Tu, C. H. (2005). From presentation to interaction: New goals for online learning technologies. *Educational Media International, 42*(3), 189–206. doi:10.1080/09523980500161072

Tu, C. H., & Cory, M. (2003). Building active online interaction via a collaborative learning community. *Computers in the Schools, 20*(3), 51–59. doi:10.1300/J025v20n03_07

Wang, Q., & Woo, H. L. (2007). Comparing asynchronous online discussions and face-to-face discussions in a classroom setting. *British Journal of Educational Technology, 38*(2), 272–286. doi:10.1111/j.1467-8535.2006.00621.x

Woods, R. H. (2002). How much communication is enough in online courses? Exploring the relationship between frequency of instructor-initiated personal email and learners' perceptions of and participation in online learning. *International Journal of Instructional Media, 29*(4), 377–394.

Yang, S. J. H., & Chen, I. Y. (2008). A social network-based system for supporting interactive collaboration in knowledge sharing over peer-to-peer network. *International Journal of Human-Computer Studies, 66*(1), 36–50. doi:10.1016/j.ijhcs.2007.08.005

KEY TERMS AND DEFINITIONS

Cognitive Presence: The development and growth of critical thinking skills.

Learning Presence: Elements such as self-efficacy as well as other cognitive, behavioral, and motivational constructs supportive of online learner self-regulation.

Mixed Methodology: A combination of quantitative and qualitative research.

Moderating Effect: A term for interaction effect of a third variable between two other variables.

Qualitative Method: A term for analysis in terms of goodness and quality.

Quantitative Research Method: A term used for analysis of research in terms of quantity measurement.

Social Presence: A measure of feeling of community that learners experience in a virtual learning environment.

Student Engagement: A psychological process, specifically, the attention, interest, investment, and effort that students expend in the work of learning to achieve their learning goals.

Teaching Presence: Teachers' three critical roles including the design and organization of the learning experience, the implementation of learning activities, and the moderations of students' learning experiences.

Virtual Environment: Computer-based worlds that can enhance and expand our ability to communicate and collaborate synchronously and/or asynchronously in a computer-mediated context with other users.

This work was previously published in a Handbook of Research on Innovative Technology Integration in Higher Education edited by Fredrick Muyia Nafukho and Beverly J. Irby, pages 303-321, copyright year 2015 by Information Science Reference (an imprint of IGI Global).

Chapter 64

Initial Adoption vs. Institutionalization of E-Procurement in Construction Firms:
The Role of Government in Developing Countries

De Chun Huang
Hohai University, China

Thi Quynh Trang Nguyen
Hohai University, China

Quang Dung Tran
Griffith University, Australia & National Civil Engineering University, Vietnam

Sajjad Nazir
Hohai University, China

ABSTRACT

This study explores the role of government in fostering construction firms move from initial adoption to institutionalization of e-procurement in developing countries' context. It proposes the research model that consists of five external environmental constructs that are considered as factors influencing the different levels of e-procurement adoption. It uses PLS-SEM to analyze the data collected from 112 construction businesses in Vietnam in 2012. It finds that the role of government has an extremely significant influence on a decision of initial adoption of e-procurement in construction enterprises through government leadership, legal and regulatory infrastructure, information and technology infrastructure (ITI), and socio-economic and knowledge infrastructure. However, the role of government is less important to a decision of institutionalization of e-procurement when only ITI significantly influences on the decision-making. As a result, useful theoretical and practical implications are proposed.

DOI: 10.4018/978-1-4666-8619-9.ch064

INTRODUCTION

E-procurement technology is referred to an advantaged method of procurement of goods, works, and services based on electronic tools, especially Internet. E-procurement alters the activities of purchasing and transforms the purchasing process from a tactical into a strategic activity. The evolution of the strategic role of a specific e-procurement is closely linked to its sophistication or integration. Literature consistently demonstrates that in order to gain full benefits and maximize potential advantages from the technology, companies must adopt and implement the technology towards a highly sophisticated level in terms of management, functions, and usage (L. Raymond, Croteau, & Bergeron, 2012). However, in both developing and developed countries, the sophisticated adoption of e-procurement in firms has fallen far below expectations. Most companies adopt the technology only at the simple but not integrated level (Le, Rowe, Truex, & Huynh, 2012; R. A. I. Raymond, Flood, & Treffinger, 2008; VECITA, 2008). Take Vietnam as an example, after nearly ten years of e-commerce infrastructure development under the master plans by the government, most enterprises are still at the first stage of adoption of Internet-based B2B e-commerce technologies (e.g. e-procurement). The rate of the sophisticated implementation of the technology is actually very low and do not match with the remarkable development of e-business infrastructure (P. Long, Pham, & Nguyen, 2010; Q. D. Tran, Vo, & Nguyen, 2011; VECITA, 2008); especially in construction industry (Umit, Jason, Murat, & Utku, 2013).

In an attempt to identify/assess determinants of adoption of e-commerce technologies, previous empirical studies considered the adoption under a general rather than process-oriented view (e.g. Chang & Wong, 2010; Le et al., 2012; Li, 2008; Teo, Lin, & Lai, 2009; Hamed Salim, Helen, & Lynne, 2013). They have focused on the adoption versus non-adoption decisions. Although these studies significantly improved our understanding of general e-commerce adoption, we also need to a better perception of the post-adoption of e-commerce technologies. In fact, there are still many practical problems have not been explained yet. For instance, given the same level of resources and the same operating environment, several firms have implemented more sophisticated e-procurement applications but others do not. In addition, several enterprises have adopted initially one or multiple simple e-procurement innovations for a long duration, and even though they have mature resources for e-commerce-based activities, but they did not conduct any subsequent implementation of the technology (Ng Kim, 2005, pg.98). According to the process-oriented view, e-commerce adoption is a complex, progressive and multi-phase process (London & Bavinton, 2006); therefore, only examining the general adoption of an innovation cannot understand well post-adoption activities (K. Zhu & Kraemer, 2005). However, the existing literature is lacking of empirical studies that pay appropriate attention on the said nature of adoption, especially in countries that are emerging as new potential markets with very high economic growth rates such as Vietnam (P. Long & Jeffrey, 2011).

In addition, a literature review of e-procurement found that the diffusion of e-procurement has been significantly improved across industries and the increasing trend of the e-procurement implementation is to move from the simple adoption to the sophistication in the near future.

In light of these, studying on the factors that speed up firms move from an initial adoption to institutionalization of e-procurement is an important consideration for more comprehensive understanding of the adoption of e-procurement in developing country's context. The present paper is to investigate empirically the role of government in decisions of e-procurement entry-level adoption and sophistication in the construction industry and to provide guidance on e-procurement institutionalization for policy-makers. The data was collected through a survey with Vietnamese construction enterprises in 2012.

LITERATURE REVIEW

Initial Adoption vs. Institutionalization of e-Procurement

Based on the process-oriented view, several studies provided empirical evidence to suggest that adoption of e-commerce technologies can be better understood by breaking it down into different levels of adoption, such as entry-level adoption and its sophistication (Molla & Licker, 2005b; Saprikis, 2013; K. Zhu & Kraemer, 2005). As mentioned earlier, sophistication (i.e. institutionalization) of an innovation should be considered through management, functions (i.e. technology and information), and its usage (L. Raymond et al., 2012).

To assess determinants of adoption and institutionalization of e-commerce in developing countries, Molla (2005) defined that a business is considered as having adopted e-commerce if it has attained an interactive e-commerce status, while a business is considered as having institutionalized e-commerce if it has attained an interactive e-commerce, transactive e-commerce or integrated e-commerce status. These e-commerce statuses are assessed or measured through functions of websites that enterprises operating. Thus, Molla's (2005) definition of the levels of e-commerce adoption fails to consider the aspects of management and usage of e-commerce. Zhu (2005) – a study on post-adoption of e-business viewed e-business adoption as a multistage process that starts at adoption and extends to usage and value creation. In which, e-business use is defined as the extent to which e-business is used to conduct value chain activities; and it can be measured by the breadth of use for different value chain activities

and the depth of use (percentage) for each activity. Thus, their definition of e-business post-adoption stage fails to consider the aspect of management of e-business. Saprikis (2013) – a study on the post-adoption stage of e-reverse auctions (e-RA) divided the adoption of this technology into three stages: trial stage, low-use stage, and commitment stage. These stages are measured through two indicators: amount of transactions are conducted via e-RA and the importance of e-RA to business' operations Saprikis, 2013. This view of adoption also fails to consider the aspects of management and function of e-RA. Therefore, there is a need to have a more rigorous definition of e-procurement adoption stages for this present study.

According to the literature of innovation adoption models (Rao, Metts, & Monge, 2003), innovation assimilation (Klein, 2012; Kevin Zhu, Kraemer, & Xu, 2006), and IT sophistication (L. Raymond et al., 2012), it can be said that sophistication of e-procurement is closely associated with the integration of e-procurement system with other systems in terms of management, function, and usage. Additionally, e-procurement includes many different innovations, such as e-tendering, e-catalog, e-payment, etc. Core procurement processes include supplier selection, order placement, order fulfillment, and payment and settlement (Rai, Tang, Brown, & Keil, 2006), and each of these activities can be supported by a specific e-procurement innovation. Therefore, we defined the entry-level adoption and its institutionalization (reflecting its level of sophistication) of e-procurement:

- **Initial Adoption of e-Procurement:** An organization is considered to have the initial adoption of e-procurement if it has deployed one or many of the e-procurement innovations for a part of their purchase, and using the static or interactive websites to make promotions and publish basis company information or receive queries, e-mail; and form entry from users.

- **Institutionalization of e-Procurement:** An organization is considered to have institutionalized e-procurement if it has:
  - ○ Deployed generally one or many of the e-procurement innovations for almost their purchases (more than 50%) and most of the procurement processes can be conducted electronically (*usage perspective*).
  - ○ Innovations deployed have a good interoperability together, with existing IT systems, and with external e-infrastructure through transactive or integrated websites that connected to e-marketplaces (*functions perspective*).
  - ○ Innovations deployed are consistent with the business strategy, organizational structure, and social environment of the enterprise (*management perspective*).

The figure 1 illustrated clearly our view of the adoption vs. institutionalization of e-procurement. For e-procurement initiatives to be most effectively applied, integration of technology, operation, strategy, structure, and human interaction must be implemented throughout the organization and integrating with external business partners in a continuously expanding network.

The Role of Government

Literature consistently agrees that the role of government is an important consideration that may affect the adoption and diffusion of innovation, especially in developing countries' context (Porter, 1990). A government can encourage and make pressures on both private and public companies to adopt e-commerce by four different ways. First, government provides a clear and strategic leadership commitment through its e-commerce

Figure 1. Adoption of e-procurement

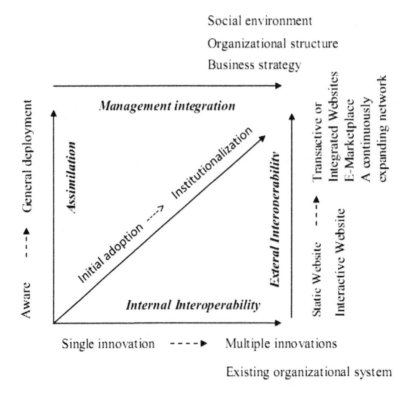

vision and directives, specific incentives (K. Zhu & Kraemer, 2005) and actual e-government actions (Neef, 2001). Second, government develops a well-defined legal and regulation infrastructure (Molla & Licker, 2005b; Oxley & Yeung, 2001). Third, government provides a well-developed IT and other supporting industries infrastructure (Molla & Licker, 2005b; Oxley & Yeung, 2001), and finally, a supportive and incentive economic environment with IT-based and skilled workforce (Oxley & Yeung, 2001; Mandana, Iman Raeesi, & Babak, 2013) and IT-oriented culture (Jessy, Reddy, & Anand, 2014).

THE CONCEPTUAL MODEL AND HYPOTHESES

The Conceptual Model

Based on the related literature, we developed a conceptual model to assess the role of government in decisions of e-procurement adoption by organizations. We firstly present the model in Figure 2, followed by explanations of the key elements of the model and postulated relationships.

The framework proposed focused on two e-procurement adoption stages: initial adoption and its extent - institutionalization. The extent of innovation adoption depends on a variety of economic, social, and political factors, including basic information infrastructure; regulatory environment; and accessibility of technical, managerial, and financial resources (K. Zhu & Kraemer, 2005). Therefore, accompany with previous studies (Molla & Licker, 2005b), we expect that there will be different impacts from government to the differences among firms in the actual adoption of e-procurement. We will use our model to examine these differences. As discussed earlier, the focus on the differences between initial adoption and its extent is motivated by the process-oriented view about the innovation adoption.

Based on the e-commerce literature, we posit that the role of government on adoption of e-procurement can be evaluated through five aspects as the followings:

- **Government Leadership Infrastructure:** It refers to the government actions in orienting, improving, promoting, and developing e-commerce environment. It includes four facets: strategic directive works (visions and commitment), practical directive works (e-Government initiates), national e-commerce supports,

Figure 2. Conceptual model

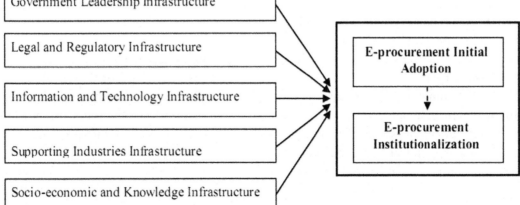

and international e-commerce supports (Ismail & Kamat, 2008; Molla & Licker, 2005b; Ruikar, Anumba, & Carrillo, 2006; Saprikis, 2013).

- **Legal and Regulatory Infrastructure:** It refers to legal requirements and regulations to stop or eliminate risks in e-business transactions. It includes four facets related to: traditional risks, e-transactions risks, international e-commerce risks, and industry-specific e-commerce risks (Kog, 2010).

- **Information and Technology Infrastructure:** It refers to technical factors required to overcome the technological challenges (i.e. Interoperability, security, inadequate software, connectivity, and reliability). It includes three technological aspects: IT applications, Internet infrastructure, B2B and G2B e-initiates. It also represents a necessary industrial information infrastructure organized by a specific industry to support the business communication, collaboration, and management between enterprises as well as the enterprises with government institutions. It includes two information aspects: across-industrial information and public administration information (Ismail & Kamat, 2008; Ruikar et al., 2006; Stephen & Brakel, 2006).

- **Supporting Industries Infrastructure:** It refers to the service level and cost structure of three major supporting industries: telecommunications, financial system, and transportation system whose activities might affect e-commerce initiatives in businesses in developing countries (Molla & Licker, 2005a).

- **Social-Economic and Knowledge Infrastructure:** It represents issues related to social culture, knowledge, and attitudes of the industry towards e-commerce. It has four facets: (1) industrial economic characteristics (competitiveness, transparency, stableness; trend of collaboration and

cooperation), (2) industrial socio-culture characteristics (trust, beliefs, concepts, judgments, expectations, and methodologies towards e-commerce) that are shared by people and enterprises within the industry. (3) They are also industrial knowledge characteristics (perception of e-procurement, skilled labor force, technicians, IT-oriented managers) that required for the development of e-procurement strategy, and (4) industrial knowledge supporting infrastructure (all initiatives, actions, and plans available that develop knowledge and positive culture for e-commerce) (Egbu, 2008; Ismail & Kamat, 2008; Schwartz & Davis, 1981; Kevin Zhu et al., 2006).

Development of Hypotheses

In developing countries, competitive environment is often determined by the relationship between business and government, and business managers often trend to be directed by government and less willing to accept changes (Nguyen, Neck, & Nguyen, 2009). A government can direct, encourage and make pressures on both private and public companies to adopt e-commerce through its e-commerce visions and directives, e-government initiatives, and specific incentives (K. Zhu & Kraemer, 2005). Empirical evidence shows government e-readiness was one of the key factors to determine the decision of institutionalization of e-commerce (Molla & Licker, 2005b).

Thus:

Hypotheses 1a&b: The performance of government leadership in the domain of e-commerce influences significantly on initial adoption (a) and institutionalization of e-procurement (b) in construction enterprises in developing countries.

As mentioned above, providing a well-defined legal and regulatory infrastructure is one of the critical contributions of government for the development of e-commerce. One of the challenges in developing any e-commerce system is converting the functionality of the traditional paper-based system to an electronic environment while maintaining legal compliance. The well-defined legal framework is positively related to ensuring the security of e-commerce activities, and then improves trust on e-transactions that is an important factor influencing using behavior of users (Chang & Wong, 2010; Ng Kim, 2005). Furthermore, it is very often that in developing countries, the law that governs electronic transactions is under-developed and lags behind the technology (Betts et al., 2006). In this case, the demand of a well-defined legal and regulatory system is extremely necessary.

Therefore:

Hypotheses 2a&b: The performance of the legal and regulatory system in the domain of e-commerce influences significantly on initial adoption (a) and institutionalization of e-procurement (b) in construction enterprises in developing countries.

Literature consistently acknowledges that IT infrastructure is an important issue for e-commerce (Aranda-Mena & Stewart, 2004; Oxley & Yeung, 2001). In developing countries, e-commerce adoption has been generally constrained by the quality, availability, and cost of accessing such infrastructure (Alzougool & Kurnia, 2008), and especially, poor industry standards and cross-disciplinary communication (Eric & M, 2009). Researchers argue that developing governments need to put in place G2B e-initiatives in order to maximize and encourage e-commerce initiatives, include common standards among both public and private sectors (Alzougool & Kurnia, 2008; MDBs, 2004). Empirical evidence also shows that IT infrastructure is positively associated to the internet-based purchasing application assimilation (Klein, 2012) and the institutionalization of

e-commerce in developing countries (Molla & Licker, 2005a).

Therefore:

Hypotheses 3a&b: The development of information and technology infrastructure influences significantly on initial adoption (a) and institutionalization of e-procurement (b) in construction enterprises in developing countries.

Accompany with IT infrastructure, other supporting industries, such as telecommunications, financial system, and transportation system are argued as factors influencing both adoption and diffusion of e-commerce technologies in developing countries. The development of such industries creates advantages by making available efficient, rapid, and sometimes preferential access to e-commerce inputs. The availability and affordability of services from the IT industry, the institutionalization and development of the financial sector, and the penetration and reliability of telecommunication and transportation facilities contribute the successful implementation and diffusion of e-commerce (Molla & Licker, 2005a). Supporting industries were empirically identified as one of the key factors determining the institutionalization of e-commerce in developing countries (Molla & Licker, 2005a).

Thus, the hypotheses seem fitting:

Hypotheses 4a&b: The development of supporting industry infrastructure (finance, telecommunication, and transportation) in the domain of e-commerce influences significantly on initial adoption (a) and institutionalization of e-procurement (b) in construction enterprises in developing countries.

Web-based procurement requires firms to share information with its business partners in the industry. Since the institutionalization of the technology is involved to facilitate streamlining and automating the entire procurement process as well as making an order and requisition information available along the entire supply chain, an information-rich economic infrastructure is indispensable (Teo et al., 2009). For such an economic environment, all its key elements (i.e. government, public administrations, private and public enterprises, and individuals) need to be well aware of the information-sharing role and have positive attitudes towards e-commerce. The economy also needs to have enough capability to provide a sustainable skilled labor force for the development of e-commerce across the industry (Oxley & Yeung, 2001). These said demands become more crucial in developing countries, such as Vietnam, where information sharing is facing the "rigidity" culture of public administration departments and officials, or even in private businesses (Le-Hoai, Lee, & Son, 2009). Empirical evidence shows that the role of professional industry associations (i.e. research institutes, universities, and other IT and human development associations) positively influences on e-commerce adoption in Vietnam (Le et al., 2012).

Therefore, the following hypotheses were made:

Hypotheses 5a&b: The development of socio-economic and knowledge infrastructure

in the domain of e-commerce influences significantly on initial adoption (a) and institutionalization of e-procurement (b) in individual construction enterprises in developing countries.

RESEARCH METHODOLOGY

Measurement Model Identification

The conceptual model proposed consists of five formatively independent variables and two reflectively dependent variables with eleven hypotheses. First, based on an existing extensive literature on e-procurement, e-commerce, and Information Systems, the set of 28 measurement items for all the independent/dependent constructs are collected. Next, two professors from Hohai University with experience in survey development were involved to assess the general structure of the instrument and edit its wordings. Then three Vietnamese e-procurement development experts refined and edited the instrument to further ensure accuracy of its professional content. Finally, the initial instrument with 23 items was gained and showed in detail in Appendix B. Information of the proposed conceptual structural model was shown as in Table 1.

Table 1. Information of the proposed conceptual model

Latent Variables	Type	Manifest variables
Government Leadership Infrastructure (GLI)	Formative	GLI1 to GLI4
IT Infrastructure (ITI)	Formative	ITI1 to ITI5
Supporting Industries Infrastructure (SII)	Formative	SII1 to SII3
Legal & Regulatory Infrastructure (LRI)	Formative	LRI1 to LRI3
Socio-economic and Knowledge Infrastructure (SEKI)	Formative	SEKI1 to SEKI3
E-procurement Institutionalization (ePI)	Reflective	ePI1 to ePI5
E-procurement Initial Adoption (ePIA)	Reflective	ePIA1 and ePIA2
A total number of items		23

Note: Manifest variables measured on a five-point Likert scale ranging from "strongly disagree" (value =1) to "strongly agree" (value =5)

Sampling and Data-Collection Procedures

Because it is often that surveys by self-administered questionnaire via post or e-mail in Vietnam gain a very low response rate, we used a questionnaire survey administered in person in this research program. Data collection was performed in two stages. The stage 1 consists of two wages, including (1) a proposal letter and the questionnaire were e-mailed by the VINAVICO Construction Consultant and Investment Company in Hanoi to introduce the research project, and then (2) calls were conducted directly to firms to making an appointment (date and time) for interview one week later. In stage 2, professional staffs of VINAVICO visited each enterprise and administered the questionnaire in person. Vietnam has been selected because many construction companies have been using simple e-procurement innovations at the initial adoption level (e.g. e-mail, e-informing, e-payment, e-tendering, etc.) (Le et al., 2012; Q. D. Tran et al., 2011; VECITA, 2008).

However, the operation of a public e-procurement system, which has been recently established and managed by the Government, could potentially have the big impact on the e-procurement state in the recent future. This makes the country become a suitable case study for the present study.

The sampling procedure involved a number of stages. First, based on a set of operational criteria, including the characteristics of the population, the comprehensiveness of the list, and its completeness in terms of contact addresses, such as the name of the top executive, a Hanoi construction business yellow-page at http://yellowpages.vnn.vn/ was identified as a sampling frame.

Ideally, the larger sample size increases the power of tests, but this is often constrained by operational limitations. In the proposed model, the construct with the largest number of formative indicators is ITI with five items and the number of independent latent variables is five too. According to a rule of thumb used in PLS-SEM (Urbach

& Ahlemann, 2010), the minimum sample size required is 50 samples. By a questionnaire survey administered in person, we hope a response rate is about 50%. Therefore, in order to obtain a minimum required returned-sample size of 50-100, a total of 200 construction businesses were selected from the sample frame using a systematic random sampling procedure (every n^{th} item).

In order to address the problem of consistency motif, the questions measuring the independent constructs were placed before the question measuring the dependent variable. The statements are designed that a response of strongly agreement will generate the highest score of 5 points in the five-point Likert scale. Respondents were key leaders who understand in depth and clearly about their enterprise as well as external context in the domain of IT and procurement activities, such as senior managers, procurement office's managers, IT managers, and marketing office's managers to provide valid and suitable data.

Response Rate and Profile of Respondents and Respondents' Organizations

After a first survey conducted in May and a fellow-up survey in July 2012, 112 completed questionnaires were collected, refined, and coded. The response rate is 56%. Of 112 responses, four were from senior managers; sixty-one were from procurement office's managers; thirty-two were from marketing office's managers; and fifteen were from IT managers. Five of them have Ph.D. degrees; fifty-seven of respondents have a Master degree; and the remaining respondents have Bachelor degrees. A majority of respondents (about 80%) has at least 5 years of experience in the construction industry. Considering the profile of the respondents and their enterprises, it can be said that the responses can be confidently relied upon. There have been thirty-seven construction contractors, fifty-four engineering and architectural design consultants, and twenty-one suppliers represent 33%, 48%, and 19% of the total of responses respectively. Most enterprises (97%) have the number of years of operation greater than 7 years. In detail, 42 firms are operating in building works (38%), 60 firms are operating in both building and civil areas (53%), remaining ones are operating in other areas. Firm size was categorized based on the number of employees. The sample consists of 98 of SMEs (83%) (the annual average number of labor is less than 300 people) and 14 of large firms (17%). In the sample, 57 enterprises have no websites, 55 remaining ones have static or interactive websites.

ANALYTICAL APPROACH AND THE RESULTS

PLS Analysis

Although our research models are not complex, but they included both reflective and formative constructs. In addition, in this study, the sample size is relatively small and normality assumption is in doubt. Therefore, we used the analytical approach of structural equation modeling (SEM) with partial least square estimation to test the models

proposed. The SEM results of the model of ePIA and ePI are shown as in Figure 3a&b, respectively.

Measurement Model

Individual Item Reliability, and Convergent and Discriminant Validity Test for Two Reflective Constructs of ePI and ePIA

To assess the individual item reliability, confirmatory factor analysis was conducted to test if all measurement items were appropriate for each construct. The results showed that all items of ePI and ePIA have factor loadings greater than the 0.707 threshold (Figure 3a&b). Convergent validity of the data was assessed by computing the Cronbach's alpha (CA) and composite reliability (CR) of the factors. Values of these indicators were greater than 0.6 and 0.7, respectively (Tables 2 and Table 3). At the indicator level, the discriminant validity is accessed by an analysis of cross-loadings. The output of Smart-PLS 2.0 M3 showed that items of ePI and ePIA have a higher correlation with their respective measured variable than with any other latent variable in the models.

Figures 3. SEM results of the full models (by Smart-PLS 2.0 M3)

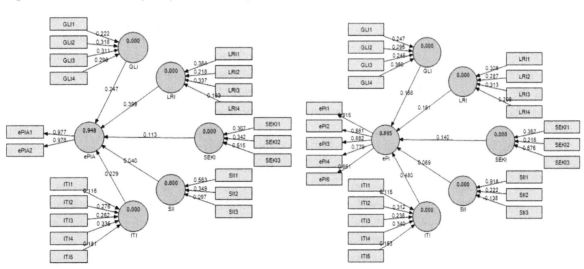

Table 2. Composite reliability (Cr), Cronbach's Alpha, inter-correlations, and square root of AVEs for the model 3a (with adopters only, n = 55)

	CR	CA	Matrix of inter-correlations and square root of AVEs					
			GLI	LRI	ITI	SII	SEKI	ePI
ePI	0.92	0.89	0.89	0.91	0.83	0.6	0.85	0.94

Table 3. Composite reliability (Cr), Cronbach's Alpha, inter-correlations, and square root of AVEs for the model 3b (with both adopters and non-adopters, n = 112)

	CR	CA	Matrix of inter-correlations and square root of AVEs					
			GLI	LRI	ITI	SII	SEKI	ePIA
ePIA	0.98	0.95	0.93	0.95	0.95	0.60	0.86	**0.977**

At construct level, the discriminant validity is accessed by an analysis of average variance extracted (AVE). The discriminant validity is adequate if the square root of AVE of each latent variable is greater than the correlation of two latent constructs. Table 2 and Table 3 show the correlation matrix for the latent factors in which the diagonal of the matrix is the square root of AVE. Generally, the results show that we experienced no problems with individual reliability, convergent validity, and discriminant validity as well.

For the assessment of formative constructs, we followed the approach proposed by Cenfetelli & Bassellier, 2009.

Test Multicollinearity of the Formative Indicators

Assessing the degree of multicollinearity among formative indicators is an important step in formative construct validation. The greater the level of multicollinearity among the indicators, the more likely many of the indicators will have low or non-significant path weights, or possibly even an opposite sign from the indicator's bivariate correlation with its construct (Cenfetelli & Bassellier, 2009).

To assess multicollinearity, variance inflation factor (VIF) was calculated (Petter, Straub, & Rai, 2007). The general statistical theory suggests that multicollinearity is not a concern if the VIF is less than 10. In this study, the result provided by SPSS shows that all VIF scores are less than the suggested threshold of 10 (Appendix A). This implies that the instrument has no multicollinearity.

Assess the Formative Indicators' Weights and Loadings and Nomological Network Effects

To assess the formative indicators' weights and loadings, a bootstrap analysis was performed with 200 subsamples and path coefficients were re-estimated using each of these samples. A specific item has both non-significant weight and loading, it implying the item is not absolutely as well as relatively important and it should be removed from the instrument (Cenfetelli & Bassellier, 2009). The output of Smart-PLS shows that all items have good weights and loadings (see Appendix A).

According to Cenfetelli & Bassellier, 2009, construct portability is important issue of formative measurements. A shortage of portability negatively influences the results of the model. A construct has a good portability if the construct's indicator weights change very little as the construct is used in different nomological networks. In this study, the two models of ePIA and ePI were used to test the portability. The result shows that there is no large change to the relative magnitudes of the indicator weights of formative constructs between the two models (Figures 3a&b). Therefore, the formative construct portability of the models is adopted.

The Structural Models

The Explanatory Power of Structural Models

According to Chin, 1998, the structural model in PLS-SEM is assessed by looking at the explanatory power of the structural model and the path coefficients. The explanatory power of the structural model can be evaluated by examining the amount of variance in the dependent variable which can be explained by the model through the squared multiple correlations (R^2). In this study, Smart-PLS 2.0 M3 provided R^2 values of two dependent variables, ePIA and ePI, are 0.948 and 0.894, respectively meaning that about 94.8% and 89.4% of the changes to the initial adoption and institutionalization of e-procurement is due to the independent latent variables of the models. The significance of the R^2 values was conducted by the F test of significance recommended by Falk & Miller, 1992, the result implies that the explanatory power of the model developed is statistically significant. The structural models were assessed by exploring the change in R^2 to see whether the effect of a particular latent variable on each of two dependent latent variables has a substantive impact. The effect size (Cohen's f^2) and the significance of f^2 statistic (Pseudo F test) were calculated (See Table 4).

Validation of the Structural Model

The path of the structural model is accessed next. Tests of each hypothesis were achieved by looking at the size and statistical significance of the path coefficient between independent and dependent variables. There are five out of the ten paths are statistically significant (Table 5).

DISCUSSION OF RESULTS

In this study, we attempted to answer to the question about the role of government on the level of e-procurement adoption in construction firms in developing countries.

E-Procurement Initial Adoption

First, the data analysis showed that *government leadership infrastructure* emerged as the most significant contribution to the entry-level adoption of e-procurement in Vietnamese construction enterprises. This is very consistent with previous empirical findings by To & Ngai, 2006; K. Zhu & Kraemer, 2005. It is also entirely consistent

Table 4. The path coefficients and t-values

Path	Path coefficients	t-values	Inference
Dependent construct: E-procurement Initial Adoption (ePIA)			
H1a: GLI->ePIA	*0.25*	*4.72*	*Supported*
H2a: LRI ->ePIA	*0.40*	*4.78*	*Supported*
H3a: ITI ->ePIA	*0.23*	*2.34*	*Supported*
H4a: SEKI ->ePIA	*0.11*	*2.36*	*Supported*
Dependent construct: E-procurement Institutionalization (ePI)			
H3b: ITI ->ePI	*0.482*	*3.78*	*Supported*

Legend: **=highly significant, *=significant; critical t-value: 1.96 P<0.05 and 2.58 P<0.01 (two-tailed).

Table 5. Results of effect size (F2) analysis

		$R^2_{included}$	$R^2_{excluded}$	f^2	Inference	F
ePIA	GLI	0.95	0.94	0.15	medium effect	3.8*
	LRI	0.95	0.93	0.28	medium to large effect	9.4**
	ITI	0.95	0.94	0.09	medium effect	3.8*
	SII	0.95	0.95	0.04	small effect	1.88
	SEKI	0.95	0.95	0.05	small effect	5.6*
ePI	GLI	0.89	0.89	0.03	small effect	1.01
	LRI	0.89	0.89	0.03	small effect	1.01
	ITI	0.89	0.88	0.15	medium effect	12**
	SII	0.89	0.89	0.03	small effect	1.01
	SEKI	0.89	0.89	0.03	small effect	1.01

Note: The effect of a predictor variable is small at the structural level if f2 is 0.02; to be medium if f2 is 0.15; and to be large if f2 is 0.35; (*) significant effect; (**) very significant effect

with the conventional wisdom that emphasizes the effects of macro-environment on initial adoption of e-commerce (Molla & Licker, 2005b). In particular, inertia forces are still strong in the Vietnamese business culture and the directive style is the common managing style of the Vietnamese thinking (JETO, 2007; Le-Hoai et al., 2009; N. D. Long, Ogunlana, Quang, & Lam, 2004; Phan & Luu, 2012), they often wait for clear e-commerce commitments and practical e-Government initiates and supports from government. In addition, at present, most Vietnamese construction enterprises are SMEs with lacking of financial, human, and technological resources (P. Long et al., 2010; Phan & Luu, 2012). SMEs have a limited control over their business environment and they tend to avoid risks taking and IT adoption (Luu, Kim, Cao, & Park, 2008). Therefore, e-commerce policies and regulations made by governments that pay especial attention to the demands of SMEs become critically necessary. Furthermore, competitive environment in Vietnam is determined by the relationship between business and government, and is mainly controlled by large and medium firms, but they tend to operate independently, and business managers often tend to be directed by government and less willing to accept the changes

(Nguyen et al., 2009). In other words, in Vietnam, there is a really big demand of the pioneering role of government in developing IT-oriented economic-social environment. Therefore, with the supporting policies from government in training and the development of innovative management skill, in the use of technologies, in disseminating new laws and government policies, and in guidance on the implications of regulatory and statutory changes on implementation and management, firms seem more willing to make the transition to e-commerce activities. This might explain these findings in this study.

Legal and regulatory infrastructure was also a significant factor influencing on the entry-level adoption of e-procurement. This finding gives an empirical support to qualitative researches that identified many legal obstacles to do e-commerce in both developed and developing countries, such as inadequate legal protection for online transactions, unclear business laws, and security and privacy concerns (APEC, 2006). This is also supported by previous empirical findings by Molla & Licker, 2005b; K. Zhu & Kraemer, 2005, etc. Particularly, this finding can be explained by the fact in Vietnam in which the legal framework for e-commerce is weak in the areas of taxation, customer protection, intellectual property rights, e-payment, public security, and human-resource development and does not take sufficiently into account the demands of private enterprises, and needs of rural users (Q. Tran, Huang, Liu, & Ekram, 2011). By implication, this result points the need for establishing a broad legal and institutional framework that makes a trustworthy e-marketplace.

Technology and information infrastructure and *socio-economic and knowledge infrastructure* were found to have considerable contributions to the initial adoption of e-procurement in Vietnamese construction enterprises. These results are completely consistent with previous results in Vietnam by Le et al., 2012. The result also supported the empirical findings in other developing countries' context by Alzougool & Kurnia, 2008; Aranda-Mena & Stewart, 2004; Eric & M, 2009; Klein, 2012. These results can be explained by the fact is that in Vietnam, the information infrastructure is poor, information sharing culture is facing the "rigidity" of public sector, or even in private businesses (Le-Hoai et al., 2009).

Supporting industry infrastructure (i.e. Finance, telecommunication, and transportation) is found not to influence on the initial adoption of e-procurement in Vietnamese construction enterprises. This result is consistent with the finding of Molla & Licker, 2005b was that supporting industries' e-readiness (i.e. telecommunication and transportation) does not appear to have any significant effect on the initial adoption of e-commerce. This finding can be resulted from the fact is that in Vietnam, e-commerce legal system and IT infrastructure are not developed and they become the overwhelming challenge to the enterprises' decision of level-entry adoption of e-procurement.

E-Procurement Institutionalization

The result of data analysis shows that among environmental determinants, only *information and technology infrastructure* has a significant

effect on the institutionalization of e-procurement adoption. This finding empirically supports a previous argument is that the factors that affect initial e-commerce adoption are different from, even opposite of, those that affect the level of institutionalization of e-commerce in an organization in developing countries' context (Molla & Licker, 2005b). This leads to the preliminary conclusion that while the initial adoption requires more institutional supports, the institutionalization focuses more on the demand of the development of IT infrastructure because of its integrated nature.

This finding is completely consistent with previous empirical evidence by Klein, 2012 and Molla & Licker, 2005a when they found that IT infrastructure contributed significantly on assimilation and institutionalization of e-commerce, respectively. In developing countries, such as Vietnam, many challenges related to IT infrastructure exist, such as the low quality, poor availability, and high cost of accessing the Internet, poor industry standards, and especially, very poor cross-disciplinary communication, etc. They together make constraints to the development of an IT-based socioeconomic environment in the country. By implication, governments need to put in place G2B e-initiatives, provide supporting policies across industries and SEMs as well in order to maximize and encourage e-commerce initiatives in both private and public sectors. An integrated e-commerce environment must be based on an advantaged IT infrastructure.

Other external factors include *government leadership infrastructure, legal and regulatory infrastructure, supporting industries infrastructure,* and *socio-economic and knowledge infrastructure* do not appear to have any significant effect on the institutionalization of e-procurement in Vietnamese construction enterprises. These findings are supported partially by the result made by Saprikis, 2013 and Molla & Licker, 2005a as they found that partners' pressure and supporting industries did not influence on the post-adoption stage of e-reverse auction use and institutionalization of e-commerce, respectively. However, these findings are not completely consistent with other results found by Molla & Licker, 2005a are that government commitments, legal system, and external market forces were significant factors influencing on institutionalization of e-commerce in developing countries. Possible explanations are that these factors are necessary but not sufficient after entry-level e-procurement adoption or an overwhelming demand of an e-commerce supportive IT infrastructure in Vietnam may have influenced on this result. This cautions future researchers not to consider all developing countries under the same perception, but pay attention to the profound differences among them. This result also indicates empirically that determinants of initial adoption are very different from those of sophistication of e-procurement.

IMPLICATIONS AND LIMITATIONS

Theoretical Implications

To the best of the authors' knowledge, the current study is one of the few empirical studies of e-procurement adoption/institutionalization based on the process-oriented view. To accomplish the objectives, this research provided the rigorous conceptual definitions of initial adoption vs. institutionalization of e-procurement based on a strong theoretical and literature review background. The study showed that consideration of e-procurement institutionalization under three key dimensions: the breadth of use for different value chain activities, the depth of use (percentage) for each activity, and the degree of interoperability is important. The present study also provided additionally empirical evidence to show that determinants of initial adoption are very different from that of institutionalization of e-procurement in developing countries' context. Therefore, the study confirms the process-based view is a necessary and effective approach to study on the adoption of e-commerce technologies in developing countries.

Practical Implications

The findings of this study present some useful directions for enhancing the institutionalization rate and beneficial use of e-procurement in construction enterprises. First, the discussion surmised that government has a stronger impact on the entry-level adoption than the institutionalization of e-procurement in firms. The role of the government in terms of commitments and supportive policies, providing legal and regulatory, IT and supporting industries infrastructures is very necessary in pushing construction enterprises to adopt e-procurement at the initial level. However, in order to convince enterprises to implement more sophisticated e-procurement, government needs to pay especial attention to the development of IT infrastructure. In more detail, government needs to pay simultaneously attention to a clear and comprehensive commitment of e-commerce, the development of e-Government initiates, and international e-commerce incentives, especially specific e-commerce supportive policies and incentives to SMEs. Related public administrations need to sit down together to develop a well-defined e-procurement legal system that considers comprehensively exclusive e-commerce risks, exclusive non-e-commerce risks and mixed e-commerce/non-e-commerce risks as well. Government, state-owned enterprises, and private firms need to more actively take responsibilities in developing B2B and G2B e-initiates, especially in improving the availability and transparency of both industrial and institutional information resources. Furthermore, government needs to promote the development of a common standard system that is extremely crucial for interfacing systems and institutionalizing e-procurement. To the Vietnamese economic environment that controlled and directed mainly by state-owned enterprises, it seems to be the most important is that its policy-makers need to implement policies to promote the development of full market-orientation in its state-owned enterprises.

Limitations and Further Research

Firstly, due to its construction industry focus, the generalizability of our results is limited. Secondly, the size of data was small with only 112 respondents. The PLS approach can solve this problem; however, a larger sample size should be collected to test whether the results obtained in this present study are replicable. The research instrument, although rigorously validated, has not been tested for test-retest reliability and external validity. Replicating the study would enable such tests. Finally, after more than twenty years of the development, the diffusion of e-procurement in both developing and developed countries has been significantly improved. Instead of simple adoption of e-procurement innovations, enterprises may be moving towards the more sophisticated implementation of the technology in terms of management, technology, information, and function because its potential full benefits. Future research should catch this trend of adoption.

CONCLUSION

In an effort to foster institutionalization of e-procurement in construction firms in developing countries, our work was pursued to assess the role of government in this context. This objective was addressed by empirically testing a research model that consists of five independent constructs represent external environmental factors, including government leadership, legal and regulatory system, information and technology infrastructure, supporting industry infrastructure, and socio-economic and knowledge infrastructure. The findings of the study suggest two conclusions: (1) in developing countries' context, government plays an extremely significant role on a decision of entry-level adoption of e-procurement in construction firms. (2) The role of government is less significant on decision-making in institutionalizing e-procurement in construction firms.

ACKNOWLEDGMENT

The authors would like to thanks to reviewers and the editor of International Journal of Enterprise Information Systems for their constructive and helpful comments. The authors are also grateful to Hohai Scholarship Program and Industrial Economics Institute, Business School of Hohai University for their financial supports to make the field survey in Vietnam from May to July 2012.

REFERENCES

Alzougool, B., & Kurnia, S. (2008). Electronic Commerce Technologies Adoption by SMEs: A Conceptual Study. *Australasian Conference on Information Systems, ACIS-0135-2008.R1.*

APEC. (2006). *The final report on transparency in procurement and e-Procurement APEC Senior Officials' Meeting (SOM III).* Viet Nam: Ha Noi.

Aranda-Mena, G., & Stewart, P. (2004). *E-business adoption in construction: international review on impediments Research Report 2003-003-A.* Brisbane: Cooperative Research Centre for Construction Innovation.

Betts, M., Black, P., Christensen, S., Dawson, E., Du, R., Duncan, W.,... González, J. (2006). Towards secure and legal e-tendering. *Information Technology in Construction, 11*(Special Issue e-Commerce in construction), 89-102.

Cenfetelli, R. T., & Bassellier, G. (2009). Interpretation of formative measurement in information systems research. *Management Information Systems Quarterly, 33*(4), 689–707.

Chang, H. H., & Wong, K. H. (2010). Adoption of e-procurement and participation of e-marketplace on firm performance: Trust as a moderator. *Information & Management, 47*(5–6), 262–270. doi:10.1016/j.im.2010.05.002

Chin, W. W. (1998). Commentary: Issues and Opinion on Structural Equation Modeling. *Management Information Systems Quarterly*, 22(1), vii–xvi.

Egbu, C. O. (Ed.). (2008). *Knowledge Management for Improved Construction e-Business Performance*. West Sussex, UK: Blackwell Publishing Ltd. doi:10.1002/9781444302462.ch13

Eric, C. W. L., & M, A. (2009). Critical success factors for e-tendering implementation in construction collaborative environments: People and process issues. [ITcon]. *Journal of Information Technology in Construction*, 14, 98–109.

Falk, R. F., & Miller, N. B. (1992). *A primer for soft modeling*. Akron: The University of Akron Press.

Hamed Salim, A.-H., Helen, M. E., & Lynne, H. (2013). The Changing Importance of Critical Success Factors During ERP Implementation: An Empirical Study from Oman. [IJEIS]. *International Journal of Enterprise Information Systems*, 9(3), 1–21. doi:10.4018/jeis.2013070101

Ismail, I. A., & Kamat, V. R. (2008). Integrated Multi-Disciplinary e-Business Infrastructure Framwork Vol. 65-80. C. J. Anumba & K. Ruikar (Eds.), E-Business in construction

Jessy, N., Reddy, D. B. S., & Anand, A. S. (2014). Conceptualizing Dimensions of Enterprise Resource Planning Systems Success: A SocioTechnical Perspective. [IJEIS]. *International Journal of Enterprise Information Systems*, 10(1), 53–75. doi:10.4018/ijeis.2014010104

JETO. (2007). *Survey of Japanese - Affiliated Firms in ASEAN and India*. from www.jetro.go.jp/en/reports/survey/pdf/2008_06_biz.pdf

Klein, R. (2012). Assimilation of Internet-based purchasing applications within medical practices. *Information & Management*, 49(3–4), 135–141. doi:10.1016/j.im.2012.02.001

Kog, Y. C. (2010). Legal Issues of Integrated Network for Construction and Real Estate Sector. *Journal of legal affairs and disputere solution in engineering and construction © ASCE*, 2(4), 228-235.

Le, V. H., Rowe, F., Truex, D., & Huynh, M. Q. (2012). An Empirical Study of Determinants of E-Commerce Adoption in SMEs in Vietnam: An Economy in Transition. *Journal of Global Information Management*, 20(3), 23–54. doi:10.4018/jgim.2012070102

Le-Hoai, L., Lee, Y. D., & Son, J. J. (2009). Partnering in Construction: Investigation of Problematic Issues for Implementation in Vietnam. *KSCE Journal of Civil Engineering*, 14(5), 731–741. doi:10.1007/s12205-010-0916-8

Li, Y. H. (2008). *An empirical investigation on the determinants of e-procurement adoption in Chinese manufacturing enterprises*. Paper presented at the International Conference on Management Science & Engineering (15th), California, USA. doi:10.1109/ICMSE.2008.4668890

London, K., & Bavinton, N. (2006). Economic, social and cultural impediments and drivers for adoption of e-business innovations within the industrial structure of the construction sector Clients driving construction innovation: moving ideas into practice (pp. 313-336). Brisbane, Qld.: Cooperative Research Centre for Construction Innovation for Icon. Net Pty Ltd.

Long, N. D., Ogunlana, S., Quang, T., & Lam, K. C. (2004). Large construction projects indeveloping countries: A case study from Vietnam. *International Journal of Project Management*, 22(7), 553–561. doi:10.1016/j.ijproman.2004.03.004

Long, P., & Jeffrey, E. T. (2011). A Success Model for Enterprise Resource Planning Adoption to Improve Financial Performance in Vietnam's Equitized State Owned Enterprises. [IJEIS]. *International Journal of Enterprise Information Systems*, 7(1), 41–55. doi:10.4018/jeis.2011010103

Long, P., Pham, L., & Nguyen, D. (2010). *Small and medium sized enterprises' e-commerce adoption model in Vietnam.* Paper presented at the *Proceedings of the Academy of Information and Management Sciences, Allied Academies International Conference, 14(2)*, Las Vegas.

Luu, T. V., Kim, S. Y., Cao, H. L., & Park, Y. M. (2008). Performance measurement of construction firms in developing countries. *Construction Management and Economics, 26*(4), 373–386. doi:10.1080/01446190801918706

Mandana, F., Iman Raeesi, V., & Babak, S. (2013). A Survey Study of Influential Factors in the Implementation of Enterprise Resource Planning Systems. [IJEIS]. *International Journal of Enterprise Information Systems, 9*(1), 76–96. doi:10.4018/jeis.2013010105

MDBs. (2004). *Electronic Government Procurement: Readiness Self Assessment. The E-GP research report.* from http://www.mdb-egp.org

Molla, A., & Licker, P. S. (2005a). E-Commerce adoption in developing countries: A model and instrument. *Information & Management, 42*(6), 877–899. doi:10.1016/j.im.2004.09.002

Molla, A., & Licker, P. S. (2005b). Perceived e-readiness factors in e-commerce adoption: An empirical investigation in a developing country. *International Journal of Electronic Commerce, 10*(1), 83–110.

Neef, D. (2001). *E-procurement from Strategy to Implementation.* Upper Saddle River: Prentice Hall.

Ng Kim, A. (2005). *Survey on electronic procurement implementation in Malaysia construction companies.* (Master thesis), University Technology Malaysia, Malaysia.

Nguyen, Q. T. N., Neck, P. A., & Nguyen, T. H. (2009). The Critical Role of Knowledge Management in Achieving and Sustaining Organisational Competitive Advantage. *International Business Research, 2*(3), http://www.ccsenet.org/journal.html

Oxley, J., & Yeung, B. (2001). E-commerce readiness: Institutional environment and international competitiveness. *Journal of International Business Studies, 32*(4), 705–724. doi:10.1057/palgrave.jibs.8490991

Petter, S., Straub, D., & Rai, A. (2007). Specifying formative constructs in information systems research. *Management Information Systems Quarterly, 31*(4), 623–656.

Phan, T. M., & Luu, H. V. (2012). *Vietnam Country Report: Vietnam National Real Estate Association.* VNREA.

Porter, M. E. (1990). *The Competitive Advantage of Nations.* Havard College.

Rai, A., Tang, X., Brown, P., & Keil, M. (2006). Assimilation patterns in the use of electronic procurement innovations: A cluster analysis. *Information & Management, 43*(3), 336–349. doi:10.1016/j.im.2005.08.005

Rao, S. S., Metts, G., & Monge, C. M. (2003). Electronic commerce development in small and medium sized enterprise: A stage model and its implication. *Business Process Management Journal, 9*(1), 11–32. doi:10.1108/14637150310461378

Raymond, L., Croteau, A.-M., & Bergeron, F. (2012). The strategic role of IT as an antecedent to the IT sophistication and IT performance of manufacturing SMEs. *International Journal on Advances in Systems and Measurements, 4*(3 and 4), 203-211.

Raymond, R. A. I., Flood, I., & Treffinger, B. (2008). Assessment of e-Business Implementation in the US Construction Industry C. J. Anumba & K. Ruikar (Eds.), e-Business in Construction

Ruikar, K., Anumba, C. J., & Carrillo, P. M. (2006). VERDICT - An e-readiness assessment application for construction companies. *Automation in Construction*, *15*(1), 98–110. doi:10.1016/j. autcon.2005.02.009

Saprikis, V. (2013). Suppliers' behavior on the post-adoption stage of business-to-business e-reverse auctions: An empirical study. *Telematics and Informatics*, *30*(2), 132–143. doi:10.1016/j. tele.2012.04.002

Schwartz, H., & Davis, S. M. (1981). Matching corporate culture and business strategy. *Organizational Dynamics*, *10*(1), 30–48. doi:10.1016/0090-2616(81)90010-3

Stephen, M. M., & Brakel, P. (2006). An evaluation of e-readiness assessment tools with respect to information access: Towards an integrated information rich tool. *International Journal of Information Management*, *26*(3), 212–223. doi:10.1016/j.ijinfomgt.2006.02.004

Teo, T. S. H., Lin, S., & Lai, K.-. (2009). Adopters and non-adopters of e-procurement in Singapore: An empirical study. *Omega*, *37*(5), 972–987. doi:10.1016/j.omega.2008.11.001

To, M. L., & Ngai, E. W. T. (2006). Predicting the organisational adoption of B2C e-commerce: An empirical study. *Industrial Management & Data Systems*, *106*(8), 1133–1147. doi:10.1108/02635570610710791

Tran, Q., Huang, D., Liu, B., & Ekram, H. M. (2011). A Construction Enterprise's Readiness Level in Implementing E-Procurement: A System Engineering Assessment Model. *Systems Engineering Procedia*, *2*(0), 131–141. doi:10.1016/j. sepro.2011.10.016

Tran, Q. D., Vo, Q. B., & Nguyen, H. D. (2011). E-commerce in construction industry in Vietnam: Barriers and drivers. *Review of Ministry of Construction*, *50*(6), 69–72.

Umit, I., Jason, U., Murat, K., & Utku, A. (2013). Data Integration Capability Evaluation of ERP Systems: A Construction Industry Perspective. [IJEIS]. *International Journal of Enterprise Information Systems*, *9*(3), 113–129. doi:10.4018/jeis.2013070106

Urbach, N., & Ahlemann, F. (2010). Structural Equation Modeling in Information Systems Research Using Partial Least Squares. *Journal of Information Technology Theory and Application (JITTA)*, *11*(2), Article 2.

VECITA. (2008). *Vietnam e-Commerce Report 2008*. Vietnam: Ministry of Industry and Trade.

Zhu, K., & Kraemer, K. L. (2005). Post-adoption variations in usage and value of E-Business by organizations: Cross-country evidence from the retail industry. *Information Systems Research*, *16*(1), 61–84. doi:10.1287/isre.1050.0045

Zhu, K., Kraemer, K. L., & Xu, S. (2006). The process of innovation assimilation by firms in different countries: A technology diffusion perspective on e-business. *Management Science*, *52*(10), 1557–1576. doi:10.1287/mnsc.1050.0487

This work was previously published in the International Journal of Enterprise Information Systems (IJEIS), 10(4); edited by Madjid Tavana, pages 1-21, copyright year 2014 by IGI Publishing (an imprint of IGI Global).

APPENDIX A

Table 6. Vif, weights, loadings, and t-values of the formative indicators

	VIF	The model of ePIA		The model of ePI (adopters only, n = 55)	
		Weights (*)	Loadings (*)	Weights (*)	Loadings (*)
GLI1 -> GLI	2.29	0.22	0.84	0.25	0.84
GLI2 -> GLI	2.37	0.32	0.87	0.30	0.87
GLI3 -> GLI	2.47	0.31	0.87	0.25	0.85
GLI4 -> GLI	2.71	0.30	0.89	0.36	0.90
ITI1 -> ITI	2.12	0.12	0.75	0.12	0.75
ITI 2 -> ITI	3.58	0.28	0.90	0.31	0.91
ITI 3 -> ITI	3.11	0.25	0.88	0.24	0.87
ITI 4 -> ITI	2.88	0.34	0.89	0.34	0.89
ITI 5 -> ITI	2.62	0.18	0.80	0.15	0.79
SII1 -> SII	1.93	0.56	0.82	0.92	0.99
SII2 -> SII	1.96	0.35	0.63	0.22	0.97
SII3 -> SII	1.89	0.10	0.79	-0.14	0.96
LRI1 -> LRI	2.94	0.38	0.91	0.33	0.90
LRI 2 -> LRI	2.49	0.22	0.87	0.29	0.89
LRI 3 -> LRI	2.36	0.33	0.88	0.31	0.87
LRI 4 -> LRI	2.86	0.19	0.85	0.21	0.85
SEKI1 -> SEKI	1.76	0.31	0.81	0.36	0.83
SEKI2 -> SEKI	1.71	0.34	0.82	0.22	0.76
SEKI3 -> SEKI	1.91	0.51	0.90	0.58	0.93
(*) Statistically significant					

APPENDIX B

Table 7. The measurement instrument

Constructs	Measurement Items/survey questions
Government Leadership Infrastructure(GLI)	**GLI1:** I believe that Government has a strong strategic commitment to general e-commerce across the nation with a comprehensive vision, effective action plans, and incentive policies. **GLI2:** I believe that Government is effectively playing its pioneering role in facilitating the market demand for e-commerce through e-Government initiatives (e.g. public e-procurement, public websites); reengineering in state organizations is being undertaken; officials are well trained and have positive attitudes towards public e-services. **GLI3:** I believe that the Government has been making many efforts to the development of e-commerce towards the regional and international scope; many bilateral and multi-parties agreements with international governments and organizations that related to legal issues, standards, security, etc. have been signing. **GLI4:** I believe that the Government has paid especial attention on the development of e-commerce in the construction industry and SMEs.
Legal and Regulatory Infrastructure (LRI)	**LRI 1:** I believe that our paper-based procurement legal system is well-defined to address traditional legal risks (e.g. corruption, bureaucracy, fraudulent, jurisdiction, intellectual property rights) **LRI 2:** I believe that our e-procurement legal system is well-defined to address e-transactions risks (e.g. software agents contracting, authentication, online security, privacy, etc.) **LRI 3:** I believe that e-commerce legal and regulatory system is unified with international legal defines; **LRI 4:** I believe that our e-commerce legal and regulatory system takes sufficiently into account the needs of both public vs. private enterprises and large vs. SMEs as well in the industry.
Information Technology Infrastructure (ITI)	**ITI1:** I believe that supporting IT applications and Internet is available and good enough to support well e-procurement activities with regards to interoperability, reliability, security, and standardization in the industry. **ITI2:** I believe B2B e-initiatives have been developed well in the industry (websites, e-marketplaces). **ITI3:** I believe that e-Government initiatives have been developed well (e.g. public e-communication, e-bank system, public e-certificate service, e-tax declaration and clearance, and public e-procurement). **ITI4:** I believe that across-industrial information sources are available and transparency equally; **ITI5:** I believe that public administration institutions have established e-databases of economic and administration information; they are available and fair for enterprises.
Supporting Industries Infrastructure (SII)	**SII1:** I believe national financial system are improved and institutionalized well to handle e-commerce; **SII2:** I believe telecommunications system is improved & institutionalized well to support e-commerce; **SII3:** I believe that the transportation system is improved and institutionalized well to support e-commerce.
Socio-economic and knowledge Infrastructure (SEKI)	**SEKI1:** I believe that the socio-cultural environment is now very incentive and supportive for e-procurement because of improved trust on e-transactions; improved e-payment activities; enhanced active and independent style of working and managing within the industry; **SEKI2:** I believe that the enterprise community in the industry is well aware of short-time vs. long-term benefits; has positive attitudes towards e-procurement; has enough skilled labor force, technicians, and managers that required for the development of e-procurement strategy; **SEKI3:** I believe that the economic environment is very good in terms of competitiveness, transparency, stableness; and has a strong trend of collaboration and cooperation.
E-procurement initial adoption (ePIA)	**ePIA1:** Our enterprise has been implementing one or several e-procurement innovations separately for a very small part of the total purchase. **ePIA2:** Our enterprise has been using the static or interactive websites to make promotions and publish basis company information or receive queries, e-mail, and form entry from users.
E-procurement Institutionalization (ePI)	Our enterprise has implemented or planned to, in the near future,: **ePI1:** Implement major amount of our purchases through e-procurement innovations; **ePI2:** Implement most procurement processes (from informing to payment) in electronic format; **ePI3:** Improve higher interoperability between e-procurement innovations together and with other IT systems; **ePI4:** Improve higher interoperability between e-procurement innovations with external IT infrastructure through transactive or integrated websites, and participating e-marketplace; **ePI5:** Implement e-procurement innovations more consistent with our business strategy, organizational structure, and social environment within our enterprise.
Note: Manifest variables measured on a five-point Likert scale ranging from "Strongly Disagree" (value =1) to "Strongly Agree" (value =5). E-procurement Innovations include e-Informing, e-Catalog, e-Tendering, e-Bidding, e-Reverse Auctioning, e-Awarding, e-Contracting, e-Invoicing, and e-Payment.	

Chapter 65
A Linguistic Approach to Identify the Affective Dimension Expressed in Textual Messages

Sandro José Rigo
University of Vale do Rio dos Sinos (UNISINOS), Brazil

Isa Mara da Rosa Alves
University of Vale do Rio dos Sinos (UNISINOS), Brazil

Jorge Luis Victória Barbosa
University of Vale do Rio dos Sinos (UNISINOS), Brazil

ABSTRACT

The digital mediation resources used in Distance Education can hinder the teacher's perception about the student's state of mind. However, the textual expression in natural language is widely encouraged in most Distance Education courses, through the use of Virtual Learning Environments and other digital tools. This fact has motivated research efforts in order to identify feelings expressed by students in textual messages. A significant part of the known approaches in this area apply textual analysis without a deep linguistic representation, which can lead to some weakness in the results obtained. This paper reports an approach using theories of Computational Lexical Semantics for the representation of the lexicon of emotion. The methodology was developed through studies regarding corpus analysis, lexical unit description, and the implementation of a computational system to identify the feelings expressed in the textual messages in natural language, using the lexicon of emotion. This system was used in evaluation experiments that indicate improvements when comparing the adopted approach with other similar approaches.

INTRODUCTION

The dynamics of digital mediation used in Distance Education (DE) generates contexts that can drive to student isolation or little integration with colleagues. However, the use of subsidies generated in this digital mediation interaction process in Virtual Learning Environments (VLE) allows the creation of resources that can promote closer student-teacher relations. Some examples of these situations are the use of the students' textual production and their interaction data in order to

DOI: 10.4018/978-1-4666-8619-9.ch065

generate profiles of these students that can help in the diagnosis of their difficulties and in the identification of subjectivity elements.

The aim of this paper is to describe and evaluate mechanisms to improve the identification of the students' emotional state, by identifying feelings and emotions expressed in textual messages by the students in the different tools available in a VLE. This is an objective described in some works as a possible way to foster the effectiveness and the quality of the interactions between teachers and students in DE (Bercht, 2001; Jaques & Vicari, 2005; Desmarais & Baker, 2012). Some studies on the relationship between emotion and memory indicate a positive relationship between the students' state of mind and cognitive activities like memorization and learning (Le Doux, 2001; Pergher et al., 2006).

Given the large and recent development and expansion of Distance Education, the analysis of students generated textual messages and the processing of the interaction data can contribute significantly to identify evidences about feelings or to report significant facts about the students learning process.

The automatic analysis of students' feelings based on their textual messages is the objective of several works. The methodologies and techniques adopted to reach this objective are very diverse. In some cases these works describe initiatives to identify pupils' emotional states based on the occurrence of specific textual terms in the students' natural language messages (Longhi, 2009; Azevedo, 2011; Edécio, 2011). In other cases, statistical tools or machine learning resources are applied to identify important textual elements and generate evidences and confirmation using the textual production (Macedo, 2009; Klemman, 2009; Oliveira et al., 2011). These initiatives demonstrated that the adopted approaches effectively promote the generation of resources to support some activities regarding the teacher's analysis of the state of mind of students. Nevertheless, the great diversity of writing styles observed in natu-

ral language messages present some challenges not yet fully meet by these approaches, fostering therefore new research efforts.

In the present paper we describe the methodological choices and the results obtained from a linguistic representation approach dedicated to the analysis of emotions expressed in the textual messages in VLEs. This work is motivated by the possible improvements in the textual treatment of these messages considering linguistic elements. The textual treatment approaches without the support of linguistic elements present some errors in the identification of situations involving figures of speech, synonyms and different writing styles. One of the improvements obtained in the use of linguistic elements is related to the more precise identification of textual sentences in natural language.

The approach described in this paper is the result of an interdisciplinary research effort involving the integrated use of Computational Lexical Semantics and Natural Language Processing (NLP) resources. With respect to language analysis oriented tasks, we adopted the principles of Cognitive Linguistics as a theoretical basis for the description of the text corpus. Thereby, this corpus description is done with information such as lexical-conceptual relations and semantic frames. This organization of the lexicon integrates description of meaningful relations and frames, therefore making the representation capable to support the proposals of the WORDNET (Miller, 1995; Fellbaum, 1998) and FRAMENET (Fillmore, 2003), facilitating future studies regarding multi-domain and multi-language requisites. From the computational point of view, the main challenges were the design and validation of a software tool to support the identification and classification of subjective textual statements made by students in the VLEs.

The adopted methodology is based on linguistic knowledge, focusing in the analysis of the studied corpus, which consists of textual messages collected in disciplines in Distance Education.

These linguistic studies originated the elements of a lexicon of emotion, which provides subsidies for the developed computational tool. The main contributions of this work are the construction of a lexicon of emotion and a computational system that implements the analysis of the textual messages from a linguistic point of view, including language resources as determinant elements for the identification of affective aspects contained in textual messages. The comparative tests performed allow the identification of improvements obtained with this approach when comparing with existing approaches that do not consider the linguistic aspects.

The text is organized into six additional sections. The next two sections describe some aspects of learning and emotions, together with analysis of related approaches, in order to provide a background and a context to our proposal. After, a section discusses the methodology applied and another section describes the system developed. The experiment conducted and the results are both described in the next section. Finally, in the last section, we draw some conclusions and plans for future work.

ASPECTS OF EMOTION AND LEARNING

Several authors, such as Picard and Healey (1997), Le Doux (2001) and Pergher (2006), present reflections that are useful for understanding the importance of the emotions and their relationship to learning. These approaches allow a better understanding about the roles of the interlocutors in virtual learning environments, in addition to a better understanding of the information regarding who they are, what they want and what motivates them to reflect, to act and to discuss. Therefore, these studies are essential elements for the reflection on who are the students arriving at university in Distance Education courses and what they look for. There are also elements, in these studies, that

help to recognize the reasons why certain experiences in the VLEs do not motivate the students or do not facilitate the understanding of the concepts needed for some academic activity.

The teacher should identify how their students are feeling about the incentives and stimulus received in the VLEs (Pergher, 2006). Also is important to look for elements to understand these feelings not only regarding specific knowledge necessities from the academic activity demands, but also regarding the profile of the student and their possibilities. It is worth emphasizing that we meant here student profile as something that denotes the understanding of what traditionally is called the reality of the student, which is composed with personal information, but that has also cultural reflexes and is therefore collective in a way. This type of reflection is fostered in the context of Distance Education, situation where the teacher's contact with the pupil occurs almost exclusively through digital mediation, mostly through texts.

It is in this scenario that the Distance Educations courses exist today and this is the culture in which live our students. Thereby, to identify their feelings becomes an essential task to help in the development of the teacher activities. To discuss strategies for teaching and learning is not the focus of this paper, however, to contribute to the qualification of this process is among the motivations for the definition of the lexicon of emotion and the proposition of the computational tool presented.

RELATED APPROACHES

According to Pang and Lee (2008) the use of the Web to identify the opinions expressed by people is a fact that has been growing and that is self-evident. One of the general motivators for such context is the search for automatic analysis of reputation of companies aiming to understand the acceptance of its products among consumers (Liu, 2012).

In the educational context there is a similar process, partly made possible by the wide adoption of VLEs, particularly in Distance Education. Students are encouraged, during the teaching-learning processes, to the use of interaction mechanisms that allow the generation of textual messages. These messages can occur in objective or subjective situations. The first situation occurs when textual messages are related to answers for objective questions, such as in exercises. The second situation occurs when the student describes personal and subjective situations. These second kind of textual messages may correspond to a diversity of situations, ranging from student feedback about their performance, personal observations about comments of colleagues and teachers, indication of the degree of satisfaction and acceptance for the teaching processes, or the description of encountered difficulties.

Given the large amount of data existing in this format, the analysis of subjective aspects on textual messages tends to become impractical and costly when individually and manually done. At the same time, the treatment of these aspects presents fundamental importance to allow the teacher to achieve improvements in the relation with students, through the use of the material generated in interactions and related to the textual expressions of the students. The techniques used for automatic messages treatment are still subject of research and experimentation, being known with various names, such as Opinion Mining, Sentiment Analysis, Subjectivity Analysis Appraisal Extraction (Pang & Lee, 2008).

These techniques implement processes that allow to analyze texts and to extract phrases denoting opinion in order to categorize these phrases and to associate it to polarity attributes. Thus, texts containing positive or negative opinions regarding certain subjects can be identified. In addition to this, other approaches seek to describe more specifically the kind of feeling expressed in the text. In certain contexts this task has a considerable complexity, as in texts where different opinions are exposed and compared, or in diverse writing styles.

The known approaches to deal with this problem use well-identified steps. Initially, the identification of subjectivity expressions is performed in elements or sentences composing the text. These results are then treated in the characteristics extraction step, through the use of different classification resources, according to the approach in question. Examples of supporting information are the specific lexicons containing textual terms and their polarity, the sets of expressions of interest or the description of grammatical classes of terms. In general these steps are handled with the support of preprocessing techniques that enable the treatment of stop-words and stemmer, among other features (Pang et al, 2002). The final step involves sorting the obtained results with a wide range of techniques from the artificial intelligence area (Chen, 2011; Tang, Tan & Cheng, 2009).

The choice of the classification resources is of high importance and can determine the possible results in the methods. Some approaches adopt the use of lexicons describing the polarity of terms found in texts (Liu, 2012). Although this approach allows adequate results in some textual organizations, in many situations it is observed an inappropriate interpretation of information related with the term and its polarity. In general these situations can be avoided with a broader linguistic treatment, such as the one proposed in this paper.

The importance of lexical bases, as the one proposed in this article, for the automatic processing of natural language is consensual in the Natural Language Processing area. One of the difficulties for the practice of this approach is the construction cost of this linguistic feature and the identification of the best theoretical-methodological strategies for its conception. In Brazil, in particular, the sentiment analysis is a challenging task, due to the scarcity of linguistic resources for the Portuguese language, demonstrating the importance of research in the area and the relevance of this work to the scientific community.

METHODOLOGY

The proposal presented here aims to facilitate the task of identifying feelings and emotions expressed with textual messages by the students in the different tools available in a VLE. Initially we undertook the construction of a lexical database, containing syntactic information of lexical items that are indicators of feelings and emotions. To this end we adopted the Cognitive Lexical semantics theory. This choice was made due to the fact that this is a sufficiently comprehensive theory to allow the necessary rules descriptions and also has descriptive power suited to the representation of the semantics of emotion in a manner useful for computational purposes. Due to this option, the description of the lexicon of emotion allows linguistic representation, because it characterizes a phenomenon that manifests itself on the surface of the language; enables the computational linguistic representation, as it admits a description of linguistic information; and allows the linguistic-cognitive representation, because it has the status of functional isomorphism, here considering that the psychological reality of a representation is not immediate, but may be representative of what we have in mind (Dominiek & Rice, 1995).

The texts analyzed for the construction of this lexicon were obtained from actual data generated by students in Distance Education courses in an assessment tool about the student's learning process. For the analysis of texts the following activities were performed: (i) compilation of corpus with texts extracted from the VLE MOODLE; (ii) pre-processing of those texts, involving conversion to compatible language corpora management tools; (iii) extracting nouns, adjectives and verbs from those texts with the use of the parser PALAVRAS (Bick, 2000); (iv) the use of concordance system

for handling the corpus, specifically the Word Smith Tools; (v) description of the lexical units that compose the lexical database.

This lexicon consists in the fundamental component of the computational tool dedicated to map, analyze and automatically present to the teacher a report of emotions and sentiments expressed by students. This aspect is being explored as an methodological differential, with the use of syntactic rules in conjunction with the polarity information. This approach allows some improvement in the results, avoiding problematic situations observed, for example, when the terms of polarity are associated with modifiers components. To validate the approach in an exploratory study, we follow the methodological steps described below.

First, some components where chosen to enable the comparison of results between polarity information based approaches and the linguistic approach proposed here. The chosen lexicon, the SentiLex-PT, consists of a lexicon for the Portuguese language, with adjectival annotated and inferred forms (http://dmir. inesc - id. en / reaction / SentiLex – PT). At the time of the execution of these tests, the SentiLex-PT base contained 6.321 adjectival annotated forms and 25.406 inferred forms. Each entry of this lexicon provides information about polarity and the polarity identification method used (annotated or inferred). This last information is important, because part of this lexicon is annotated by hand, however part has its attributes automatically generated (Silva, 2010).

Second, a set of texts was selected from a VLE (MOODLE), containing messages related to the expression of students' feelings related to their performance in courses in Distance Education. The texts are handled by the parser PALAVRAS (Bick, 2000), to obtain the necessary syntactical information. This allows the use of these texts together with syntactic rules. These texts are then treated with a lexicon developed within the context of this work, from which such elements are described as adjectives with important potential for identifying feelings, associated in turn with syntactic rules that allow a more precise identification of their contexts of occurrence. The two classification methods (i.e., adjectives, syntactic rules) give two different decisions on corresponding emotion. Therefore, the combined use of these two resources can lead to better results in the identification of the emotional state in the textual messages.

Finally, this set of resources was organized from an overall architecture so we could carry out experiments validating the approach. The syntactic rules used are generated by linguistic analysis. The rules used n the first tests were identified in a way that some textual components, such as adjectives, for example, were treated properly in steps of identification and classification. Some examples that implement these rules can be seen in the sentences shown in Table 1.

An example of these rules is described and commented below. In this case, two configurations are described in which the first is composed of an article that is an optional element, followed by a noun and the verb "to be" or the verb "to seem", complemented by an adjective. The format of these rules is exemplified as follows. For both configurations, we have the format: [article] + Noun + Verb (be/seem) + Adjective. The examples that implement these two rules can be those of the two sentences that follow. The first example sentence is "The discipline was excellent" and the second example is "The discipline seems excellent". In these two situations we can highlight the association between the adjective and the noun phrases. In other situations where the context of phrases

is presented with greater complexity, different rules configuration are possible, in order to deal with the appropriate components for the analysis.

The use of the rules is based on syntactic analysis performed by the parser PALAVRAS (Bick, 2000), which allows the components of each sentence to be correctly identified. As the result of the parser operation, a file in XML format is available. This allows the automatic file processing, as the basis for the implementation of matching algorithms and application of syntactic rules.

The functioning of the system developed is closely linked to the treatment of the registered rules, in order to identify the correct information about the texts analyzed in accordance with the linguistic information registered in the environment. For this purpose the environment allows rules registration and the indication of composition elements, such as optional items and items that identify reversal polarity of the terms.

SYSTEM DEVELOPED

To evaluate, in an exploratory approach, the linguistic resources developed, we implemented the system described below. Here we describe the architectural elements of the computational tool developed. To deal with the application context, we used the data model as shown in Figure 1, to allow the database to store the syntactic rules and also the lexicon Sentilex-PT, necessary to the comparisons between the two approaches.

Table 1. Examples of syntactic rules and associated phrases

Rule	Sentence
(DET) + N + VCOP + ADJ	Discipline is excellent
(DET) + N + VCOP + ADV + ADJ	The material was very good.
(DET) N + ADV + DENIAL + VCOP + (ADV) + ADJ/NAME	The material is not clear.
DET + N + THAT + VCOP + (ADV) + ADJ	The teacher, that was very cool during the semester, received a tribute.

Figure 1. Summary of modeling used base

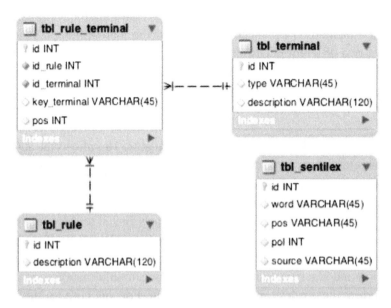

Here follows a brief description of the function of each of the tables in Figure 1. The table "tbl_sentilex" is responsible for storing the dictionary of adjectives used by the system to the initial polarity calculation. The values stored in this table are: a) the unique identifier; b) the adjective itself in its masculine singular form; c) the grammatical class, to allow the treatment of different grammatical classes; d) the polarity assigned to this term; e) the description of the source where this information was originated. The data in the table "tbl_sentilex" are initialized through an automatic load operation with the data contained in the SentiLex-PT.

The "tbl_terminal" table is intended to store the grammatical classes necessary for the description of the syntactic rules. The values stored are: a) the unique identifier; b) the grammatical shorthand class type according to the labeling pattern defined by the parser PALAVRAS (for example: "adj", "n", "v"); c) the textual description of the meaning of each item (for instance: "adjective", "noun", "verb"). The "tbl_rule" table is intended only to the registration of a syntactic rule in the system and, therefore, has only a single identifier

and a free-text description with the rule formation and meaning. The table "tbl_rule_terminal" is responsible for storing the details of a rule and the set of terminals that compose it. The data in this table are: a) the unique identifier; b) an identifier describing to which rule it belongs; c) an identifier relating to the terminal type it represents; d) an optional key parameter, which allows to specialize the criterion for use a rule in situations when one wishes not to use all verbs, but only one specific verb; e) the order in which this terminal has within a rule.

The application for testing this approach was developed using PHP programming language and the framework MVC (Model-View-Controller) designated Yii (Yes, It Is!) (YII SOFTWARE LLC, 2011) (http://www.yiiframework.com/), running on the Apache http server and applying MySQL database. Figure 2 represents an overview of the architecture of the application developed. The models "Sentilex", "Terminal", "Rule" and "ruleTerminal" work with the database and other models related to the administration of the application. The Input template is responsible for loading the data from the corpus, in addition to owning the

Figure 2. System architecture developed

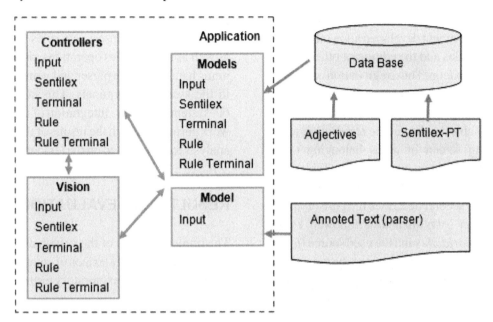

methods responsible for handling and processing of these data, as requested by its controller.

The treatment of the registered rules is one of the main functions of the system. To help in this purpose it was defined a rules registration interface, which allows the indication of elements that composes rules and also the indication of attributes for greater flexibility. This is necessary in the case of indication of optional items and items that identify reversal polarity to some specific term. For example, the rule shown in Table 2, in the header of the table, will search for occurrences of a sentence containing an adverb, a verb, an adverb and an adjective (in Portuguese:

advérbio, verbo, advérbio, adjetivo). The first occurrence of an adverb has the parameter "Terminal key" filled, so this rule will only match if the parameter value is also identical, in which case the first adverb must be the word "no" (in Portuguese: *não*). On this same item, we can observe the special attributes "[O]" and "[PI]". The attribute between brackets "[O]", determines that this terminal is optional and an occurrence in the corpus containing the following finite verb, adverb and adjective is enough to match this rule. The attribute "[PI]" indicates that the occurrence of this terminal will cause the polarity reversal of the opinion detected, so if the polarity calculated

Table 2. Example of registration rules

Rule	Order ▲	Terminal	Terminal Key
Advérbio (não) [O] [PI] + Verbo + Advérbio + Adjetivo ⬍			
Advérbio (não) [O] [PI] + Verbo + Advérbio + Adjetivo	1	adv	não [O] [PI]
Advérbio (não) [O] [PI] + Verbo + Advérbio + Adjetivo	2	v-fin	
Advérbio (não) [O] [PI] + Verbo + Advérbio + Adjetivo	3	adv	
Advérbio (não) [O] [PI] + Verbo + Advérbio + Adjetivo	4	adj	

according to the lexicon is positive, it becomes negative, if it is negative and becomes positive.

The environment developed allows the administration of rules and the edition of other components of the lexicon. Thus, registration options are available for the components of the SentiLex-PT and also for the registration of adjectives. For example, Table 3 indicates the registration screen and editing screen of items belonging to the SentiLex-PT components set. In the Table 3, the first column describes the registered word (*palavra*) and the second describes the part-of-speech classification (*classificação*), followed by the polarity (*polaridade*) and the used source (*fonte*).

In another component of the system administration, can be registered the terminal items considered by the parser PALAVRAS. This component is necessary to describe the basic elements to the generation of rules and further verification of these through the use of documents generated by the parser. Table 4 indicates the administration screen of these components. There are in the Table 4 some examples of these elements, such as adjectives (*Adjetivo*), noun (*Substantivo*), verb (*Verbo*), adverb (*Advérbio*), article (*Artigo*) and conjunction (*Conjunção*). The "Type" column of the table shown in Table 4 is related to the information described by the parser used.

Table 3. Lexical items management

Palavra	Classificação	Polaridade	Fonte
abafado	adj	-1	lexicon
abafante	adj	-1	lexicon
abaixado	adj	-1	lexicon
abalado	adj	-1	lexicon
aballzado	adj	1	lexicon
abandalhado	**adj**	**-1**	**lexicon**
abandonado	adj	-1	lexicon
abarcante	adj	-1	lexicon
abarrotado	adj	-1	lexicon
abastado	adj	1	lexicon
abastecido	adj	0	lexicon

The rules management is done in another component of the system, as shown in Table 5. In this case, operations to insert new rules are possible, as well as editing rules operations, on the basis of items handled by the parser and words registered in the system as terminals. This component of the system allows the integration of the linguistic work performed, with the results of the parser and analysis for texts based on the lexicon of emotion.

RESULTS AND EVALUATION

The implementation of the system described and the construction of the lexicon of emotion provided the environment for exploratory testing to support

Table 4. Administration of terminal elements

ID	Type	Description	
1	adj	Adjetivo	🔍 ✏ ✖
2	n	Substantive	🔍 ✏ ✖
3	v-fin	Verbo	🔍 ✏ ✖
4	adv	Advérbio	🔍 ✏ ✖
5	art	Artigo	🔍 ✏ ✖
6	conj-s	Conjunção	🔍 ✏ ✖

Table 5. Rules management

ID	Description	
1	Artigo [O] + Substantivo + Verbo Copulativo (ser) + Adjetivo	🔍 ✏ ✖
2	Advérbio (não) [O] [PI] + Verbo + Advérbio + Adjetivo	🔍 ✏ ✖
4	Substantivo + Verbo Copulativo (parecer) + Adjetivo	🔍 ✏ ✖
5	Verbo + Adjetivo + Substantivo	🔍 ✏ ✖
6	Substantivo + Conjunção (que) + Verbo + Advérbio [O] + Adjetivo	🔍 ✏ ✖

the validity of using linguistics based syntactic rules as elements in the analysis of feelings and emotions in texts. Here are described some of the results obtained, based on experimentation with analysis of documents collected in the VLE MOODLE, regarding the evaluation of undergraduate students in Distance Education. The performed test identified and compared specifically the polarities and feelings obtained with the two approaches supported by the software developed: (a) syntactic rules and lexicon of emotion; (b) polarity described by Sentilex lexicon-PT. In this way, some results are described in Table 6, with regard to the proportionality of occurrence.

In the data in Table 6, it can be observed that the analysis by rules has a larger index of textual messages polarized. The percentage of positive and negative occurrences has the value of 91.93% in the syntactic rules against the value of 52.32% in the polarity analysis with the use of SentiLex-PT. This result can be considered as an indication that a set of rules capable of detecting signatures of qualifiers in a sentence is more effective than pure and simple analysis of adjectives.

Another test scenario was designed to show the differences in results between analyses using polarity and syntactic rules. The sentences detected by rules (the first line in Table 6) where verified and the results were compared with those obtained with the polarity of the adjectives for these same sentences (the second line in Table 6). There

were detected differences of positive outcome, and consequently, negative ones, on the analysis done by syntactic rules.

To enable a more detailed view of the difference between the two analyses, we performed a manual verification of all cases, carried out by a linguist expert, to determine how many analysis diverged. The linguist expert was a professional with previous knowledge regarding both the distance learning context and the resources used (Sentilex-PT lexicon and linguistic rules) and the manual annotation of the results was carried out in order to allow further comparisons on the results correctness. The proportional analysis of the results showed that there was divergence in the calculation of polarities of sentences in the corpus. After the analysis in detail of each sentence treated by the system, it was found that 43 had divergent calculations and some sentences considered positive in the analysis by adjectives were classified as negative review by rules, while sentences considered negative in the analysis by adjectives was considered positive in the analysis by rules.

In the example shown, Table 7 demonstrates a detailed analysis of a sentence that has diverged in the calculation of polarity when using rules. As can be observed in Table 7, the analysis by rules generated the correct result, considering the content of the comments expressed in the sentences. It is observed that the column "Sentilex" identifies the negative polarity (-1) associated with the adjective "hard" (in Portuguese: *difícil*), whereas the rule "R-2" describes the polarity correctly, as positive.

Thus, it was possible to verify that the use of classifications based on syntactic rules, in a way, restricts the number of occurrences found in the universe of sentences that are identified with the standard registered, but also increases the reliability of the results obtained and allow a calculation of more consistent polarity in relation to techniques based only in adjectives.

Table 6. Comparison of approaches used

	Adjectives Polarity		Rules	
	Number	%	Number	%
Positive	246	42.34	92	74.19
Negative	58	9.98	22	17.74
Neutral	142	24.44	8	6.45
Not Classified	135	23.23	2	1.61
Total	581	100	124	100

Table 7. Detailed analysis of rules and lexicon

Id	Word	Lemma	Pos	Sentilex	Match	Polarity
304_1	vi	ver	v-fin			
304_2	que	que	conj-s			
304_3	não	não	adv		R-2 – Advérbio (não) [O] [PI] + Verbo + Advérbio + Adjetivo	1
304_4	era	ser	v-fin		R-2 – Advérbio (não) [O] [PI] + Verbo + Advérbio + Adjetivo	1
304_5	tão	tão	adv		R-2 – Advérbio (não) [O] [PI] + Verbo + Advérbio + Adjetivo	1
304_6	dificil	dificil	adj	-1	R-2 – Advérbio (não) [O] [PI] + Verbo + Advérbio + Adjetivo	1
304_7	de	de	prp			
304_8	acompanhar	acompanhar	v-fin			
304_9	a	o	art			
304_10	distância	distância	n			

CONCLUSION

This work describes and evaluates mechanisms meant to improve the identification of the students' emotional state expressed in textual messages. In order to fulfill this objective, the main problem addressed in this work, from the point of view of linguistic and computational linguistic, was to build a lexical database of the emotion domain using lexical items extracted from texts generated by students and posted on the different tools of the MOODLE Virtual Learning Environment. The theoretical discussions undertaken for the construction of the lexical base will contribute to the advancement of studies on the semantics of emotions and, in addition, will serve as a reference for the organization of the lexicon of emotion – in the context of Portuguese language. This is an area that needs the development of features for the Portuguese language, being that a relevant contribution of this work.

In theoretical form, some research issues were emphasized in this work. Under the linguistic and computational linguistic aspect, we have the description of the semantics of emotions to building a lexical database containing syntactic information about the lexicon of emotion. Under the computational linguistic aspect, we have the study on techniques of sentiment detection in texts and strategies for the implementation of a tool to this end. Finally, we highlight the study on the relevance of the identification and treatment of affective aspects in textual messages in the context of the target environments used in Distance Education.

The tool developed show appropriate results, as presented in the previous section, having been conceived to offer the teacher information with different degrees of interference, with the automatic recognition of expressions of emotion registered on the VLE and the exhibition of such information through a specific interface from which the teacher can access the lexicon enriched with semantic information and also the original context of student speech.

As future work some improvements to the tool are foreseen, so it will be possible the automatic recognition of reports of satisfaction, together with statistics on the frequency of each type of report, in addition to quick access to the original context of the student message and the description of how the reports can be used by teachers. Another future line of action is associated with the validation procedure adopted. One of the possibilities in study is to use criterion validity to validate your system, in such way that allow to identify independently the emotional state of a student, have them write some textual messages, and then use the developed system to classify their emotional state.

REFERENCES

Azevedo, B. F. T. (2011). *MINERAFÓRUM: A support resource for qualitative analysis in the discussion forums*. (Doctoral Thesis). UFRGS, Porto Alegre, Brazil.

Bercht, M. (2001). *Toward teaching agents with affective dimensions*. (Doctoral Thesis). UFRGS. Porto Alegre, Brazil.

Bick, E. (2000). *The parsing system words: Automatic grammatical analysis of portuguese in the constraint grammar framework*. Aarhus: Aarhus University Press.

Chen, L. N., Liu, C. H., & Chiu, H. J. (2011). The neural network based approach for sentiment classification in the blogosphere. *Journal of Informetrics*, *5*(2), 313–322. doi:10.1016/j.joi.2011.01.003

Desmarais, M. C., & Baker, R. S. J. D. (2012). A review of recent advances in learner and skill modeling in intelligent learning environments. *User Modeling and User-Adapted Interaction*, *22*(1-2), 9–38. doi:10.1007/s11257-011-9106-8

Dominiek, S., & Rice, S. (1995). Network analyses do of prepositional meaning: Mirroring whose mind-the linguist's or the user's language? *Cognitive Linguistics*, *6*(1), 89–130. doi:10.1515/cogl.1995.6.1.89

Edécio, E. F., Bercht, M., & Reategui, E. (2011, November). Detection and treatment of Affective State the student's Frustration in the discipline of algorithms. In *XXII Simpoósio Brasileiro de Informática na Educação*. Aracaju, Brazil: SBIE.

Fellbaum, C. (1998). *WordNet: An electronic lexical database*. Cambridge, MA: MIT Press.

Fillmore, C. J., Baker, C., & Cronin, B. (2003). the structure of the framenet database. *International Journal Lexicography, 16*(1), 281-296.

Jaques, P. A., & Vicari, R. (2005). Considering student's emotions in computer mediated learning environments. In Z. Ma (Ed.), *Web-based intelligent e-learning systems: Technologies and Applications* (pp. 122–138). Hershey, PA: Information Science Publishing. doi:10.4018/978-1-59140-729-4.ch006

Klemann, M., Lorenzatti, A., & Reategui, E. (2009). *The use of text mining tool SOBEK as textual production support*. Paper presented at the Brazilian Symposium on Computers in Education. Florianópolis. Brazil.

Le Doux, J. (2001). *The emotional brain: The mysterious emotional pathway foundations*. Rio de Janeiro: Objetiva.

Liu, B. (2012). *Sentiment analysis and opinion mining*. New York: Morgan and Claypool Publishers.

Longhi, M. T., Behar, P. A., & Bercht, M. (2008, November). *The challenge of recognizing the affective dimension in virtual learning environments*. Paper presented at the 19th Brazilian Symposium on Computers in Education. Fortaleza, Brazil.

Macedo, A. I., Reategui, A., Lorenzatti, & Behar, P. (n.d.). Using text-mining to support the evaluation of texts produced collaboratively: Education and technology for a better world. *IFIP Advances in Information and Communication Technology*, *302*(1), 368-388.

Miller, G. A. (1995). WordNet: A lexical database for English. *Communications of the ACM, 38*(11), 39–41. doi:10.1145/219717.219748

Oliveira, R. L., et al. (2011, November). A tool for Automatic monitoring of Forums messages in virtual learning environments. In Proceedings of the XXII Simpoósio Brasileiro de Informática na Educação. Aracaju, Brazil: SBIE.

Pang, A., et al. (2002, July). *Thumbs up? Sentiment classification using machine learning techniques.* Paper presented at the Conference on Empirical Methods in Natural Language Processing. Philadelphia, PA. doi:10.3115/1118693.1118704

Pang, B., & Lee, L. (2008). Opinion mining and sentiment analysis. *Foundations and Trends in Information Retrieval, 2*(1-2), 110–135.

Pergher, G. K., Grassi-Oliveira, R., Ávila, L. M., & Stein, L. M. (2006). Memory, mood and emotion. *Revista de Psiquatria do Rio Grande do Sul, 28*(1), 61–68. doi:10.1590/S0101-81082006000100008

Picard, R. W., & Healey, J. (1998, May). Digital processing of affective signals. In *Proceedings of ICASSP*. Seattle, WA: ICASSP.

Silva, M. (2010). *Automatic expansion of the lexicon is sentiment analysis social judgment.* University of Lisbon.

Tang, H., Tan, S., & Cheng, X. (2009). A survey on sentiment detection of reviews. *Expert Systems with Applications, 36*(7), 10760–10773. doi:10.1016/j.eswa.2009.02.063

This work was previously published in the International Journal of Information and Communication Technology Education (IJICTE), 11(1); edited by Lawrence A. Tomei, pages 44-59, copyright year 2015 by IGI Publishing (an imprint of IGI Global).

Chapter 66

What Makes Students to Participate in Online Collaborative Settings through Second Life?
Students' Views and Perspectives Based on Adult Participation Theories

Nikolaos Pellas
University of the Aegean, Greece

ABSTRACT

Motivational factors that may affect adult participation in educational activities have attracted educators' interests and probably are one of the most discussed topics in the field of adult education. The current study seeks to investigate the students' participation in collaborative online activities based on the interpretive framework of adult participation theories stapling to interpret motivational factors, and recommended by McGivney (1993). A qualitative (comprehensive) research was conducted and a voluntary sample of Higher education by eighty students (n=80) who participated in online collaborative settings through the virtual world of Second Life and wanted to share experiences from their participation. The added value of this effort is to understand the educational community theoretically based on the utilization of adult theories that might motivate adult participation in different aspects and more practically to enunciate the key factors influencing their decisions to participate in team-based activities held in Second Life.

1. INTRODUCTION

The continuous growth of technologically advanced environments in education and especially the social media Web 2.0 transactions that include also three-dimensional (3D) virtual worlds (VWs),

have brought to the front line the urgent need of educators and scholars to understand factors affecting students' participation in collaborative processes (Abbad & Albarghouthi, 2011; Liu, 2010; Persico & Pozzi, 2011). Indeed, all the above researchers set up their concerns for the

DOI: 10.4018/978-1-4666-8619-9.ch066

construction of an appropriate teaching framework in order to easily learn and sufficiently acquire all students a variety of learning materials from the Information, Communication Technology and Media Resources (ICT&MR). Even more their inclusion can empower the learning dimension with a socio-constructive framework that met students' needs and the school's requirements entirely, and it should follow a series of uniform methodological and organizational principles (Pellas, 2013).

Many educational researchers seek to effectively use these innovative sources as learning platforms in a situation to prepare students to gain innovative skills according to the 21st century demands. The international changes in social and financial conditions today demand from each student to acquire (e-) skills which can make her/him active participant and able to respond to this contemporary society demands, both in cultural or educational domains. In this postmodern period the technological, financial and social changes have made many areas of the compulsory education implement different projects in flexible course delivery modes (online or blended). Many well-known two-dimensional (2D) learning environments (see Learning Management System-LMS, such as Moodle or Blackboard or Massive Open Online Courses-MOOCs) are being used from Universities or Institutions as "warehousing of knowledge" where students and instructors share educational resources of the Web and communicate mainly asynchronously with type-based applications (messages on a specific forum and exchanging e-mails with other group members). Additionally, most recent "conventional" educational practices with 2D LMS in Higher education were primarily based on the oral or written communication tools and re-presentations of knowledge in different disciplines or answers in theoretical problems were usually delivered by the instructor who acted as an "expert" on the one side, but on the other students could not recall or take the appropriate feedback from their instructor in real

time (Pellas, 2014). Moreover, 2D technologies are not so useful for STEM (Science, Technology, Engineering and Mathematics) education disciplines and mainly for courses that needed to be done in different laboratories in order to actively be engaged and experimented students to understand practical consequences of their actions.

Several studies in the online learning area by using different 2D (two-dimensional) platforms (Lu et al., 2011; Janssen et al., 2011) have already demonstrated positive results of group comparisons, awareness or effectiveness in academic performances and students' attitudes. Although, there were some other researchers that were not found so sufficient these 2D technologies for practice-based learning tasks due to the identified reality in which students could not share experiences mainly in online settings, due to: (a) the technical problems (Rivera et al., 2002) or feelings of isolation that were provided by other participants (Contreras-Castillo et al., 2004), (b) the lack of previous online learning experiences of students causing satisfaction at low levels (Piccoli et al., 2001), (c) the lack of a persistent workflow where students together can communicate synchronously in real-time and in a common place (Pellas & Kazanidis, 2013), and (d) the absence of interaction between users-content or with students-instructor, while there are few experienced educators knowing how to equally use several communication forms or transactions that 2D technologies can replicate (Kotsilieris & Dimopoulou, 2013).

Most reliable instructional formats online and blended university-level courses have not yet replaced the traditional teaching methods. However, these two novel modes of learning (online and blended course delivery methods) were launched in different (candidate) learning platforms, such as Learning Management Systems (LMS) or Virtual Learning Environments (VLEs), but unfortunately there were emerged several significant limitations. A critical issue is that LMS (like Moodle or Blackboard) was only used as document repositories and these environments cannot easily support the learner's performance during the monitoring and knowledge management phases, basically when these are produced in team-based activities (Kemp & Livingstone 2006).

Many scholars and educators (Hadjerrouit, 2009; Kordaki, 2013) have focused their intention on the construction and transportation of the students' knowledge field in platforms, which have 2D graphical user interface (GUI). Until nowadays a growing academic literature body have started to implement collaborative scenarios in 3D technologically advanced environments, like VWs (Bouta Retalis & Paraskeva, 2013; Konstantinidis, Tsiatsos, Terzidou & Pomportsis, 2010). 3D multi-user VWs are defined as computer-generated environments in which users (students and instructors) can easily co-configure or co-manipulate a pre-constructed "virtual ecosystem" of visual primitives or artifacts that can support the conduct of online courses in collaborative and social situations. This issue is really important in different conditions where students obtain knowledge and increasingly try to conquer learning in different situations that can be combined the appropriate 3D technologies based on online course delivery methods (Petrakou, 2010; Cheryan, Meltzoff & Kim, 2011).

Until now of course, it was not found a specific framework embarked new analyzing contexts for learners' motivational factors emanating from:

1. The criteria that might be determined the status of an individual to participate in collaborative activities (where users are distributed or not),

2. The interactions that occurred among users (horizontal interaction among participants, negotiation of cognitive resources, etc.),

3. The performed operations to conquer an innovative knowledge domain, and

4. The anticipated effects of each activity in the learning process (cognitive outcome).

Another important thing is to understand the relationship with the aforementioned axes among different patterns of individualism and all cooperative factors, which can trigger cognitive mechanisms or produce cognitive effects. Through an effort to find a comprehensive theoretical approach in terms of motivational factors that led adults' (in-group) activities, McGivney (1993) has tried to investigate a theoretical framework. She argued that the participation of adults is directly related to the interaction of exogenous, i.e. environmental, situational factors and endogenous factors, mostly all of them related to the disposal or the experience of the participants. Theories relating to adults' participation can give a reasonable explanation in well-organized educational activities for the complexity and multifaceted nature of the leading causes among adults' participation in an educational program according to the participation theories that McGivney (1993) has proposed. This "vision" is also argued in the area of incentives of adults' participation connected mainly with the methods that may promote the analysis of motivational factors.

The reasons of participating adults in educational programs is today considered as a very complex issue, and therefore the present contemplation must be focused on the investigation and exploitation of motivation factors affecting their participation, learning needs and finally the reasons that someone is being involved in it. On this basis, online learning through the use of ICT&MR can provide an educational research important "framework" in which students may be active while discovering the knowledge. In recent years, higher education institutions have given high value to e-learning processes in technologically advanced environments since its potential for a variety of information at different locations is given approximately to isolated students. Until now, 3D multi-user VWs are the most remarkable candidate platforms and becoming gradually well-known in various disciplines of Higher education. Notwithstanding, there is appeared a growing number of notable studies that presented 3D multi-user VWs as valuable platforms for e-Education (Inman et al., 2010; Pellas, 2012; Wang & Burton, 2012); a more comprehensive study to determine the students' views/perspectives about the online collaborative learning activities that they participated in Second Life is still absent.

The purposeful and meaningful utilization of 3D learning environments needs a conceptual-theoretical background that could endorse psychological, cognitive and social processes. During the online learning process, it must be chosen methods currently more suitable for this socio-cognitive learning framework (Pellas, Peroutseas & Kazanidis, 2013). The use of 3D multi-user VWs can support learning activities following the adult learning theories in several learning activities (Bronack, Riedl & Tashner, 2006; Dede, 1995; Dickey, 2003). The instructor should not only have at his/her primary objectives the student's encouragement to co-construct an innovative knowledge field, but effectively support to promote the collaboration among users in which: (a) everyone can assess to various learning sources, and (b) everyone can freely study together with other peers to understand the extent implementation of the objectives which are set up each time.

Taking into account the technical functionalities of 3D multi-user VWs with the online course delivery method, it can be provided to the educational research an alternative opportunity in which students can be engaged and discovered a new knowledge field. The components of this framework may include potential correlations between knowledge, values and management practices that may lead to the social, cognitive and emotional development of each student. This case widely emphasizes on different scholars' rounds seek to investigate factors that may affect the students' participation in learning activities

(Blondy, 2007; Cross, 1981; Herod, 2002; Knox, 1986; Lieb, 1991; Merriam & Cafarella, 1991; Saad, Mat & Awadh, 2013).

The outline intention of this study is a part of the investigation and presentation of the major aspects of the issue concerning users' participation in Second Life, according to the "adult participation theories" in well-organized collaborative learning activities. Based on the above the urgent need to have a study that seeks to present the relationships of students' perceptions, attitudes and practices in Second Life through fully online course delivery methods is still absent. The main purpose of the current study is to highlight and summarize the analysis of key characteristics in online courses, which had occurred, and the problems that can be raised as a deterrent to the involvement of adults in collaborative online procedures.

This study seeks to answer two key questions arising by the literature review and relating mainly to:

Which are the features that Second Life inherently has to affect the adults' participation in collaborative activities?

How can interactive activities in Second Life motivate students to co-construct their innovative knowledge field?

2. BACKGROUND AND MAIN RATIONALE

2.1. Adult Learning Theories

According to Cross (1981), it is not obvious to formalize a unified theory of Adult Education, but it is more likely to have several concepts that may help the educational community to understand the learning process in different aspects. Connecting these concepts in a broader need to understand how to deploy adults, Hobson and Welbourne (1998) have further noted that the development of adults is not determined by specific theories, but through a theoretical approach attempted to register the degree of interaction with their internal and external forces that affected their lives. This effort should be investigated in order to be understood, how the evolution of the concepts can be used to achieve a more balanced approach and develop an adult learning approach, which will not override the existing perceptions of this area.

Houtkoop and Van Der Kamp (1992) on the other side have ratified that the adults' participation in learning processes depending not only on their initial motivation for acquiring basic skills, but interpreted in a native context in which can be created (i.e. the need for learning). Consistent to Kidd (1978), the motivation is the driving inherent force, arising from human needs and manifesting in the search for a wide variety of different incentives to their characteristics, similar to function. Adults' participation in educational programs considered as the ultimate goal of learning, which is depended on a variety of reasons or motives. These are different for each participant or each group of participants. Nevertheless, McGivney's "participation theories" seek to investigate the motives of participation in adult learning activities have organized within a broader framework of reference relative to the contact point between theory and practice in education (McGivney, 1993).

The following fundamental theoretical principles or models can pronounce the motivational factors of adult participation in team-based educational activities:

1. **Dynamic Field Theory (Force-Field Analysis):** The exponent of this theory was emanated from Miller (1967) who has argued that the relationship between socioeconomic status and participation of adult students in education programs for adults were inevitable. This argument was based on negative and positive forces in order to be created by students a strong driving force that may explain their participation in educational programs (Comings, Parrella & Soricone, 1999).

2. **Theory of the Interaction (Congruence Model):** For Boshier (1971) learning motivation is a function of interaction between internal psychological and external factors of the environment. Participation comes as a result of the interaction according to their perceptions (self-perceptions) in the educational environment.

3. **The Theoretical Example of "Promise-Vigor" (Expectancy-Valence Paradigm):** Rubenson (1994) has underlined that adults involved their feelings in educational tasks, when they learn or evaluate their learning outcomes, which are considered to fall their individual needs. In this context, participation is the result of interaction between the situation, in which they: (a) "expect" everything and (b) exemplify the "valence" (strength/hope) of the expected results from their participation.

4. **The Theory of Transition (Life Transitions Theory):** The decision of adults' participation in an educational activity is directly related to small or large changes (transitions) of an individual's life affecting them to participate in a new one (Blair, 2000).

5. **The Reference Group Theory:** According to this theory, adults coincide with social or cultural group in which they belong ("regulatory reference group") can be adapted more readily where they finally want to belong ("comparative reference group"). The characteristics are associated with this social situation of adults, and are the most determinant participation (Van Campenhout, 2007) can always be compared with those associated that passage even before adulthood (Tudor & Carley, 1998).

6. **Social Participation Theory:** Adults' participation in educational activities should be explained in relation to their social status in which they endorsed (Grubb, Hemby, & Conenly-Stewart, 1998; Illeris, 2003). Their participation is primarily related to the perception of the value that the same students have for themselves and their capabilities.

2.2. Collaborative e-Learning Processes In Second Life

Computer supported collaborative learning (CSCL) has an added value that observed by the reinforcement of users' (students and instructors) social and cultural changes (i.e. the strong interaction of people from different cultural traditions for the production and usability of knowledge) that are currently experiencing the views and practices of social action. The research of personal meanings in modern societies and reflections on what knowledge can be considered as valid and how different approaches have greater severity in the context of each situation, without canceling the other approaches (Stahl, Koschmann & Suthers, 2006; Van de Vold, 2010) were sufficiently highlighted by:

1. The importance of the dialogue and negotiation between humans.
2. The epistemological beliefs that participants in the dialogue must be tolerant to the multiplicity of interpretations. This change was not only proclaimed for skills or abilities achieved, but also for the identification of personal meaning through a learning procedure.

The CSCL approach refers to some of the most novel principles for contemporary learning environments (Dillenbourg, 1999; Wang, 2010) by:

1. Emphasizing on the social nature of learning and knowledge through the co-construction of knowledge.
2. Strengthening students' performance in these new roles as team members gained an innovative knowledge domain together.
3. Supporting communication and computational tools or artifacts that facilitate the learning process sufficiently.

In general, studies accessed to the implementation of this example have demonstrated not only opportunities but also limitations (Lehtinen, 2003). Specifically, the same students they distinguished technological, organizational and pedagogical constraints, for establishing successful collaborative environments. A socially interactive environment in which users can implement collaborative scenarios, may allow a deeper processing of knowledge through the discussion with cognitive, meta-cognitive strategies, and with the expression of emotions.

The difficulties observed during the collaborative process for education (informal/formal or blended/online instructional formats) with the use of contemporary 3D multi-user virtual environments could be effective as a teaching method, when combined with socio-cultural learning theories. In this way the boundaries and the context in which users learned by following a teaching scenario and performing alongside certain kinds of interaction and communication at that time. The key question in designing a collaborative learning scenario based on CSCL is what kind of peer interactions between students with instructors want in order to enhance their achievements in specific educational goals.

The transposition of this definition in practical-teaching context on distance collaborative learning (collaborative e-learning) in virtual environments, suggesting mainly the work carried out between distributed users, who are often employed in a learning activity or a project, giving a more social dimension to the experience. The advantages of being worked in this context, focusing on the effort to conduct a more effective education, acquisition of new social skills and intercultural relations and an end to the increase of self-esteem. Here, however, we should mention that in any collective interaction and involvement of users, the cognitive mechanisms and all operations are spent, not always guaranteed the successful production of the required knowledge and achievements of the final learning outcomes. Recent studies have suggested that collaborative learning environments with computer support (CSCL) have the ability to provide innovative opportunities for students to be adopted and experimented with others. Some of these platforms are 3D virtual environments that due to inherent design can support collaborative activities, since the students are given the opportunity to work remotely and collaboratively in a common persistent environment.

E-learning 2.0 as a novel term including both the term of CSCL and the utilization of Web 2.0 digital sources (3D multi-user virtual worlds also included) has given more emphasis on the social learning interaction and co-construction of knowledge to students by using social media sources such as blogs, wikis, and withal 3D multi-user virtual worlds, like Second Life. The available multimedia-interactive applications can be regarded as a relatively new learning tool that exalts applications of modern teaching methods and strategies for e-learning collaboratively (Boulos, Hetherington & Wheeler, 2007; Pellas & Kazanidis, 2013).

The rapid evolution of online social networks has transformed the cyberspace in a rapidly growing communication system, bringing to the fore many aspects of *networked collectivity.* Some of the most distinguished virtual platforms, which have attracted the interest social networking friends, and students from educational institutions, are 3D multi-user virtual worlds. These "worlds"

are defined as computer-generated environments that respond in real-time to user actions, in which interactions with other peers adopted in visual and auditory stimuli. The basic elements are as follows (Hew & Cheung, 2010; Duncan et al., 2009):

1. The illusion of a 3D place or space where users in the form of 3D substantial virtual characters (avatars) are interacting together in a visually "physical" environment;
2. The communication between peers by utilizing verbal (VoIP, IM, and chat text) or non-verbal forms (e.g. gestures that composed each user's emotional state with facial expressions or body and communicate others) of communication; and
3. The process that is "active" in a common virtual space (grid).

The multi-user virtual world of Second Life completes on the computer screen a 3D networked and interactive environment that supports communication and collaboration between geographically isolated (or not) users, over 18 years. Second Life is one of the most famous 3D emulators of real life, imaging the global reality and it can therefore be considered as one of the most functional platforms for the implementation of computer-supported collaborative e-learning scenarios (Franceschi et al., 2008; Nteliopoulou & Tsinakos, 2011; Pellas, 2012; Wang & Burton, 2012). An essential advantage of 3D multi-user virtual worlds is that are notably different from other conventional learning environments (see LMS) due to the utilization of the current interactive technology from the same users and the responsibility of the learning process that may offer to them an opportunity to learn without spatial or temporal restrictions. The shift of controlling students' participation in the learning process seems to have a positive impact on learning effectiveness (Burgess et al., 2010). The fundamental aspect of a 3D multi-user virtual world in this occasion is to cover the distance between the learning materials and regulate social interactions among users to make them active participants than passive recipients of information.

Pretty remarkable are the fundamental affordances of Second Life seemed to be ideal for different instructional formats (blended/online) in order to become candidate learning platform. The following reasons addressed this assumption (Pellas & Kazanidis, 2013):

1. The sense of (co-)*presence* that most users can "feel" when they immersed in a virtual grid that allow them to perceive it as a *space* where they belong to, rather than a digital environment they are interacting with, e.g. a Web site.

2. The *persistent* workflow lets users reform the space and constructs their meaningful and effortful structures.

3. The users' *embodiment* representation forms as cyber entities (avatars) allow users in a VW to efficiently interact with other peers ("being there") with verbal or non-verbal communication forms, e.g. using nonverbal forms of communication, compared to other means of 2D technologies, e.g. chat, forums, wikis etc.

4. The expressiveness of 3D animated or interactive 3D graphical representations or virtual places can be used to present abstract or complex concepts that are difficult to comprehend in a textual form using *metaphors* which help learners to interpret the environments or even construct their own interpretation and communicate with their teammates.

5. The *real-time simulation* and *3D interactive* capabilities of VWs can be exploited to implement students the appropriate tools or artifacts for experiential learning and problem solving activities.

The use of Second Life as a "canvas" of knowledge creation can be considered as a virtual environment that provides new opportunities even beyond the existing curriculum. Almost daily, new educational institutions are active in Second Life and develop e-learning programs by exploiting this platform to deliver high quality services to a global audience at a low cost. Educational institutions can use Second Life to create secured geographical areas (grids) and enhance the experiential learning process.

Although, the first conception of Second Life was not planned for a particular scientific research field, as those opposed to almost all 3D virtual learning environments, but clearly for entertainment. This issue has never prevented any University or Institute to use it as an "educational tool" for organizing, managing and transferring their "knowledge field" and as a result to understand and interpret the factual teaching statements. This was one of the most important reasons that Second Life was chosen in this research. The present study tries to articulate students' motivational factors that may be raised from the functional characteristics of this virtual environment to enhance and grow in the teaching process. This feature may prove a new promising and well-established alternative approach to the traditional academic e-learning procedure.

2.3. Indicate Previous Studies

There always appear in nowadays several investigations dealing with the introduction of new methods of teaching and learning in the virtual environment of Second Life. But, until recently, it cannot be said that there was even ahead some researches which may focused exclusively on a wide range of target group of evaluation to effectively implement e-learning activities. Thus, some of the most important are presented in the following (See Table 1).

Beyond this background, all previous research efforts have emphasized on the association of potentially useful, functional properties of Second Life with educational activities. The research gap

Table 1. Review of the relevant literature

Previous works	Researching areas
Vogel, Guo, Zhou, Tian and Zhang (2008)	Vogel, Guo, Zhou, Tian and Zhang in 2008 have conducted a survey that designed as a comparative evaluation of cooperative activities. They have introduced students in Second Life, and compared it with other media (MSN, e-mails, forums). In the participation graduate students from Hong Kong and the Netherlands took part. After 3 weeks of research, almost 55% of respondents rated Second Life as an innovative tool that can be used for other collaborative activities.
Eduserv (2008)	The investigation of Eduserv (period July 2007 - October 2008) was designed to identify and use various virtual worlds for the Higher Education United Kingdom (38 institutions took part). It was revealed that about almost half Higher Education colleges had the change to use Second Life for education, whereas three-quarters (3/4) of UK universities used in areas of Psychology, Ethnography of New Technologies education.
FitzGibbon, Oldham, and Johnston (2008)	In FitzGibbon, Oldham and Johnston (2008) study 243 students have responded to a survey, and after their engagement in role-play situations, they needed to explore how effective were activities in Second Life to understand the affordances in collaborative group-based projects.
Winter (2010)	This project included an extensive literature review regarding the potentially efforts in education. Through a case study, they assessed in several educational activities, in which they contributed to the effort of designing and upgrading the teaching process, aiming at asserting the educational project.
Sutcliffe and Alrayes (2012)	In this paper results of both studies (with overall 101 participants) were reviewed by using Salmon's model for online learning, suggesting that Second Life helped students' motivation and socialization at all stages. Although integration with other technologies is necessary for knowledge construction. Preliminary guidelines are proposed for configuration and management of Second Life in collaborative settings.
Petrakou (2010)	The multi-user virtual world of Second Life was utilized as a learning environment for online courses in higher education. The purpose of this study was to explore how this setting currently facilitates not only online course delivery method, but also to identify issues like interactivity that are essential in this context due to the synchronous communication and places in which each student has a spatial dimension.
Pellas and Kazanidis (2014)	In this study the effects of students' achievements were measured by comparing the degree of students' engagement (as a multi-dimensional construct consisting of the emotional, behavioral and cognitive factors) of two student groups (graduate and undergraduate) who enrolled in two different instructional formats (blended/online) which were held in Second Life (SL) in order to become learning content developers. The study findings from the quantitative analysis have disclosed that graduate students who participated in online courses achieved more positive learning outcomes and as a result the degree of their engagement was significantly increased than those who enrolled with the blended.

identified in this case led everyone to think that it should be investigated those potential positive or negative factors that may lead adult learners to participate in team-based activities.

2.4. The Main Rationale

A plethora of studies (Boellstorff, 2007; Bortoluzzi, 2012; McKerlich, Riis, Anderson & Eastman, 2011) have identified learner's attitudes in virtual communities, but the impact of factors that shaped their actual use was absent and not amplified adequately for the participatory tasks. The majority of these studies have shown some interesting results, which seemed to form mainly positive users' attitudes and perceptions. The stu-

dents' factors proposed to influence the attitudes and perceptions, by utilizing 3D multi-user VWs according to their functionality and utility that can promote potential results for the development of interactive activities between users. At the core of this process the quality and quantity of interaction and the sense of commitment in a learning community are the most crucial issues to be investigated.

The initial problematic assumption of this study has followed the previous one (Bearden et al., 1989; Park & Choi, 2009; Rovai, 2003) who insisted on the systematization of the factors influencing either directly or indirectly the decision of many adults to participate in collaborative educational or learning activities. However, even more are those educators who emphasized the compositional effect structural, cultural, socio-economic and psychological characteristics in understanding the adults' participation factors (Cross, 1998; McGivney, 1981). Interestingly, the inspiration behind this study was originally emerged from other case studies (Edwards, Rico, Dominguez & Agudo, 2010; Pellas & Kazanidis, 2012; Zhao & Wu, 2009) that have already revealed some positive findings regarding the novelty of Second Life through the online course delivery method in different educational fields.

Beyond the above, there is still lacking from the international literature a study to investigate the motivational factors that may affect the students' engagement through online settings in Second Life. Specifically, the present research aimed to unveil students' perspectives in Second Life, as a candidate educational platform for online processes and their experiences after the implementation of their activities. These are based on: a) the characteristics of active students in Second Life from all over the world, b) their activities or some future-driven directions that most of were implemented in STEM disciplines, and last but not least c) students' thoughts about the value of Second Life as an educational medium for online collaborative activities.

Despite the above studies were methodologically focused on case studies and less on some other comparatives (Deutschmann & Panichi, 2009); it is still needed to be done an empirical investigation of the effectiveness that is usually associated with the factors affecting students' engagement during their participation in collaborative activities. In this vein the rationale of this study emanated from all the literature review that have not yet shown some controversial results from adults' participation factors in the empirical analysis based on students' perceptions and views from their engagement in online collaborative activities. As a result it was not provided the effectiveness of Second Life as a candidate-learning platform, mainly for Higher education.

In these conditions the purpose of this study was to highlight and analyze the main features of an empirical research and to elucidate the most important factors that can motivate the adults in cooperative processes. The research methodology, results, and the conclusions of this study or other future-driven are discussed in detail in the sections that follow.

2.5. International Aspects of Problem Statements to Conduct This Study

Driving force of the effective functioning of education and particularly of higher education is the professional performance, development and improvement of the student user. To achieve these aim interpersonal improvements among users combined with other relationships in an environment relating to the genuine guidance or scientific support in e-Education. The significance and importance of different training sessions that need to support educational applications are very important because of the rapid social change and the rapid scientific development, needs and expected results obtained a direct impact on their professional development. Specifically, technological, financial and scientific developments create changes in the curriculum and the educational and teaching process. The adults' training with contemporary technology and more realistic ones that reflecting real-life situations through three-dimensional graphics may become candidate platforms for learning, adapting each time the methods and objectives of each educational practice (Pellas, 2014).

As regards the desire of adults that is connected with their participation in training programs, it is always necessary to be investigated their motivations, their expectations from this option, and perceptions of their overall participation and how satisfied feel by themselves. Moreover, how experienced the entire experiences from their participation are, the matters discussed for the reasons of their participation and criteria of how choosing educational programs that want to be satisfied with, delight at their vindicated expectations. For these reasons, it is necessary to set out from the academic literature references concerning the conceptual clarification of the term "motivation" and the theories that have been raised about the motives. The value of exploring incentives influencing students' participation in activities can be positive and lead to the individual steps for reaching and achieving it, or negative and driving each person to avoidance actions.

By exploring the incentives and the wider context emerged, it can be said that in any case it should be captured also crucial barriers in learning. With the term "obstacles" can be defined any factor in one way or another complicates the learning process and prevents adults to participate in these courses to reuse them in the future. This may be something that is currently missing whose presence or absence of adults' incentives and their participation in educational activities respectively may prevent the change causing the assimilation of new knowledge. Obstacles may arise within the same learner within an educational environment in which either alone or with others, in the natural or social in a technological environment and is known to everyone through habits, attitudes, values, behaviors or learning contents, emotional states, in the educational program that can the same person or group achieved. Barriers of adults' learning can include: (a) the constraints arising from the design and organization of educational programs (b) the potential of participatory activities with other users. It is very important that students at university-level courses must collaborate with others, since the university is a pre-stage of everyday life, and (c) internal obstacles, namely those related to personality factors of adult learners emerging by prior knowledge, experiences, attitudes, perceptions, emotions and personality traits are adult learners. Particular emphasis is placed in the third category of barriers, which presents the most difficulty dealing, because each case has its own characteristics and therefore should be treated in a different way.

Student engagement in educational activities through contemporary technological environments has been employed extensively many researchers, as many of them have believed that a desirable outcome of the involvement can be meaningful only if it could bring many more benefits that are not related only to acquire knowledge but also acquire the skills and generally have their real life. As Lee and Hammer (2011) have stressed that educational systems today have faced serious problems emphasized to the students' motivation and engagement. The evolution of technologically-advanced (multi-user) environments has showed that it could become potential through well planned activities. If through research and development of new systems harnessing the motives that these techniques and can bring to e-Education; it can help students to acquire the tools to become more performance in real life (Lee & Hammer, 2011). Therefore, a challenge to discover, identify and accept can afford the overrun or reconciliation. This, however, is not the only problem that scholars and educators are facing, but also a one is equally important to understand the context of learning that can be understood by adult students in higher education, in order to obtain a broader framework to be utilized in the future and may give answers based on what factors adults eventually make decisions to join group activities in contemporary environments.

3. RESEARCH METHODOLOGY

The present study attempted to empirically establish a voluntary sample of students ($n=80$) who were experienced in online collaborative tasks and it was decided that participants must be from all parts of the earth. Based on the above it was asked the prior experiences of learners where they involved, regardless their educational disciplines or sectors. Participants of this research were found from an e-mailing list where instructors or students promote ideas, solutions or experiments that they implemented through Second Life to other users daily with several announcements (Educators List-educators@lists.secondlife.com). After sending e-mail to instructors and students some of them want to participate in this survey, and thence it was necessary to collect any information from their virtual grids. After taking answers from voluntary participants that data was endorsed in Nvivo and it was started the correlation of all data in digital documents.

3.1. Participants

The research sample consisted of 80 voluntary participants (36 women and 44 men), who participated in different educational activities and they were found in different academic sectors. Before getting involved in this survey students need to have implemented online courses in collaborative settings. After that, they needed to be taken also the permission of students' instructors or supervisors in order to know about their participation in this survey. The sample was from students who have utilized Second Life as a candidate platform for online collaborative instructional formats and were all of them studied in Informatics or Computer science academic sectors.

3.2. Measures and Software Tools

The researcher analyzed Likert-type, open-ended or multiple-choice questions by a spreadsheet software. The content analysis technique with Nvivo (ver. 10) was conducted to be analyzed the data coming from the semi-structured questionnaire. Nvivo was used in an effort to provide a more the "holistic" establishment of data quality connection, configuration, search, and creation of templates. During the analysis, all data transcribed

and controlled any misunderstandings. Then, the researcher generated the codes and themes from the data, after completed students the entire questionnaire that enclosed open-ended and close-ended items. Also, it was coded the data separately and then compared for ensuring the consistency.

3.3. Research Design and Data Collection

The questions were based on the "average" access (Second Life) for e-learning settings and the main considerations that explain the factors of adult participation in organized educational activities that described in the theoretical part (see "Adult participation theories in educational activities"). Briefly, these are the following:

1. For *A. The users' experience in video games & ICT,* it was demanding to be adapted via the interpretation of *"Dynamical Theory of the field."* The main point of argument is the (negative or positive) forces gained by adults through their involvement with the ICT transactions. The aim was to create a strong driving force that interpreted their participation in previous distance education programs.
2. For the *B. The personal user needs for communication and social networking;* the *Transition Theory* adopted it. It is the perception that investigates the adults' behaviors and decisions in participatory activities may provoke some specific changes that might have come from but the preoccupation with social media,
3. For *C. The use of Second Life participants,* it was adopted by *Theory of the interaction.* For Boshier (1967), the adults' participation comes as a result of the alignment perception of themselves (self-perception) according to the type of program, and the educational environment that may participate,

4. For *D. Level of experience with educational activities* which can be based on the theoretical example of *Promise-Vigor*. The expectation has two main components: i) the hope of personal success through participation (specifically) and ii) the hope of successful completion of the course (generally),

5. For *E. Familiarity with the environment of Second Life*, it's considered the *Reference Group Theory*. According to this view, participants seek to acquire more benefits than they can with their own group and thus do not experience the feeling of deprivation by their peers.

6. Finally, (f) for *F. The views of students for the future of Second Life (as an educational tool)*, were adopted the *Social Participation Theory*. This theory belongs to the framework's interpretation for educational activities in relation to future activities that could be implemented by the same participants.

3.4. Procedure

This qualitative method was dictated through an "open-ended" questionnaire in which users expressed their opinions, and revealed their urgent need for the penetration and multifaceted interpretation to explain phenomena, not only those

of involving learners in cooperative activities, but also to record their personal experiences and expectations. The constitution of "formalizing" adult students' ideas, opinions and requirements relating to the courses were completed according to their operational characteristics. In fact, it was appeared as a successful effort of setting up a probabilistic sample (random groups with representation) with duration of three months (January-March 2012). The data obtained from the "target sample" that finally took part.

The framework for the collection of data held around the idea of using Second Life as an alternative e-learning platform defined as "artificial." Therefore, the conduct of research should not escape from these previous contexts and as the most appropriate place to be conducted was in Second Life. The procedures of data collection varied as the interview was taken place in several educational grids (virtual spaces) of academic sectors to meet participants (See Figure 1).

All students who participated in this survey should be previously followed projects that focused on the development and adoption of virtual grids in Second Life that have desirable, effective and sustainable effect on their participation in learning processes. This survey seeks to explore students' attitudes and opinions about studies that bolstered online collaborative learning processes.

Figure 1. Efforts to collect data information

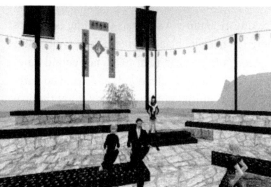

Participants of Informatics or Computer Science from all over the world who wanted to take part in this survey should firstly implement learning scenarios on the below axes:

1. The integration of students with different socio-cognitive backgrounds who wanted to strengthen the creation of their knowledge domain and share their expertise via collaborative online settings in Second Life.
2. The elicitation and capture of desired features and the degree of consensus on what is desirable or possible in the virtual world of Second Life with other peers.
3. The presentation of visual data models and interoperability issues with other 2D LMS sources as a basis for research data sharing in a stable virtual place to collaboratively learn with other users.
4. The establishment of virtual learning places in Second Life grids for learning with trained staff in administrative/organizational, pedagogical and technological aspects of e-learning/blended learning.
5. The development of a quality assurance plan and the set-up of pilot projects on the implementation of learning in order to explore the instructional affordances from the utilization of Second Life.

4. RESULTS

The questionnaire was shared where students wanted (specific places where they took their projects), orally or in chat text via Second Life. The first findings, as decoded, have proved truly the positive attitude of students towards the use of Second Life and as a result they will reuse it in the future. As it is well known, the traditional way of learning with the personal tutor-student contact is very difficult to circumvent. The excitement caused by students was based on 3D multi-user VW usage, identifying the expected positive re-

sults. In this study the evaluation of educational programs undertaken by users and brought some very interesting results, which are shown below:

1. **Demographics:** According to this research for the e-profile of students who participated, 40% lived in the United States of America (USA), while in Europe all was falling significantly (14.2%), except of course from the United Kingdom, where the participation rate raised at 26.7%. The 51.4% of the student population was female, while 48.6% male, with an average age of 24-25 years ($n=80$, M_{age} = 23-24 years old). Finally, most adults used the Second Life users from 13-36 months (64.2%). Below, we present the final results from the questions.

    a. **Users' Experience with Video Games & ICT:** All students answered that in the past have mainly played other video games, like Doom or Grand Theft Auto, (quest. 1-52.9%) which have shown their experience with 3D virtual environments. This seems to have the subsequent use of other 3D multi-user virtual worlds, although with versatile participation in online games (MOG's) (quest. 2-57.1%), they seemed to have similar experiences attending with others in distance learning environments. The main online resources (quest. 3), in which learners acquired the information into Second Life was mainly through the ISTE (24,3%) and SLED List (18,5%).

    b. **The User's Personal Needs for Communication & Social Networking:** The quest. 1 shows that 70% of students have used 1-3 hours Second Life (70%), more than any other social networking sites: (a) Facebook (64,3%), (b) YouTube (47,1%) and MySpace (32,8%). The connection of these instruments (quest. 2), reflected through the exchange of image files and audio from the Second Life to YouTube (65,7%), acquaintance with the profile of the "real" lives through Facebook (15,7%), while others worked in groups and on-line environments, such as the War of Warcraft (14,3%).

c. **The Use of Second Life from Participants:** Most students entered into the virtual environment from their home (quest. 1: 47%), while others through their workplace (27%) or university (29%) logged in it. It is striking that the majority of respondents seemed to be entered in their profile with a user account (quest. 2). However, most of them have more (38.5%), owning two or more codes for safety reasons (50%) or because they had problems with the previous (21.4%). For their e-profiles the respondents seemed to introduce facts and real life's information (38.5%), while almost half of them used only the most necessary to know others in the same (23%). Communications

between team members (quest. 4) is usually done via private message (IM) (49%), teleportation (26%) or via voice call (21%).

With the advent of virtual representations (quest. 5), many students have designed their digital entity based on their actual (external) appearance (34.3%), while others maintained their original (quest. 3-2.8%). On the overall activities that performed in Second Life for most students were using it for teaching and learning purposes (31.4%), manufacturing artifacts (21.4%), participation in meetings (7%), etc.

d. **Level of Experience with the Educational Activities in Second Life:** The education sector, in which respondents attended in on line courses (quest. 1) associated with: (a) the science of ICT (27%), (b) Economy and entrepreneurship seminars (21%), (c) Fields of Physics & Mathematics (10%) and (d) English language courses (9%) (See Figure 2).

Figure 2. Illustration of the online courses domain knowledge distribution in Second Life

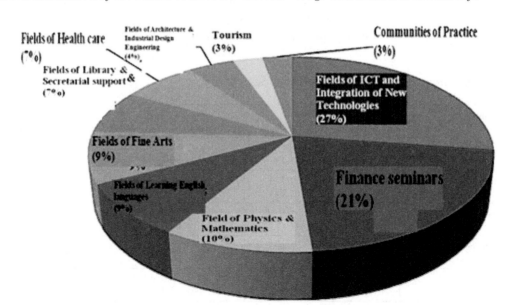

The specification of users' activities (quest. 2), is associated with the conduct of researches in Second Life (21,4%), the general student support services (17.5%) and those of e-learning skills in Second Life (texturing & scripting) (14,3%).

e. **The Familiarity of "Action Groups" with its Surroundings of Second Life:** The virtual location of visiting students are primarily educational content, with the ISTE (31,4%) are the first preferences, NMC Campus (17,1%), while many of them have also visited the International Spaceflight center (Spaceport Alpha) (11,4%). In quest. 2 it was raised the question of the following features that can support Second Life. It has been collected them in a five grade Likert scale (1=Not at all to 5=very much) in the following data (See Table 2).

On the question about the description of positive impressions in the Second Life (quest. 3), 30% answered that many the apprentices by all teams were implemented training events, in visually-rich interactive meetings with several people (25.7%), the ability of self-construction (21.4%), exploration (11.4%) in the end of their attendance at various social events except clauses (music and art). Although the ugliest experience was that students have identified problems in communication with

other people (bad behaviors) in 33%, some technical issues (31.4%) or other unauthorized who deliberately annoy others (15.7%). The following features (quest. 5) composed the overall image of Second Life and attempting to classify its availability and it was found (See Table 3).

According to the 6th question we asked from participants to evaluate the degree of ease (4-5scale) or difficulty (1-2 scale) or neutral attitude (3) some basic (personal) procedures done in Second Life (See Table 4).

Regarding now of what more learners want to learn through the processes in the virtual environment (quest. 7); it was found some ambiguous respects as (See Table 5):

f. **Students' Views for the Future of Second Life (As an Educational Tool):** In the last part of the interview, it was necessary wanted to elicit the views of users about the use of Second Life, as an educational tool in the future. In quest. 1, it can be noticed from the table the following (See Table 6).

The second question was about students' expectations for the future of Second Life and if it can eventually become a valuable tool in the educational process, the recorded views were very encouraging, as 51.4% believe that it may be the future of Web 3.0 and it will enrich with

Table 2. Amplified activities from the utilization of Second Life

Answers	1 (Not at all)	2 (Minor)	3 (Neutral)	4 (Much)	5 (Very much)
Conducting of educational seminars	1 (1,4%)	1 (1,4%)	3 (4,3%)	29 (41,4%)	46 (51,4%)
Educational researches in Second Life field	2 (2,8%)	3 (4,3%)	7 (10%)	33 (47,1%)	35 (35,7%)
Artistic expression	1 (1,4%)	1 (1,4%)	1 (1,4%)	22 (31,4%)	55 (64,5%)
Educational Simulations	0 (0%)	3 (4,3%)	6 (8,5%)	21 (30%)	50 (57,1%)
Role-play	4 (5,7%)	5 (7,1%)	8 (11,4%)	13 (18,5%)	50 (57,1%)

Table 3. General characteristics of Second Life

Answers	1 (Not at all)	2 (Minor)	3 (Neutral)	4 (Much)	5 (Very much)
Multi-user	1 (1,4%)	1 (1,4%)	1 (1,4%)	22 (31,4%)	55 (64,5%)
Interactive	0 (0%)	3 (4,3%)	6 (8,5%)	21 (30%)	50 (57,1%)
Ease of use	4 (5,7%)	5 (7,1%)	8 (11,4%)	13 (18,5%)	50 (57,1%)
Visually-rich	1 (1,4%)	3 (4,3%)	6 (8,5%)	13 (18,5%)	57 (67,1%)
Social	4 (5,7%)	5 (7,1&)	7 (10%)	19 (27,1%)	45 (50%)

Table 4. Personal uses of the virtual world

Answers	1 (Not at all)	2 (Minor)	3 (Neutral)	4 (Much)	5 (Very much)
I easily create my personal account	1 (1,4%)	3 (4,3%)	6 (8,5%)	13 (18,5%)	57 (67,1%)
I usually meet my friends in Second Life	4 (5,7%)	5 (7,1&)	7 (10%)	19 (27,1%)	45 (50%)
I learn to use multiple communication tools	1 (1,4%)	3 (4,3%)	2 (8,5%)	12 (18,5%)	63 (67,1%)
I easily create and modify my avatar	0 (0%)	2 (2,8%)	15 (2,14%)	22 (3,14%)	41 (44,3%)
I gradually teleported to other places	1 (1,4%)	1 (1,4%)	1 (1,4%)	22 (31,4%)	55 (64,5%)
I always use multimedia tools	1 (1,4%)	3 (4,3%)	6 (8,5%)	13 (18,5%)	57 (67,1%)

Table 5. Additional knowledge that is gained

Making mixed "machi-mina" with videos and sound files: 15 (18,5%)	Better educational events: 14 (17%)	More interesting places for exploring: 5 (7,1%)	Using multi-media tools for educational seminars: 5 (7,1%)	Alternative ways of identifying and meeting other avatars: 5 (7,1%)	Learning how to use communication channels: 4 (5,7%)
Multiple connection with the prims: 4 (5,7%)	Educational seminars with common assessment: 4 (5,7%)	Translator tools: 4 (5,7%)	Alternative tools for people with special need: 3 (4,3%)	Creating and using scripts and textures: 3 (4,3%)	Construct buildings: 3 (4,3%)
Learn how to promote my events: 3 (4,3%)	Creating "special" virtual places for seminars: 3 (4,3%)	Learning by doing: 3 (4,3%)	Learn how to make a special event: 2 (2,8%)	Better interaction with gestures: 2 (2,8%)	Managing communities of practice ("nomads of knowledge"): 2 (2,8%)

even more interactive features for the e-learning process. The third question was about whether it would be useful in the academic institution to hold a piece of land (grid) in Second Life, 57.1% believe that it would be a very good idea and they would like to support an effort with enthusiasm.

Regarding the benefits of this process the explanations given are:

Table 6. Second Life as a featuring "educational tool"

A special space for learning: 17 (17,1%)	Ease way to use visual tools for presentation: 17 (17,1%)	Let adults pass through to Teen Second Life: 7 (10%)	More ease way to use "open-source" subjects: 6 (8,5%)	Ease construction: 6 (8,5%)
Better communication channels: 6 (8,5%)	Modeling virtual objects: 5 (7,1%)	Easier way to utilize prims (HTML on a prim): 4 (5,7%)	Open access to educational events: 4 (5,7%)	Access to wikis or blogs tools: 3 (4,3%)
Fast repairing of lags: 3 (2,9%)	Less "techno-cratically" power of the PC hardware requirements: 1 (1,4%)	Utilizing Second Life from mobile phones: 1 (1,4%)	I don't know: 0 (0%)	

1. 7.14% of users considered that they need such an active participation in a 3D place,
2. 2.8% felt that it was very useful such a move, and would only be used as an informal learning platform,
3. 10%, held a moderate attitude, believing that such a development could only help the collaboration between academic departments,
4. 57,1%, believes that finding educational material from other universities would be useful for their research, and finally
5. It is supported by 23%, that there are hundreds of universities in SL, and as a result, they are thinking about the need to possess their own region.

5. DISCUSSION AND CONCLUSION

The main purpose of this research was to present findings from students' previous experiences in participatory activities via Second Life and in this vein to enrich the previous literature, which deals with the position of virtual environments in higher education. The conclusions that currently unveiled have some very interesting facts. Initially for the (i) research question, it seemed that in Second Life adults had a great contact with others, study together and enjoy apparently the learning process. They faced the challenge of conducting courses, mainly due to previous involvement and experience they had gained from similar with Web 2.0 (see Facebook, YouTube, WoW) seemed to significantly influence their involvement in teaching processes.

The innovative, pleasant, "open-ended" (due to participatory access) and the interactive environment of Second Life in these situations were able to support the participation, collaboration, and experiential learning among participants. It is not so coincidence that many adults found necessary to create or record videos (machinima) from their educational events. However, the relatively high degree of familiarity with ICT and the growing demands of technical equipment with various financial resources prevented as a limiting factor for the utilization of 3D multi-user VWs in the contemporary educational community.

According to Xie and Ke (2011) the interaction and autonomy that students felt can be an ally of collaborative motivation. It is also important to note that participation in discussions may offer more relative motivation and peer feedback between students (Xie, 2012). At this point, Yang, Gamble and Tang (2012) have also determined that the actions performed by students were being made through their involvement in authentic experiences and interactions. Mainly this indicated in terms of electronic game-based learning systems can improve the students' performances at high rates (Bai, Pan, Hirumi, & Kebritchi, 2012; Li, Cheng, & Liu, 2012). Childs, Schnieders and Williams (2012) have defined 3D multi-user as media sources for learning and teaching, however they did not pursue to indentify which really are the factors that engaged adults to participate in collaborative tasks. In this dimension, also Mayrath, Traphagan, Heikes and Trivedi (2011) have applied the instructional use of 3D virtual environments as more sufficient when students are motivating in learning tasks and constructing their knowledge domain. Consistent to the aforementioned one, it was proved in this study that students have better changes to be motivated, when they started to work/study with their peers in collaborative "learning-by-doing" tasks.

According to the aforementioned reasons and taking into account the present survey's findings, it can be finally overwhelmed the necessity of designing and implementing courses in Second Life to render sensorial communication. It is necessary to re-consolidate a methodological framework that can bring greater knowledge transfer, suggestive ways of presenting contemporary educational content for better learning outcomes. As for the utilization of McGivney's framework, it seemed to be equally valuable for the present of this research. Also, Von Hipell and Tippelt (2010) have established that a missing model for participation theories can prevent the research trails of learning in a team-based workshop and for this reason a "framework" was the only way that prefigured all plaits of adults' participation theories, influencing the choice to collaborate with other teammates.

The evaluation of Second Life must take into account the educational needs of teachers and learners, giving them the full control of their actions and increased the sense of responsibility. Supplementary, as an open-access environment Second Life has also advantages and disadvantages. The advantages atoned to the social interaction between users' communication through a variety of multimedia artifacts that become from the persistent virtual place. The disadvantages like bad students' behaviors from unauthorized users or lagging issues in grids were essential for further future-driven activities, but in any case cannot repudiate the whole approbation of transferring and producing a novel knowledge field.

Second Life can provide a comfort and safety place for participants, as many adult learners seek to learn from each other, worked together and enjoyed the learning process. Inasmuch the easy use of this environment that students faced, mainly was purposeful due to previous involvement and experience they had gained from similar "media" which seems to have greatly influenced for their involvement in the learning process. In the innovative, "open" (due to multi-stakeholder access), immersing and open-ended environment of Second Life, students were able to attend in the participation, cooperation, communication and experiential learning phases. There is no coincidence that many adults have found necessary even to create virtual universities for distance courses. However, the relatively high degree of familiarity with ICT and the increased demands on technical requirements or other financial costs can be a limiting factor for its utilization.

It was also pretty remarkable the fact that the research findings obtained from various educational applications in Second Life has answered in the (ii) question. It was shown that students could be gained thoughtful, critical understanding of the acquisition of knowledge through research and personal beliefs of the project them, gradually coming to realize:

1. The beneficial functional characteristics can support an instructional knowledge framework to underpin and implemented innovative teaching interventions.
2. The effective ways in which they learn together.
3. The discovery inconsistencies and misrepresentations of "person-centric visas" in relation to their educational practices.

The participants have answered crucial principles governed their educational practices. They have paid particular attention to the "why" and "how", penetrating in the learning process, abandoning thereby "behavioral" positions and have practically used new ICT sources synchronously or asynchronously. On the other hand, instructors' fortitude or exhortation by using innovative environments and learning approaches can easily overcome the "technocratic" methodological concerns that cannot be ignored. It should be also concerned about the ethical and cultural implications that may be created, especially in the levels of the learning processes and general aimed to organize a more careful way for actions. Therefore, adults should aim to achieve an understanding of life and conduct at the "denaturation" in the best possible ways to create other future-driven activities which make social change actions as part of a long professional career.

To summarize the foregoing results from the convergence of this data it can be said that Second Life can become a candidate platform for the university campus, offering another aspect of what it is called today "sustainable" education including:

1. A mass scale of learners' needs the continuous enrichment of their knowledge field.
2. The learning practices which may be guided by the participatory practices and the concept of social learning practices through similar goals, values and principles that may govern other users.
3. The development of a critic-reflective thought and the emergence of a new dimension between teachers and learners for the identification and discovery of sustainable learning sources, reflecting on users' real needs or interests.
4. The development and evaluation expedient or consubstantial conversions for collaborative action-based activities, opening the gates of a more "sustainable" educational and professional future.

Certain recommendations that can be raised and revealed the significance of the study directly or indirectly have some of most fundamental

theoretical and practical significance, which are analyzed through the following points:

1. Educational programs supporting learning in Higher Education through the use of Second Life appear to meet the real needs of the students in order to make the best possible use of their values, ideas of the same people mobilized to a greater extent and to respond more appropriately to the demands of modern educational system.
2. The recognition of the ways in which students need to be connected to create a safe, comfortable, pleasant environment, in order to provide appropriate stimuli for engaging in activities primarily need to take account of the values and ideals opinions only through experiences of users identified by adults' participation theories.
3. The positive attitude that can be cultivated in students during their active involvement in participatory activities in conjunction with the interpretation derived from the theories of adult participation could best make education understand the positive or negative attitude to use, to gain skills for professional and personal development.

The aim of this study was to highlight and emphasize both the incentives and barriers to educational ventures, and the training needs of adult students in this modern era in which are active members. The analysis and interpretation of the results showed series findings that could be useful to instructional technologists, educators and managers of training programs, where their real goal is the efficient and effective training.

The utilization of Second Life for online course delivery methods and long-term educational applications can be used by the academic institutions on the principles that define distance learning as a continuous process, which tries to meet the needs of a dynamically evolving education system, and learners' personal needs, by reducing the space-time constraints of face-to-face settings. In conclusion, it is truly understood that the need for the introduction, development and recognition of an "alternative" and "flexible" educational platform can enhance the final value of learning.

REFERENCES

Abbad, M., & Albarghouthi, M. (2011). Evaluate students' perceptions of the virtual learning environment at Paisley University. *International Journal of Emerging Technologies in Learning*, *6*(3), 28–34.

Bai, H. Pan, W. Hirumi, A., & Kebritchi, M. (2012). Assessing the effectiveness of a 3-D instructional game on improving mathematics achievement and motivation of middle school students. *British Journal of Educational Technology*. doi:10.1111/j.1467-8535.2011.01269.x

Bearden, O., Richard, G., Netemeyer, M., & Teel, J. (1989). Measurement of consumer susceptibility to interpersonal influence. *The Journal of Consumer Research*, *15*(2), 473–481. doi:10.1086/209186

Blair, S. (2000). The centrality of occupation life transactions. *British Journal of Occupational Therapy*, *63*(5), 231–237.

Blondy, L. C. (2007). Evaluation and application of andragogical assumptions to the adult online learning environment. *Journal of Interactive Online Learning*, *6*(2), 116–130.

Boellstorff, T. (2007). *Coming of age in second life: An anthropologist explores the virtually human*. Princeton University Press.

Bortoluzzi, M. (2012). Second Life for virtual communities in education: Sharing teaching principles? *Journal of e-Learning and Knowledge Society*, *8*(3), 119-128.

Boshier, R. (1971). Motivational orientations of adult education participants: A factor analytic exploration of Houle's typology. *Adult Education*, *21*, 3–26. doi:10.1177/074171367102100201

Boulos, M. N. K., Hetherington, L., & Wheeler, S. (2007). Second Life: An overview of the potential of 3D virtual worlds in medical and health education. *Health Information and Libraries Journal*, *24*(4), 233–245. doi:10.1111/j.1471-1842.2007.00733.x PMID:18005298

Bouta, H., & Paraskeva, F. (2013). The cognitive apprenticeship theory for the teaching of mathematics in an online 3D virtual environment. *International Journal of Mathematical Education in Science and Technology*, *44*(2), 159–178. doi:10.1080/0020739X.2012.703334

Bronack, S., Riedl, R., & Tashner, J. (2006). Learning in the zone: A social constructivist framework for distance education in a 3-dimensional virtual world. *Interactive Learning Environments*, *14*(3), 219–232. doi:10.1080/10494820600909157

Burgess, M., Slate, J., Rojas-Lebouef, A., & Laprairie, K. (2010). Teaching and learning in Second Life: using the community of inquiry (CoI) model to support online instruction with graduate students in instructional technology. *The Internet and Higher Education*, *13*(1), 84–88. doi:10.1016/j.iheduc.2009.12.003

Cheryan, S., Meltzoff, A., & Kim, S. (2011). Classrooms matter: The design of virtual classrooms influences gender disparities in computer science classes. *Computers & Education*, *57*(1), 1825–1835. doi:10.1016/j.compedu.2011.02.004

Childs, M., Schnieders, L., & Gweno, W. (2012). This above all: to thine own self be true": ethical considerations and risks in conducting Higher Education learning activities in the virtual world Second Life™. *Interactive Learning Environments*, *20*(3), 253–269. doi:10.1080/10494820.2011.641679

Comings, J., Parrella, A., & Soricone, L. (1999). *Persistence among adult basic education students in pre-ged classes.* Retrieved from http://www.ncsall.net/fileadmin/resources/research/report12.pdf

Contreras-Castillo, J., Favela, J., Perez-Fragoso, C., & Santamaria-del-Angel, E. (2004). Informal interactions and their implications for online courses. *Computers & Education, 42*(2), 149–168. doi:10.1016/S0360-1315(03)00069-1

Cross, K. P. (1981). *Adults as learners: Increasing participation and facilitating learning.* San Francisco, CA: Jossey-Bass.

Dalgarno, B., & Lee, M. (2010). What are the learning affordances of 3D virtual environments?'. *British Journal of Educational Technology, 40*(1), 10–32. doi:10.1111/j.1467-8535.2009.01038.x

Dede, C. J. (1995). The evolution of constructivist learning environments: Immersion in distributed, virtual worlds. *ETR&D, 35*(5), 4–36.

Deutschmann, M., & Panichi, L. (2009). Instructional design, teacher practice and learner autonomy. In J. Molka-Danielsen & M. Deutschmann. Learning and teaching in the virtual world of Second Life (pp. 27-44). Tapir akademisk forlag.

Dickey, M. (2003). Teaching in 3D: Pedagogical affordances and constraints of 3D virtual worlds for synchronous distance learning. *Distance Education, 24*(1), 105–121. doi:10.1080/01587910303047

Dillenbourg, P. (1999). Introduction: What do you mean by "collaborative learning"? In P. Dillenbourg (Ed.), *Collaborative learning: Cognitive and computational approaches* (pp. 1–19). Amsterdam, The Netherlands: Pergamon, Elsevier Science.

EDUCAUSE. (2007). *The horizon report* (2007 ed.). Austin, TX: The New Media Consortium & Boulder, Co. Retrieved September 3, 2013, from http://www.nmc.org/pdf/2007_Horizon_Report.pdf

Edwards, P., Rico, M., Dominguez, E., & Agudo, J. E. (2010). Second language e-learning and professional training with Second Life. In H. Hao Yang & S. Chi-yin Yuen (Eds.), Collective intelligence and e-learning 2.0: Implications of web-based communities and networking. Hersey, PA: IGI Global.

FitzGibbon, A., Oldham, E., & Johnston, K. (2008). Are Irish student-teachers prepared to be agents of change in using IT in education? In K. McFerrin et al. (Eds.), *Proceedings of Society for Information Technology and Teacher Education International Conference* (pp. 1397-1404). Chesapeake, VA: AACE.

Franceschi, K. G., Lee, R. M., & Hruds, D. (2008). Engaging e-learning in virtual worlds: Supporting Group Collaboration. *Journal of Management Information Systems, 26*(1), 73–100. doi:10.2753/MIS0742-1222260104

Grubb, R., Hemby, E., & Connly-Stewart, G. (1998). Adult education & human resource development: A symbiotic relationship? *PAACE Journal of Lifelong learning, 7,* 57-66.

Hadjerrouit, S. (2009). Didactics of ICT in secondary education: Conceptual issues and practical perspectives. *Issues in Informing Science and Information Technology, 6*(2), 153–178.

Heckhausen. (1991). *Motivation and action.* Springer.

Herod, L. (2002). *Adult learning from theory to practice.* Retrieved from http://www.nald.ca/adultlearningcourse/glossary.htm. Retrieved 17/03/2009

Hew, F. K., & Cheung, S. W. (2010). Use of three-dimensional (3-D) immersive virtual worlds in K-12 and higher education settings: A review of the research. *British Journal of Educational Technology, 41*(1), 33–55. doi:10.1111/j.1467-8535.2008.00900.x

Hobson, P., & Welbourne, L. (1998). Adult development and transformative learning. *International Journal of Lifelong Education, 17*(2), 72–86. doi:10.1080/0260137980170203

Houtkoop, W., & Van Der Kamp, M. (1992). Factors influencing participation in continuing education. *International Journal of Educational Research, 17*(6), 537–548.

Huber, E., & Blount, Y. (2010). Using virtual world efficiently in a post-graduated business courses: Designing an exploratory study. In *Proceedings ASCILITE 2009 Auckland,* Sydney, Australia (pp. 444-449).

Illeris, K. (2003). Towards a contemporary and comprehensive theory of learning. *International Journal of Lifelong Education, 22*(1), 396–406. doi:10.1080/02601370304837

Inman, C., Wright, V. H., & Hartman, J. A. (2010). Use of Second Life in K-12 and higher education: A review of research. *Journal of Interactive Online Learning, 9*(1), 44–64.

Janssen, J., Erkens, G., & Kirscher, P. (2011). Group awareness tools: It's what you do with it that matters. *Computers in Human Behavior, 27*(3), 1046–1058. doi:10.1016/j.chb.2010.06.002

Kemp, J., & Livingstone, D. (2006). Putting a Second Life "metaverse" skin on learning management systems. In Livingstone, D. (Ed.), *Proceedings of the Second Life Education Workshop at the Second Life Community Convention*, San Francisco, CA (pp. 13–18).

Kidd, J. R. (1978). *How adults learn.* Cambridge, MA: Prentice Hall.

Knox, A. B. (1986). *Helping adults learn.* San Francisco, CA: Jossey-Bass.

Konstantinidis, A. T., Tsiatsos, T., Terzidou, T., & Pomportsis, A. (2010). Fostering collaborative learning in Second Life: Metaphors and affordances. *Computers & Education, 55*(2), 603–615. doi:10.1016/j.compedu.2010.02.021

Kordaki, M. (2013). High school computing teachers' beliefs and practices: A case study. *Computers & Education, 68*(1), 141–152. doi:10.1016/j.compedu.2013.04.020

Kotsilieris, T., & Dimopoulou, N. (2013). The evolution of e-learning in the context of 3D virtual worlds. *The Electronic Journal of e-Learning, 11*(2), 147-167.

Kotsilieris, T., & Dimopoulou, N. (2013). The evolution of e-Learning in the context of 3D virtual worlds. *The Electronic Journal of e-Learning, 11*(2), 147-167.

Lee, J., & Hammer, J. (2011). Gamification in education: What, how, why bother? *Academic Exchange Quarterly, 15*(2).

Lehtinen, E. (2003). Computer-supported collaborative learning: An approach to powerful learning environments. In E. De Corte, L. Verschaffel, N. Entwistle, & J. Van Merriënboer (Eds.), *Powerful learning environments: Unraveling basic components and dimensions* (pp. 35–53). Amsterdam, The Netherlands: Elsevier.

Li, Z., Cheng, Y.-B., & Liu, C.-C. (2012). A constructionism framework for designing game-like learning systems: Its effect on different learners. *British Journal of Educational Technology.* doi:10.1111/j.1467-8535.2012.01305.x

Lieb, S. (1991). *Principles of adult learning.* Retrieved from http://honolulu.hawaii.edu/intranet/committees/FacDevCom/guidebk/teachtip/adults-2.htm

Liu, Y., Chen, H., Liu, C., Lin, C., & Chan, H. (2010). A model to evaluate the effectiveness of collaborative online learning teams – Self-disclosure and social exchange theory perspective. *International Journal of Cyber Society and Education, 3*(2), 117–132.

Lu, J., Chiu, M., & Law, N. (2011). Collaborative argumentation and justifications: A statistical discourse analysis of online discussions. *Computers in Human Behavior, 27*(2), 961–969. doi:10.1016/j.chb.2010.11.021

Mayrath, M. C., Traphagan, T., Heikes, E. J., & Trivedi, A. (2011). Instructional design best practices for Second Life: A case study from a college-level English course. *Interactive Learning Environments, 19*(2), 125–142. doi:10.1080/10494820802602568

McGivney, V. (1983). Participation and non-participation: A review of the literature. In R. Edwards, S. Sieminski, & D. Zeldin (Eds.), *Adult learners, education and training* (pp. 11–30). London, UK: Routledge/OUP.

McGivney, V. (1993). *Women, education and training. Barriers to access, informal starting points and progression routes*. Leicester, UK: National Institute of Adult Continuing Education.

McKerlich, R., Riis, M., Anderson, T., & Eastman, B. (2011). Student perceptions of teaching presence, social presence, and cognitive presence in a virtual world. *MERLOT Journal, 7*(3), 324–336.

Merriam, S. B., & Cafarella, R. S. (1991). *Learning in adulthood*. San Francisco, CA: Jossey-Bass.

Miller, H. L. (1967). *Participation of adults in education: A force-field analysis*. Boston, MA: Center for the Study of Liberal Education for Adults/Boston University.

Nteliopoulou, S., & Tsinakos, A. (2011). The path from first to Second Life. In T. Bastiaens & M. Ebner (Eds.), *Proceedings of World Conference on Educational Multimedia, Hypermedia and Telecommunications 2011* (pp. 3807-3814). Chesapeake, VA: AACE.

Park, J., & Choi, H. (2009). Factors influencing adult learners' decision to drop out or persistence in online learning. *Journal of Educational Technology & Society, 12*(4), 207–217.

Pellas, N. (2012). A conceptual "cybernetic" methodology for organizing and managing the e-learning process through [D-] CIVEs: The case of "Second Life". In P. Renna (Ed.), Production and manufacturing system management: Coordination approaches and multi-site Planning. IGI Global.

Pellas, N. (2014). Unraveling a progressive inquiry script in persistent virtual worlds: Theoretical foundations and decision processes for constructing a socio-cultural learning framework. In Z. Jin (Ed.), *Exploring implicit cognition: Learning, memory, and social-cognitive processes*. Hershey, PA: IGI Global.

Pellas, N. (2014). The influence of computer self-efficacy, metacognitive self-regulation and self-esteem on student engagement in online learning programs: Evidence from the virtual world of Second Life. *Computers in Human Behavior, 35*(1), 157–170. doi:10.1016/j.chb.2014.02.048

Pellas, N., & Kazanidis, I. (2013). e-Learning quality through Second Life: Exploiting, investigating and evaluating the efficiency parameters of collaborative activities in Higher Education. In V. Bryan & V. Wang (Eds.), Technology use and research approaches for community education and professional development (pp. 250-273). Hershey, PA: IGI Global.

Pellas, N., & Kazanidis, I. (2013). *Engaging students in blended and online collaborative courses at university level through Second Life: Comparative perspectives and instructional affordances.* New Review of Hypermedia and Multimedia Journal.

Pellas, N., & Kazanidis, I. (2013). On the value of Second Life for students' engagement in hybrid and online university-level courses: A comparative study from Higher education in Greece. *Education and Information Technologies.* doi:10.1007/s10639-013-9294-4

Pellas, N., Peroutseas, E., & Kazanidis, I. (2013). Virtual communities of inquiry (VCoI) for learning basic algorithmic structures with Open Simulator & Scratch4(OS): A case study from the Secondary education in Greece. In K. Diamantaras, G. Evangelidis, Y. Manolopoulos, C. Georgiadis, P. Kefalas, & D. Stamatis (Eds.), *Proceedings of the Balkan Conference in Informatics (BCI '13)* (pp. 187-194). Thessaloniki, Greece: ACM Press.

Persico, D., & Pozzi, F. (2011). Task, Team and Time to structure online collaboration in learning environments. *World Journal on Educational Technology, 3*(1), 1–15.

Petrakou, A. (2010). Interacting through avatars: virtual worlds as a context for online education. *Computers & Education, 54*(3), 1020–1027. doi:10.1016/j.compedu.2009.10.007

Piccoli, G., Ahmad, R., & Ives, B. (2001). Web-based virtual learning environments: A research framework and a preliminary assessment of effectiveness in basic IT training. *Management Information Systems Quarterly, 25*(4), 401–426. doi:10.2307/3250989

Rivera, J., McAlister, K., & Rice, M. (2002). A comparison of student outcomes & satisfaction between traditional & web based course offerings. *Online Journal of Distance Learning Administration, 5*(3), 151–179.

Rovai, A. P. (2003). In search of higher persistence rates in distance educational programs. *The Internet and Higher Education, 6*, 1–16. doi:10.1016/S1096-7516(02)00158-6

Rubenson, K. (1994). Adult education: Disciplinary orientations. In T. Husén & T. N. Postlethwaite (Eds.), *The international encyclopedia of education* (Vol. I, pp. 120–127). Oxford, UK: Pergamon Press.

Saad, A., Mat, B., & Awadh, A. (2013). Review of theory of human resources development training (learning) participation. *Journal of WEI Business and Economics,* 47-58.

Stahl, G., Koschmann, T., & Suthers, D. (2006). Computer-supported collaborative learning: An historical perspective. In R. K. Sawyer (Ed.), *Cambridge handbook of the learning sciences* (pp. 409–426). Cambridge, UK: Cambridge University Press.

Sutcliffe, A., & Alrayes, A. (2012). Investigating user experience in Second Life for collaborative learning. *International Journal of Human-Computer Studies, 70*, 508–525. doi:10.1016/j.ijhcs.2012.01.005

Tudor, R., & Carley, S. (1998). *Reference group theory revisited.* Retrieved from http://www.sbaer.uca.edu/research/sma/1998/pdf/06.pdf

van Aalst, J. (2006). Rethinking the nature of online work in synchronous learning networks. *British Journal of Educational Technology, 37*, 279–288. doi:10.1111/j.1467-8535.2006.00557.x

Van Campenhout, G. (2007). Mutual fund selection criteria and determinants of individual fund flours. *Tijdschrift voor Econome en Management, LII, 4*, 617–671.

Vogel, D., Guo, M., Zhou, P., Tian, S., & Zhang, J. (2008). In search of second life. Nirvana. *Issues in Informing Science and Information Technology, 5*, 11–28.

Von Hipell, A., & Tippelt, R. (2010). The role of adult educators towards (potential) participants and their contribution to increasing participation in adult education - insights into existing research. *European Journal for Research on the Education and Learning of Adults, 1*(1-2), 33–51. doi:10.3384/rela.2000-7426.rela0012

Wang, F., & Burton, J. (2012). Second Life in education: A review of publications from its launch to 2011. *British Journal of Educational Technology.* doi:10.1111/j.1467-8535.2012.01334.x

Wang, M.-J. (2010). Online collaboration and offline interaction between students using asynchronous tools in blended learning. *Australasian Journal of Educational Technology, 26,* 830–846.

Winter, M. (2010). *Second Life education in New Zealand: Evaluation research final report.* Retrieved October 30, 2013, from http://slenz.wordpress.com/2010/03/11/slenz-project-evaluation-vlenz-165-mar-10-2010/

Xie, K. (2012). What do the numbers say? The influence of motivation and peer feedback on students' behavior in online discussions. *British Journal of Educational Technology.* doi:10.1111/j.1467-8535.2012.01291.x

Xie, K., & Ke, K. (2011). The role of students' motivation in peer-moderated asynchronous online discussions. *British Journal of Educational Technology, 42*(6), 916–930. doi:10.1111/j.1467-8535.2010.01140.x

Yang, Y.-T., Gamble, J., & Tang, S.-Y. (2012). Voice over instant messaging as a tool for enhancing the oral proficiency and motivation of English-as-a-foreign-language learners. *British Journal of Educational Technology, 43*(3), 448–464. doi:10.1111/j.1467-8535.2011.01204.x

Zhao, Y., & Wu, L. (2009). Second Life: A new window for e-learning. In *Proceedings of the 9th International Conference on Hybrid Intelligent Systems*, Shenyang (pp. 191-194).

This work was previously published in the International Journal of Digital Literacy and Digital Competence (IJDLDC), 5(1); edited by Antonio Cartelli, pages 21-44, copyright year 2014 by IGI Publishing (an imprint of IGI Global).

Chapter 67
From Adoption to Routinization of B2B e-Commerce:
Understanding Patterns across Europe

Tiago Oliveira
Universidade Nova de Lisboa, Portugal

Gurpreet Dhillon
Virginia Commonwealth University, USA

ABSTRACT

The authors present an in depth understanding of B2B e-commerce adoption and routinization across Europe. The research was informed by the technology, organization, and environment (TOE) framework. A sample of 7,172 firms across Europe was used. A seven factor model is presented that includes technology readiness, technology integration, firm size, obstacles, education level, competitive pressure, and trading partner collaboration, which inform B2B adoption and routinization. Based on adoption and routinization, clusters of European countries, are identified and factors presented that ensure movement from one cluster to the other.

INTRODUCTION

Business-to-business (B2B) transactions have become a major part of all e-commerce transactions (Albrecht, Dean, & Hansen, 2005; Hung, Tsai, Hung, McQueen, & Jou, 2011; Sila, 2013). In this paper we define B2B e-commerce in accordance with Teo and Ranganathan (2004, p.90) as "the use of the Internet and Web-technologies for conducting inter-organizational business transactions". Firms using B2B e-commerce obtain substantial returns through efficiency improvements, inven-

tory reduction, sales increase, customer relationship enhancement, new market penetration, and financial returns (Amit & Zott, 2001; Barua, Konana, Whinston, & Yin, 2004; Zhu & Kraemer, 2005; Zhu, Kraemer, Xu, & Dedrick, 2004). The development of B2B e-commerce capability is crucial because not only it is rapidly changing the way companies buy, sell, and deal with customers, it is also becoming a more central part of their business strategies (Abu-Musa, 2004). B2B e-commerce adoption and routinization becomes a noteworthy research topic since it enables firms

DOI: 10.4018/978-1-4666-8619-9.ch067

to perform electronic transactions along the value chain activities (Straub & Watson, 2001; Zhu & Kraemer, 2002) and it represents a new way to incorporate Internet-based technologies with core business potentially affecting the whole business (Zhu et al., 2004).

The European Commission (2005) claims that more efforts are needed to improve business processes in European firms if the targets of competitiveness prescribed in the Lisbon treaty are to be achieved. Under the pressure of their main international competitors, European firms need to find new opportunities to reduce costs, improve performance, and identify the extent to which there are common behaviors across them (European Commission, 2010). The 27 European Union (EU) members have very different patterns of e-business readiness (Castaings & Tarantola, 2008; Cruz-Jesus, Oliveira, & Bacao, 2012). To the best of our knowledge very limited empirical research has been undertaken to evaluate the determinants of B2B e-commerce usage, among the 27 European countries (hereinafter, referred EU27). This study seeks to fill this gap, by improving our understanding of B2B e-commerce across EU27. This paper addresses three research questions. They are:

RQ1: What are the factors driving B2B adoption and routinization across EU?
RQ2: How many clusters of countries are there in terms of adoption and routinization, and what are the countries that belong to each cluster?
RQ3: What are the different drivers for B2B adoption and routinization across the clusters found in answering RQ2?

To address these research questions we develop a conceptual model based on the technology, organization, and environment (TOE) framework (Tornatzky & Fleischer, 1990). We empirically evaluate the integrated model through a large-scale survey (7,172 firms) across EU countries (in

methods and data analysis section). In sub-section B2B adoption and routinization, we estimate two regressions (one for adoption and the other for routinization) for the full sample to answer the first RQ. To answer the second RQ we apply a cluster analysis of countries to identify how many groups are in the EU context, in terms of adoption and routinization, and what are the countries that belong to each group (in sub-section clusters analysis of countries). In sub-section B2B adoption and routinization, we estimate six more regressions to answer the last RQ - one for adoption and one for routinization for each of three groups of countries revealed in answering RQ2. In the discussion and conclusion section we suggest a fresh understanding of B2B e-commerce adoption and routinization among countries, and provide guidelines to policymakers and practitioners.

LITERATURE REVIEW AND MODEL DEVELOPMENT

The TOE framework (Tornatzky & Fleischer, 1990) identifies three features of a firm's that may influence adoption of technological innovation. The first is the technological context that describes both the existing technologies in use and new technologies relevant to the firm; second, the organizational context, which refers to characteristics of the organization such as scope and size; third, the environmental context in which a firm conducts its business, referring to its industry, competitors, and dealings with the government.

The TOE framework has been examined in a number of empirical studies across various information system (IS) domains. It was used to explained IS adoption and use (Thong, 1999); electronic data interchange (EDI) adoption (Kuan & Chau, 2001); enterprise resource planning (ERP) adoption (Pan & Jang, 2008); cloud computing adoption (Low, Chen, & Wu, 2011; Oliveira, Thomas, & Espadanal, 2014); and interorganizational business process standards (IBPS) adoption (Venkatesh & Bala, 2012). This framework was also used to explain e-business adoption (Nguyen, 2013; Oliveira & Martins, 2010; Sila, 2013; Zhu, Kraemer, & Xu, 2003; Zhu & Kraemer, 2005) and routinization (Lin & Lin, 2008; Zhu & Kraemer, 2005; Zhu, Kraemer, & Xu, 2006). Empirical findings from these studies confirm that the TOE is a valuable framework in which to understand the adoption of IT innovations. For this reason we developed a research model for B2B e-commerce adoption and routinization based on the TOE framework (see Figure 1) in which the dependent variable is the B2B e-commerce adoption and routinization and we stipulated seven hypotheses for each of the dependent variables. In this study, adoption is a binary variable reflecting a one-time decision, that is, the decision to use the Internet for conducting or supporting value chain activities (i.e., allocating resources and physically acquiring the technology) (Zhu, Kraemer, et al., 2006). Adoption is the first step toward technology routinization. Routinization is the stage where B2B e-commerce is widely used as an integral part of the firm's value

chain activities (Zhu, Kraemer, et al., 2006), and is usually measured by the online order volume. Apparently, the effect of a factor is not necessarily the same on B2B e-commerce adoption versus routinization. A distinction between the two helps to gain an in-depth understanding.

Technology Context

Technology context is defined in terms of 1) technology readiness and 2) technology integration. The technology readiness and technology integration constructs are discussed in paragraphs below.

Technology readiness can be defined as technology infrastructure and IT human resources (Mata, Fuerst, & Barney, 1995). Technology infrastructure establishes a platform on which Internet technologies can be applied to institute a web presence for the business. IT human resources provide the knowledge and skills to develop web applications (Zhu & Kraemer, 2005). B2B e-commerce can become an integral part of the value chain only if firms have the requisite infrastructure and technical skills. These factors can

Figure 1. Research model

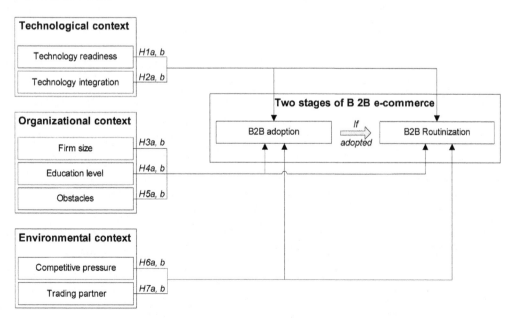

facilitate and enable the technological capacity of the firm to adopt and routinize B2B e-commerce. However, firms that do not have robust technology infrastructure and broad IT expertise may not wish to risk the adoption of B2B e-commerce. This means that firms with greater technology readiness are in a better position to adopt and use B2B e-commerce. Several empirical studies have identified technological readiness as an important determinant of IT adoption (Armstrong & Sambamurthy, 1999; Hong & Zhu, 2006; Iacovou, Benbasat, & Dexter, 1995; Kwon & Zmud, 1987; Pan & Jang, 2008; Zhu, 2004; Zhu et al., 2003; Zhu & Kraemer, 2005; Zhu, Kraemer, et al., 2006). Therefore, we postulate the following:

H1a: Higher level of technology readiness is a positive predictor for B2B e-commerce adoption.

H1b: Higher level of technology readiness is a positive predictor for B2B e-commerce routinization.

Evidence from literature suggests that technology integration helps improve firm performance through reduced cycle time, improved customer service, and lowered procurement costs (Barua et al., 2004). As a complex technology, B2B e-commerce demands close coordination of various components along the value chain. Correspondingly, a greater integration of existing applications and the Internet platforms represent a greater capacity for conducting business over the Internet (Al-Qirim, 2007; Mirchandani & Motwani, 2001; Premkumar, 2003; Zhu, Kraemer, et al., 2006). Technology integration enables firms to continuously improve and innovate by identifying and sharing information across products/services/ business units to enhance organizational knowledge and readiness (Barua et al., 2004). Therefore, the success of B2B e-commerce adoption and routinization depends on the level of technology integration. Some empirical studies have found that technology integration is positively related to e-business adoption and routinization (Zhu, Kraemer, et al., 2006) and also to e-commerce adoption (Hong & Zhu, 2006). Hence, we postulate the following:

H2a: Higher level of technology integration is a positive predictor for B2B e-commerce adoption.

H2b: Higher level of technology integration is a positive predictor for B2B e-commerce routinization.

Organizational Context

In IS and organizational research literatures, the importance of size as a predictor of IT adoption and the direction and nature of the causal influence of size has been a persistent controversy (Ettlie & Rubenstein, 1987). Some empirical studies indicate that there is a positive relationship between the two variables (Grover, 1993; Hsu, Kraemer, & Dunkle, 2006; Pan & Jang, 2008; Premkumar, Ramamurthy, & Crum, 1997; Soares-Aguiar & Palma-Dos-Reis, 2008; Thong, 1999; Zhu et al., 2003). However, there is also empirical evidence suggesting otherwise (Dewett & Jones, 2001; Harris & Katz, 1991; Martins & Oliveira, 2008; Zhu, Dong, Xu, & Kraemer, 2006; Zhu & Kraemer, 2005; Zhu, Kraemer, et al., 2006). The actual adoption of B2B e-commerce may entail bringing about a radical change in firms' business processes and organization structures, which might be hindered by the structural inertia of large firms (Damanpour, 1992). The notion of structural inertia leads us to expect that large firm size may deter B2B adoption and routinization. Hence, we postulate the following:

H3a: Larger firm size is a negative predictor for B2B e-commerce adoption.

H3b: Larger firm size is a negative predictor for B2B e-commerce routinization.

The overall capacity of the organization to evaluate technological opportunities (for example B2B) in the areas of its activity depends primarily on human capital and knowledge of the organization (Cohen & Levinthal, 1989). The profound changes that IT introduces call for workers with a higher level of education, as these have a greater ability to absorb and make use of an IT innovation (Martins & Oliveira, 2008). Education is expected to exert a positive impact on the adoption and routinization of IT (Battisti, Hollenstein, Stoneman, & Woerter, 2007; Bresnahan, Brynjolfsson, & Hitt, 2002; Brynjolfsson & Hitt, 2000; Giunta & Trivieri, 2007; Martins & Oliveira, 2008) since usually the successful implementation of B2B e-commerce requires complex skills. The diffusion of technological innovations´ (as the case of ICT) theory claims that technological complexity is one major obstacle to adopt those technologies (Rogers, 2005). Thus, the ease of use of a technology, is important to its adoption rate (Katz & Aspden, 1997). Indeed educational level of individuals plays an important role. This is because when one is facing a difficult challenge, educated individuals are more likely to be flexible and hence effectively overcome complexity. Thus, when interacting with an ICT, the relatively higher educational attainment should make it easier to cope with complex technologies, thus minimizing the impact of the difficulties (Hsieh, Rai, & Keil, 2008). In this sense education facilitates the absorption and comprehension of information. We hypothesize the following:

H4a: Workers' with higher level of educational level is a positive predictor for B2B e-commerce adoption.

H4b: Workers' with higher level of educational level is a positive predictor for B2B e-commerce routinization.

Obstacles are particularly important because these can be critical in making the adoption and routinization process seem more complicated and costly (Hong & Zhu, 2006; Pan & Jang, 2008; Zhu, Kraemer, et al., 2006). The adoption of B2B e-commerce requires a substantial degree of technical and organizational competence for smooth transition (Hong & Zhu, 2006); and these obstacles can result in resistance from users. As a consequence, it is essential to reduce the obstacles. The greater the top management support, the easier it is for the organization to overcome difficulty and complexity of IT adoption (Bajwa, Garcia, & Mooney, 2004; Cho, 2006; Hwang, Ku, Yen, & Cheng, 2004; Premkumar & Ramamurthy, 1995; Umble, Haft, & Umble, 2003). Cho (2006) concluded that firms having fewer obstacles to the adoption of a technology will be more likely to adopt the IT. Other empirical studies found that obstacles are a significant negative factor to e-business adoption and usage (Zhu, Kraemer, et al., 2006), e-commerce migration (Hong & Zhu, 2006), and to ERP adoption (Pan & Jang, 2008). Accordingly, we hypothesize the following:

H5a: Higher level of perceived obstacles is a negative predictor for B2B e-commerce adoption.

H5b: Higher level of perceived obstacles is a negative predictor for B2B e-commerce routinization.

Environment Context

Competitive pressure is a recognizable driving force for new technology usage; it tends to stimulate companies to seek competitive edge by introducing innovations (Gatignon & Robertson, 1989). Several studies have identified competitive pressure as a powerful determinant of degree of computerization (Dasgupta, Agarwal, Ioannidis, & Gopalakrishnan, 1999); adoption and routinization of interorganizational systems (Grover, 1993); EDI adoption (Iacovou et al., 1995), or EDI routinization (Ramamurthy, Premkumar, & Crum, 1999); green information technology initiation (Bose & Luo, 2011); e-commerce adoption (Dholakia & Kshetri, 2004; Huy, Rowe, Truex, & Huynh, 2012) or e-commerce routinization (Gibbs & Kraemer, 2004); e-procurement systems (Soares-Aguiar & Palma-Dos-Reis, 2008); and e-business adoption (Zhu et al., 2003) or e-business routinization (Lin & Lin, 2008; Zhu, Dong, et al., 2006; Zhu & Kraemer, 2005). Furthermore, B2B facilitates inter-firm collaboration to improve transactional efficiencies, expand existing channels, and maximize advantages from new opportunities. Firms that are first-movers in deploying B2B have tended to derive the greatest advantages. Hence, highly competitive pressures promote the implementation and operation of most successful B2B adoption and routinization. Therefore, we hypothesize that:

H6a: Higher level of competitive pressure is a positive predictor for B2B e-commerce adoption.

H6b: Higher level of competitive pressure is a positive predictor for B2B e-commerce routinization.

Trading partner collaboration is an important factor because the value of B2B e-commerce can be maximized only when many trading partners are using B2B e-commerce (Iacovou et al., 1995). As suggested by empirical evidence, the success of B2B e-commerce depends on trading partner readiness to use the internet jointly to perform value chain activities (Barua et al., 2004). In a trading community with greater partner readiness, individual adopters reveal higher levels of e-business usage due to network effects (Shapiro & Varian, 1999). Some empirical research suggests that trading partner is an important determinant for EDI, e-procurement, and e-business adoption and routinization (Iacovou et al., 1995; Lin & Lin, 2008; Soares-Aguiar & Palma-Dos-Reis, 2008; Zhu, Dong, et al., 2006; Zhu et al., 2003). Thus, we expect that:

H7a: Higher level of trading partner collaboration is a positive predictor for B2B e-commerce adoption.

H7b: Higher level of trading partner collaboration is a positive predictor for B2B e-commerce routinization.

Control Variables

In addition to the above mentioned factors, we included control variables to account for the variation of B2B e-commerce adoption and routinization that is caused by other factors. Specifically, we controlled the effect of industries and countries. Following the standard practice in IS research, dummy variables are included in the regression analyses (Bresnahan et al., 2002; Ciganek, Haseman, & Ramamurthy, 2014; Ruivo, Oliveira, Johansson, & Neto, 2013; Ruivo, Oliveira, & Neto, 2014; Soares-Aguiar & Palma-Dos-Reis, 2008; Zhu, Dong, et al., 2006; Zhu et al., 2003).

METHODS AND DATA ANALYSIS

Our data source is e-Business W@tch, which collects data across European firms. Pilot interviews were conducted with 23 companies in Germany in order to test the questionnaire (structure and comprehensibility of questions). A random sample of firms that used computers was drawn from the respective sector populations in each of the countries. The objective was to fulfill minimum strata with respect to company size class per country sector cell. Strata were to include a 10% share of large companies (250+ employees), 30% of medium sized enterprises (50-249 employees), 25% of small enterprises (10-49 employees), and up to 35% of micro-enterprises (fewer than 10 employees). We studied EU27 members (excluding Bulgaria and Malta) in eight sectors (food and beverages, footwear, pulp and paper, ICT manufacturing, consumer electronics, construction, tourism and telecommunications). Our data include 7,172 telephone interviews, which were conducted with decision-makers in firms using computer-aided telephone interview (CATI) technology. These data was collected by local institutes (one in each country). The response rates varied from country to country, ranging from 7.1% to 32.0%. About 80 percent (78.7%) of the data were collected from owners, managing directors, heads of IT, and other senior members of IT, confirming the high quality of the data source (Appendix A).

Validity and Reliability

As a first step we performed a factor analysis (FA) with varimax rotation (see Table 1, where we presented the questions used in interviews for FA) of multi-item indicators to reduce the number of variables of the survey and to evaluate the validity. Four factors presented eigenvalues greater than one. The first four factors explain 69.2% of variance contained in the data. Kaiser-Meyer-Olkin (KMO) measures the adequacy of sample; general KMO is 0.96 (KMO ≥ 0.90 is excellent (Sharma, 1996)), which reveals that the matrix of correlation is adequate for FA. The KMO for individual variables is also adequate. All the factors have a loading greater than 0.50 (except item TI4). This indicates that our analysis employs a well-explained factor structure. The four factors found are: obstacles, technology readiness, trading partner collaboration, and technology integration. The factors obtained are in accordance with the literature review.

Reliability measures the stability of the scale based on an assessment of the internal consistency of the items measuring the construct. It is assessed by calculating the composite reliability for each composite independent variable. Most of the constructs have a composite reliability over the cutoff of 0.70, as suggested by Nunnally (1978). Obstacles, technology readiness, and trading partner collaboration have a Cronbach's alpha value of 0.98, 0.77, and 0.81 respectively. The last factor - technology integration, comprises four items and has a Cronbach's alpha value of 0.58, which may be adequate for exploratory research, which is in the early stages of basic research. Nunnally

(1978) suggests reliabilities of 0.50 to 0.60 to suffice. We decided to retain this factor as it relates to the important issue of technology integration in B2B e-commerce adoption and routinization. Thus, constructs developed by this measurement model could be used to test the conceptual model and the associated hypotheses.

Cluster Analysis of Countries

To understand the pattern of ICT adoption and routinization across the EU27 members (excluding Malta and Bulgaria), we used data from the EU information society statistics (ISS) firm survey, provided by Eurostat. We measured the ICT readiness index using two score variables related to ICT adoption and routinization (Castaings & Tarantola, 2008) for each country. Cluster analysis was used to identify how many groups of countries exist with similar ICT patterns. We began by performing a hierarchical cluster analysis, which suggests an optimal number of clusters equal to three (see Appendix B). The results were validated by a non-hierarchical method (k-means). According to Sharma (1996) this is the best solution to obtain clusters. We also performed a Kruskal-Wallis test to verify if ICT adoption and routinization presented statistically significantly different values in each cluster. The results of the Kruskal-Wallis test show that there are significant statistical differences in the levels of ICT adoption and routinization for each cluster at a significant level of 1% (see Appendix C). The three clusters of countries are depicted in Figure 2. The first group can be identified as the "high ICT readiness group". It contains eleven countries coming from the EU15: Denmark (DNK), Netherlands (NLD), Ireland (IRL), Germany (DEU), Finland (FIN), Sweden (SWE), Austria (AUT), France (FRA), Belgium (BEL), United Kingdom (GBR), and Luxemburg (LUX). It excludes the southern European countries. The second, labeled "medium ICT readiness group", contains eleven countries: Greece (GRC), Italy (ITA), Estonia

Table 1. Factor and validity analysis and description of multi-item indicators used in FA

Items Measure	F1	F2	F3	F4
Obstacles				
Important obstacles for not practicing e-business in your company? (0-not at all; 1-not important; 2-important)				
EO1 - My company is too small to benefit from any e-business activities	0.93			
EO2 - E-business technologies are too expensive to implement	0.95			
EO3 - The technology is too complicated	0.95			
EO4 - Our systems are not compatible with those of suppliers or customers	0.95			
EO5 - We are concerned about potential security risks and privacy issues	0.95			
EO6 - We think that there are important unsolved legal issues involved	0.96			
EO7 - It is difficult to find reliable IT suppliers	0.96			
Technology Readiness				
TR1 - Sum of the following network applications: a Local Area Network (LAN); Wireless LAN; Voice-over-IP; Fixed line connections; Wireless-Local-Area-Networks or W-LANs, Mobile communication networks; Virtual Private Network (VPN)		0.75		
TR2 - Sum of the following questions ICT skills: your company currently employs ICT practitioners; your company regularly sends employees to ICT training programs		0.70		
TR3 - Sum of the following security applications: secure server technology, for example SSL, TLS or a comparable technical standard; digital signature or public key infrastructure; a firewall		0.65		
TR4 - Sum of the following technologies: Internet; intranet; web site;		0.62		
TR6 - Percentage of employees that have access to the internet		0.53		
Trading Partner Collaboration				
Does your company use online applications other than e-mail, to support any of the following business functions (0- no, and not use internet; 1-no; 2-yes)?				
TPC1 To collaborate with business partners to forecast product or service demand			0.88	
TPC2 To collaborate with business partners in the design of new products or services			0.89	
Technology Integration				
Does your company use any of the following systems or applications for managing information in the company (0- do not know what this is; 1-no; 2-yes)?				
TI1 - an EDM system, that is, an Enterprise Document Management System				0.67
TI2 - a SCM system, that is, a Supply Chain Management System				0.67
TI3 - an ERP system, that is, Enterprise Resource Planning System				0.66
TI4 - Knowledge Management software				0.46
Eigenvalue	6.49	2.37	1.86	1.74
Percentage of variance explained	36.04	13.18	10.32	9.68
Note: variables are marked according to factor loading; loadings greater than 0.40 are reported.				

(EST), Czech Republic (CZE), Spain (ESP), Slovakia (SVK), Slovenia (SVN), Lithuania (LTU), Cyprus (CYP), Portugal (PRT), and Poland (POL). It includes Southern European countries and some of the recent EU-27 members. Finally, the "low ICT readiness group" includes Latvia (LVA), Hungary (HUN), and Romania (ROM), all of which are relatively recent EU27 members. These results are to some extent quite similar to those obtained by Cruz-Jesus *et al.* (2012) in their

Figure 2. Pattern of ICT adoption and routinization by EU-27 countries (excluding Bulgaria and Malta)

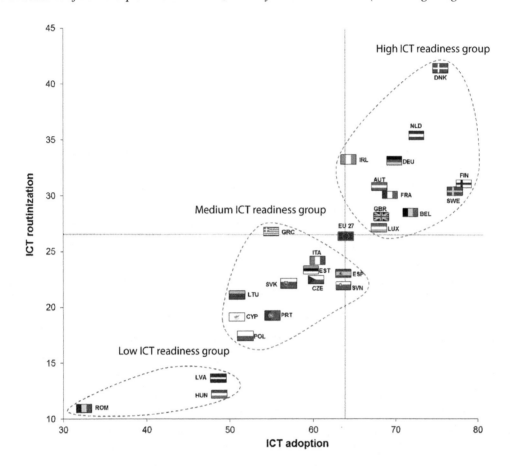

study about the digital divide across the EU-27. Although the composition of the countries is not entirely equal – they extracted five clusters while we retained three – in both studies the northern European countries tend to present higher levels of ICT adoption, while southern countries present generally lower adoption levels.

B2B E-commerce Adoption and Routinization

The dependent variables are B2B e-commerce adoption and routinization. B2B e-commerce adoption is a binary variable, which is equal to 1 if firms adopt B2B e-commerce, otherwise and zero. Since the dependent variable is binary (to adopt or not), a logistic regression is developed.

Similar regressions have been used in the IS literature to study open system adoption (Chau & Tam, 1997), EDI adoption (Kuan & Chau, 2001), IT outsourcing (Bajwa et al., 2004), e-business adoption (Oliveira & Martins, 2010; Pan & Jang, 2008; Zhu et al., 2003), and e-commerce adoption (Huy et al., 2012).

For firms that adopt B2B e-commerce (4,355 firms), we analyzed B2B e-commerce routinization, which is an ordered variable that ranges between 0 to 4 according to the percentage of online order volume as of total order volume (Y_2 = 0 – less than 5% (1,259 firms); Y_2 = 1 – 5 up to 10% (822 firms); Y_2 = 2 – 11 up to 25% (688 firms); Y_2 = 3 – 26 up to 50% (603 firms); Y_2 = 4 – more than 50% (983 firms)). An ordered logistic regression is developed (we have 115 missing observations for B2B e-commerce routinization). This is because the dependent variable is also ordered. The ordered logistic regression is not common in IS research, but it is adequate for an ordered dependent variable.

The independent variables are in accordance with our research model. As we have seen, the obstacles, technology readiness, trading partner collaboration, and technology integration were obtained by factor analysis. All the other variables were obtained directly by the questionnaire, i.e., firm size is the logarithmic number of employees, education level is the percentage share of employees with a college or university degree in the firm, and competitive pressure is equal to 1 if firms think that ICT has an influence on competition in their sector. For control we used 24 dummies for 25 countries and 7 dummies for 8 industries.

Goodness-of-fit for both regressions were analyzed. For B2B e-commerce adoption we computed likelihood ratio (LR) test, which is statistically significant (p-value<0.001 for full sample and for each group of countries); Hosmer-Lemeshow (1980) test, which is not rejected (p-values are 0.23, 0.30, 0.16, and 0.34, respectively for full sample, high, medium, and low ICT readiness group); AUC, which is equal to 0.80, 0.77, 0.79, and 0.78 respectively for B2B e-commerce adoption in full sample, high, medium, and low ICT readiness groups of countries. The prediction accuracy, which is 74.3%, 76.6%, 72.2%, and 72.9% respectively; and the adoption by random choices:

$$\left(\left[\frac{adopters}{adopters + non\text{-}adopters} \right]^2 + \left[\frac{non\text{-}adopters}{adopters + non\text{-}adopters} \right]^2 \right)$$

would result in 53.0%, 60.8%, 50.1% and 50.2% respectively for B2B e-commerce in full sample and each group, the values of which are much

lower than in the case of our regressions. Thus, we were able to conclude that the logistic regression has much higher discriminating power than the random choice. We also analyzed goodness-of-fit for B2B e-commerce routinization. The LR test is statistically significant (p-value<0.001 for the full sample and for each group of countries). The statistical procedures reveal a substantive model fit, a satisfactory discriminating power, and there is evidence to accept an overall significance of the models.

As can be seen in Table 2, in the full sample for B2B e-commerce adoption and routinization, the technology readiness, technology integration, education level, competitive pressure, and trading partner collaboration confirm their role as significant adoption and routinization facilitators; whereas the significantly negative coefficients show that firm size and obstacles inhibit B2B adoption and routinization. All of the stipulated hypotheses are supported, which reveals that the research model is adequate.

For B2B e-commerce adoption in each group of countries within the technology context, technology readiness is significant for all groups ($p<0.01$ in all), and technology integration is significant only for the high ICT readiness group (p<0.05). Within the organization context, firm size is the only significant inhibitor in the high ICT readiness group ($p<0.01$), education level is not statistically significant, and obstacles is a significant inhibitor for all groups ($p<0.01$ in all). Within the environment context, competitive pressure is significant for the high and medium ICT readiness groups ($p<0.05$ in both), and trading partner collaboration is significant for the three groups ($p<0.01$ in all). To summarize, in the high ICT readiness group, only H4a (education level) is not supported; in the medium ICT readiness group H2a (technology integration), H3a (firm size), and H4a (education level) are not supported; and in the low ICT readiness group H2a (technology integration), H3a (firm size), H4a (education level), and H6a (competitive pressure) are not supported.

Table 2. Results of the logistic regression for B2B e-commerce adoption and ordered logistic regression for B2B routinization for full sample and in each group of countries

Independent variables	B2B e-Commerce Adoption (Logistic Regression)				B2B e-commerce Routinization (Ordered Logistic Regression)			
	Full	Group of ICT Readiness			Full	Group of ICT Readiness		
		High	Medium	Low		High	Medium	Low
Technology readiness	0.537***	0.591***	0.483***	0.561***	0.450***	0.461***	0.434***	0.450***
Technology integration	0.095***	0.134**	0.062	0.125	0.101***	0.050	0.130**	0.275***
Firm size	-0.054**	-0.092***	-0.019	-0.063	-0.200***	-0.201***	-0.177***	-0.230***
Education level	0.002*	0.002	0.002	0.001	0.003***	0.002	0.005**	0.009**
Obstacles	-0.603***	-0.628***	-0.576***	-0.652***	0.415***	-0.471***	-0.342***	-0.425***
Competitive pressure	0.248***	0.236**	0.271**	0.180	0.279***	0.327***	0.291**	-0.297
Trading partner collaboration	0.541***	0.520***	0.515***	0.648***	0.279***	0.275***	0.272***	0.322***
Country dummies	Included	Included	Included	Included	Included	Included	Included	Included
Industry dummies	Included	Included	Included	Included	Included	Included	Included	Included
Sample size	7,172	3,404	3,016	752	4,355	2,430	1,532	393

Note: *p-value<0.10; **p-value<0.05; ***p-value<0.01.

For B2B e-commerce routinization in each group of countries, we found different relationships (as can be seen in Table 2). Within the technology context, technology readiness is significant for all groups (p<0.01 in all), and technology integration is significant for medium and low ICT readiness group (p<0.05 and p<0.01 respectively). Within the organization context, firm size and obstacles are a significant inhibitors for all groups (p<0.01 in all); firm size is a greater inhibitor for B2B e-commerce routinization than for B2B e-commerce adoption. Education level is significant in the medium and low ICT readiness groups (p<0.05 in both). Within the organization context, competitive pressure is significant for high and medium ICT readiness groups (p<0.01 and p<0.05 respectively), trading partner collaboration is significant for the three groups (p<0.01 in all). In summary, we found that only H2b (technology integration) and H4b (education level) are not supported in the high ICT readiness group; all hypotheses are supported in medium ICT readiness group; and

only H6b (competitive pressure) is not supported in the low ICT readiness group.

There are variables that hold diverse significance depending on B2B e-commerce adoption or routinization. On one hand, larger firm size is an inhibitor for B2B e-commerce routinization, while on the other, higher education level is a facilitator for B2B e-commerce routinization. This reveals that when firms are in a more advanced level of B2B, the firms with higher education levels of employees and smaller size are facilitators. There is one variable from each context that is statistically significant in B2B e-commerce adoption and routinization for all groups of countries. This is the technology readiness in the technology context, obstacles in the organizational context, and the trading partner collaboration in the environment context. This reveals that the main drivers of B2B e-commerce adoption and routinization are technology readiness, obstacles, and trading partner collaboration. Moreover, all three contexts are relevant for B2B e-commerce adoption and routinization.

DISCUSSION

Implications for B2B Strategic Choices in Europe

To increase B2B e-commerce adoption and routinization in Europe, our study reveals that it is important to enhance the following variables: technology readiness, technology integration, education level, competitive pressure, and trading partner collaboration. It is also important to reduce the obstacles of B2B e-commerce. Our study also reveals that smaller firms have advantage in B2B e-commerce adoption and routinization when compared to larger firms, provided the other variables analyzed in our model are on the same level. This reveals a business opportunity for small firms in the EU27 context for adoption and routinization of B2B e-commerce. This is extremely important since there are 20 million small and medium sized enterprises (SMEs) in the EU27, representing 99% of businesses (Audretsch, Horst, Kwaak, & Thurik, 2009). This fact makes them a key driver for economic growth, innovation, employment and social integration (European-Commission, 2010).

Defining Strategic Option Within and Amongst Clusters

Based on the cluster analysis in the EU27, there are three distinct groups that present specific patterns of ICT readiness. For this reason, different policies should be developed for each ICT readiness group.

In the technology context, technology integration is important only for B2B e-commerce routinization in low and medium ICT readiness groups. This means that in these contexts when firms wish to achieve a higher level of B2B e-commerce (routinization), the use of technology integration is necessary.

In the organizational context, education level of employees is not important to explain B2B e-commerce adoption in ICT readiness group and is important for B2B e-commerce routinization in the medium and low ICT readiness group. This means that the higher education level of employees is needed for firms that wish to use B2B e-commerce intensively; this is particularly relevant in the medium and low ICT readiness groups where the population has a lower education level when compared to the high ICT readiness group (especially within Nordic countries), where the level of education of the population is the highest (Eurostat, 2009).

In the context of the environment, competitive pressure is not important for B2B e-commerce adoption and routinization in the low ICT readiness group. In our opinion, when the level of B2B e-commerce increases in this group, perhaps the competitive pressure will become more important for this group. In Figure 3, we present the main drivers of B2B e-commerce, independently of the context and the variables that need to be enhanced or reduced to help it move to a higher level of B2B e-commerce.

For B2B e-commerce adoption, firm size (organizational context) is a statistically significant inhibitor only for the full sample and high ICT readiness group. Firm size is a strong inhibitor in all ICT readiness groups for e-business usage. This means that B2B e-commerce is not a phenomenon dominated by large firms, especially in the high ICT readiness group and for B2B e-commerce routinization. Small firms have the advantage of close collaboration, coordination and less bureaucracy. In addition, for the high ICT readiness group, there commonly exist more available technology and services providers, which help to lower the adoption risk. This is the reason why small firms probably have advantages in adopting B2B e-commerce. On the contrary, for eight European countries, Zhu et al. (2003) found that

Figure 3. Factors that help to move for a higher ICT readiness group

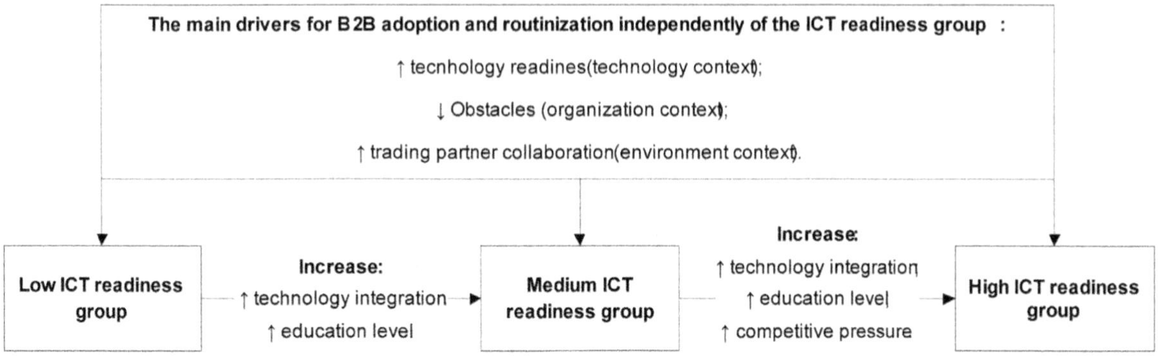

---

in 1999, larger firm size was a facilitator of e-business adoption. This difference can be due to the decreasing costs of IT over time. Moreover, when firms adopt B2B e-commerce, small firm size is a facilitator for B2B e-commerce routinization in all ICT readiness groups.

Social Responsibility with Respect to B2B Variations

The international digital divide is largely the consequence of the social and economic inequalities between countries. Countries with lower income and lower educational attainment tend to reveal lower rates of ICT access and usage when compared with higher income and better education attainment countries (Cuervo & Menendez, 2006; Kiiski & Pohjola, 2002; Pohjola, 2003). Special attention must be paid to countries in the low ICT readiness group to avoid a more pronounced digital divide across EU27 members. Our study suggests that it is necessary to increase the education level of the population and consequently the employees' readiness for IT adoption. It is also essential to promote the increased level of technology integration used by firms. For the medium ICT readiness group, it is also important to increase the level of competitive pressure.

Contributions

B2B e-commerce has become an increasingly important topic for both researchers and practitioners (Teo & Ranganathan, 2004). To promote B2B adoption and routinization it is critical to clarify the factors that explain these and conduct a deep analysis to understand if different levels of adoption and routinization have the same drivers for B2B e-commerce. We developed a model based on Tornatzky and Fleischer (1990) to study the factors that explain B2B e-commerce adoption and routinization. Based on a large sample of EU27 members, we tested our conceptual model and developed a measurement model satisfying various reliability and validity conditions. In general, our hypotheses are confirmed. Our research model is seemingly appropriate. As the sample was not limited to data from a single country, this helps to strengthen the generalization of the model and findings. The major contributions of this study are the following:

- First, we demonstrated and showed that our model is useful for identifying facilitators and inhibitors of B2B adoption and routinization.
- Second, we identified seven drivers of B2B e-commerce adoption and routinization, five facilitators and two inhibitors.

- Third, based on Eurostat country data, we found three different groups of ICT readiness.
- Finally, technology readiness in the technology context, obstacles in the organization context, and trading partner collaboration in the environment context are important drivers for B2B e-commerce adoption and routinization in all ICT readiness groups.

Our findings reveal that all three proposed dimensions are fundamental and intricate.

Limitations and Future Research

As in most empirical studies, our work has some limitations. First, the cross-sectional nature of this study does not allow us to predict how these relationships will change over time. To overcome this limitation, future research should involve panel data. Second, we did not include the government regulation variables in our model because data were not available for these variables. Further research should include these variables, if possible.

While explicitly not explored in this research there is a tendency in IS research (Gibbs & Kraemer, 2004; Hsu et al., 2006; Zhu, Dong, et al., 2006; Zhu & Kraemer, 2005; Zhu, Kraemer, et al., 2006) to aggregate B2B and B2C e-commerce together. Clearly further research is needed to understand the different drivers between B2B and B2C e-commerce. Future research can also seek additional information to evaluate the impact of B2B adoption and routinization on a firm's turnover, market share, and productivity. Finally, confirmatory studies of our research model, need to be undertaken, in different contexts. Other studies and samples should be used for the validation of our model. For example: analyzing the same industry in different countries, or industries comparison.

CONCLUSION

In this paper we have analyzed B2B e-commerce adoption and routinization at firm level in the EU27. We concluded that different countries belonging to the EU27 do not have the same level of ICT adoption and diffusion. In fact, there are three different levels or clusters, all with their own set of challenges with respect to B2B e-commerce adoption and routinization. Identification and appreciation of the different clusters helps to fine tune policy initiatives, at both the macro and micro level. While such a call may seem obvious, it has not been adequately addressed in the literature. More often than not, the focus has been on defining grand strategic choices for countries, without understanding particular nuances or differences. This is particularly true of policy initiatives that get formulated at a federal level (such as the European Union) with regions having to implement or adopt them. Typically a lack of such appreciation can lead to regional imbalances in technology adoption, which risks failure or complete abandonment of the initiative.

REFERENCES

Abu-Musa, A. A. (2004). Auditing e-business: New challenges for external auditors. *Journal of American Academy of Business*, 4(1), 28–41.

Al-Qirim, N. (2007). The adoption of eCommerce communications and applications technologies in small businesses in New Zealand. *Electronic Commerce Research and Applications*, 6(4), 462–473. doi:10.1016/j.elerap.2007.02.012

Albrecht, C. C., Dean, D. L., & Hansen, J. V. (2005). Marketplace and technology standards for B2B e-commerce: Progress, challenges, and the state of the art. *Information & Management*, 42(6), 865–875. doi:10.1016/j.im.2004.09.003

Amit, R., & Zott, C. (2001). Value creation in e-business. *Strategic Management Journal*, *22*(6-7), 493–520. doi:10.1002/smj.187

Armstrong, C. P., & Sambamurthy, V. (1999). Information technology assimilation in firms: The influence of senior leadership and IT infrastructures. *Information Systems Research*, *10*(4), 304–327. doi:10.1287/isre.10.4.304

Audretsch, D., Horst, R. d., Kwaak, T., & Thurik, R. (2009). First Section of the Annual Report on EU Small and Medium-sized Enterprises, EIM Business & Policy Research Brussels

Bajwa, D. S., Garcia, J. E., & Mooney, T. (2004). An integrative framework for the assimilation of enterprise resource planning systems: Phases, antecedents, and outcomes. *Journal of Computer Information Systems*, *44*(3), 81–90.

Barua, A., Konana, P., Whinston, A. B., & Yin, F. (2004). Assessing Internet enabled business value: An exploratory investigation. *Management Information Systems Quarterly*, *28*(4), 585–620.

Battisti, G., Hollenstein, H., Stoneman, P., & Woerter, M. (2007). Inter and Intra firm diffusion of ICT in the United Kingdom (UK) and Switzerland (CH): An internationally comparative study based on firm-level data. *Economics of Innovation and New Technology*, *16*(8), 669–687. doi:10.1080/10438590600984026

Bose, R., & Luo, X. (2011). Integrative framework for assessing firms' potential to undertake Green IT initiatives via virtualization - A theoretical perspective. *The Journal of Strategic Information Systems*, *20*(1), 38–54. doi:10.1016/j.jsis.2011.01.003

Bresnahan, T. F., Brynjolfsson, E., & Hitt, L. M. (2002). Information technology, workplace organization, and the demand for skilled labor: Firm-level evidence. *The Quarterly Journal of Economics*, *117*(1), 339–376. doi:10.1162/003355302753399526

Brynjolfsson, E., & Hitt, L. M. (2000). Beyond computation: Information technology, organizational transformation and business performance. *The Journal of Economic Perspectives*, *14*(4), 23–48. doi:10.1257/jep.14.4.23

Castaings, W., & Tarantola, S. (2008). The 2007 European e-Business Readiness Index. *JRC Scientific and Technical Reports*, 1-35.

Chau, P. Y. K., & Tam, K. Y. (1997). Factors affecting the adoption of open systems: An exploratory study. *Management Information Systems Quarterly*, *21*(1), 1–24. doi:10.2307/249740

Cho, V. (2006). Factors in the adoption of third-party B2B portals in the textile industry. *Journal of Computer Information Systems*, *46*(3), 18–31.

Ciganek, A. P., Haseman, W., & Ramamurthy, K. (2014). Time to decision: The drivers of innovation adoption decisions. *Enterp. Inf. Syst.*, *8*(2), 279–308. doi:10.1080/17517575.2012.690453

Cohen, W. M., & Levinthal, D. H. (1989). Innovation and learning: The two faces of R&D. *The Economic Journal*, *99*(397), 569–596. doi:10.2307/2233763

Cruz-Jesus, F., Oliveira, T., & Bacao, F. (2012). Digital divide across the European Union. *Information & Management*, *49*(6), 278–291. doi:10.1016/j.im.2012.09.003

Cuervo, M. R. V., & Menendez, A. J. L. (2006). A multivariate framework for the analysis of the digital divide: Evidence for the European Union-15. *Information & Management*, *43*(6), 756–766. doi:10.1016/j.im.2006.05.001

Damanpour, F. (1992). Organization Studies. *Organizational Size and Innovation*, *13*, 375–402.

Dasgupta, S., Agarwal, D., Ioannidis, A., & Gopalakrishnan, S. (1999). Determinants of information technology adoption: An extension of existing models to firms in a developing country. *Journal of Global Information Management*, *7*(3), 30–53. doi:10.4018/jgim.1999070103

Dewett, T., & Jones, G. R. (2001). The role of information technology in the organization: A review, model, and assessment. *Journal of Management, 27*(3), 313–346. doi:10.1016/S0149-2063(01)00094-0

Dholakia, R. R., & Kshetri, N. (2004). Factors impacting the adoption of the Internet among SMEs. *Small Bus. Econ. Group, 23*(4), 311–322. doi:10.1023/B:SBEJ.0000032036.90353.1f

Ettlie, J. E., & Rubenstein, A. H. (1987). Firm size and product innovation. *Journal of Product Innovation Management, 4*(2), 89–108. doi:10.1016/0737-6782(87)90055-5

European-Commission. (2005). *Information Society Benchmarking Report*. Retrieved 29 Jan, 2009, from http://ec.europa.eu/information_society/eeurope/i2010/docs/benchmarking/051222%20Final%20Benchmarking%20Report.pdf

European-Commission. (2010). *Small and medium-sized enterprises (SMEs)*. Retrieved 19/02/2010, from http://ec.europa.eu/enterprise/policies/sme/index_en.htm

European Commission. (2010). *Europe 2020 – A Strategy for Smart*. Brussels: Sustainable and Inclusive Growth.

Eurostat. (2009). Europe in figures. In S. Books (Ed.), *Eurostat yearbook 2009*. Luxembourg: European Commission.

Gatignon, H., & Robertson, T. S. (1989). Technology diffusion: An empirical test of competitive effects. *Journal of Marketing, 53*(1), 35–49. doi:10.2307/1251523

Gibbs, L. J., & Kraemer, K. L. (2004). A cross-country investigation of the determinants of scope of e-commerce use: An institutional approach. *Electronic Markets, 14*(2), 124–137. doi:10.1080/10196780410001675077

Giunta, A., & Trivieri, F. (2007). Understanding the determinants of information technology adoption: Evidence from Italian manufacturing firms. *Applied Economics, 39*(10-12), 1325–1334. doi:10.1080/00036840600567678

Grover, V. (1993). An empirically derived model for the adoption of customer-based interorganizational systems. *Decision Sciences, 24*(3), 603–640. doi:10.1111/j.1540-5915.1993.tb01295.x

Harris, S. E., & Katz, J. L. (1991). Firm size and the information technology investment intensity of life insurers. *Management Information Systems Quarterly, 15*(3), 333–352. doi:10.2307/249645

Hong, W. Y., & Zhu, K. (2006). Migrating to internet-based e-commerce: Factors affecting e-commerce adoption and migration at the firm level. *Information & Management, 43*(2), 204–221. doi:10.1016/j.im.2005.06.003

Hosmer, D. W., & Lemeshow, S. (1980). A goodness-of-fit test for the multiple logistic regression model. *Communications in Statistics, A10*(10), 1043–1069. doi:10.1080/03610928008827941

Hsieh, J. P.-A., Rai, A., & Keil, M. (2008). Understanding digital inequality: Comparing continued use behavioral models of the socio-economically advantaged and disadvantaged. *Management Information Systems Quarterly*, 97–126.

Hsu, P. F., Kraemer, K. L., & Dunkle, D. (2006). Determinants of e-business use in US firms. *International Journal of Electronic Commerce, 10*(4), 9–45. doi:10.2753/JEC1086-4415100401

Hung, W. H., Tsai, C. A., Hung, S. Y., McQueen, R. J., & Jou, J. J. (2011). Evaluating Web Site Support Capabilities in Sell-Side B2B Transaction Processes: A Longitudinal Study of Two Industries in New Zealand and Taiwan. *Journal of Global Information Management, 19*(1), 51–79. doi:10.4018/jgim.2011010103

Huy, V. L., Rowe, F., Truex, D., & Huynh, M. Q. (2012). An Empirical Study of Determinants of E-Commerce Adoption in SMEs in Vietnam: An Economy in Transition. *Journal of Global Information Management*, *20*(3), 23–54. doi:10.4018/jgim.2012070102

Hwang, H. G., Ku, C. Y., Yen, D. C., & Cheng, C. C. (2004). Critical factors influencing the adoption of data warehouse technology: A study of the banking industry in Taiwan. *Decision Support Systems*, *37*(1), 1–21. doi:10.1016/S0167-9236(02)00191-4

Iacovou, C. L., Benbasat, I., & Dexter, A. S. (1995). Electronic data interchange and small organizations: Adoption and impact of technology. *Management Information Systems Quarterly*, *19*(4), 465–485. doi:10.2307/249629

Katz, J., & Aspden, P. (1997). Motivations for and barriers to Internet usage: Results of a national public opinion survey. *Internet Research*, *7*(3), 170–188. doi:10.1108/10662249710171814

Kiiski, S., & Pohjola, M. (2002). Cross-country diffusion of the Internet. *Information Economics and Policy*, *14*(2), 297–310. doi:10.1016/S0167-6245(01)00071-3

Kuan, K. K. Y., & Chau, P. Y. K. (2001). A perception-based model for EDI adoption in small businesses using a technology-organization-environment framework. *Information & Management*, *38*(8), 507–521. doi:10.1016/S0378-7206(01)00073-8

Kwon, T. H., & Zmud, R. W. (1987). In I. J. Wiley (Ed.), *Unifying the fragmented models of information systems implementation. In critical issues in Information Systems Research (Boland RJ and Hirschheim RA* (pp. 227–251). New York.

Lin, H. F., & Lin, S. M. (2008). Determinants of e-business diffusion: A test of the technology diffusion perspective. *Technovation*, *28*(3), 135–145. doi:10.1016/j.technovation.2007.10.003

Low, C., Chen, Y., & Wu, M. (2011). Understanding the determinants of cloud computing adoption. *Industrial Management & Data Systems*, *111*(7), 1006–1023. doi:10.1108/02635571111161262

Martins, M. F. O., & Oliveira, T. (2008). Determinants of information technology diffusion: A study at the firm level for Portugal. *The Electronic Journal Information Systems Evaluation*, *11*(1), 27–34.

Mata, F., Fuerst, W., & Barney, J. (1995). Information technology and sustained competitive advantage: A resource-based analysis. *Management Information Systems Quarterly*, *19*(4), 487–505. doi:10.2307/249630

Mirchandani, D. A., & Motwani, J. (2001). Understanding small business electronic commerce adoption: An empirical analysis. *Journal of Computer Information Systems*, *41*(3), 70–73.

Nguyen, H.-O. (2013). Critical factors in e-business adoption: Evidence from Australian transport and logistics companies. *International Journal of Production Economics*, *146*(1), 300–312. doi:10.1016/j.ijpe.2013.07.014

Nunnally, J. C. (1978). *Psychometric theory*. New York: McGraw-Hill.

Oliveira, T., & Martins, M. F. (2010). Understanding e-business adoption across industries in European countries. *Industrial Management & Data Systems*, *110*(8-9), 1337–1354. doi:10.1108/02635571011087428

Oliveira, T., Thomas, M., & Espadanal, M. (2014). Assessing the determinants of cloud computing adoption: An analysis of the manufacturing and services sectors. *Information & Management*, *51*(5), 497–510. doi:10.1016/j.im.2014.03.006

Pan, M. J., & Jang, W. Y. (2008). Determinants of the adoption of enterprise resource planning within the technology-organization-environment framework: Taiwan's communications. *Journal of Computer Information Systems*, *48*(3), 94–102.

Pohjola, M. (2003). *The Adoption and Diffusion of Information and Communication Technology across Countries: Patterns and Determinants* (Vol. 4). New York: Elsevier Academic Press.

Premkumar, G. (2003). A meta-analysis of research on information technology implementation in small business. *Journal of Organizational Computing and Electronic Commerce, 13*(2), 91–121. doi:10.1207/S15327744JOCE1302_2

Premkumar, G., & Ramamurthy, K. (1995). The role of interorganizational and organizational factors on the decision mode for adoption of interorganizational systems. *Decision Sciences, 26*(3), 303–336. doi:10.1111/j.1540-5915.1995.tb01431.x

Premkumar, G., Ramamurthy, K., & Crum, M. (1997). Determinants of EDI adoption in the transportation industry. *European Journal of Information Systems, 6*(2), 107–121. doi:10.1057/palgrave.ejis.3000260

Ramamurthy, K., Premkumar, G., & Crum, M. R. (1999). Organizational and interorganizational determinants of EDI diffusion and organizational performance: A causal model. *Journal of Organizational Computing and Electronic Commerce, 9*(4), 253–285. doi:10.1207/S153277440904_2

Rogers, E. M. (2005). *Diffusion of Innovations* (5th ed.). New York: Free Press.

Ruivo, P., Oliveira, T., Johansson, B., & Neto, M. (2013). Differential effects on ERP post-adoption stages across Scandinavian and Iberian SMEs. *Journal of Global Information Management, 21*(3), 1–20. doi:10.4018/jgim.2013070101

Ruivo, P., Oliveira, T., & Neto, M. (2014). Examine ERP post-implementation stages of use and value: Empirical evidence from Portuguese SMEs. *International Journal of Accounting Information Systems, 15*(2), 166–184. doi:10.1016/j.accinf.2014.01.002

Shapiro, C., & Varian, H. R. (1999). *Information rules: A strategic guide to the network economy.* Boston: Harvard Business School Press.

Sharma, S. (1996). *Applied multivariate techniques.* New York: John Wiley & Sons, Inc.

Sila, I. (2013). Factors affecting the adoption of B2B e-commerce technologies. *Electronic Commerce Research, 13*(2), 199–236. doi:10.1007/s10660-013-9110-7

Soares-Aguiar, A., & Palma-Dos-Reis, A. (2008). Why do firms adopt e-procurement systems? Using logistic regression to empirically test a conceptual model. *IEEE Transactions on Engineering Management, 55*(1), 120–133. doi:10.1109/TEM.2007.912806

Straub, D. W., & Watson, R. T. (2001). Research commentary: Transformational issues in researching IS and net-enabled organizations. *Information Systems Research, 12*(4), 337–345. doi:10.1287/isre.12.4.337.9706

Teo, T. S. H., & Ranganathan, C. (2004). Adopters and non-adopters of Business-to-Business electronic commerce in Singapore. *Information & Management, 42*(1), 89–102. doi:10.1016/j.im.2003.12.005

Thong, J. Y. L. (1999). An integrated model of information systems adoption in small businesses. *Journal of Management Information Systems, 15*(4), 187–214.

Tornatzky, L., & Fleischer, M. (1990). *The Processes of Technological Innovation.* Lexington, MA: Lexington Books.

Umble, E. J., Haft, R. R., & Umble, M. M. (2003). Enterprise resource planning: Implementation procedures and critical success factors. *European Journal of Operational Research, 146*(2), 241–257. doi:10.1016/S0377-2217(02)00547-7

Venkatesh, V., & Bala, H. (2012). Adoption and Impacts of Interorganizational Business Process Standards: Role of Partnering Synergy. *Information Systems Research*, *23*(4), 1131–1157. doi:10.1287/isre.1110.0404

Zhu, K. (2004). Information transparency of business-to-business electronic markets: A game-theoretic analysis. *Management Science*, *50*(5), 670–685. doi:10.1287/mnsc.1040.0226

Zhu, K., Dong, S. T., Xu, S. X., & Kraemer, K. L. (2006). Innovation diffusion in global contexts: Determinants of post-adoption digital transformation of European companies. *European Journal of Information Systems*, *15*(6), 601–616. doi:10.1057/palgrave.ejis.3000650

Zhu, K., Kraemer, K., & Xu, S. (2003). Electronic business adoption by European firms: A cross-country assessment of the facilitators and inhibitors. *European Journal of Information Systems*, *12*(4), 251–268. doi:10.1057/palgrave. ejis.3000475

Zhu, K., & Kraemer, K. L. (2002). e-Commerce metrics for net-enhanced organizations: Assessing the value of e-commerce to firm performance in the manufacturing sector. *Information Systems Research*, *13*(3), 275–295. doi:10.1287/ isre.13.3.275.82

Zhu, K., & Kraemer, K. L. (2005). Post-adoption variations in usage and value of e-business by organizations: Cross-country evidence from the retail industry. *Information Systems Research*, *16*(1), 61–84. doi:10.1287/isre.1050.0045

Zhu, K., Kraemer, K. L., & Xu, S. (2006). The process of innovation assimilation by firms in different countries: A technology diffusion perspective on e-business. *Management Science*, *52*(10), 1557–1576. doi:10.1287/mnsc.1050.0487

Zhu, K., Kraemer, K. L., Xu, S., & Dedrick, J. (2004). Information technology payoff in e-business environments: An international perspective on value creation of e-business in the financial services industry. *Journal of Management Information Systems*, *21*(1), 17–54.

This work was previously published in the Journal of Global Information Management (JGIM), 23(1); edited by Choon Ling Sia, pages 24-43, copyright year 2015 by IGI Publishing (an imprint of IGI Global).

APPENDIX

Table 3. Sample characteristics

Country	Obs.	(%)	Respondent's position	Obs.	(%)
Austria	272	3.79%	Owner/Proprietor	2,122	29.59%
Belgium	232	3.23%	Managing Director/Board Member	1,474	20.55%
Cyprus	102	1.42%	Head of IT/DP	1,396	19.46%
Czech Republic	412	5.74%	Other senior member of IT/DP Department	655	9.13%
Denmark	222	3.10%	Strategy development/organization	355	4.95%
Estonia	174	2.43%	Other	1,170	16.31%
Finland	395	5.51%	Total	7,172	100%
France	523	7.29%			
Germany	525	7.32%			
Greece	226	3.15%	**Industry**	**Obs.**	**(%)**
Hungary	384	5.35%	Food and beverages	904	12.60%
Ireland	225	3.14%	Footwear	489	6.82%
Italy	411	5.73%	Pulp and Paper	714	9.96%
Latvia	164	2.29%	ICT Manufacture	1,096	15.28%
Lithuania	215	3.00%	Consumer electronics	403	5.62%
Luxembourg	69	0.96%	Construction	1,236	17.23%
Netherlands	280	3.90%	Tourism	1,308	18.24%
Poland	355	4.95%	Telecommunications	1,022	14.25%
Portugal	235	3.28%	Total	7,172	100%
Romania	204	2.84%			
Slovakia	197	2.75%			
Slovenia	293	4.09%			
Spain	396	5.52%			
Sweden	237	3.30%			
UK	424	5.91%			
Total	7,172	100%			

Table 4. Descriptive statistics for the identified clusters

High ICT readiness group		Medium ICT readiness group		High ICT readiness group		Kruskal-Wallis
Average	St. Dev.	Average	St. Dev.	Average	St. Dev.	p-Value
71.21	4.34	57.26	4.51	42.17	8.62	0.0000475
31.66	4.06	21.86	2.58	12.32	1.35	0.0000477

Figure 4. Dendrogram of Ward's method

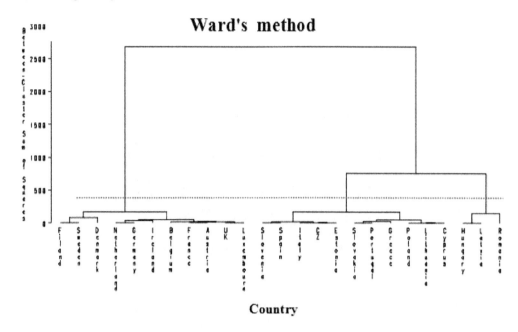

Chapter 68

The Impact of On-Line Consumer Reviews on Value Perception:
The Dual-Process Theory and Uncertainty Reduction

Hsin Hsin Chang
National Cheng Kung University, Taiwan

Po Wen Fang
National Cheng Kung University, Taiwan

Chien Hao Huang
National Cheng Kung University, Taiwan

ABSTRACT

This study combines the dual-process theory (DPT) and the uncertainty reduction theory (URT) to examine how on-line consumer reviews affect consumer uncertainty reduction and value perceptions in order to understand whether consumer attitudes will be influenced by on-line consumer reviews and if relationships are built between consumers and companies as a result. The results indicated that argument quality, recommendation sidedness, source credibility, confirmation of prior beliefs, and recommendation ratings have a positive effect on the uncertainty reduction of consumers towards the businesses under consideration. Since uncertainty reduction has an effect on value perception, this study suggests that companies provide on-line consumer reviews on their websites to increase consumer uncertainty reduction and to improve consumer value perception of their companies.

INTRODUCTION

As an information source, the Internet has hugely expanded the scope of pre-purchase information searches by providing easy access to the advice offered from thousands of individuals. Considering that people can access such information anytime and anywhere through the use of the Internet, it is reasonable to state that people may navigate on the Internet to search for product information before they conduct transactions. One of the most popular information receiving sources is online

DOI: 10.4018/978-1-4666-8619-9.ch068

reviews. Online reviews consist of word of mouth spread through online review platforms that can enhance business benefits, such as revenue and long-term relationships (Kim & Son, 2009; Lu, Ba, Hung, & Feng, 2013). In other words, online users can offer their opinions to other online users by posting their word of mouth in the form of reviews. These online reviews thus become a platform by which to spread word of mouth. As a result, many firms are making use of on-line consumer reviews by regularly posting their product information, by sponsoring promotional chats on on-line forums, such as USENET, and by proactively prompting their consumers to provide reviews of their products online (Mayzlin, 2006). Hence, online reviews not only provide a platform through which customers can express their opinions but also provide a method by which businesses can improve their products/services. Some firms even strategically manipulate online reviews in an attempt to influence consumers' purchasing decisions (Dellarocas, 2006; Lee, Kim, & Peng, 2013). As described above, online consumer reviews play an important role in the marketing activities of companies.

Social networking sites, brand websites, internet forums, product review websites, and personal blogs are all types of online consumer review platforms (Chang & Chuang, 2011). Online consumer reviews on consumer attitudes and product sales have been shown to have significant positive effects on books sales (Chevalier & Mayzlin, 2006; Saeed, Hwang, & Yi, 2003), box office revenue (Liu, 2006), and sales in the video game industry (Zhu & Zhang, 2010). Prior online consumer review studies have also explored the characteristics of online consumer reviews, such as argument quality (Bhattacherjee & Sanford, 2006; Cheung, Lee, & Rabjohn, 2008; Lee, Park, & Han, 2011), recommendation framing (Chevalier & Mayzlin, 2006; Hennig-Thurau & Walsh, 2003; Xue & Zhou, 2010), recommendation sidedness (Crowley & Hoyer 1994; Eisend, 2006; Kao, 2011; Lee et al., 2013), source credibility (Brown, Broderick,

& Lee, 2007; Cheung et al., 2008), confirmation of prior beliefs (Cheung, Luo, Sia, & Chen 2009), consistency (Benedicktus, Brady, Darke, & Voorhees, 2010; Khare, Labrecque, & Asare, 2011; West & Broniarczyk, 1998), and ratings (Chevalier & Mayzlin, 2006; Khare et al., 2011; Mudambi & Schuff, 2010). These characteristics were integrated by Cheung et al. (2009) through the dual-process theory (DPT).

The DPT posits two distinct types of influences (informational and normative) on the persuasiveness of on-line consumer reviews. Informational influence is derived from the review's messages, such as the content, source, and receiver, determined by argument quality, recommendation framing, recommendation sidedness, source credibility, and confirmation of prior beliefs. Normative influence is a result of the norms or expectations of others that are implicit or explicit in the choice preference of a group or community (Cheung et al., 2009). Normative determinants include recommendation consistency and recommendation ratings.

Based on the discussion above, this study adopts the DPT's concepts to explore the effects of characteristics of online consumer reviews on consumer uncertainty reduction. Adjei, Noble, and Noble, (2010) and Chang and Chuang (2011) proved that online customer-to-customer (C2C) communication can increase uncertainty reduction for products, which in turn can lead to an increase in consumer purchase behavior. Accordingly, online consumer reviews can be used as a method of C2C communication, and consumer uncertainty reduction can be viewed as one type of consumer attitude. Online consumer reviews can affect consumer preference toward a product (Lee et al., 2011). Indeed, the reviews of others can determine customer evaluations. For instance, a customer can evaluate information about a specific restaurant in a review. Customers can refer to the reviewer's experience and then, based on this evaluation, may change their opinions. Even though customers may be unfamiliar with a restaurant, they can evaluate the characteristics of the restaurant by referring to an online review in order to decrease their uncertainty about a decision to purchase and ultimately escalate their value perceptions. Consequently, this study argues that the characteristics of online reviews may determine the level of customer uncertainty reduction with regard to purchasing products.

The sense of uncertainty is an important concept in the uncertainty reduction theory (URT). Online information, such as is contained in online reviews, provides an efficient method for customers to gather product/service information. In fact, because customers may have no idea about the quality of restaurant, especially one with which they are unfamiliar, they can refer to an online review and easily and effortlessly gather product/service information. Hence, customers can rely on online reviews to get information upon which future decisions will be based. Further, prior URT studies have been showed that people can acquire on-line information to reduce their uncertainty about a product. In other words, online information, such as online reviews, can enhance customer knowledge about a restaurant. Their pre-purchase uncertainty will thus be decreased (Gibbs, Ellison, & Lai, 2012; Pauley & Emmers, 2007; Ramirez, Walther, Burgoon, & Sunnafrank, 2002; Tidwell & Walther, 2002). However, prior studies on this topic merely used different information-seeking strategies to explore the URT. Antheunis, Valkenburg, and Peter (2010) indicated that people can use passive, active, and interactive strategies to increase uncertainty reduction related to members of social networking sites.

Prior studies have seldom adopted characteristics of consumer reviews as antecedents to explore their impact on customer uncertainty reduction. Because online consumer review characteristics can be effectively classified into informational and normative determinants based on the dual-process theory (DPT), this study also explores the effect of online consumer review character-

istics on uncertainty reduction as built upon the URT. In addition, while most URT studies have explored interpersonal relationships, including initial interactions, development, and maintenance of interpersonal relationships (Antheunis et al., 2010; Berger & Calabrese, 1975), few studies have used the URT to explore the relationship between customers and companies (Adjei et al., 2010; Pollach, 2006). In order to extend the application of the URT, this study adopts value perception to measure the relationship between consumers and companies because the beginning of a relationship stems from value perception.

Value perception is the opinions, attitudes, and thoughts that consumers hold in regard to a particular store or product. Value perception can affect consumer purchase intentions (Munnukka, 2008; Chang & Wang, 2011), purchase decision making (Chang & Chen, 2008), loyalty toward an e-retailer (Chang & Wang, 2011), or brand equity (Hansen, Samuelsen, & Silseth, 2008). Therefore, value perception is a suitable construct by which to explore the relationship between customers and companies.

Cheung et al. (2009) applied the DPT to examine the effects of informational and normative determinants of online consumer reviews on the perceived credibility of reviews. Nonetheless, up to the present, few studies have applied the DPT to explore the effects of informational and normative determinants of online consumer reviews on consumer product attitudes. What is more, there have been no studies combining the DPT and URT into one research model. Only a few studies have used the URT to explore the relationship between consumers and companies (Adjei et al., 2010; Pollach, 2006).

To address the research gaps referenced above, this study follows Cheung et al. (2009) by using the DPT to examine online consumer review characteristics and taking the URT as the theoretical basis of an exploration into how online consumer reviews affect consumer uncertainty reduction.

This study also uses value perception as a dependent variable to explore whether uncertainty reduction can enhance the relationship between consumers and companies.

The following questions reflect our concerns in this study about online consumer reviews: How do the characteristics of online consumer reviews influence receiver uncertainty? Does consumer uncertainty reduction lead to value perceptions toward a company?

As a result, the main purposes of this study are:

1. To combine the dual-process theory (DPT) and the uncertainty reduction theory (URT) in one model to extend the application of these two theories;
2. To investigate the influence of online consumer review characteristics (divided into informational and normative determinants) on receiver uncertainty reduction;
3. To examine the influence of consumer uncertainty reduction on consumer value perceptions of a company;
4. To extend the application of the URT in the relationship between consumers and companies.

THEORETICAL BACKGROUND AND HYPOTHESES DEVELOPMENT

Over the years, many theories have been advanced to explain how people are influenced by information they receive, such as the Yale model, the Elaboration Likelihood model (ELM) (Johnston & Warkentin, 2010) and the dual-process theory (DPT). The Yale model posits that three major factors, message, source and audience, can affect people's attention, comprehension, and acceptance of a message that could in turn influence their opinions, perceptions, and actions. The ELM posits two information processing routes (central and peripheral). Individuals who have the motiva-

tion or ability to process persuasive information are more likely to follow the central route. In contrast, individuals who lack motivation or the ability to process persuasive information are more likely to use the peripheral route (Park, Lee, & Han, 2007; Martin, Carneb & Jose, 2011). In the DPT, informational influence (the content of the reviews) and normative influence (the impact of social aggregation mechanisms) work together to shape a reader's information-credibility judgments. In this research, the DPT is applied as the theoretical foundation to explore how and to what extent informational determinants and normative determinants affect the influence of online consumer reviews.

Online consumer reviews are helpful for a consumer in the process of purchase decision making (Mudambi & Schuff, 2010; Lee et al., 2013). Lee et al. (2011) proved that negative online consumer reviews can affect consumer attitudes toward a product. This research adopts the URT to explore the variations in consumer attitudes and the way informational and normative determinants of online consumer recommendations influence the uncertainty reduction of consumers in the online communication environment. The URT proposes that people will use communication to increase uncertainty reduction and to reinforce a relationship when they initially meet each other (Berger & Calabrese, 1975). URT studies have mostly been used to explore relationships between two people, such as initial interactions, development, maintenance of interpersonal relationships, relationship building in face-to-face scenarios, and relationships in computer-mediated communication (CMC) environments (Antheunis et al., 2010; Carlson, Carlson, Hunter, Vaughn, & George, 2013).

This study combines the DPT and the URT to examine and discuss the relationship between uncertainty reduction and the value perceptions related to online consumer reviews. The proposed research model is depicted in Figure 1.

Figure 1. Research framework

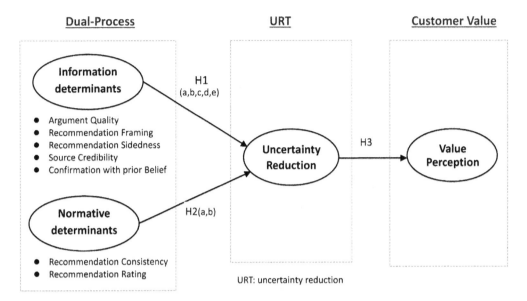

THE UNCERTAINTY REDUCTION THEORY (URT)

Berger and Calabrese (1975) proposed the URT to explain the role of communication in regard to the increase of uncertainty reduction in initial interactions and in the development of interpersonal relationships (Dimoka, Hong, & Pavlou, 2012). People use communication to increase uncertainty reduction and raise predictability regarding the behavior of both the self and the communicative partner in initial interactions, and the resulting uncertainty reduction can aid in regard to increasing relational intimacy (Drennan, Sullivan, & Previte, 2006; Pollach, 2006). Morgan and Hunt (1994) defined uncertainty as *"the degree of confidence that a customer has in his or her ability to make predictions about the firm he or she is dealing with."* Uncertainty can be arranged into two categories: cognitive uncertainty and behavioral uncertainty. Cognitive uncertainty refers to the uncertainty associated with beliefs and attitudes. Behavioral uncertainty refers to the uncertainty regarding the possible behavior occurring in a specific situation (Berger, 2002). Such catego-

rization helps researchers identify the origins of uncertainty, which results in an increased ability to address the discomfort produced by uncertainty.

Antheunis et al. (2010) indicated that uncertainty reduction is the gathering of information that allows the information seeker to predict someone's attitudes and behavior. Uncertainty reduction is critical to relational development, maintenance, and dissolution (Berger, 2002). Individuals are less likely to engage in relational maintenance when high uncertainty exists in the relationship (Matin et al., 2011). Therefore, the URT is not only important for initial interactions and the development of interpersonal relationships, but also for the maintenance of interpersonal relationships. This study defines uncertainty reduction as *"the degree of confidence that a customer has in his or her ability to make predictions about the firm he or she is dealing with."*

The URT can be applied in different countries or cultures. Gudykunst, Yang, and Nishida (1985) conducted a study using students enrolled in universities in the United States (considered to be a low-context culture), Japan, and Korea (considered to be high-context cultures). The

URT was applied in face-to-face interactions in its early stage, but with the rapid development of the Internet, some studies have extended it to CMC (computer mediated communication) (Ramirez et al., 2002; Tidwell & Walther, 2002), online romantic relationship development (Pauley & Emmers-Sommer, 2007), and online dating (Gibbs et al., 2012).

Few studies have explored the URT in the customer relationship. Customers will tend to engage in increased information seeking to increase uncertainty reduction toward a service. To increase Internet users' uncertainty reduction about data handling practices and to help companies build stable relationships with users in World Wide Web interactions, privacy policies need to explain not only the data collection and sharing practices companies engage in but also those practices in which these companies do not engage (Pollach, 2006).

Information-seeking strategies can be used on the Internet (Gibbs et al., 2012; Pauley & Emmers-Sommer, 2007; Ramirez et al., 2002; Tidwell & Walther, 2002). In CMC environments, people can use information-seeking strategies to increase uncertainty reduction between members of online social network sites (Antheunis et al., 2010). Customers can use information-seeking strategies to get information about a company's products or services on the Internet. This study focuses on consumers' information-seeking behavior that is, the degree to which they read other consumers' recommendations in an online environment.

As a result of using different information-seeking strategies to acquire information (online consumer reviews), the characteristics of online consumer reviews will have different effects on consumers' uncertainty reduction. However, prior URT studies about how online consumer review characteristics affect uncertainty reduction have not been through enough. Specifically, we will explore how consumers use active information-seeking strategies (reading online consumer reviews) to acquire information to increase un-certainty reduction about products and services. After consumers read online consumer reviews, we use the DPT to explore the effects of online consumer reviews.

DUAL-PROCESS THEORY (DPT)

The dual-process theory (DPT) is a psychology theory that has been applied in many fields, including the study of learning, memory, attention, social cognition, thinking, reasoning, and decision making (Evans, 2010; Gurrea, Orús, & Flavián, 2013). The DPT deals with the persuasion of information, the ELM and the Heuristic Systematic Model (HSM). Lee et al. (2011) adopted the ELM as his theoretical foundation to explore the effect of negative online consumer reviews on product attitudes. By adopting HSM, Koh and Sundar (2010) explored why specialist sources are more persuasive than generalist sources.

This study adopts informational influence and normative influence as two variables in the DPT to explore the effect of online consumer reviews on consumer attitude as used by Cheung et al. (2009). The DPT can influence the persuasiveness of messages, and Shen, Huang, Chu, and Liao (2010) applied this idea to explore member loyalty in virtual communities and the effect of online consumer recommendations on consumers' perceived credibility of online consumer reviews.

Informational Determinants

Informational influence is defined as the tendency to accept other people's information and consider that information to be true (Shen et al., 2010). The characteristics of online consumer reviews that can affect consumers are important. As stated in Yale's model, source, message, and receiver are three major informational components in message evaluations. This study inherits his idea, considering source credibility in the source dimension, argument quality, recommendation framing, recommendation sidedness in the message dimension, and confirmation of the receiver's prior beliefs in the receiver dimension. Informational determinants include argument quality, recommendation framing, recommendation sidedness, source credibility, and confirmation of prior beliefs as used by Cheung et al. (2009). These factors will be examined in the following paragraph.

Argument Quality

Online consumer reviews come from the experiences, evaluations, and opinions of consumers who have bought and used a product (Park et al., 2007). Chen and Xie (2008) considered online consumer reviews to be one type of product information which is created by consumer experiences rather than by the experiences of the sellers. Online consumer reviews can be positive or negative statements from potential, actual, or former customers about a product and are available to a lot of people via the Internet (Park & Kim, 2008). Mudambi and Schuff (2010) explained that online customer reviews are peer-generated product evaluations, which are posted on company or third party websites. This study defines online consumer reviews as *"reviews created by consumers from their experiences, evaluations, and opinions about products or services and posted on websites."*

Argument quality refers to the persuasive strength of arguments in an informational message (Bhattacherjee & Sanford, 2006). Negash, Ryanb, and Igbariab (2003) measured the quality of information in terms of its credibility, objectivity, timeliness, understandability and sufficiency (Li, Rong, & Thatcher, 2012; Wakefield & Whitten, 2006). Lee et al. (2011) reviewed the quality of online consumer review content in terms of relevance, reliability, understandability, and sufficiency. Argument quality contains relevance, timeliness, accuracy, and comprehensiveness (Cheung et al., 2008). Online consumer reviews offer a consumer perspective, and they help po-

tential consumers to make purchase decisions by supplying understandable, relevant, and believable recommendations with sufficient reasons to support such recommendations.

Online customer reviews are a form of online C2C communication. C2C communication quality includes relevance, frequency, duration and timeliness, and has been shown to be positively related to uncertainty reduction (Adjei et al., 2010). This study proposes that high-quality online consumer reviews can increase uncertainty reduction because the information is relevant to an evaluation of a product because it contains understandable, reliable, and sufficient reasoning. When consumers receive high-quality information about products and services that help them understand the products and services of a company to a greater degree, their uncertainty will be lower. Therefore, in order to the increase consumer uncertainty reduction, high quality online consumer reviews may be more effective than those that are of low quality:

H1a: Argument quality has a positive effect on uncertainty reduction.

Recommendation Framing

Consumers are affected by both positively framed messages and negatively framed messages they receive at the same time. Positively framed online consumer reviews stress the strength of a product or a service; on the contrary, negatively framed online consumer reviews emphasize the weakness or problems of a product or a service (Grewal, Gotlieb, & Marmorstein, 1994). The persuasive effect of online consumer reviews is created from the compound effect of positively and negatively framed messages. This study defines recommendation framing, including positively framed (e.g., a praise message) and negatively framed (e.g., a complaint message), as the valence (positive or negative) of online consumer reviews.

Valence is one of the most important message characteristics. Liu (2006) and Lee et al. (2011)

indicated that negatively framed information has a more powerful influence than positively framed information. Hennig-Thurau and Walsh (2003) investigated the motives and the consequences of reading customer reviews on the Internet and compared negative and positive information, showing that negative customer reviews tended to have a greater impact on consumer buying behavior. Negative online reviews have been shown to have more impact than positive ones with regard to decreasing book sales (Chevalier & Mayzlin, 2006). Similarly, negative reviews have been shown to hurt box office performance more than positive reviews. This contributes to an understanding box office performance. However, this effect was only demonstrated to be effective for the first week after the release of a film (Basuroy, Chatterjee, & Ravid, 2003).

Xue and Zhou (2010) compared positive and negative messages and indicated that the latter had greater impact on consumers, leading to higher credibility, less brand interest, weaker purchase intention, and stronger forward intention. A company wouldn't hire people to write about disadvantages of the company's product; therefore, consumers trust negative messages more than positive messages. This means negatively framed online consumer reviews lead to better consequences on consumer uncertainty reduction than positively framed online consumer reviews. In addition, if consumers exert more effort toward processing information, they will have a deeper impression and more ability to predict the performance of a product or service (Gurrea et al., 2013).

Lee et al. (2011) mentioned that according to prospect theory, the pain brought by an experience of loss is greater than the pleasure associated with gaining an amount equivalent to the loss. Adjei et al. (2010) indicated that consumers weight losses more heavily than gains. In the case of consumers, negative reviews are more effective and convincing than positive reviews. To sum up, negatively framed online consumer reviews have more positive effects on uncertainty reduction

than positively framed online consumer reviews. Therefore, we propose the following hypothesis:

H1b: Negatively framed online consumer reviews have a positive effect on uncertainty reduction.

Recommendation Sidedness

Crowley and Hoyer (1994) and Pechmann (1992) indicated that two-sided online consumer reviews have both positive and negative components. Two-sided product information is more persuasive than one-sided product information (Pechmann, 1992; Crowley & Hoyer, 1994). Eisend (2006) found that two-sided messages in advertising can enhance source credibility in regard to consumer communications, can reduce the negative cognitive responses of consumers, and can have a positive impact on brand attitudes and purchase intention.

Most recommendation-sidedness-related studies have focused on advertising themes and the way consumers process the information they receive. Two-sided online consumer reviews provide a more comprehensive view of a product or service than one-sided online consumer reviews. When consumers get more information about a product or service, they will increase their uncertainty reduction about the product or service being offered by a company. Cheung et al. (2009) indicated that online consumer reviews don't simultaneously point out the positive and negative features of a product or service. Kao (2011) found that two-sided messages are more persuasive than one-sided messages when high need-for-cognition (NFC) individuals are under low/moderate time pressure and when low-NFC individuals are under moderate time pressure (Crossland, Herschel, Perkins, & Scudder, 2000).

Dubois, Rucker, and Tormala (2011) also indicated that consumers' feel more assured when they perceive their attitudes as having a balanced outcome after considering both sides of an issue rather than just a single side. To sum up, two-sided online consumer reviews have more effect on uncertainty reduction than one-sided online consumer reviews, so we posit that two-sided online consumer reviews have a positive effect on uncertainty reduction:

H1c: Two-sided online consumer reviews have a positive effect on uncertainty reduction.

Source Credibility

The source of a message can be thought of as credible if the writer is perceived as professional or trustworthy and can in turn elicit more persuasiveness as compared with low credibility sources (Tormala & Petty, 2004). Source credibility is comprised of two separate concepts: source expertise and source trustworthiness. Source expertise refers to a source's ability to provide correct information, and source trustworthiness refers to the intention of the source to provide correct information (Lemanski & Lee, 2012).

Information expertise and information receiver's perceptions of the trustworthiness are elements that affect the credibility of an information source (Brown et al., 2007; Cheung et al., 2008). This study adopts the trustworthiness dimension from the definition by Brown Broderick, and Lee (2007) to examine the influence of source credibility on consumer uncertainty reduction. Because information receivers can't identify an information providers' level of expertise, receivers can only determine the degree of trustworthiness based on the content of online consumer reviews. The information receiver can therefore only feel that the writer has told the truth. Tormala and Petty (2004) indicated that participants are more certain of their attitudes in high-credibility situations than they are in low-credibility situations when the cognitive load is low. Consumers feel more certain when the source of their information is high rather than low in regard to credibility (Clarkson, Carlson, Hunter, Vaughn, & George, 2008).

People can use information-seeking strategies to increase their uncertainty reduction, but information from different information-seeking strategies needs to be processed. In information processing, source credibility can lead to different impacts on consumer attitudes. When people perceive a source as credible, the information will have a greater positive influence on uncertainty reduction because the information can be trusted. On the contrary, low source credibility means consumers don't trust the content of the message, so the effect on consumer attitude will be lower. Thus, the hypothesis of source credibility and uncertainty reduction is as follows:

H1d: Source credibility has a positive effect on uncertainty reduction.

Confirmation of Prior Belief

When consumers perceive the received information to be consistent with their prior knowledge or expectations, they have more confidence in the received information and are willing to rely on it to make purchase decisions (Cheung et al., 2009). Consumers are able to identify the level of confirmation or disconfirmation between the received information and their prior beliefs through various direct or indirect experiences. This study defines confirmation of prior belief as *"the level of confirmation between the received information and prior beliefs."*

People can increase their uncertainty reduction by getting more information most of the time, but this doesn't apply to some situations, for example, when the received information isn't consistent with a consumer's prior beliefs. Planalp and Honeycutt (1985) accepted the URT's basic premise that the central goal in communication is to acquire adequate information to increase uncertainty reduction, but they argued that not all information increases uncertainty reduction. They suggested that information-exchange can also result in an increase in uncertainty between two people in a relationship if one of the two people acquires new information about the other that is inconsistent with existing beliefs.

If the received information isn't consistent with consumers' prior beliefs, consumers will feel confused. They won't know what they can believe, and they must spend more time and energy to process the information. In other words, if the current online consumer review advice confirms the reader's existing beliefs, the reader will be more likely to believe the information, which can increase uncertainty reduction:

H1e: Confirmation of the receiver's prior beliefs has a positive effect on uncertainty reduction.

Normative Determinants

The informational determinants discussed before above are not enough to explain how online consumer reviews affect consumers' uncertainty reduction. These determinants neglect the importance of normative influence. Normative influence is as the tendency to follow or conform to other people's expectations (Shen et al., 2010). After consumers read online consumer reviews, they're affected not only by the information but also by other readers' opinions. In this study, the normatively determinants include recommendation consistency and recommendation rating.

Recommendation Consistency

Based on the research by Cheung et al. (2009), this study refers to recommendation consistency as the extent which a current online consumer review is consistent with other providers' experiences with regard to the same product or service evaluation. Consistency refers to the level of agreement across the opinions on a certain target provided through online consumer reviews (West & Broniarczyk, 1998). When reviewers have similar opinions,

the consistency will be increase, which will enhance the persuasiveness of the online consumer reviews. For example, if every online consumer review indicates that a company has good products but bad service, consistency will be high. Otherwise, if reviewers have largely diversified opinions, consistency will be low. For example, if some online consumer reviews accuse a company of bad products but others don't, consistency is considered to be low.

The DPT views consistent information as an important factor, and therefore, consumers should agree with the majority. Planalp and Honeycutt (1985) proposed that in a relationship, if a person acquires new information about another that is inconsistent with existing knowledge, it will increase uncertainty. Ba and Pavlou (2002) found that sellers with perfect consistency records are trusted more. Consistent information has been found to exhibit large effects on judgment under conditions of both high and low levels of motivation even if the information source is relatively unreliable (Benedicktus et al., 2010).

Online consumer reviews are often submitted by more than one experienced consumer in consumer discussion forums. Consumers can easily gather online consumer reviews about the same product or service through the Internet. Thus, they can compare the consistency among online consumer reviews. If a current online consumer review is consistent with the opinions of other online consumer reviews, consumers are more likely to trust the current online consumer review and will experience increases in uncertainty reduction, since people tend to follow and believe normative opinions. In contrast, if an online consumer review is inconsistent with most of the other online consumer reviews on the same product, readers will be confused and will exhibit increases in uncertainty:

H2a: Recommendation consistency has a positive effect on uncertainty reduction.

Recommendation Rating

Whether ratings can affect buyer trust in a seller's credibility depends on whether the seller has positive or negative ratings in electronic markets (Ba & Pavlou, 2002). Chevalier and Mayzlin (2006) indicated that online amateur book ratings can affect consumer purchase behavior. Cheung et al. (2009) demonstrated that recommendation ratings have a positive effect on the perceived credibility of online consumer reviews.

This study defines a recommendation rating as *"the overall rating given by online consumer review authors on a product or service."* Numerical star ratings for online customer reviews normally range from one to five stars. A very low rating (one star) indicates an extremely negative view of the product; a very high rating (five stars) reflects an extremely positive view on the product; and a three-star rating reflects a moderate view.

There are many websites which provide a star rating function for consumers to use to evaluate a product, like Amazon and Yahoo, among others. Consumers can give the product high or low rating scores according to their usage experience. The aggregate rating is another representation of how previous consumers have reacted to the product. If most consumers give a high-level rating to the product, this implies that most users agree and think the product is good.

Conversely, if most consumers give a very low rating to a product, this indicates that most people feel unsatisfied with the product. Based on the star rating, people can determine the average ratings of other consumers. The fact that a product or service can be examined by other consumers through a rating system can increase consumer uncertainty reduction towards a product or service. Thus, this study expects that:

H2b: Recommendation ratings have a positive effect on uncertainty reduction.

Value Perception

This study adopts value perception to explore the relationship between customers and companies. Perception is the process in which people select, organize, and interpret information in order to draw out a meaningful picture in the mind (Matook & de Heijden, 2013; Munnukka, 2008). Chang and Chen (2008) indicated that consumers' perceptions are built from attitudes, opinions, and situations and are experience-dependent. Sirdeshmukh, Singh, and Sabol (2002) defined value as consumer perceptions of the benefits minus the costs to maintain an ongoing relationship with a service provider, and they show that value can influence consumer loyalty toward a service provider. This study defines value perception as *"the opinions, attitudes, and thoughts that consumers hold in regard to a particular store or a product."*

Customer value perception has been shown to have a positive relationship with purchase intentions (Munnukka, 2008). Value perception increases the likelihood that a supplier will be recommended and reduces the tendency to seek substitute service providers in a B2B context (Hansen et al., 2008). Value perception has significant effects on customer loyalty intention toward an e-retailer (Chang &Wang, 2011). Currás-Pérez, Ruiz-Mafé, and Sanz-Blas (2003) suggested that sociability and entertainment gratifications and perceived risks are the main drivers of user attitude towards social networking sites. Uncertainty reduction has been shown to increase the social attraction between two people on social network sites (Antheunis et al., 2010).

This study explores the relationship between customers and companies. Like interpersonal relationships, the more information consumers know about a company, the more they increase uncertainty reduction, and the more willingness they have to build a relationship with the company. Reducing exchange uncertainty can increase consumer value perceptions (Sirdeshmukh et al., 2002).

Through increasing uncertainty reduction, consumers will feel that a company will provide them with good products and services, and then consumer value perceptions will grow. Uncertainty reduction can increase sales (Adjei et al., 2010). Before consumers start to consider buying a product from a company, a relationship must be built between them. Munnukka (2008) pointed out that customer value perceptions can be an antecedent of purchase intention. Therefore, the following hypothesis is proposed:

H3: Uncertainty reduction has a positive effect on value perception.

METHODOLOGY AND RESULTS

The constructs of this study are composed of informational determinants (argument quality, recommendation framing, recommendation sidedness, source credibility, and confirmation of prior beliefs), normative determinants (recommendation consistency and recommendation rating), uncertainty reduction, and relationship quality. Table 4 in Appendix A shows the constructs and their respective definitions adopted for the purposes of this study.

A list of measurement items is shown in Table 5 of Appendix B. Using 30 items to measure nine constructs and eight hypotheses, measurements for the questionnaire are adopted from related literature, with some changes made to fit the context of the present research. All items use a seven-point Likert scale. Participants were asked to indicate how much they agree with the statements in the questionnaire from 1 "strongly disagree" to 7 "strongly agree".

The method used in this study was chosen because it permitted the gathering of information from people who had recently used an online consumer review website and had a clear impression, thus enhancing the reliability of the research. We chose iPeen as our research platform, where

online consumer reviews are available. iPeen is an online platform that provides a functional online review discussion especially for restaurants. In other words, the characteristics of the iPeen review board have functional features, such as a review platform, a review rating system, and pictures. Hence, the features of iPeen provide the characteristics of the restaurant being considered. Moreover, the effects of online consumer reviews should be similar among industries. Consequently, the results of iPeen thus can be generalized to other online review boards and topics, so online consumer reviews of the restaurant industry (iPeen) are acceptable.

The respondents who could complete our questionnaire were individuals who had previous review experience with a restaurant review board. Due to the fact that it was necessary to ensure the respondents had previous experience with reviewing restaurants using iPeen, at the beginning of the questionnaire, we provided a situation in which we asked participants to read an online consumer review on iPeen. Afterwards, four questions were presented to confirm that the participants actually read the online consumer review. The questions were "What's the restaurant's name?", "What type of restaurant is it?", "How many online consumer reviews did you read?", and "How many stars (recommendation rating) did the restaurant get?" We carried out two pilot tests for this study because the results from the first pilot test were not good. The first results showed two constructs to have quite low values in regard to item-to-total correlations and Cronbach's alpha. Therefore, we modified the items and carried out a second pilot test. In the second pilot test, with 50 respondents, we retained a total of 45 valid questionnaires after eliminating the invalid questionnaires.

The results of the second pilot test were encouraging. The Cronbach's alpha for each construct ranged from .815 to .942, with all constructs exceeding the standard of .70. Item-to-total correlations ranged from .486 to .922, and only UR4 (.468) didn't exceed the standard of .50. Since item

UR4 was only a little below the standard of .50, we kept the item. All items in the questionnaire for the second pilot test were adopted in the formal questionnaire.

Conducting a field survey of a reviewing experience through the iPeen restaurant board provided the empirical data. An online survey was published on the iPeen restaurant board (www.ipeen.com. tw), which yielded 536 collected questionnaires in total, with a total of 450 valid questionnaires determined as suitable for further analysis. As for the demographic variables, respondents were 56% male and 44% female; the majority of respondents were between 21 and 25 years old (53.8%); almost all respondents' education level was either college or university (58%), followed by graduate school (37.8%). 34.2% of the respondents spend about 2 to 4 hours per day using the Internet. 61.3% of the respondents read one to three online consumer reviews before they answered the questionnaire. The number of rating stars for restaurants was between 4.5 and 5 (64.4%).

Common Method Variance (CMV) usually exists in information technology survey research. Hence, a Harmon's one factor test was employed in this study for common method variance (Podsakoff, MacKenzie, Lee, & Podsakoff, 2003). We used an un-rotated principle components factor analysis in which all of the measurement items were combined into a single factor. All measurements were generated with eigenvalues greater than 1. The results showed a 38.85% total variance; factor one accounted for 12.04% of the variance. Thus, this study is unlikely have concerns with CMV.

The results of the descriptive and confirmatory factor analysis are presented in Table 1. The mean value of the variable items ranged from 4.70 to 5.68, and the standard deviations ranged from .850 to 1.456. The value of tem-to-total correlation ranged from .561 to .902; factor loading ranged from .673 to .966; the Cronbach's alpha coefficient ranged from .719 to .943; the CR ranged from .719 to .942, and the AVE values exceeded .50. The

results implied that each variable displayed high convergent validity, high internal consistency, and high reliability.

In the discriminant validity test (see Table 2), all the square root values of AVE were higher than the correlation of the variables, revealing that all variables were unique and had high validity in the measurement model.

The model fit indices for the SEM model were checked to ensure good model-data fit and appropriateness for further analysis. The results were as follows: the chi-square (χ^2) = 1063.854 (p = .000); the degree of freedom (df) = 376; Chi-square/df = 2.829 (<3); the GFI = .863 (>.80); the AGFI = .830 (>.80); the CFI = .927 (>.90), and the RMSEA = .064 (<.08). All model fit index values reached the recommended values, indicating the model-data fitted well. Among the eight hypotheses, there were seven hypotheses (H1a~H1e, H2b, and H3) which proved to be significant (p<.05). The path diagram of the SEM model is shown in Figure 2. Among the eight hypotheses, only H2 was not supported. The summarized results of the hypotheses testing are shown in Table 3 and are discussed in the following section.

DISCUSSION AND CONCLUSION

The results of data analysis provide more details about the findings of this study.

Effects of Informational Determinants on the Uncertainty Reduction

According to the URT, information-seeking strategies can increase people's uncertainty reduction (Antheunis et al., 2010; Berger, 2002; Gibbs et al., 2012; Ramirez et al., 2002). This study adopts the DPT to explore the effect of online consumer review characteristics on uncertainty reduction. The results of the data analysis show that all of

Table 1. Confirmatory factor analysis (N = 450)

Constructs	Mean	S.D.	Item-to-Total	Factor Loading	VE	CR	α
Argument Quality					.608	.860	.860
AQ1	5.14	.850	.710	.784			
AQ2	4.70	1.046	.677	.743			
AQ3	5.13	1.043	.761	.852			
AQ4	5.33	1.012	.675	.735			
Recommendation Framing					.749	.856	.855
RF1	5.68	.910	.747	.898			
RF2	5.67	.909	.747	.832			
Recommendation Sidedness					.562	.719	.719
RS1	4.70	1.456	.561	.719			
RS2	5.05	1.268	.561	.780			
Source Credibility					.767	.942	.943
SC1	5.04	.984	.845	.883			
SC2	4.95	.946	.855	.888			
SC3	5.12	.932	.846	.871			
SC4	5.08	.907	.873	.905			
SC5	5.20	.951	.802	.833			
Confirmation of Prior Belief					.629	.834	.822
CB1	5.21	1.010	.708	.816			
CB2	5.31	.946	.746	.875			
CB3	5.45	1.020	.577	.677			
Recommendation Consistency					.682	.811	.811
RC1	5.14	.966	.682	.842			
RC2	5.27	.871	.682	.810			
Recommendation Rating					.754	.902	.899
RR1	5.61	1.017	.785	.842			
RR2	5.52	1.027	.850	.928			
RR3	5.59	1.030	.768	.833			
Uncertainty Reduction					.528	.870	.870
UR1	5.12	1.023	.709	.772			
UR2	5.20	1.052	.698	.714			
UR3	4.93	1.117	.642	.681			
UR4	5.61	.890	.610	.673			
UR5	5.36	1.006	.719	.797			
UR6	5.26	1.047	.639	.718			
Value Perception					.823	.932	.930
VP1	4.76	1.161	.872	.925			
VP2	4.89	1.178	.902	.966			
VP3	5.01	1.166	.797	.825			

S.D.: Standard Deviation; VE: Variance Extracted; CR: Composited Reliability; α: Cronbach's alpha

Table 2. Results of discriminant validity analysis

Variable	AQ	RF	RS	SC	CB	RC	RR	UR	VP
Argument Quality (AQ)	**.779**[a]								
Recommendation Framing (RF)	.532	**.865**[a]							
Recommendation Sidedness (RS)	.336	.092	**.750**[a]						
Source Credibility (SC)	.628	.401	.401	**.876**[a]					
Confirmation of Prior Belief (CB)	.602	.571	.227	.572	**.793**[a]				
Recommendation Consistency (RC)	.536	.624	.106	.484	.693	**.826**[a]			
Recommendation Rating (RR)	.536	.509	.248	.446	.561	.497	**.868**[a]		
Uncertainty Reduction (UR)	.676	.357	.423	.577	.564	.452	.581	**.727**[a]	
Value Perception (VP)	.380	.366	.228	.308	.414	.344	.444	.491	**.907**[a]

Note: [a] = Square Root of Average Variance Extracted (AVE)

Figure 2. Path diagram of the SEM

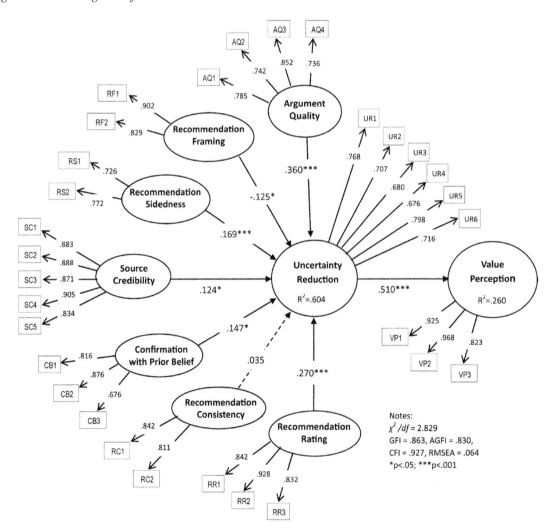

Table 3. Results of SEM paths analysis and summaries of hypotheses testing

	Hypotheses/Predictions	Path Coeff.	t-Value	Results
H1a	Argument Quality→ Uncertainty Reduction	.360***	5.409	Supported
H1b	Recommendation Framing → Uncertainty Reduction	-.125*	-2.118	Supported
H1c	Recommendation Sidedness→ Uncertainty Reduction	.169***	3.343	Supported
H1d	Source Credibility → Uncertainty Reduction	.124*	2.277	Supported
H1e	Confirmation of Prior Belief → Uncertainty Reduction	.147*	2.074	Supported
H2a	Recommendation Consistency → Uncertainty Reduction	.035	0.493	Not Support
H2b	Recommendation Rating → Uncertainty Reduction	.270***	5.142	Supported
H3	Uncertainty Reduction → Value Perception	.510***	10.292	Supported

Note: *: $p<.05$, ***: $p<.001$

these informational determinants have a significant effect on uncertainty reduction.

Adjei et al. (2010) proposed that online C2C communication quality is positively related to uncertainty reduction. In this study, argument quality is shown to have a positive effect on uncertainty reduction. Therefore, the quality of online consumer reviews can affect uncertainty reduction in consumers. They may obtain useful information from high-quality reviews which will help them better understand the food and services offered by a specific restaurant. As consumers know more about the food and service, their uncertainty becomes lower. The results support the study of Lee et al. (2011), which suggested that online consumer review quality can affect consumer attitudes toward products.

Basuroy et al. (2003), Chevalier and Mayzlin (2006), Hennig-Thurau and Walsh (2003), Lee et al. (2011), Xue and Zhou (2010) indicated that negatively framed information has a more powerful influence than positively framed information. This study shows that negatively framed online consumer reviews have a positive effect on uncertainty reduction. As predicted, consumers weight losses more heavily than gains, so they spend more time and energy processing negatively framed online consumer reviews and are as a result able to increase their uncertainty reduction about the food and services offered by a restaurant.

Crowley and Hoyer (1994), Eisend (2006), Kao (2011), and Pechmann (1992) indicated that two-sided product information is more persuasive than one-sided product information. We use their ideas to prove that two-sided online consumer reviews have a positive effect on uncertainty reduction. When consumers get two-sided reviews containing a more comprehensive view of a food or service than is the case with one-sided reviews, they increase their uncertainty reduction about the food or service provided by a restaurant. This finding supports Dubois et al. (2011), who indicated that consumers feel more certain when they perceive their attitudes as having a balanced consideration of both sides of an issue. Although most of the prior studies on this topic have used this idea with regard to advertising, this study proved that the idea could be suitable for online consumer reviews as well.

Tormala and Petty (2004) indicated that high credibility sources elicit more persuasiveness than low credibility sources and suggest that participants are more certain of their attitudes in high-credibility situations than they are in low-credibility situations. Clarkson et al. (2008) indicated that consumers feel more certain when the source of their information is high rather than low in regard to credibility. Our results support their findings. Source credibility has a positive effect on uncertainty reduction. When consumers think the source is credible, reviews will have greater influence on their level of uncertainty because they feel that they can trust the information. On the contrary, low source credibility means consumers don't trust the content of the reviews, so the effects on consumer uncertainty reduction will be lower. This means that higher source credibility will result in higher confidence on the part of consumers with regard to their judgments.

Cheung et al. (2009) indicated that confirmation of a receiver's prior beliefs has a positive effect on perceived online consumer reviews credibility. We extend their study and prove that confirmation of a receiver's prior beliefs also has a positive effect on uncertainty reduction. If the advice from current online consumer reviews can confirm consumers' existing beliefs, they will be more likely to believe the information and thus will experience increases their uncertainty reduction. The difference between Planalp and Honeycutt (1985) and our study lie in the method by which this argument is proven. We demonstrate that if information is consistent with existing beliefs, this will increase people's uncertainty reduction.

In this study, the informational determinants follow the factors chosen by Cheung et al. (2009). In Cheung et al. (2009), recommendation framing and sidedness were the two unsupported determinants of informational influence; however, in this study, all five hypotheses of informational determinants were supported. We think this is due to the difference in the size of the sample because Cheung et al. (2009) indicated that there were data for only a few negatively framed or one-sided reviews. Online consumer reviews contain either positively or negatively framed information or both one-sided and two-sided online consumer reviews in this study.

Effects of Normative Determinants on Uncertainty Reduction

This study posited that two determinants of normative influence would affect consumer uncertainty

reduction. Recommendation consistency was not supported, but recommendation rating was. Prior research has shown that higher consistency in information can increase the persuasiveness of online consumer reviews (West & Broniarczyk, 1998). Recommendation consistency has been demonstrated to have a positive effect on perceived online consumer review credibility (Cheung et al., 2009). In this study, the results showed recommendation consistency and uncertainty reduction to be positively correlated, but recommendation consistency did not have a significant effect on uncertainty reduction, and therefore, (H2a) was not supported. One plausible reason for this might be that respondents only read one online consumer review before they answered the formal questionnaire.

In the total of 450 valid questionnaires, there were 276 (61.3%) respondents who answered they read one to three online consumer reviews. It's possible there were some respondents who only read one review. In other words, if respondents only read one online consumer review, this study was unable to effectively measure recommendation consistency. Therefore, the insignificant findings on recommendation consistency could be due to the fact that most respondents only read one online consumer review.

In order to examine the applicability of this research to recommendation consistency, future research can require respondents to read more than one online consumer review before they answer the questionnaire or replicate the study using an experimental design that manipulates high vs. low consistency in online consumer reviews. Nevertheless, it is believed that the current model does provide an overall picture of consumer uncertainty reduction through the use of online consumer review characteristics.

Recommendation ratings can affect consumers' purchasing behavior (Chevalier & Mayzlin, 2006), buyers' trust in seller credibility (Ba & Pavlou, 2002), helpfulness of online customer reviews (Mudambi & Schuff, 2010), and consumers' perceived credibility of online consumer reviews (Cheung et al., 2009). This study proves that recommendation ratings can affect consumers in a different manner. The results showed that recommendation ratings have a positive effect on uncertainty reduction. Based on a recommendation rating system, consumers can determine the average rating of a restaurant based on the opinion of other consumers who have visited the restaurant. The fact that the food and service of a restaurant can be examined and rated by other consumers can increase consumer uncertainty reduction with regard to that restaurant. This result extends the effects of recommendation ratings.

Effects of Uncertainty Reduction on Value Perception

Sirdeshmukh et al. (2002) indicated that reducing exchange uncertainty can increase the perceived value of consumers. This study obtained similar results. By increasing uncertainty reduction about a restaurant, consumers can determine that the restaurant will provide good food and service, and then the perceived value of the restaurant will in turn grow. We proposed H3 based on the two statements: uncertainty reduction can increase consumer purchase behavior (Adjei et al., 2010), and customer value perceptions can serve as an antecedent of purchase intention (Munnukka, 2008). The results extend the application of the URT to the relationship between consumers and companies.

Theoretical Implications

Prior studies have already proven that information-seeking strategies can increase uncertainty reduction (Antheunis et al., 2010; Berger, 2002; Gibbs et al., 2012; Ramirez et al., 2002). This means that people can increase uncertainty reduction by acquiring information. However, there is no research that has deeply explored how online consumer review characteristics can increase

uncertainty reduction. This study adopts the DPT to bridge this theory gap.

In the DPT, informational influence contains five types of online consumer review characteristics. Informational determinants in prior URT studies have shown that people can acquire online information in order to increase their uncertainty reduction (Gibbs et al., 2012; Pauley & Emmers-Sommer, 2007; Ramirez et al., 2002; Tidwell & Walther, 2002). The results of this study show that all five of these informational determinants can increase consumer uncertainty reduction for both the products and services of a company. Therefore, not only information-seeking strategies but also different online consumer review characteristics can increase uncertainty reduction. This is a new research direction for future URT studies.

In situations characterized by normative influence, people tend to conform to the expectations of other people. We use this idea to explore the URT and to explain that uncertainty reduction is affected not only by information but also by other people's opinions. In this study, the normative determinants are recommendation consistency and recommendation rating. Recommendation consistency and uncertainty reduction are positively correlated, but recommendation consistency was not shown to have a significant effect on uncertainty reduction. On the other hand, recommendation ratings exhibited a positive effect on uncertainty reduction.

Prior studies have indicated that uncertainty reduction can be increased by face-to-face (Berger & Calabrese, 1975) and computer-mediated communication environments (Adjei et al., 2010; Antheunis et al., 2010). This study proves that consumer uncertainty reduction can likewise be increased by online consumer reviews, meaning that to increase uncertainty reduction doesn't necessarily require direct communication, as indirect communication methods can also increase uncertainty reduction. This is a new research direction by which future URT studies can explore the effects of advertising on uncertainty reduction in consumers.

Finally, most URT studies have explored relationship building between two people, such as that occurring during initial interactions, relationship development, and the maintenance of interpersonal relationships (Berger & Calabrese, 1975). There have only been a small number of studies that have used the URT to explore the relationship between customers and companies. Therefore, the results of this study provide a new research direction for future URT studies.

Managerial Implications

The current study examines how consumers are influenced by online consumer reviews. There are some implications for websites and companies managing online consumer reviews. In the case of website managers of online consumer reviews, understanding the effects of online consumer reviews is particularly important for the survival and development of their websites because when consumers feel that they are helped through the website, they will tend to visit the website again. This study shows that argument quality, recommendation framing, recommendation sidedness, source credibility, confirmation of prior beliefs, and recommendation ratings can help increase uncertainty reduction in consumers.

There are some managerial implications for online review platforms. Firstly, this study suggests that website managers establish interactive review platforms as customer referral review systems that interact with product information, such as those that offer 3D picture interaction. Hence, the vividness of the online review platform will be established in the perception of the customer. After that, as customers have shopping experience in the business under consideration, they can evaluate the gap between the online reviews and their experiences. If these two perceptions are consistent, customers will evaluate the online review platform to be trustworthy and will experience reduced levels of uncertainty about their purchases.

Secondly, website managers can invite an expert in a specific area to introduce their products in order to allow the reviewer to understand the characteristics of the product. This not only enhances argument quality but also elaborates on source credibility. For instance, if a customer reviews an evaluation of a restaurant from a gourmet chef, the customer will perceive the review is trustworthy. Hence, a trustworthy review will reduce customer uncertainty about purchase decisions.

Thirdly, website managers of online consumer reviews can encourage users to publish more high quality reviews by the means of offering bonuses, for instance, by distributing coupons. The more reviews that are available, the higher the chances of having two-sided (positive and negative) reviews are on their websites. Customers must have two-side reviews in order to feel that the information they are accumulating is reliable, and thus, uncertainty will be reduced.

Fourthly, this study suggests that companies should establish positions such as a replier, who replies to the customers' positive/negative reviews right away. In other words, the replier responds to the review sincerely and copes with any problems quickly. A sincere response will cause the customer believe that the business has invested the resources necessary to indicate that it has placed value on the customer. This strategy will enhance customer uncertainty reduction.

Finally, an online review platform is a platform through which customers can express their opinions and create discussion about their experiences. Hence, businesses should concentrate on online reviews. In other words, online review platforms provide a functional method by which to hear the voice of the customers. Businesses should make use of reviews to improve the level of products or services, and as a result, the level of products/services will escalate.

Company managers should pay more attention to online consumer reviews since they can affect both consumer uncertainty reduction and their value perceptions of a company's products or services. In practice, companies can provide online consumer reviews on their corporate websites to increase consumer uncertainty reduction and to improve consumer value perceptions. Companies don't need to control their reviews and display only the positive ones, because two-sided online consumer reviews have been shown to have a positive impact on consumer uncertainty reduction. However, our results also indicate that negatively framed online consumer reviews have a positive effect on uncertainty reduction, which means companies need to carefully handle negative reviews, such as consumer complaints. Companies need to assign staff to verify reviews about their companies on websites. If they find negative reviews, they can reply to consumers and in turn provide valuable advice that companies can use to improve the performance of their products.

CONTRIBUTIONS AND FUTURE RESEARCH

There are four theoretical contributions in this study. Firstly, Antheunis et al. (2010), Berger (2002), Gibbs et al. (2012), and Ramirez et al. (2002) mentioned that information-seeking strategies can increase uncertainty reduction. This proves that online consumer review characteristics can increase consumer uncertainty reduction. Secondly, prior studies have only adopted either the URT (Gibbs et al., 2012; Pauley & Emmers-Sommer, 2007; Ramirez et al., 2002; Tidwell & Walther, 2002) or the DPT (Cheung et al., 2009; Shen et al., 2010) in one model, while the model in this study consists of a combination of the DPT and the URT. Thirdly, Berger and Calabrese (1975) showed that uncertainty reduction can be increased by face-to-face communication. The results of this study prove that consumer uncertainty reduction can be increased by online consumer reviews. In other words, consumer uncertainty reduction can be increased by not only direct communication but also by indirect communication. Finally,

Antheunis et al. (2010), Berger and Calabrese (1975), and Chang and Chuang (2001) agreed that uncertainty reduction has a positive effect on interpersonal relationships. The results of this study prove that uncertainty reduction has a positive effect on value perception, thus successfully extending the application of the URT to the relationship between consumers and companies.

Further, there are some limitations in this study. Firstly, the sample source for this study was limited to one online consumer review website (iPeen). Future research can deeply explore different online consumer review websites in order to examine different industries. Moreover, this study only discusses the content of a restaurant board. Future studies should integrate different kinds of content into an understanding of the moderating effects or control effects that impact the customer uncertainty reduction issue, thus leading to more robust results.

Secondly, this study extends online review characteristics in regard to their impact on customer uncertainty reduction in order to ultimately discuss their impact on customer value perceptions. However, the future behavior of consumers is an important factor by which to understand the characteristics of online reviews. Once customer uncertainty is reduced, and customer value perceptions are improved, it may be possible to determine whether the future behavior of customers, such as loyalty and purchase intention, are affected. Hence, future researchers can further use future consumer behavior as the dependent variable in order to obtain more robust results.

Finally, future research can add moderating variables between the information/normative determinants and uncertainty reduction, such as online shopping experience (Xue & Zhou, 2010) and need for cognition (Lin, Lee, & Horng, 2011). The moderating variables can include level of involvement, prior knowledge of the review topic, and prior knowledge of the online consumer reviews website, among others.

REFERENCES

Adjei, M. T., Noble, S. M., & Noble, C. H. (2010). The influence of C2C communications in online brand communities on customer purchase behavior. *Journal of the Academy of Marketing Science*, *38*(5), 634–653. doi:10.1007/s11747-009-0178-5

Antheunis, M. L., Valkenburg, P. M., & Peter, J. (2010). Getting acquainted through social network sites: Testing a model of online uncertainty reduction and social attraction. *Computers in Human Behavior*, *26*(1), 100–109. doi:10.1016/j.chb.2009.07.005

Ba, S., & Pavlou, P. A. (2002). Evidence of the effect of trust building technology in electronic markets: Price premiums and buyer behavior. *Management Information Systems Quarterly*, *26*(3), 243–268. doi:10.2307/4132332

Basuroy, S., Chatterjee, S., & Ravid, S. A. (2003). How critical are critical reviews? The box office effects of film critics, star power, and budgets. *Journal of Marketing*, *67*(4), 103–117. doi:10.1509/jmkg.67.4.103.18692

Benedicktus, R. L., Brady, M. K., Darke, P. R., & Voorhees, C. M. (2010). Conveying trustworthiness to online consumers: Reactions to consensus, physical store presence, brand familiarity, and generalized suspicion. *Journal of Retailing*, *86*(4), 322–335. doi:10.1016/j.jretai.2010.04.002

Berger, C. R. (2002). Strategic and non-strategic information acquisition. *Human Communication Research*, *28*(2), 287–297. doi:10.1111/j.1468-2958.2002.tb00809.x

Berger, C. R., & Calabrese, R. J. (1975). Some explorations in initial interaction and beyond: Toward a developmental theory of interpersonal communication. *Human Communication Research*, *1*(2), 99–112. doi:10.1111/j.1468-2958.1975.tb00258.x

Bhattacherjee, A., & Sanford, C. (2006). Influence processes for information technology acceptance: An elaboration likelihood model. *Management Information Systems Quarterly*, *30*(4), 805–825.

Brown, J., Broderick, A. J., & Lee, N. (2007). Word of mouth communication within online communities: Conceptualizing the online social network. *Journal of Interactive Marketing*, *21*(3), 2–20. doi:10.1002/dir.20082

Carlson, J. R., Carlson, D. S., Hunter, E. M., Vaughn, R. L., & George, J. F. (2013). Virtual team effectiveness: Investigating the moderating role of experience with computer-mediated communication on the impact of team cohesion and openness. *Journal of Organizational and End User Computing*, *25*(2), 1–18. doi:10.4018/joeuc.2013040101

Chang, H. H., & Chen, S. W. (2008). The impact of online store environment cues on purchase intention: Trust and perceived risk as a mediator. *Online Information Review*, *32*(6), 818–841. doi:10.1108/14684520810923953

Chang, H. H., & Chuang, S. S. (2011). Social capital and individual motivations on knowledge sharing: Participant involvement as a moderator. *Information & Management*, *48*(1), 9–18. doi:10.1016/j.im.2010.11.001

Chang, H. H., & Wang, H. W. (2011). The moderating effect of customer perceived value on online shopping behavior. *Online Information Review*, *35*(3), 333–359. doi:10.1108/14684521111151414

Chen, Y., & Xie, J. (2008). Online consumer review: Word-of-mouth as a new element of marketing communication mix. *Management Science*, *54*(3), 477–491. doi:10.1287/mnsc.1070.0810

Cheung, C. M., Lee, M. K., & Rabjohn, N. (2008). The impact of electronic word-of-mouth: The adoption of online opinions in online customer communities. *Internet Research*, *18*(3), 229–247. doi:10.1108/10662240810883290

Cheung, M. Y., Luo, C., Sia, C. L., & Chen, H. (2009). Credibility of electronic word-of-mouth: Informational and normative determinants of online consumer recommendations. *International Journal of Electronic Commerce, 13*(4), 9–38. doi:10.2753/JEC1086-4415130402

Chevalier, J. A., & Mayzlin, D. (2006). The effect of word of mouth on sales: Online book reviews. *JMR, Journal of Marketing Research, 43*(3), 345–354. doi:10.1509/jmkr.43.3.345

Clarkson, J. J., Tormala, Z. L., & Rucker, D. D. (2008). A new look at the consequences of attitude certainty: The amplification hypothesis. *Journal of Personality and Social Psychology, 95*(4), 810–825. doi:10.1037/a0013192 PMID:18808261

Crossland, M. D., Herschel, R. T., Perkins, W. C., & Scudder, J. N. (2000). The impact of task and cognitive style on decision-making effectiveness using a geographic information system. *Journal of Organizational and End User Computing, 12*(1), 14–23. doi:10.4018/joeuc.2000010102

Crowley, A. E., & Hoyer, W. D. (1994). An integrative framework for understanding two-sided persuasion. *The Journal of Consumer Research, 20*(4), 561–574. doi:10.1086/209370

Currás-Pérez, R., Ruiz-Mafé, C., & Sanz-Blas, S. (2003). Social network loyalty: Evaluating the role of attitude, perceived risk and satisfaction. *Online Information Review, 37*(1), 61–68.

Dellarocas, C. (2006). Strategic manipulation of internet opinion forums: Implications for consumers and firms. *Management Science, 52*(10), 1577–1593. doi:10.1287/mnsc.1060.0567

Dimoka, A., Hong, Y., & Pavlou, P. A. (2012). On product uncertainty in online markets: Theory and evidence. *Management Information Systems Quarterly, 36*(2), 395–A15.

Drennan, J., Sullivan, G., & Previte, J. (2006). Privacy, risk perception, and expert online behavior: An exploratory study of household end users. *Journal of Organizational and End User Computing, 18*(1), 1–22. doi:10.4018/joeuc.2006010101

Dubois, D., Rucker, D. D., & Tormala, Z. L. (2011). From rumors to facts, and facts to rumors: The role of certainty decay in consumer communications. *JMR, Journal of Marketing Research, 48*(6), 1020–1032. doi:10.1509/jmr.09.0018

Eisend, M. (2006). Two-sided advertising: A meta-analysis. *International Journal of Research in Marketing, 23*(2), 187–198. doi:10.1016/j.ijresmar.2005.11.001

Evans, J. (2010). Intuition and reasoning: A dual-process perspective. *Psychological Inquiry, 21*(4), 313–326. doi:10.1080/1047840X.2010.521057

Gibbs, J. L., Ellison, N. B., & Lai, C. H. (2012). First comes love, then comes google: An investigation of uncertainty reduction strategies and self-disclosure in online dating. *Communication Research, 38*(1), 70–100. doi:10.1177/0093650210377091

Grewal, D., Gotlieb, J., & Marmorstein, H. (1994). The moderating effects of message framing and source credibility on the price-perceived risk relationship. *The Journal of Consumer Research, 21*(1), 145–153. doi:10.1086/209388

Gudykunst, W. B., Yang, S., & Nishida, T. (1985). A cross-cultural test of uncertainty reduction theory: Comparisons of acquaintances, friends, and dating relationships in Japan, Korea, and the United States. *Human Communication Research, 11*(3), 407–455. doi:10.1111/j.1468-2958.1985.tb00054.x

Gurrea, R., Orús, C., & Flavián, C. (2013). The role of symbols signaling the product status on online users' information processing. *Online Information Review, 37*(1), 8–27. doi:10.1108/14684521311311603

Hansen, H., Samuelsen, B. M., & Silseth, P. (2008). Customer perceived value in B-to-B service relationships: Investigating the importance of corporate reputation. *Industrial Marketing Management*, *37*(2), 206–217. doi:10.1016/j.indmarman.2006.09.001

Hennig-Thurau, T., & Walsh, G. (2003). Electronic word-of-mouth: Motives for and consequences of reading customer articulations on the Internet. *International Journal of Electronic Commerce*, *8*(2), 51–74.

Johnston, A. C., & Warkentin, M. (2010). The influence of perceived source credibility on end user attitudes and intentions to comply with recommended IT actions. *Journal of Organizational and End User Computing*, *22*(3), 1–21. doi:10.4018/joeuc.2010070101

Kao, D. T. (2011). Message sidedness in advertising: The moderating roles of need for cognition and time pressure in persuasion. *Scandinavian Journal of Psychology*, *52*(4), 329–340. doi:10.1111/j.1467-9450.2011.00882.x PMID:21752025

Khare, A., Labrecque, L. I., & Asare, A. K. (2011). The assimilative and contrastive effects of word-of-mouth volume: An experimental examination of online consumer ratings. *Journal of Retailing*, *87*(1), 111–126. doi:10.1016/j.jretai.2011.01.005

Kim, S. S., & Son, J. Y. (2009). Out of dedication or constraint? A dual model of post-adoption phenomena and its empirical test in the context of online services. *Management Information Systems Quarterly*, *33*(1), 49–70.

Koh, Y. J., & Sundar, S. S. (2010). Heuristic versus systematic processing of specialist versus generalist sources in online media. *Human Communication Research*, *36*(2), 103–124. doi:10.1111/j.1468-2958.2010.01370.x

Lee, J., Park, D. H., & Han, I. (2011). The different effects of online consumer reviews on consumers' purchase intentions depending on trust in online shopping malls. *Internet Research*, *21*(2), 187–206. doi:10.1108/10662241111123766

Lee, M., Kim, M., & Peng, W. (2013). Consumer reviews: Reviewer avatar facial expression and review valence. *Internet Research*, *23*(2), 116–132. doi:10.1108/10662241311313277

Lemanski, J. L., & Lee, H. S. (2012). Attitude certainty and resistance to persuasion. *International Journal of Business and Social Science*, *3*(1), 66–75.

Li, X., Rong, G., & Thatcher, J. B. (2012). Does technology trust substitute interpersonal trust? Examining Technology trust's influence on individual decision-making. *Journal of Organizational and End User Computing*, *24*(2), 18–38. doi:10.4018/joeuc.2012040102

Lin, C. L., Lee, S. H., & Horng, D. J. (2011). The effects of online reviews on purchasing intention: The moderating role of need for cognition. *Social Behavior & Personality: An International Journal*, *39*(1), 71–81. doi:10.2224/sbp.2011.39.1.71

Liu, Y. (2006). Word of mouth for movies: Its dynamics and impact on box office revenue. *Journal of Marketing*, *70*(3), 74–89. doi:10.1509/jmkg.70.3.74

Lu, X., Ba, S., Hung, L., & Feng, Y. (2013). Promotional Marketing or Word-of-Mouth? Evidence from Online Restaurant Reviews. *Information Systems Research*, *24*(3), 596–612. doi:10.1287/isre.1120.0454

Martin, S. S., Carneb, C., & Jose, R. S. (2011). Dual effect of perceived risk on cross-national e-commerce. *Internet Research*, *23*(2), 116–132.

Matook, S., & der Heijden, H. V. (2013). Goal abstraction, goal linkage dependency, and perceived utilitarian value of information systems: A mixed-method study. *Journal of Organizational and End User Computing, 25*(2), 41–58.

Mayzlin, D. (2006). Promotional chat on the internet. *Marketing Science, 21*(1), 46–66.

Morgan, R. M., & Hunt, S. D. (1994). The commitment-trust theory of relationship marketing. *Journal of Marketing, 58*(3), 20–38. doi:10.2307/1252308

Mudambi, S. M., & Schuff, D. (2010). What makes a helpful online review? A study of customer reviews on amazon.com. *Management Information Systems Quarterly, 34*(1), 185–200.

Munnukka, F. (2008). Customers' purchase intentions as a reflection of price perception. *Journal of Product and Brand Management, 17*(3), 188–196. doi:10.1108/10610420810875106

Negash, S., Ryanb, T., & Igbariab, M. (2003). Quality and effectiveness in web-based customer support systems. *Information & Management, 40*(8), 757–768. doi:10.1016/S0378-7206(02)00101-5

Park, D. H., & Kim, S. (2008). The effects of consumer knowledge on message processing of electronic word-of-mouth via online consumer reviews. *Electronic Commerce Research and Applications, 7*(4), 399–410. doi:10.1016/j.elerap.2007.12.001

Park, D. H., Lee, J., & Han, I. (2007). The effect of online consumer reviews on consumer purchasing intention. *International Journal of Electronic Commerce, 11*(4), 125–148. doi:10.2753/JEC1086-4415110405

Pauley, P. M., & Emmers-Sommer, T. M. (2007). The impact of internet technologies on primary and secondary romantic relationship development. *Communication Studies, 58*(4), 411–427. doi:10.1080/10510970701648616

Pechmann, C. (1992). Predicting when two-sided ads will be more effective than one-sided ads. *JMR, Journal of Marketing Research, 29*(4), 441–453. doi:10.2307/3172710

Planalp, S., & Honeycutt, J. M. (1985). Events that increase uncertainty in personal relationships. *Human Communication Research, 11*(4), 593–604. doi:10.1111/j.1468-2958.1985.tb00062.x

Podsakoff, P. M., MacKenzie, S. B., Lee, J. Y., & Podsakoff, N. P. (2003). Common method biases in behavioral research: A critical review of the literature and recommended remedies. *The Journal of Applied Psychology, 88*(5), 879–903. doi:10.1037/0021-9010.88.5.879 PMID:14516251

Pollach, I. (2006). Privacy statements as a means of uncertainty reduction in WWW interactions. *Journal of Organizational and End User Computing, 18*(1), 23–49. doi:10.4018/joeuc.2006010102

Ramirez, A., Walther, J. B., Burgoon, J. K., & Sunnafrank, M. (2002). Information-seeking strategies, uncertainty, and computer-mediated communication. *Human Communication Research, 28*(2), 213–228.

Saeed, K. A., Hwang, Y., & Yi, M. Y. (2003). Toward an integrative framework for online consumer behavior research: A meta-analysis approach. *Journal of Organizational and End User Computing, 15*(4), 1–26. doi:10.4018/joeuc.2003100101

Shen, Y. C., Huang, C. Y., Chu, C. H., & Liao, H. C. (2010). Virtual community loyalty: An interpersonal interaction perspective. *International Journal of Electronic Commerce, 15*(1), 49–73. doi:10.2753/JEC1086-4415150102

Sirdeshmukh, D., Singh, J., & Sabol, B. (2002). Consumer trust, value, and loyalty in relational exchanges. *Journal of Marketing, 66*(1), 15–37. doi:10.1509/jmkg.66.1.15.18449

Tidwell, L. C., & Walther, J. B. (2002). Computer-mediated communication effects on disclosure, impressions, and interpersonal evaluations. *Human Communication Research, 28*(3), 317–348. doi:10.1111/j.1468-2958.2002.tb00811.x

Tormala, Z. L., & Petty, R. E. (2004). Source credibility and attitude certainty: A metacognitive analysis of resistance to persuasion. *Journal of Consumer Psychology, 14*(4), 427–442. doi:10.1207/s15327663jcp1404_11

Wakefield, R. L., & Whitten, D. (2006). Examining user perceptions of third-party organizations credibility and trust in an e-retailer. *Journal of Organizational and End User Computing, 18*(2), 1–19. doi:10.4018/joeuc.2006040101

West, P. M., & Broniarczyk, S. M. (1998). Integrating multiple opinions: The role of aspiration level on consumer response to critic consensus. *The Journal of Consumer Research, 25*(1), 38–51. doi:10.1086/209525

Xue, F., & Zhou, P. (2010). The effects of product involvement and prior experience on Chinese consumers' responses to online word of mouth. *Journal of International Consumer Marketing, 23*(1), 45–58. doi:10.1080/08961530.2011.524576

Zhu, F., & Zhang, X. M. (2010). Impact of online consumer reviews on sales: The moderating role of product and consumer characteristics. *Journal of Marketing, 74*(2), 133–148. doi:10.1509/jmkg.74.2.133

This work was previously published in the Journal of Organizational and End User Computing (JOEUC), 27(2); edited by Tanya McGill, pages 32-57, copyright year 2015 by IGI Publishing (an imprint of IGI Global).

APPENDIX

Table 4. Construct definitions of this study and number of items

Constructs	Definitions	Reference	Items
Informational Determinants			
Argument quality	Persuasive strength of arguments in an online consumer review.	Bhattacherjee & Sanford (2006)	4
Recommendation framing	Positive or negative of the online consumer reviews. Negatively framed online consumer reviews emphasize a product or service's weaknesses or problems.	Grewal et al. (1994)	2
Recommendation sidedness	Recommendation sidedness includes one-sided and two-sided online consumer reviews. Two-sided online consumer reviews indicate both positive and negative components.	Cheung et al. (2009)	2
Source credibility	A source has credibility when the information receiver can feel the writer has told the truth as he or she sees it.	Brown et al. (2007)	5
Confirmation of prior belief	To identify the level of confirmation between the received information and prior beliefs through various direct or indirect experiences.	Cheung et al. (2009)	3
Normative Determinants			
Recommendation consistency	The extent to which a current online consumer review is consistent with other providers' experiences concerning the same product or service evaluation.	Cheung et al. (2008)	2
Recommendation rating	The overall rating given by online consumer review authors on a product or service.	Cheung et al. (2009)	3
Uncertainty reduction	Degree of confidence that a customer has in his or her ability to make predictions about the firm he or she is dealing with.	Morgan & Hunt (1994)	6
Value perception	Opinions, attitude, and thoughts that consumers hold in regard to a particular store or product.	Munnukka (2008)	3

Table 5. List of measurement items

Theoretical Constructs		Items	Reference
Informational Determinants			
Argument Quality	AQ1	The review arguments are convincing.	Cheung et al. (2009)
	AQ2	The review arguments are strong.	
	AQ3	The review arguments are persuasive.	
	AQ4	The review arguments are good.	
Recommendation Framing	RF1	Overall, the review stresses positive implications about the discussed restaurant.	Cheung et al. (2009)
	RF2	Overall, the review stresses a favorable appraisal of the discussed restaurant.	
Recommendation Sidedness	RS1	The review doesn't include only one-sided comments (positive or negative).	Cheung et al. (2009)
	RS2	The review includes both pros and cons about the discussed restaurant.	

continued on following page

Table 5. Continued

Theoretical Constructs		Items	Reference
Source Credibility	SC1	I think the writer is trustworthy.	Chang & Chen (2008), Ohanian (1990)
	SC2	I think the writer is dependable.	
	SC3	I think the writer is honest.	
	SC4	I think the writer is reliable.	
	SC5	I think the writer is sincere.	
Confirmation of Prior Belief	CB1	Information from the review didn't contradict prior knowledge I had before reading it.	Cheung et al. (2009)
	CB2	The review supported my impression of the discussed restaurant.	
	CB3	The review reinforced prior information I had about the discussed restaurant.	
Normative Determinants			
Recommendation Consistency	RC1	Comments in the review are consistent with other reviews.	Cheung et al. (2009)
	RC2	Comments in the review are similar to those of other reviews.	
Recommendation Rating	RR1	Based on the review rating, the discussed restaurant was found to be favorable by other consumers.	Cheung et al. (2009)
	RR2	Based on the review rating, the discussed restaurant is highly rated by other consumers.	
	RR3	Based on the review rating, the discussed restaurant is good.	
Uncertainty Reduction	UR1	You recognize the discussed restaurant.	Adjei et al. (2010), D'Ambra & Wilson (2004)
	UR2	You have understood the informational content about the discussed restaurant adequately.	
	UR3	Your question for the discussed restaurant can be resolved by reading the online consumer review.	
	UR4	That relevant review they discussed restaurant information is available and can be found on the online consumer review.	
	UR5	I am confident that I can predict the quality of the discussed restaurant's food.	
	UR6	I am confident that I can predict the performance of the discussed restaurant's consumer services.	
Value Perception	VP1	The food offered by the discussed restaurant will be an excellent buy for the money.	Burman & Biswas (2004), Chang & Wang (2011)
	VP2	The price charged by the discussed restaurant for the food will be an extremely fair price.	
	VP3	The food offered by the discussed restaurant will be an extremely good value for the money.	

Chapter 69
Sleep Disorder Diagnosis:
An Analytical Approach

Jacqueline Blake
University of the Sunshine Coast, Australia

Don Kerr
University of the Sunshine Coast, Australia

ABSTRACT

Sleep disorders are a significant and growing problem, both for the economy of the nation and for the physical and psychological well-being of individual sufferers. Physicians are under pressure to find ways of dealing with the backlog of patients. The purpose of this chapter is to investigate the operational, administrative, and medical environment within which sleep physicians diagnose patients with sleep disorders and develop an online support system that would efficiently gather patient history data and improve the effectiveness of patient-physician consultations, the diagnoses, and patients' self-management of any subsequent treatment plans. Investigations confirm that the physicians spend a large portion of the available consultation time on routine questions. In the new system, the patient information is captured by the patient completing an online questionnaire. Due to the reduction in time given for data collection, the physician can spend time with the patients discussing patient-specific symptoms and life-styles.

INTRODUCTION

Sleep disorders are a significant and growing problem, both for the economy of the nation and for the physical and psychological well-being of individual sufferers. Physicians, who deal with sleep disorders, and their administrative support staff and facilities, are under constant pressure to find more efficient ways of dealing with the back-log of patients, many of whom face significant wait times before being able to attend a consultation.

The main symptom of a sleep disorder is excessive daytime sleepiness there are a number of lifestyle consequences associated with this. Deloitte Access Economics (2011) state that 8.9% of the Australian population are affected. The direct and indirect costs of sleep disorders to the Australian society in 2010 was 36.4 billion dollars

DOI: 10.4018/978-1-4666-8619-9.ch069

(Deloitte Access Economics 2011). The indirect costs include co-morbidities[1] such as hypertension, lost production, transport and workplace accidents and social costs, such as learning difficulties. Physically, sleep deprivation may be associated with an increased risk of myocardial infraction (heart attack), type two diabetes, depressed immune response (Akerstedt & Nilsson 2003) and may present as depression. However treatment for sleep disorders reduces the direct and indirect costs restoring productivity and well-being to the individual and any organisation they are involved with. Sleep disorders are a chronic condition, so that for most conditions a treatment plan must be enduring requiring a considerable on-going commitment from the sufferer and partnership with their physician.

The estimate of 8.9% of the Australian population who have a sleep disorder is in all probability an underestimate with sleep disorders underdiagnosed in Australia (Deloitte Access Economics 2011), other countries report similar statistics (Young, Peppard & Gottlieb 2002) with the people who are referred for treatment being strongly symptomatic (Kramer et al. 1999). This means that there remains a sector of the population who are yet to seek treatment demonstrated by the direct costs of sleep disorders comprising only two per cent of the total cost. Sleep disorders commonly affect people around middle-age so as the population ages there are an increased number of people with sleep disorders with risk factors in adults being obesity, alcohol, smoking, nasal congestion and menopause (Young et al. 2002). The wait times for a consultation in a publically funded facility may be significant (Flemons et al. 2004). The wait times demonstrate a gap between demand for sleep disorder assistance and the ability of the most health services to provide for the current level of people referred to sleep clinics. Australia in common with other developed countries is also facing an aging population in which sleep disorders will become more prevalent (Alzougool, Chang & Gray 2008).

INCREASING DEMAND FOR SERVICES

This increasing service demand and a shortage of sleep disorder specialists (Australian Medical Workforce Advisory Committee 2000; Patlak 2005) have driven the sleep community interest in changing the traditional model of care for sleep disorders to one that leverages information systems to provide efficiencies and timely communication flows (Colten & Alterogt 2006). Abidi (2001) refers to the strategic use of knowledge derived from healthcare data as being "... *pertinent towards the improvement of the operational efficiency of the said healthcare enterprise"* (Abidi 2001, p. 6) while Hirakis & Karakounos *(2006)* and Haux (2010) state that knowledge management in healthcare allows the development of best practice models, making guidelines explicit and encourages innovation through development of the resultant knowledge base.

The term health informatics was developed by the International Medical Informatics Association (IMIA). They defined the term as "a combination of computer science, information science and health science designed to assist in the management and processing of data, information and knowledge to support healthcare and healthcare delivery (Conrick 2006, p. 4). Health informatics now forms part of the infrastructure for the delivery of healthcare with one of the major fields of research being decision support (Haux 2010). Health informatics allows the timely retrieval and filtering of patient and disorder information so that care givers have appropriate information in a quickly assimilated format within their work flow. Health informatics is the overarching domain within which this project lies as this project aims to use information systems to assist in providing knowledge to support both the patient and physician in the diagnosis of sleep disorders.

One important avenue to leverage the capabilities of this project and its collection of sleep disorder data is that of business analytics. Chen,

Chiang and Storey (2012, p. 1166) defined business analytics as "techniques, technologies, systems, practices, methodologies and applications that analyse critical business data to help the enterprise better understand its business and market and make timely business decision." In this instance we can consider a sleep clinic's business of being the most efficient means of diagnosing and helping a patient deal with the lifestyle implications of a chronic disorder diagnosis.

The purpose of this research was to investigate the operational, administrative and medical environment within which sleep physicians currently diagnose patients with sleep disorders and develop an online support system that would more efficiently gather patient history data, and so improve the effectiveness of patient–physician consultations, the diagnoses, and patients' self-management of any subsequent treatment plans. The research used observations and a participatory research process based on inputs from two sleep physicians and a sleep psychologist to guide the development for the information technology artefact. This process ensured that the resultant online tools fitted into the physician's work flow with the patient information in the required format.

RESEARCH OBJECTIVES

A design science approach was taken to building the online tools. The resultant online tools incorporates four sub-applications,

1. An online sleep diary, with an output of a physician report showing a graph of the patients sleep patterns and sleep statistics and the online presentation to the patient of the sleep pattern graph.
2. An online patient history questionnaire, asking lifestyle, medical history and sleep disorder specific questions.
3. A decision support system using as an input data from the patient history questionnaire.

4. A report generator summarising and presenting the output from the decision support system.

These tools aim to remove responsibility for form filling from the physician to the patient, Give the patient access to sleep disorder specific questions earlier in their interaction with the sleep investigation unit to aid self-discovery of sleep disorder information. Another outcome is presenting the patient information to the physician within the natural workflow of a consultation in a format which the physicians find useful.

One of the critical factors for physicians to accept a clinical decision support system is openness and transparency of how the decision was derived therefore an explanation of how a decision is reached by the system must be provided. The provision of an explanation module and the diagnostic environment of heterogeneous sleep disorder sufferers drove the adoption of small rule based decision support systems at every decision point in the argument toward diagnosis as described by Stranieri et al. (1999). Graber and Mathew (2008) found that to increase acceptance of clinical decision support systems, reducing physician time to input data and fitting the system into physician work flow were key factors.

THE IT ARTEFACT

The IT artefact will aid physicians by presenting them with relevant patient information within the natural workflow of a consultation, and in a format that the physicians finds useful, while the individual who has a sleep disorder is able to fill in the questionnaire at their leisure and in their own home.

The development of an online application gives the form designer control over the sequence in which the form must be filled in, which means that the user can be constrained to provide information according to a required pattern. An online application also provides an opportunity to validate the entered data at the point of entry. Using validation in the sleep tool application means that the physician does not need to question the patient about the data contained in the application, but instead has time to talk about what the information means to the patient, for instance the impact of smoking on sleep disorders.

A well-developed sleep tool web application can be cost effective. The data sets from large numbers of respondents represent many repeated iterations of the form; consequently, as the data is captured, it can be automatically stored, manipulated and analysed. Thus data analysis is low cost and happens in real time for each form (Haynes et al. 2006). The automatic storage of collected information also provides an opportunity for good quality, validated data to be used for future research. This is important as at the moment no aggregated analysis is carried out on the present pen-and-paper patient history forms. Anecdotal evidence suggests that manually computing the data from a paper-based patient history, and the data entry of the information into a database, requires a large time commitment from clinic staff. This means that the routine collection of sleep diary information to build an evidence base is unlikely to be given a priority outside of a specific research project.

During 2009, there was strong growth in internet access in Queensland homes, reaching 87.6 per cent, which was an increase of 2½ per cent above the 2008 figure (Queensland Government Chief Information Office 2010). Minimal difference was shown in internet use between genders. The survey showed growth in computer access by people aged over 65; their internet use had grown strongly during the year to 61.1 per cent – a 6 per cent increase (Queensland Government Chief Information Office 2010). These percentages show that online forms are a viable alternative to paper-based forms for a large proportion of the population.

THE DEVELOPMENT

One of the difficulties in constructing an online information system is the need to design the application for unknown users. Users of an online system will have a range of technical skill levels, and will access the system through a variety of connection mechanisms, using an assortment of hardware. This diversity contrasts sharply with the development of an organisational system, which requires standardised connections and hardware, and whose operators have known, minimum technical standards (Taylor, Wade & England 2003). Useability must be a primary objective of an online tool, Guenther (2004) stating that having a clear set of objectives for the user helps to make the online system a high value one. This project had two sets of users: physicians and patients. Consequently, the online tool had to meet two different sets of objectives and expectations. Calongne (2001) argues that what the user wants to achieve from the site must also be considered. In this project the online systems were tools, so that to achieve user satisfaction the online tools had to look and feel like a solid health orientated implement. In the patients' case, the tool needed to feel like a device that would provide good information to them and to their physician, while in the physicians' case, the tool needed to provide a set of quality information in an easy to assimilate format.

To display information online, equity of access had to be considered, so that online tools had utility for the sight, hearing and physically impaired; users with little technical expertise had also to be catered for. Wagner, Hassanein, and Head (2010) suggest a number of guidelines for older users of web sites, including making sure visual elements are large enough to be seen and deciphered. They suggest using elements that contrast highly with the background, such as black elements on a white background. An uncluttered web page without too many elements claiming attention helps the user to make sense of the page. Also, graphics should be used only when necessary to illustrate or add to the site's function (Yen, Hu & Wang 2007). For the online sleep tool application, the expected age range of the users was expected to be fairly broad and computer literacy to be variable. Most of the potential patients would be older than 45 and reasonably computer literate, but to improve equity of access the sleep diary had to be as accessible as possible across the whole spectrum of potential patients.

In the sleep tool application, the user interface was given the maximum contrast of black sans serif text on a plain white uncluttered background. The uncluttered background means that the sleep tool application can be personalised – with, for example, an organisation's logo – without disturbing the readability of the questions. The plain background also helps to minimise the file size of the web application, so that patients whose computers have slow download speeds are not penalised by having to wait for a graphic to appear.

A user tries to make logical sense of a displayed web page at first glance, so the design of the page must make logical sense; for instance, headings should be in a larger font. Design elements that are related need to be gathered together graphically; for example a question is contained within a frame. The graphical treatment of these elements needs to be consistent and predictable throughout the web site to aid usability (Willems 2000). A linear web site plan, where the user moves through the web application page by page, helps to orientate the user so that they are aware of where in the web site they are (Guenther 2004; Yen et al. 2007). These requirements were carried out in the application.

The heuristic evaluation rules for websites detailed by Sharp, Rogers and Preece (2007) were employed. The website has internal consistency, with terms carrying the same meaning throughout the web site, using simple language. To aid internal consistency, formatting of pages, fonts, font sizes and font colours were made consistent. Shortcuts were not used, as the sleep tool application has a simple linear format which must be followed to gather complete information. The user's memory load is minimised with no information being required to be remembered from one part of the web-page or web-site to the other. Entries into the web form are validated; for example in the sleep diary, a wake time before a sleep time cannot be chosen, and throughout, each page is checked for completeness. The user is given feedback in two forms: for the sleep diary, the user is presented with a sleep pattern graphic that represents the entered sleep patterns; for the patient history questionnaire, the user receives a message that their information has been sent to their sleep clinic.

One of the complications with implementing this application is the need to build the application in accordance with guidelines set by the government for patient privacy; for instance, a patient number cannot be used as an identifier. A different number is required to satisfy the National Privacy Principles stated in the Queensland Government's information architecture for the Department of Health (Queensland Government 2001). This was last reviewed in April 2008 (Queensland Government Chief Information Office 2008), and states that an identifier that has been assigned by an agency cannot be adopted by an outside application. Consequently, for this project, a user number that was unique, and different from the patient number, was required to be system assigned.

Purpose of the Web Application

One of the most important factors in the design of the sleep tool web application was the role the patient history played during a consultation. Physicians have clear expectations about what they consider to be best practice at this time, so patient history was included as an input to the system. In order to facilitate the knowledge acquisition process, the researcher formed a team with two sleep physicians and a psychologist. All three were considered to be experts in the field of sleep disorder diagnosis, and a collaborative approach was taken to help gain insights into their shared knowledge and experience in the sleep disorder domain and in order to develop the knowledge base for the DSS. All stakeholders (physicians and patients) provided approval for the process (as required by ethics). Gaining the physician stakeholders' approval of the output from the sleep tool application and its utility as a data gathering instrument for the patient history was essential. This approval meant the project gained access to the sleep physicians' patient knowledge and gave the medical team a vested interest in the success of the project (Cornwall & Jewkes 1995). The two sleep specialists provided expertise on the diagnostic criteria and process, while the psychologist specialised in psychological sleep disorders such as insomnia, the psychology impacts of sleep disorders and compliance with sleep disorder treatment by patients. The researcher acted as team leader to keep the team focused on the required outcome, researched questions from the team, set agendas, produced questionnaire drafts, scheduled meetings and kept records of the meetings.

Structure of the Web Application

The sleep tools application has three main areas of functionality (see Table 1).

There are four main categories of user in the sleep tools application (see Table 2).

The entry page of the online sleep application is a log-on page providing the facility to differentiate between different types of users and the means to authenticate users through the use of an identification number and user name. Differentiating between users is important to customise their interaction with the web site. To facilitate the physician's use of the tool the physician goes directly from log-on to the sleep statistic page for the entered patient number, which allows for the entry of a user name and password. The next page has a different menu, depending on the class of user.

The patient menu page shown in Figure 1 allows the user to choose between either the sleep diary or the patient history areas of functionality or, alternatively, to return to the log-on page.

The main administrator or super-user menu screen is shown in Figure 2. This shows that the

Table 1. Sleep tools application main areas of functionality

Functionality	Output
An online sleep diary, which records 14 days of a person's sleep habits and mood.	*Patient:* A graphical representation of their sleep habits. *Physician:* A graphical representation of a patient's sleep habits and a report containing sleep statistics showing the averages of sleep data.
An online patient history questionnaire	Data stored in database.
A knowledge-based decision support system	Data retrieved from database, manipulated according to logic embedded in decision support system and presented as a report to the physician detailing if the person's patient history meets the criteria for the main sleep disorders.

Table 2. Types of user in the web based sleep tools application

Type of user	Function
A super-user or administrator	Limited to one user – has overall administration responsibility.
Hospital administration staff	Add or edit patients and doctors. They may also access patient results for their clinic, to print out results for patient files.
Physicians	Review and print their patients' results.
Patients	Complete sleep diary and patient history questionnaire.

Figure 1. Patient menu from the sleep tools application

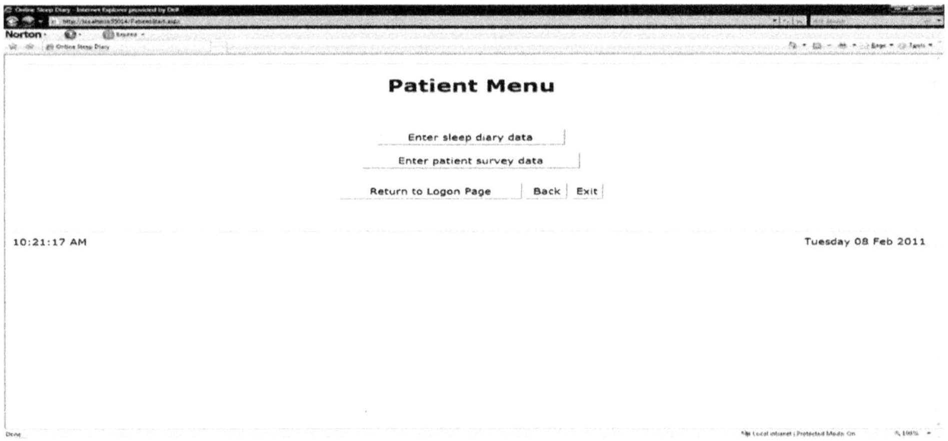

Figure 2. Super-user menu screen

main administrator can access all areas and has overall responsibility for administering the system.

The physician administration menu screen is shown in Figure 3. A physician must be linked to a clinic in order for this screen to be created. This function can be completed by an administration officer (clinic administrator) or the super-user.

The clinic administrator's menu screen is shown in Figure 4. The clinic administrator must also be associated with a clinic. Their role is to create patient records and support the physicians by printing patient reports. They may also create other administrator screens. These figures showing the management screens demonstrate

the overlay of administration and security which controls the views that users have of the main areas of functionality.

Online Sleep Diary

A sleep diary is used to record sleep patterns, usually for fourteen nights. The person notes the details of their night's sleep day-by-day, building up a picture of sleep habits (known as *sleep hygiene*). Poor sleep hygiene, or insufficient time made available for sleep, may be a cause of excessive daytime sleepiness, the main symptom of a sleep disorder. Therefore, a sleep diary can be used to

Figure 3. Physician administration screen

Figure 4. Administration officer screen

identify a cause for daytime sleepiness, lifestyle reasons or a sleep disorder. Sleep diaries are used by a number of health professionals, including psychologists, physicians and sleep specialists and is the primary diagnostic tool for identifying insomnia. It is a very useful aid in the diagnosis of other sleep disorders, as relatively short periods of time taken to fall asleep or frequent awakenings are indicators of poor quality sleep, and of sleep disorders.

During an exploratory interview early in a project to review sleep diagnosis, the remark was made by a director of a large public health clinic that "… sleep diaries were a good tool which were not being used efficiently due to the timing and the short length of time available in the consultation to extract information from the data" (pers. Comm. 23 Sept.). The current format of the sleep diary used in the sleep investigation unit study was a pen-and-paper questionnaire in which the patient coloured in a square between two printed times – for example, nine and ten o'clock – to indicate bed time and waking up time.

This created a situation that requires the sleep physician to clarify which time the patient actually meant to mark. The data contained in the completed

sleep diary required manual calculation to extract daily entries, aggregate the data and calculate the required sleep statistics and was in a format that was difficult to quickly assimilate within a time limited consultation. Due to the low utility of this model of use, the physician had difficulty in using a sleep diary effectively. The information in the sleep diary was also in a format from which a patient cannot extract information without physician assistance. An online literature search was carried out for Internet or web and online sleep diaries for evidence of previous peer reviewed papers. This search was periodically carried out throughout this project, the last being undertaken on 30 March 2012. No peer reviewed papers focusing on online sleep diaries were found.

Patient access to the information contained in an online sleep diary means the patient gains increased self-knowledge of their sleep hygiene, which has been shown to improve health outcomes (Smith et al. 2004). Patients should be able to self-monitor their sleep patterns. Wilde and Garvin (2007, p. 343) define self-monitoring as "awareness of symptoms or bodily sensations that is enhanced by periodic measurements recordings and observations to provide information

Figure 5. Flowchart of how sleep tool web application is accessed

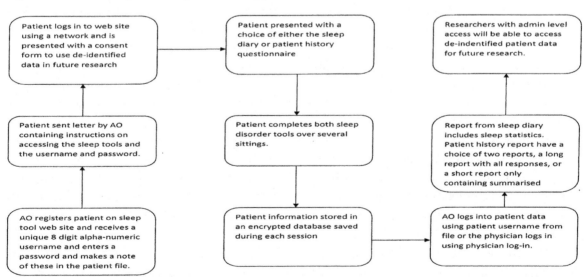

for improved self-management". Self-monitoring of sleep patterns means that the patients have an opportunity for shared decision making with their physician on the management of their sleep disorder. Shared decision making is a significant factor in compliance with treatment plans (Sheppard et al. 2009). This is important in a chronic condition such as a sleep disorder, which has an ongoing treatment burden

With this on-line system, the physician gains earlier access to patient sleep hygiene information and can therefore prioritise those patients who need to be seen first, ensuring that those in most need of the service will have the shortest wait times. It is also forecasted that patient satisfaction with the service will increase as during the wait time for an appointment they are able to self-monitor their condition. Therefore, the online sleep diary has a number of benefits, namely:

1. The data contained within the diary is presented in a summarised, readily accessible format for both physicians and patients.
2. The diary contents are available at any internet access point and in real time (subject to security precautions).
3. The diary facilitates the easy development of a database of sleep patterns and this can be used for historical data analysis.
4. The online diary has all the advantages of digital data such as reuse, multiple storage locations, easier transferability of data to other medical professionals and availability for statistical analysis.

Better quality sleep information is obtained when a sleep diary is filled out every day. This ensures that the person has the best recall of sleep quality and timing of sleep, Libman, Fichten, Bailes, and Amsel (2000) stated that questionnaires that look at respective sleep patterns are susceptible to memory distortion, whereas a sleep diary filled in every day has the ability to capture day-to-day variations, highlighting variations that

may indicate problems such as sleep deficits in sleep patterns. This means that the recording of a person's sleep habits over a two-week period in a sleep diary gives a baseline of a person's sleep patterns with greater precision than retrospective sleep quality questionnaires.

One disadvantage of a sleep diary is that subjects may change their sleep patterns in reaction to the self-monitoring and the imposition of filling in the diary day-to-day (Libman et al. 2000). However, Lacks and Morin (1992) comment that a sleep diary is the most widely used, practical and economical method of gauging sleep patterns.

An online sleep diary has a number of benefits: the data contained within the diary are presented in a summarised, readily accessible format for both physicians and patients, and are available in real time, while the database of sleep patterns is being built.

ONLINE SLEEP DIARY OUTPUTS

The online sleep diary will produce a summary report which may be printed both for the person filling in the diary and for a physician. This summary report gives access to sleep statistics (see Table 3).

Also reported is a count of the number of times that reasons for waking were checked, and the reasons given for the patient being kept awake. An average of the morning's mood and feeling are also given. The report is presented in a quickly assimilated format that has direct utility for assisting in a diagnosis of a sleep disorder. The summary report may also be filed in a patient record to provide a baseline for future sleep diary reports for the physician and patient.

A summary report of sleep hygiene practices may also be useful for the user to take to their primary care physician if the user is concerned about excessive daytime sleepiness. Potentially, this means that primary care physicians may refer patients with moderate symptoms of a sleep dis-

Table 3. Sleep statistics in report for physician

Name	Description
Mean sleep duration	Average time spent asleep.
Range of sleep duration	The minimum and maximum time spent asleep over the sleep diary time period.
Number of nights with fewer than seven hours sleep.	A count of the number of nights where fewer than seven hours of sleep were achieved.
Mean for sleep onset.	Average length of time taken between settling in bed ready for sleep; for example, light off, television off, and time that sleep was achieved.
Range of sleep onset	The minimum and maximum times spent getting to sleep over the sleep diary period.
Mean wake up time	Average time that the person wakes for the last time.
Mean sleep efficiency	Sleep efficiency is the proportion of time spent asleep in the time available for sleep; for example, of the nine hours spent in bed, eight hours were spent asleep. The sleep efficiency is 8/9 = 0.89.

order to a sleep specialist, as sleep disorders are under-diagnosed in all but the most symptomatic patients (Kramer et al. 1999). The online sleep diary may also be used by primary physicians to consider diagnosing a sleep disorder in patients who describe symptoms such as fatigue or lack of energy (Chervin 2000) which traditionally lead to a diagnosis of depression. Shepertycky, Banno and Kryger (2005) state that approximately 90% of women with moderate to severe obstructive sleep apnoea are undiagnosed or misdiagnosed as having depression – leading to significant health impacts and costs to the health system.

The facility to export the data contained in the online sleep diary in an eXtensible Markup Language (XML) format was also provided. This means that organisations other than that hosting the sleep diary can receive patient data in an electronic format, facilitating use of electronic record keeping.

CURRENT SLEEP DIARY MODEL

The current paper-based sleep diary, as stated above, does not present information in a format that the lay person can understand. The online sleep diary in this project presents sleep patterns as an easy to understand multi-coloured horizontal bar graph, with time along the x-axis.

Midnight is the centre of the x-axis to allow the comparison of the regularity of bed and waking up times important in sleep hygiene. This graph builds day by day as the patient completes each day's diary entry. The different colours within the bars represent different states, such as awake during sleep time, sleep latency and sleep time. Therefore, the physician can gain a view of the patient's sleep patterns quickly, while the patient gains access to the information on their sleep patterns presented in a simple graphical format.

The current model of a pen-and-paper sleep diary denies the patient an opportunity to self-monitor their sleep patterns and adopt functional analysis of lifestyle changes such as reducing caffeine intake. With the online sleep diary, patients gain a tool to use in self-monitoring their sleep patterns. Wilde and Garvin (2007, p.343) define self-monitoring as awareness of symptoms that is facilitated by periodic measurements or recordings to provide information for improved self-management. The use of the online sleep diary to self-monitor gives patients the opportunity for shared decision making with their physician on the management of their sleep disorder. Vermeire and Hearnshaw (2001) found that shared decision making is an important factor in compliance to treatment; it is important because compliance to CPAP requires commitment from the user.

The online sleep diary is a sub-application of the sleep tool web application, with the printed graph and sleep statistics providing a hard copy report for the physician.

Patient History Questionnaire

There are a number of questionnaires that are designed to diagnose specific sleep disorders, such as the Sleep Decisions Questionnaire (SDQ) and the Pittsburgh questionnaire. However, these questionnaires are not designed to act as a complete information gathering point for a physician consultation about sleep or designed for future automated data collection. The increasing burden of these disorders on the medical community – caused by a higher profile and aging population – has led to interest by the sleep community in changing the traditional model of care for sleep disorders to one that leverages information systems to provide efficiencies and timely communication flows (Colten & Alterogt 2006,p. 26). Within the Queensland Health system researched in this project, anecdotal evidence suggests that sleep laboratory time is available to perform more polysomnography tests. However, there is an insufficient number of appointment slots for a patient to see a sleep physician before undertaking a polysomnography sleep study. Consequently, the efficient use of a physician's time during a consultation is critical to maintaining the sleep unit's work flow and an appropriate wait time for patients before seeing a physician.

Development of the Questionnaire

The questionnaire is required to act as an information gathering point for input into the intelligent decision support system standard and a validated tool for patient appraisal in sleep disorder consultations. This will provide the sleep physician with good quality data before the first consultation with the patient. The responsibility for filling out the forms is transferred to the patient. This shift from the current practice will potentially free up physician time during the consultation and remove the need for the physician to ask information gathering closed-ended questions during the consultation; for example, "How many caffeine containing drinks did you consume during the day?" Instead, the physician will already have access to the patient's background information, so can use the limited consultation time to focus on the patient's sleep problem and to suggest lifestyle changes. This also has the potential to increase the patient's satisfaction with the provided service.

The outline of the proposed data gathering system for the decision support system for the diagnostic process was driven by a series of three one-hour interviews with the director of a Sleep Investigation Unit, Brisbane, Australia to discuss the sleep disorder diagnostic process. convergent interviewing method as described in the methodology chapter was used to discover initial requirements. This informal interviewing technique is useful when the researchers are in some doubt about the information which is to be collected. Notes and impressions from the interviews were written in a journal and emailed to the interviewee for confirmation that these were aligned with the information they intended to convey. These meetings established the outline of the patient–physician interaction and discovered that there were two main types of consultations. The first was an exploratory consultation where the physician was investigating the current symptoms and patient history; the second was a shorter, confirmatory consultation where the physician discussed the diagnosis with the patient.

Domain Specialist Knowledge Acquisition

The researcher formed a team with two sleep physicians and a psychologist. A collaborative approach was taken with the medical staff to gain their shared knowledge and experience in the sleep disorder domain as knowledge acquisition for the knowledge base of the decision support system. Gaining these stakeholders' approval of the instrument was essential to gain access to sleep investigation clinic patients so as to test the instrument, and to give these team members a vested interest in the success of the project (Cornwall & Jewkes 1995). The team members were two sleep specialists, a sleep psychologist; and the researcher. The two medical doctors provided expertise on the diagnostic criteria and process; the psychologist specialised in psychological sleep disorders such as insomnia, the psychological impacts of sleep disorders, and compliance with sleep disorder treatments by patients. The researcher led the team and in addition had domain experience in constructing questionnaires and providing information systems in knowledge management. The researcher was also responsible for keeping the team focused on producing a data gathering tool for the decision support system, for undertaking research activities outside the meeting, for checking the literature for parameters, and for confirming decisions. The researcher was also responsible for producing the hospital ethics application, producing questionnaire drafts, scheduling meetings and keeping records of the meetings.

A participatory approach was taken to the development of the questionnaire as this can form "knowledge used in action" (Cornwall & Jewkes 1995, p. 1667), while Macaulay (2007) promotes its use by physicians to produce relevant research. White, Suchowierska & Campbell (2004) agree that participatory research can produce relevant research, resulting in the development of user friendly instruments. University of British Columbia Institute of Health Promotion Research (1996) describes participatory research as "systematic inquiry, with the collaboration of those affected by the issue being studied, for purposes of education and taking action or effecting change". In this instance the community being studied comprised sleep specialists who worked within the Queensland Health public system, and who showed concern about the problem by approach-

ing the university with the research concept. The participatory research approach ensured that there was a collegial power sharing approach with a mutual respect of each participant's expertise in their field. The interaction of the team using this approach meant that once a clear definition of the problem under study was made, a solution that was technically possible and immediately useful to the physicians could be designed (White et al. 2004). The technical aspect of the solution was made accessible to the team members by using pen-and-paper and PowerPoint prototypes to make explicit the outcome of the system (Pilemalm & Timpka 2008).

RESULTS

Physician Evaluation of Sleep Tools Instrument

Investigations confirmed that the physicians spend a large portion of the available consultation time on routine questions such as capturing details on smoking habits and caffeine consumption. One of the physician's initial comments on seeing a patient history report was that at least they could read it demonstrating how important how important information which is easy to assimilate is within the confines of a consultation.

The sleep tool web application is intended to be used first, by patients with potentially limited computer literacy, and then by physicians who will use the application for diagnostic purposes. It was therefore essential to ensure that the application was usable. The International Standards Organisation (ISO) defines usability in standard 9241–11 as "extent to which a product can be used by specified users to achieve specified goals effectively, efficiently and with satisfaction in a specified context of use" (Zikmund 2003). The online sleep tools was evaluated by sleep physicians, in terms of their perception of how the use of the tools would benefit their practice, the consultation and patient information. A sample of 267 people from a general population used the sleep tools and then completed a usability questionnaire, finally a technical expect evaluated the sleep tools in terms of their usability.

The physicians were sent ten outputs from the sleep tools from randomly selected sleep disorder patients who completed the sleep tools. This is equivalent to the patient information which the physician's will receive before a consultation when the proposed sleep tool consultation interaction is implemented. The physicians were then asked a set of questions focusing on any impact that receiving the information in this format and before a patient consultation would have of their practice. The operational impacts of using the sleep tools were also investigated.

The physicians stated that the application was usable and useful, that it could improve their communication with their patients, and that it provided efficiencies during the patient–physician diagnostic interaction. Importantly use of the sleep tools did not impose a change of the physician's workflow except that they had access to good quality patient information before the patient consultation. There was still an opportunity for physician's to clarify patient information with the sleep tool report acting as an objective second opinion according to established international disorder criteria.

For the validity of the sleep tools instrument, the ten outputs from sleep disorder people were considered by the sleep physicians. The physicians concurred that the patient outputs fell within the expected range of patient responses.

Patient Evaluation of Sleep Tools Instrument

A total of 267 users entered their information in the sleep tools web application and then completed a questionnaire developed by the researcher based upon the Technology Acceptance Model (TAM). The questions from this questionnaire were pre-

tested on colleagues who had previously used TAM for evaluating applications (Soroush, Hafeez-Baig & Gururajan 2010) The questionnaire focused upon the two different areas of functionality: the online sleep diary and the online patient history questionnaire. The usability questionnaire was completed when the person's interaction with the application was finished. The questionnaire was a short pen-and-paper document that was easy to fill in.

The 269 users who evaluated the sleep tools web application indicated that it is easy to use, easy to understand and easy to read. The results demonstrated that the interface of the sleep tools web application is suited to users with low computer literacy and can be considered relatively easy to read and understand. The users' responses indicated that filling in the application resulted in them thinking about and understanding the pattern of their sleeping habits indicating that this tool is usable for users over a range of ages, education and computer literacy. This agrees with Calongne (2001) who postulated in an opinion paper that usability should be a primary objective in web site design, suggesting that knowing the audience and their objective in using a web site should be considered to achieve usability. Guenther (2004) also agreed that for successful web site usability, one should focus on end user objectives in using the application This study also agrees with Williams (2000) that a simple clean design with high contrast between elements that stand out clearly against their background are important. This also agrees with the findings from the technical evaluation that the layout of the web application was in a simple linear layout. The layout of the application in a linear design also agreed with another of Guenther (2004) principles. Yen et al. (2007) in a review of literature and the proposal of a model for web design also agreed that a linear layout assisted user's navigation.

The user evaluation that the sleep tool web application was usable agrees with previous studies that the Internet administration of questionnaires offers a valid mode of delivery (Buchanan 2003; Carlbring et al. 2007; Johnson 2005). Buchanan (2003) reviewed the administration of three online medical questionnaires and found that with the exception of using norms gathered from online questionnaires to compare against those gathered in pen and paper questionnaires, online delivery of questionnaires was a valid delivery mode. Johnson (2005) found that for protocol validity, respondents to an online questionnaire were as consistent as those respondents using a pen and paper questionnaire. Carlbring et al. (2007) investigated the psychometric properties of online questionnaires in a test retest study using online and pen and paper questionnaires. The finding was that online administration of questionnaires was reliable and valid. The outcome from this study is that an online questionnaire offers a mode of delivery which respondents find comfortable and usable.

Technical Evaluation of Sleep Tools Instrument

The technical evaluation revealed the sleep tools web application to be easy to use with a simple linear design. However, a number of usability issues were noted that were not identified by the patient usability research. Some of these issues, such as the minimalist observation, reflected the following of access considerations and a desire for regional patients with slower Internet access not to be penalised. This evaluation shows that this desire for equity of access may impact on the feel of the instrument, and the input of a graphical user interface expert should requested for the next iteration of the application.

IMPLICATIONS

In this system the collection of routine patient information is done by the patient completing an online questionnaire. Due to the removal of data collection in a consultation, the physician can spend time with the patient discussing patient-specific symptoms and life-style. This will enable the physician to see more patients or they can perform a more in-depth consultation with each patient. The implication is that a shorter consultation will allow the sleep physician to see more patients and thereby lessening the consultation wait time. In this case a shorter consultation times maximises the use of physician time and represents a saving to the service provider while the patient still receives a good quality service.

The output from the sleep tools web application will allow an efficient, consistent triage process before seeing a patient for the first time. The operational implication of this is that a patient with a high risk of sleep apnoea can be sent to have a polysomnography before a consultation with a sleep physician. This acts to shorten the diagnostic interaction by at least one consultation freeing the physician to see more new patients and reducing the cost of treating each of these patients. As the sleep disorder clinic is government funded this offers a direct saving to the government health budget and will help to alleviate wait times to be seen for patients. The patient is also saved the burden of having to travel to one consultation. Dement (2008) suggests that an aging population will exacerbate that shortage finding time gains and efficiencies within the sleep disorder consultation interaction is important for patient wait times and the cost of treating the disorder.

The sleep tools web application automatically saves the patient history and sleep diary data in a database. This database will then form a valuable resource for researchers in aggregated patient history data, with the facility to export unidentified data in a eXtensible Markup Language (XML) format. This aggregated information is not currently available within this health service as hard copy patient records are used. One of the most important characteristics of the sleep disorder population is that it is heterogeneous, future data mining of the aggregated patient history data may lead to a discovery of a combination of factors which may be used to screen for individual sleep disorders in the wider population. This analytic approach has implications for screening of populations in whom an undetected sleep disorder poses a risk not only to themselves but also to other members of the community such as commercial drivers.

One of the problems with the management of chronic conditions such as sleep disorders is to gain collaboration between health providers, such as sleep specialist and primary care physicians. The collection of electronic patient data allows an ease of patient information transfer. This means that the primary care physician is able to reinforce the need for life style changes suggested by the specialist to improve patient treatment.

CONCLUSION

The sleep tool objectives – that of devolving the responsibility for form filling from the physician to the patient, and giving the patient access to sleep disorder specific questions earlier in their interaction with the sleep investigation unit – have been met. This will aid patients in their self-discovery of their own sleep disorder information, as the literature shows that a more knowledgeable patient receives a more personalised consultation and is better able to comply with treatment plans. However the primary objective which was met was to improve the communication flows between the patient and physician. This objective meant the consultation could change from one where the patient was required to answer a series of questions to a consultation where there was time for a discussion on how a patient's condition might be best managed and fitted into their lifestyle. This type of discussion is important for treatment compliance for patients with a chronic condition such a sleep disorder.

ACKNOWLEDGMENT

The authors would like to thank the anonymous reviewers and the editor for their insightful comments and suggestions.

REFERENCES

Abidi, S. S. R. (2001). Knowledge management in healthcare: towards 'knowledge-driven' decision-support services. *International Journal of Medical Informatics*, *63*(1-2), 5–18. doi:10.1016/S1386-5056(01)00167-8 PMID:11518661

Akerstedt, T., & Nilsson, P. M. (2003). Sleep as restitution: an introduction. *Journal of Internal Medicine*, *254*(1), 6–12. doi:10.1046/j.1365-2796.2003.01195.x PMID:12823638

Alzougool, B., Chang, S., & Gray, K. (2008). Towards a comprehensive understanding of health information needs. *Electronic Journal of Health Informatics*, *3*(2), e15.

Australian Medical Workforce Advisory Committee. (2000). *The Specialist Thoracic Medicine Workforce In Australia*. Retrieved 31 March 2008, from http://www5.health.nsw.gov.au/amwac/amwac/pdf/thoracic_medicine_2000.1.pdf

Buchanan, T. (2003). Internet-based questionnaire assessment: Appropriate use in clinical contexts. *Cognitive Behaviour Therapy*, *32*(3), 100–109. doi:10.1080/16506070310000957 PMID:16291542

Calongne, C. M. (2001). Designing for web site usability. *Journal of Computing Sciences in Colleges*, *16*(3).

Carlbring, P., Brunt, S., Bohman, S., Austin, D., Richards, J., Öst, L.-G., & Andersson, G. (2007). Internet vs. paper and pencil administration of questionnaires commonly used in panic/agoraphobia research. *Computers in Human Behavior*, *23*(3), 1421–1434. doi:10.1016/j.chb.2005.05.002

Chen, Hsinchun, Chiang, Roger H L, & Storey, Veda C. (2012). Business intelligence and analytics: From big data to big impact. *Management Information Systems Quarterly*, *36*(4), 1165–1188.

Chervin, R. D. (2000). The multiple sleep latency test and Epworth sleepiness scale in the assessment of daytime sleepiness. *Journal of Sleep Research*, *9*(4), 399–400. doi:10.1046/j.1365-2869.2000.0227a.x PMID:11123526

Colten, Harvey R, & Alterogt, MBruce M. (2006). *Sleep disorders and sleep deprivation: An unmet public health problem*. Retrieved from http://books.nap.edu/catalog.php?record_id=11617#toc

Conrick, Moya. (2006). *Health informatics: transforming healthcare with technology*. Melbourne: Thomson Social Science Press.

Cornwall, A., & Jewkes, R. (1995). What is participatory research? *Social Science & Medicine*, *41*(12), 1667–1676. doi:10.1016/0277-9536(95)00127-S PMID:8746866

Dement, W. C. (2008). History of sleep medicine. *Sleep Medicine Clinics*, *3*, 147–156. doi:10.1016/j.jsmc.2008.01.003

Economics, D. A. (2011). *Re-awakening Australia: The economic cost of sleep disorders in Australia, 2010*. Australia: Sleep Health Foundation.

Flemons, W., Douglas, N. J., Kuna, S. T., Rodenstein, D. O., & Wheatley, J. (2004). Access to diagnosis and treatment of patients with suspected sleep apnea. *American Journal of Respiratory and Critical Care Medicine*, *169*, 668–672. doi:10.1164/rccm.200308-1124PP PMID:15003950

Graber, M. L., & Mathew, A. (2008). Performance of a Web-Based Clinical Diagnosis Support System for Internists. *Journal of General Internal Medicine*, *23*(Supplement 1), 37–40. doi:10.1007/s11606-007-0271-8 PMID:18095042

Guenther, K. (2004). Know the fundamentals and good design will follow. *Online*, *28*(1), 54–56.

Haux, R. (2010). Medical informatics: Past, present, future. *International Journal of Medical Informatics*, *79*(9). doi:10.1016/j.ijmedinf.2010.06.003 PMID:20615752

Haynes, R. B., Sackett, D. L., Guyatt, G. H., & Tugwell, P. (2006). Clinical epidemiology: How to do clinical practice research (3rd ed.). Philadelphia: Lippincott Williams & Wilkins

Hirakis, O., & Karakounos, S. (2006). Goals and benefits of knowledge management in healthcare. In A. A. Lazakidou (Ed.), *Handbook of Research on Informatics in Healthcare and Biomedicine* (pp. 193–200). Idea Group Reference. doi:10.4018/978-1-59140-982-3.ch025

Johnson, J. A. (2005). Ascertaining the validity of individual protocols from Web-based personality inventories. *Journal of Research in Personality*, *39*(1), 103–129. doi:10.1016/j.jrp.2004.09.009

Kramer, N. R., Cook, T. E., & Carlisle, C. C., Corwin, R. W., & Millman, R. P. (1999). The role of the primary care physician in recognizing obstructive sleep apnea. *Archives of Internal Medicine*, *159*(9), 965–968. doi:10.1001/archinte.159.9.965 PMID:10326938

Lacks, P., & Morin, C. M. (1992). Recent advances in the assessment and treatment of insomnia. *Journal of Consulting and Clinical Psychology*, *60*(4), 586–594. doi:10.1037/0022-006X.60.4.586 PMID:1506506

Libman, E., Fichten, C. S., Bailes, S., & Amsel, R. (2000). Sleep Questionnaire Versus Sleep Diary: Which Measure Is Better? *International Journal of Rehabilitation and Health*, *5*(3), 205–209. doi:10.1023/A:1012955423123

Macaulay, A. C. (2007). Promoting Participatory Research by Family Physicians. *Annals of Family Medicine*, *5*(6), 557–560. doi:10.1370/afm.755 PMID:18025494

Patlak, M. (2005). *Tips to help you detect common sleep disorders*. Retrieved 31 March 2008, from http://www.acpinternist.org/archives/2005/03/sleep.htm#pool

Pilemalm, S., & Timpka, T. (2008). Third generation participatory design in health informatics–Making user participation applicable to large-scale information system projects. *Journal of Biomedical Informatics*, *41*(2), 327–339. doi:10.1016/j.jbi.2007.09.004 PMID:17981514

Queensland Government. (2001). *Information Standard No 42A: Information privacy for the Queensland Department of Health*. http://www.qgcio.qld.gov.au/02_infostand/standards/is42a.pdf

Queensland Government Chief Information Office. (2008). *Current information standards, guidelines and reviews*. Retrieved from http://www.qgcio.qld.gov.au/02_infostand/standards.htm

Queensland Government Chief Information Office. (2010). *2009 Queensland Household Survey - Computer and Internet Use*. Retrieved 7 February 2011, from http://www.qgcio.qld.gov.au/SiteCollectionDocuments/Resources/householdsurvey2009.pdf

Sharp, H., Rogers, Y., & Preece, J. (2007). *Interaction design: Beyond human-computer interaction* (2nd ed.). Chichester, UK: John Wiley and Sons Limited.

Shepertycky, M. R., Banno, K., & Kryger, M. H. (2005). Differences between men and women in the clinical presentation of patients diagnosed with Obstructive Sleep Apnea Syndrome. *Sleep*, *28*(3), 309–314. PMID:16173651

Sheppard, V. B., Williams, K. P., Harrison, T. M., Jennings, Y., Lucas, W., Stephen, J.,... Taylor, K. L. (2009). Development of decision-support intervention for Black women with breast cancer. *Psycho-Oncology*.

Smith, S., Lang, C., Sullivan, K., & Warren, J. (2004). Two new tools for assessing patients' knowledge and beliefs about Obstructive Sleep Apnea and Continuous Positive Airway Pressure therapy. *Sleep Medicine*, *5*(4), 359–367. doi:10.1016/j.sleep.2003.12.007 PMID:15222992

Soroush, L., Hafeez-Baig, A., & Gururajan, R. (2010). *Clinicians' perception of using digital stethoscopes in telehealth platform: Queensland telehealth preliminary study*. Paper presented at the 21st Australasian Conference on Information Systems. Brisbane, Australia. Retrieved from http://aisel.aisnet.org/acis2010/43/

Stranieri, A., Zeleznikow, J., Gawler, M., & Lewis, B. (1999). A hybrid rule – neural approach for the automation of legal reasoning in the discretionary domain of family law in Australia. *Artificial Intelligence and Law*, *7*(2-3).

Taylor, M. J., Wade, S., & England, D. (2003). Informing IT system web site design through normalisation. *Internet Research: Electronic Networking Applications and Policy*, *13*(5), 342–355. doi:10.1108/10662240310501621

University of British Columbia Institute of Health Promotion Research. (1996). *Guidelines and categories for classifying participatory research projects in health*. Retrieved from http://www.lgreen.net/guidelines.html

Wagner, N., Hassanein, K., & Head, M. (2010). Computer use by older adults: A multi-disciplinary review. *Computers in Human Behavior*, *26*(5), 870–882. doi:10.1016/j.chb.2010.03.029

White, G. W., Suchowierska, M., & Campbell, M. (2004). Developing and systematically implementing participatory action research. *Archives of Physical Medicine and Rehabilitation*, *85*(Supplement 2), 3–12. doi:10.1016/j.apmr.2003.08.109 PMID:15083417

Wilde, M. H., & Garvin, S. (2007). A concept analysis of self-management. *Journal of Advanced Nursing*, *57*(3), 339–350. doi:10.1111/j.1365-2648.2006.04089.x PMID:17233653

Willems, D. (2000). Managing one's body using self-management techniques: practicing autonomy. *Theoretical Medicine and Bioethics*, *21*(1), 23–38. doi:10.1023/A:1009995018677 PMID:10927967

Williams, T. R. (2000). Guidelines for designing and evaluating the display of information on the web. *Technical Communication*, *47*(3), 383–397.

Yen, B., Hu, P. J.-H., & Wang, M. (2007). Toward an analytical approach for effective Web site design: A framework for modeling, evaluation and enhancement. *Electronic Commerce Research and Applications*, *6*(2), 159–170. doi:10.1016/j.elerap.2006.11.004

Young, T., Peppard, P. E., & Gottlieb, D. J. (2002). Epidemiology of Obstructive Sleep Apnea: A population health perspective. *American Journal of Respiratory and Critical Care Medicine*, *165*(9), 1217–1239. doi:10.1164/rccm.2109080 PMID:11991871

Zikmund, W. G. (2003). Business research methods (7th ed.). Mason, OH: Thomson South-Western.

KEY TERMS AND DEFINITIONS

Online Tool: A web-based application capable of accepting, storing and manipulating data so that the output can easily understand and add value to a task.

Polysomonography: Is a gold standard test for some sleep disorders and consists of sensors monitoring a person's vital information such as brain waves, breathing, blood oxygen levels during an overnight sleep text.

Sleep Disorder: A collection of physical and mental disorders which impact upon a person's sleep quality. The main symptom of a sleep disorder is excessive daytime sleepiness.

Sleep Hygiene: The following of habits to promote continuous sleep – such as increasing exercise, avoiding caffeine in the evening and adopting regular times to go to sleep and wake up. Controlling the sleep environment so that it is dark, cool and quiet is also considered part of sleep hygiene.

Sleep on-Set Latency: The length of time between the person settling for sleep – for example, turning off the light – and the time when sleep occurred. Sleep latency is used as an indicator of a sleep disorder. A short sleep latency time indicates a sleep deficit, while a long sleep latency time may indicate insomnia.

Sleep Study: An overnight test performed in a sleep laboratory where a person undergoes a polysomnography.

Sleep Tool Web Application: A web application which presents a patient with a patient history questionnaire to be completed and receives 14 days of sleep hygiene information. This information is then processed and the physician can receive a patient report detailing patient history, sleep hygiene information and if a person has met the criteria for a sleep disorder.

ENDNOTES

[1]   Co-existing or additional diseases with reference to an initial diagnosis.

Chapter 70
Democratic Potentials of UN Climate Change Conference Host Government Websites

Catherine Candano
National University of Singapore, Singapore & Ateneo de Manila University, Philippines

ABSTRACT

E-government discourse implicates state-produced Websites to enable opportunities and citizen spaces on policy issues, subject to demands to be inclusive, engaging, and free from commercial interests. Policy-making for a global issue like climate change takes place at the inter-governmental United Nations Climate Change Conference (UNCCC). It becomes critical to examine if and how the governments hosting this restrictive global policy-making space may engage citizens through their online presence–host country conference outreach Websites. The chapter explores relational underpinnings between states and citizens in such Websites by examining the values privileged by designers using mixed methods. Among UNCCC Websites from 2007 to 2009, the Danish government Website's enhanced features may have contributed to potential inclusivity for the inter-governmental process online compared to previous government's efforts. However, findings have shown such interactive Website's inherent design aspects may potentially shape the manner that climate conversations are limited in an assumed democratized space online.

INTRODUCTION

E-government applies information communication technologies (ICTs) mainly for public sector's benefit and improvement (Heeks, 2004). Bekkers and Homburg (1997) found in their multi-country study of government policies, 'ICT's contribution to a better government' is one of the underlying myths that propel e-government discourse. As a contemporary anecdote, it is no surprise, for example, for one to see a new United States government's web-portal, USA.gov, from the Obama administration claim "Better websites. Better government" (USA.gov, 2009). 'Better websites' understood by the GSA office of Citizen Services, the division responsible for U.S. Government's online presence includes social media or Web 2.0 (platforms such as blogs, social networking sites, etc.). Applications of Web 2.0 technologies found in various agency websites such as Environment

DOI: 10.4018/978-1-4666-8619-9.ch070

Protection Agency's (EPA) Facebook page and National Aeronautics and Space Administration's (NASA) wiki were listed side-by-side with potential outreach gains for better government: blogs, for example, were cited to provide a 'human face' for government with an 'informal tone' (Table 1).

As an illustration, the U.S. government's own web redesign efforts implicitly heralds the potentials of interactive websites for governance purposes, and that such can do no wrong. In fact, studies note that growing rhetoric sees promising directions for e-government (de Kool & van Wamelen, 2009; Horrocks, 2009). With governments rallying behind the democratic potential of enhanced interactivity with online audiences, it is worthwhile to assess the democratic potential of

Table 1. Online Web 2.0 use of U.S. Government at USA.gov (2008)

Technology	Simple Definition	Examples	Opportunity/Potential in Government
Blogs	Journal or diary with social collaboration (comments)	33 federal agencies have public blogs, USA.gov_government.blog.library Webcontent.gov.advice GovGab.gov	Govt info to new audiences. Puts human face on govt using informal tone. Opens public conversations. Surface issues & solve them.
Wikis	Collaborative authoring & editing	GSA.Collab.Environment, Core.gov, MAX, NASA, US Courts, Intellipedia, PTO, Diplopedia, PeaceCorps, Utah Politicopia	Workgroup or public collaboration for project management, knowledge sharing, public input. Contributions to 3rd party sites e.g. Wikipedia
Video Sharing (and Multimedia)	Videos, images, & audio libraries (YouTube, AOL Video, Yahoo Video, tubemogul, heyspread…)	USA.gov_multimedia library, NOAA & NASA YouTube, Coast Guard, CA&VA YouTube Channels, Americorps contest, Tobacco Free Florida contest	Public outreach, education, training, other communication for "connected" and on-line audiences. How-To videos & audios to improve service and achieve mission.
Photo-Sharing	Photo libraries	USA.gov.fed/state.photo.libraries, LoC & USGS galleries, Flickr, API EPA contest	Cost savings potential. New audiences awareness.
Podcasting	Multimedia content syndicated out for use on iPod™ Mp3 players, & computers	White House, NASA, USA.gov.federal.podcast. library. Webcountent.gov, PeaceCorps, Census daily podcasts	More ways to get message out. Build trust with conversational voice. Use for updates, live govt deliberations, emergencies, how-to messages
Virtual worlds	Simulations of environments & people (Webkinz, Club Penguin, Neopets, Stardoll, Whyville, Second Life, Active Worlds, Kaneva, ProtoSphere, Entropia Universe, uWorld)	NASA, NOAA, CDC in SL & Whyville, VA, Natl Guard, Wnergy, DoD, National Defense Univ Federal Consortium for Virtual Worlds, Real Life Govt in 2nd Life Google group	Public outreach & other communication for kids and niche Internet audiences. Virtual Town Halls, Education, Training. Ability to bring people together worldwide for meetings, lectures, etc.
Social Networking Sites	Connecting people globally	EPA.Facebook group, NASA colab, USAgov Facebook page, Myspace, LinkedIn	Intranet use to cross internal stovepipes. Cross government coordination. Public communities. Viral impact, Knowledge mgmt. Recruitment. Event announcements.
Syndicated Web Feeds	Automated notifications of frequently updated content (think RSS)	USA.gov Federal RSS library, NOAA Watch	Do more with RSS, SML/Web feeds. Expand reach. Pull content togerher across government. Authoritative source. Reduce duplication.

continued on following page

Table 1. Continued

Technology	Simple Definition	Examples	Opportunity/Potential in Government
Mashups	Combine content from multiple sources for an integrated experience.	USA Search, USGS, NASA, EPA, Virual Earth, Google Earth, Google Maps	Lots of potential. Improved govt reach, service, usefulness, and functionality. Integrate external data. Get licenses, stay vendor neutral. Make content available to others who create mashups
Widgets, Gadgets, Pipes	Small applications & code in Web pages or for desktop use	FBI widgets, Veterans affairs, Census Population Clock & NASA Planet Discoveries, Desktop widgets	Increase awareness, use, and usefulness of gov sites, information, and service. Bring content to the user's home page (iGoogle, netvibes, etc.)
Social Bookmark & News (sharing, tagging) sites	Ways of sharing content with others	USA.gov, NASA, Govt blogs, Digg, Delicious, Technorati, AddThis	Increase the popularity and use of gov pages, information, and services. Viral marketing
Micro-blogging Presence Networks	Form of blogging which allows brief (instant message size) text updates.	Twitter, Jaiku, Cromple, Pownce, NASA Edge, USA.gov. GovGab. Univ of Mich	Seek input. Broadcast msgs: emergencies, news, announcements. Real time reporting. Recruiting.

July 18, 2008 Bev Godwin, USA.gov and Web Best Practices, GSA Office of Citizen Services

*Note: it is understood that government policy, procedures, standards, and guidance are needed for many of these technologies.

government-created websites, particularly in the context of an issue with global policy scope and domestic ramifications, where its offline policy process may be inherently exclusive. One such issue and policy-making process to consider is that of climate change. The United Nations Framework Convention on Climate Change (UNFCCC) convenes United Nations Climate Change Conference (UNCCC), the primary venue for states to engage in global climate change governance. The UNCCC is open only to convention parties (members of the state duly part of the delegation), UN system observers, and pre-accredited press and civil society such as business, trade, academic or NGOs groups (UNFCCC, 2009). Due to the restricted and privileged access to UNCCC space subject to UNFCCC Secretariat accreditation, the sessions are not open to public.

Examining offline state-focused policy context, the study assessed democratic potential of UNCCC outreach websites produced by host governments from 2007 to 2009. Assessment parameters included potential to engage citizens,

be accountable to and promote the legitimacy for the UNCCC process. Structural relations between state and citizens implied within the new web design elements were explored also. Due to the location of these government websites representing the year's UNCCC, it can be said that these websites' may be exposed to audiences larger than the real-world public with offline-access to the highly restricted policy-making forum. Characterizing the nature of this digital space created by governments, as an online extension of such an exclusive policy process on a shared global issue, is, therefore, of value to examine.

BACKGROUND

ICT's Democratic Potentials

Participatory democracy scholars have identified that citizen's engagement and deliberation would invigorate polity, as a response to apathy (Barber, 1984; Pateman, 1970; Fishkin, 1991).

Barber (1984; in Wright and Street, 2007) has emphasized the legitimizing function of discussion, emphasizing the value for 'talk' on-going between public citizens regarding meaningful issues of the day as constituting the heart of a democratic process. Burt & Taylor (2008) identified the three essential roles for public actors to perform in a democratic context: enabling citizens' engagement, legitimacy and accountability. They defined "citizen engagement" to include citizens being publicly informed and participating in issue discussions, while being open to divergent points of view, reflective and actively pursuing public issues (Barber, 2003 in Burt & Taylor, 2008). They defined "legitimacy of actors" within democracies as derived from regulation, representation, ethical or moral grounds, expertise, level of autonomy, and independence that may be financial in nature (Varra, E., Tienaria, J. & Laurila, J., 2006; Lister, 2003 in Burt & Taylor, 2008). "Demonstration of accountability" is defined by the authors to include providing citizens information about organizations and activities as a political agent of democracy, as a democratic actor (Dunn, 1999; Laver & Shepsle, 1999 in Burt & Taylor 2008).

With perspectives that ICTs, particularly the internet, enable user-interactivity and participation (Rheingold, 1993), functional interest in the literature focused on harnessing such for public sector gain. Literature has defined democratic interventions by government on such platforms under various terms. Previous work by Macintosh (2004) identified e-democracy preoccupations functionally: ICT application for citizen's engagement, democratic decision-making processes, strengthening representative democracy. The term digital democracy was preferred by Van Dijik (2000), discussing instead of specific technologies, the collection of attempts to practice democracy mediated through digital networked communications as addition to (not replacement for) traditional practices without limitations of time and space.

Since then, government's use of technology, particularly ICT, to enable public life has been the cause of celebration and criticism. Positivist understandings of electronic democracy (e-democracy) could be synthesized into four areas that ICT contributes towards: addressing barriers of time-demands, size of participants, knowledge-distribution, and access for government engagement with citizens (Street 1997). Abramson et al. (1998) believed similarly ICT's promise did not lie in public opinion's passive transparency for the benefit of policy-makers. Instead, he believed the greatest promise lay within a direct mode of an ICT-enabled participation, such as in a futuristic town hall meeting, where low barriers to information sources enabled discussion on public affairs at local, national, regional levels. Hence, imperatives existed for government investment in technologies to bring about this vision, without the commercial intervention prevalent in consumer media markets. These conceptions signified merely providing ICT solutions did not suitably enable citizen participation in the government policy-making proceedings; instead, importance would need to be given for technologies and initiative to approach and motivate citizens to engage in the policy-making process, that was lacking in most cases (Macintosh, 2007 in Kamal, 2009).

Proposals of technology as a "fix" for both governments' and democracies' problems were of concern to some authors, especially in the context of ICT conceptions such as the internet as strategic inventions of the powerful (Street, 1997). Abramson, et al. (1988) argued new technologies could conceivably influence governance through citizen lobbying, government mobilization for support from the general public for policies, communications between levels and branches of government, and citizen participation. They found only limited uses at that time, which tended to reinforce preexisting power relationships between interest groups. Salter (2004) acknowledged such potentials exist, however, as a result of the dominant influencers of internet's technological development, and, therefore, identified a deliberate effort required by creators and publics to harness the internet's potential as a "democratic tool, or one that enhanced non-commercial civil society" (Salter, 2004, p.185).

Dahlberg (2001) echoed concern that any ICT intervention requires independent flows of political information and a virtual space for public debate from interests, both administrative and corporate; otherwise the space become suspect to their hand, echoing the perspective of optimists such as Abramson et al. (1998) in defense of the technology's positive effects. Further, there were caveats proposed by other scholars that the only robust assessment of government's top-down approach to ICT's democratic potentials was mainly in its value to affect offline governance, and citizen engagement processes organically, as exemplified by online consultation and discussion processes that fed into and constituted citizen's on-going input into the policy-making process, such as a case in U.K. legislature (Chadwick & May, 2003).

Bekkers and Homburg (2007) cautioned that the "e" in e-government activities does not guarantee positive political effects manifested in offline governance space. Assessing policy documents related to e-government in western practices, specific myths propelling policies were identified, including improved government service provision and activities; progressive technological application; rationalist' approach to information planning; and empowerment of citizens as consumers of public service. While the associated myths painted a technologically- deterministic portrait of association between ICT and participatory governance, some adopted a critical view of ICTs democratic potential.

The way that the state framed ICT-solutions in its toolbox is only not telling of underlying myths (Bekkers & Homberg, 2007) but also of the modality that e-government activities are conceptualized, created and carried out. Chadwick and May (2003) studied policy documents regarding e-government web-portals in U.S., Britain and the E.U., finding interaction between states and citizens largely managerial at the expense of possible consultative and participatory forms. They concluded that government framing of technology's managerial value dampens its democratic potentials. A summary of e-governance models of interaction between state and government is found in the following (Chadwick & May, 2003):

1. Managerial model
   a. "Efficient" delivery of government/state information to citizens and other groups of "users"/information dissemination.
   b. Improving flows of information within and around the state.
   c. "Control" as defining logic.
   d. Importance of "service delivery."
   e. Speeding up of information provision is "opening up" government.
   f. Regulatory, law making; responding to the needs of the "new economy."
   g. User resource issues (ability to receive and interpret information) largely absent.
   h. Unilinear model of information.
2. Consultative model
   a. Polling, access of voters and other interested parties to government, representation of views, advisory referendums.
   b. "Push-button democracy," "e-voting" – direct democracy – instantaneous opinion polling.
   c. Access as a technical issue, problems of self-selection of citizen respondents.
   d. Direct and unmediated contact between citizen and state.
   e. "Electronic town meetings."
   f. Agenda framing as critical issue.
   g. Technological lag among citizens and their representatives.
   h. Unilinear model of information.
3. Participatory model

a. Civil society exists away from the state and (will be) mediated electronically.

b. Organic emergence of democracy.

c. Voluntary associations, spontaneous interactions within cyber-space.

d. Access is enough to encourage wider political participation.

e. State protects free speech and rights of expression.

f. Participatory model will replace the other two through the *logic* of information society.

g. Discursive model of information.

Technological neutrality cannot be easily assumed due to contexts surrounding technologies' innovation and diffusion. Perspectives that technological design (such as the internet's architecture and its consequential shaping by creators' choices) had disparate effects on its democratic potentials exist is expressed in tension between concepts of surveillance and openness (Lessig, 1999; Wright &Street, 2007). Apart from detailing the politics of gatekeeping behind powerful search-engines online, Hindman (2008) discusses a barrier to internet's democratic potential in dominant websites and weblogs that remain at the top tier of search engine results, bringing to mind the difference between speaking up (and having a voice online), versus having your voice heard by readers.

Advancing consideration of ICT technological design, Wright and Street (2007) found that, in their analysis of EU, UK online forums, website interface and design tended to bear implicit choices in the matter of operationalizing certain discussion modes; these web design decisions had impacts on the resulting character of the online discussion. Examples of implicit design choices affecting the nature of deliberation include focused and structured online forums (with pre-read policy documents to gather feedback), highly unstructured ones (that may enable audience-focused agenda-setting effects but with limited policy

feedback loop) such as "Have Your Say" corners, or having a mix of both on the same website (Wright & Street, 2007).

A specific analytical framework was developed by Burt and Taylor (2008) on to understand democratic potential of online presences for U.K voluntary bodies. Burt & Taylor (2008) derived their framework from earlier work to ascertain democratic potential of outward-facing U.S. non-profit websites (Kenix, 2007 in Burt & Taylor, 2008). They proposed that the active engagement of citizens is vital to democracy, as well as citizens' perception of legitimacy and accountability. As such the authors explored performance along three dimensions of a democratic potential which theoretically underscored democratic values of citizen engagement, legitimacy, and public accountability. Specifically, the three research questions explored in the 2008 study included: (RQ1) Were the websites used to engage citizens, people in a democratic polity? (RQ2) Were the websites used to appear as legitimate democratic actors? (RQ3) Were the websites used to enhance public accountability as democratic actors?

After two researchers scrutinized the websites sequentially, authors found that the studied organizations' websites performed variably across this normative evaluation, with no exemplars among the sample in any of the three parameters of a democratic potential. Although there seemed to be an underlying discourse promoting the legitimacy of the organizations represented by the websites, it was noted, however, that the websites propensity for enabling accountability and discussion with citizens was low. For example, it was noted that interactivity was limited within the sampled websites, which may be due to its investment requirements in terms of manpower, technical expertise and design as well as moderating content. At the same time, however, this find was of concern for the researchers in that they believed that low interactivity may not just be a symptom of limited resources but may indicate a preferred relationship between the organizations and the general public as decided by the organizations creating the website. It was concluded that such organizations were underutilizing the potentials their websites has 'in respect of their pursuit of democratic goals' and providing opportunities for voice and activism among citizens (Burt & Taylor, 2008, p.1063).

The key strength of Burt & Taylor's 2008 study lay in the conceptual framework they had developed, that operationally allows analysis of complex websites that contain various types of design and content elements. The authors identified new pathways for deeper, long-term research upon which this current study on UNCCC outreach websites democratic potentials will examine. Specifically, five research questions will be explored in this study. The first three are adapted from Burt & Taylor's study of a comparative, longitudinal approach to comparing performance of website democratic potentials by directing the object of study towards the UNCCC process' online presence (via the host government outreach websites).

RQ1: Which among the websites were used by the host governments to enhance public accountability of UNCCC?

RQ2: Which among the websites were used by host governments to engage citizens in UNCCC?

RQ3: Which among the websites were used by host governments to portray UNCCC as legitimate?

The last two research questions seek to understand the nature of state-citizen interactions within the UNCCC online spaces. It is aimed to map user relationships with design decisions that affect democratic potential and ultimately conclude on the type of interactions promoted within the online.

RQ4: What are the specific website user-website producer dynamics for the strongest performing (potentially democratic) UNCCC host government website?

RQ5: What mode of online interaction between state and citizens in UNCCC is enabled by the host government websites?

METHODS

This study explores UNCCC host government websites' democratic potential and aims to map the extent of its democratic features through three-tier qualitative content analysis. UNCCC hosting is decided on a rotation among UN regional groups; since 2007, the role has been passed to Indonesia, Poland and Denmark. Each host government provided an outreach website, serving as an online presence of the UNCCC global governance process being held in their country to general public and conference participants (UNFCCC, 2009). Images of the sampled websites of UNCCC host countries from 2007 to 2009 are shown in Figures 1, 2, and 3.

In this context, a three-tier approach of structured qualitative content analysis will be undertaken. In the first tier of the qualitative content analysis, the respective UNCCC website features will be evaluated against dimensions of legitimacy, accountability and citizen engagement (adapted from Burt & Taylor, 2008). The first core value of citizen engagement explored how organizations can be considered as engaging based on their websites. This is expressed by authors to consist of sub-dimensions relating to:

1. Enabling dialogic informed discussion (talk),
2. Enabling information about issues and engaging with institutions (inform),
3. Connecting to independent institutions such as government, business, other sectors (hear),

Figure 1. Indonesian government host website COP 13 in 2007, Indonesia (www.climate.web.id)

4. Suggesting actions to address issues, and
5. Provide emotive appeals (affect).

The second core value of legitimacy explored how organizations can be considered legitimate based on their websites. This is expressed by authors to consist of:

1. Legislative/regulatory legitimacy,
2. Legitimacy of representativeness,
3. Legitimacy of moral authority/ethics,
4. Legitimacy derived from expertise, and
5. Legitimacy from independence and autonomy.

The third core value of accountability explored on how the organizations can be considered ac-

countable based on their websites, is expressed by authors in terms of providing enough information about activities in order to enable people (whether potential donors or volunteers) to sign up or walk away. They authors defined accountability in the context of three sub-dimensions:

1. Ability to give an account,
2. Ability to take account of, and
3. Being accountable to.

Table 2 provided the details of the three core values and operationalized parameters that express these in terms of particular website features, as well as elements of technical design and textual or visual content. Presence of the specific content or design features as indicated in the table criteria

Figure 2. Polish government host website COP 14 in 2008, Poland (www.cop14.pl)

set were coded for each of the websites; as such its absences were noted but not coded. Since analysis was undertaken on the unit of the website itself, multiple presences of various types of content or design features counted in favor of one criterion within the tool. A secondary researcher was asked to review the content analysis in the same sequential order of the website pages.

In Burt & Taylor (2008), the object of legitimacy analysed was the voluntary organization represented by the website; the websites studied were organizational websites. However, in this comparative application, the websites being studied were set up by different host-governments as organizations to represent one and the same governance process. The object of scrutiny that legitimacy is applied to in this context becomes the governance process, in this case, the UNCCC.

As an outcome of the methodology's first phase, the first three research questions will be addressed. In addition, the UNCCC website assessed to have the most democratic potential on performance against Burt & Taylor's analytical framework will be identified and compared to the other UNCCC websites. Compared to Burt & Taylor's original use of the tool as the primary analytical framework, this study will use this tool as a preliminary framework in the first phase of analyses, serving as a foundation for subsequent triangulation of qualitative analysis to address remaining research questions.

To address the fourth research question, a case-level focus will be applied on the identified potentially most democratic UNCCC website, where analysis of a design feature not present in the other sampled websites will be undertaken

Figure 3. Danish government host website COP 15 in 2009, Denmark (en.cop15.dk)

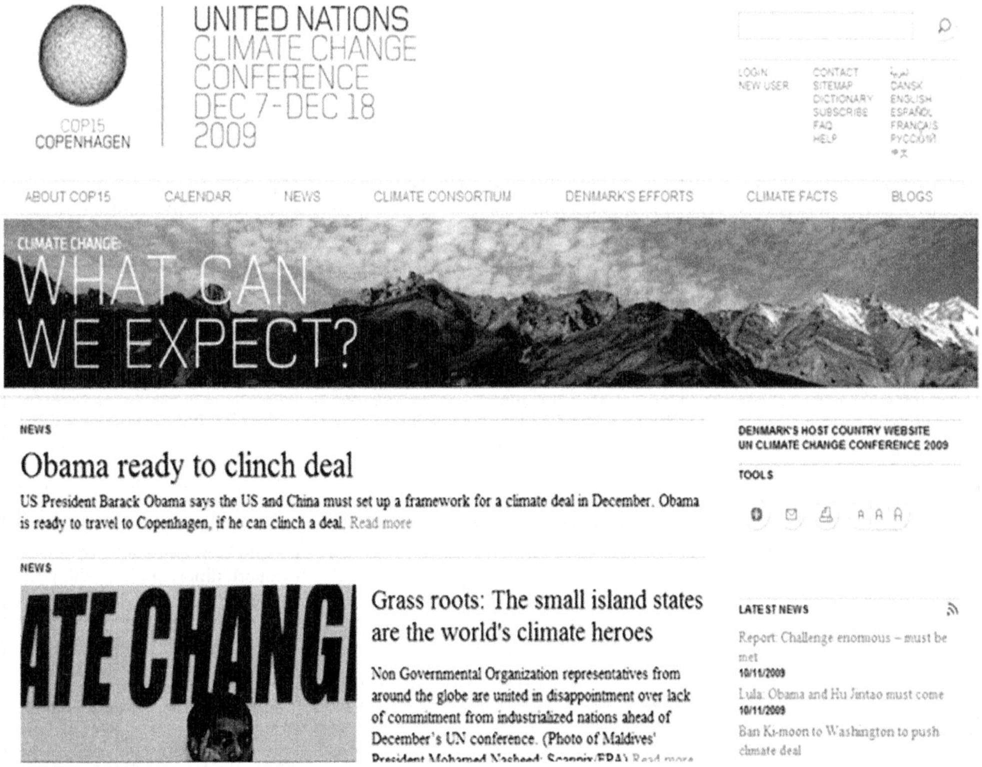

as a second tier of qualitative content analysis. This unique website feature will be qualitatively analyzed through mapping corresponding website producer's practices complicit in the design feature against corresponding website user-experience and content, to ascertain implied interrelationships between state and citizens inherent in design aspects (adapted from Wright & Street, 2007). So finally to address the fifth research question, as a third tier of analysis, interaction modes between state and citizens in the online version of UNCCC, typologies of state-citizen relationship in e-government will be ascertained (adapting from Chadwick & May, 2003).

By focusing on UNCCC websites as virtual sites of the democratic potential for environmental governance the paper identifies from the tradition of the methodology, there exist limits to the study. The project is unable claim in its analysis

to be able to represent actual users (citizens) perceptions of the online space, nor guarantee the actualization of democratic potential charted by the researcher. While it is acknowledged that resources available for each state to create the host country websites may indicate various levels of complexity in the resulting websites, it was also considered that advancements in open-access web development tools within the narrow three year timeframe may indicate less variation in the supply-side technologies available to developers of the e-governance portals. As such, the narrow sampling in terms of time period, instead of selecting a broader time period, provided rationale to investigate the manner of variance in web features developed by the UNCCC host governments in such a time span, assuming all other things equal particularly relatively similar production frontiers for possible web-features and

Table 2. Analytical instrument to assess potential as democratic actors (Burt & Taylor, 2008)

Accountability	Citizen Engagement	Legitimacy
Giving account/informative	**Affective/engaging**	**Legal/governance/procedural**
General about the org sections	Personal blogs	Declarations of interest
Mission statement	Emotive imagery	Information about the internal governance process
Constitution/governance information	Local group info	**Representative/consent based**
How funded	**Listening**	Membership profile
Campaign performance reports	Solicit views of site users on campaign/policy/approach	Thinking/reflective/informed about issue set
Annual reports/reviews/accounts	Thinking/reflective/informed about issue set	Links to info by other bodies (govt, voluntary org, research institute)
Evidence of walking the talk	Links to info by other bodies (govt, voluntary org, research institute)	**Moral/value-based, including through example**
Taking account of/welcoming comment	**Active/action participation**	Sets out moral/ethical position on issue
Contact information	Info about/register for training/attendance	Moral/ethical practice (i.e., green workplace, internally democratic, equal opportunities, employment policy and practice)
Invitation to provide feedback	Email alerts, listserves (RSS)	**Scientific/expert/experiential knowledge-base**
Being accountable to/answerable/seeking to be transparent/open/responsive	Cyber-activism (petitions, e-postcards, email message links)	Scientific/expert/experiential research
Complaint process offered/explained	Model letters	**Independence/affiliation**
Information about external bodies exercising oversight	Diary (Behind the Scenes Perspective)	Financial Sources/sponsors
	Timetable	How organization engages with the political process
	Events	Contact links to supportive elected representative
	Contact details/hotlinks for elected representatives	Statements from political parties written for the organization (N/A)
	How to communicate with elected representative	
	How the government (intergovernmental) process works	
	Getting messages across to external stakeholders (contacts, links, info)	
	Speaking	
	Discussion forums	

web-development technologies. More critically, however, the study can map the landscape of the democratic potential that the UNCCC's virtual presence, via the outreach websites, may possess vis-à-vis the restricted real-world presence of important governance process, hence stimulating future work related to audience interactivity with other virtual governance presences.

UNCCC HOST GOVERNMENT WEBSITES' DEMOCRATIC POTENTIALS

Website Feature Comparative Analysis

From 2007 to 2009, UNCCC host government websites show increased content and design features (Figures 4, 5, and 6). Increased web design features elicit questions on the potential impact: does this imply increasing democratic space for citizens within the process hosted by these governments. Step-by-step analyses of website features (structure and content) may indicate the contribution to democratic potential.

Notwithstanding geopolitical factors surrounding website creation (and creation capabilities) by comparing the websites produced by the different host governments across different years above, the evolutionary path of potential online democratic space from 2007-2009 is charted. It is noted that these websites served as the only online official extensions of the UNCCC process.

Figure 5. Site map Polish government host website COP 14 in 2008, Poland (www.cop14.pl)

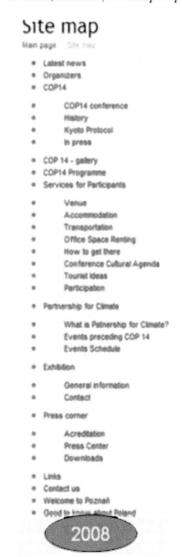

Figure 4. Site map Indonesian government host website COP 13 in 2007, Indonesia (www.climate. web.id)

Figure 6. Site map Danish government host website COP 15 in 2009, Denmark (en.cop15.dk)

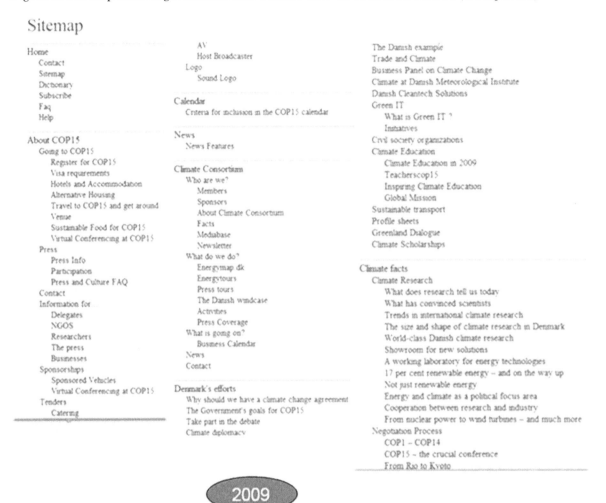

Table 3 shows top-level results addressing the first three research questions identify the Danish Government website to exhibit the most democratic potential in its online representation of the UNCCC. With consideration of uneven productive capacity considering the host governments (Indonesia, Poland and Denmark) are representing difference levels of economic development, it is acknowledged that website features may be affected by practicalities of host governments producing the site, including technical and financial capacity available echoing earlier hypothesis (Burt &Taylor, 2008). However in the case of this ap-

plication across various host governments within a narrow time period and assuming a similar access levels to open web development technologies, it is also possible that political implications regarding the intended relationship with citizens and state-produced websites stem from consideration of differing political traditions of the UNCCC host governments themselves.

The first research question asked which among the websites were used by the host governments to enhance public accountability of UNCCC? To address the potential these websites have to enhance the UNCCC's public accountability, the presence

Table 3. Percentage ratings for democratic potential parameters (UNCCC Websites 2007-2009)

Democratic Potential	UNCCC Websites 2007-2009		
	COP 13 Website (Indonesia, 2007)	COP 14 Website (Poland, 2008)	COP 15 Website (Denmark, 2009)
Accountability	36%	45% (Δ.09)	63% (Δ.18)
Citizen Engagement	27%	38% (Δ.11)	94% (Δ.56)
Legitimacy	27%	36% (Δ.09)	100% (Δ.64)

of web-features that promote information-sharing, welcoming commentary and transparency are presented in Table 4.

Table 4 shows UNCCC host websites are on par regarding potentials for transparency and accountability from 2007 to 2009, by providing information about the conference and policy-making process, but stopped short of providing detail on the inner workings of UNCCC host government (such as the host state's contribution in terms of performance reports, evidence of walking the talk, etc.). Indonesia's and Poland's web-content showed activities related to tree-planting near the conference grounds, rather than meaningful eco-friendly changes in internal organizing of the conference itself.

Danish Government's website performs better in discussing distribution and funding mechanisms for UNCCC, as well as initiatives offered as "evidence for walking the talk" on how organizers are trying to lower their own carbon footprint, promote multi-stakeholder engagement by providing video-conferencing services for free, provide climate change graduate scholarships to developing countries instead of delegate gift bags, and detail behind the scenes preparations like NGO-art project and emissions offset scheme in a blog (UNCCC COP 15, 2009).

All websites prioritized providing contact information and feedback mechanism to UNCCC host government conference organizers; however the level of detail and manner of interface with

Table 4. Do the host government websites enhance public accountability of the UNCCC?

Accountability		COP 13 (36%)	COP 14 (45%)	COP 15 (63%)
Giving Account/Informative	General about the org sections	⊙	⊙	⊙
	Mission statement	⊘	⊘	⊘
	Constitution/governance information	⊙	⊙	⊙
	How funded	⊘	⊘	⊙
	Campaign performance reports	⊘	⊘	⊘
	Annual reports/reviews/accounts	⊘	⊘	⊘
	Evidence of walking the talk	⊘	⊘	⊙
Taking Account of/Welcoming Comment	Contact information	⊙	⊙	⊙
	Invitation to provide feedback	⊘	⊙	⊙
Being Accountable to/Answerable/ Seeking to be Transparent/Open/ Responsive	Complaint process offered/explained	⊘	⊘	.
	Information about external bodies exercising oversight	⊙	⊙	⊙

⊙awareness of indicator ⊘absence of indicator

Adapted from Burt and Taylor (2008)

users are different across the three government websites. This nuance for the level of granularity and manner of providing information to solicit user feedback is not reflected in the analytical parameters adapted from Burt and Taylor's 2008 study. Indonesian Government website had a general contact (email, telephone, postal address) from the Ministry of Environment (the host ministry within the government). Polish Government website had detailed contact information for various ministries collaborating on the UNCCC (e.g. Ministry of Foreign Affairs, Ministry of Environment), and cited a number of primary and secondary contact persons for concerned areas. A general interactive feedback form was also available on the same page. On the other hand, Danish Government website had a more interactive yet centralized interface with a feedback form as well as contact information listed for the general secretariat and to the committee handling logistics, programme, website, etc. for a one-stop helpdesk approach (Figures 7, 8, and 9). Further, transparency in identifying the award of government tenders (i.e. to develop and maintain the website, provide catering services) is also a noted difference in the Danish Government website.

The second research question addressed which websites were used by host governments to engage citizens in UNCCC? To address the websites' potential to support citizen's engagement in the largely restrictive UNCCC process, presence of web-features contributing to affect, speaking and listening to citizens, enabling action/interaction are presented in Table 5. Clearly, potential for citizen's engagement within the Danish Government's website is more pronounced than the Indonesian and Polish Government's (which at minimum provide information related to the UNCCC operations such as the event timetable and practical information for participants like government delegations, civil society accredited observers and press).

Structural features found in Danish Government's website may promote than hinder inclusiveness (i.e. language localization of content into English, Danish, French, Spanish, Chinese, Russian versus the previous bilingual websites) and sociality among readers, peers and other actors (Tip a Friend; Vote on Top Thoughts, Climate Greetings, Commenting Feature in Blogs and News Items, Climate Quiz the AddIt Toolbar enables bookmarking and sharing on various platforms including Digg, and the Danish Gov-

Figure 7. Feedback format for Indonesian government website http://www.climate.web.id/cat/kontak_kami/

Figure 8. Feedback format for Polish government website http://www.cop14.gov.pl/index.php?mode=a rtykuly&action=main&id=4&menu=33&lang=EN

ernment own Facebook Page, Twitter Account and Youtube channels for the UNCCC). There are also font-size settings for users with difficulty viewing the website content (UNCCC 15, 2009). Polish Government website maintained a largely educational interactive feature that was more individual than social – a link to an external carbon footprint calculator (UNCCC 14, 2008).

The third research question examines which websites were used by host governments to portray UNCCC legitimacy? Table 6 presents outcomes that address UNCCC website's potential to shape the intergovernmental governance event's legitimacy, in terms of legality, representativeness, moral/ethical basis, expertise and affiliation.

Danish Government's website complied with all parameters, indicating deliberate website use to enhance the legitimacy of the UNCCC process online. Notable was the website content showcasing techno-science and legal expertise possessed by the country in the field of renewable energies,

numerous links to external think-tanks, experts-celebrities in climate change arena, and an ethical argument proposing that an intergovernmental agreement known as a "climate deal," should be reached during UNCCC that year. Further, the emphasis on Danish industry leadership in renewable energy also legitimized business efforts within meeting the partnership model touted at UNCCC, indicating an economic narrative and inclusion of industry stakeholders in a more direct fashion not present in previous websites.

Web-feature Climate Thinkers on the Danish government's UNCCC website is portrayed as an inclusive and accessible space, by presenting multi-sectoral arguments in climate policy via blog format that enable first-person voices. Frequently updated as of the time this study was undertaken in 2010, the web feature has showcased various experts of aspects of climate change issue addressed by the UNCCC process. Maldivian negotiator talking about sinking island threats; economist Stern

Figure 9. Feedback format for Danish government website http://en.cop15.dk/about+cop15/contact

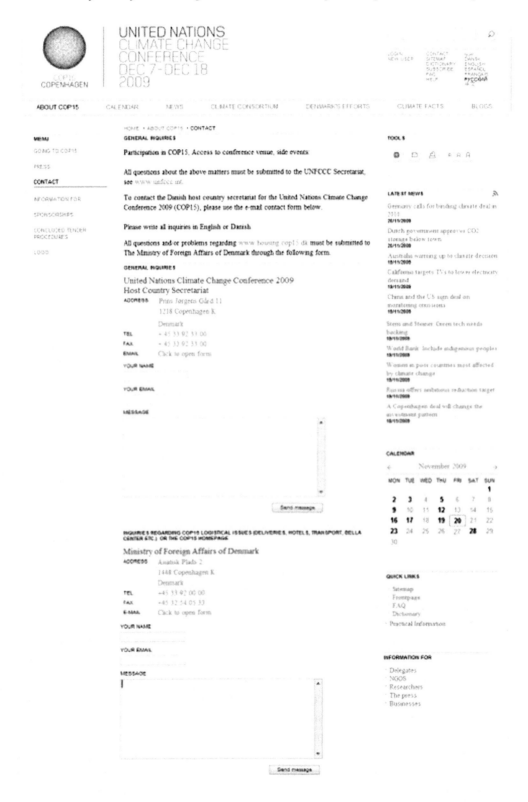

Table 5. Do the host government websites support or nurture active citizen's engagement of the UNCCC?

Civic Engagement		COP 13 (27%)	COP 14 (38%)	COP 15 (94%)
Affective/Engaging	Personal blogs	⊘	⊘	⊙
	Emotive Imagery	⊘	⊘	⊙
	Local group info	⊙	⊙	⊙
Listening	Solicit views of iste users on campaing/policy/approach	⊘	⊘	⊙
	Thinking/reflective/informed about issue set	⊘	⊙	⊙
	Links to info by other bodies (govt, voluntary org, research institute)	⊙	⊙	⊙
Active/Action Partcipation	Info about/register for training/attendance	⊙	⊙	⊙
	Email alerts, listserves(RSS)	⊘	⊙	⊙
	Cyber-activism (petitions, e-postcards, email message links)	⊘	⊘	⊙
	Model letters	⊘	⊘	⊘
	Diary (behind the scenes perspective)	⊘	⊘	⊙
	Timetable	⊙	⊙	⊙
	Events	⊙	⊙	⊙
	Contact details/hotlinks for elected representatives	⊘	⊘	⊙
	How to communicate with elected representative	⊘	⊘	⊙
	How the government (intergovernment) process works	⊘	⊘	⊙
	Getting message across to external stakeholders (contacts, links, info)	⊘	⊘	⊙
Speaking	Discussion forums	⊘	⊘	⊙

⊙awareness of indicator ⊘absence of indicator
Adapted from Burt and Taylor (2008)

Table 6. Do the host government websites shape public perceptions of legitimacy of the UNCCC?

Legitimacy		COP 13 (27%)	COP 14 (36%)	COP 15 (94%)
Legal/Governance/Procedural	Declarations of interest	⊙	⊙	⊙
	Information about the internal governance process	⊘	⊘	⊙
Representative/Consent based	Membership profile	⊘	⊘	⊙
	Thinking/reflective/informed about issue set	⊘	⊘	⊙
	Links to info by other bodies (govt, voluntary org, research institute)	⊘	⊙	⊙
Moral/Value-based, including through example	Sets out moral/ethical position on issue	⊘	⊘	⊙
	Moral/ethical practice (i.e., green workplace, internally democratic, equal opportunities, employment policy and practice)	⊘	⊘	⊙
Scientific/Expert/Experiential Knowledge-Base	Scientific/expert/experiential research	⊙	⊙	⊙
Independence/Affiliation	Financial sources/sponsors	⊘	⊘	⊙
	How organizations engage with the political process	⊙	⊙	⊙
	Contact links to supportive elected representative	⊘	⊘	⊙
	Statements from political parties written for the organization (N/A)			

⊙awareness of indicator ⊘absence of indicator
Adapted from Burt and Taylor (2008)

on future cost of climate policy inaction; Danish climate naysayer-statistician Bjorn Lomborg; and even musician Paul McCartney's on veganism as a solution (UNCCC 15, 2009). This approach differs from previous websites that emphasized promotional host-related news released during the conference.

Case Analysis: Mapping Features, User Experience, Producers' Practices

Innovative web features for Danish Government's website were mapped in terms producer's practices (in this case producer refers to both the host government, as well as the company that received the tender to develop the website) and nature of user-experience and interaction (Table 7). Particularly, the unique feature Climate Thoughts was examined. Examination of this feature was undertaken, considering perspectives by Wright & Street (2007) cognizant that implicit design

choices by creators may promote or hinder such democratic potential.

"Thinking about climate change? Don't keep it to yourself! A new web-based initiative allows people from the entire world to share their thoughts on climate change up to COP15" (Sauer-Johansen, 2009 in UNCCC, 2009). The web feature consists of a feedback form to gather the respective "climate thoughts" of internet-based users, added to a collection of expert writings quoted in the existing archive of blogs post published in the Danish Government website. By inviting user's thoughts on climate change to be collected and represented back on the web, it seems an enhancement of the feedback form as it enables a conversational aspect posted publicly between experts of the Climate Thinkers blog alongside non-expert in a more accessible manner (Figures 10 through 13).

In terms of the producer's practice, however, the Climate Thoughts Web 2.0 application design implies a certain degree of control in the relationship between state and citizens. A built-in data

Table 7. Innovative Web features of Danish government's website mapping

Design Features	Producer Practices	Nature of User-Generated Content
News Feed	Selection/synthesis of news from various news sources	Self-selecting users due to log-in/ registration required
Climate Blogs	Selection of bloggers, content	Expression of thoughts via open comments section for news, blogs, climate thoughts (*content from clime at naysayers to those critical of Al Gore Flying everywhere to give talks)
	Censorship (deletion by moderator)	
Climate Thoughts (support thought, visualization of thoughts)	Terms and conditions	
	Registration	
	Visualization of source of thoughts (also size based on supporters)	Rating system for climate thoughts (popularity)
Climate Quiz	Trivia made fun	Education on clime at change policy trivia
Content Sharing (RSS)	Third Party Application	Self-sharing of website content (via various aggregator and rating platforms digg, etc.
Renewable Energy Solution Database	External website of public-private partnership	
Climate Greetings	Limited characters in message (150)/name (30), anti-spam	Presence within collective art project via climate greeting
Twitter Account	Link to COP 15 news feed	Subscription to twitter, Facebook fanpage, YouTube
Facebook Fanpage	Link to COP 15 news feed	
Channel on YouTube	Competition for top 2 videos	Creation of user videos

Figure 10. Feature welcome page /Main menu. 1ˢᵗ level content after homepage.

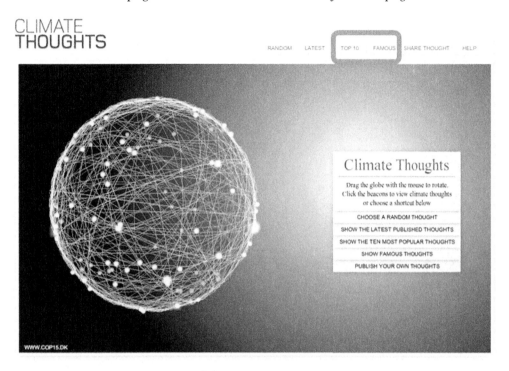

Figure 11. Top 10 thoughts in climate thoughts. 2ⁿᵈ level content after homepage.

Figure 12. Top 1 thought in climate thoughts / Meatless Mondays keep the warming away. 3rd level content after homepage.

Figure 13. Top 1 thought in climate thoughts / Meatless Mondays keep the warming away. 4th level content after homepage.

visualization tool indicated each post's source, and number of supporters represented associate with a particular Climate Thought by a networked sphere with shining points on its surface. Larger and brighter shining nodes on the surface of the sphere indicate greater popularity among internet audiences for a particular blog post–whether published by the website creators or ordinary internet audiences. The application's popularist perspective is built-into the data visualization, showing how the Climate Thoughts application's splash page automatically shows the spherical flash application once users enter– predisposing a new user to click (and see) top ranked thoughts first via the data visualization acting as a filter. 'Supporting' a thought of a public user or an expert blog poster is akin to indicating concurrence or voting on a poll by simply clicking a button.

Hindman's argument that search-engine-results' gatekeeping based on historical popularity implies a designed bias for popularity and recency among pre-determined choices, instead of meaningful or substantive generation of for users from internet wilderness (Hindman, 2008). The design philosophy behind the architecture of pre-selection is important for a critical interpretation of this seemingly inclusive and open Climate Thoughts application.

The pre-selected filtering method (and pre-defined options offered for generating a post sample) designed prioritizes currency, popularity and celebrity (instead of the potential contribution of the user-generated thoughts in terms of offline climate change policy-making or practices) clearly shows that this application is not connected to the offline UNCCC decision-space. Rather it serves as an online repository where click-through engagement of citizen's is possible to the benefit of other citizens online. Tabs on the right also indicate website producer's active structural filtering (based not on substance or diversity of posts) but mainly by value of posts' currency (Most Recent Thoughts), popularity (Top 10 Thoughts), and celebrity (Famous Thoughts). To filter a selec-

tion of posts in this way indicates little critical appreciation for substantive posts relative to the real-world, restrictive UNCCC process with potential for engagement. The 'share-and-support' mentality makes it no surprise that the current top climate thought is attributed to ex-Beatle, Paul McCartney. In "Meatless Mondays keep the warming away," he is quoted in the website's news section about going vegan to curb climate change emissions. McCartney's is a valid argument that is currently not a key policy issue on the table at actual UNCCC 2009. From June 2010, 1078 unique users support this climate thought to bid up this content to first place in the web feature.

Furthermore, the application is subject to particular terms and conditions (i.e. limits to criminal offenses under Danish law, pre-moderation) and a pre-registration process (a non-enforceable request for real name; use of appropriate tone in postings and use of English language only) before people can post thoughts. The pre-registration (and terms and conditions agreement part of this pre-registration) belies government's moderating power to pre-screen messages as a form of surveillance underlying what externally seems like an inclusive and potentially democratic space to 'share and support climate thoughts. The top climate thought from McCartney is not exempt from user-comments deemed inappropriate and therefore removed (Table 8).

Although Danish Government's website leads the pack (particularly citizen's engagement parameter) in terms of presence of potentially democratic website features, a managerial model is implicit in the design of its unique interactive web feature, Climate Thoughts. While Denmark was likely in possession of adequate state resources to utilize website production possibilities, and had the benefit of the passage of time to learn from past e-governance efforts of previous UNCCC host governments, it is noted that despite the provision of increased interactivity the case indicates that its website's features were not designed to be as participatory as it seemed. It emerged that

Table 8. Classification for model of interaction between state and citizens (UNCCC Websites 2007-2009) (Adapted from Chadwick & May 2003)

Model of State-Citizen Relations	UNCCC Websites 2007-2009		
	COP 13 Website (Indonesia, 2007)	COP14 Website (Poland, 2008)	COP 15 Website (Denmark, 2009)
Managerial	X	-X	-
Consultancy	-		X (partially)
Participatory	-	-	-

the built-in state-citizen relations model of the website can be seen as implicitly less dialogic and inclusive than it promises to be. Specifically, under Chadwick & May's framework (2003), the democratically-promising feature may be considered partially consultatory at best and managerial at worst, as it did not fully express the parameters of participatory engagement.

CONCLUSION

E-government discourse implies state-produced websites possess opportunities to bring public issues to its citizens online, and to create spaces for its citizens to engage on such issues important to public life, subject to demands to be inclusive, engaging, and free from commercial interests. At this critical juncture just after the intergovernmental UNCCC 2010 in Mexico, interest exists in the future of a global climate policy regime. It becomes even more critical to examine if, how and where states and citizens can express their different stories about what type of policy solutions are needed to address the global issue (and listen to each other), even if there is little physical space to do it face-to-face at the UNCCC.

Results address the first three research questions using Burt & Taylor's 2008 analytical framework. It was found that Danish Government's UNCCC website topically possesses the most democratic potential, representing comparatively more inclusivity for the UNCCC process online

than previous host government outreach websites. Enhanced website features possibly contributed to this potential, compared to previous government's online efforts to represent the UNCCC online by creating the outreach websites. Notwithstanding state resources, the study found that, in a limited time frame within the UNCCC process, it may be that consideration of state's political commissions for the website and its deliberate designs were factors to shape the nature of e-governance online spaces for public engagement in global climate policy.

In order to investigate such comparisons across UNCCC host country websites, the presence-absence coding scheme for potentially democratic website features (Burt & Taylor, 2008) had been reconsidered in the study as a preliminary rather than a primary analytical framework in order to address the research questions. Instead of highlighting increased opportunities to join conversations per se, it was found helpful to explore relational underpinnings between state-citizens and values privileged by designers using further qualitative analysis. Findings have shown these inherent design aspects embedded within the ICT have characteristics that while not necessarily evident to users, may potentially shape the manner wherein climate conversation are limited or enabled (or not) in an assumed 'democratized space online.'

In this age that Web 2.0 platforms capably generate personal online soapboxes to broadcast views, it is critical to ask what actual impacts to offline policy process and earnest attempts at dialogic engagement, exist within such if any. For the 2009 UNCCC website, some earnest citizens who hoped to be heard and to be responded to online, have gone as far as to leave real-world contact information in their website remarks and comments, in the hopes of taking the talk offline. Although the discourse of the citizen comments was not analyzed in this study, it would be fruitful to explore the nature of the discourse that is left on record for public viewing, vis-à-vis the items that were stricken out or deleted by moderators in Climate Thoughts web feature for example.

Considering the highly restricted political real-space of the UNCCC process that limits state-citizen interaction in parallel with the far-reaching and global impacts of the climate change issue it tackles, there is a genuine value to challenge the notion any website that deploys Web 2.0 tools is automatically open, engaging, and participatory. While the choice of technology in itself does promises democratic potential, delivering against the democratic potentials depend on the technology- shaping hand of the website producers, in this case, states. Indeed, the study illustrates that websites, no matter how highly interactive in design elements and abundant in content, may be actually be highly static in terms of facilitating online deliberation and further exercises in participation depending on procedural norms set forth by the producers, giving only the semblance of fulfilling democratic potential.

When user-generated content mechanisms are disjointed from actual policy spaces in the real world of institutional politics because a feedback loop between the online and offline presence of the governance process does not exist, these democratic potentials are mere potential. In this case there is cause for concern these voices from their online soapboxes wired to PC's all over the world, end up becoming background noise easily ignored on just another forgotten website in the corner of internet dinosaurs when the next UNCCC comes around. This is a genuine pitfall that may blindside the rhetoric of openness and

engagement that comes with generous intent to build-in interactive features and user-generated design within the next generation UNCCC host government websites.

In the case of the Danish Government's website, the abundance of user-generated content and social media platforms from a design perspective created a semblance of inclusivity that was bounded by a strong state surveillance that may have moderated (to put it lightly) or controlled (to put it pragmatically) citizen's engagement. Although Denmark has a strong political tradition of representative democracy, it is interesting that the harsh manner that they had managed state-citizen relations during the real-world UNCCC in Copenhagen, in the real world mirrors the underlying principles of management that is present in the virtual UNCCC outreach website. An alternative people's forum called KlimaForum set up by the government as a legitimate 'alternative UNCCC' ended up housing most people when the UNCCC itself turned away people from the venue despite having official badges to enter the space. Some civil society representatives who staged non-violent protests ended up in makeshift jails set up by the police who believed them to cause disturbance. And in the last days of the UNCCC, the halls were silent as all civil society actions were prohibited by the UNFCCC Secretariat and the host government in an effort to focus member states to decide on a conference agreement.

Ironically, the 2009 UNCCC had a pre-event monicker, Hope-nhagen, a result of an industry partnership of the United Nations Secretariat to generate public support for a new global climate deal. Despite the attendees from various organizations accredited to observe the policy process, who had converged onto Copenhagen to pressure states to an agreement on action, the civil society tokenism within the UNCCC process in 2009 became evident, both offline and online. Public support was of minimal value in terms of policy meaningfulness if states were not willing to listen to those inside the physical space of the

Bella Center in Copenhagen (offline) or logged-onto the Climate Thoughts application from a PC at home (online). Adapting Chadwick & May's terminology of state-citizen relations, Denmark was consistent in its offline and online hosting of the UNCCC, adopting a partially-consultative managerial style that was subtle in its application both in real and virtual world.

REFERENCES

Abramson, J., Arterton, C., & Orren, G. (1988). *Electronic Commonwealth, the Impact of New Media Technologies on Democratic Politics.* New York: Basic Books.

Barber, B. (2003). *Strong Democracy: Participatory Politics for a New Age.* Berkley, CA: University of California Press.

Bekkers, V., & Homburg, V. (2007). The myths of E-Government: Looking beyond the assumptions of a new and better government. *The Information Society, 23*(5), 373–382. doi:10.1080/01972240701572913

Burt, E., & Taylor, J. (2008). How well do voluntary organizations perform on the web as democratic actors? Towards an evaluative framework. *Information Communication and Society, 11*(8), 1047–1067. doi:10.1080/13691180802109055

Chadwick, A., & May, C. (2003). Interaction between states and citizens in the age of the Internet: 'E-government' in the United States, Britain and the European Union. *Governance: An International Journal of Policy, Administration and Institutions, 16*(2), 271–300. doi:10.1111/1468-0491.00216

Dahlberg, L. (2001). Democracy in cyberspace. *New Media & Society, 3*(2), 157–177. doi:10.1177/14614440122226038

Dahlberg, L. (2005). The corporate colonization of online attention and marginalization of critical interaction. *The Journal of Communication Inquiry, 29*(2), 160–180. doi:10.1177/0196859904272745

de Kool, D., & van Wamelen, J. (2009). Web 2.0: A new basis for e-government? In *Proceedings of 2008 3rd International Conference on Information and Communication Technologies: From Theory to Applications.* IEEE.

Dunn, D. (1999). Mixing elected and non elected officials in democratic policy making: Fundamentals of accountability. In A. Przeworski, S. Stokes, & B. Manin (Eds.), *Democracy, Accountability, and Representation* (pp. 297–326). Cambridge, UK: Cambridge University Press. doi:10.1017/CBO9781139175104.011

Fishkin, J. (1991). *Democracy and Deliberation.* New Haven, CT: Yale University Press.

Heeks, R. (2004). *Basic definitions page.* eGovernment for Development Information Exchange. Commonwealth Telecommunications Organisation. Retrieved on November 10, 2009 from http://www.egov4dev.org/egovdefn.htm

Hindman, M. (2008). *The Myth of Digital Democracy.* Princeton, NJ: Princeton University Press.

Horrocks, I. (2009). 'Experts' and e-government. *Information Communication and Society, 12*(1), 110–127. doi:10.1080/13691180802109030

Iversen, J. E., Vedel, T., & Werle, W. (2004). Standardization and the democratic design of information and communication technology. *Knowledge, Technology & Policy, 17*(2), 104–126. doi:10.1007/s12130-004-1027-y

Kamal, M. (2009). An analysis of e-participation research: Moving from theoretical to pragmatic viewpoint. *Transforming Government: People. Process & Policy, 3*(4), 340–354.

Laver, M., & Shepsle, K. A. (1999). 'Government accountability in parliamentary democracy. In A. Przeworski, S. C. Stokes, & B. Manin (Eds.), *Democracy, Accountability, and Representation* (pp. 279–296). Cambridge, UK: Cambridge University Press. doi:10.1017/CBO9781139175104.010

Lessig, L. (1999). *Code: and Other Laws of Cyberspace*. New York: Basic Books.

Lister, S. (2003). NGO legitimacy: technical issue or social construct. *Critique of Anthropology, 23*, 175–192. doi:10.1177/0308275X03023002004

Macintoch, A., & Angus, W. (2006). *Evaluating How Eparticipation Changes Local Democracy*. Paper presented at eGovernment Workshop '06 (eGOV06). London, UK.

Pateman, C. (1970). *Participation and Democratic Theory*. Cambridge, UK: Cambridge University Press.

Rheingold, H. (1993). *The Virtual Community: Homesteading on the Electronic Frontier*. New York: Harper.

Salter, L. (2004). Structure and forms of use: A contribution to understanding the 'effects' of the Internet on deliberative democracy. *Information Communication and Society, 7*(2), 185–206. doi:10.1080/1369118042000232648

Sauer-Johansen, M. (2009). *Thinking about Climate Change? Don't Keep it to Yourself!* Paper presented at United Nations Climate Change Conference 15 Hosted by Danish Government. Retrieved on October 15, 2009 from http://en.cop15.dk/blogs/view+blog?blogid=132

Street, J. (1997). Remote control? Politics, technology and `electronic democracy. *European Journal of Communication, 12*(1), 27–42. doi:10.1177/0267323197012001003

UNFCCC. (2009). *United Nations Framework Convention on Climate Change*. Retrieved on November 8, 2009 from http://www.unfccc.int

UNFCCC COP 13. (2007). *United Nations Climate Change Conference 13 Hosted by Indonesian Government*. Retrieved on October 15, 2009 from http://www.climate.web.id

UNFCCC COP 14. (2008). *United Nations Climate Change Conference 14 Hosted by Polish Government*. Retrieved on October 15, 2009 from http://www.cop14.pl

UNFCCC COP 15. (2009a). *United Nations Climate Change Conference 15 Hosted by Danish Government*. Retrieved on October 15, 2009 from http://en.cop15.dk

UNFCCC COP 15. (2009b). *Send your greetings to COP15*. United Nations Climate Change Conference 15 Hosted by Danish Government. Retrieved on October 15, 2009 from http://en.cop15.dk/climate+greetings

USA.gov. (2008). *Matrix of Web 2.0 Technology and Government*. Retrieved on November 4, 2009 from http://www.usa.gov/webcontent/documents/Web_Technology_Matrix.pdf

USA.gov. (2009). *Better Websites, Better Government*. Retrieved on November 4, 2009 from http://www.usa.gov/webcontent/technology/other_tech.shtml

Varra, E., Tienaria, J., & Laurila, J. (2006). Pulp and paper fiction: on the discursive of global industrial restructuring. *Organization Studies, 27*, 789–810. doi:10.1177/0170840606061071

Wright, S., & Street, J. (2007). Democracy, deliberation and design: The case of online discussion forums. *New Media & Society, 9*, 849–869. doi:10.1177/1461444807081230

KEY TERMS AND DEFINITIONS

Citizen Engagement: Occurs when citizens are being publicly informed and participate in issue discussions, while being open to divergent points of view, and while being reflective and actively pursuing public issues.

Digital Democracy: Collection of attempts to practice democracy mediated through digital networked communications as addition to (not replacement for) traditional practices without limitations in space and time.

Legitimacy of Actors: Acceptability derived from regulation, representation, ethical or moral grounds, expertise, level of autonomy, and independence which may be financial in nature.

Public Accountability: Occurs when citizens are provided information about organizations and activities as a political agent of democracy, as a democratic actor.

United Nations Conference on Climate Change: Annual meeting for conference of parties (states) under the United Nations Framework Convention on Climate Change, the 1992 global agreement to address the environmental issue of climate change through the UN system.

This work was previously published in E-Governance and Social Inclusion edited by Scott Baum and Arun Mahizhnan, pages 97-126, copyright year 2014 by Information Science Reference (an imprint of IGI Global).

Chapter 71
Examining Design Pattern Strategies as a Means to Achieve Social Presence in the Online Classroom

Araminta Matthews
University College – University of Maine System, USA

Robert M. Kitchin Jr.
University College – University of Maine System, USA

ABSTRACT

Design patterns have received much attention across multiple design domains where social interaction is a central goal because they have great potential for capturing and sharing design knowledge. Design patterns, design pattern language, and design pattern libraries demonstrate potential benefits to novice and expert online course designers. Trends affecting the growth of online courses and resultant pitfalls negatively affecting students and instructors indicate the need for social presence design. A literature review addresses the importance of social interaction, differentiated design, learning-oriented social networking, and Web design structures in an effort to assuage the experience of isolation reported by the majority of online students. The authors argue that design patterns are a method of overcoming many of these apparent obstacles to quality online course design and learning engagement. Additionally, they present example design patterns to solve specific social interacting problems.

INTRODUCTION

Armed with a host of Web-connected devices, today's students and instructors crave more from their online courses than guided textbook tours or a stack of assigned texts and writing activities. Through repeated experiences of high quality in-teraction design in regular Web-based activities, such as shopping, banking, playing, socializing and informal learning etc., we are becoming more expectant of satisfaction in our encounters with formal online learning environments. There is, however, a discrepancy between student and instructor expectations and the achievement of

DOI: 10.4018/978-1-4666-8619-9.ch071

satisfying social interaction in an online course, and part of that discrepancy rests in a resource deficit of time, support, technological proficiency, and design knowledge. Design pattern strategies, originally conceptualized to democratize architectural design resources and empower ordinary people to participate in designing the spaces they physically lived in (Alexander, 1979; Goodyear, de Laat, & Lally, 2006), have received much attention for their value as a means for capturing and sharing design knowledge relevant to online course design (Frizell & Hübscher, 2011). Within the context of online learning, design patterns and their collection in pattern libraries offer shareable, accessible and proven solutions to the problem of creating contextually relevant social presence in online courses, promising a potent and efficient means of overcoming these deficits of time, support, technological proficiency, and design knowledge.

It is important to note that the effects of these resource deficits come from a complex of causes with no single root source. However, we know instructors who are untrained in online course or website design may assume social presence will mimic the engagement of a face-to-face course, and use the same materials, strategies and schedules they are accustomed to (Allen, & Seaman, 2013; Smith, Ferguson, & Caris, 2001). This default design strategy–to replicate the physical course online–breaks the experience for the student and contributes to degraded satisfaction and the experience of isolation, disconnectedness and technological problems in online courses (Alman, Frey, & Tomer, 2012; Willging, & Johnson, 2004). Online courses require participants to develop new literacies, attitudes and expectations related to social interaction in this digital media environment. The tools, physical boundaries, and forces are not driven by the principles of proximity, time, and technology (DePoy, & Gilson, n.d.; Jordan, 2012). Digital spaces contain forces and problems related to digital technology literacy, Web use culture, and more abstract concerns about how

mediated connections and media cultures affect the needs and preferences of learners (Reigeluth, 2012). Student and instructor both experience dissonance when these forces are not considered and successfully addressed in the design of an online course.

Social presence in the digital environment relates directly to our ability to experience social encounters that both affirm self-perception and the perception that there are other people in the online course with us (Heim, 1998). Social interaction in physical spaces is founded on design patterns (such as podiums, desks arranged in horse-shoe patterns or clustered into small groups, and spacious hallways for chatting between classrooms). For example, details are coded to define each facet of this purposive environment, from how wide the halls should be to how lecture spaces will be used and shared. The same design patterns do not inform the blueprint for interaction in an online course. Online, activities for connecting and learning are made possible through digital whiteboards rather than physical whiteboards, and principles of proximity, time, and technology enable different requirements for interaction. Design patterns traditionally applied to fields outside of education, such as those from architecture and social interface design, help to address both the resource deficits previously mentioned and the knowledge gap between the design of online and face-to-face learning environments.

Introduced by architect Christopher Alexander, (1979), design patterns are intended to make repeated problems encountered in architectural design situations and their relevant solutions more accessible. Alexander's conceptual framework of design patterns was conceived to empower untrained people to design the environments where they live, learn, play, work and even learn together (Alexander, Ishikawa, Silverstein, Jacobson, Fiksdahl-King, & Angel, 1977). These patterns are socially derived, componential and empirical strategies that describe:

- Functional design problems inherent to a given environmental context (virtual or physical), and
- The configuration of concepts that, when actualized through a design process, solves the problems. (Alexander, 1979, p. 283)

While the application of design patterns to pedagogy and elearning is only now beginning to emerge, their utility has been endorsed by a long list of professionals in divergent fields (Pauwels, Hübscher, Bargas-Avila, & Opwis, 2010) including: architecture, software engineering, human-computer interface design, and social interface design. Most recently, elearning and pedagogy design pattern scholarship has emerged (Crumlish, & Malone, 2009; Dearden, & Finlay, 2006; Goodyear, 2005; Goodyear, de Laat, & Lally, 2006;).

On its own, a design pattern is componential to a greater set of patterns termed a pattern language (Alexander et al., 1977). A pattern language is generally understood as the collection of design patterns related to a specific domain of design, and the collection of these individual patterns are referred to as a pattern library (see Figure 1). With a pattern library and general literacy in the pattern language of that domain, the utility of the concept can be leveraged by anyone to solve design problems they encounter in that domain. Multiple pattern libraries representing multiple design domains converge, which is often the case in any elearning design project (Hixon, 2008). In the context of e-learning, multiple domains are germane to online course design, and multiple professional skills are required, including content and learning management systems expertise, instructional design, instructional technology and Web design. In short, design patterns can be applied to online course design as a best practice measure to improve the overall quality of social presence and elearning structure for both instructor and student.

Figure 1. Example pattern library, language and single pattern model

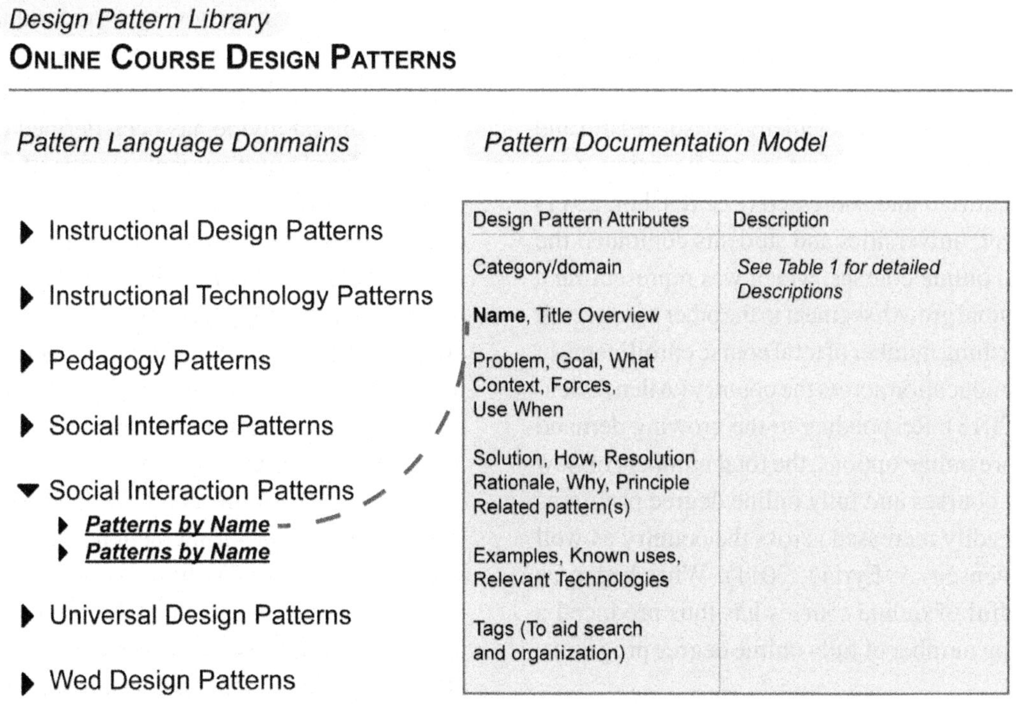

Design Pattern Library
ONLINE COURSE DESIGN PATTERNS

Pattern Language Donmains

- ▶ Instructional Design Patterns
- ▶ Instructional Technology Patterns
- ▶ Pedagogy Patterns
- ▶ Social Interface Patterns
- ▼ Social Interaction Patterns
  - ▶ *Patterns by Name*
  - ▶ *Patterns by Name*
- ▶ Universal Design Patterns
- ▶ Wed Design Patterns

Pattern Documentation Model

Design Pattern Attributes	Description
Category/domain	*See Table 1 for detailed Descriptions*
Name, Title Overview	
Problem, Goal, What Context, Forces, Use When	
Solution, How, Resolution Rationale, Why, Principle Related pattern(s)	
Examples, Known uses, Relevant Technologies	
Tags (To aid search and organization)	

BACKGROUND

Colleges and universities are rushing to establish online learning opportunities for students. Higher education has chosen the bet that online learning will be critical to the long-term strategy of universities and colleges; a perception that reached "its highest level in 2012 (69.1%)" (Allen & Seaman, 2013, p. 16). Recognizing this trend of increasing value potential for online learning environments has led to marketing investments selling the benefits of distance education and online learning (Rovai & Downey, 2010). Those benefits are typically and somewhat ubiquitously touted as:

- Technology allows faculty to teach many more students in online courses, lowering teaching costs and raising profits and efficiencies;
- Technology allows more students to participate in online courses;
- Teaching and learning can happen anywhere there is an Internet connection;
- Learning and teaching can happen at the convenience of the learner or instructor.

As a result of this marketing campaign, attractive business model, and promise of conveniences, significant and varied challenges to successful and satisfying experiences of online learning were not identified and addressed (Lee & Choi, 2011) however, universities and students continued the rush to online courses, which was representing a substantial growth segment in the otherwise overall diminishing number of total course enrollments in higher education across the country (Allen & Seaman, 2013). Responding to the growing demand for more online options, the total numbers of new online courses and fully online degree programs has steadily increased across the country as well (Christensen, & Eyring, 2011). What began as a handful of online courses has thus produced a growing number of fully online degree programs.

In a study tracking a decade of online educational trends, researchers Allen and Seaman found that:

... a major change has also occurred in the nature of the online offerings–a far larger proportion of higher education institutions have moved from offering only online courses to providing complete online programs (62.4% in 2012 as compared to 34.5% in 2002). (p. 20)

With both courses and degree programs moving to the cloud, a greater demand for technological literacy for faculty and online learners arises in order to realize satisfactory social interaction in this Web-based environment. The rush to claim a stake in the terrain of online education seems to be slowing though, while still trending up (Allen & Seaman, 2013).

Such undeniably rapid growth in the demand for educators and learners to teach and learn online carries with it its own set of problems perhaps best exemplified by concepts inherent to the digital divide. The concept of the digital divide was conceived to describe "the existing gap in [information and communication technology] access and in the ability of individuals and economies to participate in the global information society" (Bruno, Esposito, & Genovese, 2011, p. 16). The digital divide has been defined through several related but divergent streams of research (Bruno, Esposito, & Genovese, 2011). It is the concept of the gap "between those who have access to information and communication technologies (ICTs) and are using it effectively, and those who are not using it effectively" (p. 17) that is in focus here. The thrust to increase the magnitude of online course development upon faculty and students in haste appears to have increased social isolation (Arbaugh, 2000; Kuh, 2005; Weller, 2007), the exact opposite of social interaction and satisfaction with online learning. We have overwhelmed many of the faculty and exacerbated the number and the divide between those faculty members who can effectively use the ICTs to design quality social interaction into their online courses and those who cannot. The irony is, though we seem to have more online courses and flexible options, we have less successful interaction through the technology.

As technological options increase, complexity also increases, creating an apparent gap in operationalizing skills between individuals who are raised with consistent access to technology and those who come to integrate technology later in life (Epstein, Nisbet & Gillespie, 2011). The digital divide is non-discriminating in that it exists between faculty and their colleagues, faculty and students, and students and their peers. As a result, the benefits of online education have not yet been wholly realized as institutions scramble to get online and compete by encouraging faculty to develop their diverse design talents to include skills traditionally viewed as secondary to content mastery and expertise: Social networking, cloud computing, human-computer interaction, Web design, and more (Halstead, Phillips, Koller, Hardin, Porter, & Dwyer, 2011). The lack of these skills represents a resource deficit in our educational workforce that has a direct impact on their ability to design social presence into their online course. Students in online courses then encounter limited social interaction and an experience of isolation (Weller, 2007).

DESIGN PATTERNS: HISTORY, LOGIC, AND USE

Online instructors and designers require conceptually easy-to-use-and-reuse building blocks to design interactive, learner-centered social experiences in online courses. These experiences must be mapped to instructional objectives that are broadly accessible to diverse students. We refer to these building blocks as design patterns. Unlike a complex and abstract theory, patterns are conceptually easier to apply, requiring fewer leaps of creative connection between theory and practice on the part of the designer. Rather than

prescribe a theory-based solution, patterns shorten the distance between design strategy and outcome by demonstrating rather than declaring the total value of the solution. Because design patterns are "customizable, re-usable ideas, not fixed, pre-packaged solutions" (Goodyear, 2005, p. 2), they have the potential to save time-related resources, particularly through repeated use.

As explained at the outset, Alexander's conceptual framework of design patterns was founded on the belief that the people who live in a place should be empowered to design it (Alexander et al., 1977). Users are as equipped to inform the design of their experience: "Sound design is not only within the reach of a small set of uniquely talented individuals, but can be achieved by virtually all designers" (Lidwell, Holden, & Butler, 2010, p. 11). Fundamentally, a design pattern is located within an interactive social context (Alexander et al., 1977) and observes the pattern of needs of the people who inhabit that context before forming a solution, and then explains the solution. Design patterns are collaboratively created, iterative, interactive, and empirical structures that describe (a) functional design problems inherent to a given environmental context (virtual or physical) and (b) the configuration of concepts that solves the problems when actualized through a generative design process (Alexander, 1978). Design patterns take on this general form: "context → conflicting forces → configuration" (p. 182). More recently, Alexander (2002) reinforces the principle concepts behind design patterns:

Each pattern describes a problem which occurs over and over again in our environment, and then describes the core of the solution to that problem in such a way that you can use this solution a million times over, without ever doing it the same way twice. (para. 1)

Alexander's (1978) original definition of a design pattern has remained unchanged across the spectrum of design domains that have adopted the concept. This does not mean implementation has been without its challenges. Kohls and Uttecht (2009) found several obstacles to large-scale implementation of design patterns and pattern libraries. Currently there is little agreement among scholars as to how design patterns should be defined, categorized by domain, or organized into an accessible repository, or validated through systematic analysis (Kohls & Uttecht, 2009). Troubling potential academic course designers further are issues related to the role of values in design pattern implementation (Dearden, & Finlay, 2006). We see this problem play out at several axiological intersections:

- Individual course design and curriculum design;
- Between team members in a course design project; and
- Intersecting values between cultures, communities and academic disciplines.

Still, the benefits of implementation may outweigh the challenges. Even only a few well defined patterns can offer an approach to design that promises potential to improve online social interaction between learners and instructors, learners and content, and learners and their peers (Caeiro, Llamas, & Anido, 2004).

Before exploring social-interaction design patterns, it is necessary to clarify a model for documenting a design pattern, often referred to as *pattern mining*. This model documentation process allows patterns to be shared by a community of designers, representing a usable pattern library, accessible to both course design experts and non-experts (Alexander, 1979; Coutinho, Talarico, & Neris, 2009; Dearden, & Finlay, 2006; Eckstein, Bergin, & Sharp, 2002). Furthermore, a model for documenting design patterns is useful to interdisciplinary course design teams as it improves communication and explication of instructional goals and their solutions (Hixon, 2008).

Based upon Crumlish and Malone (2009, p. 28), the following documentation model provides an example and definition: interactive online learning design pattern: *Interactive Online Learning Design Pattern Documentation Model*. Additionally, Pauwels et al. (2010) provides guidance for documenting an interactive online learning design pattern, as shown in Table 1:

Table 1. Interactive online learning design pattern documentation model

Design Pattern Attributes	Description (Underline Text Signals Links to other Patterns Guidance)
Category/domain	The taxonomy of categories organizes the patterns into a library of resources. The category should clearly communicate what problem the pattern is most intended to address.
Name, Title Overview	Gives the pattern a unique and meaningful name hinting at the solution. Makes it immediately obvious to the reader what the solution is about. If possible this should contain images, such as screenshots or illustrations.
Problem, Goal, What Context, Forces, Use When	Describes the problem that has to be solved or a goal that one wants to achieve with the design. When should the pattern be used? Provides clear description of the context in which the given solution is applicable. This is often stated as a set of "forces" that influence design solutions in the context.
Solution, How, Resolution Rationale, Why, Principle Related pattern(s)	How does this pattern solve the problem? Is this design pattern part of a higher-level pattern? What other component patterns are necessary to complete this pattern? Are there similar design patterns that achieve the same goal in similar contexts?
Examples, Known uses, Technologies Options	Where has this pattern already been implemented? Include <links><images>
Tags (To aid search and organization)	Keywords, Terms

At the beginning of each pattern, there is relevant background information to support the rationale and context with greater depth. Though useful, such detailed background is not typically necessary to adequately document a design pattern as there is flexibility. A design pattern should be actionable and explained in a brief document to avoid becoming prescriptive. The interpretation of the pattern is creative and is leveraged with what the designer, no matter their proficiency, already knows. The potential efficiencies are actualized as the designer finds actionable guidance in the pattern without needing to become an expert all at once in the entire design domain. Even if multiple design patterns are necessary to design the entire solution to a specific problem, design patterns combine to reveal a path to a solution.

Online Interaction Design Problems to Solve

Because designing for social presence may require learning various technologies used to connect to, participate in, and create meaningful learning artifacts through digital learning environments (Arbaugh, 2000), many stakeholders find themselves in a constant balancing act between remaining current in their fields of expertise and remaining current with the upward trend of technology and course design principles. This creates an inadvertent impact on the quality of online courses, as noted by Allen and Seaman (2013), who have observed "the prototypical online course in U.S. higher education over the past decade has not been structured to provide large increases in efficiency. "Most online courses are very similar in design to existing face-to-face courses" (p. 22). A major problem with the design of social presence for an online course seems to stem from the assumption that an online course should mirror the traditional instructional framework of faculty as the key transmitter of knowledge rather than emphasizing the needs of learners to work in a flexible process

model (Weller, 2002). If instructors inadvertently fail to recognize the flexibility of the Web-based classroom, as well as the additional scaffolding necessary to construct a meaningful social interaction in a virtual environment (Baran, Correia, & Thompson, 2011), students may become disgruntled and experience further isolation. The Web is malleable and social; it is likely they have the same expectation for their own empowerment in a Web-based classroom. They come to online courses at first apprehensive, but additionally expecting (or at least hoping for) a more empowered and flexible learning environment (Phelan, 2012). They wish to have their apprehensions assuaged by an intuitive learning design that incorporates a sense of community (social presence) to help with the feeling of disconnectedness they experience (Kuh, 2005). This lack of social presence, sensation of disconnectedness, and the experience of isolation parroted by so many students is a systemic design error.

Fortunately, this error can be solved. The solution lies in a paradigm shift, a model of quality design considerations and targeted skill-development, and a reflection on the design patterns of countless successful social spaces that exist on the Web today. With a few simple changes, elearning can be everything faculty and students want: an inspiring space where instructors are delighted by the innovative approaches their students take when they feel a sense of ownership over their work in an empowered, social, virtual classroom.

Provide Flexible Means of Interaction

Version 2.0 of The National Center on Universal Design for Learning Guidelines provides principles that are nearly design patterns in their own right. Universal design principles are intended to meet the needs of all people regardless of their range of abilities. These principles assist course designers by "providing a framework for understanding how to create curricula that meets the needs of all learners from the start" (National Center on Universal Design for Learning Guidelines, 2013, para. 1), and thus they fit seamlessly within any design pattern for elearning. The value of universal design principles to focus on learners' broad needs are well known to most special education scholars because the populations they serve are typically more vulnerable to rigid formats of instruction (Gargiulo, & Metcalf, 2013).

Like design patterns, universal design has its historical origins in architecture and the design of physical places (The Center for Universal Design, 2013). Architect, Ronald L. Mace, coined the term *universal design* (2013), and its concepts are largely applied to overcoming interaction barriers between disabled bodies and environments and cultures (Shneiderman, 2000), but the full intention of universal design is to better design for all (Lidwell, Holden, & Butler, 2010).

Expanding on the design complexity, DePoy and Gilson (n.d.) offer Disjuncture Theory as a lens through which we can understand how bodies and environments (physical, virtual, and social) achieve degrees of fit. These degrees of fit range from complete disjuncture, with no chance for successful interaction, to full juncture, where opportunities for successful interaction are plentiful and nearly guaranteed. Designing online learning environments to ensure the best opportunity for complete juncture in the online course requires a flexible design pattern where social interaction is broadly defined. The Flexible Means of Social Interaction Design Pattern is documented in Table 2.

The Benefits of Meaningful Social Interaction

Educators have long realized that social development and networking are fundamental components of positive educational outcomes (Cleveland-Innes & Emes, 2005). Social supports and networks serve students in many positive ways (Alman, Frey, & Tomer, 2012). Often, for example, the greatest value of a college education in the eyes

of students is the social network they have when they leave. Interpersonal and group connections engage students in deeper learning (Cleveland-Innes & Emes, 2005), pave the way for cohorts that extend beyond the classroom, and open networking opportunities between classmates well into each student's future.

While social presence and networking may be on faculty radar, instructors unused to teaching online may have difficulty understanding how to create online courses that leverage the parts of teaching they typically love most, social contact with students, in the online environment (Meera, Sergey, & Gargi, 2010). Students unused to learning online may also experience many challenges, including difficulties creating social experiences in a virtual classroom after a semester of interacting with a few names (no faces) of their cohort in a text-based discussion forum or email exchange. In this void of missing social gestures, faces, and personal expressions students and faculty often struggle to connect with one another (Alman, Frey, & Tomer, 2012). In these online courses, the walls of text that rise up around faculty and students, paradoxically connecting them through technology, often isolate them from authentic and satisfying interaction. The future of online courses requires "interactive design that combines computer-enhanced perception with the gift of self-perception" (Heim, 1998, p. 73).

In order to achieve this interactive design, faculty and students need support to describe the problems and solutions to participating and co-creating social presence in online courses, an environment still foreign to many, and students also need to cultivate a Web-social-intelligence to foster tangible relationships in a virtual world beyond the course. When applied to elearning, design patterns can provide a metacognitive space in which faculty feel supported and students observe intuitive designs. In this supportive design-space, students and faculty can foster an improved social exchange in the online environment (see Table 3).

Table 2. Flexible means of social interaction design pattern

Design Pattern Attributes	Description (Underline Text Signals Links to other Patterns Guidance)
Category(ies)/domain(s)	Universal Design, Social Interaction
Name, Title Overview	Flexible Means of Social Interaction
Problem, Goal, What Context, Forces, Use when	Use this pattern to design appropriate and suitable options for interaction, production of deliverables, and assessing the range of learners' needs and preferences. No two learners are exactly alike in their abilities to engage in social interaction through online interfaces, technologies, and environmental configurations. Some expectations for interaction in an online course are beyond the reach of some students because of literacy with the new technology or preferences for expression. **Forces in Play:** technology literacy, skills, preferences, personal learning goals, and barriers to interacting through one mode of expression or another. This could include learning preferences, technology available and familiar to the learner, or embodied abilities ranging from able to not able (e.g. blind or hard of hearing). Other forces related to strengths and weakness may also be applicable. **Note:** Too much flexibility can decrease usability by providing too many options. To counter this concern, consider limiting flexibility to only the best options rather than all options. Also consider providing ample explanation about the intended learning goals for the social interaction. This will improve conceptualization in the generation of interaction encounters with the online course.
Solution, How, Resolution Rationale, Why, Principle Related pattern(s)	When designing interaction requirements, provide flexibility for acceptable modes of expression with guidance. Consider multiple formats such as video, audio, and text. Provide multiple technology solutions including any the learners may already know that may have been unknown to course designers. Consider patterns that provide interaction with either the instructor or peers. At the top of the list are patterns related to formative or summative assessments, introductions, collaborative assignments, and small group discussion. When possible, design flexibility into assessments that require social interaction. Consider the benefits and means of peer assessments and public performance of knowledge.
Examples, Known uses, Technology Options	**An Example:** In asking for introductions, provide the options of using video, audio or textual formats. Using a webcam or smart phone camera, students can record their introduction video to a streaming service such as Youtube™, Facebook™, Google+™ and other services. Promote commenting on introductions. Demonstrate, either through rubrics or ready-made exemplars expectations and elements of a successful introduction in the context of the course. Because some learners may not be able to interact with any of these formats as they are typically configured, be prepared to include support for text only versions or ask for text transcripts to accompany video and audio formats. Though this may take a bit more effort, the affordance of multiple formats provides benefits to all learners in the course.
Tags	Flexibility, Multiple Formats, Personal Expression, Social Interaction, Accessibility

Shifting the Paradigm

Even though many students believe they can find the answer to any question by punching it into a search engine and waiting a few seconds, students continue to arrive in both physical and virtual classrooms excited to learn, eager to be challenged to accomplish and discover new ways of learning, and motivated to be involved in the process of their own education in a social and critical context (Halaway, 2011). Perhaps more empowered than their face-to-face counterparts, online learners tend to have a preconceived view that the path of online education is one of convenience rather than the quality they may expect from a traditional course (Callaway, 2012). At the same time, while a minority of online learners place a greater value on the asynchronous independence afforded by virtual classrooms, a vast majority "value opportunities to interact and be part of a learning community" (Phelan, 2012, pp. 33-34). If students come to elearning environments with a desire to interact socially and yet perceive online learning to be lower-quality than face-to-face classes, then perhaps it is possible that students are not experiencing design patterns for social exchange that are useful and integrative. This begs the question: do these students feel that they are sacrificing social presence and a quality education in order to achieve an end goal on a tighter time scale?

Table 3. Collaborative online writing design pattern

Design Pattern Attributes	Description (Underline Text Signals Links to other Patterns Guidance)
Category(ies)/ domain(s)	Social Interaction, Collaborative Writing
Name, Title Overview	*Collaborative Online Writing:* Collaborative writing assignments can promote cognitive engagement, social interaction and professional development, by leveraging peer review and instructor feedback within a structured asynchronous writing space.
Problem, Goal, What Context, Forces, Use when	Use this pattern when the learning context requires the development of writing skills, interpersonal professional group communication skills, and distance group collaboration skills. Given that writing proficiency is relevant to all undergraduate and graduate programs of study this pattern is generalizable across academic disciplines. Learners and instructors have a continuum of instructional activities available to activate literacy skill development through engaging cognitive and social experiences. These interaction options range from instructor-student writing activities where exchanges are limited between instructor and students, to group writing activities where peer review and collaboration "team-teach" writing skills. *Forces in play:* In online courses students and instructors are distributed geographically and across different schedules. This necessarily means interaction will be mostly asynchronous and require a means for organizing and documenting the collaborative process. Because skills and comfort with online collaborative writing will vary among students, successful interaction will depend partly on how well the activity is defined and supported technologically. Requisite exposure to training with the chosen technology may be necessary to scaffold learner ability to successfully participate in the learning activity. The particular learning objectives related to writing and collaboration, and the desired rigor are key factors to consider in choosing which collaborative writing technology is best suited to promote learning. As with other group work activities, fairness and equity of workload can be a challenge for both students and instructors. Through instruction and assessment strategies, these issues should be addressed and structured into the activity.
Solution, How, Resolution Rationale, Why, Principle Related pattern(s)	Learning objective: Define measurable learning objectives that: • Focus on student behavior • Use simple, specific action verbs • Select appropriate assessment methods • State desired performance criteria Clearly define the assignment learning objectives and provide instructional materials to use the technology. Include expectations for frequency and required means of interaction. Choose a technology that will document interaction by author, provide a revision history, and facilitate commenting/markup within the collaborative writing space. Ideally, the technology should allow collaborators to "mention" or "ping" their fellow collaborators individually or as a group. This provides virtual, social notification alerting collaborators to respond or take action in a timely way. Instructors should explicitly detail how they will participate in the assignment, be accessible to students to answer questions. Clarify how and when *feedback* will be provided. Assessment strategies should include both group and individual performance factors and be clearly stated at the outset. *Related patterns include:* mentioning, pings, notifications, time management strategies, synchronous online meetings, rubrics, differentiated assignments, and Flexible Means of Social Interaction.
Examples, Known uses, Technology Options	*Example objectives:* • Students will be able to apply the elements of APA style, 6th edition to create a professional, annotated bibliography on an assigned topic. • Students will demonstrate proficiency using collaborative writing technologies to create an annotated bibliography as a team by using commenting and markup features within the software to provide feedback to each other on quality of contribution to the document. • Students will demonstrate the ability to use the Mention feature within the software to alert teammates in a timely way of feedback specific to their work. • Using a rubric based evaluation tool provided by the instructor, students will demonstrate the ability to evaluate their peers using a rubric. • Responding to two open ended essay questions, students will **A**: demonstrate the ability to reflect on their collaborative-writing using online technology *B:* demonstrate the ability to reflect on their needs for collaborative-writing improvement using online technology. *Possible Technologies:* Google Docs, wikis, collaborative blogs, group discussion boards, rubrics
Tags	Flexibility, Multiple Formats, Personal Expression, Social Interaction, Accessibility, Rubric

Though students initially presume online learning will be convenient, the sacrifice of social presence in poorly designed online courses has a lasting impact. This sentiment of social disconnectedness claimed by students is pervasive, and students continue to report "missing familiar teacher immediacy, and likewise missing interpersonal interactions and social cues they more typically have when learning face to face" (Slagter Van Tryon & Bishop, 2009, p. 291). Because social presence plays such a potent role in students' enjoyment regardless of the potential impact it may have on cognitive and affective learning outcomes, it is not surprising that students who perceive and engage with social presence in their online courses report increased interaction, improved satisfaction and self-confidence, and possible connections between immediate feedback loops and improved knowledge retention (Mackey & Freyberg, 2010). Students who enjoy their courses are more likely to engage deeply with the content, which may also impact instructor satisfaction.

Achieving Social Satisfaction

Social presence has the potential to improve the virtual classroom, but to accomplish this goal, learners and instructors must first shift their focus from

the face-to-face lecture of physical classrooms to a more active and interactive discovery-based model afforded by Web-based classes. Web-based technology affords instant collaboration, interaction, discovery and exposure. Where "computers handle high-speed transmission to-and-fro, the separating line between sender and receiver, viewer and producer, begins to blur" (Heim, 1998, p. 75). One way to exemplify this is through the concept of *Sage on the Stage* versus *Guide on the Side* (King, 1993), which expands upon constructivist and connectivist learning theories that are directly applicable to online learning and social presence in the virtual classroom..

In Figure 2, the first model (pictured left), the sage on the stage delivers content in a one-way conduit with knowledge transmitted by the instructor for the student to receive and reassemble later for assessment (King, 1993). In the second model, the guide on the side enters into an almost Arthurian round-table pedagogy, or *andragogy*, where the instructor is an expert participant in the learning process alongside students, and knowledge is gathered, processed, and shared collaboratively through maximized social engagement for empowered and differentiated assessment (Abrami, Bernard, Bures, Tamim, & Tamim; Knowles, 2011). Students coordinate their own cognitive events under the

Figure 2. A comparison of instructor-focus vs. learner-focus strategies in online course design

 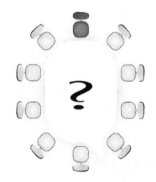

<u>Traditional:</u> Face-to-face Pedagogy
Model of Instructor-led Learning
"Sage on the Stage"

<u>Innovative:</u> Online Andragogy
Model of Collaborative Learning
"Guide on the Side"

facilitation of an expert instructor, which leverages the user experience and agency to motivate learner retention and foster social engagements. Students used to scanning a website selectively to determine what to test now are able to interact similarly within the framework of an a-la-carte style course design that includes options for assessments and entry-points within the course. As a role-model for social presence, choice-empowered students reach out to one another and to professors to obtain guidance and to explore creative *outputs*, the highest level of the new Bloom's Taxonomy where students demonstrate lasting, integrated cognitive skills and abilities (Forehand, 2005). This quality model begins first with a transition in:

... learners' identity to that of a knowledge builder and a shift of teachers' identity to that of a critical colleague or co-learner...Students need to embrace empowerment given the space to construct learning, while teachers need to become comfortable with fluidity and uncertainty. (Lim, So, & Tan, 2010, p. 208)

This transition is the first step to supporting social presence in the online classroom because, without this concept, students may continue to be socially stymied by old paradigms of the lecture-led class, looking for permission and directions for every step without the familiar social cues of the physical classroom. A successful design leverages the knowledge that the pattern of social interaction in the online class cannot simply be borrowed from the face-to-face course. Rather, it needs to emerge from problems and solutions proven to work in the online design domain (Crumlish & Malone, 2009; Goodyear, 2005; Heim, 1998; Kohls, & Uttecht, 2009).

How Does Participation Improve Social Presence?

The Web is poised to optimize equitable social presence for elearning. The very nature of the word

Web implies interconnectedness between contributors. As exemplified in the now iconic Web-film "Web 2.0: The Machine is Us/ing Us," by Kansas State University associate professor of cultural anthropology, Michael Lee Wesch (2007), the Web is constructed on a constantly moving target of content that is changed, modified, obliterated and elevated by each new user who interacts with it regardless of education, authority, expertise, or skill level. The Web is an open-source education which comes with the benefit of information and the risk of misinformation. As the exquisite depiction within the film implies, the unilinear nature of text is paper-driven, much like the traditional face-to-face classroom; the virtual classroom is as fluid and living as the Worldwide Web, a structure that is constantly reinventing itself through the direct manipulation of the people who engage with it. As such, the Web is no longer just information; the Web is evidence of social presence in a virtual environment (Wesch, 2007). Therefore, creating social presence for Web-based classes using design patterns derived from face-to-face models is like using a computer only for the purposes of word-processing or calculating sums when it is capable of so much more than that. Because design patterns are customizable (more-so than templates), it is easy for instructors to integrate the Web tools to a higher potential than perhaps they are currently used.

Interaction Matters

Research regarding student-instructor and student-student relationships in online courses confirms a number of designable, socially constructed value points to student learning. Student retention and satisfaction within an online course along with student performance, rapport, engagement, interaction, and sense of community unites all participants (Abrami et al., 2011; Picciano, 2002; Sher, 2009). Designing a solution to social interaction on the Web, however, requires an objective gap analysis as the first step: what is the gap between the existing outcome and the desired outcome? This starting place is essential to ensuring the outcome matches the design goal. Only after addressing the questions can a course designer ensure purposive and authentic interaction will be achieved. Interaction must be purposeful, motivational, learner-centric and rigorously executed with quality and skill in order to achieve effective and satisfying instructional means to accomplish course objectives (Abrami et al., 2011; Kehrwald, 2010; Picciano, 2002; Sher, 2009). Just because email is an effective means of communication between distant parties, for example, does not mean that it is the most effective social interaction tool

for frequently asked questions or student collaborative work. Designing for social presence begins with asking the goal-oriented questions. Figure 3 illustrates an instructional design model that facilitates goal-oriented questions in the design of purposive social interaction in online learning.

The APPLIES Model, developed by the authors of this chapter, is informed by existing instructional design models. Based on the ADDIE (Analysis → Design → Development → Implementation → Evaluation) Model, developed by Florida State University in 1975, and supported by The Dick and Carey Systems Approach Model (1978) (which demonstrates many of the same components as

Figure 3. The APPLIES Model. Goal-oriented questions in the design of purposive social interaction in online learning.

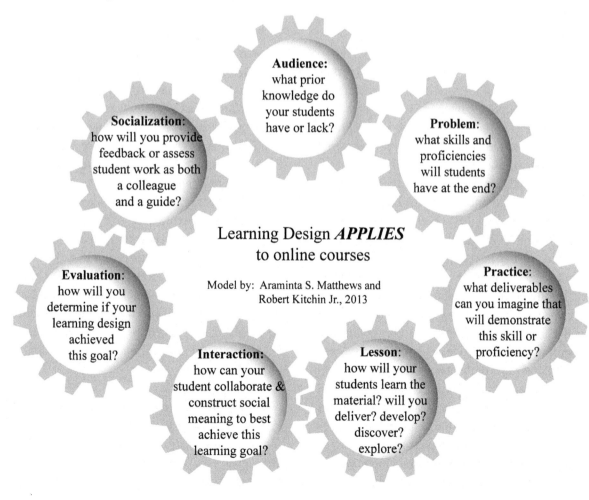

ADDIE with more emphasis on analytical feedback loops), APPLIES offers a similar model with a greater emphasis placed on social interaction design. Working through the APPLIES Model, faculty are now able to see how audience and problem analyses inform the development of assessment, knowledge acquisition (whether by didactic or discovery-based learning), and social interaction. Each of these components is integral to a fully functional online learning experience, and the strategy of inquiry posed by this model is accessible regardless of the skill level of the course designer. The design is a feedback loop where one element informs the next and previous. As such, it is possible to begin at any point along the APPLIES wheel, but it is often best to start with Audience (as the ADDIE model recommends).

Patterns of Interaction Design Already Exist

The APPLIES method of empowering learners as Web users to foster social presence is supplemented by a variety of proven interaction design patterns employed through social media Web applications of many types. Regardless of the controversy that surrounds the theories about individual learning preferences, students, as Web users, have preferences cultivated from experiences using professionally designed social interfaces on the Web (Crumlish & Malone, 2009). Examples of these social Web landscapes include Facebook™, Twitter™, Google+™ whose combined audience numbers are estimated as of June 2013, at a non-trivial billion-plus people. Alongside these well-known social networks are scores of others, where the same interactive design patterns are used to solve the same problems we face in elearning: how to foster social presence online.

To provide an example of such an interaction design pattern, consider the ability to *ping* a specific person within a post, page or comment on any of the previously mentioned social networks, notifying the person that they have been acknowl-

edged. The problem the pattern addresses is the need to gesture to another person (like a wave or a thumb's up), in the online environment. This emulates the interactive, physical situation of looking at a person or nodding in their direction. Still, whether on Google+™, Twitter™, Facebook™, or other Web-based environments, the pattern shows that making use of the ability to ping is a solution when the problem is a need to notify and acknowledge others online.

In advanced social media applications this is accomplished in multiple ways. In some cases preceding a typed username with a plus sign (+) or at sign (@) will generate a notification to that individual's inbox or phone while also linking back to a post that contains the ping to improve the response. In other applications where this automatic function is not present, typing the person's name into the post or treating it with a color or different font can signal a ping. Although it doesn't push a notification automatically to the individual, this method functions as a visual cue when that person returns to the post (see Table 4).

Pinging is an example of web functionality that online learners may experience in one area of the social Web and expect to experience in elearning environments as another area of the social Web. These previous interaction successes impact how learners expect to interact with screens, whether those screens provide access to social networks or online courses, and how they expect to interact with the software, tools, and people they find there (Crumlish & Malone, 2009: Tidwell, 2009). Crumlish and Malone reinforce this point that previous expectations of social interfaces contains benefits for users that should be leveraged and requires us to be thoughtful and consistent in our design of social Web spaces:

With the growing expectation of seamless experiences, it is important for designers to see the emerging standards and to understand how one experience of a site and its interactions affects expectations for the next site. By working with

Table 4. Ping or mention design pattern

Design Pattern Attributes	Description (Underline Text Signals Links to other Patterns Guidance)
Category/domain	Ping/Mention, Social Interaction
Name, Title Overview	Ping or Mention to Engage Others.
Problem, Goal, What Context, Forces, Use When	In asynchronous online interaction, the rhythm of interaction can be slowed if participants are unaware that activity of interest has occurred. Furthermore, in physical environments we can mention the name of someone in the room we want to notice in a public interaction. Online, this function has to be performed using technology.
Solution, How, Resolution Rationale, Why, Principle Related pattern(s)	Using social Web tools that allow mentioning or pinging course participants calls them to act on a post or document markup. Per the user's configuration, pings and mentions will send a notification to the individual mentioned, calling them to attend to the activity in a timely way.
Examples, Known uses, Technologies Options	In Google™ application use +Name in posts or document comments. On Facebook™, precede the name with the @Name. Though most LMS applications do not provide this opportunity, highlighting the other user's name in a post or replying with a comment approximates the pattern.
Tags (To aid search and organization)	Notifications, Pings, Mentions, Interaction

standard and emerging best practices, principles, and interaction patterns, the designer takes some of the burden of understanding how the application works off the user, who then can focus on the unique properties of the social experience she is building. (p. 9)

By presenting Web spaces with relevant and often ubiquitous design options for social engagement, faculty begin to notice an upward curve in their students' levels of self-regulated involvement based on increased familiar opportunities for successful and satisfying social interaction in the online learning environment (Dabbagh, Kitsantas, & Social Media in Higher Education, 2012; Dahlstrom & EDUCAUSE Center for Applied Research, 2011; Sher, 2009). Technophobic students are encouraged by the more tech-savvy members of their cohort to try new technologies, as "[the] computer establishes a reciprocal relationship between sender and receiver, viewer and producer" (Heim, 1998, p. 75). This exposure to one another begins to blur the line between instructor and learner and technology produces outcomes meaningful to the learner and admired by the learner's cohort. Figure 4 illustrates the metaphor of the reciprocal relationship between sender and receiver, viewer and producer.

Improving Digital Literacy and Attrition with Social Cohorts

National policy has included benchmarks of digital literacy in the Common Core Standards now influencing education across our nation (National Governors Association Center for Best Practices et al., 2010). These additions to the standards are reminiscent of Turner's argument for purposive agency in design that is both a function of predetermined structure and transaction between internal and external forces (2007). Technocentric students explore a variety of tools that are directly applicable to the workforce and, perhaps just as importantly, to how they view their own skill-set within a future workforce. Technophobic students, meanwhile, reap similar benefits by means of exposure. As the rapport of the cohort begins to gel, the social presence designed into the course may foster a cross-pollination of digital literacy between students and instructors.

At the same time, course designers tend to presume that the intention of social presence is to generate a sensation in the Web user that the instructor is omnipresent in the virtual classroom, but social presence is broadly intended to extend to all contributors within an online space and should not be considered on the same terms of

Figure 4. The metaphor of the reciprocal relationship between sender and receiver, viewer, and producer

proximity, time, and technology as physical spaces (Heim, 1998).

When we scan the status updates or micro-blogs that stream on social networks, readers can suspend their disbelief just as they do in movie theatres and experience the blogger's words as if they are being spoken directly to them. Suddenly, each status update is not just text on a screen but observable evidence of a living, breathing, three-dimensional identity who is communicating directly with us despite being potentially hundreds of miles away. This is the very definition of social presence (Short, Williams, & Christie, 1976), and this concept, therefore, extends to relationships between all Web users in a virtual space, students and instructors alike. Heim (1998) explains that presence through virtual environments requires this experience of being part of something purposive with others and where some choreographing is required. Heim explains in his book *Virtual Reality*:

Our full presence in the world comes not only from manipulating things but also from recognizing and being recognized by other people in the world. Our involvement increases dramatically when we feel that we are, in fact, in a drama (the

word drama in ancient Greek originally meant action or deed)....drama broadens to include dramatic situations where someone–an agent in our world who recognizes us as an agent in the world–watches what we do and responds to our actions. (p. 23)

When Web users are provided pathways to send and receive recognizable social signals amongst each other, they are able to develop relationships and produce lasting shared experiences. Sharing, collaborating, and mutual recognition allow online learners to observe how others within a cohort solved a particular problem. This may have an equally lasting effect on student self-esteem and confidence with digital technologies.

Furthermore, cohorts of students experience the reciprocal benefits of social presence beyond digital literacy. Students who work together within a cohort model, grouped into the same or similar classes throughout their college careers, are arguably more likely to complete a college degree based on the perception of the strong familial ties created within the members of the group (Lei et al., 2011). According to one study conducted by Alman, Frey, and Tomer (2012), because students in online learning cohorts with strong pathways to social presence report deeper satisfaction which may lessen attrition, an overwhelming majority of students in such course designs report "that learning activities and discussions increased their interest in course issues" (p. 300). The cohort model's success is partly attributable to the perception of increased social presence, as students in cohort-styled classrooms are almost ten times more likely than non-cohort-styled classrooms to reach out to their classmates for support and collaborative study (p. 299). When social presence is properly scaffolded within design patterns, students are given means to experience one another as salient, three-dimensional beings which, in turn, increases their overall course satisfaction.

While online course designers tend to attribute social presence to telecommunication systems that allow students to see or hear each other synchronously on the screen, this is likely due to the intrinsic nature of social presence in face-to-face classes. That is, social presence in a face-to-face class is an expected component, but online social presence and networking is more opaque and necessitates new design habits. Social networking is so important to course design, in fact, that students in face-to-face classes attend to their social-environment needs before any other needs, inventorying the participants of a new class to determine where they fit in and what skills, assets, or resources their peers possess: "The purpose of these initial status assessments is to collect and synthesize social information about others in the newly forming class group in order to form a knowable pattern of interactions that can reduce stress and confusion while learning" (Slagter Van Tryon & Bishop, 2009, pp. 293-294). This experience is largely instinctive when students walk into physical classrooms. They scan, assess, and choose a place to sit and make small talk with their neighbors, all in the interest of developing a social space within the framework of a physical course's design. This is a pattern so innate to the face-to-face classroom that few recognize it as a pattern at all.

Crumlish and Malone (2009) explain that design patterns of presence take many forms and design solutions rely on the functions or goals of presence. Do users need a way to see who else is online at the same time to take a similar participant inventory as they do in face-to-face courses? Do users need to see a history of activity, such as revisions to a document? Do users need an easy way to know who is available, when and by what means? These problems represent only a handful of design issues related to communicating presence in online courses. Crumlish and Malone offer a growing online pattern library on presence on a website ancillary (2013) to their book, *Designing Social Interfaces* (2009), which can be found in the additional reading section at the end of this chapter.

The Teaching Motivation Matters

Ongoing research into the design pattern elements that create interactive online learning habitats is needed to find definitive answers; still, there are a few considerations available now. Professors who have been teaching online for several semesters, for example, may have become effectively stale with regard to their expected routines, roles, and methods perhaps because "their ability to cope with [these expectations] is guaranteed and with it the need to grow as an online teacher fades" (Baran, Correia, & Thompson, 2011, p. 432). As a result, instructors not adequately prepared for reflection and instructional design in a pre-existing online course may fall prey to replicating "the same class material and content each time it is taught, without the adoption of new methods and technologies into the learning context" (Baran, Correia, & Thompson, 2011, p. 432). If the Web is constantly in a state of evolution, online courses may benefit from evolving design patterns, as well.

Alternatively, instructors new to teaching online may suffer an almost inverse effect. Without the aid of a competent instructional designer, an experienced faculty mentor, or other qualitative support, these new online instructors will "tend to transfer traditional approaches to the online classroom, and perpetuate approaches that have been proven to be ineffective in the face-to-face classroom" (Baran, Correia, & Thompson, 2011, p. 422). These new online instructors are no rarity, given the intense demand for online programming (Allen & Seaman, 2013), and it is not uncommon for a professor to be asked to develop an online course scheduled to start relatively soon, leaving no time to design quality.

Additionally, both seasoned and novice online instructors are limited first by what they know technology can do, what technology they believe their students can make work, and what technology they view as comfortable. Often, text is viewed as a kind of lowest common denominator for technological integration. An instructor's attitudes toward technology, whether favorable or unfavorable, impact his or her willingness to use technology and explore use-cases in an e-learning environment (Yuen & Ma, 2008). This is particularly true of social software which, "From both learners' and teachers' perspectives... may be perceived as disruptive technology due to the clash between working alone versus working collaboratively and between fixed teaching frameworks versus open learning opportunities" (Lim, So, & Tan, 2010, p. 205). Social software, such as blogs, videos, wikis, discussion boards, and social networks, may be underutilized and contribute to an adverse effect on the cognitive and affective performance of students. Because many faculty experienced with face-to-face teaching patterns may assume that their students will simply find each other without intervention or purposeful design, the necessary scaffolding to foster this social interaction is effectively misplaced. After all, students mysteriously find one another in a face-to-face classroom without instructors creating specific spaces for them to form relationships. In the digital space, students are in a foreign habitat where social interaction happens through interface allowances and instructional strategies that must be designed.

Crafting a connection between students in a virtual space may not seem like the task of the instructor, but a frequent complaint of students working in collaborative online course environments is a lack of understanding or motivation to interact with classmates. For example, wikis, collaborative learning tools which allow students to work together to create a single document or website, may cause friction in the learner experience. With wiki use, "learners seem to be lost and want more structure" (Lim, So, & Tan, 2010, p. 205). Not only do these social tools create a sense of confusion, but students also fail to fully realize the collaborative nature of cloud-based social technologies. When confronted with such collaborative tasks, "learners read very little of the content created by their peers. It is argued that while the new generation of learners use social networking programs in their daily lives, using them for learning across formal and informal learning spaces seems remote and difficult" (p. 205). Social presence and interaction on the Web is an evolving field and students necessarily need additional design supports to implement its utility to the fullest extent.

Other tools pose similar problems to interaction. For example, blogs can create another host of barriers to social presence. Faculty, used to marking up documents with feedback and corrections, may view blogs as unfit for formative assessment:

Fearing that the content of [student] blogs might not be presentable, an instructor might take the role of an editor, sanctioning and editing the learners' work before it is allowed to be published. This very act destroys learners' agency for learning and learners' voice in blogging. (Lim, So, & Tan, 2010, p. 214)

Because social interaction in any dimension requires some modicum of confidence, students and instructors engaging in Web-based social constructs need to feel safe. A blog, often connoting a more informal assessment than a research paper or presentation, may require a more hands-off approach with regard to feedback (particularly public feedback) and a wiki may require explicit instruction and demonstration to be successful.

There are several logical strategies for implementing collaborative tools, like wikis and blogs, in elearning environments. One pattern is to scaffold the social-collaborative learning environment with details about how students will interact with the tool and one another. Another pattern is to provide low-stakes, experimental assignments designed to increase the learner's confidence in using the tool and exploring its capabilities while simultaneously addressing entry-level content in the upward pedagogy of a course's design. Yet another pattern is to role-model both practical and experimental use of technology through carefully-structured examples, either selected from previous students or hand-crafted to demonstrate how others have interacted using the tool. Until one can reconcile the tool to its use within a learning goal, technology merely makes connection possible. There is no educational tension through which meaning can be made amid other people (Heim, 1998).

A Pattern for Introductions

A classroom is a social environment where most participants arrive with a common goal: to learn and succeed. This setting affords learners the opportunity to construct and connect chains of meaning within a social context, which offers opportunities for lasting knowledge acquisition. The social environment allows students to model and observe others modeling behaviors, skills, and abilities and exchange social reinforcement that creates stronger associations for improved recall (Bandura, 1977). Face-to-face classes have demonstrated this method for centuries, grouping students by perceived peer or age groups and ability levels to create cohorts where the likelihood of meaningful interaction seems greater.

Unlike face-to-face classes where human interaction is largely transparent, Web-based interaction offers a layer of anonymity or creativity. Almost like a work of fiction, Web-spaces allow people the flexibility to expose their true selves or alternate versions of themselves. This flexibility allows Web users to develop "'Real Life' identities through fantasy associations with imagined realities and with other people" (Conrad, 2002, p. 199). Identity is a key component in learning and in the virtual space. Even in the online classroom where the stakes are higher, students must craft or otherwise expose their identities to their peers, which may pose some interesting complications. Expression through body language, social gestures, and boundaries are limited to virtual, non-tangible demonstrations. In a text-based classroom, this requires not only a mastery of one's own diction, but an ability to comprehend the nuances of another's diction through textual exchanges. In a virtual classroom using multiple technologies, this is further complicated by the nature of production: few people produce video, audio, or other dynamic Web assets without forethought and perhaps editing. As such, the identities of our peers in a virtual classroom become somewhat opaque. Our Web identities are not the same as our face-to-face identities, just as our business identities may vary from the identity we possess in the company of our friends, family members, or neighbors.

The stakes of a virtual class are similar to those of an online career profile: boundaries and professionalism are important. Students are aware of the need for creating relationships in this environment and how it differs from the face-to-face social environment. In a study by Diane Conrad (2002) into the etiquette of online learners in virtual spaces, it was found that:

When learners were restricted to learning solely in online environments, however, they realized the importance of building online relationships and they promoted them with functional respect and etiquette. In fact, online learners sought clear boundaries in establishing their relationships with each other and agonized over the inauguration of those boundaries. (p. 200)

Students recognize that establishing identity and boundaries early in a course is vital to the online learning process, but where to start, how much to expose, and how to engage is often a mystery of bland, text-only communications, lost after the first read, never to be revisited. Without a design schema that invites or permits these opportunities, students will either avoid these interactions (as they will be unsure how to engage), or "in the absence of typically available verbal and nonverbal social cues, it seems that students will inevitably interject personality and personal characteristics by revealing personal information about themselves during online interactions, even without being told to do so" (Slagter Van Tryon & Bishop, 2009, p. 300). Thus, if educators and course designers are to direct the safety of their students, provide appropriate boundaries, and create meaningful social interaction, it is imperative that ice breakers and house rules are established early on.

Designing ice breakers or low-stakes entrances to course content promotes both the initial establishment of social identity and an opportunity to present the first event of instruction: gaining the learner's attention (Gagne, 1977). Examples of attention-gaining design patterns for introduction include student profiles, personal photographs, video tiles, and dynamic or text-based activities.

Breaking the virtual ice in an online social domain affords educators two additional benefits. Firstly, the mere activity of engaging with the software to complete the initiation task creates an early interaction with the technology necessary to succeed in the course. The added bonus of establishing early social presence is that students will more likely develop confidence in their own techno-literacy by experimenting with the software. Secondly, this experimentation with social software can be quantifiable. By using hash-tags, tags, keywords, and transcript searches, professors and students can easily develop a sense of the scope and network of the course's content. Aggregating blog posts, web links, micro-blogs, and other content produced by participants in an e-learning environment can demonstrate the nodes or connection points between the different domains of a course (Kop & Fournier, 2011, p. 82). Not only do students get to increase their technological self-esteem, but faculty can create a pattern for aggregating data around the course to determine an overall trajectory for student and course success. The Design Pattern of Introductions is documented in Table 5.

FUTURE RESEARCH DIRECTIONS

The idea that social interaction needs a place in our virtual learning spaces must be further explored. Design patterns as applied to pedagogy and elearning strategies necessarily requires further investigation and analysis. Within the instructional design domain, what appears to create the greatest barrier to implementation relates to leadership modeling the way forward. A connected, online, pattern library that is accessible to members of a given instructional design network, such as a university system, may address this limitation. Additionally, a clear documentation interface that allows for collaborative social contribution and stewardship to populate the pattern library with a healthy starter repository or patterns would provide additional implementation support.

Interaction in online courses between instructors and learners, learners and content systems, and learners and learners represent a new world with which we do not yet know how to interact with confidence, academic rigor and with social skill. That social interaction needs to occur is not in question. How and in what new ways is in question.

Table 5. Introductions design pattern

Design Pattern Attributes	Description
Category(ies)/domain(s)	Instructional Design
Name, Title Overview	Introductions
Problem, Goal, What Context, Forces, Use when	Use this pattern to conceptualize introduction activities between learners and orientation to course technology, materials and interactive features. Introductions online quickly fade away and appear to be irrelevant and of extremely low value in establishing presence. Contributions by learners take on a persona of anonymity without easy to follow, reviewable connection to a persistent personalized profile, linked to the produced learning artifact. Admiration and reciprocal learning is diminished when social interaction is dimmed or absent from the online learning environment. Learners' ability to purposefully interact with the course environment is disadvantaged without a guided introduction to the course configuration, and technology holds greater intimidation when there is no guidance nor demonstration by a trustworthy and capable other person. Forces in play: technology literacy, skills, preferences, and personal learning goals. Web application capabilities used must provide for profiles that persist and allow for multi-media content use such as pictures, links and video. What to share, how and when is a convergence between learner choice and instructional goals germane to the topic of the course.
Solution, How, Resolution Rationale, Why, Principle Related pattern(s)	When designing introduction prompts and interface components, provide both ample explanation and demonstration about how introductions should be executed and accessed throughout the course. This activity by the instructor of introducing the prompt parallels the method and demonstrates a "way" of introducing oneself and produced materials through the technology. Consider exposing this parallel process, making explicit that it is a bona fide demonstration as well as the utility of introduction on its own. Other patterns that may be relevant here: Professional Development, Personal Brand, and Personal and Professional Boundaries.
Examples, Known uses	As an example: Use a well-known social network such as Google+™ to create a course community. Describe and introduce through demonstration what kind of interaction and sharing will occur. Make use of the user profile by detailing with some specificity quality ways that a profile can be completed and how the profile should be used throughout the course. Be sure that a thorough review of privacy settings and ways to share privately, with select group members, the whole course and the general public is done.
Tags	Personal Expression, Social Interaction, Online Profiles, Persistent Presence, Authorship.

Moving forward we need to expand our access to study online courses, specifically the interaction patterns that are emerging through online and blended learning environments. Currently there are many barriers given the array of institutional norms of intellectual property, union sanctions related to critique of faculty work and students rights to privacy. Each barrier is complex but worth overcoming. The full rewards of online learning cannot be adequately realized absent access to study and analyze real time online learning environments. In fact, absent the on-going development of verifiable knowledge the online course may well present costly perils in learning over time.

CONCLUSION

This chapter presents a method for understanding how the forces affecting successful person-to-person and person-to-system interactions in online e-learning environments are fundamentally different from those located in the physical places of traditional learning environments. These forces, though different in each domain, carry potential not yet fully realized to improve learning through the design of satisfying, learner-centered, and purposive social engagement in online learning environments.

We have argued that sound online course design is not only within reach; it can be achieved by virtually all designers. Through well-conceptualized, easy to access, use, and share design patterns we can assist even novice online course designers to understand recurring problems related to the design of interactive learning environments and execute solutions that are relevant to the context and solve the problem with a high degree of success. What follows is innovative practice in learning design and an evolution toward new habits and online learning habitats.

REFERENCES

Abrami, P. C., Bernard, R. M., Bures, E. M., Tamim, R. M., & Tamim, R. M. (2011). Interaction in distance education and online learning: Using evidence and theory to improve practice. *Journal of Computing in Higher Education*, *23*(2-3), 2–3. doi:10.1007/s12528-011-9043-x

Alexander, C. (1979). *The timeless way of building*. New York, NY: Oxford University Press.

Alexander, C. (2001). *A pattern language sampler*. Retrieved from: http://www.patternlanguage.com/apl/aplsample/aplsample.htm

Alexander, C., Ishikawa, S., Silverstein, M., Jacobson, M., Fiksdahl-King, I., & Angel, S. (1977). *A pattern language: Towns, buildings, construction*. New York: Oxford University Press.

Allen, I. E., & Seaman, J. (2013). *Changing course: Ten years of tracking online education in the United States*. Newburyport, MA: Sloan Consortium.

Alman, S. W., Frey, B. A., & Tomer, C. (2012). Social and cognitive presence as factors in learning and student retention: An investigation of the cohort model in an ischool setting. *Journal of Education for Library and Information Science*, *53*(4), 290–302.

Arbaugh, J. B. (2000). Virtual classroom characteristics and student satisfaction with internet-based MBA courses. *Journal of Management Education*, *24*(1), 32–54. doi:10.1177/105256290002400104

Bandura, A. (1977). *Social learning theory*. Englewood Cliffs, N. J: Prentice Hall.

Baran, E., Correia, A. P., & Thompson, A. (2011). Transforming online teaching practice: Critical analysis of the literature on the roles and competencies of online teachers. *Distance Education*, *32*(3), 421–439. doi:10.1080/01587919.2011.610293

Bruno, G., Esposito, E., Genovese, A., & Gwebu, K. L. (2011). A critical analysis of current indexes for digital divide measurement. *The Information Society*, *27*(1), 16–28. doi:10.1080/01972243.2010.534364

Caeiro, M., Llamas, M., & Anido, L. (2004). *E-Learning patterns: An approach to facilitate the design of e-learning materials*. Monterrey, México: RIBIE.

Callaway, S. K. (2012). Implications of online learning: Measuring student satisfaction and learning for online and traditional students. *Insights to a Changing World Journal*, 67-94.

Center for Universal Design. (2013). Retrieved from http://www.ncsu.edu/ncsu/design/cud/about_ud/udprinciples.htm

Christensen, C. M., & Eyring, H. J. (2011). *The innovative university: Changing the DNA of higher education from the inside out*. San Francisco: Jossey-Bass.

Cleveland-Innes, M. F., & Emes, C. (2005). Social and academic interaction in higher education contexts and the effect on deep learning. *NASPA Journal*, *42*(2), 241–262.

Conrad, D. (2002). Inhibition, integrity and etiquette among online learners: The art of niceness. *Distance Education*, *23*(2), 197–212. doi:10.1080/0158791022000009204

Coutinho, A. J., Talarico, N. A., & Neris, V. P. A. (2009). Cog-learn: An e-learning pattern language for Web-based learning design. *eLearn, 2009*(8). Retrieved from http://dl.acm.org/citation.cfm?id=1595437

Crumlish, C., & Malone, E. (2009). *Designing social interfaces: Principles, patterns, and practices for improving the user experience*. Beijing: O'Reilly Media.

Dabbagh, N., & Kitsantas, A. (2012). Personal learning environments, social media, and self-regulated learning: A natural formula for connecting formal and informal learning. *The Internet and Higher Education, 15*(1), 3–8. doi:10.1016/j.iheduc.2011.06.002

Dahlstrom, E., & EDUCAUSE Center for Applied Research. (2011). *ECAR national study of undergraduate students and information technology, 2011*. Boulder, CO: EDUCAUSE Center for Applied Research.

Dearden, A., & Finlay, J. (2006). Pattern languages in HCI: A critical review. *Human-Computer Interaction, 21*(1), 49–102. doi:10.1207/s15327051hci2101_3

Depoy, E., & Gilson, S. (n.d.). Disability design and branding: Rethinking disability within the 21st. *Disability studies quarterly*. Retrieved from http://dsqsds.org/article/view/1247/1274

Dick, W., & Carey, L. (1978). *The systematic design of instruction*. Glenview, IL: Scott, Foresman & Company.

Eckstein, J., Bergin, J., & Sharp, H. (2002). Patterns for active learning. In *Proceedings of the 9th Congress of Pattern Language of Programs (PloP) 2002*. Monticello, IL: PloP.

Epstein, D., Nisbet, E., & Gillespie, T. (2011). Who's responsible for the digital divide? Public perceptions and policy implications. *The Information Society, 27*(2), 92–104. doi:10.1080/01972243.2011.548695

Forehand, M. (2005). Bloom's taxonomy: Original and revised. In M. Orey (Ed.), *Emerging perspectives on learning, teaching, and technology*. Retrieved from http://projects.coe.uga.edu/epltt/

Frizell, S. S., & Hübscher, R. (2011). Using design patterns to support e-learning design. *Instructional Design: Concepts, Methodologies. Tools and Applications, 1*(1), 114.

Gagne, R. M. (1977). *The conditions of learning*. New York: Holt, Rinehart & Winston.

Gargiulo, R. M., & Metcalf, D. (2013). *Teaching in today's inclusive classrooms: A universal design for learning approach* (2nd ed.). Belmont, CA: Wadsworth, Cengage Learning.

Goodyear, P. (2005). Educational design and networked learning: Patterns, pattern languages and design practice. *Australasian Journal of Educational Technology, 21*(1), 82–101. Retrieved from http://www.ascilite.org.au/ajet/ajet21/goodyear.html

Goodyear, P., de Laat, M., & Lally, V. (2006). Using pattern languages to mediate theory–praxis conversations in design for networked learning. *Association for Learning Technology Journal, 14*(3), 211-223. Retrieved from http://repository.alt.ac.uk/120/

Halstead, J. A., Phillips, J. M., Koller, A., Hardin, K., Porter, M. L., & Dwyer, J. S. (2011). Preparing nurse educators to use simulation technology: A consortium model for practice and education. *Journal of Continuing Education in Nursing, 42*(11), 496–502. doi:10.3928/00220124-20110502-01 PMID:21553700

Heim, M. (1998). *Virtual realism*. New York: Oxford University Press.

Hixon, E. (2008). Team-based online course development: A case study of collaboration models. *Online Journal of Distance Learning Administration, 11*(4). Retrieved from http://www.westga.edu/~distance/ojdla/winter114/hixon114.html

Jordan, J. M. (2012). *Information, technology, and innovation: Resources for growth in a connected world*. Hoboken, NJ: Wiley.

Kehrwald, B. (2010). Being online: Social presence as subjectivity in online learning. *London Review of Education*, *8*(1), 39–50. doi:10.1080/14748460903557688

King, A. (1993). From sage on the stage to guide on the side. *College Teaching*, *41*(1), 30–35. doi:10.1080/87567555.1993.9926781

Knowles, M. S. (1980). *The modern practice of adult education: From pedagogy to andragogy*. Wilton, CT: Association Press.

Kohls, C., & Uttecht, J.-G. (2009). Lessons learnt in mining and writing design patterns for educational interactive graphics. *Computers in Human Behavior*, *25*(5), 1040–1055. doi:10.1016/j.chb.2009.01.004

Kuh, G. D., & Documenting Effective Educational Practice (Project). (2005). *Student success in college: Creating conditions that matter*. San Francisco: Jossey-Bass.

Lee, Y., & Choi, J. (2011). A review of online course dropout research: Implications for practice and future research. *Educational Technology Research and Development*, *59*(5), 593–618. doi:10.1007/s11423-010-9177-y

Lidwell, W., Holden, K., & Butler, J. (2010). Universal principles of design: 125 ways to enhance usability, influence perception, increase appeal, make better design decisions, and teach through design. Beverly, MA: Rockport.

Lim, W. Y., So, H. J., & Tan, S. C. (2010). elearning 2.0 and new literacies: Are social practices lagging behind? *Interactive Learning Environments*, *18*(3), 203–218. doi:10.1080/10494820.2010.500507

Mackey, K. R. M., & Freyberg, D. L. (2010). The effect of social presence on affective and cognitive learning in an international engineering course taught via distance learning. *The Journal of Engineering Education*, *99*(1), 23–34. doi:10.1002/j.2168-9830.2010.tb01039.x

Meera, K., Sergey, M., & Gargi, B. (2010). Role of student–faculty interactions in developing college students' academic self-concept, motivation, and achievement. *Journal of College Student Development*, *51*(3), 332–342.

National Center on Universal Design for Learning Guidelines. (2013). *About UDL: Learn the basics*. Retrieved from http://www.udlcenter.org/aboutudl/udlguidelines

Pauwels, S. L., Hübscher, C., Bargas-Avila, J. A., & Opwis, K. (2010). Building an interaction design pattern language: A case study. *Computers in Human Behavior*, *26*(3), 452–463. doi:10.1016/j.chb.2009.12.004

Phelan, L. (2012, May). Interrogating students' perceptions of their online learning experiences with Brookfield's critical incident questionnaire. *Distance Education*, *33*(1), 31–44. doi:10.1080/01587919.2012.667958

Picciano, A. (2002). Beyond student perceptions: Issues of interaction, presence, and performance in an online course. *Journal of Asynchronous Learning Networks*, *6*(1), 21–40. Retrieved from http://faculty.Weber.edu/eamsel/Research%20 Groups/On-line%20Learning/Picciano%20 %282002%29.pdf

Reigeluth, C. M. (2012). Instructional-design theories and models: A new paradigm of instructional theory (Vol. 2). Hoboken, NJ: Taylor and Francis.

Rovai, A. P., & Downey, J. R. (2010). Why some distance education programs fail while others succeed in a global environment. *The Internet and Higher Education*, *13*(3), 141–147. doi:10.1016/j.iheduc.2009.07.001

Sher, A. (2009). Assessing the relationship of student-instructor and student-student interaction to student learning and satisfaction in Web-based online learning environment. *Journal of Interactive Online Learning, 8*(2), 102–120. Retrieved from http://www.ncolr.org/jiol/issues/pdf/8.2.1.pdf

Shneiderman, B. (2000). Universal usability. *Communications of the ACM, 43*(5), 84–91. doi:10.1145/332833.332843

Short, J., Williams, E., & Christie, B. (1976). *The social psychology of telecommunications*. New York, NY: John Wiley & Sons.

Slagter Van Tryon, P. J., & Bishop, M. J. (2009). Theoretical foundations for enhancing social connectedness in online learning environments. *Distance Education, 30*(3), 291–315. doi:10.1080/01587910903236312

Smith, G. G., Ferguson, D., & Caris, M. (2001). Teaching college courses online versus face-to-face. *T.H.E. Journal, 28*(9), 18–22.

Tidwell, J. (2009). *Designing interfaces: Patterns for effective interaction design*. Sebastopol, GA: O'Reilly Media, Inc.

Turner, J. S. (2007). *The tinkerer's accomplice: How design emerges from life itself*. Cambridge, MA: Harvard University Press.

Weller, M. (2002). *Delivering learning on the net: The why, what & how of online education*. London, UK: Kogan Page. doi:10.4324/9780203416969

Weller, M. (2007). The distance from isolation: Why communities are the logical conclusion in e-learning? *Computers & Education, 49*(2), 148–159. doi:10.1016/j.compedu.2005.04.015

Wesch, M. L. (2007). *Web 2.0: The machine is us/ing us*. Retrieved from http://www. youtube.com/watch?v=NLlGopyXT_g

Yuen, A. H. K., & Ma, W. W. K. (2008). Exploring teaching acceptance of e-learning technology. *Asia-Pacific Journal of Teacher Education, 36*(3), 229–243. doi:10.1080/13598660802232779

ADDITIONAL READING

Alberta Education. (2010). *Making a difference: Meeting diverse learning needs with differentiated instruction*. Edmonton, AB: Alberta Education.

Aragon, S. R. (2003). Creating social presence in online environments. *New Directions for Adult and Continuing Education, 100*, 7–68. Retrieved from http://insdsg602-s13-manning.wikispaces.umb.edu/

Borchers, J. (2001). *A pattern approach to interaction design*. Chichester, England: Wiley.

Chih-Yuen Sun, J., & Rueda, R. (2012). Situational interest, self-efficacy and self-regulation: Their impact on student engagement in distance education. *British Journal of Educational Technology, 43*(2), 191–204. doi:10.1111/j.1467-8535.2010.01157.x

DePoy, E., & Gilson, S. F. (2004). *Rethinking disability: Principles for professional and social change*. Belmont, CA: Thomson/Brooks/Cole.

Designing Social Interfaces. (2013*). Patterns.* Retrieved from http://www.designingsocialinterfaces.com/patterns/Main_Page#What.27s_a_pattern.3F

Di, T., Lin, L., Yongjian, L., Hanping, L., Xiaoyuan, X., & Jingyun, L. (2012). Genetic and environmental influences on the relationship between flow proneness, locus of control and behavioral inhibition. *PLoS ONE, 7*(11), 1–8. PMID:23133606

Dirksen, J. (2012). *Design for how people learn*. Berkeley, CA: New Riders.

Faiola, A., Newlon, C., Pfaff, M., & Smyslova, O. (2013). Correlating the effects of flow and telepresence in virtual worlds: Enhancing our understanding of user behavior in game-based learning. *Computers in Human Behavior*, *29*(3), 1113–1121. doi:10.1016/j.chb.2012.10.003

Fichter, D., & Wisniewski, J. (2009). Patterns, pattern libraries, and other good stuff. *Online*, *35*(5), 54–57.

Floyd, K., Hughes, K., & Maydosz, A. (2011). A toolkit for Web-based course creation and conversion. *Rural Special Education*, *30*(4), 32–39.

Frenette, M., & Statistics Canada. (2003). *Access to college and university: Does distance matter?* Ottawa: Statistics Canada, Analytical Studies Branch.

Gu, X., Yuankun, Z., & Guo, X. (2011). Meeting the "digital natives": Understanding the acceptance of technology in classrooms. *Journal of Educational Technology & Society, 16*(1), 392-402. Retrieved from http: http://www.ifets.info/journals/16_1/34.pdf

Gunkel, D. (2003). Second thoughts: Toward a critique of the digital divide. *New Media & Society*, *5*(4), 499–522. doi:10.1177/146144480354003

Halawah, I. (2011). Factors influencing college students' motivation to learn from students' perspective. *Education*, *132*(2), 379–390.

Jung, I., Choi, S., Lim, C., & Leem, J. (2002). Effects of different types of interaction on learning achievement, satisfaction and participation in Web-based instruction. *Innovations in Education and Teaching International*, *39*(2), 153–162. doi:10.1080/14703290252934603

Kotzé, P., Renaud, K., Koukouletsos, K., Khazaei, B., & Dearden, A. (2006). Patterns, anti-patterns and guidelines–effective aids to teaching HCI principles. In *Proceedings of the First Joint British Computer Society/International Federation for Information Processing Working Group 3, 1*. New York, NY: Springer.

Krug, S. (2006). *Don't make me think! A common sense approach to Web usability*. Berkeley, CA: New Riders.

Krug, S. (2010). *Rocket surgery made easy: The do-it-yourself guide to finding and fixing usability problems*. Berkeley, CA: New Riders.

Norman, D. A. (2002). *The design of everyday things*. New York, NY: Basic Books.

Norton, P., & Hathaway, D. (2008). Exploring two teacher education online learning designs: A classroom of one or many? *Journal of Research on Technology in Education*, *40*(4), 475–495. doi:10.1080/15391523.2008.10782517

Reilly, J. R., Gallagher-Lepak, S., & Killion, C. (2012). 'Me and my computer': Emotional factors in online learning. *Nursing Education Perspectives*, *33*(2), 100–105. doi:10.5480/1536-5026-33.2.100 PMID:22616408

Rourke, A. J., & Coleman, K. S. (2010). A learner system: Scaffolding to enhance digital learning. *The International Journal of Technology. Knowledge in Society*, *6*(1), 55–70.

Ruey, S. (2010). A case study of constructivist instructional strategies for adult online learning. *British Journal of Educational Technology, 41*(5), 706-720. doi:. 2009.00965.x10.1111/j.1467-8535

Saulnier, B. M. (2009). From "sage on the stage" to "guide on the side" revisited: (Un)Covering the content in the learner-centered information systems course. *Information Systems Education Journal, 7*(60), 3–10. Retrieved from http://proc.isecon.org/2008/3114/ISECON.2008.Saulnier.pdf

Sherman, R. C., End, C., Kraan, E., Cole, A., Campbell, J., Klausner, J., & Birchmeier, Z. (2001). Metaperception in cyberspace. *Cyberpsychology & Behavior: The Impact of the Internet. Multimedia and Virtual Reality on Behavior and Society, 4*(1), 123–129.

Silverman, S. C. (2007). *Creating community online: the effects of online social networking communities on college students' experiences. How can student affairs professionals best respond to this emergent phenomenon* (Doctoral dissertation). University of Southern California, Los Angeles, CA.

Tomlinson, C. A. (1999). Mapping a route toward differentiated instruction. *Educational Leadership, 57,* 12–16.

Tufte, E. R. (2006). *The cognitive style of PowerPoint: Pitching out corrupts within.* Cheshire, CT: Graphics Press.

Willging, P. A., & Johnson, S. D. (2004). Factors that influence students' decision to drop out of online courses. *Journal of Asynchronous Learning Networks, 8*(4), 105–118.

KEY TERMS AND DEFINITIONS

Andragogy: Andragogy is a theory developed by Knowles (1913-97) which differentiates the needs of adult learners from those of juveniles and uses the term andragogy to describe the specific methods which should be employed in the education of adults.

Design Pattern: Describes an optimal solution to a common problem within a specific context.

Design Pattern Language: Many design patterns used together to solve a complicated design problem. The components of the design language are individual design patterns, like words in a sentence are use together with a rationale or grammar to create meaningful action.

Design Pattern Library: A collection of design patterns related to a specific design domain. This collection is most often maintained in a searchable database and patterns are found using key words, titles, tags and categories.

Digital Divide: The concept of the gap between those who have access to information and communication technologies (ICTs) and are using it effectively, and those who are not using it effectively.

Pattern Mining: The process of documenting new design patterns and adding them to a pattern library.

Scaffolding: the idea that specialized instructional supports need to be in place in order to best facilitate learning when students are first introduced to a new subject.

Universal Design For Learning: A set of principles for curriculum development that give all individuals equal opportunities to learn.

This work was previously published in Student-Teacher Interaction in Online Learning Environments edited by Robert D. Wright, pages 22-49, copyright year 2015 by Information Science Reference (an imprint of IGI Global).

Chapter 72

Theoretical Foundations of a CSCL Script in Persistent Virtual Worlds According to the Contemporary Learning Theories and Models

Nikolaos Pellas
University of the Aegean, Greece

ABSTRACT

Computer-Supported Collaborative Learning (CSCL) has proved to be one of the reliable contemporary approaches to education that is based on the fundamental principles of collaborative learning procedures between users (instructor and students) in electronic learning environments or Virtual Worlds (VWs). This approach to education has resulted in many considerable changes in the traditional "status quo" of e-Education. This chapter presents a literature review of major revamped principles of Learning Theories and Models that occurred in the early 21st century and reinforced the vast majority of CSCL pursuits and capabilities. It adopts Stahl's (2000) theoretical model to articulate a novel framework for e-Education in VWs. The meaning and contribution of this approach to education will be more understandable through the analysis of collaborative learning climate conditions in the 3D technologically advanced environments based on the interests, demands, and needs of trained users.

INTRODUCTION

The fact is well known that e-learning is one alternative and innovative way for teachers and students to use information technology. Many ways to facilitate such an adoption of information technology have resulted in a wave of supporting educational applications. The new knowledge gained from this approach to education mainly for distance learning (computer, internet, e-learning platforms) can create different theoretical structure, in which students are asked to co-exist and co-construct their own concepts of new knowledge. Thus, this approach prompts researchers to generally resolve and determine collaborative practices that are generally facilitating a more sustainable

DOI: 10.4018/978-1-4666-8619-9.ch072

future of e-Education. Through these procedures a system of education can be establiahed for formal or informal learning within a shared action reasoning and thinking framework. The intergration of e-education tools in education reduces of the distance and the spatio-temporal constraints that may hinder education and result in the formation of a solid structure for the institutionalization of various types of education like adult education, and provide additional material in universities (Trentin, 2004).

Previous experiences of researchers on the issue of e-learnign and adults education revealed some interesting principles (Trushell, Byrne & Simpson, 2012; Tsai, 2007; Tsai & Chuang, 2005; Wang Reeves, 2005; Wang, H, Wang, H., Wang, L., & Huang, 2006), such as:

- The conformation of a common ground in which members use multimedia sources in online learning environments.
- The principle of active learning process through an educational context, in which users convoke the planned teaching practice through the active construction of knowledge for each group and expended energy of each student through students' needs and formulate their own experiences to achieve a common goal.
- The principle of cooperativeness, which will foster the interaction between students and with the instructor, in order to provide the necessary feedback on their actions.
- The management of team's flexibility in interactive learning environments in conjunction with models derived from the field of the contemporary education and theories advocated as models of Constructionism (Papert, 1980b) that brought to the fore new learning models that involve the "trinity" Personal Computer-Internet-Collaborative knowledge field.

- The principles of "internal" (user-based) and "external" (team-based) evaluation involving new packages for innovative educational programs for all levels of education, aimed at satisfying the principle of all-round development of students' personality.
- The gradual dissociation (fading scaffolding) through active processes and active supply construction of an innovative "knowledge field" with its own forces.
- The distribution of projects and constructive standards of learning through the collaborative exchange of knowledge and experience of users necessary for successful program implementation.

The diversity of this educational area has already provided various systems for e-learning since the early formative stages. On the other hand, the diversity should be treated with great skepticism, because various CSCL trends have emerged. Indicative of the growing concern that one of the main dilemmas for the future is whether we will accept the theoretical variety, diversity and the need for the integration and synthesis of these theories in order to create a common theoretical framework. Notwithstanding that computer-assisted activities supports collaborative learning and it was one of the most promising and widespread examples of learning in the history of ICT, there is still a lacking of a general theoretical framework in the field of CSCL with 3D technologically-advanced environments.

The purpose of this chapter is twofold: (a) to present the review of the literature for the most reliable contemporary learning theories and models that can be endorsed in a CSCL enviroment, and (b) to articulate a novel methodological framework according to the Stahl's (2002) model for CSCL procedures in virtual worlds.

BACKGROUND

Computer-Supported Collaborative Learning

CSCL as a practical-teaching paradigm reinforced by social and cultural changes (strong interaction of people from different cultural traditions, burst production and usability of knowledge), have several experiences in alternative worldviews and practices of social life's action. In modern societies, reflections on which knowledge considered as valid and how many different approaches we can use to conquer it, highlighting according to (Van Aalst, 2006; Van de Vold, 2010): (a) the importance of the dialogue, and (b) the epistemological beliefs that participants in a dialogue must be tolerant to the multiplicity of interpretations. Prospective students should communicate not only for information or as a "lobbying" tool, but also as a mean for solving problems and for constructing a "common ground" for the creation of knowledge. This change has proclaimed not only in skills or abilities, but also a sense of identity and identification of personal meaning.

The novel principles of a CSCL approach can be implemented in electronic learning environments with (Bransford, Brown, & Cocking, 1999; Wang, 2006) by:

- Emphasizing on the social nature of learning or knowledge and the co-construction of knowledge.
- Strengthening students' performance in these new roles.
- Supporting communication and computational tools.

In general, previous studies that access to the implementation of this example demonstrate not only opportunities, but also limitations (Lehtinen et al, 1999). Specifically, they have been distinguished as the technological, organizational and pedagogical constraints in order to establish successful collaborative environments. By focusing on pedagogical factors, we should highlight requirements that the instructor sitting with CSCL main principles. The social interaction of CSCL scripts, allowing a deeper processing through the discussion with cognitive and meta-cognitive strategies of dialogue ownership practices to suit with other courses from different disciplines, but the expression of emotions and responsibilities remain capable. The conditions for the realization of the above are aware of the educational function of each student's prior knowledge on epistemological bases in different subjects, for the creation of norms and procedures in a classroom routine. Otherwise, the acquisition of knowledge is no longer the center of the class activity, and the argument degenerates to quote opinions and software that supports a CSCL approach is a modern way to communicate with other classmates. This premise frequently recapitulates to the empowerment of new students' roles accompanied by the implementation of multiple team responsibilities, including (Tsai, Shen & Tsai, 2011; Tung & Chang, 2007; Turhan, Yaris & Nural, 2005; Twedden Levinsen, 2007):

- Designing of the joint action of the class (including projects and roles).
- Modeling practices knowledge creation, care for the individual needs of participants, individual assessment.
- Receiving information resources and tools and knowledge configuration of the natural environment of the classroom.
- Identifying moral leadership between other tutors.
- Negotiating with other teammates.

Figure 1. The circle of an e-collaboration approach

SOCIO-CULTURAL COLLABORATIVE PRINCIPLES WITH MEDIA SOURCES

Collaborative learning (CL) has seen a great proliferation in the last three decades and characterized by a plenary of research aimed to test the efficacy and generally the contribution of cooperativeness in contrast to the individual learning. The key question was whether and under which circumstances CL is superior to individual learning. Although, there is a growing consensus among researchers about the positive effect of cooperation in learning, while most scholars are still debating for a meaningful question of the mechanisms and reasons that further studies should implement this type of process (Halverson, 2002; Land & Hanafin, 2000). According to the above, from the review of the literature, we can distinguish different approaches of CL in two sub-categories:

1. Incentive-motivation and social cohesion (Wang & Lin, 2007).
2. Cognitive approaches, i.e. socio-constructivist approach (based on the theory of

Piaget and mechanism of cognitive conflict) and socio-cultural approach (influenced by Vygotsky's theory and approach of the Distributed Learning theory).

On the other hand, Dillenbourg (1996) distinguished three broods of concepts and mechanisms through which CSCL attempts to interpret the cognitive progress in collaborative learning with impact, conditions and interactions. Multi-pointedness (usually this word is recognized by many distributed spaces hosted on one virtual machine) of the space is given as a measurement scale, defining the notion of learning and even more the concept of cooperation (Järvelä, Volet, & Järvenoja, 2010). The development in the field of cognition and cognitive development - which will be discussed below - led to an awareness of the social nature of learning and the importance of the framework for mental activity. By extension, the interest shifted both in the organization of cooperative activities (Littleton & Light, 1999; Thompson & Lynch, 2004) and collaborative learning framework through the computer (Li et al. 2011; Wang, 2010). Also, the cognitive theory stressed to the need of designing innovative learning environments, which will support the interaction between students and facilitate collaborative learning (Järvenoja & Järvelä, 2009).

At this stage of our work we did not need to refer the behavioral learning approaches (see Pavlov, Skinner theories), as this could not (theoretically) support activities in modern (collaborative) learning environments. Instead, theories that support CSCL scripts can be used as a "substrate" to implement these courses between the dipole "human-society." Moreover, we would say that the "socio-cognitive theories, "revolve around to the pole of the "human" and the "socio-cultural considerations of society." In general, these theories argue that the construction of knowledge takes place in collaborative environments through discussions that include the creation and understanding of communication and joint (between individuals or groups) the implementation of various activities. In socio-cultural approaches, where we give more emphasis, the basic assumption is that when a person participates in a social system, then the "culture" of this system and tools for communication (especially the tongue) are formed as cognitive set-up a source of learning and development. The characteristics of these approaches are summarized on the (Pellas, 2013):

- The active cognitive construction that contributes to in-depth understanding.
- The learning progression that takes place in context with autonomous activity, mental and social support (situated cognition).
- The community, through which learning takes place, helping students to disseminate students' cultures and practices.
- The conversation (discourse), which enables the participation and negotiation in the community.

The combination of social, psychological and biological factors has led the modern pedagogi-

cal research to explore a new field of scientific approaches and educational practices related to the redefinition of learners' "action-based framework" for the recruitment of knowledge with the use of new technologies. Although, the main founders of Adult learning theories, they placed the phenomenon of learning in the social experience, responsibilities and roles of adults in the socio-cultural environment, in relation to current theories that explain learning with multimedia has no difference. Nowadays, the integration of ICT in the field of Education can really contribute to the learning process, but only when are used properly through well-structured activities with clearly defined objectives.

The change of the theoretical background and the shift to a more "constructivist" methods, has dictated the movement from the teacher-centered (instructive) approach in a more exploratory, independent and collaborative learning approaches (students as seekers of knowledge). Many teaching procedures granted in traditional education merit some valuable review and adjustment to new technological and communication data. Therefore, in order to be effective in various educational applications of computers should be based explicitly or implicitly on theories of learning and psycho-pedagogical principles that reflects to the real needs of an educational community (Huang, 2002).

Social Constructivism Theory

The Social constructivism, as it drafted by Lev Vygotsky (1896-1934) placed the internal principles of the individual thought in collaborative action and external communication with other people. A person's mental development is an inseparably linked process of the historical, social dimension and the cultural context in which the operation occurred and displayed firstly at the social, and secondly at the personal level (Vygotsky, 1978). The core of Vygotsky's theoretical structure about the social interaction determines a fundamental role in the development of knowledge. The importance of social factors and human environment in the development and direction of learning activities, defined as an evolution, based on:

- The guided learning is understandable as the construction of knowledge by means of discussion, under the instructor's guidance.
- The supporting scaffolding framework referred to the support and assistance of the teacher to trainees in order to build their new "knowledge field". The teacher in this case is not someone that simply gives the student a rich learning environment by helping to self-development (see theory of Piaget), but an active agent of social and cultural meanings that negotiates with the student and helps him internalize all that support its development.

The contribution of Vygotsky's theory in the teaching process, made two important consequences:

- The establishment of circumstances under the principle of cooperativeness among groups with different skill levels (social, cognitive and communication etc.)
- The prominent principles of the gradual reduction among "experienced" people called "assisted or (descending) discovery" (or fading scaffolding).

Distributed Learning Theory

The Distributed learning theory focuses more on social and material context (i.e. artifacts, tools and environment), in which an activity takes place for the individual (Brown & Cole, 2000; Salomon, 1993). This theory can play an important role in understanding the interactions between people and technology. The term of "distributed learning", is primarily a form of distance education provided in a wide geographic area and the form of 'mixed' methods in which learning and teaching resources are allocated to different media types and communication forms (synchronously and asynchronously). The intent of the term describes the process and not a particular learning theory that usually refers to a form of education delivery in distributed sites and learning resources (Resnick, Pontecorvo, Saljo, & Burge, 1997). The two basic principles of the theory that can distinguish it from the 'traditional' (like Constructivism) is:

- The wider unit of learning analysis of learning and cognitive processes is no longer just those occurring in a human brain, but also those between people-machines. In many cases, the unit of analysis can be an entire techno-social system.
- The cognitive (under study) system, involving all the "ingredients" of cognitive process (composite environment) (Perkins, 1993), as participants in cognitive processes are very broad and include even signals, electronic or mechanical external tools (Zhang & Patel, 2006).

Situated Learning Theory

According to the Situated Theory, learning is a process associated with activities, objectives and the socio-cultural environment in which it occurs (Lave & Wenger, 1991). Two main points of this approach we can distinguish are:

- The importance of the framework for the cognitive and mental activity. According to this position, the mind is closely interwoven with the context in which it occurs, and therefore the framework is a component of cognitive activity.
- Learning is not a function of the individual human mind, but a socio-cultural function, carried out through communication and interaction with other people.

The interaction and social participation, take place through a process of "cognitive apprenticeship," which integrated into wider communities of practice (Lave & Wenger, 1991). Learning is no longer associated with the activities, content and culture, within which occurs by incorporating certain beliefs and behaviors, which should get it. As students move from the periphery of the "community of practice" to the center, they become more active by using cognitive tools available within authentic activities (Wilson & Myers, 2000).

Activity Theory

Activity Theory is a "philosophical" (conceptual) framework for the study of human existence, whereby the most appropriate unit of analysis is human activity that consists with other several components that interact with each other (subject, object, division of labor, etc.). Activity theory extends the key mediating to the triangle (Subject-Object-Tool), where the tool mediates the relationship subject-object in a broad triangle composed of interrelated triangles (Engeström, 1987).

This new figure (or system), represents a broader context and practice in which learning is accomplished and includes apart from the subject (Cole & Engeström, 1993; Engeström, Y., Engerstom R. & Karkkainen, 1995; Engeström, Miettinen, & Punamaki, 1999; Engeström, 2001):

- Conciliators tools. The tools can be classified into two categories: a) "physical" & b) "psychological". However, the distinctions between "natural" and "psychological" tools are not always clear. This can be seen on a web site, which is a "natural" tool, but the interactivity that makes it includes a communication tool. The "symbolic" (technical) tool where people interact with these tools and express their filings or emotions consisting with various parts such as text, audio, video, etc., and

these as "entire system" can transform it as a "psychological" tool. These tools foster to a richer understanding of messages and interactive communication forms among people based on their experience, knowledge and culture.

- The object of activity, which can be either pre-designed artifact from the teacher and guide the students to create
- A community is the investigative component of learning, where students hatching the knowledge simultaneously with other students. It's a unit of analysis over the context in which the subject acts, and by extending the frame as a unified system activity.
- The rules and division of roles between the subject and the other members of the community. The unit of analysis is the whole context in which the subject acts and therefore the framework are consolidated as an activity "system."

The artifacts that used in each activity are mainly standards for setting up the new unique or produced them by using a more general artifact. This activity is a driven-process by incentives and consists of objective-led activities and functions provided.

Social Theory of CSCL

The CSCL is a part of default in socio-cultural approaches. A great literature body (Lakkala, Rahikainen & Hakkarainen, 2001; Hoadley, 2010; Stahl, 2011; 2012) suggested that for CSCL, the socio-cultural approach is more of a theoretical substrate; a general framework within it bounded or can adequately be determined. Despite the frequent references to concepts from the socio-cultural tradition, in practice it cannot show any systematic use according to this cognitive tradition. Similarly noteworthy, the socio-cultural background field of CSCL is exposed by the dialogue between members, despite that this process may hasn't yet systematically been exploited for a study of the social nature of cognition and interactive elements. The socio-cultural psychology can contribute further in the conceptualization and a study of the interaction.

In the case of Stahl's CSCL model, students work individually and can enter their notes or comments in a shared basis data. Externally, such process is indicative of a more individual work and learning with students' social interactions and activities. The "cooperation" and "interaction" is refereed from each note introduces students to develop a dialogue, while the "cooperation" refers to discussion-debate between his tutors. A prior version of the social construction and collaboration for knowledge acquisition was the social theory of Stahl (2011) that has recently introduced its own version of social theory elements for collaborative learning with computer support, as users selectively acted in an attempt to synthesize insights from the ongoing dialogue on these issues. The social theory based on extensive analysis of high school students in a learning activity with simulation software (Stahl, 2012). The proposed model provides an examination of how social interactions through concepts such as tools, status, performances, intuitive knowledge, and perspectives which are negotiable.

The model examines (Stahl, Koschmann, & Suthers, 2006; Stahl, 2012; Suthers, 2006):

- The sequence and interrelationship between individual and social processes.
- The reason through which knowledge shared and students that develops interactive knowledge the same group.
- The negotiation of meanings tools.
- The conjunction of these meanings that make up the social world in which we operate and we learn to understand through collaborative learning. The model includes issues of epistemology, semiotics, hermeneutics and ontology.

TEACHING MODELS

It is essential that with time pass we are able to understand the difference between learning theories and models. The learning theories are philosophical theorems, any depth after years of research leading to some conclusions. The models on the other side are:

- Clarifying the quintessence process of learning pathways.
- Unraveling the effective use that requires specialized knowledge from the teacher's knowledge and seeking to implement and has mirrored (e.g. two interdependent poles of society-and behavior-person organization).
- Prototyping the theory through an energetic gait to be followed by the teacher and students as a continuous sequence that describes the flow of activities.

Also teaching models support an encounter subject to the systematic investigation in the past and consist of core epistemologies mainly perceptions of learning that refer to the implementation and teaching level. We should also note that for the purposes of this chapter we refer them as models because these teaching approaches combine learning theory and teaching practice (Thomas & Storr, 2005). Meanwhile, Lipponen and Lallimo (2004) had as a starting point that it is particularly difficult to interpret and synthesis research results on collaborative learning with computer support focused on the successful examples of collaborative learning, in order to identify common elements between them. In particular, they focused on developing knowledge and authentic learning. The analysis shows that on the successful use of collaborative technologies has a common denominator: the emphasis on proper design practice in which cooperativeness is already used.

A starting point of this study was the fact that learning and design learning environments can promote learning in different forms, making available both theory and empirical research-based knowledge. The need for tailor activities as well as the consequent importance attached to the culture of learning environment suggests that the issue of collaborative computer-supported learning is primarily a matter of learning element that often tends to escape our attention (Thompson, Jeffries, & Topping, 2010).

Although, the phenomenon of learning by using computers and exploring the area that particularly involved with the online collaborative learning, at least in the last decade characterized by a series of developments that have shaped a different landscape in the area of intelligence. There have been many developments, both in theoretical and research level with (Brown, Collins & Duguid, 1989; Gunawardena, et al. 2010; Lee & Tan, 2010; Stacey, 2002):

- The failure of education systems, which do not yield expected results, can approximately motivate students.
- The awareness of learning differences and practices inside and outside school in parallel activities directly mirrored to the needs and interests of students.
- The highlighting limitations of the dominant paradigm of cognitive science. Limiting this period tends to eliminate the study's data that are now starting to be associated with psychological theories that explain the energetic situation of students and cooperation between them (Social-Constructivism).
- The variety of empirical findings on how the context is interdependent and inextricably connected with the intellect, supporting the importance of social interaction on cognitive development.
- The obvious interest on how people learn other cultures, the search and study models of teaching and learning cultures out-

side the Western world (e.g. communities of practice and studied and translated the work of Vygotsky in English and led to the renewal of relevant interest.

VIRTUAL WORLDS (VWs): VIRTUAL ENVIRONMENTS (VEs)

Virtual (desktop) environments are the most popular category of virtual environments from previous MUDs (Multi-user Dimensions) with user-friendly system and low economic demands (Slater & Steed, 2002). In three-dimensional (3D) immersive environments the great importance of the quality of the user's immersion, using devices, likes keyboard and mouse. The user's presence in the virtual environment is enhanced by the co-existence of other with a three-dimensional representation in the virtual space. This representation can be derived from a three-dimensional model synthesis of the computer or even from user's image (Selan dos Santos, 2002).

The term "virtual world" should not be confused with the term "virtual reality" that has more specific meaning. The term "virtual environment" in the literature very often identified with the term virtual reality, describing in this way data and processes that make up a virtual reality system, while in other cases used to describe depicted elements or objects (dimensional model) of an environment (Bishop, Gary, Henry, & Fuchs, 1992). Virtual reality is presenting primary mechanisms through which people can interact with computer simulations. Virtual worlds (VWs) often considered as being simple 3D multiplayer games or chat rooms, but in reality are increasingly powerful tools for educational and business purposes.

It is crucial to observe that there is no clear and strict definition of the term *"virtual world"* or *"virtual environment,"* and so we try to give below, some of the most prevalent. The term itself is controversial and of course leads to misunderstandings and hours of philosophical discussions. On this occasion, we truly believe that we must construct a definition about virtual environments and finally re-think the applications that can be included on these. With the average *"Virtual Environment"* (VE or 3D VE) we mean a computer system based on newer three-dimensional applications of VR technology, which simulates in the personal computer (PC) screen a "physical" space or place, like this in real life and aims to present a visually interactive and multi-sensory "world," which is exclusively for users and influence their actions in a positive way.

On the other side, a *"Virtual World"* (VW) is the result of a virtual environment's operational structure, which includes the representation of a natural environment and its "variants" in conjunction with a fantastic placement, where users' "virtual rooms" are freely without restrictions and commitments. This distinction very clearly indicates that virtual world's rules for building and interpreting data is supported by the operation of a "physical" environment as a computer system. A 3D environment is hosted on a server or even in a form of software, which is stored on the PC's hard disk, giving users the impression that is to be established on a "solid state," where everything looks and moves normally. The absolute connection between them is the users' capacity for the upcoming changes and developments that are promoted by the time and place. Moreover, the most important contribution that 3D VR lays is the ease managing for one or more subjects, even when it involves hazardous or inadequate processes, which could not be performed in a real environment. In this context, students learn from their mistakes, without dangerous effects on their actions, and as a result they "produce" their own "knowledge field" and the system provides the appropriate feedback, according to their actions. Although, in this contemporary "reality" that is depicted though virtual worlds, we can distinguish two major pillars that enroll all of them:

1. **Social Virtual Worlds (SVWs):** In the first category these types of virtual environments created for the communication between social media and social networking friends. The social aspects and interaction of an SVW (Second Life, The Sims online, and WeeWorld) attracts more and more cyber entities (avatars), and doesn't offer a streaming isolation in front of a computer screen, but it has many characteristics of *"persistence co-presence."* This concept refers to the collaborative action effort, coexistence and common presence between distributed users in a virtual community which continues to exist, even after a user exits from the environment.

2. **Open Source Virtual Worlds (OSVWs):** The polymorphic dimension of an OSVW (Open Simulator, Realxtend, Reaction Grid etc.) and structural requirements refer to a "technocratic infrastructure" that is being depicted through to its freeware open source server platform. Many of these worlds are working in a tandem compatibility also with the Second Life's client. OSVWs are written in visual C+ and is designed to be easily expanded through the use of plug-in. It can operate in one of two modes: (a) *standalone* or (b) networked *grid mode*. In *standalone* mode is the single process that handles the entire simulation. In grid mode, various aspects of the simulation are separated among multiple processes, which can exist on different machines. Standalone mode is simpler to configure, but is limited to a smaller number of users. *Grid mode* has the potential to scale as the number of users grows. Approximately, the user is the administrator of the server, and creates objects or introduces new things, like sounds, pictures or textures that are free of charge. Each user has access to the virtual world created by the administrator.

CATEGORIES OF VIRTUAL WORLDS AND E-EDUCATION

At the conceptual approach the importance of construction and development of a system for virtual reality training application focuses on cognitive, spiritual, social and emotional situations of students (Yamashita, 2006). Surveys have found that teachers who use interactive teaching methods designed to promote interaction and sense of community among students (Rovai, 2001). A virtual learning environment exploits the characteristics of productive principles of teaching and of course the theory of social constructivism that paves the way for the development of new teaching approaches and theories. In an attempt to approach such environments, we will see the following:

1. The multi-user virtual environments (MUVEs), introduced in the educational process to improve activities such as Distance Learning (Addison & O 'Hare, 2008), which was initially adopted as a poor education, one-way model of content delivery. The contribution of MUVEs in education has proved in practice, following an investigation (Sharpe, et al., 2006; Eduserv, 2008), which found that the upper and Higher education institutions provide education in general, e-learning services in 3 ways (Hobbs et al., 2006):

    a. The traditional (common) or by providing access to lesson's notes and supporting material.
    b. The metamorphic (innovative) that use technology to radically change the design of the educational process, with emphasis on interaction and communication.
    c. The holistic (emerging), that use technology from any source where students choose where to learn, using the services of the institution, and learn largely through external sources.

A MUVE is a popular form of multimedia with an initial aim to please to entertain users (Normand, et al., 1999). MUVEs designed for the educational community incorporating learning objects or problems in a virtual environment or context (Jones & Bronack, 2007). Users can explore the environment and examine digital objects. In such an environment there are modern means of communication between users (Schroeder, 2008). Educational MUVEs are designed to support research into learning and conceptual understanding (Delwiche, 2006). Usually there is no one right way of completion of work or solving a problem, something that makes many teachers reject their practices. Various solutions are justified, as in real life, some solutions may be better than others. Great importance is placed on students' cooperation (Peachy, 2007).

Unlike MUVEs designed solely for entertainment, educational MUVEs are usually enhanced by students according to their experience. The MUVEs in education are used for:

*   Creating of online communities and initial teacher training and after the training in their professional development (Bull & Kajder, 2004).
*   Engaging in actions on scientific issues, promoting social behavior (Kafai, 2006).
*   Promoting social development through enrichment cultures (Koleva et al, 2000).
*   Providing an environment for programming and collaboration (Vadillo & Matute, 2009).
*   Exploring and instigating for new mathematical concepts (Elliott, 2005).
*   Promoting scientific research (Clarke, 2006).

2. Collaborative virtual environments [CVEs], is collaborative learning environments, from a distance, where students work in teams with great communication. CVEs can transform PCs in three-dimensional navigable and populated places, supporting collaborative work and social play. These types of environments are a shared virtual world through a server that works as a virtual machine, where users can participate regardless of age. Research in the area of Epistemology; place the acquisition of knowledge within a system of interactions among individuals, social and material context (Curtis & Lawson, 2001). The acquisition of knowledge is no longer depending only on the stimuli or cognitive processes of the individual, but by a set of factors consistent with the interaction of the individual with the environment (Stenkuehler & Williams, 2006). CVEs can be an area of convergence and implementation of learning theories, cognitive psychology and developments in educational technology. The valuation of options during the learning process is revealed through the social interactions of disparate and anonymous teammates, both in a game-based approach, and beyond its limits.

The research in cognitive performance suggests that learning requires the reorganization of prior knowledge, the revision of old beliefs and new representations. The additional investigations lead to the development of computer visualization learning environments, or otherwise intelligent 3D VR micro-worlds. A CVE is an environment that can be considered to consist of two main elements:

- Cyber entities (avatars) that interact with the environment, objects, other participants, etc.

- The status of the cooperative activity that is the subject of cooperation and collaborative pedagogy (the style of teaching / learning which are used).

The awareness of a situation must be constantly updated on changes in the environment (Heath & Luff, 1996). Awareness is knowledge of a situation arising from the exploration and interaction with the environment (Dourish & Bellotti, 1992). The awareness of a situation is a secondary objective; specific objective is to complete the learning goal. Just briefly users need to know what happens (Dede, 2005) by supporting the dialogue and communication (negotiation and co-ordination). The necessary transfer of information is essential to support cooperation, and has eventually to do with achieving this goal and strengthen the social activities that support the ongoing collaboration.

However, a CVE that supports these factors is a demanding task. The main factors contributing to this problem, during are that Gutwin and Greenberg (2001):

- A CVE reproduce only a part of the perceptual information available in a "real" 3D "ecosystem" environment.
- The potential interaction in a CVE is limited by the "physical" workplace, and often, of the supplied information in a natural environment is not available in a CVE.

In addition to the collaborative environment that supports this type of systems, the CVE is designed to provide flexibility and many possibilities of the 3D environmental or personal representation. Because the understanding of science concepts is difficult and time consuming, students can only explore a few basic concepts. The strategy focuses on depth rather than to cover all the material in depth. A CVE facilitates the meta-cognitive awareness by allowing students to express their comments and representations of knowledge about an object and then compare it with other (Dexter & Riedel, 2003). Students are made aware of what they know and what to learn. Moreover, the variety and type of information you can offer them to see complex problems from different perspectives (Wilson & Harris, 2004).

A RATIONALE TO "TRANSFER THE KNOWLEDGE" IN VIRTUAL WORLDS

Many of the applications mentioned above draw their ideas from distributed constructionism scattered while allowing multiple users to be in a public place and simultaneously create the same time representation of the object investigated (Resnick, 1996). From 1990 onwards, it seems that the baton was taken by Koster (2004), where firstly introduced the terms:

1. Of the "persistence" in an environment (i.e. a virtual world that continues to exist even after a user exits from the world and that user-made changes to its state are, to some extent, permanent).
2. The concept of multi-participation, where multiple users are entering a public place or area (3D cyberspace) at the same time and are represented by cyber entities.

The element of "persistence," beyond the present reference of the symmetric multi-style, which is achieved by simultaneous and independent use of communication channels that allow the surface of the interface, also referred to the functional structure that governs to the organizational design, which must, however be defined by users, and finally the existence of a 3D multi-channel system consisting of digital formats of real life situations. In this case, although it appears the phenomenon of the evolution of a virtual world, which relentlessly mutating life sources even when the user

retired and turns off the personal computer. Also, the concept of "persistence" involves efforts of others to foster self-organization, collective action frameworks and co-responsibility for finding solutions to problems they encounter (Gamor, 2012). The plurality of interactive and multimedia elements make us describe a virtual world as an "eco-system", which is based on an environment that gives to user an action-based field, and also enhances human intuitive and "kinesthetic" interactive communication and interaction of its members. It should not be denied that most users enter in such worlds, more daring, friendships, inclusion in community practice, which in real life if they could do.

Of course, the usual practice of educational activity in virtual environments, we see that now lies in so-called networked virtual environments like Second Life, Open Simulator, Reaction Grid, which draw and produce content through databases. Pellas and Kazanidis (2012) referred VWs as "descendants" of the 2D [A-] LMS ([Asynchronous] Learning Management Systems) and a basic derivative of the 3D VR provides to users an educational platform through multiple channels of communication or gestures to facilitate non-verbal actions prototyping and modeling of knowledge infrastructures as the needs of each user.

At this point we believe it is now imperative the need to analyze decision superiority of the use of virtual worlds over that of the conventional 2D LMS. Thus, points that seem to outweigh the virtual environments are:

*   The use of multimedia tools and much-channel communication for users who are dispersed either by their physical space or in the virtual environment.
*   The utilization of different friendly-tailored virtual spaces to the needs of users. This occurs particularly in the pre-designed virtual worlds, where the user has the authority to define the framework for action constant and no (or minimum) maintenance of

a virtual unit with support from successive supports each company indefinitely.

- The dynamic contribution of each student through an iconic figure, not caricatured himself, but to acquire a new personality that helps individuals to overcome fears and anxieties.
- The acquisition of skills for future applications that meet future demands. More specific skills that deserve mention are the so-called original techniques: the ability to handle a window environment and general functions of the system has installed the virtual world (MS Windows or OSX etc.), to investigate possible in many places with a tele-transportation, receipt, and response messages. Secondarily is the empirical related to improving typing speed and use input devices, ability to send attached files and the possibility for solving complex problems that are harder to find than just surfing the web.
- The promotion of the principles governing the implementation framework of contemporary learning theories. As mentioned virtual worlds while encouraging the active construction of knowledge and follow the footsteps of the theory of building micro worlds (Papert, 1980), but the newest have the element of interdependence and greater communication among dispersed users, something that brings them closer the meaning and importance of dipole-man society.
- The increasing association with the "germane" cognitive load, associated with the individual and collective effort of users to contribute to the creation and operation of sign shapes and automation of the knowledge provided in the virtual environment.
- The management of the "intrinsic" cognitive load, which occurs from the very early

stages of introducing students to a new learning environment, and later by the large volume of information and interactive data needed to acquire new knowledge.

RESEARCH METHODOLOGY

Emerging Problems and Research Questions

The success of a collaborative learning scenario is always depending to a large extent on the possibility of data processing relating to teamwork, and uses them to achieve an efficient model in cooperative activity. This issue focuses to the attention of many researchers and designers of collaborative environments (Tynjälä & Häkkinen, 2005). In the literature, however, in our opinion, not yet identified a comprehensive and well-rounded approach to provide efficient management and processing activities that take place in a cooperative group activity. A first step involves the use of feedback in online learning environments, and overall impact on teamwork (Thurmond, 2003) and a second proposed active construction of knowledge in online learning environments (Tsai, 2008).

In this study, the data generated by the teamwork components considered as knowledge communicated to partners in a group, but the process of collecting, analyzing and exporting the necessary information is not described. The lack of a theoretical reflection of awareness and concepts will allow researchers and scholars:

- Watching new phenomena of social interaction and learning in the classroom.
- Managing the change of roles and responsibilities.
- Monitoring the course of creating new knowledge courses with different epistemological backgrounds.

As a result, our approach provides a detailed framework for establishing an effective collaborative practice, as well as studying and analyzing the cooperative behavior of cooperative groups. The result of this process allows a better understanding of the interactions within the group, and determines the best way to monitor and evaluate individual and team performance in order to support a collaborative activity. Specifically, we propose a methodological design that guides the process of collaborative learning (i.e., and the teachers and students) throughout its duration. Providing a well-designed methodology is important for individual and team-based success achieved at different levels: team composition, development of collaborative activity, monitoring, evaluation and support. The unique design of each of these levels depends on the specific scenario of learning taking place.

Nowadays, it is a common premise that the evolution of technological power of PCs and Internet (Web-based technologies) has given the opportunity to create innovative electronic environments for both entertainment and learning. The new technological infrastructure in conjunction with the rapid spread of broadband networks and additional developments, such as Web 2.0 applications (blogs, wikis, and virtual worlds) and interactive distributed 3D virtual environments (3DVEs) have changed far beyond the traditional methods of e-Education. Moreover, the rapid development of electronic social networking has changed the "cyberspace" in a rapidly growing communication system, bringing to the front many facets of *"networked collectivity."*

The new technological infrastructure that virtual environments support can transform the existing distributed networks, into habitable and navigable three-dimensional locations. These collaborative works and simulated sharing experiences can be supported by participants with the average age, showing the new emerging relationship between human and computer communications. The pedagogical value in recent years

became even more useful for distance learning, were segregated spatially and temporally users engage in cooperative and collaborative types of action, group-based learning, and coexisting in common virtual spaces and interact via synchronous or asynchronous communication formats, which are often offered (bulletin board, written text, dialing voice, etc.).

Previous studies on the cognitive performance of students by using VWs have shown that during the teaching process, they achieve a more easily reorganization of prior knowledge, to revise old beliefs and new representations of learning (Girvan & Savage, 2010; Pellas, 2012; Pellas & Kazanidis, 2012). Even though, the most recent findings (Dalgarno & Lee, 2010; Kluge & Riley, 2008; Pellas & Kazanidis, 2013) showed the need of using new teaching methods that may be applied in any "innovative" learning environment. However, the abundance that is delighted, is difficult to derive a common pedagogical model that can implement and incorporate the designing process. In this view, it is necessary to present the innovative methods that we can use to establish an evaluation framework with educational terms for each virtual environment.

The fact that the expanded use of ICT in Higher Education in conjunction with modern pedagogical theories that emphasized the inquiry-based learning, problem-solving and decision-making processes, are influenced most strongly across the range of teaching and learning process and tend to change the traditional way (e-) educational practice. Still, it's necessary to be mentioned that "the transferring of knowledge" through virtual environments, in a contemporary practical-teaching framework for collaborative e-learning processes, suggests the primarily jointly carried out work between distributed users. They usually employed in a learning activity or a project, giving a more social interactive dimension to their experience.

The advantages of cooperation in this effort are focused on conducting an effective training, acquiring new social skills and intercultural relations, and finally increasing their self-esteem. However, here we should note that in any collective interaction and involvement of users' cognitive mechanisms and the whole cycle that is spent, there is always some sort of "warranty" to produce the required knowledge, and achieve the final learning outcome.

Emerging questions that are raised in the field of e-Education are as follows:

- Which learning trends should be followed by the CSCL model with persistent virtual environments to become more effective?
- Have the developments of technology and online applications changed the e-Education or contemporary "technocratic" learning theories used simply as "educational tools"?
- Can an integrated approach of contemporary theories or models be the answer for a valuable educational approach?

Current research interests in the field of ICT and especially the e-learning environment should be taken seriously into account for educational use. Thus, within the empirical investigation and dealing with such environments are covering the area of modern science have created a wider field of technological education, divided into:

1. **The Educational Field:** Includes criteria of the educational process (such as support different teaching methodologies presentation of knowledge, etc.) and pedagogical principles inherent axes system management. In this study the term "pedagogical model" we mean key principles followed in organizing a system for distance learning activities. The broader sense is used to identify all forms of information presentation and interaction with the audience.

2. **The Organizational Field:** The organization of courses, study and application of differ-

ent strategies for implementing curricula, support and coordination.

3. **The Operating Field:** Pump research topics for the architectural structure of the supported e-learning process, differential forms of communication, cognitive mechanisms and tools that help improve the learning path.

4. **The Social Field:** The socio-cultural field endorses applications that can be incorporated into the overall cultural and social development of individuals addressed. The universal nature of education, puts the idea of "global student body" and "e-twinning", and winning over a greater interest in how to bridge the differences that are not achievable by conventional type of education.

THE DESCRIPTION OF A CASE STUDY

The case study that we described was under the actual use conditions of distance learning courses in the undergraduate curriculum of *"Project-based case Studies in e-learning in virtual worlds."* These courses take place over a period of 4 weeks, and involve at least two (2) instructors and over fifty (50) students, spread across more than four (4) online working groups of five (5) to six (6) people. In the first collaborative experience, students are required to work in a scenario that represents a real problem of a business or organization (collaborative learning through case studies). The second method is based on the experience of collaborative learning through activity. The design methodology of collaborative practice consists of five well-separated and structured processes and sub-processes (phases): inquiry-based definition, design, implementation, testing, and documentation and delivery of exchangeable virtual objects.

In this chapter, we explain the methodological design based collaborative practice that offers a progressive investigation, conducted for the course, while in the second case study students aimed at completing collaboratively certain objectives (phases) conducted (except the first phase is to study and understand the case study). The design of teaching each objective includes several interrelated processes appropriate learning, which students are required to complete individually (e.g. reading) or collaboratively (e.g. exercises, texturing and scripting), in order to achieve the teaching goal. At the beginning of the course we shared a document explaining to students the process of teamwork that must be followed to achieve specific objectives. The success of the coordinator's (instructor) role depends on the degree of integration of the processes undertaken, including:

- Planning and identifying the cooperative goals.
- Setting and monitoring of virtual meetings.
- Organizing and management of joint working in the virtual environment.
- Monitoring of process integration, information about team members for any delays or possible failure of the collaborative process.
- Mediating and support team members when necessary.
- Preparing the final version of the product at the end of the phase.
- Ensuring stability and cohesion of the initial workplace.
- Delivering the final product and report on the operation of the collaborative team.

The final result of all members, describes how together as a team can implement the product, and contains all the important events that occurred during the cooperative interaction. This agenda is mostly achieved via asynchronous - synchronous communication that takes place in a few cases. All asynchronous interactions take place via the FreeSWITCH module (http://wiki.freeswitch. org/wiki/Installation_Guide#Compiling_and_ Installation), a Groupware tool that supports asynchronous and synchronous communication via the Internet. The platform is a Groupware system based on the web where users can share information on common workplace, as well as organize and coordinate their actions. A server FreeSWITCH module manages a number of shared workspaces (places where there is shared information), which are accessible to members of a group through a common browser. Generally, the server FreeSWITCH module manages many common workspaces for different groups, and users can belong to different shared workspaces (e.g. there is a workspace for each project which includes a user).

A workspace can contain different types of information, which typically represent data objects that organized in a hierarchical structure. These objects have different types, such as folders, links to web pages, files, graphics, sex work, discussion areas, or objects specified by the user (address book, calendars, etc.). The system allows users various functions (which depend on the type of object) that can be applied to objects, such as renaming or deleting objects, keeping versions of files, or a user can insert a comment in a chat room, etc. The FreeSWITCH module keeps members informed of a group for the actions of their partners in a shared workspace, and provides detailed information on the history of cooperation.

In order to structure the process of collaboration through the Internet, we determined two shared workspaces in the system FreeSWITCH module. The first is a workplace that is accessible to all students. The main objective of this area of cooperation is to enable students to interact to form cooperation groups. Indeed, it is used for specific discussions involving all students, and that is needed to complete the project as well as to exchange information between teachers and students. The second workplace is personal space for each cooperative group, which records the information and constructs and interactions between members of the team that designed the integration of collaborative processes.

DECISIONS FOR THE FORMATION AND CONSOLIDATION OF ACTION GROUPS

The formation of groups co-efficient is becoming more important in our case, since the group cooperation must be created from scratch, which means that their members do not know each other, and should create their teams and collaborative processes through a common virtual workplace. Thusly, we consider the formation and consolidation of a group as dynamic processes, guided by the following two goals and inspired our research:

- Explore the different processes involved in creating effective teams in cooperation aimed at learning, especially when, why and how these processes affect the formation of a group, and the extent to ensure the creation of teams that work effectively at the level of cooperation and learning.

- Establishment of the educative function and structure of cooperative learning groups, identifying individual and group learning and social goals, relationships between members, their interactions and roles that define the nature and temperament of the group.

- Implement the composition of the group suggest a figure four phases consisting of well-defined processes (Figure 2), performed by the bottom (bottom-up), and

Figure 2. Synthenizing an action-group

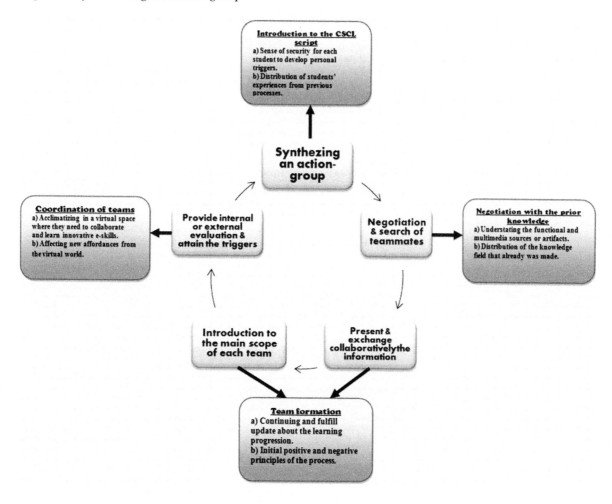

aims to involve students in activities that lead to the creation well-organized learning groups.

THEORETICAL FOUNDATIONS AND DECISIONS PROCESSES OF THE PROPOSED CSCL MODEL IN VIRTUAL WORLDS

The organization of activities in a virtual environment should be done in a way that users (cyber-entities) can deal with it as an "ecosystem" and interact with it. In this way they try to lead an economy of time and fatigue to achieve learning objectives. The central question of a learning activity is the cognitive framework, the search and matching the most effective ways, means, experiences and needs of supply, treatment and construction of new knowledge. Inasmuch as we construct the following table (Table 1) a methodological framework for describing the procedure of a learning progression in a virtual world, which inspired by the CSCL model (Stahl, 2000).

Table 1. The proposed CSCL framework in virtual worlds

Initiatives for Designing a Methodological Framework	Flowchart of a Proposed CSCL Model	Decisions Processes in a CSCL Script
Phase 1: Distribution and interrelation of a new "knowledge field" with socially constructed processes in a virtual world	1. Distributed expertise is a central concept in the model. The CSCL model intends to engage the community in a shared process of knowledge advancement, and to convey, simultaneously, the cognitive goals for collaboration. 2. Acting as a member in the community includes the sharing cognitive responsibility for the success of its inquiry. This responsibility essentially involves not only completing tasks or delivering productions on time, but also allow learners taking responsibilities for discovering what needs to be known, like goal setting, planning, and monitoring the inquiry process.	Students' decisions process in a CSCL script: Introduction to the virtual world - Students must understand metaphors and affordances from the interactive VW. Instructor's decision processes in a CSCL script: Presenting and discussing new concepts, scope of introduction and describing activities that should be followed.
Phase 2: Creating the contextual background and explaining members the meaning of the "shared" knowledge field	The process begins by creating the context to anchor the inquiry on central conceptual principles of the domain or complex real-world problems. The learning community is established by joint planning and setting up common goals.	Students' decisions process in a CSCL script: Transferring the knowledge field in the VW, and exploiting the differences of a traditional and a 3D classroom. Instructor's decision processes in a CSCL script: Reinforcement students' views for learning by sharing artifacts and tools, facilitating the learning progression.
Phase 3: Describing and negotiating the situation of a learning progression	An essential element of progressive inquiry is setting up research questions generated by students themselves to direct to the inquiry. Explanation-seeking questions (how? what?) are especially valuable. It is crucial that students come to treat studying as a problem-solving process that includes addressing problems in understanding the theoretical constructs, methods, and practices of scientific culture.	Students' decision process in a CSCL script: Using functional artifacts and tools that a client viewer provide or even instructor provide to them. Instructor's decision processes in a CSCL script: Presenting different tools, teaching units that are emerging from a traditional classroom.

continued on following page

Table 1. Continued

Initiatives for Designing a Methodological Framework	Flowchart of a Proposed CSCL Model	Decisions Processes in a CSCL Script
Phase 4: The conjunction of novel gaits of this framework and designing further actions	It is also important that students explain phenomena under study with their own existing background knowledge by constructing working theories before using information sources. This serves a number of goals by: 1. Making visible the prior (intuitive) conceptions of the issues at hand. 2. Trying to explain to other students effectively test the coherence of their own understanding, and make gaps and contradictions in their own knowledge more apparent. 3. Serving a collaborative "culture" in which knowledge is treated as essentially evolving objects and artifacts. Thoughts and ideas presented are not final and unchangeable, but rather utterances in an ongoing discourse.	Students' decision process in a CSCL script: Participate in collaborative activities. Instructor's decision processes in a CSCL script: First evaluation internal (individual or team-based), as students need to find more information about the project.
Phase 5: The engagement of students with the learning material	Students should be engaged in searching deepening knowledge in order to find answers to their questions. Furthermore, searching for relevant materials provides an excellent opportunity for self-directed inquiry and hands-on practice in struggling to grasp the differences between various concepts and theories.	Students' decision process in a CSCL script: Exploiting and exploiting the initial students' workflow-Organize and present heterogeneous group for learning competencies. Instructor's decision processes in a CSCL script: The teacher must decide how the materials should be offered to the students and how much they should actually utilize them. Questions stemming from true wonderment on the part of the students can easily extend the scope of materials beyond what a teacher can foresee or provide suggestions for.
Phase 6: Final knowledge fairs and reports	Developing new working theories and evaluate practice-based achievements raised out of new questions and scientific knowledge that the participants attain. If all productions in the shared database in a collaborative environment have been meaningfully organized them, participants should have an easy access to prior productions and theories, making the development of conceptions and artifacts a visible process.	Students' decisions process in a CSCL script: Manipulation and configuring collaborative tools of the VW and construction of appropriate 3D artifacts. Students learning is a process of understanding the cognitive value of social collaboration and gaining the capacity to utilize socially distributed cognitive resources

DISCUSSION POINTS

New technologies as we like it or not, shaping a new global reality. On the other hand, VWs seem to become more valuable in nowadays and this notion can be configured because the quality enhancement or improvement of the teaching practice in a direction where students will investigate, discover, and learn how to set goals for each action is sufficient. On the other hand the role of the instructor in our time, which is no longer important the role to facilitate the knowledge, because there is accumulated in many sources. The leverage of media literacy can help users to explore and develop these resources and hence relevant to interactive teaching, and provide instructional support in teaching the individual subjects of the course with creative and easy access to information, such as images and multiple representations by combining text. Accordingly, the learning progression and teaching negotiation object with the help of new technologies:

1. Documentation of all the cognitive elements and media sources.
2. Students recreate-discover-learn the lessons in a variety forms of learning procedures.

The e-learning by putting to a practical level and perform their role as a teacher and educator now need to:

- Be familiar as much as possible with new forms of 3D scripts in VWs, which are characterized multimodal.
- Make use of training scenarios, software, packages containing different types of exercises for homework.
- The knowledge is built and transmitted with the assistance of tools and symbols available in each community. The language, books, computers, internet, media are the tools that students and teachers use for building, negotiation and "transmission" of knowledge.
- Learning communities are a major part of learning, teachers must continually offer new opportunities for students in order to become shareholders of learning communities within and outside the classroom. Within these communities there is a close link between knowledge and action.
- Strengthening the phenomenon that takes place between the two subjects is a well-known phenomenon of social interaction. Features of this interaction are the dura-

tion, stability and the emotional dimension of the relationship and not the surface of everyday human relationships.

The aim of the pedagogical process as its aforementioned outlines can encapsulate the formation, stabilization, or change trainee users' behaviors and predetermine goals or applicable norms in a social group. The educational process is always carried out within a specific socio-cultural context in which they attempted in a synthesis of old and union attitudes to the beliefs of the new generation of demands of society with the individual's needs.

Similarly noteworthy, the CSCL model to be successfully implemented must be based on two basic principles:

1. The knowledge plait contained within this environmental framework, the abstract or general nature. It is necessary that the knowledge is applied and learned in collaborative environments, authentic contexts, and i.e. contexts include knowledge through empirical conditions.
2. The learning plait of the new knowledge in communities and learning requires the social interaction and teamwork.

This, of course, raises many questions for both the first and the second principle. For example, there is always the possibility that learning happens in a way that does not necessarily relate to a specific context or personal experience. However, generally speaking, the model of resident learning can provide good ideas for new teaching practices. This chapter focused on three such ideas:

1. Learning is accomplished through the interactions of atoms and experiential (Li, Finley, Pitts, & Guo, 2008; Rickel & Jonshon, 1997). Traditionally, learning is assessed based on the assumption that it is an individual achievement and is "inside" the mind of each student.

2. The instructors must continuously offer new opportunities for students in order to become shareholders of learning communities within and outside the classroom (Zhao & Kuh, 2004).

3. To be a close link between knowledge and action (Krause & Coates, 2008). Obviously, problem solving and learning through experience is basic knowledge of established procedures. In other words, learning is not insulated from the world of action but is located within complex social environments, which are composed of people, actions and situations.

In any occasion we need to find the pillars that consist an effective learning progression that has two aims, firstly to enhance the teaching skills of the teacher and secondly the design of the teaching acts so that the knowledge is essential, comprehensive, understandable and interesting. Effective learning (meaningful learning) based on:

1. The relevant prior knowledge that learners need to correlate with the previous and the new knowledge,

2. The substantive material, the new knowledge that should be associated with the old and should include concepts and proposals and substantive sense,

3. The trainee user chooses to learn effectively (Keskitalo, Pyykkö, & Ruokamo, 2011).

CONCLUSION

From all the aforementioned reasons, we can finally conclude the necessity of designing and implementing a virtual environment that offer a multi-sensorial communication, thereby meeting the needs of modern teaching techniques and learning theories. It is necessary to have a methodological framework to transfer a greater

knowledge field, suggestive ways of presenting educational content and better learning outcomes. Since the implementation and evaluation of the proposed model has presented a serious role of instructor must take into account. It is underlined by giving them full control and an increased the sense of responsibility for the development of the learning process by providing an educational tool for teaching, learning and self-study with the simultaneous consolidation of the concepts of programming, covering all types of learning (visual, auditory, kinesthetic). We stressed that the implementation of collaborative learning in a VW is enough currently evidence to suggest that the collaborative distance learning has significant advantages compared with the individual training version of the web, but also with the classical approach to education. These above include:

1. The significant increase in the participation of students.

2. The satisfaction of participants from the process and higher motivation.

3. The best combination of features and presentation of personal interaction among learners. He has also conducted research indicating that cooperative distance learning increases academic performance in several cases (Lehtinen, et al., 1999). The issue of the lack of a single general theoretical framework or coherent theory in the field of collaborative learning with computer support has been emphasized sufficiently in the literature (e.g. Lipponen, 2002; Lehtinen, 2003; Lipponen, Hakkarainen & Paavola, 2004). In conclusion, despite the problems with the synthesis of research results and theoretical diversity, the example of collaborative learning with computer support is a very considerable improvement according to the previous examples. In particular, elements of the approach, such as:

a. The emphasis on development and meaning.

b. The focus on social interaction and communication.

c. The examination of tools and mediated nature of cognition.

d. The emphasis on learning as opposed to the first years of educational technological infrastructure paved the way for a better quality and more complete study of collaborative learning with computer support.

Foremost, the diversity is seen as an advantage in the early stages of formulating paradigm diversity is legitimate. On the other hand, diversity is viewed with great skepticism, because if they continue all the different trends develop in divergent manner, the sector will end up being much decayed, and even without the prospect of exit from the fragmentation. Indicative of growing concern is the fact that Lipponen, Hakkarainen, and Paavola (2004) consider that one of the key dilemmas for the future is whether to accept the theoretical range and diversity of a need for integration and synthesis.

The contribution of social-cultural psychology in VWs enhances the phenomenon of collaborative computer-supported learning, but it is not limited to the above. A basic concept in the field of cooperative learning is computer-supported social interaction. This concept can include many different elements, the most obvious (e.g. collaboration between students' cognitive performance of a project) to the less obvious (e.g. collaboration with a mental tool). It can also refer to situations which are contrary to common sense (e.g. someone working alone). CL may include all or some of the above. In all these circumstances this requires an adequate theoretical framework for describing the interactions which include both social interaction with others (present or not) and with natural, artificial or mental tools (present or not). Given that social interaction is engraved on everything around the world, the general theoretical framework delineated by the socio-cultural psychology can contribute as a catalyst for the study of such phenomena and thereby to promote and further evolution of collaborative learning with computer support.

FUTURE RESEARCH DIRECTIONS

Generally virtual worlds can be used as an educational platform by many educational institutions, like colleges, libraries and urban services. We also should note that the essential e-learning may now enter the e-learning 2.0 - term that emerged after the advent of Web 2.0 and the term used to describe new ways of thinking about e-learning. The e-learning 2.0 is based on models of cooperation and the theory of social constructivism, uses virtual classrooms in real time (real time virtual classrooms) in combination with virtual (learning) environments. These developments highlight the need for a strong first develop a methodology for utilization of both virtual worlds and other services of Web 2.0, which is already known and used to co-ordinate students, offering new dimensions in their knowledge field.

In these circumstances interoperability issues and integration with other [A-] LMS, like Blackboard and Moodle will be a serious future-driven research. Currently, most users will be focused on utilization between Sloodle modules (Second Life + Moodle) and the interactive scripts in a virtual world. In this matter of e-Learning should pre-focus more attention on the part of the learning and less one. The training methods that used should be chosen with great care and educational staff is adequately trained not only in using the techniques but also some available features.

REFERENCES

Addison, A., & O'Hare, L. (2008). How can massive multi-user virtual environments and virtual role play enhance traditional teaching practice? In *Proceedings of Researching Learning in Virtual Environments* (pp. 7–16). London: The Open University.

Barab, S., Thomas, M., Dodge, T., Carteaux, R., & Tuzun, H. (2005). Making learning fun: Quest Atlantis, a game without guns. *Educational Technology Research and Development*, *53*(1), 86–107. doi:10.1007/BF02504859

Bishop, G., & Fuchs, H. (1992). Research directions in virtual environments: Report of an NSF invitational workshop. *SIGGRAPH Computers Graphics*, *26*(3), 153–177. doi:10.1145/142413.142416

Bricken, W. (1990, May). *Learning in virtual reality*. Retrieved from http://www.wbricken.com/pdfs/03words/03education/02vr-education/01learn-in-VR.pdf

Brown, K., & Cole, M. (2000). Socially-shared cognition: System design and organization of collaborative research. In D. Jonassen & S. Land (Eds.), *Theoretical foundations of learning environments* (pp. 197–210). Hoboken, NJ: Lawrence Erlbaum Associates.

Bruckman, A. S. (1997). *MOOSE crossing: Construction, community, and learning in a networked virtual world for kids*. (Unpublished Doctoral Dissertation).

Bull, G., & Kajder, S. (2004). Tapped in. *Learning and Leading with Technology*, *31*(5), 34–37.

Chen, W. (2005). *Supporting teachers' intervention in collaborative knowledge building*. Retrieved from http://halshs.archives-ouvertes.fr/docs/00/19/01/63/PDF/Chen_2004.pdf

Clarke, J., Dede, C., Ketelhut, D. J., & Nelson, B. (2006). A design-based research strategy to promote scalability for educational innovations. *Educational Technology*, *46*(3), 27–36.

Cole, M., & Engeström, Y. (1993). A cultural-historical approach to distributed cognition. In G. Salomon (Ed.), *Distributed cognitions: Psychological and educational considerations* (pp. 1–45). New York: Cambridge University Press.

Conole, G., & Fill, K. (2005). A learning design toolkit to create pedagogically effective learning activities. *Journal of Interactive Media in Education*. Retrieved from http://www-jime.open.ac.uk/2005/08/conole-2005-08-paper.html

Curtis, D., & Lawson, L. (2001). Exploring collaborative online learning. *Journal of Asynchronous Learning Networks*, *5*(1), 21–34.

Dalgarno, B., & Lee, M. (2010). What are the learning affordances of 3-D virtual environments? *British Journal of Educational Technology*, *41*(1), 10–32. doi:10.1111/j.1467-8535.2009.01038.x

De Jong, T. (2006). Computer simulations-technological advantages in inquiry learning. *Science*, *312*, 532–533. doi:10.1126/science.1127750 PMID:16645080

Dede, C. (2005). Planning for neomillenial learning styles: Implications for investments in technology and faculty. In Oblinger & Oblinger (Eds.), *Educating the net generation*. Retrieved from http://net.educause.edu/ir/library/pdf/pub7101o.pdf

Delwiche, A. (2006). Massively multiplayer online games (MMO's) in the new media classroom. *Journal of Educational Technology & Society*, *9*(3), 160–172.

Dexter, S., & Riedel, E. (2003). Why improving pre-service teacher educational technology preparation must go beyond the college's walls. *Journal of Teacher Education, 54*(4), 334–346. doi:10.1177/0022487103255319

Dillenbourg, P. (1996). Some technical implications the distributed cognition approach on the design of interactive learning environments. *Journal of Artificial Intelligence in Education, 7*(2), 161–180.

Dourish, P., & Bellotti, V. (1992). Awareness and collaboration in shared workspaces. In *Proceedings of the ACM Conference on Computer-Supported Cooperative Work (CSCW'92)* (pp. 107-114). Toronto, Canada: ACM Press.

Eduserv. (2008). *The Autumn 2008 snapshot of UK higher and further education: Developments in Second Life*. Retrieved from http://www.eduserv. org.uk/foundation/sl/uksnapshot102008

Elliot, J., Adams, L., & Bruckman, A. (2002). No magic bullet: 3D video games in Education. In *Proceedings of 5th ICLS 2002*. Seattle, Washington: ICLS. Retrieved from http://www.cc.gatech. edu/~asb/papers/aquamoose-icls02.pdf

Elliot, J., & Bruckman, A. (2002). Design of a 3D interactive math learning environment. [London: DIS.]. *Proceedings of DIS, 2002*, 64–74.

Elliott, L. (2005). *AquaMOOSE 3D: A constructionist approach to math learning motivated by artistic expression*. (Unpublished Doctoral Dissertation). Georgia Institute of Technology, Atlanta, GA.

Engeström, E. (1987). *Learning by expanding: An activity-theoretical approach to developmental research*. Helsinki, Finland: Orienta-Konsulait.

Engeström, E. (1996). Developmental work research as educational research: Looking 10 years back into the zone of proximal development. *Nordisk Pedagogik, 16*(3), 131–143.

Engeström, E., Engerstom, R., & Karkkainen, M. (1995). Polycontextuality and boundary crossing in expert cognition: Learning and problem solving in complex work activity. *Learning and Instruction, 5*, 319–336. doi:10.1016/0959-4752(95)00021-6

Engeström, Y. (1987). *Learning by expanding: An activity theoretical approach to developmental research*. Helsinki, Finland: Orienta-Konsultit Oy. Retrieved from http://lchc.ucsd.edu/MCA/Paper/ Engestrom/expanding/intro.html

Engeström, Y. (2001). Expansive learning at work: Toward an activity theoretical re-conceptualization. *Journal of Education and Work, 14*(1), 133–156.

Engeström, Y., & Miettenin, P. (1999). Introduction. In Y. Engeström, R., Miettinen, & R.L. Pumanaki (Eds.), Perspectives on activity theory (pp. 1-18). New York: Cambridge University Press.

Engeström, Y., Miettinen, R., & Punamaki, R. (1999). *Perspectives on activity theory*. Cambridge, UK: Cambridge University Press. doi:10.1017/CBO9780511812774

Gamor, K. I. (2012). Exploiting the power of persistence for learning in virtual worlds. In B. Khan (Ed.), *User interface design for virtual environments: Challenges and advances* (pp. 142–155). Hershey, PA: IGI Global.

Girvan, C., & Savage, T. (2010). Identifying an appropriate pedagogy for virtual worlds: A communal constructivism case study. *Computers & Education, 55*(2), 342–349. doi:10.1016/j. compedu.2010.01.020

Good, R. (2004). *3D virtual spaces for learning and collaboration*. Retrieved from http://www. masternewmedia.org/2004/09/27/3d_virtual_ spaces_for_learning.html

Gunawardena, C. N., Hermans, M. B., Sanchez, D., Richmond, C., Bohley, M., & Tuttle, R. (2009). A theoretical framework for building online communities of practice with social networking tools. *Educational Media International, 46*(1), 3–16. doi:10.1080/09523980802588626

Hakkarainen, K. (2003). Progressive inquiry in a computer-supported biology class. *Journal of Research in Science Teaching, 40*(10), 1072–1088. doi:10.1002/tea.10121

Hakkarainen, K., & Paavola, S. (2005). *From monological and dialogical to trialogical approaches to learning*. Retrieved from http://escalate.org.il/construction_knowledge/papers/hakkarainen.pdf

Hartikainen, A. (2008). Making meanings: Pupil talk in inquiry-oriented instruction. *NORDINA, 4*(1), 64–76.

Heikkila, S. (2004). *Process inquiry challenges product challenges*. Retrieved from http://www.el-earningeuropa.info/files/media/media13769.pdf

Hoadley, C. (2010). Roles, design, and the nature of CSCL. *Computers in Human Behavior, 26,* 551–555. doi:10.1016/j.chb.2009.08.012

Hobbs, M., Gordon, M., & Brown, E. (2006). *A virtual world environment for group work*. Cambridge, UK: Formatex. Retrieved from http://www.formatex.org/micte2006/Downloadable-files/oral/A%20Virtual%20World.pdf

Hollan, J., Hutchins, E., & Kirsh, D. (2000). Distributed cognition: Toward a new foundation for human- computer interaction research. *ACM Transactions on Human-Computer Interaction, 7*(2), 174–196. doi:10.1145/353485.353487

Hollins, P., & Robbins, S. (2008). The educational affordances of multi user virtual environments (MUVE). In *Proceedings of Researching Learning in Virtual Environments* (pp. 172–180). London: The Open University.

Järvelä, S., Volet, S., & Järvenoja, H. (2010). Research on motivation in collaborative learning: Movingbeyond the cognitive-situative divide and combining individual and social processes. *Educational Psychologist, 45,* 15–27. doi:10.1080/00461520903433539

Järvenoja, H., & Järvelä, S. (2009). Emotion control in collaborative learning situations - Do students regulate emotions evoked from social challenges? *The British Journal of Educational Psychology, 79,* 463–481. doi:10.1348/000709909X402811 PMID:19208290

Jones, G., & Bronack, C. (2007). Rethinking cognition, representations and processes in 3D online social learning environments. In D. Gibson, C. Aldridge, & M. Prenky (Eds.), *Games and simulations in online learning: Research and development Frameworks* (pp. 1–20). Hersey, PA: Information Science Publishing.

Kafai, Y., & Resnick, M. (1996). *Constructionism in practice: Designing, thinking, and learning in a digital world*. Mahwah, NJ: Lawrence Erlbaum.

Kafai, Y. B. (2006). Playing and making games for learning: Instructionist and constructionist perspectives for game studies. *Games and Culture, 1*(1), 36–40. doi:10.1177/1555412005281767

Keskitalo, T., Pyykkö, E., & Ruokamo, H. (2011). Exploring the meaningful learning of students in Second Life. *Journal of Educational Technology & Society, 14*(1), 16–26.

Kluge, S., & Riley, L. (2008). Teaching in 3D-virtual worlds: Opportunities and challenges. *Issues in Informing Science and Information Technology, 5*(1), 127–135.

Koleva, B. N., Schnadelbach, H. M., Benford, S. D., & Greenhalgh, C. M. (2000). Developing mixed reality boundaries. In *Proceedings of Designing Augmented Reality Environments* (DARE 2000) (pp. 155–157). Elsinore, Denmark: DARE.

Koster, R. (2004). *A virtual world by any other name?* Retrieved from http://terranova.blogs.com/terra_nova/2004/06/a_virtual_world.html

Krause, K., & Coates, H. (2008). Students' engagement in first year university. *Assessment & Evaluation in Higher Education, 33*(5), 493–505. doi:10.1080/02602930701698892

Kreijns, K. (2004). *Sociable CSCL environments: Social affordances, social ability and social presence.* Retrieved from http://wenku.baidu.com/view/3ddc7c848762caaedd33d452.html

Lakkala, M. IIomaki, L., Lallimo, J., & Hakkarainen, K. (2003). Virtual communication in middle school students' and teachers' inquiry. In *Proceedings of the CSCL* (pp. 443-452). Maastricht, The Netherlands: Maastricht McLuhan Institute.

Lakkala, M. (2008). Principles of progressive inquiry. *EAAIL.* Retrieved from http://deafed-childabuse-neglect-col.wiki.educ.msu.edu/file/view/Lakkala+M+-+2008+-+Progressive+inquiry+model_introduction.pdf

Lakkala, M., Rahikainen, M., & Hakkarainen, K. (Eds.). (2001). D2.1 perspectives of CSCL in Europe: A review. Helsinki, Finland: ITCOLE-project.

Land, S., & Hannafin, M. (2000). Student-centered learning environments. In D. Jonassen & S. Land (Eds.), *Theoretical foundations of learning environments* (pp. 1–23). Hoboken, NJ: Lawrence Erlbaum Associates.

Lave, J., & Wenger, E. (1991). *Situated learning: Legitimate peripheral participation.* New York: Cambridge University Press. doi:10.1017/CBO9780511815355

Lee, C., & Cheen, T. (2010). Scaffolding writing using feedback in students' graphic organize-novice writers' relevance of ideas and cognitive tools. *Educational Media International, 47*(2), 135–152. doi:10.1080/09523987.2010.492678

Lehtinen, E. (2003). Computer-supported collaborative learning: An approach to powerful learning environments. In E. De Corte, L. Verschaffel, N. Entwistle, & J. Van Merriënboer (Eds.), *Powerful Learning Environments: Unravelling Basic Components and Dimensions* (pp. 35–53). Amsterdam: Elsevier.

Lehtinen, E., Hakkarainen, K., Lipponen, L., Rahikainen, M., & Muukkonen, H. (1999). *Computer supported collaborative learning: A review.* Retrieved from http://www.kas.utu.fi/papers/clnet/clnetreport.html

Li, J., Peng, J., Zhang, W., Han, F., & Yuan, W. (2011). A computer-supported platform based on clouds. *Journal of Computer Information Systems, 7*(11), 3811–3818.

Li, L., Finley, J., & Guo, R. (2008). *Which is a better choice for student-faculty interaction: Synchronous or asynchronous communication?* Retrieved from http://www.aabri.com/manuscripts/10682.pdf

Ludvidgsen, S., & Morch, A. (2006). *Categorization in knowledge building: Task specific argumentation in co-located CSCL environment.* Retrieved from http://halshs.archives-ouvertes.fr/docs/00/19/05/22/PDF/ludvigs_morch.pdfv1.pdf

Malamos, A., Mamakis, G., Sympa, P., Kotanitsi, E., Gonel Crespo, A., & Zubizarraeta Lopez, A. (2008). Technical aspects in using X3D in virtual reality mathematics Education (EViE-m platform). In *Proceedings of 5th WSEAS/IASME International Conference on engineering education (EE'08)*. Herakleion, Greece: WSEAS.

Michail, N., Teal, G., & Basta, J. (2006). Progressive learning processes model-interpretive methodological framework for human systems inquiries. In *Proceedings of the 50th Annual Meeting of the International Society for the Systems Sciences (ISSS)* (pp. 34-39). Sonoma, CA: ISSS.

Muukkonen, H., Hakkarainen, K., & Lakkala, M. (1999). Collaborative technology for facilitating progressive inquiry: The future learning environment tools. In C. Hoadley & J. Roschelle (Eds.), *The Proceedings of the CSCL '99 Conference* (pp. 406-415). Mahwah, NJ: Lawrence Erlbaum.

Normand, V., Babski, C., Benford, S., Bullock, A., Carion, S., & Farcet, N. … Kladias, N. (1999). The COVEN project: Exploring applicative, technical and usage dimensions of collaborative virtual environments. In Proceedings of Presence: Teleoperators and Virtual Environments, 8(2), 218–236.

Onrubia, J., & Engel, A. (2012). The role of teacher assistance on the effects of a macro-script in collaborative writing tasks. *IJCSCL, 7*(1), 161–186.

Papert, S. (1995). *Mindstorms: Children, computers, and powerful ideas*. New York: Basic Books.

Pea, R. (1995). Practices of distributed intelligence and designs for education. In *Distributed cognitions: Psychological and educational considerations* (pp. 47–87). Cambridge, UK: Cambridge University Press.

Peachy. (2007). *MUVE history*. Retrieved from http://www.open.ac.uk/wikis/muve_teaching_and_learning/MUVE_history

Pellas, N. (2012). Towards a beneficial formalization of cyber entities' interactions during the e-learning process in the virtual world of Second Life. In P. Renna (Ed.), *Production and manufacturing system management: Coordination approaches and multi-site planning* (pp. 242–277). Hershey, PA: IGI Global.

Pellas, N. (2013). An innovative cybernetic organization improvement plan through participatory action research in persistent open source virtual worlds. In T. Issa, P. Isaias, & P. Kommers (Eds.), *Information systems and technology for organization in a Networked society* (pp. 107–129). Hershey, PA: IGI Global. doi:10.4018/978-1-4666-4062-7.ch007

Pellas, N., & Kazanidis, I. (2012). Utilizing and evaluating the virtual world of Second Life for collaborative activities: A primary case study. In C. Karagiannidis, P. Politis, & I. Karasavvidis (Eds.), *Proceedings of the 8th Pan-Hellenic Conference with International Participation ICT in Education*. University of Thessaly.

Pellas, N., & Kazanidis, I. (2013). E-learning quality through Second Life: Exploiting, investigating and evaluating the efficiency parameters of collaborative activities in higher education. In V. Bryan & V. Wang (Eds.), *Technology use and research approaches for community education and professional development* (pp. 250–273). Hershey, PA: IGI Global.

Poldga, H., Valyataga, T., Leinomen, T., Ellonen, A., & Priha, M. (2006). Progress inquiry learning object templates (PILOT). *International Journal on E-Learning, 5*(1), 103–111.

Preece, J. (2000). *Online communities: Designing usability, supporting sociability*. New York: John Wiley & Sons.

Rahikainen, M., Jarvela, S., & Salovaara, H. (2000). Motivational processes in CSILE-based learning. In B. Fishman & S. O'Connor-Divelbiss (Eds.), *Fourth International Conference of the Learning Sciences* (pp. 50-51). Mahwah, NJ: Erlbaum.

Rahikainen, M., Lallimo, J., & Hakkarainen, K. (2001). Progressive inquiry in CSILE environment: Teacher guidance and students' engagement. In P. Dillenbourg, A. Eurelings, & K. Hakkarainen (Eds.), *European Perspectives on Computer-Supported Collaborative Learning: Proceedings of the First European Conference on CSCL* (pp. 520-528). Maastricht, The Netherlands: Maastricht McLuhan Institute.

Resnick, L. B., Pontecorvo, C., Saljo, R., & Burge, B. (1997). Discourse, tools, and reasoning. In L. B. Resnick (Ed.), *Perspectives on socially shared cognition* (pp. 1–20). Washington, DC: Springer Verlag.

Resnick, M. (1996b). Towards a practice of constructional design. In L. Schauble & R. Glaser (Eds.), *Innovations in learning: New environments for education* (pp. 161–174). Mahwah, NJ: Lawrence Erlbaum.

Rickel, J., & Johnson, L. (1997). Mixed-initiative interaction between pedagogy agents and students in virtual environments. *AAAI Technical report SS-97-04,* 128-134.

Rogers, J. (2000). Communities of practice: A framework for fostering coherence in virtual learning communities. *Journal of Educational Technology & Society, 3*(3), 384–392.

Rogoff, B., Radziszewska, B., & Masiello, T. (1995). Analysis of developmental processes in socio-cultural activity. In L. Martin & K. Nelson (Eds.), *Sociocultural psychology: Theory and practice of doing and knowing* (pp. 125–149). New York: Cambridge University Press. doi:10.1017/CBO9780511896828.008

Rovai, A. (2001). Building classroom community at a distance: A case study. *Educational Technology Research and Development Journal, 49*(4), 35–50.

Salomon, G. (1993). No distribution without individual's cognition: A dynamic interaction view. In G. Salomon (Ed.), *Distributed cognitions: Psychological and educational considerations* (pp. 111–138). Cambridge, UK: Cambridge University Press.

Scardamalia, M., & Bereiter, C. (1994). Computer support for knowledge-building communities. *Journal of the Learning Sciences, 3*(3), 265–283. doi:10.1207/s15327809jls0303_3

Scardamalia, M., & Bereiter, C. (1999). Schools as knowledge building organizations. In D. Keating & C. Hertzman (Eds.), *Today's children, tomorrow's society: The developmental health and wealth of nations* (pp. 274–289). New York: Guilford.

Schroeder, R. (2008). Defining virtual worlds and virtual environments. *Virtual Worlds Research: Past, Present & Future, 1*(1). Retrieved from http://www.journals.tdl.org/jvwr/article/download/294/248

Schuler, D. (1996). *New community networks: Wired for change.* New York: Addison Wesley.

Selan dos Santos, R., & Letícia, S. F. (2002). Using a multi-user desktop-based virtual reality system to recreate the São Miguel das Missões ruins. *Cyberpsychology & Behavior, 5*(5), 471–479. doi:10.1089/109493102761022896 PMID:12448784

Sharpe, R., Benfield, G., Roberts, G., & Francis, R. (2006). *The undergraduate experience of blended e-learning: A review of UK literature and practice.* The Higher Education Academy. Retrieved from http://www.heacademy.ac.uk/assets/York/documents/ourwork/research/literature_reviews/blended_elearning_exec_summary_1.pdf

Shea, P., & Bidjerano, T. (2010). Learning presence: Towards a theory of self-efficacy, self-regulation, and the development of a communities of inquiry in online and blended learning environments. *Computers & Education, 55,* 1721–1731. doi:10.1016/j.compedu.2010.07.017

Sherman, W. R., & Craig, A. C. (2003). *Understanding virtual reality–Interface, application, and design.* New York: Elsevier Science.

Slater, M., & Steed, A. (2002). Meeting people virtually: Experiments in shared virtual environments. In R. Schroeder (Ed.), *The Social Life of Avatars* (pp. 145–171). Berlin: Springer. doi:10.1007/978-1-4471-0277-9_9

Stacey, E. (2002). Learning links online: Establishing constructivist and collaborative learning environments. In S. McNamara & E. Stacey (Eds.), *Untangling the web: Establishing learning links*. Retrieved from http://www.aset.org.au/confs/2002/stacey.html

Stahl, G. (2000). A model of collaborative knowledge-building. In B. Fishman & S. O'Connor-Divelbiss (Eds.), *Fourth International Conference of the Learning Sciences* (pp. 70-77). Mahwah, NJ: Erlbaum.

Stahl, G. (2011). The structure of collaborative problem solving in a virtual math team. In Proceedings of iConference 2011 (pp. 606-613). New York: iConference.

Stahl, G. (2012). Cognizing mediating: Unpacking the entanglement of artifacts with collective minds. *IJCSCL, 7*(2). doi:10.1007/s11412-012-9148-x

Stahl, G., Koschmann, T., & Suthers, D. (2006). Computer-supported collaborative learning: An historical perspective. In R. K. Sawyer (Ed.), *Cambridge handbook of the learning sciences* (pp. 409–426). Cambridge, UK: Cambridge University Press.

Steinkuehler, A., & Williams, D. (2006). Where everybody knows your (screen) name: Online games as third places. *Journal of Computer-Mediated Communication, 11*, 885–909. doi:10.1111/j.1083-6101.2006.00300.x

Strohecker, C. (2006). *Embedded microworlds for a multiuser environment (MERL TR95-07)*. Cambridge, MA: Mitsubishi Electric Research Laboratory.

Suthers, D. (2006). Technology affordances for inter-subjective meaning making: A research agenda for CSCL. *International Journal of Computer-Supported Collaborative Learning, 1*(3), 315–337. doi:10.1007/s11412-006-9660-y

Takyana, K., & Wilson, J. (2006). Mapping student learning through toy the collaborative inquiry process: The progressive e-poster. *CALaborate*, 24-32.

Thomas, A., & Storr, C. (2005). WebCT in occupational therapy clinical education: Implementing and evaluating a tool for peer learning and interaction. *Occupational Therapy International, 12*, 162–179. doi:10.1002/oti.3 PMID:16398204

Thomas, R., & Macgregor, K. (2005). Online project-based learning: How collaborative strategies and problem solving processes impact performance. *Journal of Interactive Learning Research, 16*, 83–170.

Thompson, L., Jeffries, M., & Topping, K. (2010). E-mentoring for e-learning development. *Innovations in Education and Teaching International, 47*, 305–315. doi:10.1080/14703297.2010.498182

Thompson, L. F., & Lynch, B. J. (2004). Web-based instruction: Who is inclined to resist it and why? *Journal of Educational Computing Research, 29*, 375–385. doi:10.2190/3VQ2-XTRH-08QV-CAEL

Thurmond, V. A. (2003). Defining interaction and strategies to enhance interactions in Web-based courses. *Nurse Educator, 28*, 237–241. doi:10.1097/00006223-200309000-00013 PMID:14506357

Trentin, G. (2004). E-learning and the third age. *Journal of Computer Assisted Learning, 20*, 21–30. doi:10.1111/j.1365-2729.2004.00061.x

Trushell, J., Byrne, K., & Simpson, R. (2012). Cheating behaviors, the internet and education undergraduate students. *Journal of Computer Assisted Learning, 28*, 136–145. doi:10.1111/j.1365-2729.2011.00424.x

Tsai, C. (2007). The relationship between Internet perceptions and preferences towards Internet-based learning environment. *British Journal of Educational Technology, 38,* 167–170. doi:10.1111/j.1467-8535.2006.00627.x

Tsai, C. (2008). The preferences toward constructivist internet-based learning environments among university students in Taiwan. *Computers in Human Behavior, 24,* 16–31. doi:10.1016/j.chb.2006.12.002

Tsai, C., & Chuang, S. (2005). The correlation between epistemological beliefs and preferences toward Internet-based learning environments. *British Journal of Educational Technology, 36,* 97–100. doi:10.1111/j.1467-8535.2004.00442.x

Tsai, C.-W. (2011). Achieving effective learning effects in the blended course: A combined approach of online self-regulated learning and collaborative learning with initiation. *Cyberpsychology, Behavior, and Social Networking, 14,* 505–510. doi:10.1089/cyber.2010.0388 PMID:21288076

Tsai, C.-W., Shen, P.-D., & Tsai, M.-C. (2011). Developing an appropriate design of blended learning with web-enabled self-regulated learning to enhance students' learning and thoughts regarding online learning. *Behaviour & Information Technology, 30,* 261–271. doi:10.1080/0144929X.2010.514359

Tung, F., & Chang, S. (2007). Exploring adolescents' intentions regarding the online learning courses in Taiwan. *Cyberpsychology & Behavior, 10,* 729–730. doi:10.1089/cpb.2007.9960 PMID:17927546

Turhan, K., Yaris, F., & Nural, E. (2005). Does instructor evaluation by students using a web-based questionnaire impact instructor performance? *Advances in Health Sciences Education : Theory and Practice, 10,* 5–13. doi:10.1007/s10459-004-0943-7 PMID:15912280

Tweddell Levinsen, K. (2007). Qualifying online teachers – Communicative skills and their impact on e-learning quality. *Education and Information Technologies, 12,* 41–51. doi:10.1007/s10639-006-9025-1

Tynjälä, P., & Häkkinen, P. (2005). E-learning at work: Theoretical underpinnings and pedagogical challenges. *Journal of Workplace Learning, 17,* 318–336. doi:10.1108/13665620510606742

Vadillo, M. A., & Matute, H. (2009). Learning in virtual environments: Some discrepancies between laboratory- and Internet-based researches on associative learning. *Computers in Human Behavior, 25,* 402–406. doi:10.1016/j.chb.2008.08.009

van Aalst, J. (2006). Rethinking the nature of online work in synchronous learning networks. *British Journal of Educational Technology, 37,* 279–288. doi:10.1111/j.1467-8535.2006.00557.x

van de Vord, R. (2010). Distance students and online research: Promoting information literacy through media literacy. *The Internet and Higher Education, 13,* 170–175. doi:10.1016/j.iheduc.2010.03.001

Van Joolingen, W., De Jong, T., & Dimitrakopoulou, A. (2005). Issues in computer supported inquiry learning in science. *Journal of Computer Assisted Learning, 23,* 111–119. doi:10.1111/j.1365-2729.2006.00216.x

Vygotsky, L. (1935/1978). *Mind in society: The development of higher psychological processes.* Cambridge, MA: Harvard University Press.

Wang, C.-M., & Reeves, T. C. (2007). Cyberspace and online education: The influences of global cyber culture on international students. In K. Amant (Ed.), *Linguistic and cultural online communication issues in the global age* (pp. 239–252). Hershey, PA: Information Science Reference/IGI Global. doi:10.4018/978-1-59904-213-8.ch015

Wang, H. (2007). Performing a course material enhancement process with asynchronous interactive online system. *Computers & Education, 48,* 567–581. doi:10.1016/j.compedu.2005.03.007

Wang, K. H., Wang, T. H., Wang, W. L., & Huang, S. C. (2006). Learning styles and formative assessment strategy: Enhancing student achievement in web-based learning. *Journal of Computer Assisted Learning, 22,* 207–217. doi:10.1111/j.1365-2729.2006.00166.x

Wang, M.-J. (2010). Online collaboration and offline interaction between students using asynchronous tools in blended learning. *Australasian Journal of Educational Technology, 26,* 830–846.

Wang, S., & Lin, S. (2007). The effects of group composition of self-efficacy and collective efficacy on computer-supported collaborative learning. *Computers in Human Behavior, 23,* 2256–2268. doi:10.1016/j.chb.2006.03.005

Wenger, E. (1991). *Communities of practice: Leaning, meaning and identity.* Cambridge, UK: Cambridge University Press.

Wilson, B., & Myers, K. (2000). Situated cognition in theoretical and practical context. In D. Jonassen & S. Land (Eds.), *Theoretical foundations of learning environments* (pp. 57–67). Hoboken, NJ: Lawrence Erlbaum Associates.

Wilson, V., & Harris, M. (2004). Creating change? A review of the impact of design and technology in schools in England. *Journal of Technology Education, 15,* 46–65.

Yamashita, S. (2006). What makes for effective online community building? 10 field-tested strategies you can use to boost student success. In *Proceedings of World Conference on E-Learning in Corporate, Government, Healthcare, and Higher Education.* Honolulu, HI: IEEE.

Yeh, A., & Nason, R. (2004). *Knowledge construction of 3D geography concepts and processes within a virtual reality learning environment.* Retrieved from http://eprints.qut.edu.au/1382/1/QUTpgconf2003paper.pdf

Yeh, A., & Nason, R. (2004). Knowledge building of 3D geometry concepts and processes within a virtual reality learning environment. In *Proceedings of World Conference on Educational Multimedia, Hypermedia and Telecommunications* (pp. 2175-2182). Orlando, FL: IEEE.

Zhang, J., & Patel, V. L. (2006). Distributed cognition, representation, and affordance. *Pragmatics & Cognition, 14*(2), 333–341. doi:10.1075/pc.14.2.12zha

Zhao, C., & Kuh, G. (2004). Adding value: Learning communities and student engagement. *Research in Higher Education, 45,* 115–138. doi:10.1023/B:RIHE.0000015692.88534.de

ADDITIONAL READING

AitSahlia, F., Johnson, E., & Will, P. (1995). Is concurrent engineering always a sensible proposition? *IEEE Transactions on Engineering Management, 42*(2).

Anthony, R. (1965). *Planning and control systems: A framework for analysis.* Boston: Division of Research, Graduate School of Business Administration, Harvard University.

Beebe, S., & Masterson, J. (2006). *Communicating in small groups principles and practices* (8th ed.). Boston: Pearson Education, Inc.

Blomqvist, E. (2012). *The use of semantic web technologies for decision support - A survey.* Semantic Web Journal.

Bouyssou, D. (2001). Outranking methods. Encyclopedia of Optimization, 4, 249-255.

Bramham, J., Maccarthy, B., & Guinery, J. (2005). Managing product variety in quotation processes. *Journal of Manufacturing Technology Management, 16*(4), 411–431. doi:10.1108/17410380510594507

Brans, J., Vincke, P., & Mareschal, B. (1986). How to select and how to rank projects: The promethee method. *European Journal of Operational Research, 24*(2), 228–238. doi:10.1016/0377-2217(86)90044-5

Branson, L., Clausen, T. S., & Sung, C.-H. (2008). Group style differences between virtual and F2F teams theoretical analysis and anecdotal evidence. *American Journal of Business, 23*(1), 65–70. doi:10.1108/19355181200800005

Buckingham-Shum, S. J. (2006). Sensemaking on the pragmatic web: A hypermedia discourse perspective. In *Proceedings of the 1st International Conference on the Pragmatic Web*. State College, PA: The Pennsylvania State University.

Chen, J., Damanpour, F., & Reilly, R. R. (2010). Understanding antecedents of new product development speed: A meta-analysis. *Journal of Operations Management, 28*, 17–33. doi:10.1016/j.jom.2009.07.001

Cooper, R. (2011). *Winning at new products: Creating value through innovation.* New York: Basic Books.

Cooper, R. G. (2008). Perspective: The stage-gate idea-to-launch process: Update, What's new, and nexgen systems. *Journal of Product Innovation Management, 25*(3), 213–232. doi:10.1111/j.1540-5885.2008.00296.x

Cooper, R. G. (2011). *Winning at new products: Accelerating the process from idea to launch.* Cambridge, MA: Perseus.

Cray, D., Mallory, G. R., Butler, R. J., Hickson, D. J., & Wilson, D. C. (1988). Sporadic, fluid and constricted processes: Three types of strategic decision making in organisations. *Journal of Management Studies, 25*(1), 13–39. doi:10.1111/j.1467-6486.1988.tb00020.x

DeSanctis, G., & Gallupe, R. B. (1987). A foundation for the study of group decision support systems. *Management Science, 33*(5), 589–609. doi:10.1287/mnsc.33.5.589

Eaglestone, B., Lin, A., Nunes, M. B., & Annansingh, F. (2003). Intention and effect of IS solutions: Does risk management stifle creativity? *Journal of Information Science, 29*(4), 269–278. doi:10.1177/01655515030294004

Edmondson, A. (1999). Psychological safety and learning behavior in work teams. *Administrative Science Quarterly, 44*(2), 350–383. doi:10.2307/2666999

Edmondson, A. C. (2008). Managing the risk of learning: Psychological safety in work teams. In *International Handbook of Organizational Teamwork and Cooperative Working* (pp. 255–275). Hoboken, NJ: John Wiley & Sons Ltd. doi:10.1002/9780470696712.ch13

Edmondson, A. C., & Nembhard, I. M. (2009). Product development and learning in project teams: The challenges are the benefits. *Journal of Product Innovation Management, 26*(2), 123–138. doi:10.1111/j.1540-5885.2009.00341.x

Edmondson, A. C., Roberto, M. A., & Watkins, M. D. (2003). A dynamic model of top management team effectiveness: Managing unstructured task streams. *The Leadership Quarterly, 14*(3), 297–325. doi:10.1016/S1048-9843(03)00021-3

Eisenhardt, K., & Tabrizi, B. (1995). Accelerating adaptive processes: Product innovation in the global computer industry. *Administrative Science Quarterly, 40*(1), 84–110. doi:10.2307/2393701

Fabbe-Costes, N., & Jahre, M. (2008). Supply chain integration and performance: A review of the evidence. *The International Journal of Logistics Management, 19*(2), 130–154. doi:10.1108/09574090810895933

Gebert, D., Boerner, S., & Kearney, E. (2010). Fostering team innovation: Why is it important to combine opposing action strategies? *Organization Science, 21*(3), 593–608. doi:10.1287/orsc.1090.0485

Hayes, R., Pisano, G., Upton, D., & Wheelwright, S. (2005). *Operations, strategy, and technology: Pursuing the competitive edge.* Hoboken, NJ: John Wiley and Sons Ltd.

Hickson, D. J., Miller, S. J., & Wilson, D. C. (2003). Planned or prioritized? Two options in managing the implementation of strategic decisions. *Journal of Management Studies, 40*(7), 1803–1836. doi:10.1111/1467-6486.00401

Hornecker, E. (2010). Creative idea exploration within the structure of a guiding framework: The card brainstorming game. In *Proceedings of the Fourth International Conference on Tangible, Embedded, and Embodied Interaction* (pp. 101-108). New York: ACM.

Janis, I. L. (1971). Groupthink. *Psychology Today, 5*(6), 43–46.

Johansen, R., & Bullen, C. (1988). *Computer-supported cooperative work: A Book of readings.* San Francisco, CA: Morgan Kaufmann Publishers Inc.

Johansson, C., Hicks, B., Larsson, A. C., & Bertoni, M. (2011). Knowledge maturity as a means to support decision making during product-service systems development projects in the aerospace sector. *Project Management Journal, 42*(2), 32–50.

Karacapilidis, N., & Papadias, D. (2001). Computer supported argumentation and collaborative decision making: The hermes system. *Information Systems, 26*, 259–277. doi:10.1016/S0306-4379(01)00020-5

Kessler, E. H., & Chakrabarti, A. K. (1996). Innovation speed: a conceptual model of context, antecedents, and outcomes. *Academy of Management Review*, 1143–1191.

Krishnan, V., & Ulrich, K. T. (2001). Product development decisions: A review of the literature. *Management Science*, 1–21. doi:10.1287/mnsc.47.1.1.10668

Kunz, W., & Rittel, H. (1970). *Issues as elements of information systems.* Berkeley, CA: Center for Planning and Development Research, University of California at Berkeley.

MacCarthy, B., & Atthirawong, W. (2003). Factors affecting location decisions in international operations--A delphi study. *International Journal of Operations & Production Management, 23*(7), 794–818. doi:10.1108/01443570310481568

Mankins, J. C. (2009). Technology readiness assessments: A retrospective. *Acta Astronautica, 65*(9-10), 1216–1223. doi:10.1016/j.actaastro.2009.03.058

Mintzberg, H., Raisinghani, D., & Theoret, A. (1976). The structure of unstructured decision processes. *Administrative Science Quarterly, 21*(2), 246–275. doi:10.2307/2392045

Nunamaker, J. F., Applegate, L. M., & Konsynski, B. R. (1987). Facilitating group creativity: Experience with a group decision support system. *Journal of Management Information Systems, 3*(4), 5–19.

Paulk, M. C., Curtis, B., Chrissis, M. B., & Weber, C. V. (1993). *Capability maturity model for software, version 1.1*. Pittsburgh, PA: Carnegie Mellon University.

Power, D. J. (2004). Specifying an expanded framework for classifying and describing decision support systems. *Communications of the Association for Information Systems, 13*(1).

Ramesh, B. (1999). Supporting collaborative process knowledge management in new product development teams. *Decision Support Systems, 27*(1-2), 213–235. doi:10.1016/S0167-9236(99)00045-7

Rittel, H., & Webber, M. (1973). Dilemmas in a general theory of planning. *Policy Sciences, 4*(2), 155–169. doi:10.1007/BF01405730

Saaksvuori, A., & Immonen, A. (2002). *Product lifecycle management*. Berlin: Springer-Verlag.

Schmidt, J. B., Montoya-Weiss, M. M., & Massey, A. P. (2001). New product development decision-making effectiveness: Comparing individuals, face-to-face teams, and virtual teams. *Decision Sciences, 32*(4), 575–600. doi:10.1111/j.1540-5915.2001.tb00973.x

Simon, H. A. (1977). *The new science of management decision*. Upper Saddle River, NJ: Prentice Hall PTR.

Spanjol, J., Tam, L., Qualls, W., & Bohlmann, J. (2011). New product team decision making: Regulatory focus effects on number, type, and timing decisions. *Journal of Product Innovation Management, 28*(5), 623–640.

Turner, M. E., & Pratkanis, A. R. (1998). Twenty-five years of groupthink theory and research: Lessons from the evaluation of a theory. *Organizational Behavior and Human Decision Processes, 73*(2/3), 105–115. doi:10.1006/obhd.1998.2756 PMID:9705798

Valle, S., & Vázquez-Bustelo, D. (2009). Concurrent engineering performance: Incremental versus radical innovation. *International Journal of Production Economics, 119*(1), 136–148. doi:10.1016/j.ijpe.2009.02.002

Warkentin, M., Sayeed, L., & Hightower, R. (1997). Virtual teams versus face to face teams: An exploratory study of a web-based conference system. *Decision Sciences, 28*(4), 975–996. doi:10.1111/j.1540-5915.1997.tb01338.x

Weick, K. E. (1993). The collapse of sensemaking in organizations: The Mann Gulch disaster. *Administrative Science Quarterly, 38*(4). doi:10.2307/2393339

Wheelwright, S., & Clark, K. (1992). *Revolutionizing product development: Quantum leaps in speed, efficiency, and quality*. New York: Free Press.

KEY TERMS AND DEFINITIONS

E-Learning 2.0: The term "e-learning 2.0" is a "neologism" for distributed collaborative learning through PCs & Web-based technologies ([D-] CSCL), using the Web 2.0. This definition has begun for the initial transformation of conventional distance learning systems, which are used widely through the Internet. Unlike that of the application of "traditional" e-learning, the impulse that gives us this new generation of e-learning, focusing on cooperation and the social production of knowledge. However, it is useful to mention that e-learning and e-learning 2.0, is a single bit of distance learning.

Multi-User Dimensions (MUDs): MUDs began to make their appearance in the early '90s, providing network support to games-playing, in a wide range of users worldwide. The continued use of partitioning-infinite imaginary world and the global mass turnout of users to servers such games were the reason for the genesis of many virtual worlds beyond.

Multi-User Virtual Environments (MUVE's): Virtual multi-user environments and are the continuation of MUDs. Also are found in the literature with the term "Networked Virtual Environments" (NVE) or "virtual worlds" (VWs) where users are dispersed spatially and temporally to interact with others and in a common place in real time.

Open Simulator (OS Grid): OS grid is characterized as a multi-functional server or multi-user 3D distributed virtual environment platform. It frequently recapitulates the "equipment" one of the most well-known simulated virtual environments, like those of Second Life (SL). The "open-ended" architecture of this world can be used as a social virtual world or for specific applications such as education, training, and visualization.

Scaffolding: An instructional technique involving the provision of supportive assistance or learning guidance, particularly when they are first introduced to new concepts and skills, with the aim of limiting the complexities of the learning context. It comes from Vygotsky's "Zone of Proximal Development" (ZPD). This concept refers to the gap between learners' current knowledge and also with the ability level (i.e. what they can perform without assistance) and his/her emerging or potential knowledge and ability level (i.e. what he or she can be challenged to accomplish with assistance in the form of scaffolding).

Simulation Linked Object Oriented Dynamic Learning Environment (Sloodle): It is an open source project, which integrates multiuser environment to that of SL Moodle, especially for the management of learning. It provides a set of tools that are embedded in web-based learning management system and can be used by teachers. Sloodle integrates a multi-user environment in the Second Life environment Moodle. Through its commitment to an active community of developers and users, the Sloodle project hopes to develop valid and workable pedagogy for teaching Web-based 3D virtual learning environments.

Web 2.0: Most experts talk about a new way of web design which is based on user interaction, allowing the user to change the environment, according to his demands and needs. Typical applications of Web 2.0 are social networking media, such as wikis and weblogs. Many of the commands of interactions that characterize the operation of Web 2.0 are already known from various social networking sites like Facebook or YouTube.

This work was previously published in Collaborative Communication Processes and Decision Making in Organizations edited by Ephraim Nikoi and Kwasi Boateng, pages 72-107, copyright year 2014 by Business Science Reference (an imprint of IGI Global).

Chapter 73

Librarian without Building in an E–Learning Environment:
Needed Skills, Challenges, and Solutions

Jerome Idiegbeyan-Ose
Covenant University – Canaan Land, Nigeria

Ugwunwa Chinyere Esse
Covenant University – Canaan Land, Nigeria

ABSTRACT

This chapter discusses e-learning, its advantages and challenges, the concept of a librarian without a building, and the characteristics and skills of a librarian without a building in an e-learning environment. The chapter empirically looks at the need for an e-librarian in an e-learning environment, the needed skills for such a librarian, and their challenges. Possible solutions to identify challenges are also discussed. The survey method was used for the study; the questionnaire was designed and administered to 138 librarians from Academic libraries in the six geo-political zones of Nigeria. 127 questionnaires were returned and used for analysis. The study reveals that there is a great need for e-librarians in e-learning environments, and that the librarians must possess such skills as high computer literacy, ability to learn fast, teach, and evaluate others. It was also discovered that e-librarians are faced with technical, administrative, financial, and capacity building challenges. Based on these, the authors recommend that e-librarians should be supported at all levels; they should be ready to develop themselves, strive at all cost to acquire more knowledge and skills in order to stand the changing nature of their job. It is also recommended that government agencies that accredit programmes at tertiary institutions should make sure that any institution that offers e-learning must also have a well organized e-library, and a well trained e-librarian must man the library. The study concludes that e-library and e-librarian without building must be recognized and empowered as part of the e-teaching and learning processes.

DOI: 10.4018/978-1-4666-8619-9.ch073

INTRODUCTION

Education is the bedrock of any nation. No nation can develop without proper and effective educational systems. Libraries from the ancient time to present day are always part of any educational system. No educational system can be effective without library as supporting instrument. With the advent of Information and Communication Technologies in education, E- learning platforms have been created to provide students with the opportunity to continue their education and career development without the rigidity and rigorous life of the school system. The creation of the E-learning platforms has placed additional roles on the library and the librarian whose responsibility will now include rendering services to the E-learners. Thus the concept of E- library, Virtual library, and E- librarian, librarian without building come to place.

In the last few decades, the world has gone through significant change in terms of advancements in technology and the information exchange. These advancements in information and communication technology have led to e-learning becoming a focus of global attention. E-learning", in simple terms, is Electronic Learning or any learning facilitated by electronic means which would include computer-based training (CBT) with modules, CD-ROM training, web-enabled, and Internet learning. Advent of E-learning has provided students with an opportunity to continue their education or personal pursue and career development without the rigidity and rigorous life of the school environment. This online format of Learning, offers the students a great deal of flexibility in terms of when they study, how they study, and how quickly they cover and master any given material.

OBJECTIVES OF THE STUDY

The objectives of the study are to find out:

1. Whether there is need for E- Librarian in an E- Learning environment.
2. The skills that would be needed by librarian in an E- Learning environment.
3. The challenges of E-librarian in an E-Learning environment.
4. Prefer solution to the challenges.

BACKGROUND

Over the years, there have been conflicts in the definitions of E-Learning; some authors have explicitly defined e-learning, others have implied a specific definition, but these definitions have materialize, some through conflicting views of other definitions, and some just by simply comparing defining characteristics with other existing terms. Ellis (2004) disagrees with authors like Nichols (2003) who defined e-Learning as strictly gaining access to knowledge using technological tools that are web-based, web-distributed, or web-capable. Ellis believes that e-Learning does not only cover content and instructional methods delivered via CD-ROM, the Internet or an Intranet. Tavangarian, D., Leypold, M. E., Nolting, K., Roser, M., & Voigt, D. (2004), stated that e- Learning is not only procedural but also shows some transformation of an individual's experience into the individual's knowledge through the knowledge construction process. Ellis (2004) and Triacca, L., Bolchini, D., Botturi, L., & Inversini, A. (2004) believe that some level of interactivity needs to be included to make the definition truly applicable in describing the learning experience, even though Triacca et al. (2004) added that e- Learning was a type of online learning. However, some authors have made reference to other terms such as online course/learning, web-based learning, web-based training, learning objects or distance learning believing that the terms can be used synonymously (Dringus & Cohen, 2005; Khan, 2001; Triacca et al., 2004; Wagner, 2001). Clark & Mayer, (2003), states that E-learning can be defined as instruction delivered via a computer that is intended to promote learning.

E-learning is a term that means something different to almost everyone who uses it. Some use it to refer to packaged content pieces and others to technical infrastructures. Some think only of asynchronous self-study while others realize e-learning can encompass synchronous learning and collaboration. Almost all also agree that E-Learning is an effective method that should be blended into current learning mix. So what is e-learning? According to Marc Rosenberg (2001) "E-Learning refers to the use of internet technologies to deliver a broad array of solutions that enhance knowledge and performance. It is based on three fundamental criteria:

- E-Learning is networked; which makes it capable of instant updating, storage / retrieval, distribution and sharing of instruction or information.
- It is delivered to the end user via a computer using a standard internet technology.
- It focuses on the broadest view of learning – learning solutions that go beyond the traditional paradigms of training.

In this context, we will consider E-learning as the use of new multimedia technologies and the internet to improve the quality of learning by facilitating access to resources and services as well as remote exchange and collaboration. E-learning is an umbrella that covers learning almost anytime, anywhere on a computer, connected to a network. E-learning isn't expected to replace the known conventional methods of training which is the classroom teaching; it is expected to create an augmented learning environment where technology is used to deliver a combination of teaching techniques and also aiming to maximize the participation and learning process of the individual.

Education is an important component of life because it equips us with all that is needed to make our dreams come true. One of the most promising paradigms for education is e-learning. It is commonly referred to the intentional use of networked information and communications technology (ICT) in teaching and learning. Some other terms are also used to describe this mode of teaching and learning including online learning, virtual learning, distributed learning, network and web-based learning. Since the last decade, there is a growing interest in e-learning from several directions. The growth of E-learning is directly related to the increasing access to ICT, as well as its decreasing cost. The capacity of ICT to support multimedia resource-based learning and teaching is also relevant to the growing interest in e-learning. Growing numbers of teachers are increasingly using ICT to support their teaching. Educational organizations see advantages in making their programs accessible via a range of distributed locations, including on campus, home and other community learning or resource centres. With ICT, the dream of learning anywhere and at anytime has become true. Gray Harriman (2010) states that there are different types of E-Learning resources:

- **Online Learning:** This is learning that takes place via the Web and may include text, graphics, animation, audio, video, discussion boards, e-mail, and testing. Online learning is typically "on demand" and self-directed but may include synchronous chat, web based teleconferencing (audio graphics), or similar technology.
- **Distance Learning:** This is learning that takes place when the instructor and the learner are not in the same physical location. It can also take place if the instructor and the learner are in the same location but not at the same time. Today distance learning is carried out via a number of media ranging from postal mail to teleconferencing or the Internet. "Distance Learning"

(learner focus) and "distance education" (instructor focus) are often used as interchangeable terms.

- **Blended Learning:** This combines online with face-to-face learning. The goal of blended learning is to provide the most efficient and effective instruction experience by combining delivery modalities. The term "blended learning" is used to describe a solution that combines several different delivery methods, such as collaboration software, Web-based courses, Electronic performance support systems (EPSS), and knowledge management practices. Blended learning also is used to describe learning that mixes various event based activities, including face-to-face classrooms, live E-Learning, and self-paced instruction.

- **M-Learning:** The term M-Learning or Mobile Learning refers to the use of handheld devices such as PDAs, mobile phones, laptops and any other handheld information technology device that can be used in teaching and learning.

We are all familiar with classroom-based learning which is face-to-face group learning led by an Instructor/Teacher. In E-learning environments, learners interact with learning materials, their instructors and other learners from various locations and often at various times using networked communication technology gadgets. So by its nature, E -learning offers significant flexibility as to when and how learning occurs. E-learning can include independent, facilitated, or collaborative approaches to learning. Independent learning refers to each individual learner completing learning activities or modules on their own, in their own environment, on their own schedule. The learner is independent of an instructor/teacher and the other learners. This does not mean that the learner does not have access to other resources such as an instructor/teacher, but the learner is in control of whether they contact them, when they

contact them, and for what. E-learning intersects numerous fields of thought and practice such as training and education, learning and knowledge and technology. It is essentially the computer and network-enabled transfer of skills and knowledge, which include applications and processes such as Web-based learning, computer-based learning, virtual education opportunities and digital collaboration. E-learning can therefore be categorized into two main groups: synchronous and asynchronous. With synchronous e-learning, students can be involved in a course that meets online with the faculty member through streaming audio and video at a predetermined time. With asynchronous learning, a student can participate in the learning activities at the most suitable time for him or her but this also means that the faculty member will not be available for immediate replies.

SYNCHRONOUS E-LEARNING

Synchronous training is a real-time method of e-Learning with live interaction between the instructors and the students. It is called such because students have to log in at a specified time and the classes will be held for a specified period of time. Lessons can take the form of single sessions to several sessions over a few years. Synchronous training is the e-Learning method that is nearest to classroom-style learning as students can raise their 'electronic hands', view a common blackboard and interact with each other. Synchronized training sessions are usually held in AV conferencing media, websites or internet telephony media Synchronous learning comes to the rescue of students facing geographical barriers, by aiding face to face interactions with the instructor. It has been observed that most learners find it difficult to learn without real time conversation with either the instructor or peers. This interaction, combined with access to web based courseware, augments comprehension. But, an in-depth look at the process reveals that synchronous learning has only been able to remove the physical barriers without actually adding much value to the traditional classroom based training. It supports all the learning methods that conventional learning hails, only with an added advantage of a wider student base.

ASYNCHRONOUS E-LEARNING

Asynchronous learning is learning that takes place independent of time and space. Learners are able to interact with course materials and with each other at a time of their choice. A discussion thread is an example of an asynchronous learning. One learner can post a thought, and hours (or days) later, another learner can comment on the posting. Asynchronous learning gives E-learning much of its appeal. Traditionally, students needed to be physically present to engage in learning with other students. Now, learners can engage each other when it is most convenient and a knowledge trail of discussions is left. In synchronous learning, the discussion vanishes (unless it is recorded and indexed) but asynchronously, students that are trailing behind in course work still receive the benefit of being able to read discussion posts. Asynchronous learning frees E-learning from the requirements of time and space. This is perhaps the most revolutionary aspect of e-learning. Learners across different time zones and different continents can now participate in the same courses. Content can be explored and discussed in great depth -allowing learners the time to reflect and formulate thoughtful responses. Asynchronous tools like email and discussion forums have transformed how people communicate and share knowledge.

Asynchronous training may include computer-based training, using CD-ROMs and more frequently web-based training (in which a trainee logs into an online training system with a user name and password to begin an interactive course). The course can be easily updated, is accessible from anywhere and can be used with all kinds of computer systems. This type of training is most suitable to structured content-questions that have right and wrong answers. The content may vary according to circumstances. An example of structured content would be a series of steps to be followed in formatting a document in a particular computer program. The asynchronous environment is most appropriate for those who learn best by thinking about content on their own, and who can structure their time to accommodate instruction.

E-LEARNING TOOLS

Virtual Learning Environments/Learning Management Systems: These are web applications that run on a server and are accessed via a web browser (Internet Explorer, Firefox, Safari, etc.) They are designed to assist with the delivery and organization of courses. They often contain discussion forums, chat areas, areas for delivering content, tests, quizzes and grade books. Courses can be delivered entirely online but by and large, courses are 'blended'; traditional lectures and seminars supported and enhanced by use of a Virtual Learning Environments.

Virtual Learning Environments generally have two ways of being viewed; as a student or as a teacher/instructor. The student view shows the courses the student is enrolled in and all the relevant material for those courses. The teacher/instructor view allows materials to be created, added and edited. Teachers/Instructors don't need to know about web design in order to use a Virtual Learning Environments as they include all the features required in one relatively easy to use package.

Blackboard Learning Technology: This helps you make learning more effective in and beyond the traditional walls. Breathing life into educational content, bringing efficiency to day-to-day tasks, empowering instructors with tools to engage every learner, motivating them on the devices they rely on, promoting collaboration and streamlining processes.

Moodle is a course management system (CMS): A software package designed to help educators create quality online courses and manage learner outcomes. Moodle is Open Source software, which means you are free to download it, use it, modify it and even distribute it. Moodle has features that allow it to scale to very large deployments and hundreds of thousands of students. Many institutions use it as their platform to conduct fully online courses, while some use it simply to augment face-to-face courses (known as blended learning). It has been discovered that many of Moodle users love to use the activity modules (such as forums, databases and wikis) to build richly collaborative communities of learning around their subject matter (in the social constructionist tradition), while others prefer to use Moodle as a way to deliver content to students and assess learning using assignments or quizzes.

ADVANTAGES OF E-LEARNING

E-learning is beneficial to education, organizations and to all types of learners. It is affordable, saves time, and produces measurable results. E-learning is more cost effective than traditional learning because less time and money is spent travelling. Since e-learning can be done in any geographic location and there are no travel expenses, this type of learning is much less costly than doing learning at a traditional class room. Flexibility is a major benefit of e-learning. E-learning has the advantage of taking class anytime anywhere.

Education is available when and where it is needed. E-learning can be done at the office, at home, on the road, 24 hours a day, and seven days a week.. E-learning also has measurable assessments which can be created so that both the teachers and students will know what the students have learned, when they've completed courses, and how they have performed. E-learning accommodates different types of learning styles. Students have the advantage of learning at their own pace.

Students can also learn through a variety of activities that apply to the many different learning styles available. Learners can fit E-learning into their busy schedule. If they hold a job, they can still be working with e-learning. If the learner needs to do the learning at night, the option is available. Learners can sit in their home and do the learning if they so desire. E-learning encourages students to peruse through information by using hyperlinks and sites on the worldwide Web. Students are able to find information relevant to their personal situations and interest.

E-learning allows students to select learning materials that meet their level of knowledge, interest and what they need to know to perform more effectively in an activity. E-learning is more focused on the learner and it is more interesting for the learner because it is information that they want to learn. E-learning is flexible and can be customized to meet the individual needs of the learners'; learning helps students develop knowledge of the Internet. This knowledge will help learners throughout their careers.

E-learning encourages students to take personal responsibility for their own learning. When learners succeed, it builds self-knowledge and self-confidence in them. Educators and Universities really benefit from E-learning. Students enjoy having the opportunity to learn at their own pace, on their own time, and have it less costly.

PROBLEMS OF E-LEARNING

For the student, several disadvantages exist in the virtual classroom. According to Burbles (2004) there are "hidden barriers to access" of a virtual classroom to students; there are limitations to making an online course accessible to all. Some communication tools may not suit some students; for example, the streaming of audio cannot be heard by a hearing impaired student and thus this tool is not accessible to all. Another disadvantage of the virtual classroom is that it can only be successful if the communication tools used in the classroom are "in the student's possession, accessible to the student (and) operable by the student" (Lehmann, 2004). Although synchronous communication tools are usually perceived as an advantage because of their similarity to communication in the traditional classroom, they can also be a disadvantage. This is because they consist of real-time, text-based communication in which responses are often "out of sequence" as a consequence of varying typing abilities among students (Fetterman, D., 1998). Students must have adequate typing skills and communication skills as the majority of learning is text-based and self-paced, and if they are used to being in a structured, scheduled environment, they will be disadvantaged and most likely get confused and fall behind.

Teachers are not as readily available in the virtual classroom as they are in the traditional classroom, therefore students who usually need continual support of the teacher may feel isolated. The fact that there are technological requirements to enable full participation in the virtual classroom is also another disadvantage to students. For example, if the student does not have a high bandwidth and adequate computer memory needed to access the internet and hence the virtual classroom as well as download course material, they will be disadvantaged. Also, the technological dependence of the virtual classroom can be a disadvantage if there is an internet connection failure or a similar technological problem that prevents students to complete a task. If there is no "back up plan" in the case of a technological hindrance, students will miss out on the learning activity that was scheduled.

Difficulties with software: The disadvantage of E-learning is the managing of computer files, software compatibility and learning new software, including e-Learning. For learners with beginner-level computer skills, it can sometimes seem complex to keep their computer files organized. The lesson points you to download a file which the learner does and later he or she may not find the file. The file is downloaded to the folder the computer automatically opens to, rather than a folder chosen by the learner. This file may be lost or misplaced to the learner without good computer organizational skills. In our institution, the students have the requisite level of working with the computers and the software platform, which they acquire in a first course in the discipline of Informatics.

High motivation: E-Learning also requires time to complete especially those with assignments and interactive collaborations. This means that students have to be highly motivated and responsible because all the work they do is on their own. Learners with low motivation may not complete modules.

Isolation: Another disadvantage of E-learning is that students may feel isolated and unsupported while learning. Instructions are not always available to help the learner so learners need to have discipline to work independently without assistance. E-Learners may also become bored with no interaction. It needs to be stressed that blended learning is not just a mixture of strategies and technologies, but a holistic didactical method that combines "the effectiveness and socialization opportunities of the classroom with the technologically enhanced active learning possibilities of the online environment, rather than ratio of delivery modalities" (Dziuban, Hartman, Moskal, 2004). By applying blended learning, we overcome some proven disadvantages for both form of education - distance e-learning and traditional class room learning. All collaborative learning theory contends that human interaction is a vital ingredient to learning. Consideration of this is particularly crucial when designing e-learning, realizing the potential for the medium to isolate learners. With well-delivered synchronous distance education, and technology like message boards, chats, e-mail, and tele-conferencing, this potential drawback is reduced.

However, E-learning detractors still argue that the magical classroom bond between teacher and student, and among the students themselves, cannot be replicated through communications technology. Kruse (2004) outlined the following ways in which e-learning may not excel over other methods of training:

- Technology issues of the learners are most commonly technophobia and unavailability of required technologies.

- Portability of training has become strength of e-learning with the proliferation of network linking points, notebook computers, PDAs, and mobile phones, but still does not rival that of printed workbooks or reference material.

- Reduced social and cultural interaction can be a drawback. The impersonality, suppression of communication mechanisms such as body language, and elimination of peer-to-peer learning that are part of this potential disadvantage are lessening with advances in communications technologies.

CONTEMPORARY TRENDS IN E-LEARNING AND WHAT IT AFFORDS

The growing interest in e-learning seems to be coming from several directions. These include Educational institutions that have traditionally offered distance education programs either in a single, dual setting. They see the incorporation of online learning in their repertoire as a logical extension of their distance education activities.

The growth of e-learning is directly related to the increasing access to information and communications technology, as well as its decreasing cost. The capacity of information and communications technology to support multimedia resource-based learning and teaching is also relevant to the growing interest in e-learning. Growing numbers of teachers are increasingly using information

and communications technology to support their teaching. The contemporary student population (often called the "Net Generation", or "Millennials") who have grown up using information and communications technology also expect to see it being used in their educational experiences (Brown, J. S., Collins, A., & Duguid, P. (2005).).

A key attribute of information and communications technology is its ability to enable flexible access to information and resources. Flexible access refers to access and use of information and resources at a time, place and pace that are suitable and convenient to individual learners rather than the teacher and/or the educational institution. Access to information and communication technologies offers a range of possibilities for capturing and delivering all types of subject matter content to learners and teachers in distributed educational settings. This means access to subject matter content and learning resources via networked information and communications technologies across a range of settings such as conventional classrooms, workplaces, homes, and various forms of community centers (Dede, 2000).

Contemporary educational institutions, including conventional distance education providers, often pride themselves in being able to meet the learning needs of their students and staff at a time, place and pace that are most convenient to them. They have been able to do this with the help of information and communications technologies which afford learners access to up-to-date information as and when they need them, and also the opportunity to discuss this information with their peers and teachers at their convenience. This is becoming increasingly affordable and palatable with a wide range of software applications and computer conferencing technologies for collaborative inquiry among students and asynchronous discussion. These applications enable learners and teachers to engage in synchronous as well as asynchronous interaction across space, time, and pace.

CONCEPT OF LIBRARIAN WITHOUT BUILDING

The concept of Librarian without building is not new in the 21st century libraries. The dawn of this century witnessed a dramatic change in the information profession. The beginning of this century witnessed revolution in the library environment. The concept of digital, virtual, electronic, library, library without wall/building and so on, had made it important for librarians to be in charge of these libraries. Hence we now have the concept digital librarian, virtual librarian, electronic librarian, librarian without wall or building and so on.

Libraries are changing from traditional librarianship with books, journals, catalogue cabinet with cards, shelves loaded with books to E-libraries with e-books and e-journals, OPAC database and so on. So also librarians are changing and adding more value from traditional librarianship to E-librarianship/librarian without building. With the advent of new fields of study and the emergence of virtual learning (E-Learning), there are additional demands for libraries and librarians. Faculty scholarship and student's learning will suffer in an e-learning environment without e-learning librarian (Digital Librarian/ virtual librarian/Librarian without building).

All over the world, E-learning has become integral feature of higher education, and no educational system can succeed without library; it is always said that library is the heart of any institution. Therefore for an E-learning system to survive, there must be functional E- library and for any E- library to function, there must be an E- librarian (Librarian without building) manning it. Rowley (1998) cited Oppenheim (1997) who described library without building as an organized and managed collection of information in a variety of media in digital format. The materials are organized and managed for the benefit of actual and potential user population. Trolley (1995) posits that library without building or electronic library is the vision of librarians, publishers, technology experts and researchers on how users can have access to information anytime anywhere.

Pujar and Kamat (2009) explained that E- Librarians support access to crucial resources in an E- learning environment. The E- Librarian organizes online tools to provide metadata for online materials for the E- learners, and E-teachers in the following areas: E- resources, content management, Digital library/ Institutional Repository, Courseware, Digital/ Virtual Reference Services, Electronic Discussion Forums, and so on. Librarian can provide access to various services to the E-Learners and E- teachers in an E-learning environment. E-Librarians make access and use of e-resources easier and faster because of the traditional skills which the librarian had acquired. Such skills include ability to select, acquire, organize, disseminate and preserve the right information materials for the right user. Livonen (2005) opined that the E-librarian makes easy and fast access to electronic resources for E-Learning environment.

Gunn (2002) explained that E-libraries are designed to support the information needs of their communities (E-learners and teachers). They offer resources from many sources and in many formats to the E-learners and E-teachers. They make information resources available to the users anytime and anywhere there is an internet Connection. Nfila,(2013) opines that Digital Librarian/ E-librarian is also linked to e-learning; they provide technology based information and services to enable the E- teachers and E-learners to access relevant information and services anywhere, anytime as well as provide empowerment for innovative and lifelong teaching and learning. This enables the e- learners and e- teachers to undertake learning and research at their convenient.

CHARACTERISTICS AND SKILLS OF LIBRARIAN WITHOUT BUILDING IN AN E- LEARNING ENVIRONMENT

E- Learning as earlier defined is a process of using technology to deliver learning and training programme. Such technology includes computers, internet, intranet, wireless, CD-ROM and so on. It implies web-based learning, computer based learning, virtual learning, virtual classroom. It is the delivery of content via internet, intranet/extranet (LAN/WAN). It implies any learning that utilizes a network (LAN/WAN) for delivery, interaction and facilitation. In order for the virtual Librarian (V L) or Librarian without building (LWB) to assist patrons in making the most of innovations in an e-learning environment, he or she keep one step or more ahead in the knowledge and uses of online materials.

The librarian without building in an e-learning environment must have some understanding of the operation of personal computer (PC), this will help him to cope in a situation where there are technical problems while in the middle of reference or research project, librarian without building must have understanding on how to troubleshoot and also how to solve the most common and occurring problems. He must have knowledge of the working of a PC, such as PC repair, hardware and software installation and maintenance. He must also have understanding of computer networking. The bottom line is that the virtual librarian or librarian without building must be multi-skilled. Traditional librarianship skills are needed, technical skills are needed, managerial skills are also needed if he she must succeed in an e-learning environment and in this information age. The librarian without building must have all the knowledge and skills required to practice as a professional librarian; in addition, he must have knowledge of HTML/XML, library software and applications, license and contract

negotiation, knowledge of electronic academic publishing, knowledge of copyright, knowledge of TCP/IP, Z39.50, Library 2.0, catalogue 2.0.

He must have the drive to learn and continue learning. Clearly he will be facing a career that is full of challenges and surprises. The combination of all these skills which are very necessary in the running of a virtual Library is what will determine the success or failure of the Virtual Librarian. These skills will help the Virtual Librarian or librarian without building in an e-learning environment to enjoy a long and rewarding career. Librarians that will manage the library without building must be very educated, experienced, intelligent and resourceful. Somvir, (2010) is of the view that librarians in the 21st century must train and retrain themselves and should stop having in mind that their employer has the full responsibility of training and retraining them. They must keep on updating their knowledge and skills in order to meet up with the challenges of the E learning environment. These librarians are technology application leaders who work with other members of the information management team to make information accessible to users. Hashim and Mokhtar (2012) explained that librarian without building in the 21st century libraries in an E- learning environment are knowledge based practitioners who use research as a foundation for their own professional practice.

CARL(2010) listed the following as the competences that is required of the librarian that will manage the 21st century libraries.

- Expert knowledge of the content of information resources.
- Excellent instruction and support for library and information service users.
- Appropriate information technology to acquire, organize and disseminate information.

- Skills to evaluate the outcome of information use and conduct research related to the solution of information management problems.
- Effective communication skills

These librarians are also expected to be engaged in the exploration and implementation of new technologies needed to match with the present patrons, most of whom have become technologically savvy in the use of ICT. They must possess high level of information literacy skills, as well as knowledge of the principles and techniques of effective reference services. Librarians without building in an E- learning environment must be knowledgeable in integrated library system (ILS) web technologies such as web 2.0, twitter, face book, my space, OPAC 2.0 etc. They must also have knowledge of data management.

A librarian without building that will function in an E- Learning environment must function as a dynamic filter, who filters and take up the role of balancing the information need and use of the E- learners. Therefore, librarian without building must embrace continuous learning, not only of technology but also new ways of providing effective and efficient services to the E- Learners and E- Teachers. Such librarians must contextualized the library where he/she work and the type of work that needs to be done. (Chu, Felix T. 2003)

STATEMENT OF THE PROBLEM

The advent of ICTs in Education that led to the Introduction of E-learning, E-teaching and E-Education has brought on board the concept of E-Library, E-Librarians or Library without building. This is because education and libraries are always together; no education system can achieve its aims and objectives without libraries as partners. This is because libraries are the heart of the education systems; they provide information resources that support the teaching and learning process and they

provide the resources that support the instruction curriculum. The problem now is that, with the introduction of ICTs in education, teaching and Libraries, there are additional tasks that are required from the librarians without building in order for them to function in an e-learning environment. Then, what are the skills and knowledge that will be required from them and how can they acquire the needed skills and knowledge to support the E-learning system, these are some of the problems this chapter attempts to address.

Research Questions.

Is there need for E-librarian without building in an E-Learning Environment?

1. What are the needed skills by Librarian without building in an E-Learning environment?
2. What are the challenges of librarian without building in an E-Learning environment?
3. What are the solutions to the challenges of Librarian without building in an E-Learning environment?

METHODOLOGY

Survey research design was used for this study. Questionnaire was the instrument for data collection; the questionnaire was designed and administered to 138 librarians in Nigerian academic libraries. Random sampling method was used and 23 questionnaires were administered in each of the six geo-political zones in Nigeria (University libraries, Polytechnic Libraries and Colleges of education libraries). Out of the 138 questionnaires administered, 127 was returned and found useable and were used for data analysis and this represents 92.0% response rate. The data were analyzed using frequency, percentages and tables methods.

Table 1 shows the different institutions which the respondents are affiliated to. From the above table, it can be deduced that 69 respondents rep-

Table 1. Affiliation of respondents

Affiliation of Respondents	Frequency	Percentage
University	69	54.3%
Polytechnic	35	27.6%
College of Education	23	18.1%
Total	127	100%

Table 2. Does your institution offer e-learning

Does Your Institution Offer E-Learning	Frequency	Percentage
Yes	127	100%
No	Nil	Nil
Total	127	100%

Table 3. Does your institution have e- library for e- learners

Does your Institution have E- Library for E- Learners	Frequency	Percentage
Yes	127	100%
No	Nil	Nil
Total	127	100%

Table 4. There is need for e- librarian in an e- learning environment?

There is need for E- Librarian in an E- Learning Environment?	Frequency	Percentage
Strongly Agree	118	92.9%
Agree	9	07.1%
Un- Decided	Nil	Nil
Disagree	Nil	Nil
Strongly Disagree	Nil	Nil
Total	127	100%

Table 5. Skills needed by librarian without building to functions in an e- learning environment

Skills Needed by E- Librarian to Functions in an E- Learning Environment	Frequency	Percentage
High Computer Knowledge and Skills	127	100%
Knowledge of various Databases	123	96.7%
Multi Skilled	127	100%
Highly Intelligent	127	100%
Ability to learn very fast	96	75.6%
Good communication skills	83	65.4%
Evaluation skills	127	100%
Ability to teach others	122	96.1%

resenting 54.3% are from universities, 35 respondents representing 27.6% are from polytechnics, while 23 respondents representing 18.1% are from colleges of education.

Table 2 above shows the respondents responses as to whether their institutions offer E-Learning. From the table, the data reveals that 127 (100%) that is all the respondents agreed that their institution offer E-Learning.

The Table 3 above provides information as to whether or not the institutions under study have E- Libraries for their E- Learners. From the data in the table above, it can be summarized that all the institutions investigated for this research work had E- Library for their learners as all the respondents 127 (100%) responded in the affirmative.

Table 4 above shows the respondents opinion as to whether there is need for E- Librarian in an E- Learning environment. The results shows that 118 (92.9%) of the respondents strongly agree that there is need for E- Librarian in an E- Learning environment, in the same way, 9 (07.1%) of the respondents also agree with the assertion that there is need for E- Librarian in an E- Learning environment. It is interesting to know that no respondent disagree with the statement.

Table 5 above summarized the respondents view regarding the skills needed by librarian without building in an E- Learning environment. 127 (100%), that is, all the respondents agreed that high computer knowledge and skills are needed for a librarian to function in an E- Learning environment, in the same way, 123 (96.7%) of the respondents posit that knowledge of various data bases is required for the librarian to function in an

E- Learning environment. Also, all the respondents 127 (100%) are of the view that for any librarian to function in an E- Learning environment, the librarian must be multi- skilled, that is, he or she must have various skills. More also, 127 (100%), all the respondents believed that for a librarian to function in an E-Learning environment, such a librarian must be highly intelligent. 96 (75.6%) of the respondents are of the opinion that ability to learn very fast is another skill that is required by a librarian to function in an E- Learning environment. In the same way, 83 (65.4%) of the respondents stated that good communication skill is essential for librarian in an E-Learning environment. In relation to evaluation skill, all the respondents 127 (100%) agreed that evaluation skill is need for any librarian to function in an E- Learning environment. While 122 (96.1%) of the respondents are of the opinion that ability to teach others is a requirement for a librarian in an E- Learning environment.

Table 6 above reveals the challenges that librarian without building in an E- learning environment faces. 118 (92.9%) of the respondents stated that technical and administrative issues are parts of the challenges that librarian without building faces. 122 (96.1%) of the respondents are of the view that finance is a major challenge that librarian without building faces, 114 (89.8%) agreed that adapting to change is a serious challenge faced by librarian without building in an E- Learning environment. All the respondents 127 (100%) are of the opinion that capacity building is a major challenge facing librarian without building; also, 124 (97.6%) of the respondents believe that bottlenecks from vendors are parts of the challenges that librarian without building faces. While all the respondents again 127 (100%) agreed that the issue of copyright is a serious challenge to librarian without building in an E- Learning environment.

Table 7 above presented the possible solution to the challenges to librarian without building in an E- learning environment. 124 (97.6%) of the respondents suggested that the parent institutions

should support the library in all aspects. Also, 127 (100%), that is all the respondents suggested that adequate financial support should be given to the librarian without building in an E- Learning environment. In the same way, all the respondents 127 (100%) are of the view that capacity building in terms of training and retraining of the librarian without building is another way of achieving the goal of librarian without building in an E- Learning environment. 121 (95.3%) of the respondents suggested that the various institutions should have their policies on copyright. Also, 127 (100%), that is all the respondents suggested that librarian without building in an E- Learning environment should be ready to learn, continue learning and willing to teach others.

Table 6. Challenges of librarian without building in an e- learning environment

Challenges of Librarian without building in an E-Learning Environment	Frequency	Percentage
Technical and administrative issues	118	92.9%
Financial Challenges	122	96.1%
Adapting to Change	114	89.8%
Capacity Building	127	100%
Vendors issues	124	97.6%
Copyright issues	127	100%

Table 7. Solutions to the challenges

Solutions to the challenges	Frequency	Percentage
Institution management should support the library	124	97.6%
Adequate finance should be release for E- Library development	127	100%
Adequate capacity building for Librarian without building	127	100%
There should be institutional policies on copyright	121	95.3%
Librarian Without Building should be ready to learn and teach others	127	100%

DISCUSSION OF FINDINGS

This study revealed that all the institutions that participated in this survey provide E- Learning platforms and the different institutions have different names for the programme, such as distance learning, open learning, Open University, distance education, continue education and so on. The research work also found out that all the institutions that were involved in this research work have E- Libraries for their E- Learners. It is interesting to know that 118 (92.9%) of the respondents strongly agreed that there is need for E- Librarian in an E- Learning environment. The study also discovered that for E- Librarian to function in an E- Learning environment there is need for such librarian to build up skills and knowledge. The required skill and knowledge include high computer literacy. The E- librarian must not be computer phobic; he/she must have high knowledge of various data bases and their functionalities.

The E- librarian must be multi- skilled. He must possess the ability to do different tasks. He/she must be highly intelligent and must be above average intelligence. He/she must be able to learn very fast and teach others as well. Such a librarian must have good communication skills and must be knowledgeable in evaluation of information resources and services. The study also discovered that there are some challenges that the E- Librarian faces such as administrative and technical challenges, financial challenge, change challenge, capacity building, copyright and vendors' challenges. The study also proffered solutions to the challenges - there should be institutional support for the development of E- Library, capacity building should be intensified for E- Librarian, there should be institutional policies on copyright, E- Librarian (Librarian without building) should be ready to go the extra mile to learn and also teach others.

RECOMMENDATIONS

Information and communication Technologies have changed the educational system for better, and these changes had also imparted the library because libraries are always associated with education and development. It is therefore recommended that librarians should strive to acquire more knowledge and skills so as to stand the changing nature of their job. It is also recommended that government agencies that accredit programmes at tertiary institutions should make sure that any institution that offers E- learning must also have well organized E- library and a well trained E- librarian must be employed to manage the E- library.

This chapter also recommends that librarians should try as much as possible to attend conferences and workshops both locally and internationally, where they can acquire these new skills and knowledge that are required of them to function effectively in an E- learning environment. Training should also be organized for librarians by the various professional bodies. In most countries there are professional associations and bodies that train and equip members with necessary skills. In Nigeria for example, the Nigeria Library Association and the Librarian Registration Council of Nigeria should take it as a point of duty to organized training for librarians at a subsidized cost. At the international scene, the West Africa Library Associations (WALA), the International Federation of Library Associations (IFLA) and many others should also do same to equipped librarians for the task ahead. The study also recommends that there should be institutional support for the development of E- Library; capacity building should be intensified for E- Librarians and the parent institutions should try as much as possible to bear the cost of training, so that they can catch up with the advancements in technology. There should be institutional policies on copyright.

The E- Librarian (Librarian without building) should be ready to go extra mile to learn and also teach others. They should not rely solely on the institution to train them because E- Librarians in this age must be competent enough to handle challenges of the E-Learning Environment.

FUTURE RESEARCH DIRECTIONS

The authors recommends that further research should be carried out to investigate the relationship between E- Librarian, (librarian without building), E- Teacher and the E- Learners in an E- Learning environment. This has become important because the three actors (E- Librarian, E- Teacher, and the E- Learners) are the major components of E- Learning. The success or failure of the E-Learning system depends to a very great extent on the cordial relationship between them. Also, it is recommended that another study should be carried out to investigate the choice of librarian as regards working as a professional librarian in a traditional library system or working as an E-librarian in an E- Learning environment and the study should find out the reasons librarians prefer working as professionals in a traditional library system or as an E – Librarian in an E- Learning environment.

CONCLUSION

The introduction of Information and Communication Technologies (ICTs) in education has brought on board new methods of teaching and learning. These new method of teaching and learning has also brought on board new library, new librarian, and new roles for the librarian. Therefore, the librarian without building in this new learning environment must acquire new skills required to fit into the changing world of modern day educational system. E- learning as a learning platform has empowered so many individuals, organiza-

tions, as well as nations at one point or the other. E- Library and E- librarian or library without building must be recognized and empowered as part of the learning process because the success of any E- learner greatly depends on the E- teachers, E- libraries and the E- librarians or the librarians without building in an E- Learning environment must strive at all cost to acquire new knowledge and skills they must not rely soly on their parent organizations such training and retraining, and must continue to upgrade that knowledge and skills through capacity building, through seminars and work shop, through short and long term training in order to remain relevant in this present digital age.

There is hope for librarian without building in an E-learning environment; if they can develop themselves and know how to fly their onions, this is true because E-learning cannot function effective without E-library and E-Librarians (Librarian without building) in charge of the library just as the traditional educational system cannot survive without library attached to the institution to support the teaching, learning and Research process of their parent organization.

REFERENCES

Allen, M. W. (2013). Learning circuits. Retrieved from http://www.astd.org/LC/2004/0704_allen.htm

Brown, J. S., Collins, A., & Duguid, P. (2005, January-February). Situated cognition and the culture of learning. *Educational Researcher*, 32–42.

Burbles, N. C. (2004). Navigating the advantages and disadvantages of online pedagogy. In *Learning, Culture and Community in Online Education: Research and Practice*. New York: Peter Lang Publishing.

Canadian Association of Research Libraries. (2010). Core competencies for 21st century CARL librarians. Retrieved from www.carl-abrc.ca

Chu, F. T. (2003). The future of librarianship. In *Expectations of librarians in the 21st century.* Westport, CT: Greenwood Press.

Clark, R. C., & Mayer, R. E. (2003). *E-learning and the science of instruction.* San Francisco: Jossey-Bass.

Dede, C. (2000). Emerging technologies and distributed learning in higher education. In D. Hanna (Ed.), *Higher education in an era of digital competition: Choices and challenges.* New York: Atwood.

Dringus, L. P., & Cohen, M. S. (2005). An adaptable usability heuristic checklist for online courses. Paper presented at the 35th Annual FIE '05. New York, NY.

Dziuban, C. D., Hartman, J. L., & Moskal, P. D. (2004), Blended learning. ECAR Research Bulletin, 7.

Fetterman, D. (1998). Virtual classroom at Stanford University. Retrieved on April 3, 2013 from http://www.stanford.edu/~davidf/virtual.html

Gray Harriman Ltd. (2010). E-learning resources. Retrieved from http://www.grayharriman.com/index.htm

Gunn, H. (2002). Virtual libraries supporting student learning. *School Libraries Worldwide, 18*(2), 27–37.

Hashim, L., & Mokhtar, W. H. (2012). Preparing new era librarians and information professionals: Trends and issues. *International Journal of Humanities and Social Science, 2*(7), 151–156.

Kruse, K. (2004). Learning guru. Retrieved from http://www.e-learningguru.com/articles/art1_3.htm

Lehmann, K. J. (2004). Successful online communication. In K. J. Lehmann (Ed.), *How to be a Great Online Teacher.* New York: Scarecrow Education.

Livonen, M. (2005). University Libraries as a gateway to e-learning. Paper presented at International Conference of Information and communication Society. Tallinn, Estonia.

Nichols, M. (2003). A theory of e-learning. *Journal of Educational Technology & Society, 6*(2), 1–10.

Peljar, S. M., & Kamat, R. K. (2009). Libraries a key to harness e-learning: Issues and perspective. *DESIDOC Journal of Library & Information Technology, 29*(1), 23–30.

Rosenberg, M. J. (2001). *E-learning.* New York: McGraw-Hill.

Somvir, A. (2010). Role of librarian in the 21st century. Retrieved from http://www.scribd.com/doc/34056683/Role-of-librarians-in-the-21st-century

Tavangarian, D., Leypold, M. E., Nölting, K., Röser, M., & Voigt, D. (2004). Is e-learning the solution for individual learning?. Electronic Journal of e-Learning, 2(2), 273-280.

Triacca, L., Bolchini, D., Botturi, L., & Inversini, A. (2004). Mile: Systematic usability evaluation for e-learning web applications. *AACE Journal, 12*(4).

ADDITIONAL READING

Abdul, H. A. (2002). e-learning Is it the e or the Learning that matters? *The Internet and Higher Education, 4,* 2002.

Abdulwahab, O. (Ed.). Library and information science in developing countries Contemporary issues. Hershey, PA: Information Science Reference (an imprint of IGI Global).

Alexander, S. (2001). E-learning developments and experiences. *Education + Training, 43*(4/5), 240–248. doi:10.1108/00400910110399247

Alexander, S., & Golja, T. (2007). Using students' experiences to derive quality in an e-Learning system: An institution's perspective. *Journal of Educational Technology & Society*, *10*(2), 17–33.

Armitage, S., O'Leary, R. (2003). A good guide for learning technologists (eLearning series No.4: Learning and Teaching support Network Generic centre.

Bates, A. (2005) Technology, e-Learning and Distance Education London: Routledge.

Boff, C., & Singer, C. (2003). Academic reference librarians in the 21st Century. In BridgeKarl (Ed.). Expectations of librarians in the 21st century, Westport, Greenwood press.

Botha, M. (2004). The information deprived continent: can we do something? In Brophy, Peter, Fisher, Shelagh & Craven, Jenny (Ed.). *Libraries without walls: the distributed delivery of library and information services*. Proceeding of an international conference held on 19 – 23 September 2003, organized by the centre for research in library and information management (CERLIM), Manchester Metropolitan University. London, Facet Publishing.

Brophy, P., Fisher, S., & Craven, J. (Eds.). (2004). *Libraries without walls 5: the distributed delivery of library and information services*. Proceeding of an international conference held on 19 – 23 September 2003, organized by the centre for research in library and information management (CERLIM), Manchester Metropolitan University. London, Facet Publishing.

Carliner, S. (2004). *An overview of online learning* (2nd ed.). Armherst, MA: Human.

Carpenter, J., & Wallis, M. (2004). Research resources and the academic researchers. In Brophy, Peter, Fisher, Shelagh & Craven, Jenny (Ed.). *Libraries without walls: the distributed delivery of library and information services*. Proceeding of an international conference held on 19 – 23 September 2003, organized by the centre for research in library and information management (CERLIM), Manchester Metropolitan University. London, Facet Publishing.

Clark, R. C., & Mayer, R. E. (2003). e-learning and the science of instruction. San

Collis, B., & Moonen, J. (2001). Flexible learning in a digital world. London. Kogan Page. JISC e-Learning Models Desk Study Terry Mayes & Sara de Freitas 39 of 43 Issue 1

Collis, B., Peters, O., & Pals, N. (2000). 'A Model for Predicting the Educational Use of Information and Communication Technologies'. *Instructional Science*, *29*, 95–125. doi:10.1023/A:1003937401428

Cynthia, A. (2003). The more things change: what is a librarian today? In B. Karl (Ed.), *Expectations of librarians in the 21st century*. Westport: Greenwood press.

David Stanley, H. (2003). The 21st century librarian in Bridges Karl (Ed.). Expectations of librarians in the 21st century, Westport: Greenwood Press. education. New York: Peter Lang.

Ehlers, U. (2004). Quality in e-learning. The learner as a key quality assurance category. *European Journal of Vocational Training*, *29*, 3–15.

English, L. O. (2003). New librarians in the 21st century: The normalization of change in Bridges Karl (Ed.). Expectations of librarians in the 21st century, Westport, Greenwood press.

Goodyear, P. (2002). Psychological Foundations for Networked Learning. In C. Steeples & C. Jones (Eds.), *Networked Learning: Perspectives and Issues*. London: Springer-Verlag. doi:10.1007/978-1-4471-0181-9_4

Hanson, T., & Day, J. (Eds.). (1996). *Managing the Electronic library: A practical guide for information professionals*. London: Bowker Saur.

Hopkinson, A. (2012). Establishing the digital library: Don't ignore the library standards and don't forget the training needed. In *Tella*. Adeyinka and Issa.

Johnson, R. D., Hornik, S., & Salas, E. (2008). An empirical examination of factors contributing to the creation of successful e-learning environments. *International Journal of Human-Computer Studies*, *66*, 356–369. doi:10.1016/j.ijhcs.2007.11.003

Kasperek, S. (2003). Technology skills in libraries if the 21st century in Bridges Karl (Ed.). Expectations of librarians in the 21st century, Westport, Greenwood press.

Kearsley, G. (Ed.). (2005). *Online learning: Personal reflections on the transformation of education*. NJ: Educational Technology Publications.

Kolawole, O. O. (2004). Overcoming barriers to library use by Nigerian professionals. In Brophy, Peter, Fisher, Shelagh & Craven, Jenny (Ed.). *Libraries without walls: the distributed delivery of library and information services*. Proceeding of an international conference held on 19 – 23 September 2003, organized by the centre for research in library and information management (CERLIM), Manchester Metropolitan University. London, Facet Publishing.

Lesk, M. (2005). *Understanding Digital Libraries* (2nd ed.). Amsterdam: Elsevier.

Lomex, E. L. (2003). Electronic resources librarians in the 21st century. In B. Karl (Ed.), *Expectations of librarians in the 21st century*. Westport: Greenwood press.

Martin, A., & Madigan, D. (Eds.). (2006). *Digital Literacy for learning*. London: Facet Publishing.

McCown, R., Driscoll, M., & Roop, P. (1996). *Educational psychology. A learning-centered approach to class-room practice* (2nd ed.). Boston: Allyn and Bacon.

Moreno, R., & Mayer, R. E. (2002). Learning science in virtual reality multimedia environments: Role of methods and media. *Journal of Educational Psychology*, *94*, 598–610.

Morris, A., & Cox, A. (2004). Librarians in digital communities of practice. In P. Brophy, S. Fisher, & J. Craven (Eds.), *Libraries without walls: The distributed delivery of library and information services*. London: Facet Publishing.

Mutual, S. M. (2012). Demystifying digital scholarship. In A. Tella & A. O. Issa (Eds.), *library and information science in developing countries: Contemporary issues*. United states: Information Science Reference (an imprint of IGI Global).

Naidu, S. (2002). Designing and evaluating instruction for e-learning. In P. L. Rodgers (Ed.), *Designing Instruction for Technology-Enhanced Learning* (pp. 134–159). Hershey, PA: Idea Group Publishing.

Narciss, S., Proske, A., & Körndle, H. (2007). Promoting self-regulated learning in web-based learning environments. *Computers in Human Behavior*, *23*, 1126–1144. doi:10.1016/j.chb.2006.10.006

Obe, S. P., & Griffiths, P. (2002). *Creating a successful e- information services*. London: Facet Publishing.

Paechter, M., & Schweizer, K. (2006). Learning and motivation with virtual tutors. Does it matter if the tutor is visible on the net? In M. Pivec (Ed.), *Affective and emotional aspects of human–computer-interaction: Emphasis on game-based and innovative learning approaches* (pp. 155–164). Amsterdam: IOS Press.

Parker- Gibson. Necia (2003). Qualities of a 21st century librarian. In Bridges Karl (ed.). Expectations of librarians in the 21st century, Westport, Greenwood press.

Resource Development Press.

Richardson, J. C., & Swan, K. (2003). Examining social presence in online courses in relation to students' perceived learning and satisfaction. *Journal of Asynchronous Learning Networks*, *7*(1), 68–88.

Role of method and media. Journal of Educational Psychology, 94

Rosenberg, M. J. (2001). e-Learning. New York: McGraw-Hill.

Ross, S. (2003). The future of librarianship. In B. Karl (Ed.), *Expectations of librarians in the 21st century*. Westport: Greenwood press.

Rowley, J. (2004). The Electronic Libraries: fourth Ed. of computers for libraries.London, Facet Publishing.

Seale, J. (2006). *Disability and e-leaning in higher education: Accessiblity theory and practice*. Oxford, United kingdom: Routledge.

Selim, H. M. (2007). Critical success factors for e-learning acceptance. Confirmatory factor models. *Computers & Education*, *49*, 396–413. doi:10.1016/j.compedu.2005.09.004

Shank, R. (1997). *Virtual Learning*. New York: McGraw-Hill.

Shee, D. Y., & Wang, Y. S. (2008). Multi-criteria evaluation of the web-based e learning system: A methodology based on learner satisfaction and its applications. *Computers & Education*, *50*, 894–905. doi:10.1016/j.compedu.2006.09.005

Shotsberger, P. G. (2000). The human touch: Synchronous communication in web-based learning. *Educational Technology*, *40*(1).

Swan, K. (2001). Virtual interaction: Design factors affecting student satisfaction and perceived learning in asynchronous online courses. *Distance Education*, *22*(2). doi:10.1080/0158791010220208

Theng, Yin-Leng, Foo, Schubert, Goh, Dion & Na, Jin- Cheon (2009). *Handbook of research on digital libraries: Design, development and impact*. Hershey: Information Science Reference.

Training (pp. 33-50). Englewood Cliffs, NJ: Educational Technology Publications.

Uwaje, Chris (2010). E- Knowledge- Time is running out. Abuja, connect technology limited.

Wagner, E. D. (2001). *Emerging learning trends and the world wide web*. Web-based.

Wang, Y. S. (2003). Assessment of learner satisfaction with asynchronous electronic learning systems. *Information & Management*, *41*, 75–86. doi:10.1016/S0378-7206(03)00028-4

Wilen-Daugenti, T. (2009)..edu – Technology and learning environments in higher

KEY TERMS AND DEFINITIONS

21st Century Librarian: 21st century librarians refer to those librarians that provide services to both face and faceless patrons. Their services enable the users to access the present day virtual libraries without necessarily coming in contact with the librarians. The 21st century Librarians makes use of technologies in performing their day to day duties.

21st Century Libraries: the 21st century library is a collection of units of document in both prints and digital the resources are spread everywhere, accessible always, anytime and anywhere with the aid of Information and Communication Technologies. It is a type of library where individuals and groups such as authors, publishers, vendors and readers are linked through hyperlink technology across the global electronic network to relate in different ways.

Academic Libraries: These are libraries that are established in institutions of higher learning, such as Universities, Polytechnics and colleges of Education. They are to such the curriculum of their parent organization, in terms of teaching learning and research activities of their parent organization.

E-Learners: A student that uses e-learning to gain education.

E-Learning: Web-based training (WBT), also known as elearning and on-line learning, is training that resides on a server or host computer that is connected to the World Wide Web.

E-Library/Library without Building: It can be refers to as an electronic or online library where users can have access to information resources electronically over the net. This type of library provides 24 hours online access to digital resources to users.

Virtual Learning Environment: A virtual learning environment (VLE) is a set of teaching and learning tools designed to enhance a student's learning experience by including computers and the Internet in the learning process.

This work was previously published in E-Learning 2.0 Technologies and Web Applications in Higher Education edited by Jean-Eric Pelet, pages 45-64, copyright year 2014 by Information Science Reference (an imprint of IGI Global).

Chapter 74
A Business Motivation Model for IT Service Management

Marco Vicente
Technical University of Lisbon, Portugal

Nelson Gama
University of Lisbon, Portugal

Miguel Mira da Silva
Technical University of Lisbon, Portugal

ABSTRACT

The Enterprise Architecture (EA) approach usually considers a set of motivational concepts that are used to model the reasons and motivations that underlie the design and change of organizations, which corresponds to their Business Motivation Model (BMM). Likewise, this BMM is also present in organizations that provide IT services. However, although ITIL has become a standard for performing IT Service Management (ITSM), there is not one holistic solution to integrate EA and ITIL. Therefore, we propose to join both approaches through the definition of a specific Enterprise Architecture to design organizations according to ITIL's best practices to perform ITSM. Thus, this paper's goal is twofold: on one hand to establish that architecture's motivation model, and, on the other, to contribute for a formal identification and representation of the ITIL business motivation model itself.

INTRODUCTION

Enterprise Architecture (EA) is a coherent whole of principles, methods, and models that are used in the design and realization of an enterprise's organizational structure, business processes, information systems, and infrastructure (Lankhorst et al., 2009).

The purpose of enterprise architecture is to align an enterprise to its essential requirements, to provide a normative restriction of design freedom toward transformation projects and programs. Key elements of enterprise architecture are concerns, models, views, architecture principles and frameworks. Enterprise architecture addresses the properties that are necessary and sufficient for it to be fit for its mission (Greefhorst & Proper, 2011).

DOI: 10.4018/978-1-4666-8619-9.ch074

The Open Group Architecture Framework (TOGAF) (The Open Group, 2009) is a freely available standardized method for EA that has become a worldwide and broadly accepted standard (Greefhorst & Proper, 2011).

In the view of TOGAF, EA is divided into four architecture domains: business, data, application and technology. These domains describe the architecture of systems that support the enterprise and correspond to the "How, What, Who, Where and When" columns of the Zachman framework (Zachman, 1987). In turn, they do not cover the elements that motivate its design and operation which corresponds to Zachman's "Why" column (The Open Group, 2012).

In fact, these elements belong to what is called the Business Motivation Model (BMM) defined by the Object Management Group (OMG) as a "scheme and structure for developing, communicating, and managing business plans in an organized manner" (Object Management Group, 2010).

The BMM provides a small set of important concepts to express motivation: means, ends, influencers and directives. The model was initially created to provide the motivations behind business rules, but can also be used to find the motivation for architecture principles (Greefhorst & Proper, 2011). Accordingly, TOGAF version 9.0 also includes a business motivation model that is simpler than the OMG one and is based on the concepts of drivers, goals, objectives, and measures.

On the other hand, IT Service Management (ITSM) evolved naturally as services became underpinned in time by the developing technology. In its early years, IT was mainly focused on application development, but as time went by, new technologies meant concentrating on delivering the created applications as a part of a larger service offering, supporting the business itself (The Stationery Office, 2007).

IT Infrastructure Library (ITIL) (Hanna et al., 2008) is the de facto standard for implementing ITSM (Hochstein, Zarnekow & Brenner, 2005).

It is a practical, no-nonsense approach to the identification, planning, delivery and support of IT services to the business (Arraj, 2010). The ITIL Core consists of five publications: Service Strategy, Service Design, Service Transition, Service Operation and Continual Service Improvement. Each book covers a phase from the Service Lifecycle and encompasses various processes which are always described in detail in the book in which they find their key application (Van Bon et al., 2007).

There have been several attempts to integrate and relate EA and ITIL, because having different organizational departments or teams handling each approach independently, results on wasted resources and turns organizations less efficient or effective.

Therefore, we propose to integrate both approaches through the definition of an Enterprise Architecture for organizations that have ITSM as an architectural driver.

In fact, EA does not say anything about designing specific organizations because its goal is to be able to represent every organization. Conversely, our goal is to narrow it down, and define a specific architecture to design organizations according to best practices on specific domains, which in this case is ITSM, but could as well be purchasing or logistics.

In related work, we are already building the models and views that represent the architecture for this kind of organizations, and, in this article, we will just focus on presenting this architecture's motivation model: the set of motivations that underlie its design or change, which should match the ITIL motivations themselves.

On the other hand, when researching through ITIL literature, we noticed that ITIL is presented through textual definitions of concepts and its relationships, while its processes are usually depicted as well defined sequences of activities by flow charts.

However, the motivation behind why we need ITIL, why those were the chosen processes, the drivers, assessments, goals, principles and requirements, when not described through text, are loosely depicted by adhoc graphical diagrams that lack a formal notation and representation.

That does not surprise us, because as opposed to engineering disciplines (where modeling a system consists of constructing a mathematical model that describes and explains it), in the fields of enterprise and software architecture, it is usual to see diagrams as a form of structure that helps in visualizing and communicating system descriptions. In other words, in architecture there is a tendency to replace mathematical modeling by adhoc visualizations (Lankhorst et al., 2009).

Unfortunately, the lack of a strong symbolic and semantic model often leads to some drawbacks: there is not a clear, uniform representation of the concepts; each diagram has concepts of different conceptual levels; it is not clear which are the elements represented or its attributes and it is hard to check for coherence across the several diagrams.

This paper's goal is then twofold: on one hand to define the motivation model that guides and restricts the freedom of design when designing organizations according to ITSM best practices; and, on the other, to enhance ITIL with a formal definition and representation of its business motivation model, for knowledge sharing, stakeholder communication and to aid discussion and validation by the ITIL community itself.

To achieve this, we chose ArchiMate's Motivation extension as the modeling language for reasons that we shall later address. This work's contribution is not just a theoretical concept map between ITIL and the ArchiMate notation, but an actual set of ITIL models demonstrating the proposal value and feasibility.

Although a subset of these topics have been formerly addressed (Vicente et al., 2013), this article brings several new contributions: (1) a new, overall vision of the motivations, theoretical foundations, state of the art and problem that lead to this research work, (2) clarification on how this work will set the foundations to the definition

of a specific enterprise architecture for ITSM organizations, (3) the identification, discussion and analysis of the architecture principles that restrict its freedom of design and (4) a revised and broaden demonstration of the architecture business motivational model, with more models and examples and a thoroughly description and analysis.

The methodology applied across this paper is Design Science Research, where we develop and validate a proposal to solve our problem (Hevner et al., 2004). The following sections follow the methodology's steps: "Related Work" covers aims and objectives as the awareness and recognition of a problem from a state of the art review giving us the issues that must be addressed. The following section, "Research Problem", exposes the main problem while offering a tentative idea to how these issues might be addressed. Afterwards, "Proposal" presents a proposal as an attempt to solve the previously described problem. Next, we present a "Demonstration" followed by the "Evaluation" comparing the results with the research questions and to conclude we show our proposal applicability and themes for further work.

RELATED WORK

In this section we present a literature review of the topics related to this work. We start by introducing what is Enterprise Architecture, followed by TOGAF - an EA framework, and ArchiMate - an EA modeling language. Later, we will introduce the Business Motivation Model and ITIL, a best practice model to IT service management. Finally, we will show how ITIL representations usually only include business and informational concepts, not considering other domains.

Enterprise Architecture

The Zachman Framework (Zachman, 1987) appeared in the late 1980s with the goal of defining logical constructs (architectures) to represent organizations. It is based on the principle that an organization does not have just one architecture, but a set of them, arranged as layers. Each of these layers produce artifacts that answer six organizational questions (What, Where, When, Why, Who and How) (Zachman, 1987).

Today, business performance depends on a balanced and integrated design of the enterprise, involving people, their competencies, organizational structures, business processes, IT, finances, products and services, as well as its environment (Greefhorst & Proper, 2011).

EA is a coherent set of principles, involving the design and performance of different architectures. It specifies the components and its relationships, which are used to manage and align assets, people, operations and projects to support business goals and strategies (Lankhorst et al., 2009; Ross, Weill & Robertson, 2006), concerning those properties of an enterprise that are necessary and sufficient to meet its essential requirements (Greefhorst & Proper, 2011).

EA is based on a holistic representation of organizations, on views and the ability to map relationships between artifacts and architectures, and on the independence and connection between layered architectures (Gama, Sousa & Mira da Silva, 2012) which usually are (Lankhorst et al., 2009; The Open Group, 2009; Zachman, 1987): Business, Process, Application, Information, and Technology. The alignment between architectures allows a coherent blueprint of the organization, which is then used for governance of its processes and systems (Pereira & Sousa, 2004).

TOGAF

The Open Group Architecture Framework (TOGAF) is a framework for developing an EA (The Open Group, 2009). It was developed and is currently maintained as a standard by The Open Group (TOG). The first version of TOGAF, in 1995, was based on the US Department of De-

fense's Technical Architecture Framework for Information Management (TAFIM) (The Open Group, 2009; Van Sante & Ermersj, 2009). Each version of the standard is developed collaboratively by the members of the TOG Architecture Forum (The Open Group, 2009; Van Sante & Ermersj, 2009).

The first seven versions of TOGAF addressed technology architecture based on its adoption in businesses at the time each was written. In 2002, Version 8 was published, which expanded the scope of TOGAF from a purely technology architecture to an Enterprise Architecture, by including business and information systems architecture in the new version (Van Sante & Ermersj, 2009). In 2009, TOGAF 9 was released with new features as a modular structure, a content framework specification, extended guidance and additional detail (The Open Group, 2009).

TOGAF provides the methods and tools for assisting in the acceptance, production, use, and maintenance of an EA (The Open Group, 2009). It is one of the leading architecture frameworks worldwide, and in its latest version there is increasing reflection on the use of the architecture and its governance (Van Sante & Ermersj, 2009). It is based on an iterative process model supported by best practices and a reusable set of existing architecture assets (The Open Group, 2009). The TOGAF document focus on EA key concepts and TOGAF Architecture Development Method (ADM), a step by step approach to developing an EA (Jonkers, Proper & Turner, 2009).

ArchiMate

The ArchiMate modeling language was developed to provide a uniform representation for architecture descriptions (Jonkers, Proper & Turner, 2009; The Open Group, 2012). It offers an integrated architectural approach that describes and visualizes the different architecture domains and their underlying relationships and dependencies (Jonkers, Proper & Turner, 2009; The Open Group, 2012). The goal of the ArchiMate project is to provide domain integration through an architecture language and visualization techniques that picture these domains and their relations, providing the architect with instruments that support and improve the architecture process (Lankhorst & the ArchiMate team, 2004).

In a short time, ArchiMate has become the open standard for architecture modeling in the Netherlands; it is now also becoming well known in the international EA community, being today a TOG standard (Jonkers, Proper & Turner, 2009).

The domains of business, application and infrastructure are connected by a "service orientation" paradigm, where each layer exposes functionality in the form of a service to the layer above (The Open Group, 2012). Besides this layered structure, ArchiMate also distinguishes between active structure elements, behavior elements and passive structure elements (where the passive ones represent the architecture information domain), having also another distinction between internal and external system view. On top of this, ArchiMate is a formal visual design language, supports different viewpoints for selected stakeholders and is flexible enough to be easily extended (The Open Group, 2012).

Business Motivation Model

In the view of TOGAF, EA is divided into four architecture domains: business, data, application and technology. These domains describe the architecture of systems that support the enterprise and correspond to the "How, What, Who, Where and When" columns of the Zachman framework (Zachman, 1987). In turn, they do not cover the elements which motivate its design and operation which corresponds to Zachman's "Why" column (The Open Group, 2012).

In fact, these elements belong to what is called the Business Motivation Model defined by the Object Management Group (OMG) as a "scheme and structure for developing, communicating, and managing business plans in an organized manner" (Object Management Group, 2010).

The Business Rules Group (BRG) developed the Business Motivation Model which was later accepted as an OMG specification. BMM identifies factors that motivate the establishing of business plans, identifies and defines its elements and indicates how all these factors and elements inter-relate. In fact, there are two major areas of the BMM. First we have Ends and Means, where Ends are things that the enterprise wishes to achieve (as goals and objectives) and Means things that will be used to achieve these Ends (as strategies, tactics, business policies and business rules). The second is the Influencers that shape the elements of the business plans, and the Assessments made about the impacts of those Influencers on Ends and Means (eg strengths, weaknesses, opportunities and threats).

The model was initially created to provide the motivations behind business rules, but can also be used to find the motivation for architecture principles (Greefhorst & Proper, 2011). Accordingly, TOGAF version 9.0 also includes a business motivation model that is simpler than the OMG one and is based on the concepts of drivers, goals, objectives, and measures. It has concepts as Driver (factors generally motivating or constraining an organization), Goal (strategic purpose and mission of an organization), Objective (near to mid-term achievements that an organization would like to attain) and Measure (performance criteria).

TOGAF recommends using this extension when the architecture needs to understand the motivation of organizations in more detail than the standard business or engagement principles and objectives that are informally modeled within the core content metamodel (The Open Group, 2009). Likewise, ArchiMate 2.0 has a motivation extension which is closely linked to the developments of TOGAF, as ArchiMate does not provide its own set of defined terms, but rather follows those provided by the TOGAF standard (The Open Group, 2012).

ITIL

Enterprises need to manage the delivery of services that support users in conducting their activities in the context of business processes (Braun & Winter, 2007). ITIL was created by the Central Computer and Telecommunications Agency (CCTA), an office of the British government and was first released to the public in the late eighties (Van Sante & Ermersj, 2009). ITIL is a common-practice model possessing the character of a branch standard (Hochstein, Zarnekow & Brenner, 2005). While the first version was mainly based on experience in data centers running big mainframes, in 2000 a revised version (ITIL v2) was launched becoming the worldwide de facto standard for IT Service Management (Van Sante & Ermersj, 2009).

In 2007, ITIL v3 introduced the lifecycle principle, whereby the provisioning of services was considered to be a continuous process in which new services are brought into existence whilst others are phased out (Van Sante & Ermersj, 2009). The current version of ITIL covers the major weaknesses identified in the previous versions, namely being too focused on technology (Gama, Sousa & Mira da Silva, 2012). Now, instead of focusing on the service itself, the focus lay on this cycle of life, renewal and decommissioning of services, with a greater business-focused perspective (Van Sante & Ermersj, 2009). The ITIL Core consists of five publications: Service Strategy, Service Design, Service Transition, Service Operation and Continual Service Improvement. Each book covers a phase from the Service Lifecycle with various processes which are always described in detail in the book in which they find their key application (Van Bon et al., 2007).

ITIL Graphical Representations

ITIL is a collection of five books with the best practices related to the effective and efficient management of IT (Gama, Sousa & Mira da Silva, 2012). As already mentioned, there is an effort on these books to illustrate concepts, its relationships, framework lifecycle, processes, information management, information systems and databases through visual representations. However, it is mainly in process modeling (by flow charts or BPMN) that we see a formal representation, with a known symbolic and semantic model. The other representations to describe the remaining ITIL domains seem to lack a common, clear and formal notation and semantic.

Besides these official books, we searched for other ITIL graphical representations. We found several adhoc diagrams from distinct organizations with different notations. These were mainly in-house sketches, diagrams and flowcharts expressing the ITIL views of its authors. Because they are so many and so distinct, its description would be lengthy and hardly noteworthy. Additionally, we have also come across with some commercial solutions. Thus, we have chosen three of the most popular ones to include here as an example on how ITIL is usually represented (IT Process Maps, ITIL Process Map, Microsoft, Microsoft Visio, IDS Scheer's ARIS, iGrafx Flowcharter/ Process, foxIT, foxPRISM and Casewise are all registered trademarks).

ITIL Process Map (ITIL Process Maps, 2012) from IT Process Maps, is announced as "a complete reference process model, designed to serve as a guideline and starting point for your ITIL and ISO 20000 initiatives". The product is a set of process models mapped in the Business Process Model and Notation (BPMN) (Object Management Group, 2012), with processes, artifacts and events. The diagrams have drill-down capabilities and it also has a responsibility assignment matrix (RACI) to illustrate the participation of the ITIL roles in the various ITIL processes. It is available for several platforms, as Microsoft Visio, IDS Scheer's ARIS, and iGrafx Flowcharter/Process.

foxPRISM (FoxPRISM, 2012) from foxIT is a tool that consists of "a fully interactive web based process knowledge base that assists in the design and management of Service Management processes and the implementation of Service Management tools (...) provides a customizable framework onto which organizations can map and build their own process models". This web tool uses flowcharts in swimlane format and text to describe ITIL processes. The elements are processes, activities, roles and events. It also uses a RACI matrix to map roles to processes.

Casewise Online Visual Process Model for ITIL (Casewise, 2012) is a web tool described as "the world's first diagram-only view of all guidance for each of the five new ITIL v3 books providing organizations with the insight to simplify the alignment of business processes ensuring all ITIL standards are met by using simple frameworks and mapping tools". It has all the ITIL processes mapped in BPMN, with processes, activities and events. Also has drill-down capabilities and in each process it is possible to check each process according to Critical Success Factors (CSFs), Key Performance Indicators (KPIs), Best Practice Tips and Hints, Risks and Controls.

It is noticeable from these representations that ITIL is often depicted as just a process architecture, hence the use of flowcharts or BPMN.

The BPMN standard is restricted to process modeling, not covering application, infrastructure or motivation issues. Its main purpose is to provide a uniform notation in terms of activities and their relationships (Lankhorst et al., 2009). We acknowledge the added value of these tools and models and are not claiming they are incorrect, but pointing out instead they lack completeness, because they limit themselves to the representation of business and informational concepts, not considering other domains.

RESEARCH PROBLEM

Today, there is no fully complete framework to be used as a comprehensive off-the-shelf solution to ensure the alignment between service management and the organization's concepts and artifacts. In fact, different frameworks are often used as complementary and, most of the times, simultaneously too. Beyond the difficulties associated with the governance of both initiatives, this implies some problems (Gama, Sousa & Mira da Silva, 2012). Parallel EA and ITIL projects imply a duplication of investments and costs. In effect, even with shared infrastructures we cannot avoid a duplication of data repositories, procedures and human resources, being hard to define a way for teams not to compete together or maintain different efforts aligned (Gama, Sousa & Mira da Silva, 2012).

Although EA and ITIL describe areas of common interest, they do it from different perspectives. ITIL was developed to support Service Management and EA to support a holistic organization view. However, since services have become part of fast-changing organizations, the prediction of what will be needed tomorrow is of growing interest to the people that deliver them. Conversely, architecture has changed from a rather static design discipline to an organization-encompassing one, and is only useful if the rest of the organization is using it to enable all developments to be aligned (Van Sante & Ermersj, 2009).

There are several common benefits and components which raise the issues of relationship and integration of EA and ITIL although they have different concerns on IT service provision (Nabiollahi, Alias & Sahibuddin, 2010). EA is regarded as a pivotal concept for organizational engineering, and when ITSM is regarded as the dominant operations model for IT, ITSM must be sufficiently integrated into EA (Braun & Winter, 2007). EA guarantees consistency in building new products or services and addresses business requirements, while ITSM, on the other hand, guarantees the consistency of services, through the use of standard processes (Correia & Abreu, 2009).

In fact, EA principles remain the best way to represent organizations as a system, relating multiple architectures to their artifacts and components. The widespread scope of ITIL involves all organizational architectures, but it does not describe how to design and realize the whole organization. Currently ITIL and EA teams work in different departments with little opportunity to share expertise. Initiatives to address the alignment between IT and organizational issues have conducted to an overlap of the work developed. Therefore, both approaches should be merged (Gama, Sousa & Mira da Silva, 2012).

On the other hand, although ITIL shares the same domains as EA, they are indeed different and complementary, mainly because EA changes business processes according to business requirements and strategy, while ITIL has standard well defined processes. In fact, ITIL processes never change and the requirements from business strategy are used not to change its own processes, but to create, change or evolve the services it offers. That said, each framework have different coverage and distinct responsibilities. The scope of ITIL is just service management while EA handles all organization alignment and change, feeding ITIL with the requirements that its services should realize.

Accordingly, Radhakrishnan (2008) identifies several benefits of EA and ITSM collaboration, like organizational learning, avoiding duplication of effort, re-use of documentation and outputs, cross training, and planning and implementing the target EA and ITSM architectures with a coordinated and integrated method.

There have also been some attempts to relate and integrate EA and ITIL. In fact, Braun and Winter (2007) proposed an EA expansion to integrate ITIL v2 and Service Oriented Architectures (SOA), having EA as a pivotal concept with ITIL regarded for IT operations. EA provided an over-

view of the IT architecture to support IT services, while ITIL was assigned to the IT architecture as an essential part of management processes to services delivery (Gama, Sousa & Mira da Silva, 2012).

Nabiollahi (Nabiollahi, Alias & Sahibuddin, 2010) provides a service based framework for EA to meet the ITSM requirements of ITIL v3, suggesting an EA extension to involve service architecture layer from ITIL Service Design (Taylor, Lloyd & Rudd, 2007). The development of an architecture model for IT services is proposed, making it a service layer for EA. However, it does not clarify how to do it or the relationships between architectures (Gama, Sousa & Mira da Silva, 2012).

Gama (Gama, Sousa & Mira da Silva, 2012) recently proposed to merge both ITIL and EA initiatives in a single body restricting resources and efforts. The solution encompasses the EA principles with referred architectures and the relationship between them, following ITIL service management processes. The common concepts and interfaces between EA and ITIL were identified having services as the integration key point.

Thorn (2007) addresses the relation between ITIL and TOGAF, regarding EA as a fundamental concept for organizational engineering, in which ITIL is included as a framework to an operation model for IT delivered services. He argues that both frameworks can be used together by mapping them, TOGAF covers the development of EA, and is involved in the product's conception lifecycle whereas ITIL ensures the delivery and management of IT services to users (Gama, Sousa & Mira da Silva, 2012; Thorn, 2007).

In the same note, Sante (Van Sante & Ermersj, 2009) addresses the fact that the recent versions of ITIL and TOGAF keep converging to integration. In fact, in ITIL v3 references are made to architectural concepts, hitherto only found in publications on architecture. The same, although to a much lesser extent, applies to TOGAF 8: where references are made to IT management (Van Sante & Ermersj, 2009). The author relates the five ITIL books to TOGAFs ADM cycle, showing there are indeed several similarities, but identifying two main differences: a) developing business architecture is part of the TOGAF framework while the scope of ITIL is limited to developing an effective and efficient IT department, whilst developing business architecture is out of scope in ITIL; and b) running IT operations and delivering actual IT services are within the scope of ITIL, while TOGAF does not cover the development and maintenance of a run time environment, neither the way how services are actually produced and delivered (Van Sante & Ermersj, 2009). Figure 1 shows this vision of EA and ITIL scopes and how to use it to achieve strategic alignment.

All these integration attempts tried to answer a real problem that should not be taken lightly. However, while all these approaches seem to come close to integration, they do not propose a definitive and holistic solution. In fact, Braun's (Braun & Winter, 2007) and Thorn's (Van Sante & Ermersj, 2009) work is limited to ITIL v2, what makes it outdated, Nabiollahi (Nabiollahi, Alias & Sahibuddin, 2010) proposes a service architecture as a new architecture layer, but does not clarify the architectures relationships. As for Sante's (Van Sante & Ermersj, 2009) work, although we agree upon the approaches used and the conclusions reached, the result is not a unique body of knowledge with EA and ITIL, but two different frameworks linked by a mapping.

Moreover, none of these approaches provide models or a formal representation for the proposed solutions. In fact, what we are looking for is a holistic solution, following the EA approach but using ITIL best practices to perform IT service management. A body based on a set of principles, methods and formal models to underlie the design and change of these organizations.

On the other hand, and as we have tried to bring forth in the last section, there also seems to be a void when it comes to representing ITIL on other realms than the processes' one. In fact, there is an overall lack of representation when it comes to the elements that motivate ITIL design and operation. Indeed, we can easily find out who should perform the ITIL processes, what, how, where and when they should be executed, but we cannot find representations that address why do we actually need them in the first place. Actually, this lack of a formal representation of the ITIL motivation model may even impair ITIL communication and implementation, because if stakeholders are not fully aware of ITIL motivations, concerns, benefits, goals, objectives or requirements, resistance to change will probably increase.

Therefore, we strongly believe that like EA, we can also look at ITIL as a composition of architectures, namely business, information, application and infrastructure (Vicente et al., 2013b). And, since ITIL is about service providing and

Figure 1. Strategic alignment with EA and ITIL (adapted from Van Sante & Ermersj, 2009)

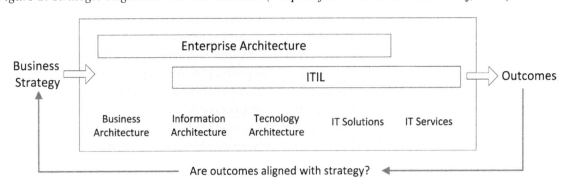

shares so many similarities to EA, it should also share the same motivation elements as defined in TOGAF: "drivers, goals and objectives that influence an organization to provide business services to its customers. This in turn allows more effective definition of service contracts and better measurements of business performance" (The Open Group, 2009).

Hence, we define our problem as the lack of a formal, coherent, consistent, concise and complete model of the motivation aspects of ITIL. Thus, in these pages we will try to contribute for the development of an ITIL business motivation model, along with its formal representation. Following Dietz (2006) reasoning, we also want to provide a system ontology: a formal, explicit specification of a shared conceptualization, where natural language is inappropriate because of its inherent ambiguity and impreciseness. And, by formal representation we mean the existence of a known symbolic and semantic model with a common, clear and formal notation and semantic.

As for future work, this model will also set the foundations to define an enterprise architecture to design organizations that choose to use ITIL best practices to perform ITSM.

PROPOSAL

To address our problem we needed the right modeling language. Here we will explain why we have chosen ArchiMate and propose a concept and relationship mapping from ITIL to it.

ArchiMate

It was our purpose, since the beginning, to use an EA modeling language, because as we have already said, this work is part of a wider effort to specify an enterprise architecture for organizations that need to manage IT services.

Therefore, this will be later used as the definition of the motivation model of that architecture,

and we will later relate our motivation models to the other EA domains, in order to show which of those domain's elements realize and implement the BMM requirements.

Hence, a BMM modeling language was not enough; we actually needed something wider that embraced several architectures while allowing to create an ITIL holistic organizational view.

In effect, Lankhorst (2009) enumerates and discusses several languages for modeling IT and business:

- IDEF (Integrated Computer - Aided Manufacturing (ICAM) DEFinition), a group of 16 methods that have a military background. Of these methods, IDEF0, IDEF3 and IDEF1X ('the core') are the most widely used. IDEF0 handles functional modeling by representing the elements that control the execution of a function, actors, objects or data consumed and relationship between functions. IDEF3 is about process modeling and uses flow diagrams to model task sequences, workflows and decision logic. As for data modeling there is IDEF1X, used to create logical and physical data models. However, although the IDEF family gives support for modeling different architecture views, there are no communication mechanisms between models, which hinders its visualization as interrelated elements of an architectural system;

- The BPMN standard defines a graphical notation that serves as a common basis for a variety of business process modeling and execution languages. It is however restricted to process modeling, not covering applications or infrastructure, and having as main purpose to provide a uniform notation for modeling business processes in terms of activities and their relationships;

- Testbed is a business modeling language and method intended for business and organization modeling and its target users are mostly business consultants. It recognizes three aspects domains: actor (resources for business activities), behavior (business processes performed by resources) and item (data objects handled by business processes). Nevertheless, the language lacks the architectural perspective of information systems and the concepts related to this;

- ARIS (Architecture of Integrated Information Systems) is a well-known approach to enterprise modeling. It is a business modeling language supported by a software tool, that documents business process types, provides blueprints for analyzing and designing business processes and supports the design of information system. To model business processes in an enterprise model, ARIS uses ordered graphs of events and functions known as event-driven process chains (EPCs), which provide connectors for alternative and parallel execution of processes. However, the semantics of EPCs are given only in verbal form, the corresponding object models are specified in a rudimentary meta-model. Moreover, the graphical notation is extensive, with quite a learning curve; the integration of perspectives does not guarantee the overall integrity of interrelated models; ARIS is limited to business modeling, specifically to organizational, functional and process modeling; and, finally it is not extensible;

- UML (Unified Modeling Language) is the most important industry-standard language for specifying, visualizing, constructing, and documenting the artifacts of software systems. It is managed by the OMG and it is meant to be used by system designers. It has a combination of 13 sublanguages with its own diagram to model a

specific aspect of a software system. These diagrams can be grouped in 3 categories: structure (package, class, object, composite structure), behavior (use case, state, sequence, timing, communication, activity, interaction overview) and implementation (component, deployment). However, these diagram types and UML meta-model are interrelated; no strict separation between views and meta-model concepts has been made, which leads to ill-defined relations between modeling concepts in different diagrams. On the other hand, UML partially has a formal basis but misses semantic and consistency, what makes difficult to define rigorous analysis techniques.

Moreover, Lankhorst also identifies common issues among them all, like poorly defined relations between domains, models not integrated, weak formal basis and lack of clearly defined semantics, and the fact that most of them miss the overall architecture vision being confined to either business or application and technology domains. It is also noticeable that none of them covers the organization's motivation or business strategy.

ArchiMate, on the other hand, provides a uniform representation for diagrams that describe EAs. It offers an integrated architectural approach that describes and visualizes the different architecture domains and their underlying relations and dependencies, and, since version 2.0, it also has a Motivation extension that introduces the elements that "provide the context or reason lying behind the architecture of an enterprise"(The Open Group, 2012).

Actually, this extension recognizes the concepts of stakeholders (persons or organizations that influence, guide or constrain the enterprise), drivers (internal or external factors which influence the plans and aims of a enterprise), assessments (an understanding of strengths, weaknesses, opportunities, and threats in relation to these drivers), goals (desired result to achieve) and requirements, principles and constraints (desired properties to realize the goals).

Therefore, it seemed to fill all the other languages' gaps and stood out as the one we were looking for to model ITIL business motivation.

Mapping ITIL Motivation to ArchiMate

Before starting to model we needed to map ITIL motivational concepts in the language's metamodel. Motivational concepts are used to model the motivations, or reasons, that underlie the design or change of some enterprise architecture. These motivations influence, guide, and constrain the design (The Open Group, 2012).

ArchiMate's Motivation metamodel (Figure 2) has motivational elements that are realized by requirements, which in turn are realized by core concepts. Stakeholders are structure elements assigned from Business Actors. The Motivation elements are driver, assessment, goal, principle and constraint.

Therefore, based on the major areas concepts of the Business Motivation Model of OMG (Ends, Means, Influencers) and also on the simpler, smaller BMM concepts' set proposed by TOGAF (drivers, goals, objectives, measures) we analyzed the ITIL literature and searched for concepts within a small semantic distance.

In effect, in ITIL there are roles, departments, business units and service owners that have interests and concerns in the outcome of the architecture. These are ArchiMate's stakeholders. Then, factors that influence the motivational elements are usually presented in the process introduction or definition, sometimes in the scope or otherwise referred as drivers or stakeholders concerns. These elements represent the ArchiMate concept driver. Later on, it is common for enterprises to take assessments of these drivers. In ITIL these are represented as a SWOT or driver analysis that is used to identify benefits, problems, mistakes, risks and opportunities. The desired results that a stakeholder wants to achieve are referred in ITIL as the organization mission, goal or objectives.

Figure 2. ArchiMate motivation metamodel (adapted from The Open Group (2012))

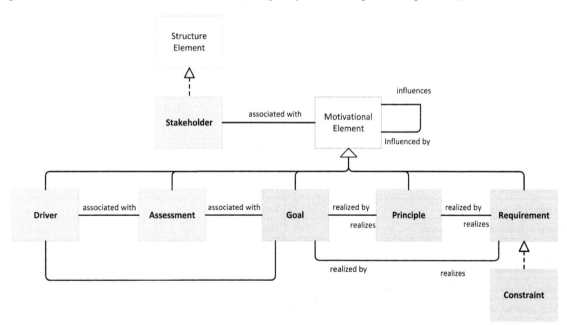

This matches ArchiMate's goal concept. Next we have desired properties of solutions – or means – to realize the goals. In ITIL we have requirements, policies, implementation and guidelines that correspond to ArchiMate's requirement. Likewise, we have in ITIL principles and implementation guidelines that map to principle and finally there is constraint that maps to its ArchiMate homonym counterpart.

On Table 1 we present a map with the summary of ITIL motivational concepts and relationships to ArchiMate's Motivation extension.

DEMONSTRATION

In this section we present the ITIL principles that will restrict the design freedom of our architecture and, afterwards, we shall present several ArchiMate models based on the last section's mapping and on our definition of the ITIL business motivation model.

Architecture Principles

We started by the identification and definition of ITIL principles, which will be our architecture's

principles. In fact, architecture principles provide a means to direct transformations of enterprises, forming the cornerstones of any architecture and bridging the gap between high-level strategic intents and concrete designs (Greefhorst & Proper, 2011).

Dietz (2006) also points out that "The notion of architecture I have in mind is one of normalized restriction of design freedom. Operationally, it is a set of design principles, concerning both the function and the construction of systems." (p. 216).

Also, according to TOGAF (2009) "Principles are general rules and guidelines, intended to be enduring and seldom amended, that inform and support the way in which an organization sets about fulfilling its mission" (p. 265).

On the other hand, as part of the specification process, architecture principles may be prioritized to determine the guiding (key) architecture principles. These are the most fundamental ones. Those that truly make a difference are the hardest to change and are closest to the drivers. Determining the guiding architecture principles is important since top-level architectures should only contain a limited number of architecture principles. A rule of thumb is to have no more than 10 guiding architecture principles. More than that decreases

Table 1. Mapping concepts and relationships

ITIL Concept	ArchiMate Concept
Role, Department, Business unit, Service Owner, Responsibility	Stakeholder
Concern, driver, scope, process introduction, process definition	Driver
Benefit, problem, mistake, risk, opportunity, SWOT analysis	Assessment
Mission, goal, objective	Goal
Requirement, policy	Requirement
Principle, implementation guideline	Principle
Constraint	Constraint
ITIL relationship	ArchiMate relationship
Is related to, assessment resulted in, stakeholder is concerned with	Association
Makes possible, implements	Realization
Benefits, prejudices	Influence

the accessibility of the architecture, and obfuscates the importance of the most important architecture principles. Other architecture principles can be documented in downstream architectures (segment architectures, reference architectures and solution architectures) (Greefhorst & Proper, 2011).

Accordingly, in ITIL we also find this principle hierarchy, where we can identify sets of principles according to the scope we chose to address. In fact, the main ITIL principle is "all services must provide measurable value to business objectives and outcomes", followed by three other fundamental principles (Van Bon et al., 2007):

- **Specialization & co-ordination principle:** The goal of service management is to make capabilities and resources available through services that are useful and acceptable to the customer with regard to quality, costs and risks. The service provider takes the weight of responsibility and resource management off the customer's shoulders so that they can focus on the business' core competence. Service management coordinates the business of service management responsibility with regard to certain resources. Utility and warranty act as a guide;
- **Agency principle:** Service management always involves an agent and a principal that seconds this agent to fulfill activities on their behalf. Agents may be consultants, advisors or service providers. Service agents act as intermediary between service providers and customers in conjunction with users. Usually, these agents are the service provider's staff, but they can also be self-service systems and processes for users. Value for the customer is created through agreements between principals and agents;
- **Encapsulation principle:** The customer's interest focuses on the value of use; he prefers to be spared from any technical details

and structure complexity. The 'encapsulation principle' is focused on hiding what the customer does not need and showing what is valuable and useful to the customer. Three principles are closely linked to this: separation of concerns; modularity: a clear, modular structure; and loose coupling: reciprocal independence of resources and users.

However, since ITIL is a five-book framework, it is possible to enumerate principles for each of the books, which guide and restrict the freedom of design on the topics they cover. They are aimed to enable service providers to plan and implement these best practices. The Stationary Office (2007b) also states that "principles are the same irrespective of the organization: however, the approach may need to be tailored to circumstances, including the size, distribution, culture and resources" (p. 23), what comes aligned to what Greefhorst and Proper (2011) have also defended: "Depending on the specific situation, different drivers will lead to the formulation (and enforcement) of design principles, and architecture principles in particular" (p. 49). As an example, we present the Service Transition book principles:

- Define and implement a formal policy for Service Transition;
- Implement all changes to services through Service Transition;
- Adopt a common framework and standards;
- Maximize re-use of established processes and systems;
- Align Service Transition plans with the business needs;
- Establish and maintain relationships with stakeholders;
- Establish effective controls and disciplines;
- Provide systems for knowledge transfer and decision support;
- Plan release and deployment packages;
- Anticipate and manage course corrections;

- Proactively manage resources across Service Transitions;
- Ensure early involvement in the service lifecycle;
- Assure the quality of the new or changed service;
- Proactively improve quality during Service Transition.

Then again, ITIL also defines sub principles for each of the above. Below we present the key principles for "Define and implement a formal policy for Service Transition":

- Policies should clearly state the objectives and any non-compliance with the policy shall be remedied;
- Align the policies with the overall governance framework, organization and Service Management policies;
- Sponsors and decision makers involved in developing the policy must demonstrate their commitment to adapting and implementing the policy;
- This includes the commitment to deliver predicted outcomes from any change in the Services;
- Use processes that integrate teams; blend competencies while maintaining clear lines of accountability and responsibility;
- Deliver changes in releases;
- Address deployment early in the release design and release planning stages.

We have presented these principles as they are stated on ITIL. However, according to Greefhorst and Proper (2011) architecture principles should adhere to a number of quality criteria; they should be specific, measurable, achievable, relevant and time framed (SMART).

Therefore, we also wanted to evaluate ITIL principles according to the SMART approach. Thus, we find them quite specific according to its depth level; on the other hand, they are definitely achievable; and, as for measurability, ITIL provides several key performance indicators (KPI) to measure these principles. There is however an obvious deficiency in the time-framed attribute, but then again we are talking about a set of best practices to apply on different organizations, so we would advise to use these principles and add time-frame properties according to the specific organization where ITIL is being applied on.

Modeling ITIL Business Motivation Model in ArchiMate

Although we had a concept mapping from the last section, we wanted to go further on and demonstrate that it really could be used to model ITIL BMM in the ArchiMate language.

Thereby, we started to analyze the official ITIL books, going through all its processes' and functions' descriptions. In fact, we had already done this on a first iteration when we were identifying the ITIL BMM concepts. This time, however, we were not looking for the concept's class, but for its instances. For example, instead of looking up for concepts that were semantically close to "goal", we were now searching for references of its ITIL counterparts "mission, goal, objective" and gathering its instances like "detect service events" or "ensure only authorized users can use services" in the Service Operation book.

Following this procedure, we eventually compiled a set of elements that are, in our opinion, the most relevant motivation items for every ITIL process.

This assumption is based on the elements' own relevance through the official books and general ITIL sources. However, being ITIL a set of best practices, built upon IT service providers' different opinions and experiences, we also concede that some practitioners could include other elements or leave some of these out.

Thereby, we do not want to claim that this is the only motivational representation of ITIL, but instead to demonstrate that based on our mapping, on the identified concepts and on our perception, this is our proposed ITIL BMM model and its ArchiMate representation. We therefore welcome (and encourage) that these BMM proposals are revised by the ITIL community itself and may eventually be adapted to reflect, as ITIL does, the majority of its practitioners' opinions.

Earlier in Figure 2 we presented the ArchiMate metamodel of motivational concepts. It included the actual motivations or intentions - i.e., goals, principles, requirements, and constraints – and

the sources of these intentions; i.e., stakeholders, drivers, and assessments. Motivational elements are related to the core elements via the requirement or constraint concept. On Figure 3 we present the ArchiMate notation for each of these concepts.

With these concepts' instances we produced several models. In this paper we shall only present a small set of them. The first (Figure 4) represents an ITIL overview with all its five books. Here we can see the main motivations for ITIL and which of its books realizes them. We can also see why

Figure 3. Notation for ArchiMate motivation concepts

Figure 4. ITIL business motivation model overview (http://db.tt/xRiyqm6Q)

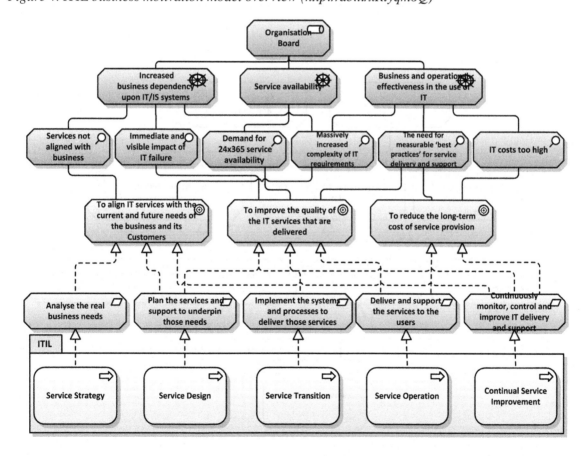

organizations need ITIL and what are the main problems that ITIL addresses and how does it proposes to solve them.

In fact, as drivers we have "Increased business dependency upon IT/IS systems", "Service availability" and "Business and operational effectiveness in the use of IT". Upon these drivers assessments were used to identify possible issues as, for instance, "Services not aligned with business", "Immediate and visible impact of IT failure" and "Demand for 24x365 service availability". All these problems lead to the definition of strategic goals that the organization needs to achieve like "Align IT services with the current and future needs of the business and its Customers", "Improve the quality of the IT services that are delivered" and "Reduce the long term cost of service provision".

These goals are realized by requirements that are the tactics on how to reach them. In this figure we show for each requirement which ITIL book

(here we informally abstract an ITIL book as a set of ITIL processes) realizes it. We have, for instance, the "Analyze the real business needs" requirement that is realized by the Service Strategy book; or the "Deliver and support the services to the users" which is realized by the Service Operation one.

In this model, each book is modeled as a black box system, where we just know that some architectural element inside it (a process, role, application component, infrastructure, et cetera) realizes the said requirement, regardless of which it is.

Afterwards, in Figure 5, we zoom into one of the ITIL books, the Service Strategy one. Now we can see an expanded set of drivers, assessments, goals and requirements that are related and realized by the Service Strategy book.

Here for the concerns of "Value creation" and "Service Assets and Strategy" the goals are now "Ensure the market is well defined" and "Ensure the offerings and strategic assets are developed". The requirements to realize these goals are, for

Figure 5. Detail of service strategy, full model available in http://db.tt/vY7xA1zx

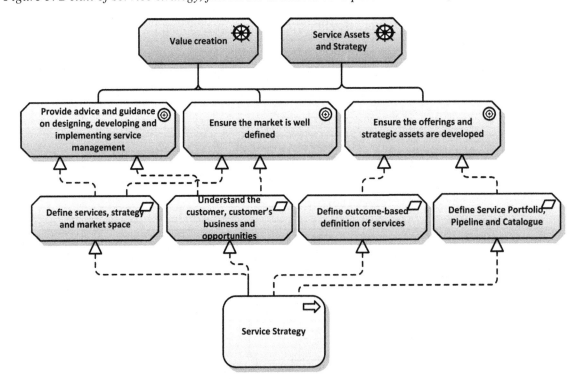

instance, "Define services, strategy and market space" or "Understand the customer, customer's business and opportunities". Again, the Service Strategy book is seen as a black box system, but now, since it is the system of interest (as opposed to the last model, which the system of interest was the whole ITIL) each motivation element is a refinement and/or specialization of the ones in the former model.

In Figure 6 we show the motivations (at the same level of depth) for another ITIL book, the Service Operation one. Here we have as drivers "IT services day-to-day operations" and "Incident handling service interruption and restore".

We have assessments like "Lack of defined processes to support SLAs", "Security breaches while accessing services" or "Events not automatically detected". These lead to formulate goals like "Ensure only authorized users can access services", "Detect service events" or "Resolve incidents and resume service as soon as possible". As we did before, we need to define requirements to realize these goals, and these are, for example, "Implement authentication, authorization and validation tools", "Use automatic monitoring tools for event detecting and report" or "Identify, log, categorize, diagnose, solve and close incidents". All these requirements are then realized by the Service Operation book.

In Figure 7 we aimed for a deeper fine-grained representation and focused on the Business Relationship Management process. This allows us to look to this process and see again which are its motivational elements and how are they realized by requirements, now in a process scope. Here we take the driver "Customer needs" we see that assessments have identified some issues: "Services are not what the customer asked for" and

Figure 6. Detail of service operation, full model available in http://db.tt/OO7r7de5

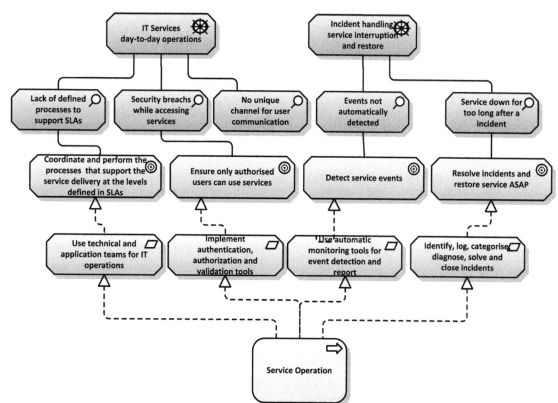

Figure 7. Detail of business relationship management, full model available at http://db.tt/MdFx9XyR

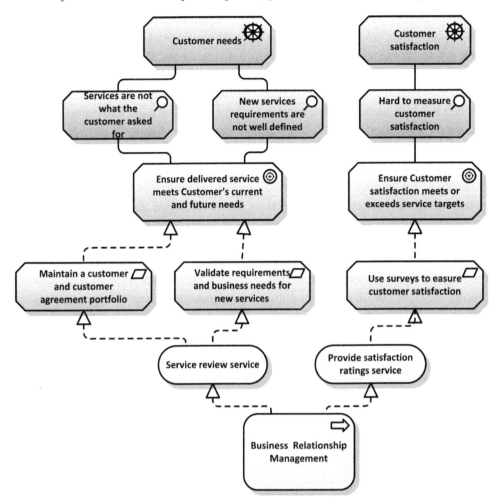

"New service requirements are not well defined". Both these problems can be solved if we achieve the goal of "Ensure delivered service meets Customer's current and future needs", which, in turn, is realized by the requirements "Maintain a customer agreement portfolio" and "Validate requirements and business needs for new services". These requirements will be realized this time by the Business Relationship Management process, which is now our black box system.

In Figure 8 we show the same set of motivational elements for the Incident Management process, from ITIL Service Operation book. Here, doing the same top-down approach, we may start at the "Service Quality" driver, for which assess-

ments have identified the "Same incidents keep happening" and "Interruptions take too long to solve" issues. To address the former we set the goal of "Ensure all incidents are recorded" and to realize this, we set the requirement "Incidents must be identified, categorized, prioritized and logged". As before, these requirements will be realized by architectural elements from the Incident Management process.

Finally, to show how we can use these models to align business and IT, we present in Figure 9, a model where we show, for several Incident Management requirements, which are the specific activities from this process that realize each one of the requirements.

Figure 8. Detail of incident management, full model available at http://db.tt/15hxwU2N

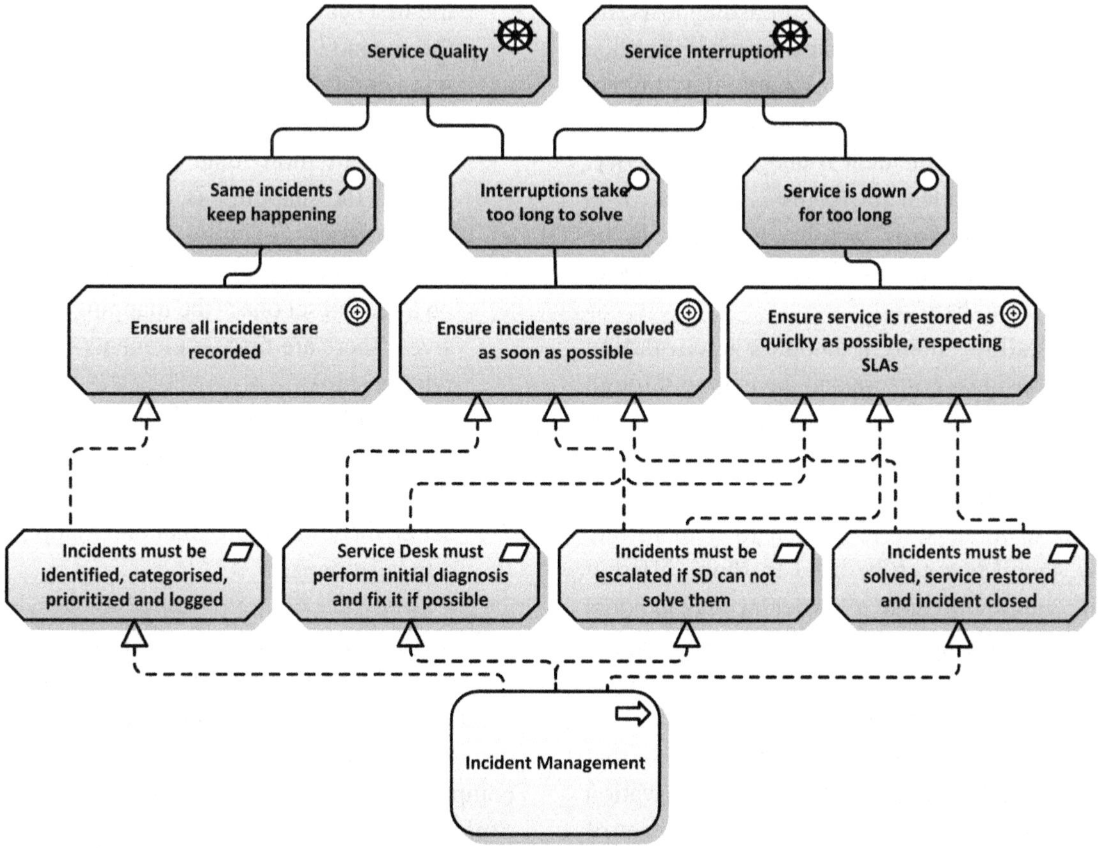

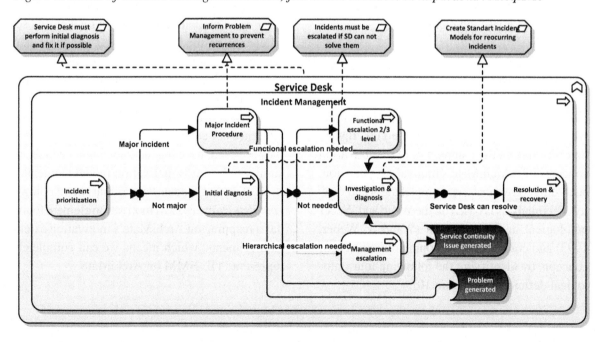

Figure 9. Detail of incident management model, full model available in http://db.tt/7MlcqXvR

We can see, for instance, that the requirement "Service Desk must perform initial diagnosis and fix it if possible" is realized by the whole Service Desk function. On the other hand, the "Inform Problem Management to prevent recurrences" is realized by a Incident Management activity: the "Major incident procedure". Likewise, it is the "Initial diagnosis" activity that realizes the "Incidents must be escalated if Service Desk cannot solve them".

This allows doing a complete trace starting from a business concern and navigating through assessments, goals and requirements until we reach the actual activity (or other core architecture element) that realizes business strategy.

These models were chosen to demonstrate how ArchiMate can be used to show different ITIL views, directed to different stakeholders with own concerns. Yet, all the models remain consistent, since the elements are similar but on different granularity levels.

Overall, we produced all the models that represent the complete ITIL business motivation model. Together, our work consists on a set of models with the whole ITIL 26 processes and 4 functions motivation model, representing for each book and each process the whole set of drivers, assessments, goals and requirements.

EVALUATION

Since one of the goals of this paper is to contribute with a formal representation of the ITIL BMM, here we analyze the mapping of ITIL motivation concepts into ArchiMate's motivation extension, according to two criteria: completeness and clarity. This analysis is based on the Wand and Weber ontological analysis method (Wand & Weber, 1993) and compares the mapping of both sets of concepts by identifying the following four ontological deficiencies (Figure 10):

- **Incompleteness:** Can each element from the first set be mapped on an element from the second? (the mapping is incomplete if it is not total).
- **Redundancy:** Are the first set elements mapped to more than a second set element? (the mapping is redundant if it is ambiguous).
- **Excess:** Is every first set element mapped on a second set one? (the mapping is excessive if there are first set elements without a relationship).
- **Overload:** Is every first set element mapped to exactly one second set element? (the mapping is overloaded if any second set element has more than one mapping to a first set one).

The amount of concepts in ITIL that have no representation in ArchiMate defines the lack of completeness, clarity is a combination of redundancy, overload and excess of concepts. Lack of completeness would be a serious issue while lack of clarity would make the mapping unidirectional and hard to reverse.

It should be again noted what we are mapping. In fact, we have on one hand ArchiMate, which is a formal modeling language, with a closed set of clearly defined concepts and, on the other, textual descriptions of IT best practices. There is not in ITIL a clear definition of a motivational elements' set that would clearly ease our task, so our identification is based on ITIL textual references of concepts that, in the context where they are used, have business meanings which are similar to business motivation model elements.

Having that, we can then say that our mapping is *complete*, as every ITIL motivation element found has a mapping on ArchiMate's motivation extension elements, which means we can completely represent ITIL BMM on ArchiMate.

Figure 10. Ontological deficiencies

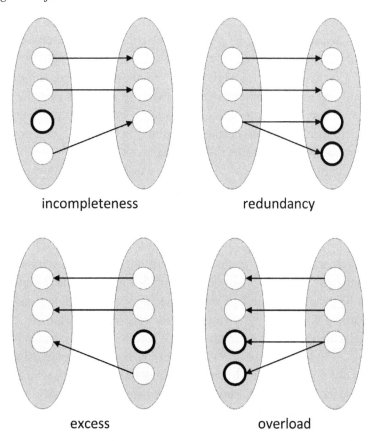

As for *redundancy*, since ArchiMate's motivation elements is a small, closed set, as opposed to ITIL richness of textual descriptions, it was expectable that there was only one ArchiMate element to represent any ITIL concept. This means it becomes straightforward to model ITIL BMM in ArchiMate as we do not have to choose between several elements to model an ITIL one.

It should however be noted that if we had found redundancy, then the "correct" ArchiMate concept would have to be chosen according to context and experience. Although this choice could be rather easy for human architects, it could be a serious problem for automated model transformations.

We also did not find *excess*, as ArchiMate concepts are all present on ITIL. This was also expected since the ArchiMate motivation elements

are aligned with the TOGAF ones, which we used as part of the guidelines when searching in ITIL.

Finally, we found one deficiency: *overload*, because there are several ITIL concepts to only one from ArchiMate. This happens because, as we have mentioned before, ITIL does not explicitly define a BMM or identifies its concepts. Therefore, since we have to derive motivation elements from ITIL textual descriptions, it was predictable that several ITIL concepts would match an ArchiMate one. This deficiency can lead to problems if we ever wanted to do the opposite process: to go from an ArchiMate ITIL motivation model back to ITIL again. To avoid this, while modeling, we should include in ArchiMate's object attributes a reference to the original ITIL concept it was mapped from, to allow an eventual reverse mapping.

To sum up, we can conclude that our mapping is complete, not ambiguous and not excessive. It is indeed overloaded, but this actually derives from the intrinsic nature of the problem we want to solve: the lack of a formal BMM for ITIL. Furthermore, by identifying and mapping these concepts, we believe we are also contributing with a tool that can help to identify and define the motivation model of future ITIL releases and to update our models accordingly.

CONCLUSION

Having two different approaches to IT governance can lead to several setbacks. In a time when organizations strive to be efficient and effective, one should not be wasting resources by having different organizational departments or teams handling both approaches independently.

Therefore, we propose to integrate the Enterprise Architecture approach and the ITIL framework through the definition of a specific EA, with its own set of principles, methods, models and views, to give the enterprise architect the tools to design specific organizations according to ITSM best practices. However, this work focuses only on that architecture's motivation model, on the motivations that constrain and underlie its design or change.

Thus, we started up with the conviction that like EA, ITIL also had a business motivation model and there was a need to define and model it through a formal graphical language.

For that task, we chose ArchiMate's Motivation extension and mapped ITIL motivation to it. In fact, the main contribution of this proposal is the definition and formalization of ITIL business motivation model for all its 26 processes and 4 functions, with the inclusion of roles, drivers, assessments, goals and requirements.

By using this approach we are able to design better organizations according to ITSM best practices, by identifying in our models what are the most relevant concerns and drivers for each organization, and trace them down through goals, principles and requirements to the specific ITIL book, process and activity that realizes them.

This way we can achieve business/IT alignment by ensuring that the ITIL processes that will be implemented in each organization have a direct match to the organization's concerns and business strategy.

For future work, we believe the next step is to expose these models to the ITIL community where they can be validated, and, in particular, can be used to promote discussion about the ITIL motivation model itself. Furthermore, we are currently working on modeling ITIL's business, application, information and infrastructure architectures in ArchiMate's core concepts, to answer the remaining Zachman's questions: the "How, What, Who, Where and When". Next, we plan to bridge both approaches using business motivation model requirements which are realized by core elements like processes, activities or databases.

In short, IT has the goal to turn organizations more efficient and effective, and to achieve this, it is fundamental that each stakeholder is aware of change, its reasons and how he will be affected by it. Communicating, designing and implementing change is therefore a key factor on agile, prone to change organizations. Furthermore, it is also our belief that when people are well informed about the whys, then resistance to change may be overcome and diminished.

Thereby, the goal of this work is twofold: on one hand to contribute to a better communication and representation of ITIL motivation concepts, to encourage ITIL discussion in its own community and to help each stakeholder realize what is to be changed and why is it being changed, through a set of complete, consistent and formal models; and, on the other, to set the motivation model of a specific Enterprise Architecture to design organizations according to ITIL best practices on IT service management.

REFERENCES

Arraj, V. (2010). *ITIL: The basics white paper.* The Stationary Office.

Braun, C., & Winter, R. (2007). Integration of IT service management into enterprise architecture. In ACM (Ed.) *ACM Symposium on Applied Computing*, New York, NY (pp. 1215-1219).

Correia, A., & Abreu, F. B. (2009). Integrating IT service management within the enterprise architecture. In *Proceedings of the 4th ICSEA*, Porto, Portugal (pp. 553–558).

Dietz, J. (2006). *Enterprise ontology–theory and methodology.* Berlin: Springer. doi:10.1007/3-540-33149-2

FoxPRISM. (2012). Retrieved Augst 26, 2012, from http: //www.foxit.net/pages/toolkits/fox-PRISM.shtml

Gama, N., Sousa, P., & Mira da Silva, M. (2012). Integrating enterprise architecture and IT service management. In *Proceedigns of the 21st International Conference on Information Systems Development (ISD2012)*, Prado, Italy.

Greefhorst, D., & Proper, E. (2011). *Architecture principles: The cornerstones of enterprise architecture.* Berlin, Germany: Springer. doi:10.1007/978-3-642-20279-7

Hanna, A., Windebank, J., Adams, S., Sowerby, J., Rance, S., & Cartlidge, A. (2008). *ITIL V3 foundation handbook.* Norwich, UK: The Stationary Office.

Hevner, A., March, S., Park, J., & Ram, S. (2004). Design science in information systems research. *Management Information Systems Quarterly, 28,* 78–105.

Hochstein, A., Zarnekow, R., & Brenner, W. (2005). ITIL as common practice reference model for it service management: Formal assessment and implications for practice. In *Proceedings of the 2005 IEEE International Conference on eTechnology eCommerce and eService* (Vol. 21, pp. 704–710).

ITIL process maps. (2012). Retrieved August 26, 2012, from http://en.it-processmaps.com

Jonkers, H., Proper, E., & Turner, M. (2009). *TOGAF 9 and ArchiMate 1.0. White Paper.* The Open Group.

Lankhorst, M., & the ArchiMate team. (2004). *ArchiMate language primer.*

Lankhorst, M. et al. (2009). *Enterprise architecture at work.* Berlin, Germany: Springer. doi:10.1007/978-3-642-01310-2

Nabiollahi, A., Alias, R. A., & Sahibuddin, S. (2010). A service based framework for integration of ITIL V3 and enterprise architecture. In *Proceedings of the 2010 International Symposium in Information Technology (ITSim),* Kuala Lumpur (Vol 1, pp. 1-5).

Object Management Group. (2010). *Business motivation model v1.1.* Object Management Group.

Object Management Group. (2011). *Business process model and notation (BPMN) version 2.0.* Object Management Group.

Pereira, C., & Sousa, P. (2004). A method to define an enterprise architecture using the Zachman framework. In ACM (Ed.), *Proceedings of the 19th Annual ACM Symposium on Applied Computing (SAC'04)*, Nicosia, Cyprus (pp. 1366-1371).

Radhakrishnan, R. (2008). *Enterprise architecture & IT service management - ITSM frameworks and processes and their relationship to EA frameworks and processes*. The Open Group.

Ross, J. W., Weill, P., & Robertson, D. C. (Eds.). (2006). *Enterprise architecture as strategy: Creating a foundation for business execution*. Boston, MA: Harvard Business School Press.

Taylor, S., Lloyd, V., & Rudd, C. (Eds.). (2007). *ITIL: Service design*. Norwich, UK: TSO.

The casewise online visual process model for ITIL version 3. (2012). Retrieved August 26, 2012, from http://www.casewise.com/itil

The Open Group. (2009). *TOGAF version 9, The open group architecture framework*. The Open Group.

The Open Group. (2012). *Archimate 2.0 specification*. The Open Group.

The Stationery Office. (2007). *The official introduction to the ITIL service lifecycle*. The Stationery Office.

The Stationery Office. (2007b). *Service transition*. The Stationery Office.

Thorn, S. (2007). TOGAF and ITIL. In The Open Group (Ed.), Vol. Catalog number W071, 26, San Francisco, CA.

Van Bon, J. et al. (2007). *Foundations of IT service management based on ITIL v3*. Van Haren Publishing.

Van Sante, T., & Ermersj, J. (2009). *TOGAF 9 and ITIL V3*. Retrieved from www.best-management-practice.com

Vicente, M., Gama, N., & Mira da Silva, M. (2013). Modeling ITIL business motivation model in ArchiMate. In J. Falcão e Cunha, M. Snene, & H. Nóvoa (Eds.), *Exploring services science, 143, Lecture Notes in Business Information Processing* (pp. 86–99). Springer Berlin Heidelberg. doi:10.1007/978-3-642-36356-6_7

Vicente, M., Gama, N., & Mira da Silva, M. (2013b). Using ArchiMate and TOGAF to understand the enterprise architecture and ITIL relationship. In X. Franch & P. Soffer (Eds.), *CAiSE 2013 Workshops, 148, Lecture Notes in Business Information Processing* (pp. 134–145). Springer Berlin Heidelberg. doi:10.1007/978-3-642-38490-5_11

Wand, Y., & Weber, R. (1993). On the ontological expressiveness of information systems analysis and design grammars. *Information Systems Journal*, *3*(4), 217–237. doi:10.1111/j.1365-2575.1993.tb00127.x

Zachman, J. (1987). A framework for information systems architecture. *IBM Systems Journal*, *26*, 276–292. doi:10.1147/sj.263.0276

This work was previously published in the International Journal of Information System Modeling and Design (IJISMD), 5(1); edited by Remigijus Gustas, pages 83-107, copyright year 2014 by IGI Publishing (an imprint of IGI Global).

Section 6
Emerging Trends

This section highlights research potential within the field of web design and development while explor-ing uncharted areas of study for the advancement of the discipline. Introducing this section are chapters that set the stage for future research directions and topical suggestions for continued debate, centering on the new venues and forums for discussion. A pair of chapters on space-time makes up the middle of the section of the final 5 chapters, and the book concludes with a look ahead into the future of the web design and development field. In all, this text will serve as a vital resource to practitioners and academics interested in the best practices and applications of the burgeoning field of web design and development.

Chapter 75

Challenges, Opportunities, and Trends in Quality K–12 Online Environments

Marius Boboc
Cleveland State University, USA

ABSTRACT

This chapter provides background information related to K-12 online education, ranging from definitions to benefits and challenges. An in-depth analysis of the virtual learning landscape reveals the multitude of dimensions by which it could be evaluated, including the range of programs, service provider types, approaches to blended learning, kinds of instruction delivery, as well as levels of interaction within cyberspace. A proposed theoretical framework identifies academic programs/curricula, student support services, and virtual program/school administration as categories that connect the relevant literature review to recommendations for future research intended to inform policy-setting efforts aimed at supporting the further development of high quality K-12 online environments.

INTRODUCTION

Online learning in the world of K-12 education has grown substantially over a rather short period of time. For instance, virtual schools have gained public interest and recognition since the first one was established in 1996. A decade later, Michigan became the first state to require that each student should have exposure to e-learning prior to graduation from high school (DiPietro, Ferdig, Black, and Preston, 2008). Today 24 states and Washington, D.C. have blended schools, while entirely online, multi-district schools in 30 states serve more than 310,000 students. At the same time, more private/independent schools include supplemental online and hybrid classes (Watson, Murin, Vashaw, Gemin, and Rapp, 2013). Over the course of last century, high school and college retention and graduation rates have increased gradually, in spite of occasional fluctuations. As societal needs change, schools have to keep up the pace of innovation, especially in terms of computer technology. There is increasing pressure on K-12 education to reform teaching and learning in ways that accommodate the development of 21st century skills required for high school and college gradu-

DOI: 10.4018/978-1-4666-8619-9.ch075

ates to be competitive in a global workforce market. Decision makers and stakeholders in education are taking into account the current achievement gap demonstrated by American students, reduced funding opportunities, the digital divide impacting students across the country, and an expected teacher shortage. Under these circumstances, online education has become a viable set of models for instruction delivery. While the field is still refining its operational terms (e-learning, virtual schooling, digital instruction, etc.), its potential as "disruptive innovation" (Horn, 2010) should be backed up by evidence-based research on the actual use of technology in the classroom along a continuum of types of instructional settings ranging from traditional, face-to-face to hybrid/blended to entirely Web-based. While there is increased legislative support for virtual learning, policy-setting structures need data designed to indicate the need for support in terms of curricula, staffing, administration, infrastructure, accountability requirements, professional development, etc.

While the current research on the effectiveness of e-learning is still insufficient, there are indications that is promotes greater access to equitable, high quality, cost-efficient learning opportunities to students that may not otherwise benefit from a wider range of formal education options. The computer technologies used in virtual settings have also evolved to become more student-centered and interactive, while supporting teachers in structuring their courses better. As the needs, interests, and characteristics of students change over time, online education is expected to play an important role in providing specialized services that are at least on par with traditional, face-to-face schools. At the same time, the shift in learner profile accommodated by e-learning implies enhanced reflection and autonomy, as students assume more responsibility in instructional sequences they are engaged in. At the same time, the roles online teachers play change accordingly, as they become more facilitating as designers, motivators, and trouble-shooters in virtual learning settings.

As the field of online learning is in its formative stage, there are several drawbacks that have been referenced by several research reports and policy briefs. On the one hand, the initial cost of setting up a high quality virtual environment, coupled with the requirements of scaling up to meet a wide range of student needs, led to the redefining/restructuring of some initiatives. As various models of e-learning have been proposed, the need for some structure and guiding standards emerged. Efforts were made to investigate how the effectiveness of traditional, face-to-face instruction could translate into equally effective online delivery systems. The quality of curricula and their associated pedagogy, the level of support for teachers, students, and parents, coupled with the multi-faceted administration of hybrid/blended courses, programs, or schools developed into topics of conversation about e-learning that are dealt with in this chapter.

Continuing the line of inquiry into what constitutes high quality online education is intended to have significant implications for future policy-setting efforts. The chapter proposes a framework within which the perceived benefits and challenges of e-learning come together to inform how institutional technology plans connect the local context, in terms of academic programs, student support services, and administration, with state, national, and global levels where online students can prove the quality of their education.

BACKGROUND

The correlation between educational opportunities for all students and their academic achievement supports the national economic development. According to a seminal study by Goldin and Katz (as cited by Picciano and Seaman, 2010), the American economy's unprecedented growth in the 20th century is in part due to increasing numbers of students being able to complete cycles of formal education, especially secondary and postsecondary. An in-depth analysis of these trends indicate consistently high enrollment and graduation rates from high school and college, primarily for the first half of the 20ᵗʰ century. There are several reasons for which the second half of last century demonstrated a fluctuation of these rates, particularly after 1970. The two researchers take into account the quality of high school curricula and pedagogy as a subset of these factors, with a direct impact on the preparedness for college and career based on a 4-year graduation model. According to the 2012 Digest of Education Statistics, about 3,376,000 students were expected to graduate high school at the end of the 2012-2013 academic year, lower than the record high in 2009-2010. The number represents 78.2 percent of high school students graduating in four years (U.S. Department of Education, 2012). In 2011, the dropout rate was 7.1 percent among 16-to 24-year olds. Though the trend had slowed down compared to the 12.1 percent rate in 1990, African American and Hispanic students were more at risk of poor academic performance compared to White students. Consequently, there have been attempts to deal with the increasing problem of students at risk of dropping out of school, both secondary and college. Among them, there are a few that are worth mentioning, such as early college programs, differentiated instruction, school day extension, and credit recovery (Picciano and Seaman, 2010).

The field of education is moving from an "industrial-age paradigm (...) to a learner-centered, information-age paradigm" (Reigeluth, Carr-Chellman, Beabout, and Watson, 2009, p. 131). The roles teachers and students play in the process of instruction have changed by placing them within a gradually less hierarchical structure. Along the same lines, students and teachers have become co-creators of knowledge. The artifacts of this teacher-mediated/facilitated learning process ground the acquisition of knowledge and the development of skills in the realities students

actually face, thus rendering learning relevant to their individual lives. Computer technology applications to classroom practice have led to the production of increasingly complex digital media artifacts that are part of a larger range inclusive of legislative, architectural, recreational, and personal products (Garner, 2013).

Given the fast-paced world of computer technology and its increasing effect on schooling, we have witnessed a variety of attempts to reform teaching and learning. These initiatives have impacted all aspects of education, ranging from curriculum to assessment to pedagogy. Whether the impetus is internal or external to schools and education professionals, the ensuing discourse has prompted all stakeholders to take a closer look at how schooling as a system is set up and how efficient it is. Part of these conversations focuses on the delivery of instruction, spurred by recent innovations in computer technologies with direct applications to classroom settings. The sense of urgency in aligning education with effective uses of technology is underscored by a policy brief issued in 2011 by the Alliance for Excellent Education (AEE). According to it, there are three factors that should be taken into account in setting policies at various decision-making levels that would govern the implementation of digital learning. The apparent gap between education attainment of American students and the global labor market demands is compounded by the emerging inability to fund educational initiatives, coupled with an expected teacher shortage from 2015 onward. All these challenges require urgent measures from the federal level all the way to that of individual school districts and school buildings, aimed at meeting the requirements of recent attempts to reform education, such as Race to the Top and Investing in Innovation. Under these circumstances, digital learning is expected to play a pivotal role in terms of increasing teacher effectiveness, providing all students with equitable access to education, documenting the progress made by each student as a way to narrow the achievement gap, as well as enabling students to make informed choices about college and/or career.

DEFINING ONLINE EDUCATION

There have been several words and phrases used to delineate the semantic realm of online education proposed by a variety of stakeholders, such as researchers, practitioners, as well as organizations, both federal/national and non-profit. Each definition relies on several characteristics of the field that attempt to be in synchronicity with the latest developments in computer technology, as identified by several researchers (Carnevale, 2001; Larreamendy-Joerns and Leinhardt, 2006; Saba, 2005). The range of identifiers includes distance education, distance learning, e-learning, Web-based education/instruction, digital learning, virtual learning, or the eponymous online education. Some of these defining terms are considered synonymous or interchangeable (Watson, Murin, Vashaw, Gemin, and Rapp, 2013). Using technology to enhance student learning is considered digital learning, inclusive of a "wide spectrum of tools and practice," based on a document released by the Alliance for Excellent Education as part of its Digital Learning Series (2012, p. 1). According to a document called *Digital Learning Now*, online instruction focuses on computer technology mediating student learning by providing "some element of control over time, place, path and/or pace" (Foundation for Excellence in Education, 2011, p. 5). While underlying the teaching and learning process on its reliance on the Internet, online instruction continues earlier iterations of distance learning (Means, Toyama, Murphy, Bakia, and Jones, 2010). Under these circumstances, online learning represents the convergence of technology, content delivered digitally, and specific pedagogical tools and strategies. Depending on the extent to which computer technology is used to support instruction, the terms used also include

blended or hybrid learning (Watson, 2008; Wicks, 2010). A more comprehensive definition of online education is used by the National Education Association by making reference to the curriculum, the location differential between students and teachers, the a/synchronous nature of communication, the increased teacher presence accommodated by the virtual environment (as opposed to the physical learning setting of traditional classrooms), a learning platform or course management system that allows for monitoring of teacher as well as student performance.

THE LANDSCAPE OF ONLINE EDUCATION

Today's students are a lot more used to computer technology than any previous generation in the history of humankind. Playing, communicating, learning, and socializing using various software applications have in common greater levels of interactivity. Consequently, school curricula have changed recently to accommodate, to varying degrees, student demands for relevant, engaging content featuring dynamic exchanges of information that require resources other than text-based (Bailey, Schneider, and Vander Ark, 2012). The potential for increased interactivity and enhanced affordable learning opportunities for all students supports the designation of online learning as disruptive innovation (Horn, 2010). The national picture of computer and Internet use in the U.S. reveals that, while the rate by which Americans can use such technology and its associated applications to daily life has grown substantially, there is a continuous digital gap (U.S. Census Bureau, 2013). Under these circumstances, in 2011 a little more than two thirds of the U.S. population had a computer in their respective households, representing a tremendous increase from less than 10% in 1984 or even a little over 61% in 2004. In tandem, household Internet use grew from 18% in 1997 to over 71% in 2011. Related to the digital gap mentioned earlier, most of non-Hispanic White and Asian households reported having access to the Internet (76.2% and 82.7%, respectively), compared to Hispanic (58.3%) and African American (56.9%) homes. In terms of distribution of census data by age, household members aged 35 to 44 reported the most common Internet access (81.9%), compared to a little over 61% for households where people over 55 live. At the same time, highly educated individuals consistently report using the Internet at higher rates than any other group categorized by level of education achieved. Concurrently, high income earners reported having access to the Internet in much greater numbers than people making less than $25,000 a year – 86% compared to almost 50%. Zooming in on the category dealing with 3-17 year-old individuals, 39.8% of them do not have any Internet connection (13.2% of which have no computer in the house, while the other 26.6% have one). By comparison, 39.1% of individuals in this age group have Internet access.

Given the expanded use of computer technology applications in all aspects of daily life, the field of education is gradually demonstrating a greater awareness of the impact such technologies have on teaching and learning. To that effect, data from a 2012 poll conducted by Project Tomorrow shows an increase of 7 percentage points in school administrators' responses to a question emphasizing the importance of technology use to student success (moving up from 43% in 2008 to 50% in 2012). By the same token, parents demonstrate an upward evolution in terms of the their perception of the same issue, increasing their rating of technology use in the classroom as "extremely important" from 49% in 2008 to 56% four years later. At the same time, there is variation within the range of actual use of computer technology applications to classroom instruction. As an illustration, data provided by the National Center for Education Statistics in 2009, as cited in the Digital Learning Imperative (2012), show that while 97% of teachers had access to a computer

in their respective classroom, only 72% of them (64% of teachers at the high school level) used computers in their teaching. Focusing on particular applications students had an opportunity to engage in, only 13% of teachers said they had used technology to design and develop products, 17% of them gave computer access to students to engage in demonstrations and simulations, while 42% of teachers provided students with the necessary technology to put together multimedia presentations.

In tandem with the various ways in which online education is defined, its practical applications demonstrate a spectrum ranging from home study (or what is traditionally known as distance or correspondence education) to instruction delivery mediated by computer technology either partially or entirely (Rice, 2006). One example of the latter category is represented by virtual high schools. By May 2009, there were 28 states that had statewide virtual high schools, 25 of which had local school districts monitoring diploma-granting processes (Bush, 2009). Of particular interest is the set of purposes such virtual secondary programs serve. To that effect, 24 state programs focused on core curricula, while 7 other programs dealt with supplemental or enrichment instruction. There were additional 24 programs that offer advanced placement opportunities to students in their respective states.

Computer-based instructional technologies have become more prevalent in K-12 settings in recent years (Cavanaugh and Blomeyer, 2007). Consequently, learning has been rendered a lot more fluid or mobile, influenced by the omnipresence of computer technology applications (Barreto and Orey, 2013). As an illustration, 53 percent of public school districts had high school students taking online classes during the 2009-2010 academic year, representing over 1.3 million high school students, a marked increase from the 222,000 students enrolled in distance education in 2002 (NCES, 2012). Moreover, state lawmakers across the country addressed "nearly 700 bills relevant to digital learning" (Foundation for Excellence in Education, 2012, p. 6). The same report references that 152 of those bills were signed into law in various states, allowing students to take courses online.

As "distance learning is becoming mainstream across the country" (Patton, 2005, p. 58), teaching and learning in virtual environments reached an important evolutionary phase. An analysis of recent literature on various ways in which students engage in technology-mediated learning reveals access to virtual resources (such as museum Web sites), tutoring, labs, as well as participation in Web-based a-synchronous discussions (Larreamendy-Joerns and Leinhardt, 2006). Table 1 outlines the dimensions of online education along several important characteristics, as identified by Varounek (2006) and later modified by Wicks (2010). The percentages associated with the various forms of instruction delivery included in the table below are referenced by Archambault and Crippen (2009), as well as by Allen and Seaman (2010). It should be noted that the face-to-face instruction, equivalent to 0 percent online components, is not listed. The learning experience typology is proposed by Means, Toyama, Murphy, Bakia, and Jones (2010, p. 5).

Recent policy briefs identify features of online learning intended to form a framework supportive of various funding options. In this light, being increasingly accessible to a wide range of users, virtual environments provide engaging learning

Table 1. Dimensions of online education; adapted from Varounek (2006) and Wicks (2010)

Range of programs	Individual/select courses			Entire program		
Focus of programs	Core curriculum		Supplemental/enrichment curriculum		Credit recovery/Remedial curriculum	
Geographic magnitude levels of program offerings	Single district	Multiple districts	Statewide	Multiple states	National	Worldwide
Provider type	District	Magnet	Contract	Charter	Private	Home environment
Location	School		Home		Other	
Synchronicity	Asynchronous			Synchronous		
Governance	Local board	Consortium	Regional authority	University	State	Vendor
Instruction delivery	Fully online (over 80%)		Blended/hybrid (30 to 79%)		Web-facilitated (1 to 29%)	
Instruction level	Elementary school		Middle school		High school	
Learning experience	Expository		Active		Interactive	
Level of teacher-student interaction	Low		Average		High	
Level of student-student interaction	Low		Average		High	
Level of student-learning platform interaction	Low		Average		High	

opportunities to a greater number of students who vary in terms of their academic and demographic backgrounds. The social dimension of online instruction, when structured and supported appropriately, should lead to personalized learning that is rigorous academically and transformative in terms of the outcomes, while mediated by very skilled instructors (Watson and Gemin, 2009).

Recent trends in K-12 education relate directly to e-learning. As more multimedia platforms support learning, there is an associated reduction in text-based instructional resources being used in the classroom, thus leading to enhanced engagement and interactivity. The latter attributes of online learning are ensured by the integration of virtual classroom components, such as online resources, synchronous chat sessions, wikis, blogs – both in text-based and audio form, etc. (Cavanaugh and Blomeyer, 2007). Moreover, according to the Southern Regional Education Board, cited by Bailey, Patrick, Schneider, and Vander Ark (2013), it is expected that around 75% of public school districts in its jurisdiction will offer online options by 2015. The same researchers comment on one benefit students have from more online course or program offerings by having flexibility in demonstrating their competency. That could be done either by accessing individualized/personalized curricula delivered entirely online or in a blended/hybrid manner. Though the latter has been slow to develop in the world of K-12 education, is it likely to "emerge as the predominant model of the future" (Watson, 2008, p. 3) by increasing equitable student access to learning opportunities while leading to effective (re)configurations/combinations of the best features of face-to-face and online instruction.

In terms of approaches to blended/hybrid learning, Staker and Horn (2012) propose four models, as follows:

1. Rotation model relies on a fixed schedule or a teacher's availability, with several options:

   a. Station-rotation that alternates among teacher-directed instruction, group work stations, and online instruction segments, for all students in a given class.
   b. Lab-rotation enhances teacher-directed instruction by allowing student to extend learning in a computer lab.
   c. Flipped-classroom includes teacher-facilitated practice sessions in the traditional classroom setting, while the actual instruction takes place online after school.
   d. Individual-rotation emphasizes customization of instructional sequences, in no specific order, one of which is Web-based.

2. Flex model implies online delivery of curricula and instruction, based on which students follow a customizable sequence of pedagogical strategies, such as supplemental instruction, collaborative work, enrichment activities, etc.

3. Self-blend model includes online courses, ranging from a single one to a few, that students enroll in as a way supplement their traditional, classroom-based curriculum. In this case, students receive instruction from the same teachers, both online and on campus.

4. Enriched-virtual model derives from the entirely online/virtual schools by providing students with opportunities for "on site/campus" learning within each class.

As the infrastructure is increasingly able to accommodate the growing number of online courses and programs, schools have reached a point where we are witnessing a shift to ensuring indicators of effectiveness assurance (McKnight, 2004). In other words, we are moving from quantity to quality (Liu and Johnson, 2004) that should align with student-centered online pedagogy.

Curricula are analyzed in terms of how they provide students with solid knowledge bases and associated skills, as well as with cross-disciplinary 21st century skills (Johnson, 2009). E-learning represents a flexible platform allowing students access to rich learning opportunities (Hayden, McNamara, and Kane, 2009) designed to support the co-construction of knowledge while expressing "their online identities" (Kazmer, 2004). The effective processes of designing, implementing, and evaluating online education rely on a variety of factors that contribute to the development of meaningful interactions in the virtual world. Three factors are quite prominent when it comes to the effective implementation of online education: interaction with content, with instructors, and with peers (Swan, 2002; Wanstreet, 2006). Keeping them in balance leads to the creation of a sustainable and engaging learning community in the virtual environment. At the same time, K-12 institutions should be cognizant of the needs of online teachers. There is an increasing body of evidence that demonstrates that supporting these instructional practitioners in the online environment includes professional development, training, as well as technical and administrative assistance (McKnight, 2004). Consequently, online instructional design should blend effective pedagogical practices with a thorough understanding of the specifics of virtual learning environments and how students interact best in there.

Given the recent rise in the profile of online education, there are several research and/or policy groups that have pointed out the need to investigate the effectiveness of teaching and learning in virtual environments. As higher education institutions have also witnessed increasing interest in courses and programs delivered online, either entirely or in a hybrid manner, there have been several research studies dealing with the effectiveness of e-learning. By contrast, there are only a few rigorous studies focused on K-12 online education, reason for which findings could be considered trends more than models for future

practice (Barbour, 2010; Cavanaugh, Gillan, Kromrey, Hess, and Blomeyer, 2004; Journell, 2012; Means, Toyama, Murphy, Bakia, and Jones, 2010; Patrick and Powell, 2009; Rice, 2006). This body of research investigates student characteristics and achievement, as well as ways in which to determine student achievement in virtual learning settings (Archambault and Crippen, 2009). There is a direct implication of this paucity of research data on the ability of the states to issue policies intended to provide guidance to the processes of implementing digital learning in K-12 classrooms (Watson and Gemin, 2009). Nonetheless, there are a few studies that point out some of the problems faced by online K-12 learners, such as content comprehension, especially if there is discontinuity in students' attendance, technical issues (Barbour, Siko, Sumara, and Simuel-Everage, 2012), communication, particularly when collaborating with peers in the virtual environment, leading to the potential for a negative attitude toward e-learning (Edwards and Rule, 2013). Additionally, off-task behavior increases under asynchronous learning circumstances, while there is little sense of community (Barbour and McLaren, 2012). On the positive side, middle school students expressed interest in having access to technologically-rich, creativity-centered learning experiences preparing them for life outside of school (Lee and Spires, 2009). The existing research, coupled with new lines of scholarly inquiries should inform the recommendations included in this chapter, as they are intended to inform initiatives aimed at developing policy and standards guiding effective K-12 online education.

In 2010, the Digital Learning Council released a set of guidelines intended to emphasize components of high quality digital learning environments centered on differentiation/customization, increased student access and success, high caliber curricula, and supporting infrastructure. In this light, student access should be coupled with personalized learning and clear opportunities for positive academic performance. At the same time, high quality requirements should underscore curricula, pedagogy, and assessment, all of which should rely on an appropriate foundation in terms of funding, hardware, software, and technical expertise and support (Foundation for Excellence in Education, 2011).

BENEFITS OF ONLINE EDUCATION

Education in the U.S. is in the early stages of implementing online learning. While virtual schooling has grown at an impressive pace recently, coupled with more investment in infrastructure, more evidence is needed to identify effective practices that could be scaled up, with a particular emphasis on maximizing student achievement and preparation for college and career in the 21ˢᵗ century. Some of the reasons behind the impetus promoting online education have been mentioned by a variety of stakeholders, including researchers, practitioners, as well as policy/decision makers and advisors. As an illustration, Bailey, Patrick, Schneider, and Vander Ark (2013), as well as Barbour (2010; 2013) underline the greater access to equitable, high quality, more cost-efficient learning opportunities that are designed to meet individual learning styles/preferences, given particular contextual factors (such as geographic location, for instance). By providing several curricular choices, students benefit from engaging in relevant learning connected to the knowledge bases and skill sets required in today's workplaces. New developments in terms of learning platforms or management systems include updates and teacher-friendly features that enhance the assessment processes used to determine student progress both formatively and summatively, thus reinforcing competence-based instruction. The same team of researchers connects their findings to the profile of the next generation learner, as outlined in a recent report called released by EDUCAUSE. The parameters of this next generation learner profile are personalization, flexibility, interac-

tivity, relevance, self-pacing, self-assessment, collaboration, challenging/intellectually stimulating/engaging (Calkins and Vogt, 2013; Next Generation Learning Challenges, 2013). These circumstances emphasize the importance of data from the U.S. Department of Education and the National Training and Simulation Association, cited by the Federal Communications Commission (2012), according to which students need 30 to 80 percent less time to master a learning objective under technology-based circumstances.

Several additional recent research studies reveal that student performance in blended/hybrid or entirely virtual courses is, on average, comparable to or better than that in traditional, face-to-face classes (Cavanaugh, Gillan, Kromrey, Hess, and Blomeyer, 2004; Means, Toyama, Murphy, Bakia, and Jones, 2010). When technology implementation is properly managed, there are financial benefits, as well as improved student learning (Federal Communications Commission, 2012). The more interactive the online exchanges of information, the more engaged students are with the content of their courses, supported by increased levels of motivation (Barbour and Reeves, as cited in Cavanaugh, Barbour, and Clark [2009]), also echoed by parents' perception of the same topic (Sorensen, 2012). The heightened degree of involvement with course content also translates into more time on task spent by student in virtual learning environment compared to face-to-face equivalents. Online instruction relies on greater reflection and learner control of the ways in which they interact with the content, peers, and instructors (Patrick and Powell, 2009).

In-depth analyses of factors leading to effective online instruction highlight enhanced learner autonomy and responsibility (Keegan and Wedemeyer, as cited in Cavanaugh, Gillan, Kromrey, Hess, and Blomeyer, 2004). While e-learning could be more time consuming than face-to-face instruction, when structured and monitored effectively, it could lead to increased awareness of self-efficacy and self-concept, thus impacting positively the internal locus of control (Rotter, as cited in Cavanaugh, Gillan, Kromrey, Hess, and Blomeyer, 2004). For online instruction to be effective, the professional skills needed rely on the congruence among pedagogy, technology, and content (Russell and Savery, as cited in DiPietro, Ferdig, Black, and Preston, 2008). That complex skill set implies a fundamental shift in the roles undertaken by teachers in traditional, face-to-face classroom environments. In addition to being able to balance one's knowledge of the academic discipline(s) with that of the full range of characteristics of the student population, effective online teachers have to be well versed in various computer technology applications, as well as how their use impacts class dynamics and the content area pedagogy (Ferdig, 2006). Consequently, effective online teachers have become designers, facilitators (Barbour, 2013), mediators of virtual exchanges of information, technical troubleshooters, motivators, and participatory researchers documenting practices that could contribute to the further development of the field. A holistic representation of the pedagogical skills online teachers use to maximize student learning focuses on the integration of instructional planning, the full range of assessment strategies, frequent opportunities for communication and collaboration, and student-centered instructional strategies that rely on relevant and engaging resources (Alliance for Excellent Education, 2012).

CHALLENGES OF ONLINE EDUCATION

Accessibility and the ability to reach a greater variety of students in different locations, some of which could not be integrated into a formal educational process before, represent salient reasons for the recent promotion of online education (Nord, 2011) supportive of a pliable learning environment (Greener, 2010). At the same time, there is still a need for quantitative and qualitative studies focused on the effectiveness of K-12 online education (DiPietro, Ferdig, Black, and Preston, 2010; Rice, 2006), as most of past research studies dealt with adult learners in college and university settings. Work conducted in K-12 virtual environments emphasized student characteristics and performance (Archambault and Crippen, 2009), time spent teaching online, content management, and student-derived issues related to motivation, interaction, and evaluation (Archambault, 2010), lack of familiarity with instructional technology, which directly impacts the rate at which distance education can evolve (Patton, 2005), as well as the need to develop a pedagogy that accommodates the particular features defining distance education that brings together technology, content, and instructional strategies (DiPietro, Ferdig, Black, and Preston, 2010). The latter group of researchers also point out that there are no standards guiding the formal preparation of online teachers, either as a program for pre-service teachers or professional development series for in-service teachers. At the same time, increasing emphasis is placed on the importance of online education in the 21st century by various federal and professional organizations at the national level. For instance, the National Education Technology Plan (U.S. Dept. of Education, 2010) urges practitioners and decision makers in the field of education to create "engaging, relevant, and personalized learning experiences for all learners that mirror students' daily lives and the reality of their futures" (p. x) by taking into account the constant access to multimedia content via a wide range of technologies students have. One of the recommendations put forth by the Federal Communications Commission in its National Broadband Plan (2010) prompts K-12 accrediting agencies and teacher certification organizations to "allow students to take more courses for credit online and to permit more online instruction across state lines" (p. 244), which would address a critical issue facing American education in the 21ˢᵗ century – the fact that students are not well prepared to compete in a global economy (Alliance for Excellence in Education, 2012).

Keeping in mind the rapid growth of online education in the U.S., some of the obstacles faced by both decision makers/administrators and practitioners have to do with the high initial cost of virtual schools, equitable access for all students who want to pursue the online or hybrid format, as well as accreditation and accountability requirements (Barbour, 2010). Additionally, there are issues pertaining to student characteristics that may help or hinder them achieve in the online environment – a sense of isolation, perceived range of opportunities for high levels of interaction based on which students could develop their social skills, readiness and motivation profile for virtual learning (Cavanaugh, Gillan, Kromrey, Hess, and Blomeyer, 2004), as well as study habits and organizational skills (Picciano and Seaman, 2010). The range of challenges also features a focus on teachers when it comes to their knowledge and experience with online instruction, classroom management in virtual environments, support systems – both administrative and technical (Archambault and Crippen, 2009), as well as professional development/training needs (Picciano and Seaman, 2009). The analysis of how these issues could impact the future of e-learning has to be coupled with input from teachers related to their awareness of what the areas of improvement are in the generic field of educational technology. In this light, a recent project involving over 100,000 teachers from more than 8,000 schools and 2,400 school districts across the country, conducted by a national education non-profit organization, reveals that the number one issue identified by teachers in terms of being able to use technology at their respective school is the fact that students do not have adequate access to computers. Moreover,

this challenge also features an increase from 31% of teachers in 2008 to 55% of them mentioning it as such four years later. A similar increase of 24 percentage points in the magnitude of a problem is found in relation to the participating teachers' need for professional development on how to use effectively computer technology applications in the classroom. One additional finding with very important implications for policy setting structures in school districts emphasizes flexibility and autonomy/support in the selection of types of technology teachers can make. To that effect, 28% of teachers identified this item as an obstacle based on the 2012 survey, representing an increase from 19% in 2008 (Project Tomorrow, 2013).

Moving American schools forward into the 21ˢᵗ century implies meeting increasing accountability requirements, dealing with diminished financial resources, and implementing the new Common Core standards, while providing students with relevant learning opportunities designed to prepare them for college and career in an ever-changing world. Well-educated high school and college graduates need well-prepared teachers, irrespective of the instruction delivery format. When it comes to online teachers, providing them with appropriate professional development will ensure their improved ability to deal with the noted issues of time management – both in terms of instructional planning and actual content delivery -, participation in curriculum development intended to promote student learning, as well as awareness of the interplay among student characteristics, technology, and pedagogy in virtual spaces (Archambault, 2010). As online education is intended to support the continued efforts to improve schools in the U.S., the guiding principles for the evaluation of effectiveness include excellence, efficiency, equity, and choice (Cavanaugh and Blomeyer, 2007), all of which have their respective place in the planning, implementation, and assessment of e-learning.

RECOMMENDATIONS AND POLICY IMPLICATIONS

In spite of the recent substantial growth of online education, the field of study and practice is still in its "nascent stages and significant growth is yet to come" (Picciano and Seaman, 2009, p. 22). Future developments should take into account the variety of factors impacting e-learning, ranging from societal changes, technological advances, and educational policies intended to promote further economic development. Recent research has shown that well-designed virtual learning is on par with high quality face-to-face instruction (Cavanaugh, Gillan, Kromrey, Hess, and Blomeyer, 2004). Consequently, a clear focus on systematic planning for online learning, coupled with research-based implementation and evaluation would be required to ensure a sustainable and effective evolution into the 21st century. The International Association for K-12 Online Learning (iNACOL) proposes an outline of principles supporting the design of quality virtual instruction, as follows:

- Stemming from the premise that e-learning has the potential to provide students with high quality curricula and pedagogy, stakeholders should be informed of its characteristics and expectations for improved learning (Cavanaugh, Gillan, Kromrey, Hess, and Blomeyer, 2004)
- All students should have equitable access to a wide range of online learning opportunities, ranging from single courses to entire programs, in entirely virtual or hybrid formats, dealing with remedial, regular, or supplemental content
- Funding formulae, as one of the most important policy issues, should be based on well-informed expectations for sustainable growth of online education in a manner that keeps up with demand

- Accountability (inclusive of teacher licensure) and accreditation requirements should be clearly communicated by using well-defined institutional structures and processes, while engaging all stakeholders in a dynamic, responsive decision making process focused on oversight, continuous improvement, and compliance with existing quality assurance standards
- Online teachers should be engaged and supported as expert practitioners in professional learning communities that would investigate pedagogical principles as they apply to a variety of types of e-learning, leading to the development of a research-informed body of literature of effective practice
- Professional development opportunities for online teachers should extend their lines of inquiry into the effectiveness of their instructional practice, while empowering them to become instructional leaders in their schools or school districts based on their e-learning expertise (Watson and Gemin, 2009).

Under these circumstances, this chapter proposes a framework (see Figure 1) intended to structure a planning process that starts with the outline of the educational system at a macro level represented by societal needs, national policies, standards, and sets of expectations set against global marketplace requirements for the 21st century. An intermediate level focuses on local and/or regional factors that influence the particular ways in which macro-level policies, mandates, as well as recommendations/guidelines apply. A micro level zooms in on the intricate nature of an educational setting supported by a dynamic technology plan that promotes online education. By outlining the various factors defining macro- and intermediate-level contexts supporting particular school cultures, strategic plans are of utmost im-

Figure 1. Investigating challenges, opportunities, and trends in quality K-12 online environments

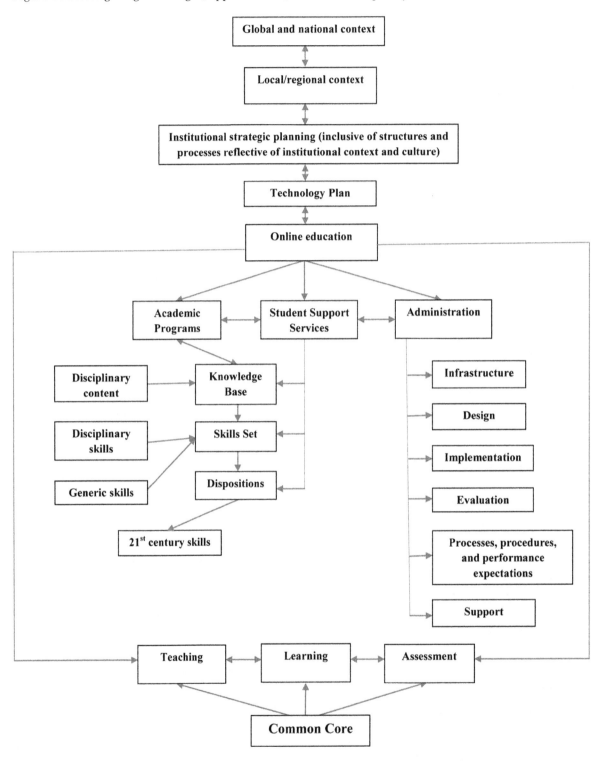

portance as they identify the parameters needed for various schools to implement online learning environments effectively. While these considerations represent the foundation for such technology plans, their core is centered on how the following components of K-12 online education work in tandem. Based on this three-pronged foundation, online curricula come to life by means of teaching, learning, and assessment, all of which rely on a range of professional guidelines and standards when it comes to academic content. As far as the specifics of online pedagogy are concerned, particular emphasis is placed on the ways in which previous professional references provide examples of effective practice bringing together cognitive presence, social presence, and teaching presence in virtual learning environments.

1. Academic programs or curricula delivered to students via virtual environments, with a particular focus on the interplay among knowledge bases, skill sets, and dispositions, all of which are intended to provide online students with opportunities to develop and apply 21st century skills. This component entails several items, as follows:

    a. Clear goals and outcomes that encompass the balanced academic, social, and emotional development of students, to which appropriate staffing levels could be determined (Bailey, Patrick, Schneider, and Vander Ark, 2013). These goals and outcomes anchor subsequent analyses and decisions made about curricula, instructional design, range of educational technology applications, assessment strategies and tools, program evaluation, as well as reporting structures and procedures (Watson and Gemin, 2009). Additionally, the implementation of academic programs in virtual learning environments needs to ensure online equity to all students, based on which

they can perform at expected levels of engagement (Rose and Blomeyer, 2007).

    b. High quality curricula and associated pedagogy fully accommodating of the characteristics of virtual instruction as well as the range of online learner needs (NAIS, 2010). Curricula should align with appropriate standards, such as the Common Core, be strongly correlated with positive student learning outcomes (Bailey, Patrick, Schneider, and Vander Ark, 2013), and involve teachers in frequent collaborative analyses of content. At the same time, curricula should present students with appropriate learning opportunities designed to promote the development of knowledge bases, skill sets, and positive dispositions within as well as across academic disciplines, leading to full participation in society as a viable and productive member (Cavanaugh, Gillan, Kromrey, Hess, and Blomeyer, 2004). Differentiated pedagogy relevant to e-learning configurations featured by today's schools should be grounded in research-based literature focused on the spectrum of student needs and interests, as well as the specific ways in which education technology can meet those needs and develop those interests (Cavanaugh and Blomeyer, 2007). Concurrently, student participation and engagement mediated by teachers and curricula in a safe learner-centered setting (Conrad and Donaldson, 2004) should result in increased student retention and readiness for college and/or career. This particular aspect of virtual instruction is very important in any initiatives attempting to balance learner characteristics, appropriate support systems, and affective learning, as a way to increase interaction and socialization patterns and structures/networks (Patrick and Powell, 2009; Watson and Gemin, 2008), while avoiding the sense of isolation reported by some students in online settings (Rice, 2006), also echoed by parents' perspectives on the same issue (Sorensen, 2012). Also related to ensuring effective e-learning, institutional strategic planning and decision making should look into hiring practices to bring in the best qualified teachers, supporting instructors to collaborate, while holding them accountable for effective curriculum implementation and positive student learning outcomes, as well as empowering and rewarding them as they drive the continuous improvement process (Public Impact, 2013). To this effect, a Gallup poll involving 1,025 adults across the U.S. conducted in October 2013 shows that online education appears to be considered "same or better" than traditional, face-to-face instruction in terms of providing a wide range of individualized/personalized curricular options that are worth the financial investment because students can experience success in the virtual format of their courses or programs (Lederman, 2013).

2. Student support services, directly correlated with academic programs, are vital in the process of implementing curricula effectively along the same lines mentioned earlier – knowledge bases, skill sets, and dispositions. Depending on the scope, reach, and focus of a given e-learning course or program, student support should address an entire spectrum of issues, such as enrollment and orientation, technical requirements, curriculum specifics (ranging from the written to the assessed

curricula, tutoring services availability), as well as counseling and mentoring (Watson and Gemin, 2009). Further analysis of the inclusive/accessible academic, social, and personal support systems (Calkins and Vogt, 2013) made available to online learners has to connect to the continuum of needs and interests students demonstrate as they acquire knowledge and develop skills as well as the associated positive dispositions. In other words, there has to be a match between the availability of resources both at the school and school district level and the full range of services required by students. Equally important in the strategic planning process is the focus on at-risk learners in virtual environments. Recent research has shown that a multi-faceted approach works well under these circumstances, necessitating establishing a cadre of trained practitioners (teachers, counselors, tutors, etc.), individualizing interventions to accommodate student needs, and identifying instructional strategies proven to promote student success (Archambault et al., 2010). Further investigation is needed to determine the degree to which virtual instruction addresses the specific needs of special education students (Vasquez and Straub, 2012).

3. Administration of online education relates to infrastructure, the design, implementation, and evaluation of curricula delivered via asynchronous and synchronous applications of technology, as well as on various processes, procedures, and performance expectations both for online teachers and students, all of which should inform the development of a focused professional development program aimed at continuous improvement. Aligning the school technology plan with that of the school district and/or the state leads to a smoother process by which to market the online instructional sequence (be it single courses or entire

programs, hybrid or all-online), recruit teachers and support personnel staff, seek funding, select learning platforms/management systems, and establish quality control procedures and indicators for content, teaching, technology, and routine organizational operations (Bailey, Patrick, Schneider, and Vander Ark, 2013). Policies guiding virtual instruction should be constantly revisited by connecting them to national, state, and local levels of decision making that coordinate the correlation between offer and demand for e-learning (Southern Regional Education Board, 2012). Concurrently, effective online schooling requires coordination and leadership (Cavanaugh, Gillan, Kromrey, Hess, and Blomeyer, 2004) that take into account the full range of the decision-making process, from understanding the profile of next generation learners, planning for instruction, involving stakeholders, and identifying all necessary resources to ensure high quality instruction (Next Generation Learning Challenges, 2013). Given the fast-paced world of technology, virtual school oversight should engage in productive negotiations about infrastructure sustainability and the necessary, scalable digital conversions (Project Tomorrow, 2013). Equally important is the support for teaching staff in the form of professional development programs. Recent research shows that such type of support is rated as very important when it comes to dealing with the significant differences between teaching in traditional, face-to-face classrooms and virtual learning settings (Watson and Gemin, 2009). In addition to the focal points on effective ways to communicate online, there is heightened interest in learning more about adapting/adopting new technologies designed to individualize instruction (Project Tomorrow, 2013), classroom and time management skills, Internet privacy and safety, developing cur-

ricula for virtual delivery, netiquette, special needs students (NAIS, 2010), psychology of online learners, tools used to design virtual curricula, assessment of online learning and behavior, as well as instructional design principles used for e-learning (Dawley, Rice, and Hinck, 2010). Given the preference for fully online facilitated professional development, where gaining a sense of ownership and autonomy are important attributes of a community of practice (Hur and Hara, 2007), national and regional organizations propose guidelines that recommend a formal context-specific plan by which to set up structures and strategies designed to transition online teachers from their pre-service stage to assuming leadership roles in their respective schools or school districts (Davis and Rose, 2007). The organizing categories used by the Southern Regional Education Board (2009) focus on academic preparation, content knowledge, skills, and dispositions related to the use of instructional technology, and online teaching and learning methods. Though there is insufficient state policy recommendations as well as research on the impact of mentoring for online teachers on their instructional performance and the learning outcomes of their students, there are several examples of mentoring programs in Alabama, Colorado, Florida, Idaho, Mississippi, Missouri, and Tennessee that encourage reflective practice and collaborative professional development within a learning community developed on shared expertise and interest areas (Wortmann, Cavanaugh, Kennedy, Beldarrain, Letourneau, and Zygouris-Coe, 2008).

Recommendations for decision makers and practitioners in the field of online education revolve around the emerging challenges, opportunities and trends that support quality delivery of instruction in virtual learning environments, as supported by the aforementioned framework. There is a growing body of evidence related to the national online education landscape that includes state-level policies guiding program offerings, funding options, enrollment benchmarks, public-private partnerships, teacher accountability requirements, etc. A report issued by the Center for Digital Education identifies the top 25 states in the U.S. based on their legislation governing e-learning, as follows (in ranking order): Florida, South Carolina, New Mexico, Hawaii, Michigan, Louisiana, Idaho, Minnesota, Oregon, Arkansas, Missouri, North Carolina, Texas, Kentucky, Iowa, West Virginia, Virginia, New Hampshire, Montana, Nevada, Colorado, Wisconsin, Utah, Alabama, and Illinois. Florida is also a national leader in terms of the number of online students served – over 124,000 in the 2008-2009 school year. Twenty-four states had online programs developed by legislation or a state-level agency, therefore being labeled "state-led." Nine of these states used the same funding formula in place for traditional schools. Colorado and New Hampshire had statewide online programs available to students throughout their respective state either via school districts of charter schools. Twenty-nine states had full-time and charter virtual schools funded in a variety of ways, one of which is the same formula used for traditional charter schools (Online Learning Policy Survey: A Survey of the States, 2009).

The following examples of virtual learning models present different ways in which states deal with challenges facing the further development of online schools, such as funding, accountability and accreditation requirements, virtual pedagogy, infrastructure sustainability, and quality assurance structures and procedures (State Education Technology Directors Association, 2008):

- Alabama Connecting Classrooms, Educators, and Students Statewide (ACCESS; available at http://accessdl. state.al.us/) – a statewide, school-based program available free of charge to 9-12 students across the state. The curriculum includes AP, dual credit, electives, remedial, enrichment, and core classes delivered via a Web-based system or interactive video-conferencing, along with some face-to-face components.

- Arizona Connections Academy (available at http://www.connectionsacademy.com/ arizona-online-school/home.aspx) – a full-time virtual charter school for any K-12 students across the state who are provided the necessary curricular materials (hard copies as well as Web-based), a computer, a printer, and a subsidy for Internet service.

- Idaho Digital Learning Academy (available at http://www.idahodigitallearning. org/) – a virtual school for traditional, home schooled, at-risk, and gifted students grades 7-12 across the state.

- Florida Virtual School (also mentioned by the Southern Regional Education Board [2009] and Davis [2012]; available at http://www.flvs.net/Pages/default.aspx) – the first statewide Web-based public high school in the country, it has developed into a virtual school that offers middle and high school students across the state as well as outside Florida. Students who take AP courses offered by this online school consistently outperform their peers at traditional schools (Southern Regional Education Board, 2009).

Additional examples of virtual schools include Commonwealth Connections Academy (available at http://www.connectionsacademy. com/pennsylvania-cyber-school/home.aspx), a free public K-12 cyber school that has some optional hybrid components based on several teaching centers across Pennsylvania; Odyssey Charter Schools (available at http://odysseyk12. org/), a tuition-free public hybrid school open to K-12 students from Clark County and Las

Vegas, Nevada, featuring a blend of on-site and virtual learning opportunities, similar to Chicago Virtual Charter (K-9) School (available at http://www.k12.com/cvcs#.Utf7A_RDv3E); as well as Omaha Public Schools eLearning (available at http://www.leadcommission.org/profile/omaha-public-schools-elearning), initially developed as a blended learning approach to credit recovery, now available to all 9-12 students in the district (Watson, 2008).

Policy makers and practitioners in the field of e-learning could also base their analyses on findings generated by a study involving 16 teachers from Michigan Virtual School (available at http://www.mivhs.org/), one of the largest non-profit, state-supported online schools in the country. The findings underline evidence-based practices based on coding along three categories: general characteristics, classroom management strategies, and pedagogical strategies. Effective participating Michigan Virtual School teachers demonstrated the following general characteristics: supportive of student learning; knowledgeable and experienced in terms of basic uses of technology, while interested in investigating the potential of emerging technologies; aware of the time demands of teaching online; aware of students' learning styles/preferences; able to establish a teaching presence in the virtual environment, designed to motivate student learning; able to demonstrate organizational skills; well-versed in using assessment data to evaluate the quality of curricula, teaching, and student learning; very knowledgeable in terms of the content area(s) they represent; able to monitor and modify the instructional pace of a class based on evidence of student engagement and learning; and committed to the mission virtual schools serve. As classroom managers, these virtual teachers seemed to use a variety of strategies to deal with student misbehavior by being aware of a wide range of triggers, including personal crises. Finally, the online instructors participating in the study demonstrated their ability to use different appropriate assessment strategies to develop a highly interactive, well-structured, safe learning environment accommodating of students' interests, needs, and motivation levels. As learning is very social, the virtual setting has to be organized in a student-centered manner that engages students in meaningful interactions supporting a community of learners in a technology-rich environment (DiPietro, Ferdig, Black, and Preston, 2008).

The findings mentioned earlier align with the standards for quality online teaching put forth by the International Association for K-12 Online Learning. These standards focus on the knowledge bases and skill sets needed to virtual learning environments, coupled with a deep understanding of one's content area(s) they teach, in a flexible manner that engages students in a setting that uses a variety of appropriate interactive technologies. Through constant, clear communication and frequent feedback, online teachers create a classroom space that takes into account student characteristics designed to facilitate learning. Each virtual instructor is also a member of a larger community, be it their respective school or a community of practice, where they observe standards that guide the profession (iNACOL, 2011). In turn, these recommendations correlate with the standards for quality online programs developed by the same organization. In this case, the emphasis is on institutional mission, purpose and commitment, governance and leadership structures, planning processes, staffing, financial plans, and quality assurance in terms of equity and access, as well as integrity and accountability. Additional standards emphasize instructional processes related to curriculum, instruction, and assessment, while others deal with support services for stakeholders (staff, students, and parents), as well as evaluation plans leading to continuous improvement for the entire institution (Pape and Wicks, 2009).

FUTURE RESEARCH

Given the substantial increase in the demand for and offer of online education in the U.S. over the past decade, several models of instruction emerged, some of which evolved over time, while others continued to establish themselves as originally conceived, leading to greater state-level legislative support, to varying degrees. One fundamental issue facing virtual schooling is that of equitable access to learning opportunities for all students, leading to growth and development, which, in turn, equates with preparedness for college and career. Scaling up successful models of e-learning needs to be supported by adequate infrastructure, and high quality technologies (perceived as "disruptive innovation" – Horn, 2010), curricula, teaching, and assessment practices. Current economic circumstances bring to the fore the additional issues of the attainment gap, diminishing funding sources, and an expected shortage of highly qualified teachers, all of which should be taken into account by stakeholders involved in decision making. As noted earlier, data-driven policy setting would benefit from evidence-based practices that could be adapted or adopted across the country. Consequently, future research agendas could be developed along the following lines:

- The intersection among content knowledge, technology, pedagogy (Archambault and Crippen, 2009), and assessment in virtual learning environments, as they differ in significant ways from traditional, face-to-face classrooms. A subsequent focal point could be devoted to the different instructional models and what makes each of them effective (Picciano and Seaman, 2009), as well as the transfer of teaching skills pertaining to the same four components mentioned above from one setting to the other.
- The goals, outcomes, and expectations of online education (Cavanaugh and Blomeyer, 2007), leading to more frequent updates to the general public and policy-setting structures, which would result in a better understanding of the various facets of the support for virtual schooling.
- The correlation between curriculum and instruction, on the one hand, and student learning outcomes, on the other hand, with a particular emphasis on increasing equitable access for all students irrespective of their needs (Bailey, Patrick, Schneider, and Vander Ark, 2013), increased interactivity and engagement (Cavanaugh and Blomeyer, 2007), leading to improved learning (Barbour, 2010), as well as higher retention and graduation rates.
- The specifics of online assessment practices that promote self-concept, self-efficacy, and self-assessment.
- The online pedagogy that leads to the transfer of knowledge and skills across disciplines in highly interactive virtual learning environments.
- The needs of online teachers as they transition into their professional role, as well as they acquire specific knowledge and experience in virtual settings.
- The various ways in which current professional standards of practice in online schools accommodate the interplay among academic programs, student support services, and administration.
- The impact of emerging technologies (such as cloud-based computing [Stein, Ware, Laboy, and Schaffer, 2013]) on virtual schooling, with a particular emphasis on sustaining the associated high quality curricula and pedagogy.

In this chapter we outlined background information related to K-12 online education by presenting various definitions, benefits, and challenges. The evolution of virtual learning has led to the current complex landscape that reveals a multitude of trends and models of e-learning. The existing body of research on the effectiveness of K-12 online instruction indicates the need for further study. However, there is emerging evidence pertaining to the fact that virtual learning promotes greater access to equitable, high quality, cost-efficient learning opportunities to students that may not otherwise benefit from a wider range of formal education options. Under these circumstances, proper planning and policy-making should take into account the drawbacks referenced by several research reports and policy briefs, such as the initial cost of setting up a high quality virtual environment, or the requirements of scaling up to meet the needs of a wide range of students. As various models of e-learning have been proposed, the need for some structure and guiding standards emerged. Efforts were pursued to investigate the degree to which the effectiveness of traditional, face-to-face instruction could translate into equally effective online delivery systems. Therefore, the proposed theoretical framework identifies academic programs/curricula, student support services, and virtual program/school administration as categories that connect the relevant literature review to recommendations for future research intended to inform policy-setting efforts aimed at supporting the further development of high quality K-12 online environments. In conclusion, this chapter dealt with indicators of curriculum quality and its associated pedagogy, support systems for teachers, students, and parents, as well as the multi-faceted administration of hybrid/blended courses, programs, or schools.

REFERENCES

Allen, I. E., & Seaman, J. (2010). *Learning on demand: Online education in the United States, 2009*. Needham, MA: Sloan Consortium.

Alliance for Excellent Education. (2011). *Digital learning and technology: Federal policy recommendations to seize the opportunity and promising practices that inspire them*. Retrieved from http://all4ed.org/reports-factsheets/digital-learning-and-technology-federal-policy-recommendations-to-seize-the-opportunity-and-promising-practices-that-inspire-them/

Alliance for Excellent Education. (2012). *The digital learning imperative: How technology and teaching meet today's education challenges*. Retrieved from http://all4ed.org/reports-factsheets/the-digital-learning-imperative-how-technology-and-teaching-meet-todays-education-challenges/

Archambault, L. (2010). Identifying and addressing teaching challenges in K-12 online environments. *Distance Learning*, 7(2), 13–17.

Archambault, L., & Crippen, K. (2009). K-12 distance educators at work: Who's teaching online across the U.S. *Journal of Research on Technology in Education*, 41(4), 363–391. doi:10.1080/1539 1523.2009.10782535

Archambault, L., Diamond, D., Brown, R., Cavanaugh, C., Coffey, M., Foures-Aalbu, D., et al. (2010). An exploration of at-risk learners and online education. *International Association for K-12 Online Learning*. Retrieved from http://files.eric.ed.gov/fulltext/ED509620.pdf

Bailey, J., Patrick, S., Schneider, C., & Vander Ark, T. (2013). *Online learning: Myths, reality & promise*. Retrieved from http://www.digital-learningnow.com/wp-content/uploads/2013/07/Online-Learning-Paper-.pdf

Bailey, J., Schneider, C., & Vander Ark, T. (2012). *Funding the shift to digital learning: Three strategies for funding sustainable high-access environments*. Retrieved from http://digitallearningnow.com/wp-content/uploads/2012/08/DLN-Smart-Series-Paper-1-Final.pdf

Bailey, J., Schneider, C., & Vander Ark, T. (2013). *Navigating the digital shift: Implementation strategies for blended and online learning.* Retrieved from http://www.digitallearningnow.com/wp-content/uploads/2013/10/DLN-ebook-PDF.pdf

Barbour, M., Siko, J., Sumara, J., & Simuel-Everage, K. (2012). Narratives from the online frontier: A K-12 student's experience in an online learning environment. *Qualitative Report, 17,* 1–19. Retrieved from http://www.editlib.org/p/55210

Barbour, M. K. (2010). Researching K-12 online learning: What do we know and what should we examine? *Distance Learning, 7*(2), 6–12.

Barbour, M. K. (2013). The landscape of K-12 online learning: Examining what is known. In M. G. Moore (Ed.), *Handbook of Distance Education* (3rd ed., pp. 574–593). New York, NY: Routledge.

Barbour, M. K., & McLaren, A. (2012). It's not that tough: Students speak about their online learning experiences. *Turkish Online Journal of Distance Education, 13*(2), 226–241.

Barreto, D., & Orey, M. (2013). Trends and issues in learning, design, and technology. Educational Media and Technology Yearbook, 37, 3-5.

Bush, M. (2009). *Virtual high schools. ECS State Notes.* Denver, CO: Education Commission of the States.

Calkins, A., & Vogt, K. (2013). Next generation learning: The pathway to possibility. *EDUCAUSE.* Retrieved from http://www.educause.edu/library/resources/next-generation-learning-pathway-possibility

Carnevale, D. (2001). It's education online. It's someplace you aren't. What's it called? *The Chronicle of Higher Education, 47*(8), A33.

Cavanaugh, C., & Blomeyer, R. L. (2007). *What works in K-12 online learning.* Eugene, OR: International Society for Technology in Education.

Cavanaugh, C. S., Barbour, M. K., & Clark, T. (2009, February). Research and practice in K-12 online learning: A review of open access literature. *International Review of Research in Open and Distance Learning, 10*(1). Retrieved from http://www.irrodl.org/index.php/irrodl/article/view/607

Cavanaugh, C. S., Gillan, K. J., Kromrey, J., Hess, M., & Blomeyer, R. (2004). *The effects of distance education on K-12 student outcomes: A meta-analysis.* Naperville, IL: Learning Point Associates.

Center for Digital Education. (2009). *Online learning policy survey: A survey of the states.* Folsom, CA: Author. Retrieved from http://media.convergemag.com/documents/CDE09_REPORT_OnlineLearning_Short_V.pdf/

Conrad, R. M., & Donaldson, J. A. (2004). *Engaging the online learner: Activities and resources for creative instruction.* San Francisco, CA: Jossey-Bass.

Davis, M. (2012, August). New laws, programs expand K-12 online-learning options. *Education Week, 32*(2), S3–S5.

Davis, N., & Rose, R. (2007). Professional development for virtual schooling and online learning. *North American Council for Online Learning.* Retrieved from http://files.eric.ed.gov/fulltext/ED509632.pdf

Dawley, L., Rice, K., & Hinck, G. (2010). *Going virtual! 2010: The status of professional development and unique needs of K-12 online teachers.* Retrieved from http://edtech.boisestate.edu/goingvirtual/goingvirtual3.pdf

DiPietro, M., Ferdig, R. E., Black, E. W., & Preston, M. (2008). Best practices in teaching K-12 online: Lessons learned from Michigan Virtual School teachers. *Journal of Interactive Online Learning, 9*(3), 10–35.

Edwards, C., & Rule, A. (2013). Attitudes of middle school students: Learning online compared to face to face. *Journal of Computers in Mathematics and Science Teaching*, *32*(1), 49–66.

Federal Communications Commission. (2010). *Connecting America: The national broadband plan*. Retrieved from http://download.broadband. gov/plan/national-broadband-plan.pdf

Federal Communications Commission. (2012). *Digital textbook playbook*. Retrieved from http:// www.fcc.gov/encyclopedia/digital-textbook-playbook

Ferdig, R. E. (2006). Assessing technologies for teaching and learning: Understanding the importance of technological pedagogical content knowledge. *British Journal of Educational Technology*, *37*(5), 749–760. doi:10.1111/j.1467-8535.2006.00559.x

Foundation for Excellence in Education. (2011). *Digital learning now!* Tallahassee, FL: Author.

Foundation for Excellence in Education. (2012). *2012 Digital learning report card*. Tallahassee, FL: Author.

Garner, G. (2013). Trends and issues: The consumption and sustainability of digital media in the modern global economy. Educational Media and Technology Yearbook, 37, 45-54.

Greener, S. L. (2010). Plasticity: The online learning environment's potential to support varied learning styles and approaches. *Campus-Wide Information Systems*, *27*(4), 254–262. doi:10.1108/10650741011073798

Hayden, K. L., McNamara, K., & Kane, D. (2009). Assessing effective strategies and design in online learning. In *Proceedings of World Conference on E-Learning in Corporate, Government, Healthcare, and Higher Education 2009* (pp. 2660-2667). Chesapeake, VA: AACE.

Horn, M. (2010). K-12 online education is increasingly hybrid learning. *Distance Learning*, *7*(2), 18–20.

Hur, J. W., & Hara, N. (2007). Factors cultivating sustainable online communities for K-12 teacher professional development. *Journal of Educational Computing Research*, *36*(3), 245–268. doi:10.2190/37H8-7GU7-5704-K470

International Association for K-12 Online Learning. (2009, July). *Funding and policy frameworks for online learning*. Retrieved from http://www. inacol.org/cms/wp-content/uploads/2012/09/ NACOL_PP-FundPolicy-lr.pdf

International Association for K-12 Online Learning. (2011). *National standards for quality online teaching* (2nd ed.). Retrieved from http://www. inacol.org/cms/wp-content/uploads/2013/02/ iNACOL_TeachingStandardsv2.pdf

Johnson, P. (2009). The 21st century skills movement. *Educational Leadership*, *67*(1), 11.

Journell, W. (2012). Walk, don't run – to online learning. *Phi Delta Kappan*, *93*(7), 46–50.

Kazmer, M. (2004). Online identity: Implications for course design. *Online Classroom*, 6-7.

Larreamendy-Joerns, J., & Leinhardt, G. (2006). Going the distance with online education. *Review of Educational Research*, *76*(4), 567–605. doi:10.3102/00346543076004567

Lederman, D. (2013). Americans' view of online courses. *Inside Higher Ed*. Retrieved from http:// www.insidehighered.com/news/2013/10/15/ american-adults-see-online-courses-least-equivalent-most-ways

Lee, J., & Spires, H. (2009). What students think about technology and academic engagement in school: Implications for middle grades teaching and learning. *AACE Journal*, *17*(2), 61–81.

Liu, L., & Johnson, L. (2004). Static and dynamic design in online course development. In R. Ferdig et al. (Eds.), *Proceedings of Society for Information Technology and Teacher Education International Conference 2004* (pp. 2946-2951). Chesapeake, VA: AACE.

McKnight, R. (2004). Virtual necessities: Assessing online course design. *International Journal on e-Learning*, 5-10.

Means, B., Toyama, Y., Murphy, R., Bakia, M., & Jones, K. (2010). *Evaluation of evidence-based practices in online learning: A meta-analysis and review of online learning studies.* U.S. Department of Education. Retrieved from http://www2.ed.gov/rschstat/eval/tech/evidence-based-practices/finalreport.pdf

National Association of Independent Schools. (2010). *K-12 online learning: A literature review.* Retrieved from http://www.nais.org/Articles/Pages/NAIS-2010-K-12-Online-Learning-A-Literature-Review.aspx

National Education Association. (n.d.a). *Guide to teaching online courses.* Retrieved from http://www.nea.org/home/30103.htm

National Education Association. (n.d.b). *Guide to online high school courses.* Retrieved from http://www.nea.org/home/30113.htm

Next Generation Learning Challenges. (2013). Rethink: Planning and designing for K-12 next generation learning. *EDUCAUSE.* Retrieved from http://www.educause.edu/library/resources/rethink-planning-and-designing-k%E2%80%9312-next-generation-learning

Nord, D. (2011). Online learning programs: Evaluation's challenging future. In S. Mathison (Ed.), *Really new directions in evaluation: Young evaluators' perspectives* (pp. 129–134). New Directions for Evaluation.

Pape, L., & Wicks, M. (2009). National standards for quality online programs. *International Association for K-12 Online Learning.* Retrieved from http://www.inacol.org/cms/wp-content/uploads/2013/02/NACOL-Standards-Quality-Online-Programs.pdf

Patrick, S., & Powell, A. (2009, June). *A summary of research on the effectiveness of K-12 online learning.* Retrieved from http://www.k12.com/sites/default/files/pdf/school-docs/NACOL_ResearchEffectiveness-hr.pdf

Patton, C. (2005). Faster, cheaper, better. *District Administration*, 58–61.

Picciano, A. G., & Seaman, J. (2009). K-12 online learning: A 2008 follow-up of the survey of U.S. school district administrators. *Sloan Consortium.* Retrieved from http://sloanconsortium.org/publications/survey/k-12online2008

Picciano, A. G., & Seaman, J. (2010). *Class connections: High school reform and the role of online learning.* New York, NY: Babson Survey Research Group.

Project Tomorrow. (2013). *From chalkboards to tablets: The digital conversion of the K-12 classroom.* Retrieved from http://www.tomorrow.org/speakup/pdfs/SU12EducatorsandParents.pdf

Public Impact. (2013). *A better blend: A vision for boosting student outcomes with digital learning.* Chapel Hill, NC: Author.

Reigeluth, C. M., Carr-Chellman, A. A., Beabout, B., & Watson, W. (2009). Creating shared visions of the future for K-12 education: A systemic transformation process for a learner-centered paradigm. In L. Moller, J. B. Huett, & D. M. Harvey (Eds.), *Learning and instructional technologies for the 21st century* (pp. 131–150). New York: Springer. doi:10.1007/978-0-387-09667-4_8

Rice, K. L. (2006). A comprehensive look at distance education in the K-12 context. *Journal of Research on Technology in Education, 38*(4), 425–448. doi:10.1080/15391523.2006.10782468

Rose, R. M., & Blomeyer, R. L. (2007). Access and equity in online classes and virtual schools. *North American Council for Online Learning.* Retrieved from http://files.eric.ed.gov/fulltext/ED509623.pdf

Saba, F. (2005). Critical issues in distance education: A report from the United States. *Distance Education, 26*(2), 255–272. doi:10.1080/01587910500168892

Snyder, T. D., & Dillow, S. A. (2013). *Digest of Education Statistics 2012 (NCES 2014-015).* U.S. Department of Education, National Center for Education Statistics, Institute of Education Sciences. Retrieved from http://nces.ed.gov/pubs2014/2014015.pdf

Sorensen, C. (2012). Learning online at the K-12 level: A parent/guardian perspective. *International Journal of Instructional Media, 39*(4), 297–307.

Southern Regional Education Board. (2006). *Standards for quality online teaching.* Retrieved from http://publications.sreb.org/2006/06T02_Standards_Online_Teaching.pdf

Southern Regional Education Board. (2009). *Overcoming doubts about online learning.* Retrieved from http://publications.sreb.org/2009/09T02_Overcoming_Doubts.pdf

Southern Regional Education Board. (2009). *Guidelines for professional development of teachers.* Retrieved from http://publications.sreb.org/2009/09T01_Guide_profdev_online_teach.pdf

Staker, H., & Horn, M. B. (2012). *Classifying K-12 blended learning.* Retrieved from http://www.christenseninstitute.org/wp-content/uploads/2013/04/Classifying-K-12-blended-learning.pdf

State Educational Technology Directors Association. (2008). *Learning virtually: Expanding opportunities.* Retrieved from http://www.setda.org/c/document_library/get_file?folderId=270&name=DLFE-292.pdf

Stein, S., Ware, J., Laboy, J., & Schaffer, H. E. (2013). Improving K-12 pedagogy via a Cloud designed for education. *International Journal of Information Management, 33*(1), 235–241. doi:10.1016/j.ijinfomgt.2012.07.009

Swan, K. (2002). Building learning communities in online courses: The importance of interaction. *Education Communication and Information, 2*(1), 23–49. doi:10.1080/1463631022000005016

U.S. Department of Commerce, Economics and Statistics Administration, Census Bureau, (2013). *Computer and Internet use in the United States: Population characteristics.* Retrieved from http://www.census.gov/prod/2013pubs/p20-569.pdf

U.S. Department of Education, National Center for Education Statistics. (2012). *The condition of education.* Retrieved from http://nces.ed.gov/pubs2012/2012045.pdf

U.S. Department of Education, Office of Educational Technology. (2010). *Transforming American education: Learning powered by technology.* Retrieved from http://www.ed.gov/sites/default/files/netp2010.pdf

Vanourek, G. (2006). *A primer on virtual charter schools: Mapping the electronic frontier.* Chicago: National Association of Charter School Authorizers.

Vasquez, E. III, & Straub, C. (2012). Online instruction for K-12 special education: A review of the empirical literature. *Journal of Special Education Technology, 27*(3), 31–40.

Wanstreet, C. E. (2006). Interaction in online environments: A review of the literature. *The Quarterly Review of Distance Education, 7*(4), 399–411.

Watson, J. (2008). Blended learning: The convergence of online and face-to-face education. *North American Council for Online Learning.* Retrieved from http://www.inacol.org/cms/wp-content/uploads/2012/09/NACOL_PP-BlendedLearning-lr.pdf

Watson, J., & Gemin, B. (2008). Socialization in online programs. *North American Council for Online Learning.* Retrieved from http://files.eric.ed.gov/fulltext/ED509631.pdf

Watson, J., & Gemin, B. (2009). Management and operations of online programs. *International Association for K-12 Online Learning.* Retrieved from http://www.inacol.org/cms/wp-content/uploads/2012/09/iNACOL_PP_MgmntOp_042309.pdf

Watson, J., & Gemin, B. (2009). Funding and policy frameworks for online learning. *International Association for K-12 Online Learning.* Retrieved from http://www.inacol.org/cms/wp-content/uploads/2012/09/NACOL_PP-FundPolicy-lr.pdf

Watson, J., Murin, A., Vashaw, L., Gemin, B., & Rapp, C. (2013). Keeping pace with K-12 online and blended learning: An annual review of policy and practice. *Evergreen Education Group.* Retrieved from http://kpk12.com/reports/

Wicks, M. (2010). A national primer on K-12 online learning (2nd ed.). Vienna, VA: International Association for K-12 Online Learning.

Wortmann, K., Cavanaugh, C., Kennedy, K., Beldarrain, Y., Letourneau, T., & Zygouris-Coe, V. (2008). *Online teacher support programs: Mentoring and coaching models.* Vienna, VA: North American Council for Online Learning.

ADDITIONAL READING

Bawane, J., & Spector, M. (2009). Prioritization of online instructor roles: Implications for competency-based teacher education programs. *Distance Education, 30*(3), 383–397. doi:10.1080/01587910903236536

Berge, Z. L. (2008). Changing instructor's roles in virtual worlds. *Quarterly Review of Distance Education, 9*(4), 407–414.

Collins, A., & Halverson, R. (2009). *Rethinking education in the age of technology: The digital revolution and schooling in America.* New York, NY: Teachers College Press.

Duncan, H. E., & Barnett, J. (2009). Learning to teach online: What works for pre-service teachers. *Journal of Educational Computing Research, 40*(3), 357–376. doi:10.2190/EC.40.3.f

Garrison, D. R. (2011). *E-Learning in the 21st century: A framework for research and practice* (2nd ed.). New York, NY: Routledge.

Hur, J. W., & Brush, T. A. (2009). Teacher participation in online communities: Why do teachers want to participate in self-generated online communities of K-12 teachers? *Journal of Research on Technology in Education, 41*(3), 279–303. doi:10.1080/15391523.2009.10782532

Jahnke, J. (2012). Student perceptions of the impact of online discussion forum participation on learning outcomes. *Journal of Learning Design*, 3(2), 27–34. doi:10.5204/jld.v3i2.48

Kennedy, K., & Archambault, L. (2012). Offering preservice teachers field experiences in K-12 online learning: A national survey of teacher education programs. *Journal of Teacher Education*, 63(3), 185–200. doi:10.1177/0022487111433651

Kim, P., Kim, F. H., & Karimi, A. (2012). Public online charter school students: Choices, perceptions, and traits. *American Educational Research Journal*, 49(3), 521–545. doi:10.3102/0002831212443078

Klein, J. D., Spector, M., Grabowki, B. L., & de la Teja, I. (2000). *Instructor competencies: Standards for face-to-face, online and blended settings*. Charlotte, NC: Information Age Publishing.

Norton, P., & Hathaway, D. (2013). Preparing teachers, building capacity: A response to K-12 online initiatives. In R. McBride & M. Searson (Eds.), *Proceedings of Society for Information Technology & Teacher Education International Conference 2013* (pp. 886-894). Chesapeake, VA: AACE.

Norton, P., & Smith, R. D. (2007). Preparing virtual teachers: Who is on the other end? In R. Carlsen et al. (Eds.), *Proceedings of Society for Information Technology & Teacher Education International Conference 2007* (pp. 456-463). Chesapeake, VA: AACE.

Rauh, W. J. (2011). The utility of online choice options: Do purely online schools increase the value to students? *Education Policy Analysis Archives*, 19(34), 1–18.

Smith, J. J., & Dobson, E. (2011). Beyond the book: Using Web 2.0 tools to develop 21st century literacies. *Computers in the Schools: Interdisciplinary Journal of Practice, Theory, and Applied Research*, 28(4), 316–327. doi:10.1080/07380569.2011.620939

Smith, R. D. (2009). Virtual voices: Online teachers' perceptions of online teaching standards. *Journal of Technology and Teacher Education*, 17(4), 547–571.

Wallace, R. M. (2004). A framework for understanding teaching with the Internet. *American Educational Research Journal*, 41(2), 447–488. doi:10.3102/00028312041002447

KEY TERMS AND DEFINITIONS

21st Century Skills: Application of knowledge related to core academic subjects, life and career, learning and innovation, as well as information, media, and technology.

Asynchronous: Occurring at various times.

Blended/Hybrid Instruction: A combination of face-to-face, synchronous and virtual, Web-based, synchronous or asynchronous teaching.

Common Core: Guidelines regarding K-12 instruction in mathematics and English Language Arts adopted by 45 states and Washington, D.C.

Curriculum: Course of study.

Instructional Technology: Design, development, use, management, and evaluation of the process of learning mediated by technology applications.

Online Education: Teaching and learning mediated by computer-based technology that features differences in how learners can have control over time, place, medium or pace of instruction.

Synchronous: Occurring at the same time.

This work was previously published in Exploring the Effectiveness of Online Education in K-12 Environments edited by Tina L. Heafner, Richard Hartshorne, and Teresa Petty, pages 19-44, copyright year 2015 by Information Science Reference (an imprint of IGI Global).

Chapter 76

Promoting Human-Computer Interaction and Usability Guidelines and Principles through Reflective Journal Assessment

Tomayess Issa
Curtin University, Australia

Pedro Isaias
Portuguese Open University, Portugal

ABSTRACT

This chapter aims to examine the challenges to, and opportunities for, promoting Human Computer Interaction (HCI) and usability guidelines and principles through reflective journal assessment by information systems students from the Australian and Portuguese higher education sectors. In order to raise students' awareness of HCI and aspects of usability, especially in the Web development process, a new unit was developed by the first researcher called Information Systems 650 (IS650) in Australia. From this unit was derived the Web Site Planning and Development (WSPD) course introduced in Portugal. The reflective journal assessment approach was employed to enhance students' learning and knowledge of HCI and its usability aspects. This study provides empirical evidence from 64 students from Australia and Portugal, based on quantitative and qualitative data derived from three sources: students' formal and informal feedback and an online survey. Students confirmed that the use of reflective journal assessment consolidated their understanding of HCI and usability guidelines and principles and improved their reading, searching, researching, and writing skills, and their proficiency with the endnote software.

DOI: 10.4018/978-1-4666-8619-9.ch076

INTRODUCTION

The Internet (Cyberspace or Information Super-highway) is a network of thousands of computer systems utilizing a common set of technical protocols to create a worldwide communication medium. These massive groups of users reach the Internet through their computers and terminals via educational institutions, commercial Internet access providers and other organizations. The Internet provides numerous benefits to consumers regarding access to information, entertainment, research, business and marketing. The Internet allows users to educate themselves and acquire knowledge at their own pace, and website information can be easily accessed by consumers who can readily obtain only the information which is relevant to their needs (Cappel & Huang, 2007; Issa, 1999; Issa & Turk, 2012; Y. Lee & Kozar, 2012).

Although the Internet offers huge opportunities, there are also many potential problems. A website must meet the users' expectations in terms of content and ease of use. Websites which meet users' expectations will enjoy many advantages as a result of their effective design. According to Donahue (cited in McCracken and Wolfe, 2004) the four most important advantages are: 'Gaining a competitive edge; reducing development and maintenance costs; improving productivity; lowering support costs' (McCracken & Wolfe, 2004, p. 1). Other advantages of good website design are that they allow the users to enjoy working with websites with minimal frustration and aggravation. Studies and research have indicated that usable websites consistently have the highest conversion rates (completion of sales and repeat visits). If users have a gratifying and enjoyable experience, this will encourage them to visit the website more frequently.

In contrast, some users search websites for an item or ways to buy it, quickly become frustrated and leave a website and most probably will never return to it, if the site is not user-friendly and easy to navigate. Website designers should anticipate their target users' needs in order to prevent the frustrations which often occur. Frustration can result from failure to complete a task when working with a website or a system, or when goals are not achieved. This failure can be take place if the users: 'spend a lot of time hitting the wrong buttons; get error messages; feel confused; curse at the screen; and need to ask customer support for help' (McCracken et al. 2004, p. xii). Website design should be driven by two key intentions: to assist people to locate information quickly, and to provide information that is well presented, readable and readily available by adopting the usability and HCI principles and guidelines (Issa & Turk, 2012; Leung & Law, 2012; Sørum, Andersen, & Vatrapu, 2011). Moreover, designers should provide clear instructions to the users concerning the purpose and limitations of the site.

However, if a website has poor usability and its design is not according to HCI principles and guidelines, the users might well ask how the creators of the website could possibly think that it would be acceptable (McCracken et al. 2004, p. xii). Often this happens because the designers are inexperienced or they disregard the users' needs. Perhaps the designer focused on the technical aspects of the project and did not pay any attention to the users' expectations and requirements. Some designers try to mimic successful sites by copying attractive images from the Internet and create their home page without a basic knowledge of design principles. Hence, the website will lack cohesion since the graphics and the texts were written and created by different writers and designers, and it will 'stay a jumble of loose parts.' However, 'If you make your own site, it is your work. It will radiate something of your personality, your preferences and your taste' (Hoekstra, 2000). For these reasons, the first researcher developed a new unit IS650 to raise awareness of usability and HCI principles and guidelines among the Information Systems students, especially in higher education sectors in Australia and Portugal. For the same reason, the IS650 unit is offered in Universidade Aberta as the Web Site Planning and Development (WSPD) unit.

To improve students' understanding, a reflective journal assessment was employed as a pedagogic tool to encourage reflection, critique and self-analysis by students and to make them aware of the importance of usability and HCI principles and guidelines. The units were intended to make students understand that a website developed using the principles and guidelines was more likely to be successful and encourage users to revisit the website as it made them comfortable, confident and satisfied by working with the site. The principle behind integrating reflective journal assessment in the IS650 and WSPD units was to allow the students to understand the importance of usability and HCI in the web development process, and to improve students' skills gained from reading, writing, searching, researching, critical thinking and using the Endnote software.

The outcomes from this chapter will contribute a new and significant theoretical, practical and methodological approach to implementing reflective journal assessment in the higher education sector, and effectively conveying to students of Information Systems in Australia and Portugal, the importance of the concepts of HCI and usability. These findings will be of benefit to both academics and practitioners in the field of information systems/technology. The researchers acknowledge that the study has limitations since it was conducted only in Australia and Portugal.

The aim of this chapter is to ascertain whether the reflective journal assessment improves students' understanding of the principles of HCI and usability, especially in the website development process and to promote professional learning, and communication skills. Furthermore, this chapter addresses ways to encourage students to think critically about usability and HCI issues. Currently, the majority of educationalists indicate that employing reflective journal assessment in the master's degree would enhance students'

confidence in their ability, mainly in terms of communication skills as this assessment approach promotes independent research and self-teaching. This chapter is organized as follows: 1) Introduction; 2) HCI and Usability; 3) HCI and Usability design and guidelines; 4) Reflective Journal; 5) Methodology and Research Question; 6) Participants and Assessments; 7) Results; 8) Discussion and Recommendations; 9) Conclusion.

HCI AND USABILITY

In order for computer-based systems -including websites- to be widely accepted and used effectively, they need to be well designed via a "user-centred" approach. This is not to say that all systems/websites have to be designed to accommodate everyone, but that computer-based systems/websites should be designed for the needs and capabilities of the people for whom they are intended. In the end, users should not even have to think about the complexity of how to use a computer/website. For that reason, computers and related devices including websites have to be designed with an understanding that people with specific tasks in mind will want to use them in a way that is seamless with respect to their work. Additionally, it is very important to 'define style, norms, roles and even mores of human and computer relationship that each side can live with, as computers become more complex, smarter and more capable,' and as we allow them to 'take on autonomous or semi-autonomous control of more critical aspects of our lives and society' (Miller, 2004, p. 34).

Systems designers need to know how to think in terms of future users' tasks and how to translate that knowledge into an executable system. This can be accomplished by creating a good interface design to let the user interact and deal with the computer without any difficulties and to have more control of the system. Alice Head (1999, p.9) stated that good interface design 'is a reliable and effective intermediary, sending us the right cues so that tasks get done – regardless of how trivial, incidental, or artful the design might seem to be'.

Recently, as we know, user-centred design has become an important 'concept in the design of interactive system[s] [including the websites]. It is primarily concerned with the design of socio-technical systems that take into account not only their users, but also the use of technologies in users' everyday activities; it can be thought of as the design of spaces for human communications and interaction'(DePaula, 2003, p. 219).

HCI 'is recognized as an interdisciplinary subject'(Dix, Finlay, Abowd, & Beale, 2004, p.4) and therefore requires input from a range of disciplines such as 'computer science (application design and engineering of human interfaces), psychology (the application of theories of cognitive processes and the empirical analysis of user behavior), sociology and anthropology (interactions between technology, work, and organization), and industrial design (interactive products)'. Therefore, HCI comprises 'science, engineering and design aspects' (Hewett et al., 1992).

The purpose of HCI is to design a computer system -including website- to match the needs and requirements of the users. The HCI specialists need to think about the above factors in order to produce an outstanding system/website. To achieve the goals of HCI, a number of approaches can be utilized. These approaches need to be studied very carefully in order to develop a system/website which provides the user with productivity and efficiency. These approaches are (Preece, Rogers, Benyon, Holland, & Carey, 1994, p. 46-47): Involving the user (involve the user as much as possible so that s/he can influence the system design); Integrating different kinds of knowledge and expertise (integrate knowledge and expertise from the different disciplines that contribute to HCI design)'; and Making the design process iterative (testing can be done to check that the design does indeed meet users' requirements).

Hence, it is obvious that HCI design should be user-centred, integrate knowledge from different disciplines, and be highly iterative. In addition, it is important to undertake effective usability evaluation. This will provide feedback regarding negative and positive aspects of prototypes. It is important that the way in which people interact with computers/websites is intuitive and clear. However, designing appropriate HCI is not always straightforward, as the many poorly designed computer systems testify.

One of the challenges of HCI design is to keep abreast of technological developments and to ensure that these are harnessed for maximum human benefit. Recent studies (Dillahunt, Mankoff, & Forlizzi, 2010; DiSalvo, Sengers, & Hronn Brynjarsdottir, 2010; Issa & Turk, 2012; Joshi, Sarda, & Tripathi, 2010; Shi, 2011; Silberman & Tomlinson, 2010) confirm that HCI design, especially in the web development process, will enhance the website presentation, layout and contents, and will meet the diversity of users who will potentially and most likely be using the website. By adopting the above concepts in the web's development process the website will be easy to use and this will encourage users to visit this website frequently.

Usability refers to the 'quality of the interaction in terms of parameters such as time taken to perform tasks, number of errors made and the time to become a competent user' (Benyon, Turner, & Turner, 2005, p. 52). Alternatively, usability 'is a quality attribute that assesses how easy user interfaces are to use. The word "usability" also refers to methods for improving ease-of-use during the design process' (Nielsen, 2003). The usability evaluation stage is crucial as it is here that a software development team can establish the positive and negative aspects of its prototype releases, and make the required changes before the system is delivered to the target users. Several studies (Davis & Shipman, 2011; Hertzum & Clemmensen, 2012; Lavie, Oron-Gilad, & Meyer,

2011; Leung & Law, 2012; Sauer, Seibel, & Rüt-tinger, 2010) indicated that usability evaluation can assist designers to observe users to identify what can be improved and what type of new aspects should include in the design, including the websites. HCI specialists 'observe and talk with participants as they try to accomplish true-to-life tasks on a site (or system), and this allows them to form a detailed picture of the site as experienced by the user' (Carroll, 2004).

From the user's perspective, usability is a very important aspect of the web development process as it can mean the difference between completing a task precisely and completely or not, and the user appreciating the process or being frustrated. Alternatively, if usability is not a priority in website design, then users will become very frustrated working with it. The main goal of a usable website is to provide users with a positive response to their research; if the website design is not user-friendly, users are likely to become frustrated (Lazar, Jones, & Shneiderman, 2006; S. Lee & Koubek, 2010; Y. Lee & Kozar, 2012; Tuzovic, 2010). A recent study by Lee and Kozar (2012) confirmed that usability can bring several benefits to the website development process or any application, including effectiveness, efficiency and satisfaction.

Effective HCI and usability design include using appropriate design elements and making the system easy to use. Nowadays, much research goes into the development and improvement of HCI and advances have been made particularly with the use of graphics and animation components – also referred to as multimedia (de Castro Lozano et al., 2011). There are several benefits of adhering to the principles of HCI and usability. These include: the interfaces are more pleasant for the users; communicability is improved because the user interface design is better able to convey the intended meaning or feeling to the target user; and lastly, a website with good usability and HCI will promote users' trust and satisfaction, and this will encourage users to revisit the website. Such a website is successful and manages to convey its message or promote its activities effectively.

HCI AND USABILITY DESIGN PRINCIPLES AND GUIDELINES

To understand the importance of HCI and Usability aspects in the web development process, it is worth examining the design principles and guidelines suggested by Te'eni, Carey, & Zhang (2007). The adoption of these principles and guidelines when developing a user interface, including a website, will improve the performance, functionality, learnability, efficiency, effectiveness, usefulness or utility; it will produce fewer errors and improve users' satisfaction and achievement of goals (Davis & Shipman, 2011; Fernandez, Insfran, & Abrahão, 2011; Leung & Law, 2012; Oztekin, 2011).

To allow our students to understand the HCI and usability concepts in the web development process, design principles and guidelines are introduced. Principles are used to formalize the high level and widely appropriate design goals, while guidelines are essential to the designers to achieve the principles. (Te'eni et al., 2007; Zhang, Carey, Te'eni, & Tremaine, 2005). The design principles are divided into seven stages (see Figure 1); each principle is mainly focused on a specific concept which should be considered initially by the designers and users in order to develop a successful user interface including a website.

The principles are:

1. **Improve Users' Task Performance and Reduce Their Effort:** This principle aims to achieve high functionality along with high usability (i.e. efficiency, ease of use, and comfort in using the system, given that the functionality has been established).
2. **Strive for Fit Between the Information Representation Needed and Presented**:

Figure 1. Design Principles – prepared by the researchers

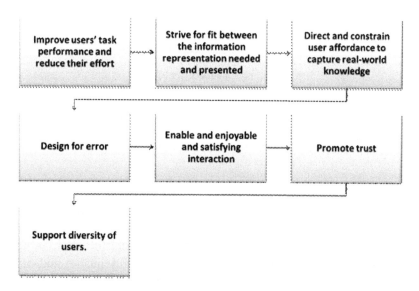

a. **Representation:** A simplified description of a real-world phenomenon.

b. **Functionality:** The set of activities.

c. **Usability:** A measure of ease.

d. **Cognitive Fit:** System's representation of the problem supports the user's strategies for performing the task.

3. **Direct and Constrain User Affordance to Capture Real-World Knowledge:** The general idea here is that the knowledge required to act effectively resides both in the person's head and in the real world around him/her.

4. **Design for Error:** A faulty action due to incorrect intention (mistake) or to incorrect or accidental implementation of the intention (slip).

5. **Designing for an Enjoyable and Satisfying Interaction:** The design of the interface or website should make the interaction enjoyable for both the designer and users.

6. **Promote Trust:** Is a critical component in developing interface or website, especially the e-commerce systems where the interactions translate directly into revenue.

7. **Support Diversity of Users:** This principle should take into consideration the diversity of populations of users.

To ensure that the user interface or website is popular and meets users' needs, users and designers must consider these design principles to prevent user frustration and to attract more users to visit the website.

Furthermore, to complete the interface or website design, designers and users must consider the design guidelines which are essential in the web development process. The design guidelines comprise five steps (see Figure 2).

1. **Consistency Guidelines:** If the interface is consistent (even if poorly designed), the end user can adapt to it.

2. **Control and Feedback go Hand in Hand:** Providing feedback is probably the most accepted guideline in the design of any interaction.

3. **Metaphor:** The use of familiar terms and associations to represent a new concept.

Figure 2. Design Guidelines - prepared by the researchers

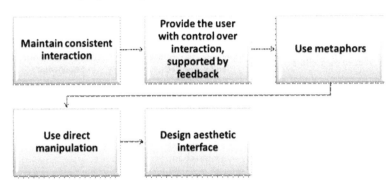

4. **Direct Manipulation:** An interaction style in which objects are represented and manipulated in a manner analogous to the real world.
5. **Design Aesthetic Interface:** Aesthetic appeal concerns the overall appearance of an application.

The integration of design principles and guidelines in the web development process will ensure that websites are successful, since they will improve functionality, learnability, efficiency, effectiveness, and accuracy; most importantly, using these websites will increase users' satisfaction. This was confirmed by students from the IS650 and WSPD units. Student 1 confirmed that learning these principles and guidelines 'allow me to think differently and be more critical when I visit any new website now. In the end, the unit made me more aware of this field and the concepts within it'. Another student (Student 2) stated '…which in my opinion are the pinnacle of the unit as it presents detailed elements to enable a high quality interaction with users and provide designers with a framework to guide their developments'.

REFLECTIVE JOURNALS

Currently, teaching in the higher education sector is a challenging exercise, as teachers attempt to use the best approaches to teaching and assessment methods, using the latest, cutting edge technology to develop and enhance students' communication, reflective thinking, research, search, critical thinking, decision making, writing and reading skills, and proficiency in using the endnote software. These skills are essential for both the academic environment and the future workplace. The reflective journal idea was introduced and developed by Dewey (1933) who maintained that reflection 'was a deliberate cognitive process, which addressed problem solving before a solution was reached' (Clarke, 2003, p.4). Several studies indicated (Bailes, Hulsebosch, & Martin, 2010; Scott, 2011; Titus & Gremler, 2010) that integrating reflective journal assessment in a higher education curriculum is essential since this assessment will enhance the level of student performance especially the critical thinking and writing skills, and this assessment will change their learning events and improve students' confidence in their communication skills (e.g. writing, research, citing). In this respect, the majority of educators indicated and confirmed that this assessment approach is considered ideal as an independent method of research and self-teaching.

Recent studies (Anderson, 2012; Clarkeburn & Kettula, 2012; Gadsby & Cronin, 2012; Knapp, 2012; Power, 2012) confirmed that using reflective journals in higher education will encourage the students to engage in critical evaluation and 'becoming more actively involved in their own professional accountability'(Gadsby & Cronin, 2012, p.2). Therefore, this assessment offers many advantages to students and teachers simultaneously since students will acquire or refine several skills and develop their confidence by completing these assessments; on the other hand, teachers will better understand what they already know by reconsidering what they have already learnt (Loughran, 2002). This will lead as to Dewey (1933, p. 78) argument that 'we do not learn from experience, we learn from reflecting on experience'. This statement confirmed that using the reflective journal assessment in IS60 and WSPD units will assist students to learn the HCI and usability concepts by using reflecting and reproducing.

To assist our students to write the reflective journal, the researchers adopted the analysis and evaluation of a reflective journal template (which was developed by the communication skills centre at the Australian University); this template contains the following steps. 1) Reading (full citation required, including author, title, date, publication details, and page numbers). 2) What is the subject/theme of this article, (3) Argument/Findings (What is the author's argument?), (4) Evidence (How do this author's views compare with what others have said on the same or a similar topic?), (5) Observations (What are your own thoughts on the subject?), and (6) Conclusion. Figure 3 demonstrate the steps which are required to write a reflective journal.

The reflective journal is marked using the following criteria developed by the researchers: 1) Reading (well presented; accurate acknowledgement of sources); 2)What is the subject/theme of this article (well presented, listing the important themes of the article(s); 3) Argument/Findings (evidence of understanding; adding up-to-date references to support evidence(s); 4) Observations (student's observations and perspective were presented, explained and demonstrated well); 5) Conclusion (sound and appropriate conclusion(s) is drawn; a full and well-written conclusion is provided based upon the foundation in the argument construction section); 6) Structure and quality of writing (well-structured, e.g. paragraphing, sentence structure, spacing; above-average standard of expression and presentation, excellent overall expression and presentation). Students use the template when completing their journal entries and refer to the assessment criteria to ensure that each is met before the final submission. In addition, although a marking guide is used for this assessment, the marking criteria focus on the ability to reflect instead of what is reflected upon; this avoids plagiarism, unlike other assessment methods (MacFarland & Gourlary, 2009). However, the assessment of the reflective journals must follow the university's policy on plagiarism; therefore, Turnitin software (http://turnitin.com/) is used to detect plagiarism in this assessment.

Therefore to improve the effectiveness of the IS650 and WSPD units in conveying HCI and Usability principles to Information Systems students,

Figure 3. The concept map for writing reflective journal – prepared by the researchers

the researchers integrated the reflective journal assessment in their curriculum and course work. This method of assessment is considered to be an appropriate means of enhancing communication skills and critical thinking. Most importantly, the intention is to promote Human Computer Interaction and Usability Guidelines and Principles among Information Systems students in Australia and Portugal, who are considered our future developers.

IS650 AND WSPD UNITS; UNIT PROGRAM AND ASSESSMENTS

In this chapter, the researchers intend to examine whether the use of reflective journals assessment can improve students' understanding of the concepts behind usability and HCI principles and guidelines for the web development process. To achieve this, the first researcher developed the IS650 unit program based on her PhD research and results, the Te'eni et al. (2007) textbook, and an up-to-date literature review of journals, e-journals, books and e-books to ensure that up-to-date knowledge and cutting edge development are delivered to the students to promote and enhance their understanding of the design and development of successful, effective websites. Teaching HCI and Usability are a challenge exercise for both authors, since these units need a lot of preparation and planning to ensure that the materials and exercises are cutting edge and enlightened. Several literature reviews (Koehne & Redmiles, 2012; Kybartaite, Nousiainen, Marozas, & Jegelavicius, 2007; Odrakiewicz, 2010) confirmed that teaching these aspects will allow students to obtain new knowledge and skills in dealing with the brand-new technology from iPad to websites. The unit program comprises the following topics: physical, cognitive and affective engineering; evaluation; task analysis; colour; navigation; prototyping; HCI methodologies; social networking and a new topic was introduced is sustainable design. As in-

dicated previously, to convey the same principles as those contained in the IS650 unit, the second researcher is currently running the IS650 unit in his university as the WSPD unit.

To promote HCI and usability aspects in IS650 and WSPD units, students must complete the following assessments: 1) mini tests, reflective journal and contribution to group discussion forum under the blackboard and Moodle respectively. These assessment methods are chosen carefully to develop students' skills of reflective thinking, research, communication, debating, writing and presenting skills using technology and information skills. These skills are essential for university life and the demands of the workplace in future. A series of recommendations is made to ensure that the completion of this unit at the university level will achieve several benefits, including: understanding the principles and guidelines of usability and HCI, which are required to develop websites successfully, analysing and synthesizing journal articles and publications and providing a literature review to identify the gaps in the literature; improving students' communication and personal skills, and matching the unit, degree and university aims and objectives. The units' assessments and syllabus are designed with mainly university graduate attributes in mind (see Table 1). In 2013, slight modifications will be made to the assessment approaches especially for IS650 unit; the three assessments are: Final Test (Individual Assessment) 40%; Reflective Journal (3) – 30% and finally, Wiki – 30%.

PARTICIPANTS

This study focused on two postgraduate units in Australia and Portugal: the IS650 unit in Australia and the WSPD unit in Portugal. The 64 participants are mainly from Australia, Asia (Including India), and Europe, Middle East, America (North and South) Mauritius and Africa. A mixture of different nationalities and cultures plays an important role

Table 1. Assessment activities for postgraduate units - Australia and Portugal (2009 – 2012)

Unit	Assessments	Unit Syllabus
IS650	Mini Tests 25% Reflective Journal (7 Individual and 3 Teamwork) 40% Contribution to Group Discussions – Blackboard (10%)	The IS unit focuses primarily on the principals of usability and human-computer interaction (HCI) design of users' interface including websites
WSPD	Six Group Activities (10% for each activity) 60% overall One final individual work 40%	The WSPD unit is mainly focused on issues relating to Website Planning and Development through a Human-Computer Interaction approach and other related issues.

in these units, as each participant interacts and shares his/her knowledge and skills, experience, and cultural perspective with their colleagues in person or via online discussion. The participant group comprised 27% females and 73% males. The researchers noted that both genders took equal part in various activities including discussions, debates, presentations, teamwork activities, and the exchange of ideas. Table 2 provides the demographic details of the IS650 and WSPD students for the 2009-2012 periods.

RESEARCH METHODS AND QUESTION

This chapter aims to examine whether the use of reflective journal assessment will enhance students' understanding of the concepts of HCI and usability in the web development process. This chapter provides experimental evidence based on quantitative and qualitative data derived from three sources: online survey, informal and formal

students' feedback from 64 student evaluations and attitudes toward the IS650/WSPD units (respectively at Curtin University and at Universidade Aberta). Both informal and formal feedback was collected during the semester to report students' perceptions of the learning experience at the university, including feedback about the unit and teaching. Informal feedback is a teaching and learning innovation. During week four of the semester, students are asked to provide their anonymous feedback regarding the unit structure, layout and assessments via an online survey. This feedback assists the lecturers to enhance/improve their teaching of the unit before the end of the semester. The second method is formal feedback, which is collected at the end of the semester through the university's formal feedback process. Students have the opportunity to provide feedback anonymously on their learning experiences and on the unit and teaching evaluation.

Finally, the third method is the online survey. This survey is divided into five parts. The purpose of each part of the survey was explained to

Table 2. Postgraduate units participants – Australia and Portugal (2009 – 2012)

Unit	Students #	Gender		Nationality						
		Female	Male	Australia	Asia (Including India)	Europe	Middle East	America (A) / North (N) and South (S)	Mauritius	Africa
IS650	*52*	*15*	*37*	*1*	*37*	*0*	*6*	*1(NA), 1 (SA)*	*2*	*4*
WSPD	*12*	*2*	*10*	*0*	*0*	*9*	*0*	*1(SA)*	*0*	*2*
Total	*64*	*17*	*47*	*1*	*37*	*9*	*6*	*2*	*2*	*6*

students. The first part pertains to background information such as participant's level of formal education; main field(s) of study, and gender. Part two aims to examine students' reactions to the unit's program; part three is intended to evaluate students' attitudes to the units' assessment approach; part four seeks students' perception of the lecturer's feedback on the various methods of assessment including the reflective journals, exam and the discussion board. Finally, part five aims to examine whether students' skills (oral presentation, writing, reading, critical thinking, research and search, use of the Endnote software, collaboration and communication) are promoted and improved after completing the IS650 and WSPD units. In the following section, the researchers discuss the results from part five of the survey. The authors used a five-point Likert scale ranging from "Strongly disagree" to "Strongly agree" for parts two to five. Besides using the Likert five-point scale for this survey, the authors provided a section where students could write down other comments regarding each part. The online survey response rate from IS650, and WSPD was 61.5% and 90% respectively.

RESULTS

To confirm the study's aims and objectives, this section presents the results from the informal and formal feedback and the results from part five of the survey. It was noted from the informal feedback (see Table 3) that students were satisfied with both the lectures (classes) and lecturer (instructor) for both IS650 and WSPD units.

Students confirmed that their lecturers had a good knowledge of HCI and usability and that the classes were engaging and not boring as lecturers used various types of teaching styles in their classes. Furthermore, students were very generous in their comments about their lecturers:

Quick response, willingness to help, friendly and approachable (Student 1)

Enthusiasm, understanding and compromise, asks our opinions (Student 2)

Lecturers are more focused on the knowledge and hot the information (Student 3)

Table 3. Informal feedback – IS650 and WSPD

Year	Unit	Question	SD/D	N	A/SA
2009	IS650	I am satisfied with the Lectures (Classes)		1	18
		I am satisfied with the Lecturer (Instructor)		1	18
2010	IS650	I am satisfied with the Lectures (Classes)		1	14
		I am satisfied with the Lecturer (Instructor)			15
2011	IS650	I am satisfied with the Lectures (Classes)		1	15
		I am satisfied with the Lecturer (Instructor)			16
2012	IS650	I am satisfied with the Lectures (Classes)	1	1	11
		I am satisfied with the Lecturer (Instructor)	1	1	11
2011	WSPD	I am satisfied with the Lectures (Classes)			10
		I am satisfied with the Lecturer (Instructor)			10

Very detailed when explaining, give good feedback that can help study improve (Student 4)

Good communications, cooperative, solves student's problems (Student 5)

Helpful, kindness (Student 6)

Lecturers give feedback and those help to improve the writing, reading and referencing skills … thank you (Student 7)

Excellent teaching style and presentation slides (Student 8)

Lecturers use many unique teaching styles to other lecturers. e.g. mp3, class activities, mind maps (Student 9)

Sharing and inform interesting issues related with HCI, such as Usability and Satisfaction, using mind map for material summarizing (Student 10)

Using different activities related to the lecture such as exercises for each week and challenge exercises and so on (Student 11)

Group discuss is really a powerful weapon, learn things quick & it is good to share ideas with each other (Student 12).

This feedback confirmed that researchers have unique teaching methods for HCI and Usability concepts, as the majority of the students acknowledged that the activities, the unit program and, most importantly, the approach to assessment including the reflective journals intended to assist them to understand the concepts of HCI and usability, together with the lecturers' feedback, all play a major role in improving their learning journey.

The informal feedback from students was invariably positive:

The journals are very dynamic as they force us to be resourceful, using textbooks, websites, and articles. Also in class reading and analysis keeps class interesting, especially cause me get to discuss in group. (Student 13)

Better understanding of HCI, information about new technologies via the reflective journals (Student 14)

I have learnt to write reflective reviews of the articles I read therefore increased my learning toward HCI and usability (Student 15)

The home work journals is a step in the right direction (Student 16)

I like the journal writing every week, bush us to study hard (Student 17)

Understand the complexity behind HCI and Usability via exercises and reflective journals (Student 18)

Practical approach to teaching than a conventional way (Student 19)

Makes are feeling like doing a post-grad course by encouraging reading articles which are related to our unit in line to write the reflective journals. (Student 20)

Class activities keep the classes interesting. The assessment style of reflective journals have helped in applying knowledge learned in class to real world occurrences (Student 21)

Involving students to read articles that related to the lecture topic to understand the unit program (Student 22)

The journal articles writing are very good to improve our reading, writing knowledge about HCI (Student 23)

I learned huge knowledge from this unit especially Human computer interaction, which I was not aware of before (Student 24)

Personal contact with the unit coordinator, interaction through presentations, improving our thinking and knowledge to HCI and Usability through critical reflection reports (Student 25)

Students were very satisfied and pleased with the reflective journal assessment and recognized that this assessment assisted them to: 1) improve their understanding and knowledge of HCI and

Usability by critically reflecting on their reading; and 2) it improved their communication skills as well as their level of critical thinking.

By the same token, the results from part five for the online survey confirmed that completing IS650 and WSPD units (see Tables 4 and 5) improved and developed a number of students' skills including oral presentation, writing, reading, critical thinking, research and search, use of the Endnote software, collaboration and communication. The online survey was used for units IS650 and WSPD during 2012.

Results depicted in Tables 4 and 5 confirm that the completion of the IS650 and WSPD units allowed the students to acquire valuable skills as a result of collaboration, writing, reading, critical thinking, research, search and communication, all

Table 4. IS650 Students 2012 – Part five – online survey (Response rate 61.5%)

Question	Strongly Disagree	Disagree	Neutral	Agree	Strongly Agree	Mean	Standard Deviation
Collaboration skills	0	0	1	3	4	4.38	0.74
Writing skills	0	0	0	2	6	4.75	0.46
Reading skills	0	0	0	2	6	4.75	0.46
Critical skills	0	0	0	2	6	4.75	0.46
Research skills	0	0	0	3	5	4.63	0.52
Search skills	0	0	1	4	3	4.25	0.71
Communication skills	0	0	1	4	3	4.25	0.71

Table 5. WSPD Students 2012 – part five – online survey (Response rate 90%)

Question	Strongly Disagree	Disagree	Neutral	Agree	Strongly Agree	Mean	Standard Deviation
Collaboration skills	0	1	1	5	2	3.89	0.93
Writing skills	0	1	4	3	1	3.44	0.88
Reading skills	0	0	4	4	1	3.67	0.71
Critical skills	0	0	1	6	2	4.11	0.60
Research skills	0	0	1	5	3	4.22	0.67
Search skills	0	0	1	6	2	4.11	0.60
Communication skills	0	0	3	5	1	3.78	0.67

of which skills are essential for university studies and life in general. Students confirmed and emphasized that IS650 and WPDS units were quite challenging and 'it improves my overall quality' and 'Very useful and interesting Units' (Student 26). By the same token, several studies (Diggins, 2004; Gadsby & Cronin, 2012; Lanning, Brickhouse, Gunsolley, Ranson, & Willett, 2011; Worley, 2008) indicate that effective communications skills will help students to build trust, respect, foster learning and attain their goals. It was acknowledged that both writing and oral skills are essential for sharing ideas, feelings and commitments. Therefore, productive communication skills will assist students to understand the assessments, including the reflective journals. Students are given the opportunity to perform well in their studies as well in the workplace, since businesses seek graduates with effective communication and collaboration skills (Cunliffe, 2004; Lanning et al., 2011; Woei & White, 2010).

DISCUSSION

The results from the informal, formal and online survey reveal that the use of reflective journal assessments in IS650 and WSPD gives students a better understanding and knowledge of Human-Computer Interaction and Usability principles and guidelines. This assessment approach is considered to be the new professional learning method in higher education intended to educate students and impart the skills which are required for both current study and the workforce in future. Moreover, students were satisfied and gratified with the unit assessments since their communication, collaboration, interpersonal, writing, reading, oral presentation, search/research, problem-solving and decision-making skills, which are required for this study and real life in the future, were improved. Also, the findings indicated that the weekly reflective journals assist students to keep track of the unit work throughout the course, as it acts as a revision of material presented during lectures and laboratory sessions.

Furthermore, students confirmed that reflective journal's assessment was one of the ways to enhance their understanding of HCI and Usability. For example, one of the students indicated that 'the first of the journal genres, analysis of current research of the HCI community' required a critical analysis of journal documents. To produce these journals, a structure was provided, which firstly required a brief account of the findings in each individual article. These findings were critically analyzed to enable students to gain an understanding of the relationship between the given articles while providing supporting evidence to justify these relationships. Following this, observations were needed, which required further polishing of current understandings of HCI. This structure represents a methodology that anyone can reproduce to construct a critical working document for a given subject matter. Student 27 endorsed that 'It was noted that through the continuous reflective journals' assessment of the academic writing, a clear improvement was achieved. Students were not only required to reach some standards, but also pushed to improve our coherence and completeness, which are fundamental for being a successful postgraduate. Although it was a great challenge writing the reflective journals, but was fundamental to allow higher performance not only in the IS650 unit, but in other units as well'. The majority of students observed that the IS650 and WSPD units gave them a new insight into HCI and usability which is essential in the web development process as most of them were previously unaware of these issues. Finally, an understanding of all aspects related to HCI and usability in the development of any information systems/technology is an incredible asset that every Information professional should possess.

Despite its challenges, the integration of the reflective journal in IS650 and WSPD units proved to be an interesting and outstanding achievement from the researchers' perspective, as the majority of the students indicated in their formal and informal feedback, as well the online survey, that this assessment approach in their units allowed them to, firstly, raise their awareness of aspects of Usability and HCI especially in the web development process, as the majority of students confirmed that these concepts are essential in the website development process. Student 28 signposted: 'I did not know and aware that HCI and Usability is a thoroughly studied and well-researched field within Information Systems'. While Student 29 pointed out that 'Conducting this subject is very important because I believe every system/web designer should know about HCI and usability how it can be adapted in the design especially the website'. By the same token, Student 30 noted that 'The journals have taught me a lot of Human Computer Interaction aspects such as the complexity of Human Computer Interaction, the importance of user involvement in the system design, the necessity of measuring usability to improve the current usability, the role of trust in e-commercial, etc. While some journals are easy to read, some of them are targeted for more experienced audience'.

Secondly, the students' comments confirmed and revealed that this assessment approach in both IS650 and WSPD units allowed them to understand the concepts behind the unit program, and that the completion of the journals was an excellent experience. Student 31 stated that 'the journal assignments have been a very satisfying experience for me, I have to learn the latest issue of Human Computer Interactions. Please keep doing the journal assignments in the future, as it will help the students to improve their reading and writing skills as well as learning new concepts of Human Computer Interactions'. However, this was not the only benefit to be derived from the reflective journals. This approach also gave students the opportunity to acquire and improve upon a wide range of communication skills which are necessary

for the purposes of study and future workplace requirements as the majority of organizations seek graduates with excellent communication skills to match the needs of both business and society in general. Finally, student 32 commented: 'I enjoyed the lecturer's teachings because it seemed obvious to me that this particular topic was of a big interest to her. I enjoy studying with lecturers who seem passionate about the field they are teaching as the enthusiasm reaches me, at least during the class. She also listened to the student feedback regarding workload and activities we wanted. Lastly, I appreciated the presentation on her thesis as, again, I like to see practical and concrete work relating to the unit I am learning. It makes the unit feel much more useful in the real world'.

In the IS650 and WSPD units, reflective journal assessment is designed to improve student(s) experience from critically, creatively and reflectively, reviewing, synthesising, analysing and recording the main key points and thoughts about material from textbook(s), journal articles and the Internet. In addition, this assessment encourages student(s) to keep up to date with their readings and their visits to WWW sites which are related to the unit. A reflective journal should not only contain a summary of the reading; it also seeks to encourage students to reflect upon the information acquired from reading these articles, to add their personal record of their educational experiences after having read these articles, and to consider how these experiences assist them to understand and follow the curriculum of units IS650 and WSPD. Lastly, on the basis of the students' outstanding overall satisfaction, the first author is now considered as a teacher-leader in reflective journal assessment in her school, and she now works with her colleagues to support and implement this assessment in the school curriculum strategy to reflect the desirable attributes of university graduates and to promote and improve students' learning skills.

The research aims were confirmed by strong student satisfaction and gratification with the reflective journal assessments in the IS650 and

WSPD units. Students were very delighted with this assessment approach; student 31 expressed that 'writing journal is good way of learning as we read the articles, then try to understand what it is about, try to find the linkage between different authors view on the subject and then write how different authors were agreeing or arguing on the same topic supporting our own point of view'. In addition, 'It is all about giving extra justification to your point of view or your way of thinking by supporting it with the articles and giving additional explanation in order to make your answer justifiable and more meaningful'. Finally, there is no doubt that this assessment approach offers numerous many benefits for higher education since students endorsed and confirmed that they learned the principles and guidelines behind HCI and Usability and above all, that their communication skills improved dramatically.

RECOMMENDATIONS FOR INTEGRATING REFLECTIVE JOURNAL IN HIGHER EDUCATION

Reflective journal assessment in higher education is considered a vehicle for reflection, acquiring new knowledge (i.e. HCI and Usability) and, most importantly, prompting and improving students' communications skills for their current studies as well as the workforce in future. This assessment enables students to document their experiences, thoughts, questions, ideas and conclusion that signboard their learning journey when undertaking the IS650 and WSPD units.

The researchers hold that reflective journal assessment is a unique tool that allows students to express their opinions and observations and later to reflect on what they learn from these articles. This assessment process will encourage students to become active learners; it fosters independent learners, since they read, analyze and synthesize,

write, observe and later reflect. To ensure the smooth integration of reflective journal assessment in a unit, the following guidelines which are based on the researchers' experience, should be followed: 1) introduce the reflective journal analysis and evaluation template to assist students to organize their ideas, thoughts, and reflection following their reading; 2) keep track of journal submissions, the first journal in particular, to ensure that students have followed the template, especially the observation section; 3) check the marking guide for the reflective journals before the final submission, to ensure that the final submission meets the marking guide and the lecturer' criteria; 4) indicate students' strengths and weaknesses of the current journal entry in order to improve the subsequent journal entry; 5) in order to promote this method of assessment among the students, especially in the first week of the semester, introduce some class exercises based on the template; students present these to the class for peer assessment and feedback from the lecturer regarding the presentation in general and any new thoughts and ideas that have emerged.

Finally, these guidelines are based on the lecturers' perspectives after implementing reflective journal assessment in IS650 and WSPD. Finally, the current studies (Bailes et al., 2010; Clarke, 2003; Lin, Hong, Wang, & Lee, 2011; Power, 2012 ; Sengers, McCarthy, & Dourish, 2006; Titus & Gremler, 2010) indicate that this form of assessment is common-used in the higher education sector as it helps to develop self-empowerment, creativity, writing skills, self-expression, and critical thinking; moreover, it encourages reflection which is associated with deep learning and meta-cognition. Therefore, the researchers' perception is that this assessment approach should and must be integrated in the higher education curriculum to foster students' learning and shift it away from - traditional teaching-learning practices to the independent learning to learn method.

CONCLUSION

This chapter aims to examine and investigate the employment of reflective journal assessment in the IS650 and WSPD units. This form of assessment was introduced in these units based on both university and business needs since university graduates should develop the communication and critical thinking skills necessary for both their current studies and for their future place in the workforce. The researchers used three sources to collect the data for this study, namely: formal and informal students' feedback, and an online survey. The study outcomes confirmed the research question and study aims, as the majority of students indicated that this method of assessment assisted them to understand the HCI and usability principles and guidelines as these concepts are essential in the web development process, especially to satisfy the users from generations X, Y, and Z. In addition, the IS650 and WSPD units provide significant knowledge regarding the HCI and Usability topics, expanding students' horizons and giving them a greater understanding of the unit program and the rationale for this approach to assessment. Furthermore, this assessment method significantly improved students' communication and time management skills, which are needed for their current studies as well as the workforce in future. A set of recommendations was developed by the researchers to implement the reflective journal as a means of assessment in the higher education sector. This study was limited to two university units; researchers are planning to employ the reflective journal assessments in other units in order to further study and compare students' attitudes to this type of assessment.

REFERENCES

Anderson, J. (2012). Reflective journals as a tool for auto-ethnographic learning: A case study of student experiences with individualized sustainability. *Journal of Geography in Higher Education*, *36*(4), 613–623. doi:10.1080/03098265.2012.692157

Bailes, C., Hulsebosch, P., & Martin, D. (2010). Reflective journal writing: Deaf pre-service teachers with hearing children. *Teacher Education and Special Education*, *33*(3), 234–247. doi:10.1177/0888406409356763

Benyon, D., Turner, P., & Turner, S. (2005). *Designing interactive systems*. Englewood Cliffs, NJ: Pearson Education Limited.

Cappel, J. J., & Huang, Z. (2007). A usability analysis of company websites. *Journal of Computer Information Systems*, *48*(1), 117–123.

Carroll, M. (2004). *Usability testing leads to better ROI*. Retrieved from http://www.theusability-company.com/news/media_coverage/pdfs/2003/NewMediaAge_270303.pdf

Clarke, M. (2003). *Reflection: Journals and reflective questions a strategy for professional learning*. Paper presented at the NZARE/AARE Conference. Auckland, New Zealand.

Clarkeburn, H., & Kettula, K. (2012). Fairness and using reflective journals in assessment. *Teaching in Higher Education*, *17*(4), 439–452. doi:10.1080/13562517.2011.641000

Cunliffe, A. (2004). On becoming a critically reflexive practitioner. *Journal of Management Education*, *28*(4), 407–425. doi:10.1177/1052562904264440

Davis, P., & Shipman, F. (2011). *Learning usability assessment models for web sites*. Paper presented at the IUI 2011. Palo Alto, CA.

DePaula, R. (2003). *A new era in human computer interaction: The challenges of technology as a social proxy*. Paper presented at the Latin American Conference on HCI. New York, NY.

Dewey, J. (1933). *How we think: A restatement of the relation of reflective thinking to the educative process*. Boston: D. C. Heath.

Dillahunt, T., Mankoff, J., & Forlizzi, J. (2010). *A proposed framework for assessing environmental sustainability in the HCI community*. Paper presented at the CHI 2010. Atlanta, GA.

DiSalvo, C., Sengers, P., & Hronn Brynjarsdottir, P. (2010). *Mapping the landscape of sustainable HCI*. Paper presented at the CHI 2010. Atlanta, GA.

Dix, A., Finlay, J., Abowd, G., & Beale, R. (2004). *Human-computer interaction* (3rd ed.). Englewood Cliffs, NJ: Pearson Education Limited.

Fernandez, A., Insfran, E., & Abrahão, S. (2011). Usability evaluation methods for the web: A systematic mapping study. *Information and Software Technology*, *53*(8), 789–817. Retrieved from http://www.sciencedirect.com/science/article/pii/S0950584911000607 doi:10.1016/j.infsof.2011.02.007

Gadsby, H., & Cronin, S. (2012). To what extent can reflective journaling help beginning teachers develop Masters level writing skills? *Reflective Practice: International and Multidisciplinary Perspectives*, *13*(1), 1–12. doi:10.1080/14623943.2011.616885

Head, A. J. (1999). *Design wise*. Thomas H Hogan Sr.

Hertzum, M., & Clemmensen, T. (2012). How do usability professionals construe usability? *International Journal of Human-Computer Studies*, *70*(1), 26–42. Retrieved from http://www.sciencedirect.com/science/article/pii/S1071581911001030 doi:10.1016/j.ijhcs.2011.08.001

Hewett, T., Baecker, R., Card, C., Carey, T., Gasen, J., Mantei, M., et al. (1992). *Human-computer interaction*. Retrieved from http://old.sigchi.org/cdg/

Hoekstra, G. (2000). *History of web design*. Retrieved from http://www.weballey.net/webdesign/history.html

Issa, T. (1999). *Online shopping and human factors*. Unpublished.

Issa, T., & Turk, A. (2012). Applying usability and HCI principles in developing marketing websites. *International Journal of Computer Information Systems and Industrial Management Applications*, *4*, 76–82.

Joshi, A., Sarda, N. L., & Tripathi, S. (2010). Measuring effectiveness of HCI integration in software development processes. *Journal of Systems and Software*, *83*(11), 2045–2058. doi:10.1016/j.jss.2010.03.078

Knapp, N. F. (2012). Reflective journals: Making constructive use of the apprenticeship of observation in preservice teacher education. *Teaching Education*, *23*(3), 323–340. doi:10.1080/10476210.2012.686487

Koehne, B., & Redmiles, D. F. (2012). *Envisioning distributed usability evaluation through a virtual world platform*. Paper presented at the Cooperative and Human Aspects of Software Engineering (CHASE). New York, NY.

Kybartaite, A., Nousiainen, J., Marozas, V., & Jegelavicius, D. (2007). *Review of e-teaching/ e- learning practices and technologies*. Retrieved from http://hlab.ee.tut.fi/video/bme/evicab/astore/ delivera/wp4revie.pdf

Lanning, S. K., Brickhouse, T. H., Gunsolley, J. C., Ranson, S. L., & Willett, R. M. (2011). Communication skills instruction: An analysis of self, peer-group, student instructors and faculty assessment. *Patient Education and Counseling*, *83*, 145–151. doi:10.1016/j.pec.2010.06.024 PMID:20638816

Lavie, T., Oron-Gilad, T., & Meyer, J. (2011). Aesthetics and usability of in-vehicle navigation displays. *International Journal of Human-Computer Studies*, *69*(1-2), 80–99. doi:10.1016/j. ijhcs.2010.10.002

Lazar, J., Jones, A., & Shneiderman, B. (2006). Workplace user frustration with computers: An exploratory investigation of the causes and severity. *Behaviour & Information Technology*, *25*(3), 239–251. doi:10.1080/01449290500196963

Lee, S., & Koubek, R. J. (2010). The effects of usability and web design attributes on user preference for e-commerce web sites. *Computers in Industry*, *61*(4), 329–341. doi:10.1016/j. compind.2009.12.004

Lee, Y., & Kozar, K. (2012). Understanding of website usability: Specifying and measuring constructs and their relationships. *Decision Support Systems*, *52*(2), 450–463. Retrieved from http://www.sciencedirect.com/science/ article/pii/S0167923611001679 doi:10.1016/j. dss.2011.10.004

Lin, H.-S., Hong, Z.-R., Wang, H.-H., & Lee, S.-T. (2011). Using reflective peer assessment to promote students' conceptual understanding through asynchronous discussions. *Journal of Educational Technology & Society*, *14*(3), 178–189.

Loughran, J. (2002). Effective reflective practice: In search of meaning in learning about teaching. *Journal of Teacher Education*, *53*(1), 33–43. doi:10.1177/0022487102053001004

MacFarland, B., & Gourlary, L. (2009). Points of departure - The reflection game: Enacting the penitent self. *Teaching in Higher Education*, *14*(4), 455–459. doi:10.1080/13562510903050244

McCracken, D. D., & Wolfe, R. J. (2004). *User-centered website development a human-computer interaction approach*. Hillsdale, NJ: Pearson Education, Inc.

Miller, C. A. (2004). Human-computer etiquette: Managing expectations with intentional agents. *Communications of the ACM*, *47*(4), 31–34.

Nielsen, J. (2003). *Usability 101*. Retrieved from http://www.useit.com/alertbox/20030825.html

Odrakiewicz, P. (2010). Managing complexity in higher education through innovative ways of integrity teaching and integrity education management using innovative case studies. *Global Management Journal*, *2*(2), 122–130.

Oztekin, A. (2011). A decision support system for usability evaluation of web-based information systems. *Expert Systems with Applications*, *38*(3), 2110–2118. Retrieved from http://www.sciencedirect.com/science/article/pii/S0957417410007797 doi:10.1016/j.eswa.2010.07.151

Power, J. B. (2012). Towards a greater understanding of the effectiveness of reflective journals in a university language program. *Reflective Practice: International and Multidisciplinary Perspectives*, *13*(5), 637–649. doi:10.1080/14623943.2012.6 97889

Preece, J., Rogers, Y., Benyon, D., Holland, S., & Carey, T. (1994). *Human computer interaction*. Reading, MA: Addison-Wesley.

Sauer, J., Seibel, K., & Rüttinger, B. (2010). The influence of user expertise and prototype fidelity in usability tests. *Applied Ergonomics*, *41*(1), 130–140. doi:10.1016/j.apergo.2009.06.003 PMID:19632666

Scott, I. (2011). The learning outcome in higher education: Time to think again? *Worcester Journal of Learning and Teaching*, *5*, 1–8.

Sengers, P., McCarthy, J., & Dourish, P. (2006). *Reflective HCI: Articulating an agenda for critical practice*. Paper presented at the CHI' 06. New York, NY.

Shi, M. (2011). *Website characteristics and their influences: A review on web design*. Paper presented at the ABIS 2011. New York, NY.

Silberman, M. S., & Tomlinson, B. (2010). *Toward an ecological sensibility: Tools for evaluating sustainable HCI*. Paper presented at the CHI 2010. Atlanta, GA.

Sørum, H., Andersen, K. N., & Vatrapu, R. (2011). *Public websites and human–computer interaction: An empirical study of measurement of website quality and user satisfaction*. Retrieved from http://dx.doi.org/10.1080/0144929X.2011.577191

Te'eni, D., Carey, J., & Zhang, P. (2007). *Human computer interaction: Developing effective organizational information systems*. Hoboken, NJ: John Wiley & Sons, Inc.

Titus, P., & Gremler, D. (2010). Guiding reflective practice: An auditing framework to assess teaching. *Philosophy and Style Journal of Marketing Education*, *32*(2), 182–196. doi:10.1177/0273475309360161

Tuzovic, S. (2010). Frequent (flier) frustration and the dark side of word-of-web: Exploring online dysfunctional behavior in online feedback forums. *Journal of Services Marketing*, *24*(6), 446–457. doi:10.1108/08876041011072564

Woei, L., & White, G. (2010). *The promotion of critical thinking through the use of an online discussion board: Asking the right questions?* Paper presented at the Global Learn Asia Pacific. New York, NY.

Worley, P. (2008). Writing skills essential in tech ed today. *Tech Directions*, *68*(2), 17–19.

Zhang, P., Carey, J., Te'eni, D., & Tremaine, M. (2005). Integrating human-computer interaction development into the systems development life cycle: A methodology. *Communications of the Association for Information Systems*, *15*, 512–543.

KEY TERMS AND DEFINITIONS

Design Guidelines: Are essential to the designers to achieve the principles.[2]

Design Principles: Are used to formalize the high level and widely appropriate design goals.[2]

Human Computer Interaction: Allocate, users, analysts, and designers (internal and external) to identify that the website design is practical. There are many specific issues that need to be taken into consideration when designing website pages, such as text style, fonts, layout, graphics, and color. (Issa 2008).[1]

Method- Formal Feedback: Is collected at the end of the semester through the university's formal feedback process.[2]

Method –Informal Feedback: Is a teaching and learning innovation to examine students' attitudes toward the unit structure, layout and assessments via an online survey.[2]

Reflective Journal: Is an essential assessment to develop students' critical thinking and communication skills, writing, reading, research, search, and using endnote software. [2]

Usability: Allow users, analysts, and designers (internal and external) to confirm that the website design is efficient, effective, safe, has utility, is easy to learn, easy to remember, easy to use and to evaluate, practical, visible, and provides job satisfaction (Issa 2008).

ENDNOTES

[1]   Issa, T. (2008). *Development and Evaluation of a Methodology for Developing Websites - PhD Thesis, Curtin University, Western Australia.* Retrieved from http://espace.library.curtin.edu.au:1802/view/action/nmets.do?DOCCHOICE=17908.xml&dvs=1235702350272~864&locale=en_US&search_terms=17908&usePid1=true&usePid2=true

[2]   Prepared by the authors.

This work was previously published in Emerging Research and Trends in Interactivity and the Human-Computer Interface edited by Katherine Blashki and Pedro Isaias, pages 375-394, copyright year 2014 by Information Science Reference (an imprint of IGI Global).

Chapter 77

Enterprise Architecture's Identity Crisis:
New Approaches to Complexity for a Maturing Discipline

Paul R. Taylor
Monash University, Melbourne, Australia

ABSTRACT

This chapter outlines the rational foundations of the enterprise architecture discipline to date and describes ways and situations in which the traditional approaches of enterprise architecture fail to account for a number of contemporary market and economic situations and organizational behaviors. It characterizes new methods and approaches loosely based on systems thinking, with examples from the Australian e-government experience, and argues that the discipline must re-invent itself to incorporate a post-rational perspective to stay relevant. The chapter concludes with narratives of how the new enterprise architecture must engage with business to stay relevant over the next decade and beyond.

ENTERPRISE ARCHITECTURE AS A MATURING DISCIPLINE

Enterprise architecture has an identity crisis. Borne of an era of escalating software development and maintenance expenditure of U.S. military and government agencies, enterprise architecture has grown over three decades to encompass a discipline of methods, tools and practices to manage information system complexity. The success of some of enterprise architecture's methods can be attributed to rational and objective analysis, classification and abstraction of selected features of complex and large-scale problems and systems. But over the last decade, paradigmatic market and business shifts such as the emergence of the information and knowledge economies bought on by the Internet, personal and pervasive computing, and the digitisation of just about everything has put pressure on enterprise architecture's foundations. It is no longer enough to apply structural tools and problem decomposition to every kind of business problem, as may have been done successfully in the past – the complexity of today's business challenges is not always amenable to a 'divide-and-conquer' approach.

DOI: 10.4018/978-1-4666-8619-9.ch077

As a consequence of this and other factors, enterprise architects need to look beyond its traditional foundations in a search for a new and more relevant identity. Like a teenager realising that the black and white world of childhood is in fact rendered in a thousand shades of grey, enterprise architecture must re-establish its identity before it can reach a new level of maturity for its next three decades. The discipline must re-evaluate its purpose, relationships, obligations and responsibilities to the organisations it serves. It must infuse new approaches and methods from outside its traditional domain of engineering to tackle the sorts of dynamic and ill-defined problems and systems rational analysis cannot solve.

To do this, enterprise architecture must embrace design as much as analysis, synthesis as much as simplification, with methods and tools drawn from systems thinking (Senge 1992), design and 'design thinking' (Brown 2008), perspective and problem negotiation, and facilitation. Enterprise architects must move closer to the business, and engage in the design of new businesses by brokering technology, vendor and product capabilities and services to meet rapidly changing business objectives. The new enterprise architecture will sit amidst the complexity and contradiction of the increasingly dynamic architecture of the organisation, serving the business' needs and being prepared to change, reconfigure or jettison established technologies and platforms without being bound by the chains of legacy or sunk cost. Not that the old methods will be abandoned – on the contrary, they continue to provide the foundation of the discipline and the main levers to understand and manage complexity. But the new enterprise architecture will be integrative – able to hold rational *and* post-rational perspectives on problems and systems in creative tension (Martin 2007), drawing on both to design technology interventions that will be effective for today's dynamic, hyper-connected and loosely-coupled enterprises.

This chapter outlines the rational foundations of the enterprise architecture discipline and describes ways and situations in which the traditional approaches of enterprise architecture fail to account for a number of contemporary market and economic situations and organisational behaviours. It characterises new methods and approaches loosely based on design and systems thinking, with examples from e-government experience, and argues that the discipline must re-invent itself to incorporate a post-rational perspective to stay relevant. The chapter concludes with narratives of how the new enterprise architecture must engage with business to stay relevant over the next decade and beyond.

FORMATIVE YEARS

Enterprise architecture's formative years are well documented. The term 'enterprise architecture' was apparently coined by Steven H. Spewak, the Chief Architect at global logistics company DHL Systems (Spewak 1992). Spewak drew on the Zachman (1987) framework to propose an Enterprise Architecture Planning methodology (Spewak 1992). (Zachman originally referred to his framework as 'a framework for information system architecture'). Enterprise architecture gained legitimacy with the 1996 Clinger-Cohen Act which required US federal departments and agencies to establish and maintain enterprise architecture programs. Shortly after, a Chief Information Officer's Council was formed, which in 1998 established the Federal Enterprise Architecture Framework as a uniform planning and design structure. Under the Office of Management and Budget, compliance with agency Information Technology Architectures (based in turn on the Federal Enterprise Architecture Framework) became mandatory for all significant IT investments. In 2002, the Office of Management and Budget initiated the development of a Federal Enterprise Architecture with the objective of technology standardisation, unified planning, identification of opportunities to simplify business processes, and avoidance of redundant technology investments across the agencies. The parallel successes of enterprise architecture in the private sector are widely documented in the enterprise architecture and information systems literature (Hagan 2004; Ross, Weill et al. 2006; Chew and Gottschalk 2009).

Other national governments adopted and continue to invest in enterprise architecture for the management of large-scale information technology investments. The Australian Government Information Management Organisation (AGIMO) developed a focus on priority areas of government technology investment, including supporting information technology investment planning and decision-making, e-government and cross-agency services. In 2007, AGIMO released the first elements of the Australian Government Architecture, a business architecture adapted from the Federal Enterprise Architecture Framework and intended to improve the consistency and cohesion of government services to citizens and cost-effective delivery of information and communications technology services by government (AGIMO 2007; AGIMO 2011). The governments of the United Kingdom followed a similar path, investing in enterprise information and technology architecture to target specific outcomes.

Definitions

For the purposes of this discussion 'enterprise architecture' needs a definition. Enterprise architecture is the combination of the capabilities, resources and structures that an enterprise relies upon to deliver value. The purpose of the discipline of enterprise architecture is to optimise the often fragmented legacy of capabilities, resources and structures into an integrated environment that supports delivery of the business strategy, while at the same time being suitably responsive to change. Most definitions recognise that today's enterprise encompass end-to-end product, service and information flows that reach beyond acknowledged

organisational boundaries to include partners, suppliers, and customers who play active roles in delivery of services and the creation of value.

Because of its all-encompassing scope, enterprise architecture is typically approached via frameworks that impose separation of domains or layers (this approach is discussed further below). One such domain is 'business architecture'. Business architecture is defined by the Object Management Group as 'a blueprint of the enterprise that provides a common understanding of the organisation and is used to align strategic objectives and tactical demands' (Object Management Group 2013). The business architecture 'blueprint' typically presents business level concerns such as services, processes and capabilities, deferring the detail of how these are realised, delivered or sustained to concerns within the application, technology and infrastructure domains or layers. This chapter challenges the relevance of enterprise and business architecture and its tools and agents (frameworks in the hands of enterprise architects) to the increasingly difficult task of tackling complexity in today's business environments.

Foundations

Enterprise architecture has always been considered a discipline based on the scientific principles of objective truth, rational analysis and repeatable processes. It is founded on the rational belief that complexity in a domain yields to the imposition of structured, objective methods. As such, it is typical of the products of the modern era, in which scientific rationalism was appropriated by planners and designers as a theory to underpin design and sweep away the informal and *ad hoc* practice of centuries of vernacularism. Until this point, much design was inseparable from making; design was a craft, exercised tacitly when a maker performed piecemeal assemblage, typically using locally available materials and resources (Alexander 1988; Lawson 1997). In pre-modern forms of designing, theory followed practice, not in the sense of being related to it or to owing its very existence to it, but as a kind of incidental by-product of making. In modern designing, theory in all its forms–from geometry to materials science to abstract representational forms–drove practice to the point of disembodying design from mind and action into inanimate, rational forms such as methodologies, processes and automata (Jones 1988). Enterprise architecture has strong ties to modernism, the primacy of theory and the pursuit of orderly frameworks and schemata.

Enterprise architecture owes some of its present-day identity on the fact that the activity of software making was first termed software *engineering*. Software creation has been profoundly shaped by the adoption of engineering as the metaphor of choice. There is no obvious point in the early history of software when the suitability of the engineering metaphor as a basis for the nascent discipline was openly debated. McIlroy (1968) demanded a hardware-like component-based software discipline to reduce risk in the mushrooming United States' Department of Defence software investment. Boehm (1976) first used the term in the context of his separation of a project into design and implementation phases, with a project management regime for each phase. McBreen (2002) claims that early systems development typically involved bespoke hardware development as well as software development, and as a result, conformance to an engineering project regime occupied the software team while the bespoke hardware was developed. Whatever the reasons, one thing is likely – the engineering metaphor was taken to imply a degree of formality and repeatability in software construction as is found in other engineering disciplines. Software creation was widely perceived as hardware engineering's undisciplined sibling. In adopting the engineering metaphor, the emerging software industry revealed its desire to appropriate engineering's legitimacy and maturity. Enterprise architecture was borne at this time and directly from this lineage.

The appropriateness of the engineering metaphor to software creation has been widely debated. Eaves (1992) argued that the essential nature of software development is, and has always been, one of code-crafting as problem and requirements discovery happen in parallel. He concludes that the 'standard model of scientific research is not applicable in the domain' and 'we are (still) dealing with a craft' (p. 15). Eaves also refers to what he calls a 'rage for order' – the 'human instinct which forces the creation of illusory or aesthetic order out of chaos, if no other order is to be had' (p. 11). Others have explored alternative metaphors, including craft (McBreen 2002), theatre (Laurel 1993) and in philosophical terms, social construction and constructivism (Floyd 1992). The late-modern perspectives of enterprise architecture's founders help to explain its early emphasis on structure, planning and optimisation. But times have changed. The heat of the debates between Zachman, Finkelstein and Spewak and their ilk on framework structure and cell semantics has long since dissipated, and the foundations of modernism have been undermined by an increasingly socially constructed view of organisations and culture over the past two decades. It is time to take the same perspective on enterprise architecture, starting with its basic construct, the framework.

Frameworks

The framework is the fundamental structuring mechanism of enterprise architecture. The framework defines and separates concerns, leading to a logical sequence of discovery and discourse on concepts, business strategy, strategy, resources, and planning. As a vehicle for communication, the enterprise architecture framework provides a flattened view of the congruence of business and IT strategies and how, at a high level, IT will implement the strategies. Proponents claim that the benefits of the framework include business-IT alignment and agreement on the value and benefits of the enterprise architecture (Chew and Gottschalk 2009; TOGAF 2012).

A framework is a structural template that can be overlayed on top of the messiness of real world problems and systems to present a semblance of order. Frameworks have mechanisms that abstract and isolate the elements of business objectives, information, process, and technology as distinct layers. By separating these layers, frameworks make it possible to manage complexity by 'dividing and conquering'. The relationship between framework layers and abstraction is not necessarily one of increasing detail, as layering suggests. In Zachman's framework, for example, successive layers can imply further detail, but each successive layer represents a distinct concern, so the transition from one layer to the next is one of transformation, not decomposition. It is possible and acceptable to deal with information model detail in Zachman's information layer. Many enterprise architects, however, understand frameworks as dictating ordering and successive decomposition.

Frameworks as planning tools for the enterprise have served us well. They are well suited to the way people have tended to think about organisations over the past two decades. Framework 'thinking' worked well in conjunction with waterfall approaches to software engineering. So pervasive was framework thinking that the vendor and services marketplace organised itself around the boundaries – technology and platforms, products and services, for example – making for alignment between problem scoping and decomposition, program structure and procurement.

But the way we think about organisations is changing. Under the broad-based forces of globalisation and market deregulation, the ubiquity of Internet and pervasive access, and rapid advances in the technology and communications infrastructure, the economic and business context in which organisations operate is shifting. Much is being written on the major themes of these shifts, including digital disruption, organisational agility and the effects of technology-mediated social movements on media, marketing, collaboration and commerce, not to mention politics and culture itself. The enterprise architecture frameworks still in use today were conceived and established before these themes had emerged or had perceivable impact. Today's enterprise architects are dealing with business and organisational realities for which established enterprise architecture frameworks offer limited help. These limitations of frameworks fall broadly into three groups – organisational, structural and temporal changes.

Changing Organisational Paradigms

Changes to how organisations are viewed have been playing out over decades and can be summarised as the evolution from the Taylorian (1911) paradigm of organisation as hierarchical and deterministic machine, to contemporary views of the organisation as an open, socially constructed, multi-agent ecosystem (Heylighen, Cilliers et al. 2007). As in all evolutionary processes, paradigm shifts occur in response to contextual changes, and environmental selection ensures ever-increasing efficiency, viability and, in business terms, profitability (Kaplan 2000). How an organisation responds to change depends on its priorities and resources, and is subject to the organisation's strategies and the complexity of its systems. In many organisations, the overhead of governance (the means of decision-making, particularly determining priorities and making effective decisions) introduces decision-making latency that means its systems are always (to some degree) legacy systems. In strategic planning and enterprise architecture, change drives the need for almost continuous planning. The approach taken to planning is therefore an important determinant of an organisation's agility.

Changing organisational paradigms dictate how complexity manifests itself and is tackled. The way an architect chooses to deal with complexity says a lot about what they believe the problem to be. Complexity has traditionally been addressed using decomposition based on function. In civic planning, this leads to zoning; in software engineering, waterfall systems; in sociology, category dilemmas. Functionalist designers argued that classification and decomposition are effective design strategies that result in highly efficient designs, and for certain systems this is undoubtedly true. But behaviourist designers counter with the claim that functionalism works only for design problems of low complexity and in well-understood, stable, closed systems. Cities, like societies, organisations and cultures, need other kinds of thinking about design (Alexander 1988).

Business-IT Alignment

Secondly, the relationship between business and information technology has moved on from a customer-provider relationship to one of co-dependency. Technology has always been driven by business demand, and strategic planning methods hold that technology exists purely to serve business objectives. Business-technology alignment is a primary value proposition of enterprise architecture. Alignment occurs when technology investment supports business objectives and the business vision. Enterprise architecture teams often invest considerable efforts to develop and maintain models of an organisation's business, structure, processes, data and technology, as a basis for planning and management.

But increasingly, new business services are enabled and defined by new technology capabilities (pervasive, location-aware services, for example), and we have reached the point where it is no longer sensible or even possible to perform strategic business planning without incorporating some kind of exploration of the capabilities of technologies to define new business services. Technology is now intrinsic to new business design. Orlov and Cameron (2007) were early observers of the dis-

solution of the business/technology boundary and 'business/IT alignment'. Recognising that technology touches every corner of business operations, from transaction automation, to mobile devices, to analytic insights, they argued that it investment in technology is not guaranteed to deliver business results or ensure maximized business benefits or use. Rather, technology and business are increasingly mutually-defining.

Timescales and Domain Stability

Thirdly, timescales for realising business-driven change and for delivering new technology-supported services are collapsing. Enterprise architecture grew out of the era of software development *in-the-large* when long (by today's standards) software development timescales were not invalidated by organisational shifts and a map of an organisation's technology could be assumed to be relatively stable over ten or more years. Enterprise architecture frameworks predate component and object-oriented development technologies, as well as (post-waterfall) rapid application development methods. Increasingly, the rate of business change outpaces the organisation's ability to respond.

Many factors have eroded the timeframes for business change. The Internet has introduced a new age of technology-mediated markets, trade and communication, the magnitude and extent of which rivals that of the printing press and electricity distribution. Globalisation of supply and labour markets has revolutionised how businesses create and distribute products. The option to dis-aggregate and distribute functional capabilities such as manufacturing and supply chain, and customer service through geographically independent services on a foundation of reliable global digital communications has revolutionised how companies resource operations. Escalating complexity is driven by other recently recognised forces including diversity, independence, ambiguity and emergence (Morowitz 2002). If it is to stay relevant, enterprise architecture must furnish tools and approaches that alleviate the problem.

Frameworks and Tools in Context

In 2004, the MITRE Group wrote that 'enterprise architecture is a discipline in its early years with the emphasis beginning to move from frameworks, modelling methods, and tools to compliance and performance issues'. The future of enterprise architecture is likely to 'focus on best practices, assessment and effective use of enterprise architecture to improve government management' (Hagan 2004). Beyond tools and frameworks, most assessments of enterprise architecture effectiveness point the finger at 'soft' factors, such as leadership and engagement style, communication, effective governance and continued commitment throughout the lifetime of systems initiatives. For the 2009 Enterprise Architecture Summit, Gartner analysts published the 'Ten Enterprise Architecture Pitfalls', headed up by 'selecting the wrong person as lead enterprise architect' and 'not engaging business people' (Gartner 2009). Their remaining traps can be summarized as follows: enterprise architecture must be business-driven, stakeholders at all levels must be engaged, the enterprise architect's efforts must be relevant, and outcomes must be promoted. Clearly, 'soft skills' are vitally important in the effective delivery of enterprise architecture (Frampton, Barrow et al. 2005).

Wrapping frameworks and tools with strong delivery skills will improve the perceived effectiveness of enterprise architecture, but as a solution to the multiple challenges facing the discipline, it is idiomatic and non-repeatable. It takes enterprise architecture into the space of performance art, the very place from which the modernists dragged it some three decades ago. A more durable overlay is needed for enterprise architecture to find a lasting form of maturity.

ADOLESCENCE

As a discipline, enterprise architecture has established itself and a level of recognition but it is now experiencing a kind of adolescent awkwardness. Something more than frameworks, methods and analytical competency is needed for the discipline to 'grow up'. To navigate its adolescent years, enterprise architecture must resolve its relationship with the business it serves. The key to this is for enterprise architects to embrace design and to start practicing it beyond the information and technology domains. This section presents some accounts of design practice by business people in the domain of business, but using some of the tools, techniques and thinking of the enterprise architect. They describe architecture lifted to the level of the business, in which enterprise and technology concerns contribute but do not dictate. In each case, the people leading these initiatives did not call themselves enterprise architects, but they performed the business designer role in a fashion that signposts the way to maturity for the discipline of enterprise architecture.

An Architecture for Government Service Delivery

Despite all of the Western world's industrial and economic progress, substantial inequities in income and standard of living remain. The government in the State of Victoria, Australia, has been providing services to support the disadvantaged for over 150 years, particularly to children at risk through family violence, victims of drug or alcohol abuse, the disabled and the homeless. The scale of this 'social safety net' is noteworthy. In 2010-11, the department employed 11,700 staff in 57 offices who managed 55,000 child protection reports, 31,000 clients with disability needs, 26,000 families with child support, 39,000 homeless people and 83,000 in publicly-funded houses.

The budget for 2011-12 was $3.4 billion, with over $1.3 billion going directly to community service organisations to deliver services.

The scale of the department's response motivates ongoing scrutiny, in terms of both financial accountability and measures of effectiveness. In recent years, research on people living in situations of social disadvantage has repeatedly shown that handing out relief to presenting problems temporarily alleviates need but often has limited impact on the cycle of poverty or disadvantage. The root causes of social problems are diffuse, and have motivated responses on many levels. Factors such as cultural diversity, social class, increasing complexity of need, and successive layers of legislation combine to limit the effectiveness of the human services sector in reducing entrenched disadvantage. With an aging and growing population base, governments have recognised the need to move on from traditional welfare approaches to new models of holistic and integrated care.

In late 2011, the Victorian government released a report (Wooldridge and Lovell 2011) that addressed some of these issues. The report recognised a fragmented and poorly coordinated support system where service providers focus on particular issues or groups of vulnerable people without a 'whole of system' view. The government's 'focus on programs rather than people', the report claims, has created a situation where individuals must make sense of services, navigate from door to door, and 'fit their particular problem to an existing program' to qualify for support. Effectiveness is also limited by failure to recognise the family circumstances of clients and the impact of relationships on their situation. The report acknowledges that the department has addressed 'solving problems after they occur rather than anticipating and intervening to prevent them'. This propensity to deliver crisis intervention rather than effecting lasting change drives dependency rather than independence. Recognising that disadvantage is not experienced in isolation but most often in families and communities by people with not one but multiple related needs, the report advocates moving from a 'problem and program' based model to one based on 'person and place'. By confronting all domains of disadvantage – personal, economic, and community – the goals of unlocking potential and enabling people to build better lives for themselves and their families can be achieved more consistently.

The antidote to crisis management, the authors argue, is to regard each individual as being on a path from dependency (with the attendant crises) through a self-realisation stage (in which workers help individuals to recognise their needs and the causes of crises) to maturity (when the individual self-manages with planned rather than unplanned assistance). The report recommends replacing the department's divisions and programs with a new structure that supports the delivery of coordinated personalised services. Case workers will form multi-specialty teams with processes and tools to respond more holistically to a client's individual circumstances.

The new model of operation recognises three categories of care delivery – 'managed', 'guided' and 'self-managed' support. 'Managed support' represents face-to-face intervention for families or individuals with high and/or multiple personal, social and economic needs over medium to long timeframes. In these cases, a client support worker will collaborate with the client (and their family wherever possible) to identify their goals and provide the comprehensive planning, support and coordination of services required to achieve their goals. 'Guided' support will be available to families and individuals requiring a moderate level of support to resolve the difficulties they are experiencing. In such situations, a case worker will support them to decide on their service and other needs so that they can progress to self-sufficiency. 'Self-managed' support will be available to the majority of clients who are capable of self-administering and managing their needs with minimal intervention, including finding and accessing information, referral options, or booking services.

There are several striking things about this proposal. The first is the way that analysis of service delivery practice and operating costs has informed a strategic plan based on a systemic perspective. At the core of the proposal is the recognition that the existing model of service delivery is broken – reactionary scheduling and delivery of services provides short-term relief but does not alter the cycle of disadvantage. This cycle is observed to be playing out regardless of the services, from youth justice to child support to disability. The recognition that disadvantage is experienced in multiple dimensions (personal, economic and community) and that individuals can be lifted through stages of self-awareness and capability to become self-sufficient is insightful. It is only by embedding this systemic model in the processes, services and work practices of the department and its agencies that the escalating demand can be met. Much detail in the new model remains to be ironed out. But the fact that the interdependent social and economic systems at work in the manifestation of disadvantage have been mapped lends credence to the proposed new model and the plan.

The second noteworthy characteristic is that the new operating model narrative paints an image of the business architecture of the new organisation, without explicitly calling out organisation, hierarchy or the mechanics of service delivery. It does this because it implies a new structure (replacement of program-focussed divisions with a services-centred cross-competency focus) and the essence of how the reconfigured business will operate. The kind of business architecture that an experienced enterprise architect would conceive of would, of course, consist of much more detail in the definitions than this – a view of organisation, capabilities, information and operation to name the mainstays. But the essence of the business architecture can be seen to

fall out of the operating model – cross-specialty case teams, prescriptive and managed care paths, a service-centric competency including service design and management, outcome monitoring, client-centricity and self-service, are some of the capabilities of the new business. The technology architecture layer of the enterprise architecture follows, and will include support for client identity, a services catalogue, a single and coordinated view of client, a common care plan, and a range of access channels. Most enterprise architects would be at home designing the identity, data, platform, security and integration architectures needed to support this new services-centric business model. But many would not be comfortable recognising and designing an intervention into the system of disadvantage.

An Architecture for Participation

In another department of the same government just across the street, a small team of business strategists was charged with up-skilling the State's workforce through increased participation in skills training. Vocational training in diverse skills such as apprenticeships, tourism services, hospitality and hairdressing is provided by a large sector of established technical institutes across the State. Skills training is widely acknowledged as being sensible and defensible government policy. A society with improved skills reduces the likelihood of skills shortages, lifts workforce participation, and stimulates employment and the economy. Government partially funds, accredits and administers the sector through its primary Skills Agency.

The strategists on the 'skills team' tackled a number of objectives, including alignment of supply with demand and policy, increased awareness and participation. The traditional way of achieving the objective of increased training participation would be to design a Website on a.gov domain and launch it with media fanfare and a ministerial press release. This typically results in a small spike in site visits but within a few months, the site is all but idle. Bureaucrats are then left with the problem of how to do better with next year's budget and the messy task of creatively interpreting Web analytics and other indicators to paint some kind of a picture of success.

The skills team recognised that for the online part of the campaign they needed to 'meet the people where they are'. First, the Skills Agency's Website was updated, but with minimal spend and only to make sure that content and links were correct and useable. Next, a marketing consultancy was engaged with the brief to identify the most effective places to engage the target audiences – males aged between 18 and 30 for building trade apprenticeships and males and females of similar age for hospitality industry training. For the prospective tradesmen, the consultancy identified a popular online football tipping competition run in partnership with one of the city's daily newspapers. For a small membership fee at the start of the season, football fans can pick and predict teams, winners and best and worst performers each week. The subscriber base is large, stable and homogeneous – sports-fanatics, average age 24, working/middle-class males. The Skills Agency placed selected trades apprenticeship advertisements on certain pages of the online tipping Website.

Recognising that the target demographic held a strong affinity with the brand and content of a long-standing metropolitan youth music FM station, and that this station cross-promoted the online football tipping game, the Skills Agency bought advertorial segments and placed skills and apprenticeship 'advocates' on the high-rating breakfast and drive shows. A few of these advocates (known by the agency as 'ambassadors') are high-profile sportsmen or personalities who supplement their on-air promotion with pre-edited tweets on twitter.com and status updates on Facebook.com. The station then launched a competition to offer a one-week placement with well-known employers. The Skills Agency repeated the formula for the hospitality targets, this time using conventional television advertising during the current series of a hugely popular reality cooking show, celebrity chef ambassadors, and a week's work experience placement with one of the city's top restaurants. The campaign resulted in record awareness and take-up of the skills offerings, leading to a measurable increase in participation rates within the target demographics. The approach intelligently recognised and leveraged established communities, going with the flow rather than trying to divert the flow. As a result, no-one was required to change their routine and nothing was forced.

On the surface, there is not much of what we might think of as enterprise architecture in this story. If anything, enterprise architects might be excused for thinking that the chosen business solution minimised technology and architecture. But the approach to designing the most effective solution to the problem of skills participation with the available means is pure architecture, because it recognises and leverages existing systems in a way that minimises friction and investment and maximises immediate outcomes. The fact that the systems are social systems driven by human behaviours such as brand loyalty and the cult of personality should not exclude enterprise architecture. When the enterprise architect thinks in terms of systems, the means by which the system operates is mostly immaterial.

Architecting Clinical Space

The systems that influence or bound how people work exist in many forms. Architects of the built world have always been engaged in a discourse on how architecture and design meets human needs in the context of space and place. While architects have long been criticised for exhibiting a public preference for the ephemeral image over usefulness and the experience of longer-term habitation, they are increasingly being challenged to bring a human-centred approach to architecture and planning. 'Old design' has delivered deterministic outcomes based on discipline, particularly in visual communications, interior spaces, products, information design, architecture and planning. 'New design' pursues purposeful and holistic outcomes – design for experiencing, for emotion, for interacting, for sustainability, for service and for transforming.

Sanders and Westerlund (2011) describe developing and applying human-centred approaches to the design of a large scale hospital campus in post-Katrina New Orleans (NBBJ 2012). The tools they used (personas, timelines and journeys, participatory modelling, experience models) are user-centric participatory techniques that ensure a level of co-creation and ownership. They used puppets and scale models of patient rooms in the hands of nurses and clinicians to optimise the design of operating theatres and recovery rooms. They role-played clinical settings to challenge how and why nurses move between patient and other fixtures during routine care delivery. Sanders describes how the role-playing dissolved the distinction between professional architect/designer and client, delivering improved designs that represented user's specific needs without compromising the architect's professional design judgement.

Traditional architects and career nurses are 'on different planets' when it comes to what they think is important in the design of a theatre or ward, she argues. Architects often ignore or defer details that nurses think is of utmost importance – where the hand sanitation stations are positioned, for example. To an architect used to designing public buildings, this detail is tertiary. But when viewed from the perspective of meeting business objectives, it can be crucial. The placement of the sanitation stations can make or break the nurses' ability to meet infection control targets, and the placement of shelves is vital when you understand that the heavily unionised workforce is required to wear tunics or gowns without pockets for infection control and nurse safety. The architects were able to move beyond their preconceptions of hospital theatres and wards to consider the workflow systems at play. By using objectives to drive design,

seemingly minor changes to a design can be hugely significant. The principle of driving design with business objectives to lay out physical spaces that support efficient workflow is equally applicable for the design of information systems.

Architecting Systems with Platforms

A final story illustrates that the business domain is not devoid of the kinds of archetypes and patterns from technology domains that architects are comfortable with. Some archetypes have important places in both business and system domains. When these can be deployed in the business architecture of a system, the alignment of the problem and solution spaces can powerfully dissolve complexity. The platform archetype is a good example, as the following story from the health informatics sector illustrates.

Information management in healthcare is undergoing a long-running transformation from paper-based records to paperless systems. Large investments in systems and infrastructure are being made in many public and private healthcare organisations to deliver a universal Electronic Medical Record (EMR). In Australia, the National E-Health Transition Authority has been governing the rollout of a national e-health infrastructure that will provide citizens with a personal electronic health record of every interaction with primary and allied health care providers, potentially over a lifetime. But the maturity and openness of the information infrastructures at the national and health provider levels have been moving at very different rates. The marketplace for health-care provider products has been, and continues to be dominated by ERP-styled offerings, some with proprietary, vendor-locked architectures and limited integration capabilities. Most of the vendors can deliver an integrated EMR but only if their proprietary modules are implemented across all of the hospital's clinical services. The experience of many healthcare providers is that ERP-class business systems provide comprehensive functionality and inter-module integration but in many cases are costly to customise or extend. Recognising this, the U.S. Health and Human Services Department awarded a research and development grant to a team at Harvard University to develop an open platform for health care applications (Mahidhar 2011).

The team from Harvard was tasked with liberating health data by designing an open and standards-based architecture so that vendors could build third-party applications capable of running on multiple platforms at low marginal cost. They recognised that a platform model was needed to deliver a health IT ecosystem, modelled on Apple's iStore or Amazon's platform services. Within a year the Harvard team developed 'Substitutable Medical Applications, Reusable Technologies' (SMART), an open-source architecture that offers a set of core services to facilitate substitutable health care applications, or plug-ins (Mandl, Mandel et al. 2012). The team published its application programming interfaces and initiated an open application development contest with a $5,000 prize. Fifteen different vendors or developer communities delivered 'apps' for use by clinicians and patients. The team also integrated the platform with Cerner APIs to deploy the SMART platform beside a leading healthcare vendor's ERP-class product.

The SMART environment, based on open standards and designed to support and encourage third-party light-weight application development, is an enabling technology platform with the potential to host a business ecosystem. The establishment of a viable ecosystem depends upon a number of much broader factors, including adoption by providers, integration support from vendors and community-based developers, and users (clinicians, allied healthcare professionals, administrators and patients and their carers). This remains SMART's biggest hurdle, but it is largely outside the influence of the Harvard team.

Enterprise architects will recognise the system archetypes underlying both NEHTA's e-health infrastructure and the SMART platform – the 'business ecosystem' built upon an enabling 'business platform'. The new business ecosystem, typified by Amazon and Apple, consists of capabilities and rules that organize and manage the commerce engine and maintain the independence and low or zero entry costs of users, authors and reviewer communities, as well as a marketplace of independent vendors who sell through the ecosystem's online stores. The platform provides and manages identity, authorisation, content, digital rights, inventory and supply chain, and publishing partners. The Amazon ecosystem facilitates a market in which the best authors and retailers do the most business and where micro-brands and reputations are made and lost. No single authority or group controls the others, and Amazon profits from each transaction on its platform. Ecosystems like these foster innovation through what has been called 'radical adjacency' – the ability for a participant to go beyond its normal business practice to seize an opportunity in widely adjacent markets. Spotting an opportunity to create a 'business ecosystem' by designing a platform rather than a point solution is a natural consequence of a systems-centric analysis.

TOWARDS MATURITY

The common theme through these stories is the application of a systems perspective to business architecture. By observing the primacy of business objectives, recognising the forces at play in the wider business and social context, and then designing and structuring interventions to most effectively meet these objectives whilst exploiting existing constraints and behaviours, the business architect can achieve the potential of enterprise architecture in a way that is not often realised.

Maturity for enterprise architecture is down this kind of path, and it goes beyond the rational foundation of enterprise architecture to include business-centric architecture, design and 'systems thinking'.

'Systems thinking' (Checkland 1981; Senge 1992) is key. It is a holistic approach to understanding complex interactions and problems, or how things influence each other within a whole. 'Systems thinking' assumes that the component parts of a closed, open, social or natural system can best be understood in the context of relationships with each other and with other systems, rather than in isolation. The approach is most suited to open, socially constructed systems 'where having good participants produces better results than having good planners' (Shirky 2012). To further illustrate the kinds of new design approaches available to enterprise architects, some cameos of business-centric design and 'systems thinking' conclude the chapter.

Designing Systems that Exploit Human Behaviours

Governments have traditionally employed broad-brush mechanisms to influence citizen behaviour to achieve desired outcomes, including regulation, enforcement, taxation and subsidy. These devices, rooted in a rational and economic world-view, constitute the main macro-economic levers for controlling an economic system. At a micro-economic level, these controls impact in different ways depending on sector-based competitive, commercial and other forces. And at the level of individuals, the cause-and-effect relationship is diffuse at best.

Most government policy has been based on the theory that people rationally seek to maximise their welfare. But this model is increasingly swamped by the escalating complexity of choice. In their quests to identify alternative mechanisms for influence, psychologists and economists have started straying into each other's fields in their

study of individual decision-making in a variety of social and everyday settings. In 'Nudge', Richard Thaler and Cass Sunstein (2008) argue that people make many more decisions reactively and in-the-moment than analytically, drawing on arbitrary factors – product packaging, convenient access, simplicity or brand familiarity – as the means of choice. Their list of the fallacies of choice includes 'anchoring' (cognitive and perceptive bias based on personal experience), skewed perspectives of representativeness (for example, the perception that the probability of a coin toss outcome changes after a sequence), and 'status quo' (a person's inbuilt bias against change).

Other authors explore similar lines. In 'Predictably Irrational', Ariely (2008) explores the multitude of social and contextual influences that supplant rational thought in personal and collective decision-making. These include the influence of relationships and the effect that a decision will have on an important relationship, price anchoring (accepting the first price you see as the benchmark for all other offers), irrational attachment to a 'free' offer regardless of what other consequences come with that choice, and how decision-making behaviour changes during certain forms of stimulation, all with the slightly ironic twist that irrational behaviours are often observed repeatedly and are therefore predictable. In 'Freakonomics' Levitt and Dubner (2005) similarly claim that people often make predictable mistakes because they rely on heuristics, fallacies, and the influence of social interactions.

Recognising this human foible affords the insightful designer an opportunity to influence choices for common and individual good by architecting sensible defaults, so that human laziness is rewarded by better individual and collective outcomes. Examples include setting savings plan enrolment and risk profile defaults to 'on' and 'conservative', and placing healthy food options at eye-level. With its promises of quick wins for seemingly simple interventions, the theory has attracted followers, including UK Prime Minister

Cameron, who established a 'Behavioural Insights Team' with the remit to 'find innovative ways of encouraging, enabling and supporting people to make better choices for themselves' (UK Cabinet Office 2010). The team initially tackled the application of behavioural insights to fraud (by designing changes that lead to higher compliance), energy efficiency (encouraging uptake of energy efficiency measures), consumer affairs (collective purchasing schemes) and health (organ donation and smoking cessation).

A subsequent review initiated by the House of Lords to determine the feasibility of using social and contextual cues to influence behaviour to complement laws and regulation, found that while 'nudging' worked at the individual level, behavioural change interventions appear to work best when they are part of a package of legislative, regulatory and fiscal measures. Useful behavioural change, the authors concluded, takes time – and typically much more than the allotted term of an elected politician. The review did little to dampen Prime Minister Cameron's support for his Behavioural Insights Team which continues down its path of designing behavioural interventions to shape social policy. For enterprise architects, behavioural insights and the ability to understand human choices has interesting implications for designing systems and interventions.

Designing Systems Based on Co-Creation of Value

The building block of the services economy is the service. In economic terms, the service or 'tertiary' sector may be defined as whatever is not agriculture or manufacturing. A service is an activity or experience provided by one person or organisation to another for the recipient's benefit. Increasingly, products are sold with services, and the services contribute as much or more revenue than do the products. In information systems, a familiar example is that of 'systems integration' in

which a vendor sells software product licenses but makes ten to one hundred times this revenue on the provision of professional services to configure, customise, integrate and operationalize the resulting business system. In recent years, escalating competition fuelled by the availability of personal devices and online services has driven increasing focus on the design of customer interactions and the value added at each 'touch-point'. As well as the intensifying focus on the quality of the user experience, organisational designers now view the continuous design of services as an essential business capability.

The terms 'service science, management, and engineering' refer to the growing academic interest in the interdisciplinary field of getting the services (the value proposition from the customer's perspective and the touch-points) right. Enterprise architects are familiar with the notion of service and its application layer analogue (enterprise services in a Services-Oriented Architecture (Chew and Gottschalk 2009)) and the methods for designing enterprise services. But the 'services science' notion of service design is broader and is motivated by the creation of value as seen by the customer and enrichment of the customer relationship. The links between the services of enterprise architecture and those of 'services science' seem obvious but nevertheless involve a fundamental shift in mindset and problem orientation. Design theorists outside of information sciences have known for a long time about the importance of an organisation's ability to define design strategy and execute its design capability (Lockwood and Walton 2008). Service reform continues to be considered a central challenge in the UK (Demos 2012) and Australia (Australian Public Service Commission 2007; Parker and Bartlett 2008).

The social media revolution and its defining phenomena of participation such as 'crowdsourcing' (Howe 2009) has moved the discussion of the relevance of services from maximising the value provided by the service provider to the customer, to co-creation of value. A branch of 'services science' called Service-Dominant (S-D) logic has emerged that portrays value creation in conjunction with (rather than for) customers as a source of competitive advantage (Vargo and Lusch 2004; Vargo and Lusch 2008). According to Vargo and Lusch, S-D logic holds to ten premises of which four are foundational. The first foundation is that service (defined as 'the application of knowledge, skills and resources') is the fundamental basis of all exchange. The second holds that the customer is always a co-creator of value (value creation is therefore interactional). The third is that all social and economic actors are resource integrators – this implies that the context of value creation is networks (and networks of networks). The fourth foundational principle of Service-Dominant logic is that value is always uniquely and phenomenologically determined by the beneficiary – that is, value is a constructed (idiosyncratic, experiential, contextual, and meaning-laden) rather than objective thing.

The co-creation concept becomes relevant to enterprise architecture when the organisational capabilities needed to execute S-D logic in practice are considered. Karpen, Bove et al. (2012) looked at the question of what capabilities an organisation should develop to exploit co-creation. They proposed a portfolio of six capabilities for facilitating and enhancing interaction and resource integration, including the ability to understand individual customer's service contexts, service processes, and expected service outcomes ('individuated interaction capability'); the ability to enhance social and emotional links with customers in service processes ('relational interaction capability'); the ability to support fair and non-opportunistic customer service processes ('ethical interaction capability'); the ability to enable customers to shape the nature and content of service processes ('empowered interaction capability'); the ability to assist customer's own knowledge and competency development in service processes ('developmental interaction capability'); and the ability to facili-

tate coordinated and integrated service processes that include customers ('concerted interaction capability').

Examples of these principles and capabilities are not hard to find. Amazon's analysis of search and purchase patterns to better understand a visitor's interests is 'individuated interaction'. Old Spice's (or any of the thousands of other prominent consumer brands') YouTube channel which facilitates dialogue with the brand and among viewers is 'relational interaction'. 'Ethical interaction' is demonstrated by an organisation's corporate responsibility strategy which mandates supplier agreements and employee training for good interaction practices with customers. 'Empowered interaction' is demonstrated by Dell's famous online notebook configurator. The provision of customer training to boost product proficiency by publishing manuals and opening up the service department demonstrates 'developmental interaction'. And any supplier that federates or orchestrates the interactions between consumers and partners to deliver superior customer service demonstrates 'concerted interaction'. Collectively, these capabilities position an organisation for value co-creation at the point of service. Not every organisation will need to provide all capabilities, and investment will need to be guided by a form of strategic planning that places customer value at its centre. With some reorientation, enterprise architects are ideally placed to play a leading role in these kinds of service planning and design dialogues.

Designing Systems using "Design Thinking"

In recent years, the methods of designers have been appropriated by some business strategists under the moniker 'design thinking', an amalgam of design-based approaches packaged for a generalist audience, and populated by authors including Martin (2007) and Lockwood (2009), consultancies such as IDEO (Brown 2008) and commentators including Nussbaum (2012). 'Design thinking' is anything but a theory-driven movement, but it does tip its hat to a broad epistemological base including ethnography, wicked problems, systems theory, participatory design and iterative innovation models. Its adaptation of 'systems thinking' is particularly relevant to enterprise architects. Tim Brown's seminal example of 'design thinking' is Thomas Edison's ability to invent and at the same time, foresee how people would use the invention and design a context in which it would be successful. So while Edison is remembered for inventing the first electric light bulb, Brown argues that equal inventive genius can be seen in his design and construction of the generators and power distribution lines so that the electric light could be laid out to illuminate the gas-lit streets. Without this 'systemic' view, Brown argues, his invention might have remained little more than a 'parlour trick'.

'Design thinking' consists of a continuous iteration of three broad types of activity – inspiration, ideation and implementation. 'Inspiration' involves examination of the business problem through intense *in situ* observation, involving many disciplines to gain multiple perspectives, uncovering constraints, resources, changes, expert or skilled behaviours, and opportunities. 'Ideation' is a brainstorming activity in which participants and designers deconstruct observations and stories, often leading to roughly conceived or *ad hoc* prototypes. Ideation cycles rapidly to avoid burning energy on unproductive options. When an idea or option emerges, 'implementation' activities such as designing the user experience, engineering and improving the prototypes, and filling in the gaps in the context of the innovation to ensure its success completes the 'design thinking' process.

Brown's consultancy (IDEO) claims many successful examples of the application of the approach. One is a new product design for a neglected market segment that has parallels with the whole-system approach taken by Edison to invent his electric light scheme. Shimano, a Japanese manufacturer of bicycle components, worked with IDEO to conceive of a new product to appeal to a large and cashed-up but widely disengaged cycling segment – Baby Boomers. Market research confirmed that although Boomers were put off by lycra-clad speedsters, modern cycle complexity and the dangers of road riding, they held fond memories of casual Sunday afternoon cycling on 'old fashioned' bikes with large mud-guarded wheels, wide seats, and upright handlebars. IDEO worked with Shimano to define a concept to reconnect American mid-age consumers with their joyous childhood experience of bikes and cycling. The multi-disciplinary design team came up with the concept of 'coasting', riding a minimalist bike built for pleasure rather than speed. The team prototyped the bikes, but went further to designate accessible cycling paths and popular, scenic precincts in many American cities, to address concerns of safety and to allow association between 'cruisers' and others engaged in causal recreation. The team worked with three leading cycle manufacturers to bring the bike to market. The launch campaign used laid back messages ('first one there's a rotten egg') and activated Websites with online and social media cross-promotion. After a successful launch in 2007, seven new cycle manufacturers signed up to produce Coasters within a year. This 'design thinking' story illustrates the focus on the designed artefact and its complete context of use. The designers created the object *and* a supportive ecosystem in which the product would succeed.

Towards Design Mastery

To grow beyond an adolescent stage of maturity, enterprise architects must engage with design outside of the technology domain. Although 'pure' business design may take the architect into foreign places, most of the design skills needed are not new. Architects have been practicing them as part of agile methodologies for a decade or more. To lead the kinds of design scenarios described in this chapter, enterprise architects could start by demonstrating some of the following kinds of designerly behaviours.

Observational Powers

Accounts of successful innovation and design projects consistently describe the power of observation. Tim Brown describes 'design thinking' as being powered by 'a thorough understanding, through direct observation, of what people want and need in their lives and what they like or dislike about the way particular products are made, packaged, marketed, sold and supported' (Brown 2008). Direct observation demands a range of techniques, from the kinds of observation and scenario-playing pioneered at Xerox ParcPlace to 'living with the tribe' as done by ethnographic researchers. The enterprise architect must become a keen and acute observer, able to step into the shoes of the people performing the tasks and using the tools at hand. This kind of observation balances impartiality and objective detachment with involved empathy, all the while seeing every detail and relating it to big-picture objectives and outcomes.

Centrality of Experience

A 'design ethos' cannot properly serve two masters. Making the user experience central may at times conflict with other business priorities – profits, return on investment, delivery timeframe, budget and quality to name a few. Design thinking incorporates iteration and failure-tolerance throughout the design process to deliver frequent and early feedback and allow constant revision in light of experience. 'Systems thinking' requires attention to the political, social and other systems that motivate behaviour. The process to perfect the human experience of a product or service is highly unpredictable, and innovation initiatives compete with other projects for resources and budget. To be motivated by user experience over profitability or other business contingencies, the enterprise architect must understand the place of the user experience amidst competing demands throughout the designing, defending it where necessary, and only compromising it when the implications are understood.

Designing for Continuous Designing

New approaches to systems-centred design recognise that designing happens not at a point in time in the studio or behind a door labelled 'R&D Department' but in the full light of the business in all its situations, places and forms. Business architects must emancipate design and employ it, or facilitate collaborative designing in all phases and activities, from discovering and negotiating business objectives, researching the experience of participants and stakeholders, envisioning, conception and scenario-playing, prototyping and development, through to system development and operation. The mature business architect considers how their systems will cope amidst inevitable change and how their systems will support ongoing redesign.

Designing with a "Systems Thinking" Perspective

Systems theoretic models (Checkland 1981; Senge 1992) tackle large-scale 'soft' problems characterised by lack of structural clarity and complex interdependencies between the parts. 'Systems thinking' promotes taking an end-to-end view of systems in context and proposes a catalogue of generic system archetypes. In systems thinking, an intervention is considered successful if it results in an improved but ultimately stable system. A stable system is one that is dynamic and can support change, growth and contraction. Business architects must recognise the wider system in which their solutions exist, designing interventions or modifications where necessary so that their changes create or preserve the enclosing system's viability and stability under normal and exceptional conditions.

Dealing with Assumptions and Constraints

Hammer and Champy (1993) kicked off the business process reengineering movement in the 1990s with the call to 'slay the sacred cows'. 'Design thinking' also advocates opening up problems, reframing definitions and challenging assumptions. The business constraints and user expectations enshrined within existing systems are constantly evolving. By questioning and challenging assumptions, valuable problem insights can be found that allow new, alternate or novel solutions. Techniques such as ideation, prototyping, iteration, incremental refinement, collaborative design, synthesis, user-centric design, full lifecycle design, and service design all provide opportunities to uncover explicit and implicit assumptions. The business architect must go beyond questioning assumptions to understand the impacts and consequences of their interventions on the complete social and technological systems.

Designing the Delivery Path

Critics of 'design thinking' have observed its failure to deliver on innovation in many organisations, partly because of the emphasis placed on training, tools and techniques at the expense of facilitating the hard slog of innovation projects (Nussbaum 2012). Tim Brown, in a reflective moment, has agreed that 'design thinking' has largely been successful in making the big leaps that large organizations cannot make for themselves but less successful when the idea is handed off to the client organisation to deliver (Brown 2009). The 'design thinker' must look down the path of implementation to delivery and operation of the innovation, preparing the path in whatever ways

can be foreseen and are possible at the time. The 'systems thinker' must articulate the system in its entire context, making changes if necessary to ensure that the system will operate as desired through all of the system's operating phases and under all conditions.

Facilitation, Not Heroics

From Le Corbusier to Frank Lloyd Wright, modern history is full of stories of heroic designers, typified by the creative genius who could single-handedly conceive a building uniquely responsive to the client's brief and the site and revolutionary in its statement in the architectural discourse at the same time. These larger-than-life characters may still be celebrated in architecture but they are the antithesis of today's systems designers. There is no doubt that design and systems thinking requires advanced design aptitude and skills but the abilities to co-design and facilitate other's designing are equally important as personal creativity and design ability. The enterprise architect must be capable of designing individually, jointly and collaboratively with others, facilitating the designing where it is most appropriate at the time, with the system or innovation project's overall goals and objectives always in mind.

Recognising Mature Practice

The established tools of enterprise architecture are still relevant to today's organisations. Modelling and proactively managing the technology environment using the frameworks, methods and tools of the established discipline is an essential practice for effective and efficient operations. But if enterprise architects do not aggressively engage in discussions, debates, analyses and executive level decision-making that forms new business services or evolves existing ones, others will in their place. Enterprise architects who stay in their technology comfort zone risk becoming marginalised as businesses adopt new networked, socially connected, open forms. If enterprise architects do not embrace these practices, they risk becoming marginalised in technology-centred corners, from where their influence diminishes. From here, the curse of irrelevance can quickly become real. As each new portion of the enterprise's information and communication technology services is modernised, outsourced or migrated to the cloud, the 'old' enterprise architecture loses a piece of its identity. Such erosion can only be countered by corresponding growth.

The future for enterprise architects is bright. But it is higher up the value chain that it has been in the past. Today's enterprise architects may increasingly use unfamiliar titles as they move primarily in business circles. Those who have practiced the discipline of enterprise architecture through their careers who are able to make this transition will know that they are doing many of the same things, thinking similar thoughts, and applying the same patterns and tools. The difference will be their demonstrated capacity to place themselves fairly and squarely in the business. Enterprise architects become business architects when they treat the objectives of the business as their number one priority and the organisation's information technology as a means to an end. With this focus, their architecting skills take on new relevance.

REFERENCES

AGIMO. (2007). *Australian government architecture: Principles. Australian Government Information Management Office.* AGIMO.

AGIMO. (2011). *Australian government architecture: Reference models. Australian Government Information Management Office.* AGIMO.

Alexander, C. (1988). *A city is not a tree.* London: Thames and Hudson.

Ariely, D. (2008). *Predictably irrational: The hidden forces that shape our decisions.* New York: HarperCollins.

Australian Public Service Commission. (2007). *Changing behaviour: A public policy perspective.* Retrieved from http://www.apsc.gov.au/__data/assets/pdf_file/0017/6821/changingbehaviour.pdf

Boehm, B. W. (1976). Software engineering. *IEEE Transactions on Computers, 25*(12), 1226–1241. doi:10.1109/TC.1976.1674590

Brown, T. (2008). Design thinking. *Harvard Business Review.* PMID:18605031

Brown, T. (2009). *Tim Brown urges designers to think big.* Retrieved from http://www.ted.com/talks/tim_brown_urges_designers_to_think_big.html

Checkland, P. (1981). *Systems thinking, systems practice.* Chichester, UK: Wiley.

Chew, E. K., & Gottschalk, P. (2009). *Information technology strategy and management: Best practices.* Hershey, PA: IGI Global. doi:10.4018/978-1-59904-802-4

Demos. (2012). *Public services and welfare.* Retrieved 23 August, 2012, from http://www.demos.co.uk/publicservicesandwelfare

Eaves, D. (1992). *The prospects of a formal discipline of software engineering.* Monash University.

Floyd, C. (1992). Software development as reality construction. In C. Floyd, R. Budde, H. Zullighoven, & R. Keil-Slawik (Eds.), *Software Development and Reality Construction.* Berlin: Springer-Verlag. doi:10.1007/978-3-642-76817-0_10

Frampton, K. Barrow, et al. (2005). A study of the in-practice application of a commercial software architecture. In *Proceedings of the Australian Software Engineering Conference (ASWEC 2005).* Brisbane, Australia: IEEE Computer Society.

Gartner. (2009). *Gartner identifies ten enterprise architecture pitfalls*. Retrieved 13 August, 2012, from http://www.gartner.com/it/page.jsp?id=1159617

Hagan, P. J. (2004). *Guide to the (evolving) enterprise architecture body of knowledge*. The MITRE Corporation.

Hammer, M., & Champy. (1993). *Reengineering the corporation: A manifesto for business revolution*. New York: Harper.

Heylighen, F., & Cilliers, , et al. (2007). Complexity and philosophy. InBogg, J, & Geyer, R (Eds.), *Complexity, Science and Society*. Oxford, UK: Radcliffe Publishing.

Howe, J. (2009). *Crowdsourcing: Why the power of the crowd is driving the future of business*. New York: Three Rivers Press.

Jones, J. C. (1988). Softecnica. In J. Thackara (Ed.), *Design after modernism*. London: Thames and Hudson.

Kaplan, S. M. (2000). Co-evolution in socio-technical systems. In *Proceedings of Computer Supported Cooperative Work (CSCW 2000)*. Philadelphia: ACM Press.

Karpen, I. O., & Bove, , et al. (2012). Linking service-dominant logic and strategic business practice: A conceptual model of a service-dominant orientation. *Journal of Service Research*, *15*(21).

Laurel, B. (1993). *Computers as theatre*. Reading, MA: Addison-Wesley.

Lawson, B. (1997). *How designers think*. Oxford, UK: Architectural Press.

Levitt, S., & Dubner. (2005). *Freakonomics: A rogue economist explores the hidden side of everything*. New York: William Morrow.

Lockwood, T., & Walton. (2008). *Building design strategy: Using design to achieve key business objectives*. New York: Allworth Press.

Lockwood, T. (2009). *Design thinking: Integrating innovation, customer experience, and brand value*. Allworth Press.

Mahidhar, V. (2011). Ecosystems for innovation: An interview with U.S. CTO Aneesh Chopra. *Deloitte Review*, 11. Retrieved 14 August, 2011, from http://www.deloitte.com/assets/Dcom-Australia/Local%20Assets/Documents/Industries/Government%20Services/Public%20Sector/Deloitte_review_issue_nine_2011.pdf

Mandl, K. D., & Mandel, , et al. (2012). The SMART platform: Early experience enabling substitutable applications for electronic health records. *Journal of American Medical Informatics*, *19*(4).

Martin, R. L. (2007). *The opposable mind: How successful leaders win through integrative thinking*. Boston: Harvard Business School Publishing.

McBreen, P. (2002). *Software craftsmanship: The new imperative*. Boston: Addison-Wesley.

McIlroy, M. D. (1968). Mass produced software components. In *Proceedings of the First NATO Conference on Software Engineering*. Garmisch, Germany: IEEE.

Morowitz, H. (2002). *The emergence of everything: How The world became complex*. Oxford, UK: Oxford University Press.

NBBJ. (2012). *NBBJ architecture and design*. Retrieved 7 May, 2012, from http://www.nbbj.com

Nussbaum, B. (2012). Design thinking is a failed experiment: So what's next? *Co.DESIGN*. Retrieved 24 August, 2012, from http://www.fastcodesign.com/1663558/design-thinking-is-a-failed-experiment-so-whats-next

Object Management Group. (2013). *Business architecture working group*. Retrieved 18 March, 2013, from http://bawg.omg.org/

Orlov, L. M., & Cameron. (2007). *Business technology defined: Technology management is changing to deliver business results*. Forrester Research.

Parker, S., & Bartlett. (2008). *Towards agile government*. State Services Authority, Government of Victoria.

Ross, J. W., & Weill, , et al. (2006). *Enterprise architecture as strategy: Creating a foundation for business execution*. Boston, MA: Harvard Business School Press.

Sanders, E., & Westerlund. (2011). *Experiencing, exploring and experimenting in and with co-design spaces*. Paper presented at the Nordic Design Research Conference. Helsinki, Finland.

Senge, P. M. (1992). *The fifth discipline: The art and science of the learning organization*. Sydney, Australia: Random House.

Shirky, C. (2012). *Clay Shirky's internet writings*. Retrieved 14 August, 2012, from http://shirky.com/

Spewak, S. H. (1992). *Enterprise architecture planning: Developing a blueprint for data, application and technology*. QED Publishing Group.

Taylor, F. W. (1911). *The principles of scientific management*. New York: Harper and Row.

TOGAF. (2012). *The open group architecture framework (TOGAF)*. Retrieved 27 July 2012, 2012, from http://www.opengroup.org/togaf/

UK Cabinet Office. (2010). *Behavioural insights team*. Retrieved 9 June 2012, from http://www.cabinetoffice.gov.uk/behavioural-insights-team

Vargo, S. L., & Lusch,. (2004). Evolving to a new dominant logic for marketing. *Journal of Marketing, 68*(1), 1–17. doi:10.1509/jmkg.68.1.1.24036

Vargo, S. L., & Lusch,. (2008). From goods to service(s): Divergences and convergences of logics. *Industrial Marketing Management, 37*(3), 254–259. doi:10.1016/j.indmarman.2007.07.004

Wooldridge, M., & Lovell. (2011). *Human services: The case for change*. Retrieved 7 August, 2012, from http://www.dhs.vic.gov.au/about-the-department/news-and-events/news/general-news/human-services-the-case-for-change

Zachman, J. A. (1987). A framework for information systems architecture. *IBM Systems Journal, 26*(3), 276–292. doi:10.1147/sj.263.0276

This work was previously published in A Systemic Perspective to Managing Complexity with Enterprise Architecture edited by Pallab Saha, pages 433-453, copyright year 2014 by Business Science Reference (an imprint of IGI Global).

Chapter 78

The Driving Machine:
Combining Information Design/ Visualization with Persuasion Design to Change Behavior

Aaron Marcus
Aaron Marcus and Associates, Inc. (AM+A), USA

ABSTRACT

The Driving Machine seeks to provide an innovative vehicle dashboard that combines information design and persuasion design to change the driver's behavior, promoting safety, fuel efficiency, and sustainability.

INTRODUCTION

A 21st-century global vehicle dashboard-design challenge is to take advantage of technology to increase safety and conserve energy. The context is this: Advances in technology increase driving distractions, and global warming increases our desire to reduce our carbon footprint. In particular, the Green movement has helped to increase people's awareness of sustainability issues and propelled development of innovative products to help decrease our ecological footprint.

The Driving Machine seeks to increase safe driving-behavior and fuel-efficient driving by offering information, overviews, social networking, just-in-time knowledge, and incentives, including gamification, that can help to reduce, even prevent, vehicular accidents and promote more

fuel-efficient driving. The question then shifts to how best to motivate, persuade, educate, and lead people to adopt safe-driving behavior and reduce their energy consumption. For our conceptual design project we researched and analyzed powerful ways to improve safe and green behavior by persuading and motivating people to become more alert drivers and to reduce their energy consumption through a vehicle dashboard application we call the "Driving Machine."

Dashboards and automotive-related applications are available to increase people's awareness of safety and the environment, but such technologies often do not focus on innovative data visualization, and they may lack persuasive effectiveness to encourage drivers to continue good driving behavior. Communicating one's carbon footprint, driving skills, and alertness, helps build awareness

DOI: 10.4018/978-1-4666-8619-9.ch078

and identity, but does not result automatically in effecting behavioral changes. The question then becomes: How can we better motivate, persuade, educate, and lead people to become safer and more efficient drivers? Aaron Marcus and Associates, Inc. (AM+A) has embarked on the conceptual design of a mobile-phone/tablet-based product, the Driving Machine, intended to address this situation.

The author's firm previously designed and tested similar concept prototypes that seek to change people's behavior: the Green Machine application in 2009, oriented to persuading home consumers to make energy-conservation behavior-changes; the Health Machine application in 2010, oriented to avoiding obesity and diabetes through behavior changes regarding nutrition and exercise; and the Money Machine in 2011, targeted to baby boomers and oriented to assisting them to manage their wealth more effectively (Marcus & Jean, 2010; Marcus, 2011; Marcus, 2012; Marcus, 2013). The Driving Machine uses similar principles of combining information design/visualization with persuasion design.

A Driving Machine key objective is to combine information design and visualization with persuasion design to help users achieve their goals of driving more safely and efficiently by persuading users to adapt their driving behavior, for example to follow traffic laws better and adopt carpooling behavior.

AM+A intends to apply user-centered design along with persuasive techniques to make the Driving Machine highly usable and to increase the likelihood of success in adopting new driving behavior. This chapter explains the development of the Driving Machine's user interface.

BACKGROUND

As the amount of computing technology continues to increase in our cars and trucks, careful consideration must be given to dashboard design to ensure the safety and reliability of drivers, passengers, and vehicles. Increasingly states are passing laws that limit drivers' abilities to operate mobile phones or to read/send text messages while driving. Recent research illustrates that even such laws may not go far enough, as cited by Paul Green (Green, 2003). Paul Green (2003) describes how driving and using a cell phone, regardless of having hands free or not, places drivers at greater risk of causing accidents than drivers who only talk to passengers inside their vehicles. The reason talking on the phone is a greater danger than talking to passengers is because passengers are more aware of current driving situations than people being communicated with on the phone. One study by Redelmeier and Tibshirani (1999), as stated by Green (2003), that using a cell phone increases the likelihood of a crash by up to 4.3 times versus those not using a cell phone while driving. Estimates for distraction-related crashes in the United States typically come from a sample of about 5,000 police-reported crashes called the Crashworthiness Data System (CDS) (Green, 2003). To overcome future problems that new technologies might have on driving, the National Highway Traffic Administration (NHTASA) proposed a set of guidelines to test the impact of a specific task on driving performance and safety. If a task is deemed too distracting to a driver's focus based on the Visual-Manual NHTSA Driver Distraction Guidelines for In-Vehicle Electronic Devices, NHTASA encourages automobile manufactures to prevent a driver's from being able to perform the interfering task (National Highway Traffic Safety Administration, 2012).

AM+A previously has done research for BMW (Marcus, Chen, Brown, & Ball, 2002) in a report titled "Future HMI Directions," in which AM+A thoroughly researched a driver-centered approach to HMI (Human-Machine Interaction). Although the report is over ten years old, the human factor issues are still highly relevant today as evidenced in Green's research and the NHTASA report.

In addition to safety, designing a system that encourages being environmentally conscious is an important attribute of our research. While fuel prices and the threat of global warming continue to rise, carpooling in the United States is at a very low 11% (Johnson, Jones, & Silverman, 2010). Services such as Zimride seek to counter the low rate of carpooling by creating a social network where people can be drivers and passengers in carpools. Zimride also offers Lyft, which helps those who would normally travel alone in a taxi request on-demand ridesharing. Honda Motors developed its Ecological Drive Assist System to encourage efficient driving by supporting behavior change, in offering visual feedback via an ambient green or blue color, and also by gamifying driving behavior through the design of virtual leaves for more sustainable driving (Honda Motors, 2008).

Our research shows that an innovative approach to vehicle dashboard design must account for the following: design for safety where a driver easily should be able to take a second glance at a display cluster and then refocus her/his attention on the road. Next, a display cluster must not increase the level of complexity that a driver encounters. For example, a focus on helpful rather than powerful features is important to ensure a reduction of complexity. A graphical user interface should not focus on visual complexity with an overabundance of graphics; rather, it must use graphics only if it enhances dynamic content that would otherwise be less visible. The user interface should not constrain the user to conform to a particular layout, but instead allow her/him to customize the available information present in the digital dashboard. Lastly, the dashboard development must follow a user-centered design process.

User-Centered User-Experience Design

The user-centered user-experience design (UCUXD) approach links the process of developing software, hardware, and user-interface (UI) to the people who will use a product/service. UCUXD processes focus on users throughout the development of a product or service. The UCUXD process comprises these tasks, which sometimes occur iteratively:

- **Plan:** Determine strategy, tactics, likely markets, stakeholders, platforms, tools, and processes.
- **Research:** Gather and examine relevant documents, stakeholder statements.
- **Analyze:** Identify the target market, typical users of the product, personas (characteristic users), use scenarios, competitive products.
- **Design:** Determine general and specific design solutions, from simple concept maps, information architecture (conceptual structure or metaphors, mental models, and navigation), wireframes, look and feel (appearance and interaction details), screen sketches, and detailed screens and prototypes.
- **Implement:** Script or code specific working prototypes or partial "alpha" prototypes of working versions.
- **Evaluate:** Evaluate users, target markets, competition, the design solutions, conduct field surveys, and test the initial and later designs with the target markets.
- **Document:** Draft white papers, user-interface guidelines, specifications, and other summary documents, including marketing presentations.

AM+A carried out many of these tasks in the development of the Driving Machine concept design, except for implementing working versions.

To better understand the demographics and to focus on creation of user-centered designs, our company incorporates the use of personas and use scenarios.

Personas are characterizations of primary user types and are intended to capture essentials of their demographics, contexts of use, behaviors, and motivations/objectives, and their impact on design solutions. Personas are also called user profiles. Typically, UI development teams define one to nine primary personas. For the Driving Machine personas, we identified three target markets: young drivers, early adopters, and elderly drivers.

Use scenarios are a UI development technique that emphasizes user-centered stories about product/service use. In the development of an initial concept prototype, a use scenario helps determine what behavior to simulate. A use scenario is essentially a sequence of task flows with actual content provided, such as the user's demographics and goals, the details of the information being exchanged, etc. Use scenarios differ from what are called "use cases." Use cases are descriptions of functions and information flows that are very specific and tied to data input and output, making them close to "pseudo-code" description of operations. Use scenarios are much more "real world" with "every-day language" descriptions.

For example, to simulate a print dialog box, a use scenario might state "an account executive wants to print out a PowerPoint presentation in landscape format, duplexed, with page numbers, as quickly as possible." The prototype developer then needs to simulate, with prototyping software, how the account executive would accomplish this task using the software.

Scenarios should have a format that includes the following:

- A descriptive and compelling title
- The background of the situation and the user
- The event or information that prompts user action
- Step-by-step listing of user actions (typically technology-independent) to reach a goal or conclusion
- A list of user benefits demonstrated by the scenario

- Optionally, reference to any supporting materials, such as existing screen designs, paper materials, information listings, or prototypes
- Optionally, a description of the current methods used to accomplish the same goal. These descriptions are good for comparison, as the new scenario is meant to be an improvement upon the existing methods

For the Driving Machine, we designed the following general use scenario topics that were drawn from the personas. Some specific examples might be relevant only to a particular age group or driving experience. Note the general usage of the terms "objective" and "goal." An objective is a general sought-after target circumstance. A goal is more specific and is usually qualified by concrete, verifiable conditions of time, quantity, etc. For example, an objective is, "I want to be reduce the likelihood of being in an accident." A related goal would be, "I want to have zero traffic accidents for the next two years."

Carbon Footprint Monitoring

- Receive up-to-date articles, advice, and tips regarding monitoring current and past driving behavior.
- Set customizable alerts for driving, whether positive or negative.
- Receive unsafe alerts.
- Establish and maintain objectives (e.g., "I want to reduce my carbon footprint").
- Establish and maintain goals (e.g., specify number of people you want to drive in a carpool). See the ramifications of this goal on current and past trends.
- Visualize and monitor the carbon footprint.

Carpooling

- Share current location with people near by.
- Alert driver of any potential passengers.

- Visualize and monitor the number of and location of carpool passengers.

Social Media

- Post green/efficient driving achievements on the users' own walls and possibly their friends' walls, similar to a merit-badge system.
- Connect with insurance agent by automatically sending them status reports on your driving behavior.
- Share tips and strategies with specific friends or family.
- Import personal information from social media sites (e.g., race, sex, age). Users not connected to a social media site can add their information manually through the Driving Machine.
- Resolve any urgent ethical issues.

Gamification

- Set and use pre-existing achievements to help reduce insurance premiums.
- Compare estimated fuel economy to actual fuel economy.
- Earn badges for being a driver in a carpool or on-demand carpool.
- Purchase carbon offsets by carpooling.
- Reward posting gas prices with gas reward cards.
- Develop an "economy of tipsterism," likes and dislikes, bribes and no bribes, objective vs. biased opinion, etc.

DRIVING MACHINE INFORMATION ARCHITECTURE AND SCREEN DESIGNS

From our investigations of dashboard and automotive-related applications, including those cited in (Marcus, 2013), AM+A concluded that usable, useful, and appealing vehicle user-interface (UI) design must include incentives to lead to behavior change. Safe and sustainable driving behavior is possible by providing incentives such as a games, and just-in-time systematic instructions to motivate people to change their behavior. The proposed Driving Machine needs to combine persuasion theory, provide better incentives, and motivate users' to achieve short-term and long-term behavior change towards a Driving Machine everyday user.

Our Driving Machine concept assumes that the primary vehicle dashboard is one of approximately six screens that might be available in a vehicle:

- Driver's dashboard,
- Central screen often containing navigation controls and climate/media controls accessible to the driver the front-seat passenger,
- Front seat passenger's screen, which might include a media-management system for the rear-seat screens,
- Back-seat left, center, and right screens often on the back of the front seats and/or overhead in the center.

The Driving Machine should be non-obtrusive, but encouraging to use. Well-designed games will serve as an additional appealing incentive to teach, i.e., to train the driver. Drivers should be able to receive badges for accomplishing certain tasks. The Driving Machine should allow users to share their experience with friends, family members and the world, primarily through Facebook and Twitter. The Driving Machine should also allow drivers to communicate their experiences with insurance companies to allow drivers to receive reduced rates, and with family/friends.

Based on these concepts and available research documents, we have proposed and are developing conceptual designs of the multiple functions of the Driving Machine. Subsequent evaluation will provide feedback by which we can improve the metaphors, mental model, navigation, interaction, and appearance of all functions and data in the Driving Machine's user interface. The resultant improved user experience will move the Driving Machine closer to a commercially viable product/service.

In particular, we believe a well-designed Driving Machine will be more usable, useful, and appealing to memory-conscious users, especially those experiencing long and short-term memory loss. Another objective is to provide a dashboard experience that can reliably persuade people to become safer and energy-conscious drivers.

Persuasion Theory

According to Fogg's persuasion theory (Fogg & Eckles 2007), to create behavioral change through the Driving Machine, we have defined four key processes:

- Increase frequency of reporting driving behavior to social networks.
- **Motivate changing some driving habits:** Talking on the phone, texting while driving, follow traffic laws, and driving over the speed limit.
- Teach how to drive efficiently (e.g., green, use less fuel).
- Persuade drivers to carpool.

Each step has requirements for the application. Motivation is a need, want, interest, or desire that propels someone in a certain direction. From the sociobiological perspective, people in general tend to maximize reproductive success and ensure the future of descendants. We apply this theory in the Driving Machine by making people understand that every action has consequences on safety and sustainability, and by providing incentives to make particular choices.

We also drew on Maslow's A Theory of Human Motivation (Maslow, 1943), which he based on his analysis of fundamental human needs. We adapted these to the Driving Machine context:

- The safety and security need is met by the possibility to visualize the amount of food expense saved.
- The belonging and love need is expressed through friends, family, and social sharings and support.
- The esteem need can be satisfied by social comparisons that display weight control and exercise improvements, as well as by self-challenges that display goal accomplishment processes.
- The self-actualization need is fulfilled by being able to visualize the improvement progress of the health mattered indexes and mood, and also by predicting the change of the users' future health scenarios.

Persuasion/Information Platform

AM+A believes that effective Machine design that combines information and persuasion requires these essential components:

- **Dashboards:** How am I doing now?
- **Overview:** What is my path, structure/process?
- Focus on social networks
- **Focus on just-in-time knowledge:** Tips and advice
- **Incentives:** Games, awards, rewards, competitions, stores

Overall Information Architecture

The following is an initial diagram of the information architecture for the Driving Machine (see Figure 1). In this diagram, the information architecture is called a concept map and uses list structures rather than more typical boxes and links.

Figure 1. Driving machine information architecture (concept map)

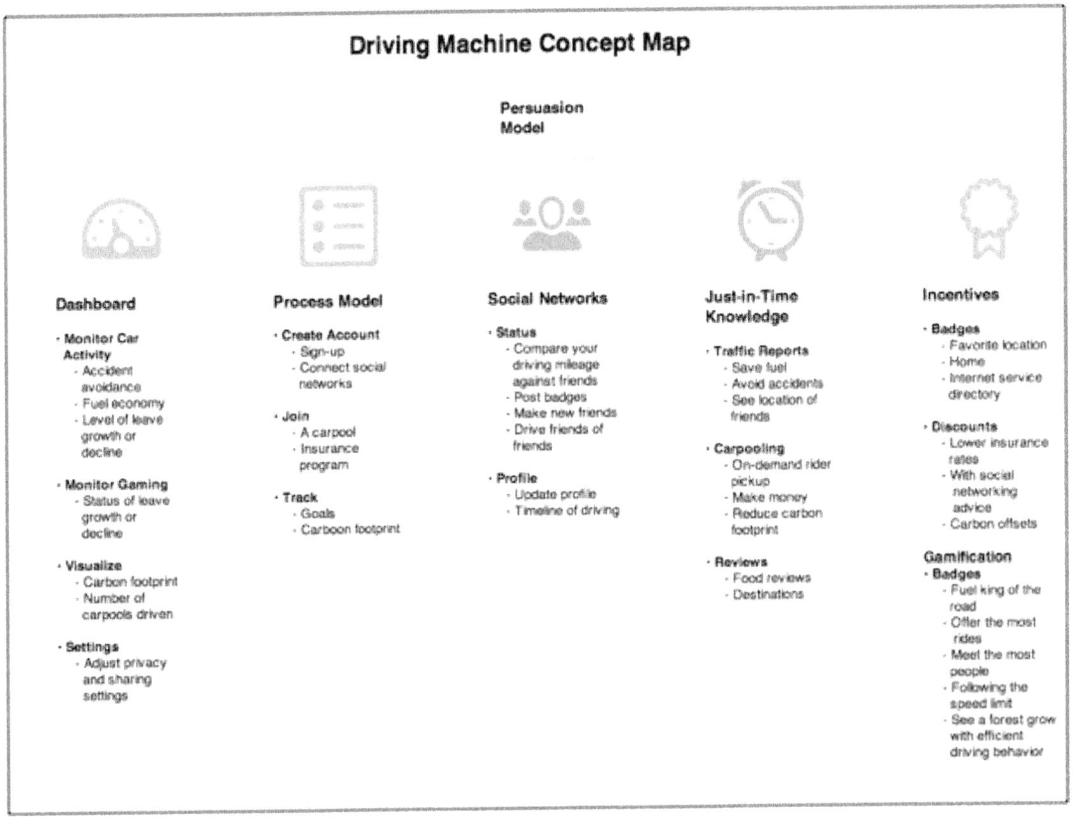

Components

Main Function

- Displays user's driving behavior such as speed (e.g., going over and under the speed), carbon footprint in tables and trend charts

Dashboard

- Records amount of money/time/fuel spent driving
- Calculates and displays money/time/fuel used so far for the day, week, month, or year
- Provides ability to see graphs comparing fuel usage and comparison to others with similar vehicles
- Ability to modify sharing and privacy settings

Safety/Driving Record

- Displays user's speeding and traffic violations
- Provides ability to see charts comparing driving record with those of similar experience/age/gender/location
- Alert family and friends of arrival to specific destinations

Green/Sustainable Driving

- Displays overall carbon dioxide emissions for daily and historic driving
- Provides ability to see more detailed expansion of contributing factors

- Provides ability to see charts comparing environmental impact to other vehicles, driving situations (e.g., weather conditions, traffic conditions, number of passengers, etc.)

Driving Advisor

- Enables quick communication between user and driving coach

Settings

- Enables user to set notification settings. Notifications are shown in email and on the landing page. They are less urgent then alerts and the user checks them on their own time
- Enables user to set alert settings. Alerts are important to know about right away and are received via text or through red exclamation points on top of the Driving Machine application icon. Examples of alerts are: speeding, breaking harshly, fuel prices

Process Model

Efficient Driving

- Displays collection of driving, travel, or other templates
- Alerts others when traffic conditions or other circumstances cause the driver/passenger to be late

Goal Setting

- Records amount of money, time, and/or fuel allocated for specific goals
- Calculates and displays money, time, and/or fuel put so far towards each goal compared to total amount needed

- Provides ability to see charts of money/time/fuel for goals or a more detailed textual view

Future Planning

- Displays collection of future planning calculators (e.g., lower carbon footprint, drive safer)
- Alerts when future plans have changed based on circumstances changing
- Enables user to fill out a new future calculator or view/edit an existing, already filled out future calculator

Social Networks

View and make social media achievement postings.

Announcements

- Displays announcements of posts from friends on the Driving Machine
- Enables user to post own updates
- Enables user to comment on posts or give them a "thumbs up"

Profile

- Displays user's profile
- Includes user's picture, comments from friends and updates from user

Friends

- Displays list of friends on the Driving Machine
- Displays privacy settings next to each friend
- Allows search for a friend, or clicking on a friend to go to their profile

Driving Machine Wall

- Displays the main Driving Machine profile/wall
- Includes updates and tips from the Driving Machine company
- Allows comments from users of the app

My Tips (e.g., These Might Be from an Insurance Agent)

Traffic Updates

- Displays updates on current traffic conditions

Tips

- Displays feed of tips from experts
- Displays rating on tips and allows users to pick "thumbs up" or "thumbs down"
- Allows filtering based on popularity, type of person posting the tip, time of posting
- Allows search for tips on specific subjects

Driving Machine Partnership

- Displays information about forming a partnership with the Driving Machine company
- If user is already in partnership, displays updates on the partnership and opportunities to each more

Contests Achievements Collection

- Displays pictures of achievements
- Displays progress on each achievement through a progress bar
- Enables clicking on picture to receive more information about a specific achievement

Competitions

- Displays current competitions and progress of each user involved
- Alerts about changes of user ahead in competition
- Allows starting of new competitions

Point Store

- Displays featured objects purchasable with points
- Displays list of all objects and associated cost in points
- Allows purchasing of objects with accumulated Driving Machine points

Circles

- Displays list of circles
- Displays user's joined circles
- Allows looking at specific pages for already joined circles

Screen Designs (Look-and-Feel)

Based on the information architecture, AM+A designed initial concept sketches of some key screens of the Driving Machine. AM+A sketched metaphor concepts, information architecture concepts, and specific screen design concepts before rendering detailed diagrams and screens. The following are representative revised screen designs with brief descriptions that help the reader to understand the approach of the Driving Machine.

This primary dashboard screen in Figure 2 illustrates all permanent, pertinent information. The outer rectangle showcases the automobile logo and the original equipment manufacturer (OEM) logo, e.g., perhaps Honda and Sony in Japan,

Figure 2. Basic, permanent information displays

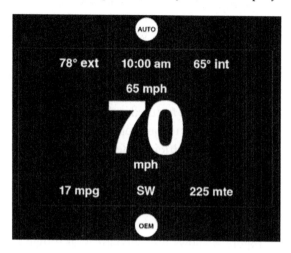

Kia and Samsung in South Korea, or Buick and Apple in the US. The inner rectangle showcases (clockwise from top left) external temperature (78 °ext), time (10:00 am), internal temperature (65 °int), miles to empty (225 mte), compass (SW), and miles per gallon (17 mpg). In the center, the current speed is shown in large numbers (70 mph) with the speed limit in smaller numbers above (65 mph). All of this information will always be present on the dashboard, and this information would be the default view in the case that nothing is wrong with the operation of the car.

Figure 3 shows the dashboard screen with all possible indicators that could appear (e.g., low gas,

emergency brake engaged, maintenance required, etc.) These icons are industry-standard, and commonly used across all automobile companies.

Figure 4 shows the dashboard with the left-turn signal on and also a red bar indicating a near-collision, both of which signs would blink. The red bar indicates that the car is close to colliding with an obstacle that may be in a blind spot. The location of the red bar indicates the location of the obstacle. In this figure, the obstacle would be to the left of the vehicle. A refinement of this design would show the red bar only along the lower left edge of the screen, which would indicate rear-left.

Figure 5 shows an alternative dashboard view, which emphasize navigation capabilities. The dashboard showcases the same elements (clockwise from top left), external temperature/internal temperature (78°/65°), time (10:00 am), compass (SE), miles to empty (225 mte), current speed (speed limit) (70 mph (65)), miles per gallon (17 mpg).

Figure 6 shows a novel concept: The information design of the dashboard would be combined with customized, personalized imagery in the form of a skin, which might be sold to the user as an optional extra. These would need to be carefully designed to maintain legibility and readability of key safety-related data. AM+A has designed

Figure 3. Emergency condition indicators

Figure 4. The dashboard with the left-turn signal on and blind-spot near-collision indicator on

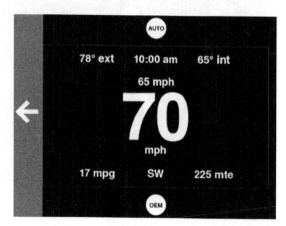

Figure 5. Alternative dashboard design with navigation map in the center

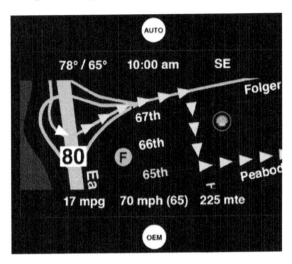

dashboard view with a themed background featuring the movie, "Avatar." Users would be able to shift and select different themed backgrounds or "skins" depending on interest. The example shows a themed background featuring the movie, "Little Shop of Horrors." (Image Credit: AM+A manipulation of public domain movie stills). A second example shows a themed background featuring the game, "Pacman." (Image Credit: AM+A design using Pac-Man-like image elements. Fair use of copyrighted materials).

Figure 7 shows an alternative design based on the pioneering work of the modern Swiss typographer, Wolfgang Weingart. His distinctive typographic style has been "adopted and adapted" to the needs of vehicle dashboard information design. This design indicates how many different designers could be featured in dashboard displays emphasizing their unique approach to visible language without sacrificing safety. In this version of the "Weingart skin," the color of the "sparkles" indicates whether the driver is speeding or not. Here, the red sparkles indicate that the driver is above the speed limit.

Figure 8 shows a dashboard with a themed background that indicates the eco-friendliness of a driver's behavior (how much the driver brakes, how quickly the driver accelerates, etc.). Here, the more eco-friendly the driving, the more trees will appear. (Image Credit: Tree image by Megan Chiou. Used with permission.). Another dashboard design indicates a driver's eco-friendliness using a simple color outline. Here, the green color indicates that the driver is eco-friendly. In other circumstances, based on driver behavior, the outline might be a warning color of yellow or a "danger" situation of red, that is, "eco-hostile" behavior The imagery or the outline can be used to encourage the driver to change her/his behavior, and drive in a

Figure 6. Personalized skins combined with information display

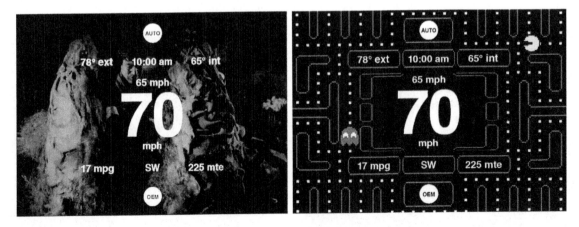

Figure 7. Personalized skin combined with information display in "high-design" style

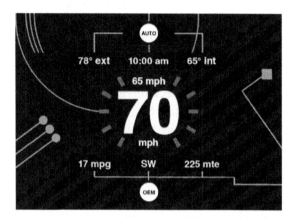

more environmentally responsible manner. This behavior could lead to rewards or awards offered by vehicle manufacturers, the government, or other sources of funding or recognition.

FUTURE RESEARCH DIRECTIONS

Following the user-centered development process described above, AM+A plans to continue to improve the Driving Machine screen designs as time/occasions permit. Significant further effort would require additional time, and funding from an outside source. Tasks include the following:

- Revise personas and use scenarios, especially for business use as well as personal.
- Conduct user evaluations.
- Revise information architecture and look and feel.
- Build initial working prototype (e.g., for iPad, or other tools, platforms).
- Evaluate the Driving Machine across different demographics and cultures.
- Research and design improved information visualizations.

The Driving Machine is an ongoing research and development project. The current screen designs may be used, together with a questionnaire, to elicit feedback from potential users.

We believe a well-designed Driving Machine will be more usable, useful, and appealing to drivers, especially those having communication/behavior challenges.

Our objective is to provide a vehicle/mobile application that can reliably persuade people

Figure 8. Indicators promoting sustainable driving behavior

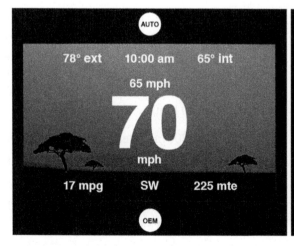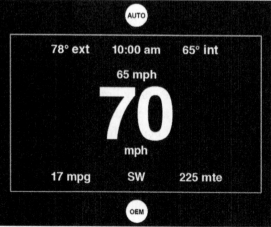

to move towards safer, more sustainable, more people-oriented interactions in order to facilitate better communication between the driver and her/his environment.

AM+A plans to continue development, as appropriate to user-centered design, with interviews, approximately ten people and approximately two advisors with expertise in vehicle systems. Through these interviews, we hope to learn what works, what doesn't, and how to refine the Driving Machine prototype further, from information architecture (metaphors, mental model, and navigation) through look-and-feel (appearance and interaction).

CONCLUSION

AM+A aimed to incorporate information design and persuasion theory for behavior change into a mobile tablet-oriented application that would constitute an advanced vehicle dashboard. This self-funded work on the Driving Machine project is current and ongoing, and was undertaken to demonstrate the direction and process for such products and services. Although the design is incomplete, AM+A is willing to share the approach and lessons learned, in the interest of helping alleviate worldwide automobile safety challenges and worldwide environmental challenges.

At this stage, AM+A is seeking to persuade other design, education, and automotive groups to consider similar development objectives. We hope that our process and concept prototypes (the self-funding of which inevitably limited the amount of research, design and evaluation) will inspire others, and that they benefit from the materials provided thus far.

The process has already been demonstrated successfully with a previous project, the Green Machine (Marcus & Jean, 2009), versions of which have been considered and used by SAP for enterprise software development (Marcus, Dumpert, & Wigham, 2011).

AM+A's long-term objective for the Driving Machine is to create a functional working prototype to test whether the application can actually persuade people who experience driving challenges to exercise greater vehicle control, increase safety, and reduce their carbon footprint. If the theories are proven to be correct, this approach could have significant implications that will benefit millions of people in the United States and abroad by reducing the number of automobile accidents and decreasing greenhouse gas emissions.

ACKNOWLEDGMENT

The author thanks the following for their assistance conducting research and in preparing the text and images for this document. Special thanks goes to Ms. Chiou for image construction/design, Mr. Scott Abromowitz Douglas, AM+A Designer/Analyst, and Ms. Megan Chiou, AM+A Designer/Analyst.

REFERENCES

Audi A8 > Audi of America. (2012). Retrieved August 10, 2012, from http://models.audiusa.com/a8

Berman, B. (2010). EV Expert Says Nissan LEAF's Dashboard Lacks Most Important Number | PluginCars.com. Retrieved August 10, 2012, from http://www.plugincars.com/ev-expert-says-nissan-leaf-dashboard-lacks-most-important-number-106590.html

Cialdini, R. B. (2001a). The Science of Persuasion. *Scientific American, 284*, 76–81. doi:10.1038/scientificamerican0201-76 PMID:11285825

Cialdini, R. B. (2001b). *Influence: Science and Practice* (4th ed.). Boston: Allyn and Bacon.

Fogg, B. J. (2003). *Persuasive technology: Using computers to change what we think and do.* Amsterdam: Morgan Kaufmann.

Fogg, B. J., & Eckles, D. (2007). *Mobile persuasion: 20 perspectives on the future of behavior change.* Palo Alto, CA: Persuasive Technology Lab, Stanford University.

Ford's Smartgauge With Ecoguide Coaches Drivers to Maximize Fuel Efficiency on New Fusion Hybrid | Ford Motor Company Newsroom. (2008, October 28). Retrieved August 10, 2012, from http://media.ford.com/article_display. cfm?article_id=29300

Green, P. (2003). The human-computer interaction handbook. In J. A. Jacko & A. Sears (Eds.), (pp. 844–860). Hillsdale, NJ, USA: L. Erlbaum Associates Inc. Retrieved from http://dl.acm.org/citation.cfm?id=772072.772126.

Hartson, R., & Pyla, P. S. (2012). *The UX Book. Process and guidelines for ensuring a quality user experience. Waltham.* Elsevier.

Hofstede, G. (2012). http://geert-hofstede.com/index.php (12.02.2012).

Johnson, T., Jones, S., & Silverman, A. (2010, August 5). Programs hope to reverse skid in car pooling - USATODAY.com. Retrieved August 9, 2012, from http://www.usatoday.com/news/nation/2010-08-04-carpooling-down_N.htm

Marcus, A. (2002). Information Visualization for Advanced Vehicle Displays. In: Information Visualization, 1, pp. 95 – 102.

Marcus, A. (2011). The MoneyMachine. User Experience Magazine, 11:2. *Second Quarter, 2012,* 24–27.

Marcus, A. (2012). The Story Machine. Workshop on Legacy Design, Proc. ACM SIGCHI, CHI 2012 conference, 1-7 May 2012, Austin, TX, unnumbered CDROM pages.

Marcus, A. (2013in press). *Mobile Persuasion Design.* London: Springer Verlag.

Marcus, A., Chen, E., Brown, K., & Ball, L. (2002). *BMW: Future HMI Directions.* Aaron Marcus and Associates, Inc.

Marcus, A., Dumpert, J., & Wigham, L. (2011). User-Experience for Personal Sustainability Software: Determining Design Philosophy and Principles. In A. Marcus (Ed.), Design, User Experience, and Usability. Theory, Methods, Tools and Practice, Lecture Notes in Computer Science (Vol. 6769, pp. 172–177). Springer Berlin/Heidelberg. Retrieved from http://www.springerlink.com/content/f8lm37795r3743v7/abstract/

Marcus, A., & Jean, J. (2010). Going Green at Home: The Green Machine. Information Design Journal, 17:3. *First Quarter, 201,* 233–243.

Maslow, A. H. (1943). A theory of human motivation. *Psychological Review, 50,* 370–396. doi:10.1037/h0054346

Maslow, A. H. (2006). *Motivazione e personalità* (11th ed.). Roma: Armando.

Motors, H. (2008). Honda Develops Ecological Drive Assist System for Enhanced Real World Fuel Economy: Implementation on All-New Insight Dedicated Hybrid in Spring 2009 (Press Release). Retrieved from http://world.honda.com/news/2008/4081120Ecological-Drive-Assist-System/

Multilayer Instrument Cluster | Johnson Controls Inc. (n.d.). Retrieved August 10, 2012, from http://www.johnsoncontrols.com/content/us/en/about/our_company/featured_stories/multilayer_instrument.html

National Highway Traffic Safety Administration. (2012). Visual-Manual NHTSA Driver Distraction Guidelines for In-Vehicle Electronic Devices.

Wagner, M., & Armstrong, N. (2003). *Field Guide to Gestures: How to Identify and Interpret Virtually Every Gesture Known to Man*. Quirk Books.

Ziegler, C. (2012). Cadillac CUE: driving is safer (and more dangerous) than ever | The Verge. Retrieved August 9, 2012, from http://www.theverge.com/2012/8/6/3220366/cadillac-c

ADDITIONAL READING

Arsenault, R., & Ware, C. (2000). Eye-hand coordination with force feedback. *CHI Letters, 2*(1).

Ashley, S. (2001, October). Driving the info highway. *Scientific American*. doi:10.1038/scientificamerican1001-52 PMID:11570042

Audi A8 > Audi of America. (2012). Retrieved August 10, 2012, from http://models.audiusa.com/a8

Baddeley, A. D. (1986). *Working Memory*. New York: Oxford University Press.

Bennett, J. (1984). Managing to meet usability requirements. In J. Bennett, D. Case, J. Sandelin, & M. Smith (Eds.), *Visual display terminals: Usability issues and health concerns*. Englewood Cliffs, NJ: Prentice-Hall.

Berman, B. (2010, December 21). EV Expert Says Nissan LEAF's Dashboard Lacks Most Important Number. *PluginCars.com*. Retrieved August 10, 2012, from http://www.plugincars.com/ev-expert-says-nissan-leaf-dashboard-lacks-most-important-number-106590.html

Bertone, C. M. (1982). Human factors considerations in the development of a voice warning system for helicopters. In *Behavioral Objectives in Aviation Automated Systems Symposium*. Warrendale, PA: Society of Automotive Engineers.

Boff, K. R., Kaufman, L., & Thomas, J. P. (1986). Cognitive processes and performance. Handbook of perception and human performance, 2.

Brewster, S. A., Wright, P. C., & Edwards, A. D. N. (2001). *Guidelines for the creation of earcons*. Glasgow Interactive Systems Group.

Briziarelli, G., & Allen, R. W. (1989). The effect of a head-up speedometer on speeding behavior. *Perceptual and Motor Skills*, 69.

Campbell, J. L., Carney, C., & Kantowitz, B. H. (1997). *Human factors design guidelines for Advanced Traveler Information Systems (ATIS) and Commercial Vehicle Operations (CVO)* (Technical Report FHWA-RD-98- 057). Washington, DC: U.S. Department of Transportation, Federal Highway Administration.

Campbell, J. L., Carney, C., & Kantowitz, B. H. (1998). *Human factors design guidelines for Advanced Traveler Information Systems (ATIS) and Commercial Vehicle Operations (CVO)*. Retrieved November 9, 2001, from http://www.fhwa.dot.gov/tfhrc/safety/pubs/atis/index.html

Campbell & Hershberger. (1988). *Automobile head-up display simulation study: Effects of image location and display density on driving performance*. Unpublished manuscript, Hughes Aircraft Company.

Carroll, J. M., & Mack, R. L. (1984). Learning to use a word processor: By doing, by thinking, and by knowing. In J. C. Thomas & M. L. Shneider (Eds.), *Human factors in computer systems*. Norwood, NJ: Ablex.

Carswell, C. M., & Wickens, C. D. (n.d.). *Lateral task segregation and the task- hemispheric integrity effect*. Manuscript submitted for publication. *Human Factors*.

Commission of the European Communities. (1999). *Commission recommendation of 21 December 1999 on safe and efficient in-vehicle information and communication systems: A European statement of principles on human machine interface*. Brussels, Belgium: European Union.

Constantine, L. L., & Lockwood, L. A. D. (1999). *Software for use: A practical guide to the models and methods of usage-centered design*. New York: ACM Press.

Cooper, A., & Saffo, P. (1999). *The Inmates are Running the Asylum: Why High Tech Products Drive Us Crazy and How to Restore the Sanity*. Indianapolis, IN: Sams Publishing.

Curbow, D. (2001). User benefits of connecting automobiles to the internet. *CHI 2001 Proceedings*.

De Waard, D. (1996). *The measurement of drivers' mental workload. Haren*. The Netherlands: University of Groningen, Traffic Research Centre.

Dennerlein, J. T., Martin, D. B., & Hasser, C. (2000). *Force-feedback improves performance for steering and combined steering-targeting tasks*. ACM. doi:10.1145/332040.332469

Dingus, T., Hulse, M., Jahns, S., Alves-Foss, J., Confer, S., Rice, A., et al. (1996). *Development of human factors guidelines for Advanced Traveler Information Systems (ATIS) and Commercial Vehicle Operations (CVO): Literature Review* (Technical Report FHWA-RD-95- 153). Washington, DC: U.S. Department of Transportation, Federal Highway Administration.

Dingus, T. A., & Hulse, M. C. (1993). Some human factors design issues and recommendations for automobile navigation information systems. *Transportation Research, 1C*(2).

Doll, T. J. (1986). *Synthesis of auditory localization cues for cockpit applications*. Human Factors Society 30th Annual Meeting. Santa Monica, CA: Human Factors Society.

Draper, S. W. (1993). *The notion of task in HCI*. New York: ACM Press.

Ewing, J., Mehrabanzad, S., Sheck, S., Ostroff, D., & Shneiderman, B. (1986). An experimental comparison of a mouse and arrow-jump keys for an interactive encyclopedia. *International Journal of Man-Machine Studies*. doi:10.1016/S0020-7373(86)80038-4

Fleming, J. (1998). *Web navigation: Designing the user experience*. Cambridge, MA: O'Reilly & Associates.

Ford. (2008, October 28). Ford's Smartgauge With Ecoguide Coaches Drivers to Maximize Fuel Efficiency on New Fusion Hybrid. *Ford Motor Company Newsroom*. Retrieved August 10, 2012, from http://media.ford.com/article_display.cfm?article_id=29300

Gaver, W. (1997). Auditory interfaces. In Human computer interaction.

Gill, J. (2000). *Which button*. London: Royal National Institute for the Blind.

Graham, R., Hirst, S. J., & Carter, C. (1995). Auditory icons for collision avoidance warnings. Intelligent transportation: Serving the user through deployment. *Proceedings of the 1995 Its America Annual Conference*. Washington, DC.

Green, P. (1998). *Visual and task demands of driver information systems* (Technical Report UMTRI-98-16). Ann Arbor, MI: The University of Michigan Transportation Research Institute.

Green, P. (2000). Crashes induced by driver information systems and what can be done to reduce them. *Convergence 2000 Conference Proceedings* (SAE Publication P-360). Warrendale, PA: Society of Automotive Engineers.

Green, P. (2001). *Safeguards for on-board wireless communications*. Paper presented at the Second Annual Plastics in Automotive Safety Conference. Troy, MI.

Green, P., Levison, W., Paelke, G., & Serafin, C. (1993). *Suggested human factors design guidelines for driver information systems* (Technical Report FHWA-RD-94-087). Ann Arbor, MI: The University of Michigan Transportation Research Institute.

Green, P., & Williams, M. (1992). Perspective in orientation/navigation displays: A human factors test. *Vehicle Navigation and Information Systems Conference Proceedings*. Oslo, Norway: IEEE.

Greenland, A. R., & Groves, D. J. (1991). *Head-up display concepts for commercial trucks. Future Transportation Technology Conference and Exposition* (SAE Technical Paper Series Number 911681). Warrendale, PA: Society of Automotive Engineers.

Greenstein, J., & Arnaut, L. (1987). Human factors aspects of manual computer input devices. In G. Salvendy (Ed.), *Handbook of Human Factors*. Hoboken, NJ: Wiley-Interscience.

Helander, M. G. (1987). *Handbook of Human Factors*. Hoboken, NJ: Wiley-Interscience.

Held, R., Estanthiou, A., & Green, M. (1966). Adaptation to displaced and delayed visual feedback from the hand. *Journal of Experimental Psychology*, 72.

Helsen, W. F., Elliott, D., Starkes, J. L., & Ricker, K. L. (1998). Temporal and spatial coupling of point of gaze and hand movement in aiming. *Journal of Motor Behavior*, *30*(3). doi:10.1080/00222899809601340 PMID:20037082

Hewett, T. T. (1998, April). *Cognitive factors in design: Basic phenomena in human memory and problem solving*. CHI.

Hoffman, P. (1999). Accommodating color blindness. *Usability interface, 6*(2). Retrieved November 17, 2001, from http://www.stcsig.org/usability/newsletter/9910-color-blindness.html

Hooey, B. L., & Gore, B. F. (1998). *Advanced Traveler Information Systems (ATIS) and Commercial Vehicle Operations (CVO): Components of the Intelligent Transportation Systems: Head-up displays and driver attention for driver navigation information* (Technical Report FHWA-RD-96-153). Washington, DC: US Department of Transportation Federal Highway Administration.

Horton, W. (1994). *The icon book: Visual symbols for computer systems and documentation*. New York: John Wiley and Sons.

Hutchins, E. L., Hollan, J. D., & Norman, D. A. (1986). Direct manipulation interfaces. In D. A. Norman & S. W. Draper (Eds.), *User centered system design: New perspectives on human-computer interaction*. Hillsdale, NJ: Erlbaum.

IBM. (n.d.). *Out of box experience guidelines*. Retrieved November 4, 2001, from http://www-3.ibm.com/ibm/easy/eou_ext.nsf/Publish/77

Jacob, R. J. K. (1996). The future of input devices. *ACM Computing Surveys, 28A*(4).

John, B. E., & Kieras, D. E. (1996, December). The GOMS Family of User Interface Analysis Techniques: Comparison and Contrast. *ACM Transactions on Computer-Human Interaction, 3*(4). doi:10.1145/235833.236054

Johnson, J. (2000). *GUI bloopers – Don'ts and do's for software developers and web designers*. Morgan Kaufmann.

Kahn, P., & Lenk, K. (1998, November/December). Principles of typography for user interface design. *Interactions Magazine*.

Kamada, T., & Kawai, S. (1991). *A general framework for visualizing*. University of Tokyo.

Kantowitz, B. H., & Sorkin, R. D. (1983). *Workspace design. Human factors: Understanding people-system relationships*. New York: J. Wiley and Sons.

Kline, D. W., & Scialfa, C. P. (1996). Visual and auditory aging. In J. E. Birren & K. W. Schaie (Eds.), *Handbook of Psychology of Aging* (4th ed.). New York: Academic Press.

Kowlaski, L. A., McMurtrey, K., & Wickham, D. P. (2001). *Improving the out of box experience: A case study*. Society of Technical Communication.

Laurienti, P. J., Burdette, J. H., Wallace, M. T., Yen, Y. A., Field, A. S., & Stein, B. E. (2001). Deactivation of sensory-specific cortices: Evidence for cross-modal inhibition. *Proceedings of the 7th Annual Meeting of the Organization for Human Brain Mapping*.

LeCompte, D. C. (1996). Irrelevant speech, serial rehearsal, and temporal distinctiveness: A new approach to the irrelevant speech effect. *Journal of Experimental Psychology*, 22. PMID:8805820

LeCompte, D. C. (1999). Seven, plus or minus two, is too much to bear: Three (or fewer) is the real magic number. *Proceedings of the Human Factors and Ergonomics Society 43rd Annual Meeting*.

Little, C. (1997). *The intelligent vehicle initiative: Advancing "Human- Centered" smart vehicles*. U.S. Department of Transportation.

Luce, P. A., Feustel, T. C., & Pisconi, D. B. (1983). Capacity demands in short-term memory for synthetic and natural speech. *Human Factors*. PMID:6840769

Lund, A. (2001, October). Measuring usability with the USE questionnaire. *Usability interface: Newsletter of the Society for Technical Communication Usability SIG*.

Maclean, K.E., Snibbe, S.S., & Levin, G. (2000). Tagged handles: Merging discrete and continuous manual control. *CHI Letters, 2*(1).

Mandel, T. (1997). *The elements of user interface design*. Wiley.

Manes, P., & Green, P. (1997). *Evaluation of a driver interface: Effects of control type (knob versus buttons) and menu structure (depth versus breadth)* (Technical Report UMTRI-97-42).

Marcus, A. (2000). User interface design for a vehicle navigation system. In E. Bergman (Ed.), *Information appliances and beyond, interaction design for consumer products*. Morgan Kaufmann.

McAteer, S. (1998). *Internet everywhere*. Jupiter strategic planning services, Web technology strategies.

McGrenere, J. (2000). *Bloat: The objective and subjective dimensions (Student Poster)*. *CHI 2000 Proceedings*. The Hague, The Netherlands: ACM.

Meier, B. J. (1988). Ace: A color expert system for user interface design. In *Proceedings of the ACM SIGGRAPH Symposium on User Interface Software*. New York: ACM Press.

Meister, D., & Sullivan, D. J. (1969). *Guide to human engineering design for visual displays* (Technical Report N0014-68-C-0278). Washington, DC: Office of Naval Research.

Micheal, S. G., & Casali, J. G. (1995). Auditory prompts: Effects on visual acquisition time and accuracy in a dashboard-mounted navigational display task. *Proceedings of the 3rd Annual Mid-Atlantic Human Factors Conference*. Blacksburg, VA.

Microsoft Corporation. (1999). *Microsoft Windows user experience: Official guidelines for user interface developers and designers*. Redmond, WA: Microsoft Press.

Miller, G. A. (1956). The magical number seven, plus or minus two: Some limits on our capacity for processing information. *Psychological Review*, 63. PMID:13289977

Mills, C., & Weldon, L. (1987). *Reading text from computer screens: Human-computer interaction laboratory*. College Park, MD: University of Maryland.

Miner, N., Gillespie, B., & Caudell, T. (n.d.). *Examining the influence of audio and visual stimuli on a haptic interface*.

Motors, H. (2008). *Honda Develops Ecological Drive Assist System for Enhanced Real World Fuel Economy: Implementation on All-New Insight Dedicated Hybrid in Spring 2009* (Press Release). Retrieved from http://world.honda.com/news/2008/4081120Ecological-Drive-Assist-System/

Mullet, K. (1995). *Designing visual interfaces: Communication oriented techniques*. New York: Prentice-Hall.

Multilayer Instrument Cluster | Johnson Controls Inc. (n.d.). Retrieved August 10, 2012, from http://www.johnsoncontrols.com/content/us/en/about/our_company/featured_stories/multilayer_instrument.html

Muratore, D. (1987). *Human performance aspects of cursor control devices (6321)*. Houston, TX: Mitre.

National Science and Technology Council (NSTC). (1997). The Human Centered Transportation System of the Future. Paper presented at ITS America 7th Annual Meeting. Washington, DC.

National Science and Technology Council's (NSTC) Human Centered Transportation Safety Team presentation at ITS America 7th Annual Meeting in Washington, D.C. (June 1997). The Human Centered Transportation System of the Future

Nielsen, J. (1994). Heuristic evaluation. In J. Nielsen & R. L. Mack (Eds.), *Usability Inspection Methods*. New York: John Wiley and Sons.

Nielsen, J. (1999). *Designing web usability: The practice of simplicity. (1999)*. Indianapolis, IN: New Riders Publishing.

Norman, D. (1988). *The psychology of everyday things*. Basic Books.

Nowakowski, C., Utsui, Y., & Green, P. (2000). *Navigation system evaluation: The effects of driver workload and input devices on destination entry time and driving performance and their implications to the SAE recommended practice* (Technical Report UMTRI-2000-20). Ann Arbor, MI: The University of Michigan Transportation Research Institute.

Paap, K. R., & Cooke, N. J. (1997). Chapter 24: Design of Menus. In Handbook of Human-Computer Interaction.

Patterson, R. D., & Milroy, R. (1979). *Existing and recommended levels for auditory warnings on civil aircraft*. Cambridge, UK: Medical Research Council Applied Psychology Unit.

Popp, M. M., & Farber, B. (1991). Advanced display technologies, route guidance systems, and the position of displays in cars. In A. G. Gale (Ed.), *Vision in Vehicles–III*. North-Holland: Elsevier Science.

Preece, J., Rogers, Y., Sharp, H., & Benyon, D. (1994). *Human-computer interaction*. Addison-Wesley.

Rober, P., & Hofmeister, J. (2001). An analysis of human computer interaction in vehicles. In *Systems, social and internationalization design aspects of human-computer interaction: Vol. 2 of the Proceedings of HCI International 2001*.

Rosenfeld, L., & Morville, P. (1998). *Information architecture for the world wide web*.

SAE. (2000). *Navigation and route guidance function accessibility while driving (SAE Recommended Practice J2364)*. Warrendale, PA: Society of Automotive Engineers.

SAE. (2001). *Calculation of the time to complete in-vehicle navigation and route guidance tasks (Technical Report SAE J2365)*. Warrendale, PA: Society of Automotive Engineers.

Salvendy, G. (1987). *Handbook of human factors*. Hoboken, NJ: Wiley Interscience.

Sanders, M. S., & McCormick, E. J. (1993). *Human factors in engineering and design* (7th ed.). New York: McGraw-Hill.

Segen, J., & Kumar, S. (1999). Dextrous interaction with computer animations using vision-based gesture interface. In H. Bullinger (Ed.), *Human-computer interaction: Ergonomics and user interfaces*.

Sheridan, T.B. (1997, May). Trains, planes and automobiles. *The Reflector*.

Shneiderman, B. (1983). Direct manipulation: A step beyond programming languages. *IEEE Computer, 16*(8).

Shneiderman, B. (1992). *Designing the user interface: Strategies for human-computer interaction*. Boston: Addison-Wesley.

Shukla, M., Denzil, J., & Jampani, A. (2001). *Measuring awareness and distraction caused by change in information density*. Blacksburg, VA: Department of Computer Science, Virginia Tech.

Simpson, C.A., & Marchionda, Frost, K. (1984). Synthesized speech rate and pitch effects on intelligibility of warning messages for pilots. *Human Factors*, 27. PMID:6241175

Simpson, C. A., McCauley, M. E., Ronald, E. F., Ruth, J. C., & Williges, B. H. (1987). Speech controls and displays. In G. Salvendy (Ed.), *Handbook of Human Factors*. New York: J. Wiley and Sons.

Smith, B. A., Ho, J., Ark, W., & Zhai, S. (2000). *Hand eye coordination patterns in target selection*. Almaden, CA: IBM Almaden Research Center. doi:10.1145/355017.355041

Snowberry, K., Parkinson, S. R., & Sisson, N. (1983). Computer display menus. *Ergonomics, 26*(7), 699–712. doi:10.1080/00140138308963390

Society of Automotive Engineers. (2000). *Navigation and route guidance function accessibility while driving (SAE Recommended Practice J2364)*. Warrendale, PA: Society of Automotive Engineers.

Solso, R. L. (1988). *Cognitive psychology*. Boston: Allyn and Bacon.

Sorkin, R. D. (1987). Design of auditory and tactical displays. In G. Salvendy (Ed.), *Handbook of human factors*. New York: J. Wiley and Sons.

Standing, L. (1973, May). Learning 10,000 pictures. *The Quarterly Journal of Experimental Psychology, 25*(2). doi:10.1080/14640747308400340 PMID:4515818

Stokes, A., Wickens, C., & Kite, K. (1990). *Display technology–Human factors concepts*. Warrendale, PA: Society of Automotive Engineers.

Stricker, A., & Shea, B. (1999). *Cognitive technologies* (Information Report CITL IR-002) Cognition and Instructional Technologies Laboratories Texas A&M. Retrieved November 18, 2001, from http://citl.tamu.edu/cognitive-tech.htm

Tarrière, C., Hartemann, F., Sfez, E., Chaput, D., & Petit-Poilvert, C. (1988). *Some ergonomic features of the driver-vehicle-environment interface* (Technical Report SAE 885051).

United States Department of Defense. (1989). *Human engineering design criteria for military systems, equipment and facilities (Military Standard MIL-STD-1472D)*. Philadelphia, PA: Naval Forms and Publications Center.

Usher, D. M. (1982). A touch-sensitive VDU compared with a computer aided keypad for controlling power generated man-machine systems. *IEEE Conference Publication No. 212.*

Walker, N., Fain, W. B., Fisk, A. D., & McGuire, C. L. (1997)... *Human Factors, 39*(3). doi:10.1518/001872097778827188 PMID:9394636

Watson, W. E. (1981). *Human factors design handbook.* McGraw-Hill.

Weintraub, D. J. (1987). HUDs, HMDs, and common sense: Polishing virtual images. Human Factors Bulletin, *30*(10).

Weintraub, D. J., Haines, R. F., & Randle, R. J. (1984). The utility of head-up displays: Eye-focus vs. decision times. *Proceedings of the Human Factors and Ergonomics Society 28th Annual Meeting.* Santa Monica, CA: Human Factors and Ergonomics Society.

Weintraub, D. J., Haines, R. F., & Randle, R. J. (1985). Head-up display (HUD) utility. II. runway to HUD transition monitoring eye focus and decision times. *Proceedings of the Human Factors and Ergonomics Society 29th Annual Meeting.* Santa Monica, CA: Human Factors and Ergonomics Society.

White, J. (2011, December 14). The Car Dashboard That Wants to be an iPad. *Wall Street Journal.* Retrieved from http://online.wsj.com/article/SB 10001424052970204903804577082203288412 734.html# Wickens, C.D. (1990). *Engineering psychology and human performance.* Glenview, IL: Scott Foresman.

Woodhead, M. (1957). *Effects of bursts of loud noise on a continuous visual task. (RNP No. 57/891).* Royal Navy.

Woodruff, A., Landay, J., & Stonebraker, M. (1998). *Constant information density in zoomable interfaces.* Berkeley, CA: Department of Electrical Engineering and Computer Sciences, University of California.

Woodson, W. E. (1981). *Human factors design handbook. Joint Army- Navy-Air Force Steering Committee.* McGraw-Hill.

Yoo, H., Tsimhoni, O., Watanabe, H., Green, P., & Shah, R. (1999). *Display of HUD warnings to drivers: Determining an optimal location* (Technical Report UMTRI-99-9). Ann Arbor, MI: The University of Michigan Transportation Research Institute.

Zerweck, P. (1999). Multidimensional orientation systems in virtual space on the basis of finder. In H. Bullinger (Ed.), *Human-computer interaction: Ergonomics and user interfaces.*

Zetie, C. (1995). *Practical user interface design – Making GUIs work.* McGraw-Hill.

Ziegler, C. (2012, August 8). Cadillac CUE: driving is safer (and more dangerous) than ever | The Verge. Retrieved August 9, 2012, from http://www.theverge.com/2012/8/6/3220366/cadillac-cue-safety

KEY TERMS AND DEFINITIONS

Culture-Centered Design: Use of culture models (patterns of signs, rituals, heroes/heroines, and values; patterns of preference and expectation) based on user analyses that are used to inform user-experience design of software-applications.

Information Architecture: Mental models and navigation of an application often represented as a diagram.

Information Visualization: Means of conveying structures and processes through tables, forms, charts, maps, and diagrams.

Look-and-Feel: Appearance and interaction characteristics of a software application.

Metaphor: Primary concept conveyed through visual, verbal, or other means.

Persuasion Theory: Philosophy, principles, and techniques of changing short-term and long-term behavior.

User-Centered Design: Philosophy, principles, and techniques oriented to gaining insight from users in order to make applications more usable, useful, and appealing.

User-Experience: All "touch points" encountered by a user during interaction/communication with a product or service.

User-Interface Components: Metaphors, mental models, navigation, interaction, and appearance.

This work was previously published in Research and Design Innovations for Mobile User Experience edited by Kerem Rizvanoglu and Görkem Çetin, pages 1-21, copyright year 2014 by Information Science Reference (an imprint of IGI Global).

Chapter 79
'Talking Tools':
Sloyd Processes Become Multimodal Stories with Smartphone Documentation

Annika Wiklund-Engblom
Åbo Akademi University, Finland

Juha Hartvik
Åbo Akademi University, Finland

Kasper Hiltunen
Åbo Akademi University, Finland

Mia Porko-Hudd
Åbo Akademi University, Finland

Marléne Johansson
Åbo Akademi University, Finland

ABSTRACT

The study presented is part of a work-in-progress project of developing a mobile application for smartphones, Talking Tools (TT). The first context TT is developed for and tested in is sloyd education [Swedish: slöjd], a compulsory subject taught in Finnish schools. In sloyd learners design and manufacture unique artifacts in various materials (textiles, wood, metal, and electronics). The process-based work flow of sloyd lends itself well to this kind of educational tool, which aids multimodal documentation, communication, and instruction. The empirical study targets what student teachers (N=11) microblogged about and the character of the blog posts during a sloyd project. A sociocultural perspective of appropriating new tools for learning is used as a theoretical frame, as well as views on multimodality and transmedia. Their sloyd process is discussed in terms of transmedia storybuilding, as learners build their own story as a flow of content through their documentation and interactions.

INTRODUCTION

Smartphones are found in the pocket of nearly every learner in Finland today. This is an untapped educational resource that could be exploited for the purpose of learning and teaching (Ilomäki, 2012). The business model of the telecom industry in Finland further allows for affordable smartphone data plans, which is critical for schools to be able to justify the use of mobile phones from a democratic perspective, but also having the financial possibility to supply phones to those who cannot afford it themselves.

DOI: 10.4018/978-1-4666-8619-9.ch079

This article presents a pilot study on a mobile application for smartphones, Talking Tools (TT), which aims at utilizing the above mentioned untapped resource by turning smartphones into learning tools with an explicit educational purpose. Developing TT is a collaborative project between sloyd education researchers, transmedia developers, user experience experts, and educational technology researchers at Åbo Akademi University, Finland, as well as software developers and coding experts at UpCode Ltd., a software company specialized in developing reading and scanning solutions for smartphones.

The pilot study of the application targets student teachers' documentation using TT. The aim is to explore *what* they chose to document in this multimodal environment. Multimodal documentation can enable transmedia storybuilding, in which the flow of dynamic content facilitates learning and allows for participation. It supports both independent and collaborative learning and allows for flexible information access, communication, and documentation (cf. Naidu, 2008). Being a learner in a multimodal blended learning environment entails both consuming and creating one's own content using a number of media sources and tools (Kress, 2003, 2010; Kress & van Leeuwen, 1996/2006; Säljö, 2012). Kress and van Leeuwen (1996/2006) have established a theory of multimodality offering concepts to analyse and understand the interplay between culture, situation and multimodality. The research aims and questions of the present study are discussed within a sociocultural framework of learning (Säljö, 2005; Vygotsky, 1978, 1986) including perspectives on multimodality and transmedia learning.

CONTEXT

In the Nordic countries, sloyd is a common free time activity in society, as well as an activity in educational contexts (Johansson & Lindfors, 2008; Nygren-Landgärds, 2003). The word sloyd etymologically stems from the old Swedish word *slöghþ*, which stands for shrewdness, diligence, skilfulness and smartness, and the word *slögher*, denoting characteristics such as being handy, being deft, having professional skills, being skilful, experienced, and resourceful (Svenska Akademins ordbok, 1981). Kojonkoski-Rännäli (1995) discusses the phenomenon of sloyd through analysing the words 'hand' and 'work' that form the Finnish word for sloyd, *käsityö*. The word 'hand' shows that the materials used in sloyd are concrete and tangible. In working the material, you use your hands, body and various tools. The concept of 'work' shows that the actor is a human being and that the work that is realized is a result of planning and modelling.

Sloyd as a core subject was established in Finland in connection with the introduction of Folk schools in the 1860s (Nurmi, 1979). Educational sloyd was, from the outset, tasked with objectives that resided outside the concrete making and practice of everyday sloyd (Peltonen, 1998). The sloyd class is learner-centred and allows everyone to work from their own ability and motivation in creating artefacts within a predefined educational and curricular frame.

The sloyd educational theory of learners' sloyd process emphasizes the learner's ability to carry out a 'whole' sloyd process from idea to finished product. The process involves phases of *planning*, *planning of manufacturing*, and *manufacturing and evaluation* (Lindfors, 1991). Learners are given the opportunity to define their idea, plan their work and carry out their plans, observe the consequences of their activities and evaluate the different stages of the work as a whole (Pöllänen & Kröger, 2006). Making a sloyd artefact takes time and the work usually stretches over several lessons. Lindström (2009) describes educational sloyd as a subject in which the learner learns *about*, *in*, *with* and *through* sloyd. The objectives of the activity can be dealing with materials and techniques (*about*), experimenting to achieve a certain effect or mood (*in*), supporting knowledge in other subjects (*with*), or risk-taking or patience (*through*). The individual process that leads to the tangible sloyd product is as important as the product itself (Lindfors, 1991). Studies have shown that learning in the sloyd classroom includes both material and immaterial dimensions in interaction with others and in interaction with mental and physical tools (Illum & Johansson, 2012; Johansson, 2002, 2006). Through the practical sloyd process the learners may access the wide spectrum of learning that the process enables beyond the practical realm.

The sloyd educational practice is an ongoing process where the learner, the group of learners and the teacher are involved and interrelate with each other when practicing sloyd (Lindfors, 1999). The learners are involved in cycles of activity (Uljens, 1997). Learners' former experiences form the basis for a new cycle of activity. The teacher creates different intentions for the activity. These are transformed into actions that provide new experiences for the learners. The experience takes its final form when the experienced activities become objects for reflection. In teacher education students practice whole sloyd processes, similar to the processes that learners carry out in school, in order to prepare student teachers for planning, carrying out and evaluating sloyd educational practice. During these processes student teachers learn knowledge about sloyd as well as knowledge in, with and through sloyd. Thus, sloyd teacher education needs to raise students' awareness of several levels of knowledge, including technical skills, instructional design of sloyd educational practices, and ideological subject values.

The artefacts made during sloyd lessons can be seen as a type of communication and storytelling (Mäkelä, 2011). Although the artefact in itself is a materialised documentation, the process cannot be detected from it and, hence, remains hidden (Johansson, 2002, 2006). The sloyd process can in a similar way be regarded as the carrier of a valuable story. Regardless of who the learner in sloyd is, there is an educational value in the story

surrounding the creative process. Until now there have been no effective tools for a smooth capturing of the ongoing process in sloyd. One purpose of TT is therefore to allow learners to describe, visualize and discuss their story connected to their own creative process (Johansson & Porko-Hudd, 2013). Learners are, thus, encouraged to capture the essence of the why, how and what within the creative sloyd process.

The purpose of TT is to encourage microblogging about work processes using text, images and short video clips. These chronological blog entries are automatically saved in individual blogs. Peers can share their blog entries and comment on each other's processes. The teacher can monitor the documentation, provide feedback and share learning objects, in order to support the learners' work. Hence, opportunities for learners, peers and teachers to reflect are provided by the transparency that is achieved through the visualisation of the work process afforded by TT. According to Gao, Luo and Zhang (2012), the learning content is not solely limited to information provided by the teacher, when learners are connected via microblogging; everyone, both teachers and learners, in the virtual learning community can serve as information providers, information consumers and knowledge constructors. The objective of the multimodal documentation tools are to stimulate learners in multiple ways; learning by watching/listening, doing, sharing, collaborating, and reflecting on one's process as a whole, as well as learning by being exposed to variations of processes through other learners' stories.

MULTIMODALITY AND MULTILITERACY

Multimodality refers to multiple modes of representation, such as text, audio, images, and moving images (Kress, 2003, 2010; Kress & van Leeuwen, 1996/2006; Säljö, 2012). The concept of multiliteracy is discussed in terms of how we are able to use multimodal communication in the ever-changing landscape of media tools and multimodal output. We have to be able to both create and interpret communication that is much more than what it used to be in a text-based, single-mode format (The London Group, 1996).

Multiliteracy in the context of TT can be defined as the ability to use the mobile application as a tool for learning how to, e.g., write about the creative sloyd process, in which multimodal affordances are used as options for complementing the text with photos, videos, drawings, etc. One aspect of this multiliteracy is also to learn how to reflect on other learners' written texts, photos, drawings etc. of their creative work process, i.e., it is not only about creating your own multimodal texts, but understanding and reflecting on other learners' achievements and being part of a conversation (Johansson & Porko-Hudd, 2013).

TRANSMEDIA STORYBUILDING

The term transmedia is usually referred to in the context of storytelling for entertainment purposes, in which the story is designed to flow between various media sources and platforms. The end-users are often engaged as participators in the transmedia storyworld (Jenkins, 2006). The concept of transmedia has also entered the learning stage. In this context it is referred to as a blended and dynamic content method to facilitate learning (Teske & Horstman, 2012). However, the storytelling feature is usually still the essential characteristic, whether it is used as a teaching method or solely for entertainment purposes.

We would like to take this a step further by introducing a new term, transmedia storybuilding, which can be defined as the learning process where the learner creates his/her own story with the help of various media tools and multimodal texts and sign systems, e.g., written texts, sketches, photos, and video (cf. Kress, 2010; Säljö, 2012). In this particular context, there is not necessarily

a predetermined storyworld. Rather, the learners build their own, be it factual or fictional. Parallels can also be drawn to the concepts of transmediation (Siegel, 1995) and its synonym transduction (Kress, 2010), which both refer to the process of translating meaning from one sign system to another. However, here we emphasize the continuous flow of the storybuilding process rather than a translation.

The current case of TT implementation serves as an example of how the concept of transmedia storybuilding can be used in sloyd education. The aim is that the learning process will flow between the design and manufacturing of tangible artefacts and a number of converging media tools and multimodal learning objects. The learning process is the learner's own story created through the transmedia learning experience enabled through the resources available. The convergence of the old and the new in this case involves the old ways of mediating sloyd tools and processes with new educational technology such as the Talking Tools application. This kind of instructional method, thus, combines the sloyd subject with multimodal literacy practice.

The idea behind using multimodal content is to make the learning situation flexible and make use of tools that can enhance and visualize materials in multiple ways. Therefore, the multimodal affordances provided by a blended learning environment may assist a transmedia storybuilding process. In this transmedia flow, learners can add their own 'voices' through their active participation, such as voices of co-creation in the sloyd conversation. The intention is to put the learner through a constructive act, not merely transmit content. The story created in this transmedia content flow is ultimately the learner's, although to some extent structured according to a specific instructional design by the teacher. Thus, the learners become more like 'directors' of their learning experiences.

One can argue that humans are by default transmedia storybuilders based on our multichannel sensory system and multimodal brain. This is similar to Stein's (2008, p. 874) claim that "all learning is multimodal". Our perceptual and sensory systems are the source of our conscious experience (Fauconnier & Turner, 2002). Sight, hearing, touch, smell, and taste are our bodies' 'tools' to experience various perceptions from a variety of perspectives, and this is particularly evident in sloyd education (Illum & Johansson, 2012). Media tools function as extensions of our bodies, McLuhan argued (1964) and, hence, educational media tools can be described as extensions of our bodies and senses to assist transformation of experiences into knowledge. It can be argued that the method of using multimodal media tools is thus similar to combining multiple features of our bodies' sensory system for interpreting our experiences.

SOCIOCULTURAL PERSPECTIVE

ICT (Information and Communications Technology) and access to the Internet have in many ways changed how Western people communicate, behave, socialize and manage their everyday lives. One of the latest additions, the smartphone, has made information online more independent of time and space. The phone is becoming a powerful tool for learning as it has rapidly developed into a pocket-size computer supporting Internet-based applications in which users can create, share, and exchange information and ideas in virtual communities.

A sociocultural perspective, in which learning is seen as based on the relation between the collective and the individual (Säljö, 2005; Wertsch, 2002), is relevant in the design of educational technology where social media often is an important ingredient. This theoretical approach sees our learning in relation to the context we live in, the tools we work with, and the social context we are a part of (Säljö & Linderoth, 2002). The external memory field is expanding, and is continuously

being created. This fact is also having an impact on educational settings (Säljö, 2012). Social learning theorists would argue that learning could even be constrained by the lack of social presence as development of knowledge is a social process (Naidu, 2008). Therefore, it is seen as essential that TT supports both individual and peer learning (Johansson & Porko-Hudd, 2013).

When technological tools change, it changes how we interact with the world around us, but also the way we learn and acquire knowledge (Säljö & Linderoth, 2002). It has long been argued that the characteristics of the medium itself will affect society (McLuhan, 1964). ICT allows for new strategies of solving problems and provides an atmosphere of trial-and-error testing for learning. This gives permission for error-making, which then is seen as a step in the process of learning instead of being judged as being right or wrong as an end-result (Säljö & Linderoth, 2002). Mistakes made during a creative process are often crucial steps in order to reach an optimal solution (Beard & Wilson, 2002). This approach towards error-making is of significance for how we learn, and learn to learn in new ways with the help of ICT. It is a sociocultural perspective for understanding how human learning functions in terms of appropriating new tools in our environment (Lave & Wenger, 1991; Säljö & Linderoth, 2002).

One such new learning tool is the smartphone. Two significant factors for understanding mobile learning and its implication for education are conversation and context. Sharples, Taylor and Vavoula (2007, p. 225) propose a tentative definition of mobile learning as "the processes of coming to know through conversations across multiple contexts among people and personal interactive technologies". They "claim that conversation is the driving process of learning" (ibid, p. 225), and that "all activity is performed in context /.../ learning not only occurs in a context, it also creates context through continual interaction" (ibid, p. 230). One affordance of TT is microblogging. This provides opportunities for creating conversations around learning tasks, such as the sloyd assignment in the present study. We want to emphasize this, since the long-term research regarding the TT application is framed by these perspectives; investigating the learning process while using new technological tools and learning objects as a means for learning – from both a learner and a teacher perspective.

RESEARCH AIMS AND QUESTIONS

The aim of the empirical study presented in this article is to find out what teacher students are documenting, in order to explore their patterns of using the multimodal microblogging tool of the Talking Tools (TT) smartphone application. Learners' understanding and actions are always part of a context, which they help to create and recreate (Lave & Wenger, 1991). In this study, the interest is not on the materials and techniques taught in sloyd, but on how learners use the TT application for documenting, reflecting, and communicating, in order for us to understand how this new tool influences their learning activities, both individually and socially, and how it can support the creative process. Finding out what learners are documenting will support the ambition of developing guidelines for teachers on how to apply TT in educational situations. The long-term objective is to explore how to maximize the added value of TT in various contexts and for different types of didactical models. Namely, how can learning activities be enhanced, facilitated, and supported by the use of TT for both formal and informal learning in different subjects?

EMPIRICAL STUDY

Background and Data Collection

The Talking Tools (TT) mobile application was piloted on eleven student teachers taking part in

a compulsory sloyd course at Åbo Akademi University in Finland. During the course the students were working on an assignment called 'The Battery Guzzler'. In this assignment, the students were challenged to solve a storage problem for batteries. They were instructed to design and manufacture a product that would function as a storage place for batteries with the purpose of keeping track of empty batteries.

Altogether eleven teacher students participated in the course; seven male and four female students. Three of them were first-year students and eight were second-year students. Blogs 1 through 10 and 13 were made by individual students as part of the assignment. Blogs 11 and 12 were made by groups of students. The 'Battery Guzzler' assignment documented in the TT application continued during six teacher-led lessons, each consisting of 3 x 45 minutes. At the beginning of the course, the students were informed about the study and asked to participate in it. All ethical measures were adhered to, in accordance with proper code of conduct. Since the mobile solution at this time only supported Android devices, some of the students could use their own devices, whereas seven students were supplied with a device. At the time of the study, only a limited number of the planned features of TT were available. Therefore, this study was limited to the documentation features.

The students were encouraged to document their work process within the course; from the first ideas to the finished artefact. They were asked to take pictures and write short texts, comments, as well as reflect and describe their work, either during or after the sloyd lesson. In addition, the students were encouraged to follow and comment on each other's blogs by giving feedback and observing each other's work process. The objective was for the students to create their own story of their learning process. The teacher students documented their sloyd processes in 13 different blogs by creating photos and text entries (Figure 1). There were 478 entries (273 photos and 205 texts) varying between 7 and 85 entries per blog

Figure 1. Number of entries in the blogs

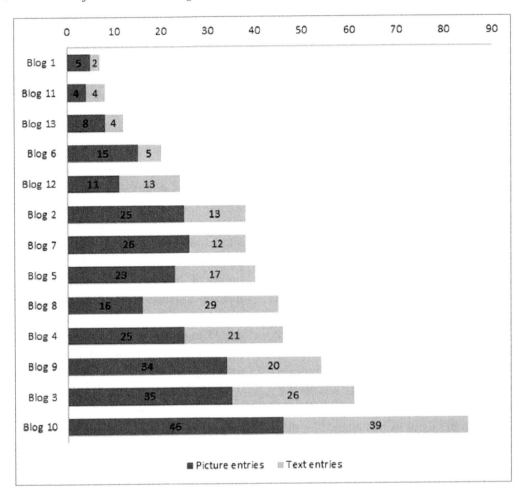

with an average of 37 entries consisting of 21 photos (57%) and 16 text entries (43%).

Analysis and Results

Content analysis was used in order to systematically identify categories of documentation practices in the multimodal blog data. As a reliability measure, all thirteen blogs were read and analysed separately by three researchers of sloyd education (one PhD and two PhD students). Their preunderstanding of the sloyd subject was useful for interpreting the blog data, and, especially, in analyzing the visual images. The analysing software NVivo (by QSR International) was used for the content analysis. NVivo allows for flexible

switching between entries in blogs and between blogs. This flexibility in manipulation of qualitative data gives an overview that makes it easier to see patterns of interest.

At first, during the process of analysis, the researchers read the material repeatedly. Secondly, the content was organized into units of meaning in an open coding process, in order to identify qualitative categories of activities. Thirdly, the units were categorized further, by analysing and interpreting the essence of the units of meaning. When the data had been analysed independently by all three researchers, the interpretations and categories were synchronized. The researchers then jointly analysed the consistency of the categories found. A consensus was reached and resulted in a final number of seven categories of documentation activities made by the student teachers during the sloyd project.

The categories consist of 1) *Concurrent Process Notes,* 2) *Retrospective Summary Notes,* 3) *Lecture Notes,* 4) *Notes of Peer Activities,* 5) *Communication with Peers,* 6) *Emotional Comments,* and 7) *Response to the Talking Tools App.* In the following, the categories are presented using illustrating excerpts. These excerpts have been translated from Swedish to English by the authors, and all names are fictive.

1. **Concurrent Process Notes**: The category *Concurrent Process Notes* consists of notes that the students have made during a work process. The notes can either be pictures of the sloyd product in progress or texts about the work process. The following excerpt exemplifies entries from a student's concurrent documentation during his sloyd process. The excerpt consists of two text entries and one picture entry (Figure 2).

Now follows an interesting experiment with the risk that the entire work is destroyed. The idea is to use a technique that my cousin Dani taught me, namely, sanding away the paper edges.

The sandpaper technique works surprisingly well. The most important thing was to always sand diagonally downwards. (Blog 13).

In the first text entry the student describes what he will do and shows his awareness about a critical phase for the work as a whole. The student exposes the fact that his work requires preparatory work in the form of information retrieval. Here, information is retrieved from a cousin who has experience of similar operations. The picture taken a few minutes later shows him using the technique. In addition, the student has engaged a fellow student to take a picture of him as he carries out the technique. The image adds value to the text since it visually shows how the technique is performed (diagonally). In the second text entry he evaluates how the method worked. Using text

Figure 2. Blog 3: Concurrent process notes

and image together he highlights the most effective work method. All three entries, made within 17 minutes, illustrate a demarcated moment of the manufacturing process.

2. **Retrospective Summary Notes:** Although the mobile device allows concurrent note-taking, some students chose to describe their activities after class, like a retrospective summary of what they had accomplished during the day. The following excerpt describes how one student summarizes what he/she has been working on. The entries within this category are generally longer than entries made during a manufacturing process. Entries also include descriptions of several different steps in the process. The excerpt below, in blog 13, includes descriptions related to all phases of *planning, planning of manufacturing,* and *manufacturing and evaluation* (Lindfors, 1991) of the artefact.

I started by sketching out what I wanted to do... Finally, I came up with the idea of a cat with LED lights as eyes.

After this I glued together pieces of wood that would be enough material to cobble together a box. Having planed boards, I would start with the box BUT the material cracked and I started from scratch with taking finished pieces of wood and screw and glue together into a box. After this I sawed out a cat face, paws and also cut out a piece of metal as a back plate for the cat. That is how far I have come at this point. [Blog 13]

The entry includes a description of different stages of the process from idea to ongoing manufacturing activities. The text is used as a retrospective description of different phases of the craft process. The student discloses that the work began with sketching, but mentions nothing about what the sketches contained. The selected idea is described briefly. After this, vari-

ous manufacturing-related stages and events are summarized. Unlike the first category, entries in this category contain much information about the manufacturing process. In addition, the sequence of actions and phases are described in the written text, whereas pictures are more commonly used in entries in the first category. In this blog the social context is not documented, which may be perceived as an indication that the student was working alone.

3. **Lecture Notes:** Entries that describe things that the teacher taught during the lesson make up a third category. Many students made text notes of things that the teacher said during the lessons. The excerpt below describes a text note of critical steps in using the circular saw. In blog 10 the student stresses some of the critical safety aspects by using capital letters.

circular saw. NEVER use both the rip fence and the crosscut fence at the SAME TIME. Cut pieces with enough supporting surface. earmuffs and face shield should be used on all type of machines. [Blog 10]

Ten out of thirteen students chose to take pictures as the teacher demonstrates a new manufacturing technique or machine. The excerpt in Figure 3 is a picture in Blog 3 representing teacher 'J' demonstrating how to use the planer.

In this entry there are no written text comments related to the picture. The image is used as a memory aid for catching work posture, grip and generally handling of the material when using the planer. In this particular situation students were encouraged to take photos about how to safely and correctly use the machine.

4. **Notes of Peer Activities:** For the most part students described their own work processes. Nonetheless, some students made entries about fellow students' processes. The fourth

Figure 3. Blog 3: Teacher 'J' demonstration

category comprises posts about what others in the group are working on. The excerpt from Blog 4 below illustrates how a student describes what his/her peers are planning to do within the assignment.

Hahaaa! Managed to measure out my hexagon! Jonathan in the background [referring to a previous picture post]. He'll do a house. [Blog 4]

While the student's own success is mentioned in the blog, the student also comments on what his/her peer students are working on.

5. **Communication with Peers:** In contrast to category 4, *Notes of Peer Activities,* in which comments about other students' work are only mentioned, category 5 describes peers as active participants who in various ways influence how the sloyd process progresses. Although most entries were about documenting a student's own process, the microblogging tool was also used to communicate with fellow students. The excerpt

in Figure 4, consisting of a picture and a text entry below from Blog 2, describes how a student thanks another student for helping with the planning during the lesson:

Here's my drawing. thanks Emma for helping with the calculation! [Blog 2]

Unlike previous categories, entries in this category show communication with classmates. In the excerpt above classmate Emma gets a thank you for her help with the planning. The image and the accompanying written text summarize a working stage in cooperation.

6. **Emotional Comments:** Some of the entries show how emotionally engaged the students are throughout their work process. Entries reveal anticipations for the task, the joy after a successful work step and disappointments when the final outcome was not as planned. The excerpt from Blog 3 below describes the anticipation and anxiety after a critical point in the work:

Figure 4. Blog 2

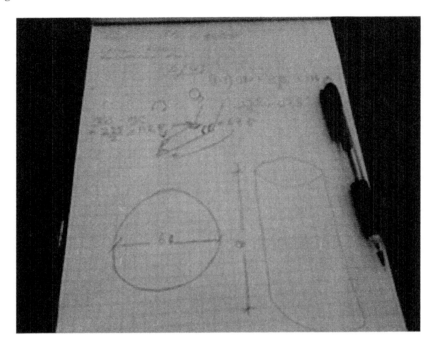

Oh no... hard to know how it will be. Doubt that the glue will hold. Hope I get rid of air bubbles ... [Blog 3]

In the excerpt below, from Blog 4, the student is in the phase of *manufacturing*. He/she points out that a certain stage of the overall work is successfully finished (in this case sawing) and it is time to go on to the next stage. Documentation that explicitly marks an ending of a phase in the work process as a whole emerges frequently in the students' blogs.

Yes, sawing check! [Blog 4]

The thumbs-up is used to reinforce the message of the text (Figure 5). In addition to writing about the successful sawing, the student has placed out the material in the background of the photo to emphasize the expression of the 'like' imagery.

7. **Response to the Talking Tools App:** The seventh category consists of posts and comments on the Talking Tools app. Students commented the application's ease of use in particular and also provided suggestions for technical improvement. The excerpt below, from Blog 4, describes a student's suggestion on how the usability of the microblogging tool could be improved.

101

A delete function for individual blog posts would be surely nice, considering my previous post. In addition, an opportunity to write titles on posts would help structure. [Blog 4]

He/she proposes developing a function that would allow deleting entries. He/she also suggests that each post could be marked with a title.

Summary of Categories

The results show that many of the notes were made after the completion of a critical step of the work

Figure 5. Blog 4: Sawing check

process, and before the next step or phase was begun (category 1). The students took a break for documenting one phase before starting a new one. The microblogging was also used for diary-like descriptions of what had happened during the day (category 2). This second category, *Retrospective Summary Notes*, contrasted with the first category with regards to both length of notes and the time of the documentation.

TT was often used for note-taking during the teacher's demonstrations (category 3). Thus, TT substituted regular note-taking methods, such as using pen and paper. The work process of sloyd education takes place in a social context where we are influenced by each other. Students found it relevant to write what other students were doing (category 4). Written text and photos show how students help each other during their work process (category 5). Students used emotional comments to reinforce their emotions related to their work process, e.g., happiness about successful operations, and anxiety about uncertainty of the outcome of operations in the work process (category 6). Finally, some technology-related reflections were described in the students' documentations (category 7).

CONCLUSION

The research interest in the development and implementation of the Talking Tools (TT) centres on how learners' learning and reflection are facilitated. We will summarize what the students' documentation showed us about the possibilities and challenges of using this smartphone application. We discuss the findings in relation to the specific conditions of sloyd education, while using perspectives of multimodality, socio-cultural learning, and transmedia.

Phases of the Sloyd Process

In sloyd education, it is desirable for learners to take notes of information that is relevant to their own work. However, creating meaning in the documentation may also include aspects that are not directly connected to sloyd. One aspect that is meaningful to one learner may not have the same value for another learner, or for the teacher (Säljö & Linderoth, 2002; Porko-Hudd, 2011). However, both the first and second category of the blog analysis (*Concurrent Process Notes* and *Retrospective Summary Notes*) show evidence of the Lindfors' (1991) system theory of phases and steps in the learner's sloyd process.

The theory conceptualizes the sloyd activity as an ongoing, holistic human process where the actor (learner, teacher and peers) is acting within the sloyd activity itself. The learner's sloyd process is a slowly progressing process of structural change, divided into three phases: the *planning phase*, the phase of *planning of manufacturing* and the phase of *manufacturing*. These steps will naturally overlap and be iterative, as the process will most likely occasionally go backward and then forward again (Lindfors, 1999). The blogs' contents easily fit into the three sloyd process phases as most entries somehow describe moments within the work process. Without going into further detail of Lindfors' theory, we conclude that the steps of the sloyd process were represented in the blogs subjected to study. It also made us aware that the phase of *manufacturing* could be further developed as the blogs clearly made visible how the phase in fact consists of several reiterative moments of planning, executing and evaluating.

Multimodal Documentation

In the social context of sloyd, multimodal documentation offers a broader picture of how teaching has shaped the learners' work (cf. situated learning, Lave & Wenger, 1991). Many students used both written text and photos in their blogs. A photo of a calculation (as documented in Blog 2) may be used as a memory aid. But it also provides possibilities for both classmates and teachers to observe and learn how the reasoned solution was developed. Similarly to a written text, a photo mediates meaning for both the photographer and the viewer of the documented information. The photo becomes a mediating resource for meaning-making (Kress & van Leeuwen, 1996/2006; Säljö, 2012; Wertsch, 2002).

Entries in categories 1 and 2 (*Concurrent Process Notes* and *Retrospective Summary Notes)* show that the written language is important in order to make reflections. As Vygotsky (1986) states, the written word is crucial to convey thinking. However, a reader with prior experience in sloyd can perhaps follow the text-based documentation of this type, while a non-experienced novice would likely benefit from additional images. The results further indicate that retrospective summaries are useful, also when modern smartphones are used as tools for documentation. This method of writing in a diary form has lately been used by students teachers at university level, as well as by learners in sloyd education in elementary school, in order to describe their sloyd processes, and to raise awareness about their work process (e.g., Johansson, 2002, 2011).

Prior research has shown that sloyd is a subject that easily touches learners emotionally, which is confirmed by category 6 (*Emotional Comments*). These emotional experiences may even be carried for a long time (Porko-Hudd, 2011). The results in this study show that multimodal documentation was used for expressing emotions, using both text and nonverbal signs through photos (see blog 4). Using the thumbs-up sign to communicate positive emotions non-verbally in a photo is perhaps representative of the multiliteracy-skilled net generation. However, this type of innovative multimodal communication may also be seen as part of the appropriating process of using TT as a new tool for learning.

The students' documentation clearly shows how smartphones enable multimodal texts, which contributes to a rich documentation of thoughts and actions. Video as a note-taking feature was not available in the early version of TT that was piloted, but it would no doubt add richness to the documentation. Moving images might provide opportunities to document complicated processes, which are difficult to reproduce in written text. Examples of such processes could be ergonomics, technology, and handgrip (Goodwin, LeBaron & Streeck, 2011). Although multimodal documentation enables sensory experiences to be described, some experiences (for instance how soft a material ought to be) need to be experienced in real life (Illum & Johansson, 2012). However, for people with these prior sensory experiences of processing materials, the documentation with TT facilitates describing and sharing such experiences through the multimodal documentation. Although no smartphone can replace sensory experiences TT can be used as a complementary resource to document the perceptions and appearance.

Open Access for Classmates and Teacher

It can be concluded that the student teachers' blog posts give a good general picture of the activities in the sloyd class. One of the great advantages of this kind of documentation is that it makes the individual work process visible to others in the group. By having access to their own processes, as well as those of their peers, learners are given the possibility to become more aware of their own performance as they can compare it to others' work processes. The opportunity to take part of each other's documentation, or share documentation, can be seen as a resource for learning as it builds up collective memory (Säljö, 2005; Wertsch, 2002).

Prior research on learning in sloyd has shown the importance of providing opportunities for reflecting on the learning (Johansson, 2002, 2006). Especially in sloyd, learners are prone to focus on the practical doing rather than the more abstract notion of what they have learned from the work process itself. When documentation is available even after class hours, learners can continue their reflective process outside of school. It provides nearly limitless opportunities for classmates to learn and communicate, as well as to be present in each other's learning processes. Thus, they can both give and get new perspectives that they otherwise would not have received. The fact that learners can easily access the notes of classmates provides an advantage over notes made on paper as the time for reflection becomes more independent of time, place and pace.

Potential Challenges

It is important to point out that all entries do not necessarily describe the correct way to perform a task or work step, as wrong practices may just as easily be documented. This might reduce the informational value of the memory aid. For example, within category 3 (*Lecture Notes*), there was a photo of the teacher standing on the wrong side of the circular saw (blog 1), which might be dangerous. This fact was not reflected on in the blog. Hence, documentation without correct reflection may even be harmful, especially since it is so easy to take a photo in every kind of situation.

Simultaneous documentation might distract learners' attention from the teacher's teaching, as well as distract the teacher. There is also a risk that the microblogging about the task becomes more interesting and time consuming than the actual task that is being documented. Another challenge might be to develop an open and positive atmosphere where learners give each other constructive feedback. An ongoing creative process is often very personal and learners may be sensitive to criticism. The question is whether learners even want to share everything. The approach needs to be carefully described, and the class should agree on a common code of conduct.

The Transmedia Story

While looking at the teacher students' documentation activities from a transmedia storybuilding perspective, a few aspects need to be highlighted. First of all, it can be concluded that the documentation process does not necessarily become a story by default. Rather, the documentation process can metaphorically be compared to a path of knowledge building as described by Scardamalia and Bereiter (2006). Secondly, the storybuilding process has several parallel stories: 1) about the artefact development (Lindfors, 1991), 2) about the learning process related to the artefact development, and in the case of teacher students there is the story 3) about developing as a teacher (Uljens, 1997). These parallel story tracks are naturally intertwined, but need to be emphasized to facilitate reflection for each of them in the documentation process.

The difference between transmedia storybuilding and storytelling is another aspect that needs to be problematized. The documentation process using TT is naturally multimodal and flows between mediating tools, similar to a mediation process of using multiple sign systems (Kress, 2010) for communication and documentation. We interpret these as transmedia affordances enabling a transmedia storybuilding learning process. However, this is from the perspective of the learner. Whenever the goal is to 'broadcast' your story to a peer, or the teacher, or even a parent, it becomes a storytelling process, and then it is not necessarily transmedia, unless multiple means of transmitting are used.

From a sociocultural perspective, the process of co-creation is seen as ubiquitous (Lave & Wenger, 1991). This aspect is especially emphasized in the way TT is designed. Its purpose is to encourage learners to communicate, collaborate, teach and learn from each other's processes, and be involved in an ongoing co-creation process without boundaries. Thus, the two perspectives of storytelling and storybuilding are not easily discerned as separate entities. From a sociocultural perspective you cannot, perhaps, even separate them. The essential affordance we would like to highlight is the possibility it brings for reflection, and for this you can use either a specific storybuilding assignment for an internal reflection on the process, its successes, failures, and end results, or you can focus the assignment on reflections through storytelling, in which learners create a story for the purpose of an external audience.

Methodological Considerations

The results represent the authors' subjective interpretations of the blogs' content. However, from this interpretive research method the teacher students'

subjective experiences cannot be fully understood. Differences can most likely be found between what the students document and what they actually did (cf. Johansson, 2002, 2006; Säljö, 2005). Also, the data often lacked descriptions of the context, which would help in understanding the activity, especially the social context.

Future Research

Research ambitions regarding the Talking Tools application and its implementation in various learning contexts are comprehensive, broad and long-term. The assumption is that learning resources allowing for multimodal learning and transmedia storybuilding in learning broaden the horizon of proximal development. There are at least three perspectives that will be covered: a sociocultural perspective of the learning experience, a contextual perspective of implementation in a variety of contexts, and a learning design perspective of how to increase the added value of TT by exploring various methods of implementation. There is no doubt that the multimodal documentation features of TT offer a new platform for reflection. However, a future challenge is how to make the documentation a resource for learners to reach a better awareness of their own learning. Future research within the project could therefore focus on what practices are needed to help learners analyse, reflect, evaluate or summarize their learning process.

REFERENCES

Beard, C., & Wilson, J. P. (2002). *Experiential learning. A best practice handbook for educators and trainers* (2nd ed.). Philadelphia, PA: Kogan Page.

Fauconnier, G., & Turner, M. (2002). *The way we think. Conceptual blending and the mind's hidden complexities*. New York, NY: Basic Books.

Gao, F., Luo, T., & Zhang, K. (2012). Tweeting for learning: A critical analysis of research on microblogging in education. *British Journal of Educational Technology*, *43*(5), 783–801. doi:10.1111/j.1467-8535.2012.01357.x

Goodwin, C., LeBaron, C., & Streeck, J. (Eds.). (2011). *Embodied interaction. Language and the body in the material world. Learning in doing: Social, cognitive & computational perspectives.* New York, NY: Cambridge University Press.

Illum, B., & Johansson, M. (2012). Transforming physical materials into artefacts – learning in the school's practice of sloyd. *TechneA Journal*, *19*(1), 2–16.

Ilomäki, L. (Ed.). (2012). *Laatua e-oppimateriaaleihin: e-oppimateriaalit opetuksessa ja oppimisessa* [The quality of e-learning materials: E-learning materials in teaching and learning]. Helsinki, Finland: Finnish Ministry of Education.

Jenkins, H. (2006). *Convergence culture: Where old and new media collide.* New York, NY: New York University Press.

Johansson, M. (2002). *Slöjdpraktik i skolan – hand, tanke, kommunikation och andra medierande redskap [Craft and design (sloyd) in school – hand, mind, communication and other mediating tools]*. Doctoral dissertation. Göteborg studies in educational science, 185. Gothenburg, Sweden: Acta Universitatis Gothoburgensis.

Johansson, M. (2006). The work in the classroom for sloyd. *Journal of Research in Teacher Education, 2–3*, 153–171.

Johansson, M. & Lindfors, E. (2008). Finland. Slöjd [Käsityö]. *Nuläge och framåtblickar – om undervisning och forskning inom det nordiska slöjdfältet* (Techne serien. Forskning i slöjdpedagogik och slöjdvetenskap B:15/2008, s. 17–30). Vasa, Finland.

Johansson, M., & Porko-Hudd, M. (2013). Smart slöjd med smarta mobiltelefoner? – om didaktiska dimensioner i digitalt lärande [Smart sloyd with smart phones? Didactical dimensions in digital learning]. In A. Marner & H. Örtegren (Eds.) KLÄM. Konferenstexter om Lärande, Ämnesdidaktik och Mediebruk [KLÄM. Conference Texts on Learning, Didactics and Media Use]. Tilde (1). Umeå, Sweden: Umeå University.

Kojonkoski-Rännäli, S. (1995). *Ajatus käsissämme. Käsityön käsitteen merkityssisällön analyysi* [The idea of our hands. A conceptual analysis of the handicraft concept]. Turku, Finland: University of Turku.

Kress, G. (2003). *Literacy in the new media age.* London, UK: Routledge. doi:10.4324/9780203164754

Kress, G. (2010). *Multimodality. A social semiotic approach to contemporary communication.* London, UK: Routledge.

Kress, G., & van Leeuwen, T. (1996/2006). *Reading images. The grammar of visual design.* London, UK: Routledge.

Lave, J., & Wenger, E. (1991). *Situated learning: Legitimate peripheral participation.* Cambridge, UK: Cambridge University Press. doi:10.1017/CBO9780511815355

Lindfors, L. (1991). *Slöjddidaktik. Inriktning på grundskolans textilslöjd* [Sloyd didactics focusing on textile sloyd in comprehensive school]. Helsinki, Finland: Finn Lectura.

Lindfors, L. (1999). Sloyd education in the cultural struggle. Part VIII. An outline of a sloyd educational theory. (Ed. Rep. No. 4). Vaasa, Finland: Åbo Akademi University, Faculty of Education.

Lindström, L. (2009). Estetiska lärprocesser om, i, med och genom slöjd [Aesthetic learning about, in, with and through sloyd]. *KRUT, Kritisk utbildningstidskrift, 133/134*, 57–70.

Mäkelä, E. (2011). *Slöjd som berättelse: Om skolungdom och estetiska perspektiv [Sloyd as a Story: On School Youth and Aesthetic Perspectives].* Doctoral dissertation, Umeå, Sweden: Umeå University.

McLuhan, M. (1964). Understanding media: The extensions of man. New York, NY: McGraw Hill.

Naidu, S. (2008). Enabling time, pace, and place independence. In J. M. Spector, M. D. Merrill, J. Van Merrienboer, & M. P. Driscoll (Eds.), *Handbook of research on educational communications and technology* (3rd ed., pp. 259–269). Routledge.

NordFo, Åbo Akademi, Pedagogiska fakulteten. Johansson, M. (2011). Dagboksmetod – att beskriva slöjdarbete med elevers och lärares egna ord [Diary method – describing sloyd work with pupils' and teachers' own words]. *TechneA Journal, 18*(1), 79–93.

Nurmi, V. (1979). Opettajankoulutuksen tähänastinen kehitys [The Development of Teacher Training]. Juva: WSOY.

Nygren-Landgärds, C. (2003). *Skolslöjd nu och då - men vad sen?* [Sloyd as a school subject in present and past - but what in the future?] Vasa: Åbo Akademi.

Peltonen, J. (1998). Käsityökasvatus Suomessa. Kouluaineesta tieteenalaksi [The science of sloyd education in Finland. From a school subject to an academic discipline]. I M. Itkonen (Red.), *Tekemisen viljeltyneisyys. Näkökulmia kulttuurin filosofiseen olemukseen* (s. 1–22). Hämeenlinna: Hämeen ammattikorkeakoulu.

Pöllänen, S., & Kröger, T. (2006). Kokonainen ja ositettu käsityö paradigmamaailmoina: Näkökulmia ja tulevaisuudensuuntia. [Whole and partial sloyd as a paradigm: Perspectives and future directions] In L. Kaukinen & M. Collanus (Eds.), *Tekstejä ja kangastuksia* [Texts and mirages]. Hamina, Finland: Akatiimi.

Porko-Hudd, M. (2011). Skriv och berätta: Lärarstuderandes minnesberättelser om slöjd [Write and tell: Teacher students' memories from sloyd education]. *TechneA Journal, 18*(1), 63-78.

Säljö, R. (2005). *Lärande och kulturella redskap. Om lärprocesser och det kollektiva minnet [Learning and cultural tools. On learning processes and collective remembering].* Stockholm, Sweden: Norstedts.

Säljö, R. (2012). Literacy, digital literacy and epistemic practices: The co-evolution of hybrid minds and external memory systems. *Nordic Journal of Digital Literacy, 1,* 5–20.

Säljö, R., & Linderoth, J. (Eds.). (2002). *Utm@ningar och e-frestelser: IT och skolans lärkultur* [Ch@llenges and e-temptations: ICT and the learning culture of our school]. Stockholm, Sweden: Prisma.

Scardamalia, M., & Bereiter, C. (2006). Knowledge building: Theory, pedagogy, and technology. In K. Sawyer (Ed.), *Cambridge handbook of the learning sciences* (pp. 97–118). Cambridge University Press.

Sharples, M., Taylor, J., & Vavoula, G. (2007). A theory of learning for the mobile age. In R. Andrews & C. Haythornthwaite (Eds.), *The SAGE handbook of e-learning research* (pp. 221–247). London, UK: SAGE.

Siegel, M. (1995). More than words: The generative power of transmediation for learning. *Canadian Journal of Education, 20*(4), 455–475. doi:10.2307/1495082

Stein, P. (2008). *Multimodal pedagogies in diverse classrooms: Representation, rights and resources.* London, UK: Routledge.

Svenska akademiens ordbok. (1981). Ordbok över svenska språket (Tjugoåttonde bandet, Sluvra – Solanin). Lund, Sweden: Svenska akademien, Gleerup.

Teske, P. R. J., & Horstman, T. (2012). Transmedia in the classroom: Breaking the fourth wall. In A. Lugmayr (Ed.), *Proceedings of the 16th International Academic MindTrek Conference* (pp. 5-9), Tampere, Finland. doi:10.1145/2393132.2393134

The New London Group. (1996). A pedagogy of multiliteracies: Designing social futures. *Harvard Educational Review, 66*(1).

Uljens, M. (1997). *School didactics and learning. A school didactic model framing an analysis of pedagogical implications of learning theory.* Hove, UK: Psychology Press. doi:10.4324/9780203304778

Vygotsky, L. (1978). Mind in society. The development of higher psychological processes. Cambridge, MA: Harvard University Press. (Original texts published 1930–1935).

Vygotsky, L. (1986). Thought and language (A. Kozulin translation). Cambridge, MA: MIT Press. (Original text published 1934).

Wertsch, J. V. (2002). *Voices of collective remembering.* Cambridge, MA: Cambridge University Press. doi:10.1017/CBO9780511613715

Wiley, D. A. (2008). The learning objects literature. In J. M. Spector, M. D. Merrill, J. Van Merrienboer, & M. P. Driscoll (Eds.), *Handbook of research on educational communications and technology* (3rd ed., pp. 345–355). Routledge.

This work was previously published in the International Journal of Mobile and Blended Learning (IJMBL), 6(2); edited by David Parsons, pages 41-57, copyright year 2014 by IGI Publishing (an imprint of IGI Global).

Index

Become an IRMA Member

Members of the **Information Resources Management Association (IRMA)** understand the importance of community within their field of study. The Information Resources Management Association is an ideal venue through which professionals, students, and academicians can convene and share the latest industry innovations and scholarly research that is changing the field of information science and technology. Become a member today and enjoy the benefits of membership as well as the opportunity to collaborate and network with fellow experts in the field.

IRMA Membership Benefits:

- **One FREE Journal Subscription**

- **30% Off Additional Journal Subscriptions**

- **20% Off Book Purchases**

- Updates on the latest events and research on Information Resources Management through the IRMA-L listserv.

- Updates on new open access and downloadable content added to Research IRM.

- A copy of the Information Technology Management Newsletter twice a year.

- A certificate of membership.

IRMA Membership $195

Scan code to visit irma-international.org and begin by selecting your free journal subscription.

Membership is good for one full year.

CPSIA information can be obtained at www.ICGtesting.com
Printed in the USA
BVOW07*1159050915

416546BV00006B/26/P